Lecture Notes in Computer Science   5653

Commenced Publication in 1973
Founding and Former Series Editors:
Gerhard Goos, Juris Hartmanis, and Jan van Lee

Editorial Board

Sophia Drossopoulou (Ed.)

ECOOP 2009 – Object-Oriented Programming

23rd European Conference
Genoa, Italy, July 6-10, 2009
Proceedings

 Springer

Volume Editor

Sophia Drossopoulou
Imperial College London
Department of Computing
180 Queen's Gate, London SW7 2AZ, UK
E-mail: scd@doc.ic.ac.uk

Library of Congress Control Number: Applied for

CR Subject Classification (1998): D.1, D.2, D.3, F.3, C.2, K.4, J.1

LNCS Sublibrary: SL 2 – Programming and Software Engineering

ISSN	0302-9743
ISBN-10	3-642-03012-2 Springer Berlin Heidelberg New York
ISBN-13	978-3-642-03012-3 Springer Berlin Heidelberg New York

springer.com

© Springer-Verlag Berlin Heidelberg 2009
Printed in Germany

Typesetting: Camera-ready by author, data conversion by Scientific Publishing Services, Chennai, India
Printed on acid-free paper   SPIN: 12717804   06/3180   5 4 3 2 1 0

Foreword

Welcome to the proceedings of ECOOP 2009! Thanks to the local organizers for working hard on arranging the conference — with the hard work they put in, it was a great success. Thanks to Sophia Drossopoulou for her dedicated work as PC Chair in assembling a fine scientific program including forward-looking keynotes, and for her efforts to reduce the environmental impact of the PC meeting by replacing a physical meeting with a virtual meeting. I would also like to thank James Noble for taking the time and effort to write up last year's banquet speech so that it could be included in this year's proceedings.

One of the strong features of ECOOP is the two days of workshops preceding the main conference that allows intense interaction between participants. Thanks to all workshop organizers.

Last year's successful summer school tutorials were followed up this year with seven interesting tutorials. Thanks to the organizers and speakers.

This year's Dahl-Nygaard award honored yet another pioneer in the field, namely, David Ungar for his contributions including *Self*. I appreciate his efforts in providing us with an excellent award talk.

The world is changing and so is ECOOP. Please contemplate my short note on the following pages entitled *On Future Trends for ECOOP*.

April 2009   Eric Jul

On Future Trends for ECOOP

The world is changing and so is the European Conference on Object-Oriented Programming (ECOOP) series. ECOOP 1998 had more than 700 attendees, many workshops, a large tutorial program, and many exhibitors. Since then many things have changed starting with the .com bust, which meant a reduction in participation from industry and consequently also a reduction in tutorial attendance and exhibits. The past decade has also seen a number of more specialized conferences in the OO area focusing on specific topics, e.g., Java, so it is perhaps natural that some move on from ECOOP to such conferences on subtopics within OO, while ECOOP still covers new, and less established OO ideas of the future.

These trends have changed ECOOP from a mix of industry and academia to mostly academia, resulting in lower attendance, significantly reduced exhibits, and a change in tutorials from fully paid introductory tutorials to an academic program of summer school tutorials.

Since the turn of the century, there has also been a slow drop in the number of workshops, which, besides the strong papers in the main conference, has been one of the hallmarks of ECOOP. A strong workshop program is important in attracting strong academics who are not only trendsetters, but also active participants willing to have lively discussions on their views.

The changing conditions for ECOOP can and should lead to changes in the conference: I encourage those of you interested in developing ECOOP to look to the future: which parts of ECOOP should be strengthened? Which should be changed? The introduction of summer school tutorials is an example of a successful change — one that has been appreciated by attendees. Perhaps the change from a larger conference to a smaller, more academic conference with intense workshops and lively summer school tutorials provides for a more intimate conference with ample oppertunity for academic interchange.

Naturally, the AITO members continually assess the focus and direction of each ECOOP. The AITO General Assembly meeting, which traditionally is held the evening before the main conference opens, includes a discussion on the upcoming ECOOP conferences. We appreciate all input from ECOOP attendees, so I will conclude by encouraging you to pass on your thoughts to any AITO member.

April 2009   Eric Jul

Preface

It is both an honor and a pleasure to be presenting the proceedings of the 23rd European Conference on Object-Oriented Programming (ECOOP 2009). This year's ECOOP was held in Genoa, Italy; it had a technical program of 25 research papers on a broad range of topics, accompanied by 14 workshops and seven summer school tutorials.

Each of the 117 submissions received at least four (and as many as seven) reviews. For PC papers five reviews were required, and higher standards applied. As in the previous two years, the authors were given the opportunity to write short responses after reading the preliminary reviews.

After that, instead of the traditional physical meeting which would have resulted in around 37 tonnes of CO_2, the PC had two weeks of intensive deliberations over CyberChairPRO and email, during which further reviews were written, and papers were hotly debated and deeply scrutinized. Our virtual meeting was complemented by four long conference calls.

Many PC members had mixed feelings about this mode of deliberarion, and I am particularly grateful to those who joined the PC despite their skepticism, and to those who had to be awake at 3:00 in the morning to participate in the calls. Although the fun of a physical meeting cannot be matched by conference calls, I firmly believe that ECOOP's high quality of selection was maintained. Consequently, I hope that future chairs will adopt and improve virtual meetings.

The PC selected 25 papers, presented in this volume, and awarded two best paper prizes: one to Davide Ancona and Giovanni Lagorio, for "Coinductive Type Systems for Object-Oriented Languages," and the other to Einar Høst and Bjarte Østvold for "Debugging Method Names."

David Ungar was this year's recipient of the Dahl-Nygaard award, and William Cook gave the banquet speech. The volume also includes summaries of the two ECOOP invited talks, namely "Classes, Jim, but not as we know them - Type Classes in Haskell: what, why, and whither," given by Simon Peyton Jones, and "Java on 1000 Cores: Tales of Hardware/Software Co-design" given by Cliff Click. The volume concludes with "The Myths of Object-Orientation," last year's banquet speech by James Noble, prefaced by Jan Vitek, last year's PC chair.

I thank the authors of all submitted papers, and the external referees who provided excellent reviews. I am grateful to AITO and in particular to Eric Jul for their trust and their advice when needed, to Richard van de Stadt for helping with and customizing CyberChairPRO to the special needs of this PC, and to the local organizers – especially Elena Zucca and Davide Ancona – for valuable input to all issues related to the program. I am particularly obliged to the PC members for their hard work, their enthusiastic debates, their support throughout the process, and their commitment to make a success of ECOOP 2009.

April 2009   Sophia Drossopoulou

Organization

ECOOP 2009 was organized by the University of Genoa and the University of Milan, Italy, under the auspices of AITO (Association Internationale pour les Technologies Objets), and in cooperation with ACM SIGPLAN and SIGSOFT.

Executive Committee

Conference Chairs

Giovanna Guerrini   University of Genoa, Italy)
Elena Zucca   University of Genoa, Italy

Program Chair

Sophia Drossopoulou   Imperial College, London, UK

Organizing Committee

Organizing Chair

Davide Ancona   University of Genoa, Italy
Walter Cazzola   University of Milan, Italy

Workshop Chairs

Ferruccio Damiani   University of Turin, Italy
Mario Südhold   Ecole des Mines de Nantes, France

Summer School Committee

Antonio Cisternino   University of Pisa, Italy
Paola Giannini   University of Piemonte Orientale, Italy
James Noble   Victoria University of Wellington,
                    New Zealand

Publicity Chair

Dave Clarke   Katholieke Universiteit Leuven, Belgium

Poster and Demo Chairs

Lorenzo Bettini   University of Turin Italy
Giovanni Lagorio   University of Genoa, Italy

Exhibition Chairs

Giovanni Rimassa   Whitestein Technologies AG, Zurich,
                                        Switzerland
Mirko Viroli   University of Bologna, Italy

Sponsor Chair

Vittoria Gianuzzi   University of Genoa, Italy

Doctoral Symposium Chair

Stephen Nelson   Victoria University of Wellington,
                                        New Zealand

Webmaster

Antonio Cuni   University of Genoa

Administrative Staff

Laura Montanari
Daniela Peghini

Sponsoring Organizations

Program Committee

Elisa Baniassad	The Chinese University of Hong Kong, China
Françoise Baude	University of Nice Sophia Antipolis, France
Bernhard Beckert	University of Koblenz, Germany
Lodewijk Bergmans	University of Twente, The Netherlands
John Tang Boyland	University of Wisconsin-Milwaukee, USA
Siobhan Clarke	Trinity College Dublin, Ireland
William Cook	University of Texas at Austin, USA
Sophia Drossopoulou	Imperical College, London, UK
Eric Eide	University of Utah, USA
Erik Ernst	University of Aarhus, Denmark
Cormac Flanagan	University of California at Santa Cruz, USA
Yossi Gil	Google Haifa and Technion, Israel
Neal Glew	Intel, USA
Kathryn E. Gray	University of Cambridge, UK
Görel Hedin	Lund University, Sweden
Atsushi Igarashi	Kyoto University, Japan
Richard Jones	University of Kent, UK
Viktor Kuncak	Ecole Polytechnique Fédérale de Lausanne, Switzerland
Doug Lea	State University of New York at Oswego, USA
Gary T. Leavens	University of Central Florida, USA
Oscar Nierstrasz	University of Bern, Switzerland
James Noble	University of Wellington, New Zealand
Nathaniel Nystrom	IBM Research, USA
Awais Rashid	Lancaster University, UK
Diomidis Spinellis	Athens University of Economics and Business, Greece
Peter Sewell	University of Cambridge, UK
Laurence Tratt	Bournemouth University, UK
Jan Vitek	Purdue University, USA
Matthias Zenger	Google, Switzerland
Elena Zucca	University of Genoa, Italy

Referees

Mehmet Akşit	Christian Bird	Richard Bubel
Brian Amedro	Christoph Bockisch	Robert Bunyan
Davide Ancona	Lidia Bonilla	Nicholas Cameron
Mike Barnett	Viviana Bono	Walter Cazzola
Yonatan Ben-Ya'akov	Johannes Borgstrom	Selim Ciraci
Ytai Ben-tsvi	Thorsten Bormer	Curtis Clifton
Robert Biddle	Chandrasekhar Boyapati	Roberta Coelho
Gavin Bierman	Pim van den Broek	Tal Cohen

David Cunningham

Ferruccio Damiani

Giorgio Delzanno

Brian Demsky

Mariangiola Dezani

Christophe Dony

Derek Dreyer

Robert Dyer

Jürgen Ebert

Torbjörn Ekman

Burak Emir

Manuel Fähndrich

Fabiano Ferrari

Lev Finkelstein

Thomas Finsterbusch

Sebastian Fleissner

Jeff Foster

Tal Franji

Stephen N. Freund

Robert Fuhrer

Tudor Gîrba

Igor Gelfgat

Michael George

Christoph Gladisch

Arda Goknil

Georgios Gousios

Phil Greenwood

Giovanna Guerrini

Arjun Guha

Ratan Guha

Gurcan Gulesir

Philip Guo

Ghaith Haddad

Philipp Haller

Scott Harmon

Tim Harris

Simon Helsen

Ludovic Henrio

Stephan Herrmann

Mike Hicks

Martin Hirzel

Christian Hofmann

Antony Hosking

Fabrice Huet

Ali Ibrahim

K.R. Jayaram

Tomas Kalibera

Tetsuo Kamina

Vassilios Karakoidas

Andrew Kennedy

Raffi Khatchadourian

Peter Kim

David Kitchin

Vladimir Klebanov

Kenneth Knowles

Krzysztof Kuchcinski

Adrian Kuhn

Ivan Kurtev

Giovanni Lagorio

Rustan Leino

Keren Lenz

Brian Lewis

Ondrej Lhotak

Adrian Lienhard

Peter Müller

Elton Mathias

Sean McDirmid

Fadi Meawad

Todd Millstein

Dimitris Mitropoulos

Clayton Goodrich Myers

Mayur Naik

Shin Nakajima

Srinivas Nedunuri

Anders Bach Nielsen

Emma Nilsson-Nyman

Lennart Ohlsson

Johan Ostlund

Matthew Parkinson

David J. Pearce

Thomas Pederson

Fabrizio Perin

Frances Perry

Leaf Petersen

Benjamin Pierce

Marco Pistoia

Filip Pizlo

Alex Potanin

Daniel Pähler

Xin Qi

David Röthlisberger

Pritam Roy

Mohan Rajagopalan

Hridesh Rajan

Lukas Renggli

Jorge Ressia

William Retert

Gregor Richards

Robby

Sven G. Robertz

Arjan de Roo

Chieri Saito

Alberto Sardinha

Jan Schäfer

Marco Servetto

Jeremy Singer

Sriram Srinivasan

Rok Strniša

Konstantinos Stroggylos

Philippe Suter

Daniel Tang

Olivier Tardieu

Ran Tavory

Ewan Tempero

Tachio Terauchi

Cheng Thao

Igor Tsvetkov

Shmuel Tyszberowicz

Naoyasu Ubayashi

Giora Unger

Peter Van Roy

Michalis Vazirgiannis

Mandana Vaziri

Toon Verwaest

Mirko Viroli

Eran Werner

Nathan Weston

Ben Wiedermann

Victor Winter

Tobias Wrigstad

Lei Zhao

Tian Zhao

Lukasz Ziarek

Steffen Zschaler

Table of Contents

Modularity

Mining and Extracting

Refactoring

Keynote 2

Concurrency, Exceptions and Initialization

Concurrency and Distribution

ECOOP 2008 Banquet Speech

Classes, Jim, But Not as We Know Them — Type Classes in Haskell: What, Why, and Whither

Simon Peyton Jones

Microsoft Research

Haskell is now quite widely used, but its most important contributions are the *ideas* that it embodies. In this talk I will focus on one of these ideas, namely type classes, with a few anecdotes and reflections along the way about the process of developing the language.

Type classes are probably Haskell's most distinctive feature. The original idea is very neat and, better still, it led to a long series of subsequent generalisations and innovations. Indeed, although the language is now nineteen years old, Haskell's type system is still in a state of furious development. For example, I am involved in adding type-level functions to Haskell, as I will briefly describe.

I will explain what type classes are, how they differ from the classes of mainstream object oriented languages, why I think they are so cool, and what the hot topics are. I'll give plenty of examples, so you don't need to already know Haskell.

S. Drossopoulou (Ed.): ECOOP 2009, LNCS 5653, p. 1, 2009.

Coinductive Type Systems for Object-Oriented Languages*

Davide Ancona and Giovanni Lagorio

DISI, Univ. of Genova, Italy
{davide,lagorio}@disi.unige.it

Abstract. We propose a novel approach based on coinductive logic to specify type systems of programming languages.

The approach consists in encoding programs in Horn formulas which are interpreted w.r.t. their coinductive Herbrand model.

We illustrate the approach by first specifying a standard type system for a small object-oriented language similar to Featherweight Java. Then we define an idealized type system for a variant of the language where type annotations can be omitted. The type system involves infinite terms and proof trees not representable in a finite way, thus providing a theoretical limit to type inference of object-oriented programs, since only sound approximations of the system can be implemented.

Approximation is naturally captured by the notions of subtyping and subsumption; indeed, rather than increasing the expressive power of the system, as it usually happens, here subtyping is needed for approximating infinite non regular types and proof trees with regular ones.

1 Introduction

In the context of object-oriented programming, many solutions have been proposed to the problem of type inference [17,16,1,21,6,20,12], but the increasing interest in dynamic object-oriented languages is asking for ever more precise and efficient type inference algorithms [3,12].

Two important features which should be supported by type inference are *parametric* and *data polymorphism* [1]; the former allows invocation of a method on arguments of unrelated types, the latter allows assignment of values of unrelated types to a field. While most proposed solutions support parametric polymorphism well, only few inference algorithms are able to deal properly with data polymorphism; such algorithms, however, turn out to be quite complex and cannot be easily specified in terms of a type system.

In this paper we propose a novel approach based on coinductive logic to specify type systems of programming languages. The approach consists in encoding programs in Horn formulas which are interpreted w.r.t. their coinductive Herbrand model. This is made possible by the notion of type constraint defined in

---

* This work has been partially supported by MIUR EOS DUE - Extensible Object Systems for Dynamic and Unpredictable Environments.

previous work on principal typing of Java-like languages [7,4] and is a generalization of the algorithm presented in [6]. In contrast with other approaches based on a unique kind of subtyping constraint, the encoding of a program into a Horn formula is allowed by constraints which are atoms (that is, atomic formulas) of different forms, each one corresponding to a kind of compound expression of the language. Coinduction arises naturally at two different levels: at the level of terms, since recursive types are infinite terms, and at the level of proofs, since recursive methods and the use of infinite types require proofs to be infinite as well.

The paper is structured as follows: In Section 2 we provide a first example by formalizing a type system for a fully annotated language similar to Featherweight Java (FJ) [14]; the example is intended as a way for gently introducing the main concepts of the approach and to prepare the reader to the idealized type system presented in Section 3 and formalized in Section 4. In Section 5 the idealized type system is extended with subtyping and subsumption, and soundness is claimed (some proofs are sketched in Appendix B). Finally, conclusion and comments on further work can be found in Section 6.

2   A Simple Example

In this section we provide a first example by formalizing a type system for a fully annotated language similar to Featherweight Java (FJ) [14]. This section is mainly intended as a way for introducing the main concepts of the approach and to prepare the reader to the more advanced type system defined in the next sections; also, it shows the approach can be used for defining different kinds of type systems.

2.1   Syntax and Operational Semantics

The syntax of the languages is defined in Figure 1. Syntactic assumptions listed in the figure have to be verified before transforming a program into a Horn formula. We use bars for denoting sequences: for instance, $\overline{e}^m$ denotes $e_1, \ldots, e_m$, $\overline{\tau\ x}^n$ denotes $\tau_1\ x_1, \ldots, \tau_n\ x_n$, and so on.

We assume countably infinite sets of *class names* c, *method names* m, *field names* f, and *parameter names* x. A program consists of a sequence of class declarations and a main expression from which the computation starts. A class declaration consists of the name of the declared class and of its direct superclass (hence, only single inheritance is supported), a sequence of field declarations, a constructor declaration, and a sequence of method declarations. We assume a predefined class *Object*, which is the root of the inheritance tree and contains no fields, no methods and a constructor with no parameters. A field declaration consists of a type annotation and a field name. A constructor declaration consists of the name of the class where the constructor is declared, a sequence of parameters with their type annotations, and the body, which consists of an invocation of the superclass constructor and a sequence of field initializations,

$$prog ::= \overline{cd}^n \; e$$
$$cd ::= \textbf{class} \; c_1 \; \textbf{extends} \; c_2 \; \{ \; \overline{fd}^n \; cn \; \overline{md}^m \; \} \quad (c_1 \neq Object)$$
$$fd ::= \tau \; f;$$
$$cn ::= c(\overline{\tau \; x}^n) \; \{\textbf{super}(\overline{e}^m); \overline{f = e';}^k\}$$
$$md ::= \tau_0 \; m(\overline{\tau \; x}^n) \; \{e\}$$
$$e ::= \textbf{new} \; c(\overline{e}^n) \mid x \mid e.f \mid e_0.m(\overline{e}^n) \mid \textbf{if} \; (e) \; e_1 \; \textbf{else} \; e_2 \mid \textbf{false} \mid \textbf{true}$$
$$\tau ::= c \mid \textbf{bool}$$
$$v ::= \textbf{new} \; c(\overline{v}^n) \mid \textbf{false} \mid \textbf{true}$$

Assumptions: $n, m, k \geq 0$, inheritance is acyclic, names of declared classes in a program, methods and fields in a class, and parameters in a method are distinct.

Fig. 1. Syntax of OO programs

one for each field declared in the class.[1] A method declaration consists of a return type annotation, a method name, a sequence of parameters with their type annotations, and an expression (the method body).

Expressions are standard; even though the conditional expression, and the constants **true** and **false** could be encoded in the language, we have introduced them for making clearer the connection with union types in Section 3.2. For making the examples easier to read, we will also use the primitive type of integers, but leave it out in the formal treatment, which would be straightforward. As in FJ, the expression *this* is considered as a special implicit parameter.

A type annotation can be either the primitive type **bool** or a class name.

Finally, the definition of values v is instrumental to the (standard) small steps operational semantics of the language, indexed over the class declarations defined by the program, given in Figure 2.

$$(\text{field-1}) \; \frac{cbody(cds, c) = (\overline{x}^n, \{\textbf{super}(\ldots); \overline{f = e';}^k\}) \quad f = f_i \quad 1 \leq i \leq k}{\textbf{new} \; c(\overline{e}^n).f \rightarrow_{cds} e_i'[\overline{e}^n/\overline{x}^n]}$$

$$(\text{field-2}) \; \frac{\begin{array}{c} cbody(cds, c) = (\overline{x}^n, \{\textbf{super}(\overline{e'}^m); \overline{f = \ldots;}^k\}) \\ \forall i \in 1..k \quad f \neq f_i \quad \textbf{class} \; c \; \textbf{extends} \; c' \; \{ \ldots \} \in cds \\ \textbf{new} \; c'(e_1'[\overline{e}^n/\overline{x}^n], \ldots, e_m'[\overline{e}^n/\overline{x}^n]).f \rightarrow_{cds} e \end{array}}{\textbf{new} \; c(\overline{e}^n).f \rightarrow_{cds} e}$$

$$(\text{invk}) \; \frac{mbody(cds, c, m) = (\overline{x}^n, e)}{\textbf{new} \; c(\overline{e}^k).m(\overline{e'}^n) \rightarrow_{cds} e[\overline{e'}^n/\overline{x}^n][\textbf{new} \; c(\overline{e}^k)/this]}$$

$$(\text{if-1}) \; \frac{}{\textbf{if} \; (\textbf{true}) \; e_1 \; \textbf{else} \; e_2 \rightarrow_{cds} e_1} \qquad (\text{if-2}) \; \frac{}{\textbf{if} \; (\textbf{false}) \; e_1 \; \textbf{else} \; e_2 \rightarrow_{cds} e_2}$$

Fig. 2. Reduction rules for OO programs

---

[1] This is a generalization of constructors of FJ, which makes the encoding compositional: a constructor declaration contained in a class c can be encoded if just the name c and the fields declared in c are known.

For reasons of space, the rule for contextual closure and the standard definition of contexts have been omitted (to be as general as possible, no evaluation strategy is fixed); furthermore side conditions have been placed together with premises. Auxiliary functions *cbody* and *mbody* are defined in Appendix A.

Rule (field-1) corresponds to the case where the field f is declared in the same class of the constructor, otherwise rule (field-2) applies and the field is searched in the direct superclass. The notation $e[\overline{e}^n/\overline{x}^n]$ denotes parallel substitution of x_i by e_i (for $i = 1..n$) in expression e.

In rule (invk), the parameters and the body of the method to be invoked are retrieved by the auxiliary function *mbody*, which performs the standard method look-up. If the method is found, then the invocation reduces to the body of the method where the parameters are substituted by the corresponding arguments, and *this* by the receiver object (the object on which the method is invoked).

The remaining rules are trivial.

The one step reduction relation on programs is defined by: $(cds\ e) \rightarrow (cds\ e')$ iff $e \rightarrow_{cds} e'$. Finally, $\rightarrow^*$ and $\rightarrow^*_{cds}$ denote the reflexive and transitive closures of $\rightarrow$ and $\rightarrow_{cds}$, respectively.

2.2 Encoding of Programs into Horn Formulas

Since Prolog is the most direct way to implement a prototype interpreter for coinductive logic programming (see the conclusion), we follow the standard Prolog syntax notation. We assume two countably infinite sets of *predicate* and *function* symbols each associated with an *arity* $n \geq 0$, and ranged over by p and f respectively, and a countably infinite set of *logical variables* ranged over by X. Functions with arity 0 are called *constants*. We write p/n, f/n to mean that predicate p, function f have arity n, respectively. For symbols we follow the usual convention: function and predicate symbols always begin with a lowercase letter, whereas variables always begin with an uppercase letter.

A Horn formula Hf is a finite conjunction (or, more abstractly, a finite set) of *clauses* (ranged over by Cl) of the form $A \leftarrow B$, where A is the *head* and B is the *body*.

The head is an *atom*, while the body is a finite and possibly empty conjunction of atoms; the empty conjunction is denoted by *true*. A clause with an empty body (denoted by $A \leftarrow true$) is called a *fact*. An atom has the form[2] $p(\overline{t}^n)$ where the predicate p has arity n and $\overline{t}^n$ are *terms*.

For list terms we use the standard notation [ ] for the empty list and [_|_] for the list constructor, and adopt the syntax abbreviation $[\overline{t}^n]$ for $[t_1|[\ldots [t_n|[\ ]]]]$.

A formula/clause/atom/term is *ground* if it contains no logical variables.

In the following simple examples terms are built in the usual inductive[3] way from functions symbols and logical variables. In particular, the Herbrand universe of a Horn formula, obtained from a program *prog*, is the set of all terms

---

[2] Parentheses are omitted for predicate symbols of arity 0; the same convention applies for function applications, see below.

[3] In Section 4 we will consider infinite terms as well.

inductively defined on top of the constant [ ] and all constants representing class, method and field names declared in *prog*, and on top of the binary function symbol [-|-].

The encoding of a program into a Horn formula intuitively corresponds to a reverse compilation procedure where the target language (Horn formulas) is at an higher level[4] of abstraction. Following this intuition, a method declaration is encoded in a Horn clause. Consider for instance the following class declaration:

```
class NEList extends List {
  Object el;
  List next;
  NEList(Object e, List n){super();el=e;next=n;}
  NEList add(Object e){new NEList(e,this)}
}
```

Method `add` can be encoded in the following clause:

$$has\_meth(nelist, add, [E], nelist) \leftarrow$$
$$type\_comp(E, object), new(nelist, [E, nelist], nelist),$$
$$override(list, add, [object], nelist).$$

The clause states that for all types E, class $NEList$[5] has a method named *add* taking one argument[6] of type E and returning a value of type $NEList$ (atom $has\_meth(nelist, add, [E], nelist)$), if the following constraints are satisfied:

- E is type compatible with *Object* (atom $type\_comp(E, object)$),
- the constructor of class $NEList$ takes two arguments, the former of type E and the latter of type $NEList$, and returns[7] an object of type $NEList$ (atom $new(nelist, [E, nelist], nelist)$),
- in case of overriding, the signature of the method is compatible with method *add* of the direct superclass *List* (atom $override(list, add, [object], nelist)$).

Note that if some of the constraints above cannot be satisfied, then the method `add` (hence, the whole program) is not well-typed (the conjunction of atoms $B_{\overline{cd}^n}$ defined in Figure 4 explicitly requires that all declared methods must be well-typed).

Each constraint corresponds to an atom which is directly generated from the method declaration: $type\_comp(E, object)$ is derived from the type annotation of the parameter of *add*, $new(nelist, [E, nelist], nelist)$ is generated from the body of *add*, and $override(list, add, [object], nelist)$ depends from the direct superclass of $NEList$, and the signature and return type of *add*.

----

[4] In this sense, our approach shares several commonalities with abstract interpretation, and a thorough comparison would deserve further investigation.

[5] Note that, to comply with the standard syntax of Horn formulas requiring constant symbols to begin with a lowercase letter, class names must be necessarily changed.

[6] We use lists to encode Cartesian products of types.

[7] The returned type is redundant here, but not in the type system defined in Section 3.2.

To encode a method body into a conjunction of constraints (that is, atoms) we follow the consolidated constraint-based approach to compositional typechecking and type inference of Java-like languages [5,7,4,15,6]: each kind of compound expression is associated with a specific predicate:

- $new(c, [\overline{t}^n], t)$ corresponds to object creation, c is the class of the invoked constructor, $\overline{t}^n$ the types of the arguments, and t the type of the newly created object (recall footnote 7).
- $field\_acc(t_1, f, t_2)$ corresponds to field access, t_1 is the type of the accessed object, f the field name, and t_2 the resulting type of the whole expression;
- $invoke(t_0, m, [\overline{t}^n], t)$ corresponds to method invocation, t_0 is the type of the receiver, m the method name, $\overline{t}^n$ the types of the arguments, and t the type of the returned value. This predicate is completely redundant here (its definition is identical to has_meth), but not in the type system defined in Section 3.2;
- $cond(t_1, t_2, t_3, t)$ corresponds to conditional expression, t_1 is the type of the condition, t_2 and t_3 the types of the "then" and "else" branches, respectively, and t the resulting type of the whole expression.

Besides those predicates needed to encode an expression, others are instrumental to the encoding, as $type\_comp$ and $override$ above.

The encoding of a program is defined in Figure 3, whereas Figure 4 contains the set of clauses $Hf_{default}$ which are shared by all programs, and the conjunction of atoms $B_{\overline{cd}^n}$ which imposes the requirement that each method declaration in $\overline{cd}^n$ must be well-typed. Note that not all formulas in Figure 4 are Horn clauses; indeed, for brevity we have used the negation of predicates dec_field and dec_meth. However, since the set of all field and method names declared in a program is finite, the predicates not_dec_field, not_dec_meth could be trivially defined by conjunctions of facts, therefore all formulas could be turned into Horn clauses.

For the encoding we assume bijections to translate class, field and method names to constants, and parameter names to logical variables (translations are denoted by $\hat{c}$, $\hat{f}$, $\hat{m}$, and $\hat{x}$, respectively). Furthermore, we assume that $\widehat{this} = This$.

The rules define a judgment for each syntactic category of the OO language:

- $\overline{cd}^n \ e \rightsquigarrow (Hf|B)$: a program is translated in a pair $(Hf|B)$, where Hf is the union of the set $Hf_{default}$ of clauses shared by any program with the set of clauses generated from the class declarations. The second component B is the conjunction of $B_{\overline{cd}^n}$ and B_m, where $B_{\overline{cd}^n}$ is the conjunction of atoms requiring that each method declared in $\overline{cd}^n$ is well-typed (see Figure 4), whereas B_m is the conjunction of atoms generated from the main expression e of the program;
- fd **in** $c \rightsquigarrow Cl$, md **in** $c \rightsquigarrow Hf$: the encoding of a field/method declaration depends on the class c where the declaration is contained;
- cn **in** $fds \rightsquigarrow Cl$: the encoding of a constructor declaration depends on the declaration of the fields contained in the class of the constructor: the encoding is defined only if all fields in fds are initialized by the constructor in the

$$(\text{prog})\ \dfrac{\forall i = 1..n\ cd_i \rightsquigarrow Hf_i \quad e \textbf{ in } \emptyset \rightsquigarrow (t\,|\,B_m)}{\overline{cd}^n\ e \rightsquigarrow (Hf_{default} \cup (\cup_{i=1..n} Hf_i)\,|\,B_{\overline{cd}^n},\,B_m)}$$

$$(\text{field})\ \dfrac{}{\begin{array}{c}\tau\,f;\textbf{ in } c \rightsquigarrow\\ dec\_field(\widehat{c},\widehat{f},\widehat{\tau}) \leftarrow true.\end{array}}$$

$$(\text{class})\ \dfrac{\forall i = 1..n\ fd_i \textbf{ in } c_1 \rightsquigarrow Cl_i \quad cn \textbf{ in } \overline{fd}^n \rightsquigarrow Cl \quad \forall j = 1..m\ md_j \textbf{ in } c_1 \rightsquigarrow Hf_j}{\textbf{class } c_1 \textbf{ extends } c_2\ \{\ \overline{fd}^n\ cn\ \overline{md}^m\ \} \rightsquigarrow \left\{\begin{array}{l} class(\widehat{c_1}) \leftarrow true.\\ extends(\widehat{c_1},\widehat{c_2}) \leftarrow true.\end{array}\right\} \cup (\cup_{i=1..n}\{Cl_i\}) \cup \{Cl\} \cup (\cup_{j=1..m} Hf_j)}$$

$$(\text{constr-dec})\ \dfrac{\forall i = 1..m\ e_i \textbf{ in } \{\overline{x{:}\tau}^n\} \rightsquigarrow (t_i\,|\,B_i) \quad \forall j = 1..k\ e'_j \textbf{ in } \{\overline{x{:}\tau}^n\} \rightsquigarrow (t'_j\,|\,B'_j)}{\begin{array}{c}c(\overline{\tau\,x}^n)\ \{\textbf{super}(\overline{e}^m);\overline{f = e';}^k\} \textbf{ in } \overline{\tau'\,f;}^k \rightsquigarrow\\ new(\widehat{c},A,\widehat{c}) \leftarrow type\_comp(A,[\overline{\widehat{\tau}}^n]),\overline{B}^m, extends(\widehat{c},P),\\ new(P,[\overline{t}^m],P),\overline{B'}^k, type\_comp([\overline{t'}^k],[\overline{\widehat{\tau'}}^k]).\end{array}}$$

$$(\text{meth-dec})\ \dfrac{e \textbf{ in } \{This{:}c,\overline{x{:}\tau}^n\} \rightsquigarrow (t\,|\,B)}{\begin{array}{l}\tau_0\ m(\overline{\tau\,x}^n)\{e\} \textbf{ in } c \rightsquigarrow\\ dec\_meth(\widehat{c},\widehat{m},[\overline{\widehat{\tau}}^n],\widehat{\tau_0}) \leftarrow true.\\ has\_meth(\widehat{c},\widehat{m},A,\widehat{\tau_0}) \leftarrow type\_comp(A,[\overline{\widehat{\tau}}^n]), extends(\widehat{c},P),\\ \qquad\qquad override(P,\widehat{m},[\overline{\widehat{\tau}}^n],\widehat{\tau_0}),B, type\_comp(t,\widehat{\tau_0}).\end{array}}$$

$$(\text{new})\ \dfrac{\forall i = 1..n\ e_i \textbf{ in } V \rightsquigarrow (t_i\,|\,B_i) \quad R \text{ fresh}}{\textbf{new } c(\overline{e}^n) \textbf{ in } V \rightsquigarrow (R\,|\,\overline{B}^n, new(\widehat{c},[\overline{t}^n],R))}$$

$$(\text{var})\ \dfrac{}{x \textbf{ in } V \rightsquigarrow (\widehat{\tau}\,|\,true)}\ x{:}\tau \in V \qquad (\text{field-acc})\ \dfrac{e \textbf{ in } V \rightsquigarrow (t\,|\,B) \quad R \text{ fresh}}{e.f \textbf{ in } V \rightsquigarrow (R\,|\,B, field\_acc(t,\widehat{f},R))}$$

$$(\text{invk})\ \dfrac{\forall i = 0..n\ e_i \textbf{ in } V \rightsquigarrow (t_i\,|\,B_i) \quad R \text{ fresh}}{e_0.m(\overline{e}^n) \textbf{ in } V \rightsquigarrow (R\,|\,B_0, \overline{B}^n, invoke(t_0,\widehat{m},[\overline{t}^n],R))}$$

$$(\text{if})\ \dfrac{e \textbf{ in } V \rightsquigarrow (t\,|\,B) \quad e_1 \textbf{ in } V \rightsquigarrow (t_1\,|\,B_1) \quad e_2 \textbf{ in } V \rightsquigarrow (t_2\,|\,B_2) \quad R \text{ fresh}}{\textbf{if } (e)\ e_1 \textbf{ else } e_2 \textbf{ in } V \rightsquigarrow (R\,|\,B, B_1, B_2, cond(t,t_1,t_2,R))}$$

$$(\text{true})\ \dfrac{}{\textbf{true in } V \rightsquigarrow (bool\,|\,true)} \qquad (\text{false})\ \dfrac{}{\textbf{false in } V \rightsquigarrow (bool\,|\,true)}$$

Fig. 3. Encoding of programs

same order[8] as they appear in *fds* (that is, as they have been declared in the class of the constructor);

- *e* **in** $V \rightsquigarrow (t\,|\,B)$: an expression is encoded in a pair $(t\,|\,B)$, where t is the term encoding the type of the expression, and B the conjunction of atoms generated from the expression. The encoding depends on the type

---

[8] This last restriction is just for simplicity.

$class(object) \leftarrow true.$
$subclass(X, X) \leftarrow class(X).$
$subclass(X, object) \leftarrow class(X).$
$subclass(X, Y) \leftarrow extends(X, Z), subclass(Z, Y).$
$type\_comp(bool, bool) \leftarrow true.$
$type\_comp(C1, C2) \leftarrow subclass(C1, C2).$
$type\_comp([\,], [\,]) \leftarrow true.$
$type\_comp([T1|L1], [T2|L2]) \leftarrow type\_comp(T1, T2), type\_comp(L1, L2).$
$field\_acc(C, F, T) \leftarrow has\_field(C, F, T).$
$invoke(C, M, A, R) \leftarrow has\_meth(C, M, A, R).$
$new(object, [\,], object) \leftarrow true.$
$has\_field(C, F, T) \leftarrow dec\_field(C, F, T).$
$has\_field(C, F, T1) \leftarrow$
    $extends(C, P), has\_field(P, F, T1), \neg dec\_field(C, F, T2).$
$override(object, M, A, R) \leftarrow true.$
$override(C, M, A, R) \leftarrow dec\_meth(C, M, A, R).$
$override(C, M, A1, R1) \leftarrow$
    $extends(C, P), override(P, M, A1, R1), \neg dec\_meth(C, M, A2, R2).$
$has\_meth(C, M, A1, R1) \leftarrow$
    $extends(C, P), has\_meth(P, M, A1, R1), \neg dec\_meth(C, M, A2, R2).$
$cond(T1, T2, T3, T4) \leftarrow$
    $type\_comp(T1, bool), type\_comp(T2, T4), type\_comp(T3, T4).$

$B_{\overline{cd}^n}$ is the conjunction of atoms generated from $\overline{cd}^n$ as follows:
$has\_meth(\widehat{c}, \widehat{m}, [\widehat{\tau_1}, \ldots, \widehat{\tau_k}], \widehat{\tau_0})$ is in $B_{\overline{cd}^n}$ iff class c is declared in $\overline{cd}^n$ and contains
$\tau_0\ m(\overline{\tau\ x}^k)\ \{\ldots\}$.

Fig. 4. Definition of $Hf_{default}$ and $B_{\overline{cd}^n}$. Negation is used for brevity, but it can be easily removed (see the comments to the figure).

environment V, assigning types to parameters, and is defined only if all free variables of e are contained in the domain of V.

Rule (class) just collects all clauses generated from the field and constructor declarations, and the Horn formulas generated from the method declarations, and adds to them the two new facts stating respectively that class c_1 has been declared and that its direct superclass is c_2.

A constructor declaration generates a single clause whose head has the form $new(\widehat{c}, A, \widehat{c})$, where c is the class of the constructor, A is the logical variable corresponding to the list of arguments passed to the constructor, and c is the type of the object[9] created by the constructor. The first atom in the body checks that the list of arguments A is type compatible w.r.t. the of parameter type annotations, that is, that A is a list of exactly n types which are subtypes of the corresponding type annotations (see the 3rd and 4th clause defining predicate $type\_comp$ in Figure 4). However, all occurrences of the parameters are directly encoded by the corresponding types as specified by the environment $\{\overline{x:\tau}^n\}$ (see

---

[9] We have already pointed out that the third argument of new is completely redundant here, but this is not true for the type system defined in Section 3.2.

rule (var) below). The atoms $\overline{B}^m$, $extends(\widehat{c}, P)$, $new(P, [\overline{t}^m], P)$ encode the invocation of the constructor of the direct superclass, where $\overline{B}^m$ and $\overline{t}^m$ are the atoms and types generated from the arguments (see the first premise). Finally, the remaining atoms check that the field $\overline{f}^k$ declared in the class are initialized correctly; $\overline{B}^k$ and $\overline{t}^k$ are the atoms and types generated from the initializing expressions (see the second premise). Finally, note that the clause is correctly generated only if: (1) the free variables of the expressions contained in the constructor body are contained in the set $\{\overline{x}^n\}$ of the parameters (therefore, *this* cannot be used); (2) all fields declared in the class are initialized exactly once and in the same order as they are declared.

Rule (meth-dec) generates two clauses, one for the predicate *dec_meth* and the other for the predicate *has_meth*. Predicate *dec_meth* specifies just the signatures and return types of all methods declared in c, and is used for defining predicates *override* and *has_meth* (see Figure 4); predicate *has_meth* specifies names, and argument and return types of all methods (either declared or inherited) of a class. The clauses generated by this rule correspond to the case when the method is found in the class, whereas there is a unique shared clause (defined in Figure 4) to deal with method look-up in the direct superclass. Atoms $extends(\widehat{c}, P)$, $override(P, \widehat{m}, [\widehat{\overline{\tau}}^n], \widehat{\tau}_0)$ ensure that the method overrides correctly the method (if any) inherited from the direct superclass P. Atoms B, $type\_comp(t, \widehat{\tau}_0)$ check that the body is correct and that the type of the returned value is compatible with the declared type. Note that the variable *this* can be accessed in the body of the method and that it has type c, as specified in the environment $\{ This{:}c, \overline{x{:}\tau}^n \}$.

Rule (var) can be instantiated only if x is defined in the environment V; the associated type t is returned together with the empty conjunction of atoms.

The other rules for expressions (except for the trivial ones on boolean constants) are very similar: premises generate types and atoms for all subexpressions, then the conclusion collects all generated atoms, adds a new atom corresponding to the whole expression, and generates a fresh variable (to avoid clashes) for the type of the whole expression.

Clauses defined in Figure 4 are quite straightforward. For instance, they state that *Object* is a predefined class which is the root of the inheritance relation and which has a default constructor with no parameters. Since *Object* cannot be redefined, it turns out that the class declares no fields and no methods.

The definition of *field_acc* is identical to *dec_field*, but this is no longer true for the type system defined in the next section (see Section 3.2).

The predicate *override* checks that methods are overridden correctly (we use the most restrictive formulation asking types of arguments and of the returned value to be all invariant); the first clause specifies that all methods of class *Object* are overridden correctly (since, in fact, *object* has no methods), the second states that a method declared in a class is overridden correctly only by a method having the same name and types of parameters and returned value, while the last clause says that a method is overridden correctly if it is not declared in the class and if it is overridden correctly in the direct superclass.

Finally, the clause defining *cond* states that a conditional expression is correct if the type of the condition is *bool* (we use *type_comp* for uniformity with the definitions given in Section 4); the corresponding type is any common super type of the expressions of the two branches.

Coinductive Herbrand Models. Well-typed programs are defined in terms of coinductive Herbrand models, that is, greatest instead of least fixed-points are considered.

As we will see in Section 3.4, coinduction arises naturally at two different levels: at the level of terms, since recursive types are infinite[10] terms, and at the level of proofs, since recursive methods and the use of infinite types require proofs to be infinite as well.

The Herbrand base of a Horn formula obtained from a program *prog* is the set of all ground atoms built from the predicates in the formula and the (ground) terms of the Herbrand universe of the formula.

A substitution θ is defined in the standard way as a total function from logical variables to terms, different from the identity only for a finite set of variables. Composition of substitutions and application of a substitution to a term are defined in the usual way. A ground instance of a clause $A \leftarrow A_1 \ldots A_n$ is a ground clause Cl s.t. $Cl = A\theta \leftarrow A_1\theta, \ldots, A_n\theta$ for a certain substitution θ.

Given a Horn formula Hf, the immediate consequence operator T_{Hf} is an endofunction defined on the parts of the Herbrand base of Hf as follows:

$$T_{Hf}(S) = \{A \mid A \leftarrow B \text{ is a ground instance of a clause of } Hf, B \in S\}.$$

A Herbrand model of a logic program Hf is a subset of the Herbrand base of Hf which is a fixed-point of the immediate consequence operator T_{Hf}. Since T_{Hf} is monotonic for any *prog*, by the Knaster-Tarski theorem there always exists the greatest Herbrand model of Hf, which is also the greatest set S s.t. $S \subseteq T_{Hf}(S)$. The greatest Herbrand model of Hf is denoted by $M^{co}(Hf)$ and called the coinductive Herbrand model of Hf.

A conjunction of atoms B is satisfiable in Hf iff there exists a substitution θ s.t. $B\theta \subseteq M^{co}(Hf)$.

A program $\overline{cd}^n$ e is well-typed iff $\overline{cd}^n$ $e \rightsquigarrow (Hf|B)$ and B is satisfiable in Hf.

Finally, we only informally state the claim and do not prove it (since it is out of the scope of this section) that the notion of well-typed program is equivalent to that given by a conventional type system (like that of FJ).

Claim (informal equivalence). A program $\overline{cd}^n$ e is well-typed w.r.t. to a standard type system iff $\overline{cd}^n$ $e \rightsquigarrow (Hf|B)$ and B is satisfiable in Hf.

3   An Idealized Type System: An Outline

In this section we present a more advanced type system supporting method and data polymorphism. The type system is idealized since it involves infinite

---

[10] However, in the simple type system defined here infinite terms are not needed.

terms and proof trees not representable in a finite way, therefore only sound approximations of the system can be implemented. Under this perspective, the system could be considered as an abstract specification for a large class of type inference algorithms for object-oriented programs which can only be sound but not complete w.r.t. the given system, and, thus, an attempt at pushing to the extreme the theoretical limits of static type analysis.

3.1 Extension of the Syntax

At the syntax level the only needed extension to the language defined in Section 2 concerns type annotations which now can be empty, that is, users can omit (partially or totally) field and method type annotations:

$$\tau ::= N \mid \epsilon$$
$$N ::= c \mid \texttt{bool}$$

This extension does not affect the operational semantics given in Figure 2.

A type annotation τ can be either a nominal type N (the primitive type `bool` or a class name c), or empty. Consider for instance the following example:

```
class EList {
  EList(){super();}
  add(e){new NEList(e,this)}
}

class NEList {
  el;
  next;
  NEList(e,n){super();el=e;next=n;}
  add(e){new NEList(e,this)}
}
```

Omitting types in method declarations allows method polymorphism: for instance, the two methods `add` are polymorphic in the type of their parameter `e`. Omitting types in field declarations allows data polymorphism: it is possible to build a list of elements of heterogeneous types and, as we will see, in the type system defined in the sequel each element of the list is associated with its exact type.

Type annotations are intended as explicit constraints imposed by the user, but do not make type analysis less precise. For instance, if the declaration of field `el` is annotated with type `Item`, then only instances of `Item` or of a subclass of `Item` can be correctly added to a list. However, if we add to a list an instance of `ExtItem` which is a subclass of `Item`, then the type system is able to assign to the first element of the list the type `ExtItem`.

3.2 Structured Types

To have a more expressive type system, we introduce structured types encoded by the following terms:

- X, which represents a type variable;
- *bool*, which represents the type of boolean values;
- $obj(\widehat{c}, t)$, which represents the instances of class c, where t is a record $[\widehat{f_1}:t_1, \ldots, \widehat{f_n}:t_n]$ which associates with each field f_i of the object a corresponding type term t_i; as in the type system of Section 2, the methods of a class are encoded as clauses, whereas the types of fields need to be associated with each single instance, to be able to support data polymorphism;
- $t_1 \vee t_2$, which represents a union type [8,13]: an expression has type $t_1 \vee t_2$ if it has type t_1 or t_2.

Note that nominal types are explicitly used by programmers as type annotations, whereas structured types are fully transparent to programmers.

The use of structured types should now clarify why predicates *type_comp* and *invoke* has been already introduced in Section 2 and why predicate *new* has arity 3.

- The difference between predicates *type_comp* and *subclass* is now evident: *type_comp*/2 (see Figure 6) defines the relation of type compatibility between structured and nominal types. For instance, the atom

$$type\_comp(obj(\widehat{c_1}, t_1) \vee obj(\widehat{c_2}, t_2), \widehat{c})$$

  is expected to hold, whenever both c_1 and c_2 are subclasses of c.
- The first and third argument of predicate *new* are now clearly different: the former is the class name of the invoked constructor, whereas the latter is the structured type of the created object. The following invariant is expected to hold: if $new(\widehat{c}, [\overline{t}^n], t)$ holds, then $type\_comp(t, \widehat{c})$ holds as well.
- Predicates *invoke* and *has_meth* are now clearly distinct: the first argument of *invoke* is the structured type of the receiver, whereas the first argument of *has_meth* is the class from which method look-up is started.

3.3   Typing Methods

As already mentioned, type annotations are intended as explicit constraints imposed by the user, but do not make type analysis less precise. For instance, if we assume that a program declares[11] classes H and P, with H subclass of P, and we annotate the parameter of method **add** of class **EList** as follows

```
add(P e){new NEList(e,this)}
```

then **new EList().add**(e) is not well-typed if $e=$**new Object()**, while it has type $obj(\widehat{NEList}, [\widehat{el}:obj(\widehat{H}, [\,]), \widehat{next}:obj(\widehat{EList}, [\,])])$ if $e=$**new H()** (hence, the type associated with field **el** corresponds to an instance of H rather than P). This means that, during type analysis, parameters are associated with a structural type (even when they are annotated) which depends on the specific method invocation.

---

[11] Note that here H and P denotes concrete names and are not meta-variables.

Similarly, the type of *this* cannot be fixed (we cannot simply associate with it the class name where the method is declared, as done in Section 2), therefore *this* is treated as an implicit parameter which is always the first of the list. The only implicit constraint on *this* requires its associated type to be type compatible with the class where the method is declared. Consider for instance the following class declaration:

```
class C { val;  C(v){super();val=v;} get(){this.val} }
```

Method `get` generates the following clause:

$$has\_meth(\widehat{C}, \widehat{get}, [This], X) \leftarrow type\_comp(This, \widehat{C}), field\_acc(This, \widehat{val}, X).$$

The head of the clause requires method `get` of class C to have just the implicit parameter *this* (indeed, no explicit parameters are declared), whereas the body requires *this* to be an instance of either C or a subclass of C, and to have a field val of type X. Hence, if e has type $obj(\widehat{C}, [\widehat{val}{:}t])$, then the expression e.`get()` has type t.

A quite standard consequence of type inference [16,17,1,21] is that no rule is imposed on method overriding. Consider for instance the following two class declarations:

```
class P { P(){super();} m(){new A()} }
class H extends P { H(){super();} m(){new B()} }
```

In this very simple example method m of class P always returns an instance of A, but is overridden by the method of H which always returns an instance of B, where A and B are two unrelated classes. The definition of method m of class H would not be considered type safe in Java, if we assume to annotate methods m in P and in H with the return type A and B, respectively. Indeed, in Java the type of an instance of class H is a subtype of the type of an instance of class P.

In the type system defined here the structural type $obj(\widehat{H}, [\,])$ is not a subtype of $obj(\widehat{P}, [\,])$; indeed, an object type $obj(\widehat{c_1}, t_1)$ is a subtype of $obj(\widehat{c_2}, t_2)$ if and only if $c_1 = c_2$ and t_1 is a record type which is a subtype of the record type t_2 (w.r.t. the usual width and depth subtyping relation, see Section 5.3 for the formal definition). In this way the two method declarations above are perfectly legal, and the method invocation e.`m()` has type $obj(\widehat{A}, [\,])$ if e has type $obj(\widehat{P}, [\,])$, $obj(\widehat{B}, [\,])$ if e has type $obj(\widehat{H}, [\,])$, and $obj(\widehat{A}, [\,]) \lor obj(\widehat{B}, [\,])$ if e has type $obj(\widehat{P}, [\,]) \lor obj(\widehat{H}, [\,])$.

3.4   Regular Types

Whereas in Section 2 types are just constants, here we take a coinductive approach by allowing types (and, hence, terms) to be infinite. This is essential to encode recursive types. Consider for instance the following class declarations:

```
class List extends Object {
    altList(i,x){
        if(i<=0) new EList()
        else new NEList(x,this.altList(i-1,x.succ()))
    }
}
```

```
class EList extends List {          class NEList extends List {
    EList() { super(); }                el; next;
                                        NEList(e,n) { super();
                                                      el=e;next=n;}
}                                   }
```

```
class A{                            class B{
    A(){super();}                       B(){super();}
    succ(){new B()}                     succ(){new A()}
}                                   }
```

The expression **new List().altlist(i,new A())** returns an empty list (an instance of **EList**) if $i \leq 0$, or, if $i > 0$, a non empty list (an instance of **NEList**) whose length is i and whose elements are alternating instances of class **A** and B (starting from an **A** instance). Similarly, **new List().altlist(i,new B())** returns an alternating list starting with a B instance.

The following two mutually recursive types t_A and t_B precisely describe **new List().altlist(i,new A())** and **new List().altlist(i,new B())**, respectively:

$$t_A = obj(\widehat{EList},[\,]) \vee obj(\widehat{NEList},[\widehat{el}:obj(\widehat{A},[\,]),\widehat{next}:t_B])$$
$$t_B = obj(\widehat{EList},[\,]) \vee obj(\widehat{NEList},[\widehat{el}:obj(\widehat{B},[\,]),\widehat{next}:t_A])$$

In fact, t_A and t_B correspond to regular infinite trees (see in the following). However, coinductive terms include also non regular trees[12] [19] (see Section 5.1).

4   An Idealized Type System: A Full Formalization

In Section 2 types are just constants, whereas here types can be infinite terms, therefore the coinductive version of the Herbrand universe and base needs to be considered. In the rest of the paper we will identify terms with trees.

The definition of tree which follows is quite standard [11,2]. A path p is a finite and possibly empty sequence of natural numbers. The empty path is denoted by ϵ, $p_1 \cdot p_2$ denotes the concatenation of p_1 and p_2, and $|p|$ denotes the length of p.

We first give a general definition of tree, parametric in the set S of nodes, and then instantiate it in the case of terms and idealized proof trees.

A tree t defined over a set S is a partial function from paths to S s.t. its domain (denoted by $dom(t)$) is prefix-closed, not empty, and verifies the following closure property: for all m, n and p, if $p \cdot n \in dom(t)$ and $m \leq n$ then $p \cdot m \in dom(t)$.

---

[12] That is, infinite trees which cannot be finitely represented.

If $p \in dom(t)$, then the subtree of t rooted at p is the tree t' defined by $dom(t') = \{p' \mid p \cdot p' \in dom(t)\}$, $t'(p') = t(p \cdot p')$; t' is said a *proper* subtree of t iff $p \neq \epsilon$.

A tree is regular (a.k.a. rational) if and only if it has a finite number of distinct subtrees.

A term is a tree t defined over the set of logical variables and function symbols, satisfying the following additional property: for all paths p in $dom(t)$ and for all natural numbers n, $p \cdot n \in dom(t)$ iff $t(p) = f/m$ (that is, $t(p)$ is a function symbol f of arity m), and $n < m$.

Note that, by definition, if $t(p) = X$, then $p \cdot n \notin dom(t)$ for all n; the same consideration applies for constants (hence, logical variables and constants can only be leaves).

Regular terms can be finitely represented by means of term unification problems [19], that is, systems of a finite number of equations [11,2] of the form $X = t$ (where t is a finite term which is not a variable). Note that Horn formulas are built over finite terms; infinite terms are only needed for defining coinductive Herbrand models.

The definition of coinductive Herbrand universe and base of a Horn formula Hf is a straightforward extension of the conventional definition of inductive Herbrand universe and base, where terms are defined as above.

A useful characterization of coinductive Herbrand models is based on the notion of *idealized proof tree* [19,18].

An idealized proof tree T (proof for short) for a Horn formula Hf is a tree defined over the coinductive Herbrand base of Hf, satisfying the following additional property: for all paths p in $dom(T)$, if $T(p) = A$, $m = \min\{n \mid p \cdot n \notin dom(T)\}$, and for all $n < m$ $T(p \cdot n) = A_n$, then $A \leftarrow A_0, \ldots, A_{m-1}$ is a ground instance of a clause of Hf.

A proof T for a Horn formula Hf is a proof of the atom A iff $T(\epsilon) = A$. It can be proved [19,18] that $\{ A \mid A$ ground, $\exists$ proof T for Hf of $A \}$ is the coinductive Herbrand model of Hf.

4.1 Encoding of Programs into Horn Formulas

The encoding of programs for the idealized type system is defined in Figure 5, whereas Figure 6 contains the set of clauses $Hf_{default}$ which are shared by all programs. For completeness, all rules and clauses have been included, even though some of them are the same as those defined in Figure 3 and Figure 4. Rules and clauses which are different are highlighted.

Soundness of the encoding is claimed in Section 5, where the system is extended with subtyping and subsumption.

For simplicity, as already done in Figure 4, in Figure 6 we have used some convenient abbreviation; besides $\neg dec\_field$ and $\neg dec\_meth$, inequality has been introduced for field names; however, since the set of all field names declared in a program is finite, $\neq$ could be trivially defined by conjunctions of facts, therefore all formulas could be turned into Horn clauses.

Before explaining some details, it is interesting pointing out the main differences with the encoding defined in Section 2.

$$(\textbf{prog}) \frac{\forall i = 1..n \ cd_i \rightsquigarrow Hf_i \qquad e \textbf{ in } \emptyset \rightsquigarrow (t \mid B_m)}{\overline{cd}^n \ e \rightsquigarrow} \\ (Hf_{default} \cup (\cup_{i=1..n} Hf_i) \mid B_{\overline{cd}^n})$$

$$(\text{field}) \frac{}{\tau \ f; \textbf{ in } c \rightsquigarrow} \\ dec\_field(\widehat{c}, \widehat{f}, \widehat{\tau}) \leftarrow true.$$

$$(\textbf{class}) \frac{\begin{array}{c} \forall i = 1..n \ fd_i \textbf{ in } c_1 \rightsquigarrow Cl_i \quad cn \textbf{ in } \overline{fd}^n \rightsquigarrow Cl \\ \forall j = 1..m \ md_j \textbf{ in } c_1 \rightsquigarrow Hf_j \quad Hf^{fds} = \cup_{i=1..n}\{Cl_i\} \quad Hf^{mds} = \cup_{j=1..m} Hf_j \end{array}}{\textbf{class } c_1 \textbf{ extends } c_2 \ \{ \ \overline{fd}^n \ cn \ \overline{md}^m \ \} \rightsquigarrow \left\{ \begin{array}{l} class(\widehat{c_1}) \leftarrow true. \\ extends(\widehat{c_1}, \widehat{c_2}) \leftarrow true. \end{array} \right\} \cup} \\ Hf^{fds} \cup \{Cl\} \cup Hf^{mds}$$

$$(\textbf{constr-dec}) \frac{\forall i = 1..m \ e_i \textbf{ in } \{\overline{x}^n\} \rightsquigarrow (t_i \mid B_i) \quad \forall j = 1..k \ e'_j \textbf{ in } \{\overline{x}^n\} \rightsquigarrow (t'_j \mid B'_j)}{c(\overline{\tau \ x}^n) \ \{\textbf{super}(\overline{e}^m); \overline{f = e;}^k\} \textbf{ in } \overline{\tau' \ f;}^k \rightsquigarrow} \\ new(\widehat{c}, [\overline{\widehat{x}}^n], obj(\widehat{c}, \overline{(\widehat{f}:t'}^k \mid R))) \leftarrow type\_comp([\overline{\widehat{x}}^n], [\overline{\widehat{\tau}}^n]), \overline{B}^m, \\ extends(\widehat{c}, P), \\ new(P, [\overline{t}^m], obj(P, R)), \overline{B'}^k, \\ type\_comp([\overline{t'}^k], [\overline{\widehat{\tau'}}^k]).$$

$$(\textbf{meth-dec}) \frac{e \textbf{ in } \{This, \overline{x}^n\} \rightsquigarrow (t \mid B)}{\tau_0 \ m(\overline{\tau \ x}^n)\{e\} \textbf{ in } c \rightsquigarrow} \\ dec\_meth(\widehat{c}, \widehat{m}) \leftarrow true. \\ has\_meth(\widehat{c}, \widehat{m}, [This, \overline{x}^n], t) \leftarrow type\_comp(This, \widehat{c}), \\ type\_comp([\overline{x}^n], [\overline{\widehat{\tau}}^n]), \\ B, type\_comp(t, \widehat{\tau_0}).$$

$$(\text{new}) \frac{\forall i = 1..n \ e_i \textbf{ in } V \rightsquigarrow (t_i \mid B_i)}{\textbf{new } c(\overline{e}^n) \textbf{ in } V \rightsquigarrow (R \mid \overline{B}^n, new(\widehat{c}, [\overline{t}^n], R))} \quad R \text{ fresh}$$

$$(\textbf{var}) \frac{}{x \textbf{ in } V \rightsquigarrow (\widehat{x} \mid true)} \quad x \in V \qquad (\text{field-acc}) \frac{e \textbf{ in } V \rightsquigarrow (t \mid B)}{e.f \textbf{ in } V \rightsquigarrow} \quad R \text{ fresh} \\ (R \mid B, field\_acc(t, \widehat{f}, R))$$

$$(\text{invk}) \frac{\forall i = 0..n \ e_i \textbf{ in } V \rightsquigarrow (t_i \mid B_i)}{e_0.m(\overline{e}^n) \textbf{ in } V \rightsquigarrow (R \mid B_0, \overline{B}^n, invoke(t_0, \widehat{m}, [\overline{t}^n], R))} \quad R \text{ fresh}$$

$$(\text{if}) \frac{e \textbf{ in } V \rightsquigarrow (t \mid B) \quad e_1 \textbf{ in } V \rightsquigarrow (t_1 \mid B_1) \quad e_2 \textbf{ in } V \rightsquigarrow (t_2 \mid B_2)}{\textbf{if } (e) \ e_1 \textbf{ else } e_2 \textbf{ in } V \rightsquigarrow (R \mid B, B_1, B_2, cond(t, t_1, t_2, R))} \quad R \text{ fresh}$$

$$(\text{true}) \frac{}{\textbf{true in } V \rightsquigarrow (bool \mid true)} \qquad (\text{false}) \frac{}{\textbf{false in } V \rightsquigarrow (bool \mid true)}$$

Fig. 5. Encoding of programs for the idealized type system (rules with underlined name in bold are those different w.r.t. Figure 3)

Here only those methods which might be invoked during the execution of the main expression are required to be type safe, and no overriding rule is imposed.

These differences stem from the fact that the encoding of Section 2 corresponds to the specification of a typechecking algorithm (since programs are fully annotated with types), whereas here we are specifying a type inference algorithm which has to work with programs which may have no type annotations at all. Earlier error detection is sacrificed in favor of a more precise type analysis. This approach is not new, indeed it is followed by most of the proposed solutions to the problem of type inference of object-oriented programs [17,16,1,12].

More in details, these two main differences are reflected by the fact that in rule (prog) only the atoms B_m generated from the main expression are considered, and that in Figure 6 no *override* predicate is defined. Note that the type system could be easily made more restrictive, by adding to B_m in rule (prog) the atoms $B_{\overline{cd}^n}$ generated from $\overline{cd}^n$ as follows: all atoms contain distinct logical variables, and $has\_meth(\widehat{c}, \widehat{m}, A, R)$ is in $B_{\overline{cd}^n}$ iff class c is declared in $\overline{cd}^n$ and declares a method m. Then it would be possible to accept only programs s.t. the formula $B_m, B_{\overline{cd}^n}$ is satisfiable (for types different from the bottom). In this way, the type system would reject programs containing methods which are inherently type unsafe, even though unused. On the other hand, a method m which is not inherently type unsafe as m(x){x.foo()} would not be well-typed in a program where no class declares a method foo.

We only comments rules and clauses which are new or significantly different w.r.t. those given in Section 2.

The clause generated from rule (constr-dec) is very similar to that in Figure 3, except for the following two differences: (1) the type returned by *new* is the structured type $obj(\widehat{c}, [\overline{f{:}t'}^k \mid R])$ where the types $\overline{t'}^k$ of the fields $\overline{f}^k$ declared in the class are determined by the initializing expressions $\overline{e'}^k$, whereas R is the record assigning types to the inherited fields, which is derived from the type $obj(P, R)$ returned by the invocation of the constructor of the direct superclass; (2) n logical variables $\overline{x}^n$ need to be explicitly introduced since such variables are used for passing the actual types each time the constructor is invoked. This difference is reflected in the environment V used in the judgments for expressions which simply contains the parameters, but no associated types (see also the rule (var)). Finally, since type annotations can be empty, we have to define $\widehat{\epsilon}$; because $type\_comp(t, \widehat{\epsilon})$ must be always true (no additional constraint is imposed), for simplicity we adopt the convention that $\widehat{\epsilon}$ always generates a fresh variable.

In rule (meth-dec) the main differences w.r.t. Figure 3 (except for those already mentioned for (constr-dec)) are that *this* has to be dealt as an implicit parameter (the first of the list) of the method, and that no rule on overriding[13] is imposed. Predicate *dec_meth* has only two arguments since the types of arguments and of the returned value are no longer needed.[14]

---

[13] Ignoring the overriding rule is safe, as explained at the end of Section 3.3.

[14] The corresponding predicate in Figure 4 has four arguments for properly defining predicate *override*.

$class(object) \leftarrow true.$

$subclass(X, X) \leftarrow class(X).$

$subclass(X, object) \leftarrow class(X).$

$subclass(X, Y) \leftarrow extends(X, Z), subclass(Z, Y).$

$type\_comp(bool, bool) \leftarrow true.$

$type\_comp([\,], [\,]) \leftarrow true.$

$type\_comp([T1|L1], [T2|L2]) \leftarrow type\_comp(T1, T2), type\_comp(L1, L2).$

$*type\_comp(obj(C1, X), C2) \leftarrow subclass(C1, C2).$

$*type\_comp(T1 \vee T2, C) \leftarrow type\_comp(T1, C), type\_comp(T2, C).$

$*field\_acc(obj(C, R), F, T) \leftarrow has\_field(C, F, TA), field(R, F, T), type\_comp(T, TA).$

$*field\_acc(T1 \vee T2, F, FT1 \vee FT2) \leftarrow field\_acc(T1, F, FT1), field\_acc(T1, F, FT1).$

$*field([F{:}T|R], F, T) \leftarrow true.$

$*field([F1{:}T1|R], F2, T) \leftarrow field(R, F2, T), F1 \neq F2.$

$*invoke(obj(C, S), M, A, R) \leftarrow has\_meth(C, M, [obj(C, S)|A], R).$

$*invoke(T1 \vee T2, M, A, R1 \vee R2) \leftarrow invoke(T1, M, A, R1), invoke(T2, M, A, R2).$

$*new(object, [\,], obj(object, [\,])) \leftarrow true.$

$has\_field(C, F, T) \leftarrow dec\_field(C, F, T).$

$has\_field(C, F, T1) \leftarrow extends(C, P), has\_field(P, F, T1), \neg dec\_field(C, F, T2).$

$*has\_meth(C, M, A, R) \leftarrow extends(C, P), has\_meth(P, M, A, R), \neg dec\_meth(C, M).$

$*cond(T1, T2, T3, T2 \vee T3) \leftarrow type\_comp(T1, bool).$

Fig. 6. Definition of $Hf_{default}$ for the idealized type system (clauses marked with an asterisk are those different w.r.t. Figure 4)

For what concerns Figure 6, new clauses have been introduced to deal with union types: invoking a method M with arguments of type A on an object of type $T_1 \vee T_2$ is correct if the same method with the same argument type can be invoked on type T_1 and on type T_2, and the resulting type is the union of the two obtained types R_1 and R_2. Note that conditional expressions can be typed in a more precise way with the union of the types of the two branches.

In the first clause of predicate *field_acc*, after retrieving the type of the field from the record part of the type of the object (a new predicate *field* has been introduced), it is checked that such a type is compatible with the type annotation associated with the field declaration. This check can be useful for analyzing open expressions (for closed expressions the check is redundant since is already done at creation time).

5   Extending the System with Subtyping

In this section we extend the idealized type system presented in Section 3 and Section 4 with subtyping and subsumption; rather than increasing the expressive power of the system, subtyping and subsumption allow sound (but not complete) implementation of the system, by supporting approximation of infinite non regular types and proof trees with regular ones.

5.1   Non Regular Types

Non regular (hence infinite) types may be inferred for quite simple expressions. For instance, assume to add to class `List` the following method declaration:

```
balList(i){
    if(i<=0) new EList()
    else new NEList(new A(),
                    this.balList(i-1).addLast(new B())))
}
```

where the obvious declarations of methods `addLast` in classes `EList` and `NEList` have been omitted. Method `balList` generates all linked lists of the form $a^i b^i$ (where $i \geq 0$, and a and b denote the instances of class `A` and `B`, respectively). It is well known that the language $\{a^i b^i \mid i \geq 0\}$ is not regular; indeed, the most precise type of **new** `List()`.`balList`(i) is the non regular term t_0 defined by the following system containing a countably infinite number of equations:

$$t_n = t_n^B \vee obj(\widehat{NEList}, [\widehat{el}{:}obj(\widehat{A}, [\,]), \widehat{next}{:}t_{n+1}])$$
$$t_0^B = obj(\widehat{EList}, [\,])$$
$$t_{n+1}^B = obj(\widehat{NEList}, [\widehat{el}{:}obj(\widehat{B}, [\,]), \widehat{next}{:}t_n^B])$$

Of course, type t_0 can be inferred with a non regular proof (see Section 5.2), while a type inference algorithm would only be able to infer a regular type,[15] like the following:

$$t = obj(\widehat{EList}, [\,]) \vee obj(\widehat{NEList}, [\widehat{el}{:}obj(\widehat{A}, [\,]) \vee obj(\widehat{B}, [\,]), \widehat{next}{:}t])$$

To infer t subtyping and subsumption have to be introduced in the type system; indeed, as explained in Section 5.3, t_0 is a subtype of t.

5.2   Non Regular Proofs

Consider the following method declaration added to class `List`:

```
duplicate(i,e,l) {
    if(i<=0) l else this.duplicate(i-1,e,new NEList(e,l)) }
```

Method `duplicate` adds n (with $n = \max(0,i)$) duplicates of the element `e` at the beginning of the list `l`.

Let us consider the expression **new** `List()`.`duplicate`(i,e,l), where i, e and l are expressions of type int, t_e, and t_l, respectively. In our system it is possible to prove that the expression has the type t_0 defined by the following infinite set of equations (where n ranges over the natural numbers):

$$t_n = t_n' \vee t_{n+1} \qquad t_0' = t_l \qquad t_{n+1}' = obj(\widehat{NEList}, [\widehat{el}{:}t_e, \widehat{next}{:}t_n'])$$

---

[15] Indeed, it can be shown that there exist infinitely many regular types which can approximate t_0 with an arbitrary precision.

Indeed, a non regular proof can be built containing the following atoms:

$$invoke(obj(\widehat{List},[\,]), \widehat{duplicate}, [int, t_e, t_0'], t_0)$$
$$invoke(obj(\widehat{List},[\,]), \widehat{duplicate}, [int, t_e, t_1'], t_1)$$
$$\cdots$$
$$invoke(obj(\widehat{List},[\,]), \widehat{duplicate}, [int, t_e, t_n'], t_n)$$
$$\cdots$$

Intuitively, each atom corresponds to a recursive call of the infinite sequence (starting from the top) which is generated when the value of i tends to $+\infty$.

However, type t_0 is provably equivalent (see Section 5.3) to the following regular type:

$$t = t_l \vee obj(\widehat{NEList}, [\widehat{el{:}t_e}, \widehat{next{:}t}])$$

But type t can be inferred with a regular proof only with subsumption. To see that, we first prove that the atom

$$(1)\quad invoke(obj(\widehat{List},[\,]), \widehat{duplicate}, [int, t_e, t], t)$$

holds. This derives from the fact that t and $t \vee t$ are equivalent and that

$$(2)\quad invoke(obj(\widehat{List},[\,]), \widehat{duplicate}, [int, t_e, obj(\widehat{NEList}, [\widehat{el{:}t_e}, \widehat{next{:}t}])], t)$$

holds. But $obj(\widehat{NEList}, [\widehat{el{:}t_e}, \widehat{next{:}t}])$ is a subtype (see Section 5.3) of t, hence, by subsumption[16], (2) holds if (1) holds, and we conclude by coinductive hypothesis. Finally, from (1) we have that $invoke(obj(\widehat{List},[\,]), \widehat{duplicate}, [int, t_e, t_l], t)$ holds by subsumption, since t_l is a subtype of t.

5.3   Formal Definitions

Subtyping is coinductively defined by the following rules, where, for simplicity, we assume that field names in object types are distinct:

$$(\text{bool})\frac{}{bool \leq bool} \qquad (\text{obj})\frac{\forall i = 1..m \; f_{\pi(i)} = f_i \quad t_{\pi(i)} \leq t_i'}{obj(c, [\overline{f{:}t}^n]) \leq obj(c, [\overline{f'{:}t'}^m])} \; \pi{:}\{1..m\}{\rightarrow}\{1..n\}$$

$$(\vee\text{R1})\frac{t \leq t_1}{t \leq t_1 \vee t_2} \quad (\vee\text{R2})\frac{t \leq t_2}{t \leq t_1 \vee t_2} \quad (\vee\text{L})\frac{t_1 \leq t \quad t_2 \leq t}{t_1 \vee t_2 \leq t} \quad (\text{tuple})\frac{\forall i = 1..n \quad t_i \leq t_i'}{[\overline{t}^n] \leq [\overline{t'}^n]}$$

$$(\text{distr})\frac{obj(c, [\overline{f{:}t}^n, f{:}t_f, \overline{f'{:}t'}^m]) \leq t \quad obj(c, [\overline{f{:}t}^n, f{:}t_f', \overline{f'{:}t'}^m]) \leq t}{obj(c, [\overline{f{:}t}^n, f{:}t_f \vee t_f', \overline{f'{:}t'}^m]) \leq t}$$

---

[16] We are applying the counter-variant rule which says that if a method invocation has a type, then it has the same type for any invocation where an argument of type t_a has been replaced with a new argument of a subtype of t_a.

Rule (obj) uses standard width and depth record subtyping, but is invariant w.r.t. the class of the object. Since all field names are assumed to be distinct, in rule (obj) π must necessarily be injective and, therefore, $n \geq m$.

Rule ($\vee$R1), ($\vee$R2) and ($\vee$L) are standard. Rule (distr) ensures that object types "distributes over" union; by (distr), ($\vee$R1), ($\vee$R2) and (obj) we prove that $obj(c, [f{:}t_1 \vee t_2]) \leq obj(c, [f{:}t_1]) \vee obj(c, [f{:}t_2])$, whereas by ($\vee$L), ($\vee$R1), ($\vee$R2) and (obj) we prove that $obj(c, [f{:}t_1]) \vee obj(c, [f{:}t_2]) \leq obj(c, [f{:}t_1 \vee t_2])$.

To avoid unsound subtyping we require some *contractiveness* conditions [9,10] on meta-proofs[17].

A type t is *contractive* iff there is no countably infinite sequence of natural numbers s for which there exists n s.t. for all finite prefix p of s, with $|p| \geq n$, $p \in dom(t)$, and $t(p) = \vee/2$. For instance, the regular type defined by the equation $t = t \vee t$ is not contractive; t is in fact the bottom type, denoted by $\perp$, that is, the least type satisfying $t = t \vee t$.

A particular care must be taken when proving subtyping between non contractive types; for instance, by coinductively applying rule ($\vee$R1) or ($\vee$R2) we can obtain $t \leq \perp$ for every t, which is clearly unsound. A similar issue arises with rule (distr). Instead of the more drastic solution of prohibiting the instantiation of rules ($\vee$R1), ($\vee$R2) and (distr) with non contractive types, we prefer to require meta-proofs to be contractive.

A meta-proof for $t_1 \leq t_2$ is *contractive* if it does not contain an infinite subtree which is obtained by instantiating only rules ($\vee$R1), ($\vee$R2) and (distr).

Finally, we say that $t_1 \leq t_2$ holds if there exists a (coinductive) contractive meta-proof for $t_1 \leq t_2$ built with the subtyping rules defined above.

We define on top of subtyping a notion of *subsumption* between atoms. To do this, we first need to annotate each predicate of arity n with a string α of length n (where $\alpha(i)$ denotes the annotation of the i-th argument), specifying whether arguments are covariant ($\leq$), contravariant ($\geq$) or invariant ($=$). For instance, we write $p/{\leq}{\geq}{=}$ to mean that predicate p has 3 arguments, and that the first is covariant, the second contravariant and the last invariant.

If p/α, then the ground atom $p(\overline{t}^n)$ *subsumes* the ground atom $p(\overline{t'}^n)$ iff for all $i = 1..n$ the relation $t_i \, \alpha(i) \, t_i'$ holds, where $t \geq t'$ holds iff $t' \leq t$ holds, and $t = t'$ holds iff t and t' are syntactically equal.

Let us consider the *invoke* predicate. Clearly it must be contravariant w.r.t. the arguments corresponding to the receiver and the arguments passed to the method, covariant w.r.t. the type of the returned value, and invariant w.r.t. the name of the method, therefore $invoke/{\geq}{=}{\geq}{\leq}$.

For instance, $invoke(obj(c_1, [\,]), m, [obj(c_3, [f_1{:}t_1, f_3{:}t_3])], obj(c_4, [\,]))$ is subsumed by $invoke(obj(c_1, [\,]) \vee obj(c_2, [\,]), m, [obj(c_3, [f_1{:}t_1])], obj(c_4, [f_2{:}t_2]))$.

The annotations for the other predicates encoding expressions are the following: $new/{=}{\geq}{\leq}$, $field\_acc/{\geq}{=}{\leq}$, $cond/{\geq}{\geq}{\geq}{\leq}$. All the remaining predicates can be invariant in all arguments.

---

[17] We use the term meta-proof since $t_1 \leq t_2$ does not belong to the coinductive Herbrand base of the Horn formula under consideration. Note that $\leq$ cannot be easily encoded as a predicate, because of the contractiveness conditions.

The immediate consequence operator T_{Hf} as defined in Section 2 can be now refined with the notion of subsumption:

$$T_{Hf}(S) = \{A' \mid A \leftarrow B \text{ is a ground instance of a clause of } Hf$$
$$A \text{ subsumes } A' \text{ and } B \in S\}.$$

The definition of idealized proof tree can be easily refined in a similar way.

5.4 Soundness of the System

Soundness follows by progress and subject reduction theorems below; the former states that a well-typed program cannot get stuck, the latter states that if a well-typed program reduces, then it reduces to a well-typed program. The proofs of these two theorems come directly from the main lemmas in Appendix B.

Theorem 1 (Progress). *If cds e $\leadsto$ (Hf, B) and B is satisfiable in Hf, then either e is a value or e $\rightarrow_{cds}$ e′ for some e′.*

Theorem 2 (Subject reduction). *If cds e $\leadsto$ (Hf, B), B is satisfiable in Hf, and e $\rightarrow_{cds}$ e′, then cds e′ $\leadsto$ $(Hf, B′)$, and B′ is satisfiable in Hf.*

We say that *cds e* is a normal form iff there exists no *e′* s.t. $(cds\ e) \rightarrow (cds\ e′)$. Soundness ensures that reduction of well-typed programs never gets stuck.

Theorem 3 (Soundness). *If cds e $\leadsto$ (Hf, B), B is satisfiable in Hf, $(cds\ e) \rightarrow^* (cds\ e′)$, and cds e′ is a normal form, then e′ is a value.*

Proof. By induction on the number n of reduction steps. The claim for $n = 0$ holds by progress. If $n > 0$, then there exists e'' s.t. $(cds\ e) \rightarrow (cds\ e'')$, and $(cds\ e'') \rightarrow^* (cds\ e′)$ in $n - 1$ steps. By subject reduction we have that *cds e″* $\leadsto$ $(Hf, B′)$ and $B′$ is satisfiable in Hf, therefore we can conclude by inductive hypothesis. $\qquad\square$

6 Conclusion and Further Developments

We have shown how type systems can be specified by encoding programs into Horn formulas and by considering their coinductive Herbrand models [19,18]. The encoding was made possible thanks to the notion of type constraint for principal typing of Java-like languages [7,4].

Coinduction arises naturally at two different levels: at the level of terms, since recursive types are infinite terms, and at the level of proofs, since recursive methods and the use of infinite types require proofs to be infinite as well.

The approach has been used for fully formalizing two quite different type systems, for the same language (the only syntactical difference being the possibility of omitting type annotations). The definitions of the two type systems are reasonably compact, and modular: despite the two systems are quite different, only

3 rules out of 12 have to be changed, while almost half of the clauses shared by all programs could be reused.

The idealized type system provides theoretical limit to type inference of object-oriented programs, since only sound approximations of the system can be implemented. From the soundness of the type system can be directly derived the type safety of any type inference algorithm which is proved to be sound w.r.t. the system.

The idealized type system has also shown how simple type annotations can be used without compromising the precision of type analysis, thus integrating smoothly the two different notions of nominal and structural type.

Finally, the followed approach allows quite naturally typing of open expressions and general queries on the program, as $has\_meth(C, m, [int], T)$ asking for all classes C and return type T of method m with exactly one argument of type int. However, because of the limitations of the logic, very simple properties can be proved independently of any program.

One of the most interesting and challenging issue left open in this paper concerns the implementation of reasonable approximations of the idealized type system. We have just started investigating possible solutions to this problem, by exploiting recent results on the operational semantics of coinductive logic programming [19,18]. We have developed a prototype[18] supporting a partial implementation of the idealized type system, based on a Prolog meta-interpreter for coinductive logic programs, which still needs to be integrated with the notions of subtyping and subsumption. Since regular types are fully supported as solutions to term unification problems interesting examples can be typed (as the one shown in Section 3.4), even without subsumption.

References

1. Agesen, O.: The cartesian product algorithm. In: Olthoff, W. (ed.) ECOOP 1995. LNCS, vol. 952, pp. 2–26. Springer, Heidelberg (1995)
2. Amadio, R., Cardelli, L.: Subtyping recursive types. ACM Transactions on Programming Languages and Systems 15(4) (1993)
3. Ancona, D., Ancona, M., Cuni, A., Matsakis, N.: RPython: a Step Towards Reconciling Dynamically and Statically Typed OO Languages. In: OOPSLA 2007 Proceedings and Companion, DLS 2007: Proceedings of the 2007 Symposium on Dynamic Languages. ACM Press, New York (2007)
4. Ancona, D., Damiani, F., Drossopoulou, S., Zucca, E.: Polymorphic bytecode: Compositional compilation for Java-like languages. In: ACM Symp. on Principles of Programming Languages 2005. ACM Press, New York (2005)
5. Ancona, D., Lagorio, G., Zucca, E.: True separate compilation of Java classes. In: PPDP 2002 - Principles and Practice of Declarative Programming. ACM Press, New York (2002)
6. Ancona, D., Lagorio, G., Zucca, E.: Type inference for polymorphic methods in Java-like languages. In: Italiano, G.F., Moggi, E., Laura, L. (eds.) ICTCS 2007 - 10th Italian Conf. on Theoretical Computer Science 2003, eProceedings. World Scientific, Singapore (2007)

---

[18] Available at http://www.disi.unige.it/person/LagorioG/J2P

7. Ancona, D., Zucca, E.: Principal typings for Java-like languages. In: ACM Symp. on Principles of Programming Languages 2004. ACM Press, New York (2004)
8. Barbanera, F., Dezani-Cincaglini, M., de'Liguoro, U.: Intersection and union types: Syntax and semantics. Information and Computation 119(2) (1995)
9. Brandt, M., Henglein, F.: Coinductive axiomatization of recursive type equality and subtyping. In: de Groote, P., Hindley, J.R. (eds.) TLCA 1997. LNCS, vol. 1210. Springer, Heidelberg (1997)
10. Brandt, M., Henglein, F.: Coinductive axiomatization of recursive type equality and subtyping. Fundam. Inform. 33(4) (1998)
11. Courcelle, B.: Fundamental properties of infinite trees. Theoretical Computer Science 25 (1983)
12. Furr, M., An, J., Foster, J.S., Hicks, M.: Static type inference for Ruby. In: SAC 2009 - 24th ACM Symp. on Applied Computing (2009)
13. Igarashi, A., Nagira, H.: Union types for object-oriented programming. Journ. of Object Technology 6(2) (2007)
14. Igarashi, A., Pierce, B.C., Wadler, P.: Featherweight Java: a minimal core calculus for Java and GJ. ACM Transactions on Programming Languages and Systems 23(3) (2001)
15. Lagorio, G., Zucca, E.: Just: safe unknown types in java-like languages. Journ. of Object Technology, 6(2) (February 2007); Special issue: OOPS track at SAC (2006)
16. Oxhøj, N., Palsberg, J., Schwartzbach, M.I.: Making type inference practical. In: Lehrmann Madsen, O. (ed.) ECOOP 1992. LNCS, vol. 615, pp. 329–349. Springer, Heidelberg (1992)
17. Palsberg, J., Schwartzbach, M.I.: Object-oriented type inference. In: ACM Symp. on Object-Oriented Programming: Systems, Languages and Applications 1991 (1991)
18. Simon, L., Bansal, A., Mallya, A., Gupta, G.: Co-logic programming: Extending logic programming with coinduction. In: Arge, L., Cachin, C., Jurdziński, T., Tarlecki, A. (eds.) ICALP 2007. LNCS, vol. 4596, pp. 472–483. Springer, Heidelberg (2007)
19. Simon, L., Mallya, A., Bansal, A., Gupta, G.: Coinductive logic programming. In: Etalle, S., Truszczyński, M. (eds.) ICLP 2006. LNCS, vol. 4079, pp. 330–345. Springer, Heidelberg (2006)
20. Wang, T., Smith, S.: Polymorphic constraint-based type inference for objects. Technical report, The Johns Hopkins University (2008) (submitted for publication)
21. Wang, T., Smith, S.F.: Precise constraint-based type inference for java. In: Knudsen, J.L. (ed.) ECOOP 2001. LNCS, vol. 2072, p. 99. Springer, Heidelberg (2001)

A   Auxiliary Functions

$$(\text{mbody-1}) \frac{\text{class } c \text{ extends } c' \{ \ldots \tau_0 \ m(\overline{\tau \ x}^n)\{e\} \ldots \} \in cds}{mbody(cds, c, m) = (\overline{x}^n, e)}$$

$$(\text{mbody-2}) \frac{\text{class } c \text{ extends } c' \{ \ldots mds \} \in cds \qquad m \notin mds}{\dfrac{mbody(cds, c', m) = (\overline{x}^n, e)}{mbody(cds, c, m) = (\overline{x}^n, e)}}$$

$$(\text{cbody}) \frac{\text{class } c \text{ extends } c' \{ \ldots c(\overline{\tau \ x}^n) \ \{\text{super}(\overline{e}^m); \overline{f = e'};^k\} \ldots \} \in cds}{cbody(cds, c) = (\overline{x}^n, \{\text{super}(\overline{e}^m); \overline{f = e'};^k\})}$$

Fig. 7. Auxiliary functions

B   Lemmas and Main Theorems of Section 5 (Some Proofs Are Sketched)

Progress. To prove progress we need the following lemmas.

Lemma 1. *If* $\mathcal{C}[e]$ *in* $V \rightsquigarrow (t \mid B)$, *then* e *in* $V \rightsquigarrow (t' \mid B')$, *with* $B' \subseteq B$.

Proof. By case analysis on the contexts and by induction on their structure. $\square$

Lemma 2. *If* $cds \rightsquigarrow Hf$, *and* $invoke(\widehat{c}, \widehat{m}, [t_1, \ldots, t_n], t)$ *is satisfiable in* Hf, *then* $mbody(cds, c, m) = (\overline{x}^n, e)$ *for some variables* $\overline{x}^n$ *and expression* e.

Proof. By induction on the height of the inheritance tree. Note that by assumption (see Figure 1) inheritance cannot be cyclic. $\square$

Theorem 1 [Progress] If $cds \ e \rightsquigarrow (Hf, B)$ and B is satisfiable in Hf, then either e is a value or $e \rightarrow_{cds} e'$ for some e'.

Subject reduction. The following lemma strongly relies on the notion of subtyping and subsumption as defined in Section 5.

Lemma 3. *If* $cds \rightsquigarrow Hf$, e *in* $V \rightsquigarrow (t \mid B)$, $B\theta \subseteq M^{co}(Hf)$, *and* $e \rightarrow_{cds} e'$, *then there exist* t', B' *and* θ' *s.t.* e' *in* $V \rightsquigarrow (t' \mid B')$, $B'\theta' \subseteq M^{co}(Hf)$, *and* $t'\theta' \le t\theta$.

Theorem 2 [Subject reduction] If $cds \ e \rightsquigarrow (Hf, B)$, B is satisfiable in Hf, and $e \rightarrow_{cds} e'$, then $cds \ e' \rightsquigarrow (Hf, B')$, and B' is satisfiable in Hf.

Proof. A corollary of lemma 3. $\square$

Checking Framework Interactions with Relationships

Ciera Jaspan and Jonathan Aldrich

Institute for Software Research,
Carnegie Mellon University,
Pittsburgh PA 15213, USA
ciera@cmu.edu, jonathan.aldrich@cs.cmu.edu

Abstract. Software frameworks impose constraints on how plugins may interact with them. Many of these constraints involve multiple objects, are temporal, and depend on runtime values. Additionally, they are difficult to specify because they are often extrinsic and may break behavioral subtyping. This work introduces *relationships* as an abstraction for specifying framework constraints in FUSION (Framework Usage SpecificatIONs), and it presents a formal description and implementation of a static analysis to find constraint violations in plugin code. We define three variants of this analysis: one is sound, one is complete, and a pragmatic variant that balances these tradeoffs. We prove soundness and completeness for the appropriate variants, and we show that the pragmatic variant can effectively check constraints from real-world programs.

1 Introduction

Object-oriented frameworks have brought many benefits to software development, including reusable codebases, extensible systems, and encapsulation of quality attributes. However, frameworks are used at a high cost; they are complex and difficult to learn [1]. This is partially due to the complexity of the semantic constraints they place on the *plugins* that utilize them.

As an example, consider a constraint in the ASP.NET web application framework. The ASP.NET framework allows developers to create web pages with user interface controls on them. These controls can be manipulated programatically through callbacks provided by the framework. A developer can write code that responds to control events, adds and removes controls, and changes the state of controls.

One task that a developer might want to perform is to programmatically change the selection of a drop down list. The ASP.NET framework provides the relevant pieces, as shown in Fig. 1[1]. Notice that if the developer wants to change the selection of a `DropDownList` (or any other derived `ListControl`), she has to access the individual `ListItems` through the `ListItemCollection` and change the selection using `setSelected`. Based on this information, she might naïvely change the selection as shown in List. 1. Her expectation is that the framework will see that she has selected a new item and will change the selection accordingly.

---

[1] As the implementation of FUSION runs on Java, we translated the examples to Java syntax.

S. Drossopoulou (Ed.): ECOOP 2009, LNCS 5653, pp. 27–51, 2009.

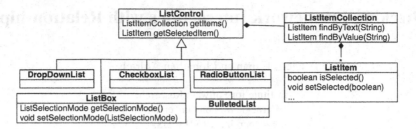

Fig. 1. ASP.NET ListControl Class Diagram

List. 1. Incorrect selection for a DropDownList

```
1   DropDownList list;
2
3   private void Page_Load(object sender, EventArgs e) {
4     ListItem newSel;
5     newSel = list.getItems().findByValue("foo");
6     newSel.setSelected(true);
7   }
```

When the developer runs this code, she will get the error shown in Fig. 2. The error message clearly describes the problem; a `DropDownList` had more than one item selected. This error is due to the fact that the developer did not de-select the previously selected item, and, by design, the framework does not do this automatically. While an experienced developer will realize that this was the problem, an inexperienced developer might be confused because she did not select multiple items.

The stack trace in Fig. 2 is even more interesting because it does not point to the code where the developer made the selection. In fact, the entire stack trace is from framework code; there is no plugin code referenced at all! At runtime, the framework called the plugin developer's code in List. 1, this code ran and returned to the framework, and then the framework discovered the error. To make matters worse, the program control could go back and forth several times before finally reaching the check that triggered the exception. Since the developer doesn't know exactly where the problem occurred, or even what object it occurred on, she must search her code by hand to find the erroneous selection.

The correct code for this task is in List. 2. In this code snippet, the developer de-selects the currently selected item before selecting a new item.

```
Cannot have multiple items selected in a DropDownList.
Stack Trace:

[HttpException (0x80004005): Cannot have multiple items selected in a DropDownList.]
   System.Web.UI.WebControls.DropDownList.VerifyMultiSelect() +133
   System.Web.UI.WebControls.ListControl.RenderContents(HtmlTextWriter writer) +206
   System.Web.UI.WebControls.WebControl.Render(HtmlTextWriter writer) +43
   System.Web.UI.Control.RenderControlInternal(HtmlTextWriter writer, ControlAdapter adapter) +74
   System.Web.UI.Control.RenderControl(HtmlTextWriter writer, ControlAdapter adapter) +291
```

Fig. 2. Error with partial stack trace from ASP.NET

List. 2. Correctly selecting an item using the ASP.NET API

```
1  DropDownList list;
2
3  private void Page_Load(object sender, EventArgs e) {
4    ListItem newSel, oldSel;
5    oldSel = list.getSelectedItem();
6    oldSel.setSelected(false);
7    newSel = list.getItems().findByValue("foo");
8    newSel.setSelected(true);
9  }
```

List. 3. Selecting on the wrong DropDownList

```
1  DropDownList listA, listB;
2
3  private void Page_Load(object sender, EventArgs e) {
4    ListItem newSel, oldSel;
5    oldSel = listA.getSelectedItem();
6    oldSel.setSelected(false);
7    newSel = listB.getItems().findByValue("foo");
8    newSel.setSelected(true);
9  }
```

This example, and many others we have found on the ASP.NET developer forum, shows three interesting properties of framework constraints.

Framework constraints involve multiple classes and objects. List. 2 requires four objects to make the proper selection. The framework code that the plugin used was located in four classes.

Framework constraints are often extrinsic. While the DropDownList was the class that checked the constraint (as seen by the stack trace), the constraint itself was on the methods of ListItem. However, the ListItem class is not aware of the DropDown-List class or even that it is within a ListControl at all, and therefore it should not be responsible for enforcing the constraint. Compare the extrinsic nature of these constraints to the intrinsic nature of a class invariant. In addition to being difficult to check, it is more difficult to document an extrinsic constraint as it is unclear where the documentation should go so that the plugin developer will naturally discover it.

Framework constraints have semantic properties. Framework constraints are not only about structural concerns such as method naming conventions or types; the developer must also be aware of semantic properties of the constraint. There are at least three semantic properties shown by the DropDownList example. First, the plugin developer had to know which objects she was using to avoid the problem in List. 3. In this example, the developer called the correct operations, but on the wrong objects. She also had to notice which primitive values (such as true or false) she used in the calls to change the selection. Finally, she had to be aware of the ordering of the operations. In List. 2, had she swapped lines 5 and 6 with lines 7 and 8, she would have caused unexpected runtime behavior where the selection change does not occur. This behavior occurs because `getSelectedItem` returns the first selected `ListItem` that it finds in the `DropDownList`, and that may be the newly selected item rather than the old item.

In previous work [2], we proposed a preliminary specification approach and sketched a hypothetical analysis to discover semantic mismatches, such as the ones described above, between the plugin code and the declared constraints of the framework. The previous work primarily discussed the requirements for such a system and explored a prototype specification. In this paper, we make three contributions:

1. We show that the concept of framework developer-defined relations across objects captures an underlying programming model used to interact with frameworks. We use these relations to specify framework constraints FUSION (Framework Usage SpecificatIONs). (Sect. 2)
2. We propose (Sect. 3) and formally define (Sect. 4) a static analysis that detects violations of constraints in plugins. We define three variants of the FUSION analysis: a sound variant, a complete variant, and a third variant that is neither sound nor complete. We prove soundness and completeness for the appropriate variants, and we argue that the pragmatic variant is better for practical use. There are only minor differences between the variants, so it is simple to switch between them.
3. We implemented the pragmatic variant of the FUSION analysis and ran it on code based on examples from framework help forums. As the FUISION does not require the entire framework to be specified, framework developers will be able to add specifications as they answer questions on these forums. We show that FUSION captures the properties described and that the pragmatic variant can handle real-world code with relatively few false positives and false negatives. (Sect. 5)

2   Developer-Defined Relations over Objects

When a plugin developer programs to a framework, the primary task is not about creating new objects or data. In many cases, programming in this environment is about *manipulating the abstract associations between existing objects*. Every time the plugin receives a callback from the framework, it is implicitly notified of the current associations between objects. As the plugin calls framework methods, the framework changes these associations, and the plugin learns more about how the objects relate. Each method call, field access, or conditional test gives the plugin more information. For example, in List. 2, when the plugin made the call to `ListItemCollection.findItemByValue`, it learned about the association between the returned `ListItem` and the `DropDownList`. These may be direct associations within code, or they may represent an abstract association with no references in memory. Even when the plugin needs to create a new object, it is frequently done by calling abstract factory methods that set up the object and its relationships with other objects. Many frameworks, including ASP.NET, also use dependency injection, a mechanism in which the framework populates the fields of the plugin based on an external configuration file [3]. When using dependency injection, the plugin simply receives and manipulates pre-configured objects. In the `DropDownList` example, all the objects are provided by the framework

List. 4. The Child relation. Every relation must define `params`, `effect`, and `test`

```
1  @Relation({ListItem.class, ListControl.class})
2  public @interface Child {
3      String[] params();
4      Effect effect();
5      String test() default "";
6  }
```

through dependency injection, and the plugin simply changes their relationships with each other.

Since the primary mechanism of interaction is based on manipulating relationships between objects, we will model it formally using a mathematical relation. A *relation* is a named set of tuples on several types τ.[2] A *relationship* is a single tuple in a relation, represented as

$$name(\ell_1, \ldots, \ell_n)$$

where each ℓ is a static representation of a runtime object with the type defined by the relation.

In this section, we introduce FUSION and three specification constructs based on relationships. The first construct in FUSION, *relationship effects*, specify how framework operations change associations between objects. The second construct, *constraints*, uses relationships to specify extrinsic and semantic constraints across multiple objects. Finally, *relation inference rules* specify how relationships can be inferred based on the current state of other relationships, regardless of what operations are used.

2.1   Relationship Effects

Relationship effects specify changes to the relations that occur after calling a framework method. The framework developer annotates the framework methods with information about how the calling object, parameters, and return value are related (or not related) after a call to the method. These annotations describe additions and removals of relationships from a relation. For example, the annotation @Item({item, list}, ADD) creates an Item relationship between `item` and `list`, while @Item({item, list}, REMOVE) removes this relationship[3]. When a relationship is removed or added, we are simply marking whether or not its existence in the relation is known. Thereby, if a relationship is "removed", but there was no prior knowledge of whether it existed, it is marked as definitely not in the relation.

Relationship effects may refer to the parameters, the receiver object, and the return value of a method. They may also refer to primitive values. Additionally, parameters can be wild-carded, so @Item({*, list}, REMOVE) removes *all* the Item relationships between `list` and any other object.

---

[2] The relations shown in this paper are only unary and binary, but n-ary relations are supported.

[3] We are presenting a simplified version of the syntax for readability purposes. The correct Java syntax for the add annotation appears as @Item(params={"item", "list"}, effect=ADD). This is the syntax used in the implementation.

List. 5. Partial `ListControl` API with relationship effect annotations

```
1   public class ListControl {
2       @List({result, target}, ADD)
3       public ListItemCollection getItems();
4
5       //After this call we know two pieces of information. The returned item is selected and it is a child of this
6       @Child({result, target}, ADD)
7       @Selected({result}, ADD)
8       public ListItem getSelectedItem();
9   }
10  public class ListItem {
11      //If the return is true, then we know we have a selected item. If it is false, we know it was not selected.
12      @Selected({target}, TEST, return)
13      public boolean isSelected();
14
15      @Selected({target}, TEST, select)
16      public void setSelected(boolean select);
17
18      @Text({result, target}, ADD)
19      public String getText();
20
21      //When we call setText, remove any previous Text relationships, then add one for text
22      @Text({*, target}, REMOVE)
23      @Text({text, target}, ADD)
24      public void setText(String text);
25  }
26  public class ListItemCollection {
27      @Item({item, target}, REMOVE)
28      public void remove(ListItem item);
29
30      @Item({item, target}, ADD)
31      public void add(ListItem item);
32
33      @Item({item, target}, TEST, result)
34      public boolean contains(ListItem item);
35
36      @Item({result, target}, ADD)
37      @Text({text, result}, ADD)
38      public ListItem findByText(String text);
39
40      //if we had any items before this, remove them after this call
41      @Item({*, target}, REMOVE)
42      public void clear();
43  }
```

In addition to the ADD and REMOVE effects, a TEST effect uses a parameter to determine whether to add or remove a relationship. For example, we might annotate the method `List.contains(Object obj)` with @Item({obj, target}, TEST, result) to signify that this relationship is added when the return value is true and removed when the return value `result` is false.

As relations are user-defined, they have no predefined semantics. Any hierarchy or ownership present, such as Child or Item relations, is only inserted by the framework developer. In fact, relationships do not have to reflect *any* reference paths found in the heap, but may exist only as an abstraction to the developer. This allows relations to

List. 6. Comments showing how the relationship context changes after each instruction

```
1   DropDownList ddl = ...;
2   ListItemCollection coll;
3   ListItem newSel, oldSel;
4   oldSel = ddl.getSelectedItem();
5       //Child(oldSel, ddl), Selected(oldSel)
6   oldSel.setSelected(false);
7       //Child(oldSel, ddl), !Selected(oldSel)
8   coll = ddl.getItems();
9       //Child(oldSel, ddl), !Selected(oldSel), List(coll, ddl)
10  newSel = coll.findByText("foo");
11      //Child(oldSel, ddl), !Selected(oldSel), List(coll, ddl), Item(newSel, coll), Text("foo", newSel)
```

List. 7. DropDownList Selection Constraints and Inferred Relationships

```
1   @Constraint(
2       op="ListItem.setSelected(boolean select)",
3       trigger="select == false and Child(target, ctrl) and ctrl instanceof DropDownList",
4       requires="Selected(target)", effect={"!CorrectlySelected(ctrl)"})
5   @Constraint(
6       op="ListItem.setSelected(boolean select)",
7       trigger="select == true and Child(target, ctrl) and ctrl instanceof DropDownList",
8       requires="!CorrectlySelected(ctrl)", effect={"CorrectlySelected(ctrl)"})
9   @Constraint(
10      op="end—of—method",
11      trigger="ctrl instanceof DropDownList",
12      requires="CorrectlySelected(ctrl)", effect={})
13  @Infer(trigger="List(list, ctrl) and Item(item, list)", infer={"Child(item, ctrl)"})
14  public class DropDownList {...}
```

be treated as an abstraction independent from code. This is a common specification paradigm; relations have a similar purpose to model fields in JML specifications [4].

To define a new relation, the framework developer creates an annotation type and uses the meta-annotation @Relation to signify it as a relation over specific types. List. 4 shows a sample definition of the Child relation from the DropDownList example.

Once the framework developer defines the desired relations, they can be used as relationship effects, as shown in List. 5. These annotations allow tools to track relationships through the plugin code at compile time. List. 6 shows a snippet from a plugin, along with the current relationships after each instruction. For example, after line 4 in List. 6, we apply the effects declared in List. 5, lines 6-8. Therefore, at line 5, we learn the two new relationships shown. This information, the *relationship context*, provides us with an abstract, semantic context that each instruction resides in. In the next section, we use this context to check the semantic parts of framework constraints.

2.2   Constraints

Framework developers can specify *constraints* on framework operations in a propositional logic over relationships. They are written as class-level annotations, but as constraints are extrinsic, they can constrain the operations on any other class. As the three examples in List. 7 show, a constraint has four parts:

1. *operation*: This is a signature of an operation to be constrained, such as a method call, constructor call, or even a tag signaling the end of a method. Notice that these constraints may be defined in another class, as in the first constraint in List. 7. This makes constraints more expressible that a class or protocol invariant.
2. *trigger predicate*: This is a logical predicate over relationships. The plugin's relationship context must determine that this predicate holds for this constraint to be triggered. If not, the constraint is ignored. While *operation* provides a syntactic trigger for the constraint, *trigger* provides the semantic trigger. The combination of both a syntactic and semantic trigger allows constraints to be more flexible and expressible than many existing protocol-based solutions.
3. *requires predicate*: This is another logical predicate over relationships. If the constraint is triggered, then this predicate must be true under the current relationship context. If the requires predicate is not true, this is a broken constraint and the analysis should signal an error in the plugin.
4. *effect list*: This is a list of relationship effects. If the constraint is triggered, these effects will be applied in the same way as the relationship effects described earlier. They will be applied regardless of the state of the requires predicate.

In the first example at the top of List. 7, the constraint is checking that at every call to `ListItem.setSelected(boolean)`, if the relationship context shows that the argument is false, the receiver is a Child of a `ListControl`, and if that `ListControl` is a `DropDownList`, then it must also indicate that the `ListItem` is Selected. Additionally, the context will change so that the `DropDownList` is not CorrectlySelected. The second constraint is similar to the first and it enforces proper selection of `ListItems` in a `DropDownList`. The third constraint ensures that the plugin method does not end in an improper state by utilizing the "end-of-method" instruction to trigger when a plugin callback is about to end.

2.3   Inferred Relationships

In some cases, the relationships between objects are implicit. Consider the `ListItem-Collection` from the `DropDownList` example. The framework developer would like to state that items in this list are in a Child relation with the `ListControl` parent. However, it does not make sense to annotate the `ListItemCollection` class with this information since `ListItemCollections` should not know about `List-Controls`.

Inferred relationships describe these implicit relationships that can be assumed at any time. In List. 7, line 13 shows an example for inferring a Child relationship based on the relations Item and List. Whenever the relationship context can show that the "trigger" predicate is true, it can infer the relationship effects in the "infer" list. Inferred relationships allow the framework developer to specify relationship effects that would otherwise have to be placed on every location that the predicate is true; this would significantly drive up the cost of adding these specifications.

It is possible to produce inferred relationships that directly conflict with the relationship context. To prevent this, the semantics of inferred relationships is that they are ignored in the case of a conflict, that is, relationships from declared relationship effects and constraints have a higher precedence. The rationale behind this is that the constraints and relationship effects are explicitly declared, and this should be reflected by the giving them precedence. Additionally, the inferred relationships are only used on an as-needed basis; to generate all possible inferred relations would be expensive for the analysis. An alternative mechanism would be to signal an error, though it is not currently clear whether this will increase the number of false positives.

3   The FUSION Analysis

We have designed and implemented a static analysis to track relationships through plugin code and check plugin code against framework constraints. The FUSION analysis is a modular, branch-sensitive, forward dataflow analysis[4]. It is designed to work on a three address code representation of Java-like source. We assume that the analysis runs in a framework that provides all of these features. In this section, we will present the analysis data structures, the intuition behind the three variations of the analysis, and a discussion of their tradeoffs. Sect. 4 defines how the analysis runs on each instruction.

The FUSION analysis is dependent on several other analyses, including a boolean constant propagation analysis and an alias analysis. The FUSION analysis uses the constant propagation analysis for the TEST effect. For this purpose, the relation analysis assumes there is a function $\mathcal{B}$ to which it can pass a variable and learn whether the represented value is true, false, or unknown.

The FUSION analysis can use any alias analysis which implements a simple interface. First, it assumes there is a context $\mathcal{L}$ that given any variable x, provides a finite set $\bar{\ell}$ of abstract locations that the variable might point to. Second, it assumes a context Γ_ℓ which maps every location ℓ to a type τ. The combination of these two contexts, $< \Gamma_\ell, \mathcal{L} >$ is represented as the alias lattice $\mathcal{A}$. This lattice must conservatively abstract the heap, as defined by Def. 1.

Definition 1 (Abstraction of Alias Lattice). *Assume that a heap* h *is defined as a set of source variables* x *which point to a runtime location* ℓ *of type* τ. *Let* H *be all the possible heaps at a particular program point. An alias lattice* $< \Gamma_\ell, \mathcal{L} >$ *abstracts* H *at a program counter if and only if*

$\forall\, h \in H \,.\, \mathrm{dom}(h) = \mathrm{dom}(\mathcal{L})$ and
  $\forall\, (x_1 \hookrightarrow \ell_1 : \tau_1) \in h \,.\, \forall\, (x_2 \hookrightarrow \ell_2 : \tau_2) \in h \,.$
   (if $x_1 \neq x_2$ and $\ell_1 = \ell_2$ then
     $\exists\, \ell' \,.\, \ell' \in \mathcal{L}(x_1)$ and $\ell' \in \mathcal{L}(x_2)$ and $\tau_1 <: \Gamma_\ell(\ell'))$ and
   (if $x_1 \neq x_2$ and $\ell_1 \neq \ell_2$ then
     $\exists\, \ell_1', \ell_2' \,.\, \ell_1' \in \mathcal{L}(x_1)$ and $\ell_2' \in \mathcal{L}(x_2)$ and $\ell_1' \neq \ell_2'$ and $\tau_1 <: \Gamma_\ell(\ell_1')$ and $\tau_2 <: \Gamma_\ell(\ell_2'))$

This definition ensures that if two variables alias under any heap, then the alias lattice will reflect that by putting the same location ℓ' into each of their location lists. Likewise,

---

[4] By branch-sensitive, we mean that the true and false branches of a conditional may receive different lattice information depending upon the condition. This is not a path-sensitive analysis.

if the two variables are not aliased within a given heap, then the alias lattice will reflect this possibility as well by having a distinct location in each location set. The definition also ensures that the typing context Γ_ℓ has the most general type for a location.

If the alias analysis ensures Def. 1 and can provide the required interface, the variants of the FUSION analysis are provably sound or complete. Additionally, a more precise alias analysis will increase the precision of the FUSION analysis.

3.1 The Relation Lattice

We track the status of a relationship using the four-point dataflow lattice represented in Fig. 3, where unknown represents either true or false and bot is a special case used only inside the flow function. The FUSION analysis uses a tuple lattice which maps all relationships we want to track to a rela-tionship state lattice element. We will represent this tuple lattice as ρ. We will say that ρ is *consistent* with an alias lattice $\mathcal{A}$ when the domain of ρ is equal to the set of relationships that are possible under $\mathcal{A}$.

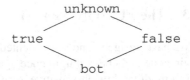

Fig. 3. The relationship state lattice

Notice that as more references enter the context, there are more possible relationships, and the height of ρ grows. Even so, the height is always finite as there is a finite number of locations and a finite number of relations. As the flow function is monotonic, the analysis always reaches a fix-point.

3.2 Flow Function

The analysis flow function is responsible for two tasks; it must check that a given operation is valid, and it must apply any specified relationship effects to the lattice. The flow function is defined as

$$f_{\mathcal{C};\mathcal{A};\mathcal{B}}(\rho, \text{instr}) = \rho'$$

where $\mathcal{C}$ is all the constraints, $\mathcal{A}$ is the alias lattice, $\mathcal{B}$ is the boolean constant lattice, ρ is the starting relation lattice, ρ' is the ending relation lattice, and instr is the instruction the analysis is currently checking. The analysis goes through each constraint in $\mathcal{C}$ and checks for a match. It first checks to see whether the operation defined by the constraint matches the instruction, thus representing a syntactic match. It also checks to see whether ρ determines that the trigger of the constraint applies. If so, it has both a syntactic and semantic match, and it binds the specification variables to the locations that triggered the match. These bindings will be used for the remaining steps.

Once the analysis has a match, two things must occur. First, it uses the bindings generated above to show that the requires predicate of the constraint is true under ρ. If it is not true, then the analysis reports an error on instr. Second, the analysis must use the same bindings to produce ρ' by applying the relationship effects.

3.3 Soundness and Completeness

Soundness and completeness allow the user of the analysis to either have confidence that there are no errors at runtime if the analysis finds none (if it is sound) or that any errors

Table 1. Differences between sound, complete, and pragmatic variants

Variant	Trigger Predicate checks when...	Requires Predicate passes when...
Sound	True or Unknown	True
Complete	True	True or Unknown
Pragmatic	True	True

the analysis finds will actually occur in some runtime scenario (if it is complete). For the purposes of these definitions, an error is a dynamic interpretation of the constraint which causes the requires predicate to fail. In the formal semantics, an error is signaled as a failure for the flow function to generate a new lattice for a particular instruction.

We define soundness and completeness of the FUSION analysis by assuming an alias analysis which abstracts the heap using $\mathcal{A}$, as described above. For both of these theorems, we let $\mathcal{A}^{conc}$ define the actual heap at some point of a real execution, and we let $\mathcal{A}^{abs}$ be a sound approximation of $\mathcal{A}^{conc}$. We also let ρ^{abs} and ρ^{conc} be relationship lattices consistent with $\mathcal{A}^{abs}$ and $\mathcal{A}^{conc}$ where ρ^{abs} is an abstraction of the concrete runtime lattice ρ^{conc}, defined as $\rho^{conc} \sqsubseteq \rho^{abs}$.

For the sound variant, we expect that if the flow function generates a new lattice using the imprecise lattice ρ^{abs}, then any more concrete lattice will also produce a new lattice for that instruction. As the flow function only generates a new lattice if it finds no errors, then there may be false positives from when ρ^{abs} produces errors, but there will be no false negatives. To be locally sound for this instruction, the new abstract lattice must conservatively approximate any new concrete lattice. Thm. 1 captures the intuition of local soundness formally. Global soundness follows from local soundness, the monotonicity of the flow function, and the initial conditions of the lattice.

Theorem 1 (Local Soundness of Relations Analysis).
> if $f_{C;\mathcal{A}^{abs};\mathcal{B}}(\rho^{abs}, instr) = \rho^{abs'}$ and $\rho^{conc} \sqsubseteq \rho^{abs}$
> then $f_{C;\mathcal{A}^{conc};\mathcal{B}}(\rho^{conc}, instr) = \rho^{conc'}$ and $\rho^{conc'} \sqsubseteq \rho^{abs'}$

If the FUSION analysis is complete, we expect a theorem which is the opposite of the soundness theorem and is shown in Thm. 2. If a flow function generates a new lattice given a lattice ρ^{conc}, then it will also generate a new lattice on any abstraction of ρ^{conc}. An analysis with this property may produce false negatives, as the analysis can find an error using the concrete lattice yet generate a new lattice using ρ^{abs}, but it will produce no false positives. Like the sound analysis, the resulting lattices must maintain their existing precision relationship.

Theorem 2 (Local Completeness of Relations Analysis).
> if $f_{C;\mathcal{A}^{conc};\mathcal{B}}(\rho^{conc}, instr) = \rho^{conc'}$ and $\rho^{conc} \sqsubseteq \rho^{abs}$
> then $f_{C;\mathcal{A}^{abs};\mathcal{B}}(\rho^{abs}, instr) = \rho^{abs'}$ and $\rho^{conc'} \sqsubseteq \rho^{abs'}$

The FUSION analysis can be either sound, complete, or pragmatic by making only minor changes to the analysis. Proofs of soundness and completeness, for the sound and complete variants respectively, can be found in our associated technical report [5]. The differences between the variants are summarized in Tab. 1 and are described below.

```
public class ListItemCollection {
    @Item({*, target}, REMOVE)
    public void clear() {...}
}
```

```
@Constraint(op = "ListItemCollection.clear()",
    trigger = "x instanceof ListItem",
    requires = "true",
    effect = {"!Item(x, target)"})
```

Fig. 4. Translating a relation effect with wildcards into a constraint. The Item relation has type `Item(ListItem, ListItemCollection)`.

Trigger condition. The trigger predicate determines when the constraint will check the requires predicate and when it will produce effects. The sound variant will trigger a constraint whenever there is even a possibility of it triggering at runtime. Therefore, it triggers when the predicate is either true or unknown. The complete variant can produce no false positives, so it will only check the requires predicate when the trigger predicate is definitely true. Regardless of the variant, if the trigger is either true or unknown, the analysis produces a set of changes to make to the lattice based upon the effects list. The pragmatic variant will work the same as the complete variant when determining whether to trigger the constraint. The rationale here is to try to reduce the number of false positives by only checking constraints when they are known to be applicable.

Error condition. The requires predicate should be true to signal that the operation is safe to use. The sound variant will cause an error whenever the requires predicate is false or unknown. The complete variant, however, can only cause an error if it is sure there is one, so it only flags an error if the requires predicate is definitely false. In this case, the pragmatic variant will work the same as the sound variant. If the analysis has come to this point, it already has enough information to determine that the trigger was true. Therefore, we will require that the plugin definitely show that the requires predicate is true, with the expectation that this will reduce the false negatives.

While the pragmatic variant can produce false positives and false negatives, we believe it will be the most cost-effective in practice based on our experience described in Sect. 5. Additionally, this variant may use inferred relationships, a feature which is not sound or complete but reduces the specification burden on the framework developer.

4   Abstract Semantics of FUSION

In this section, we present formal semantics for a simplified version of the specifications and analysis, the grammar for which is shown in Fig. 5. We do not formalize TEST effects or specialized relations for equality (==) and typing (instanceof). A semantics with TEST effects can be found in our technical report [5], and it is possible to add specialized relations by calling out to other flow analyses in the same manner as is done with both TEST effects and aliasing.

Relationship effects and wildcards are both syntactic sugar that can be easily translated into a constraint form. Relationship effects are translated by considering them as a constraint on the annotated method with a true trigger predicate, a true requires predicate, and the effect list as annotated. Wildcards are easily rewritten by declaring a fresh variable in the trigger predicate and constraining it to have the desired type. Fig. 4 shows an example effect with a wildcard translated into a constraint.

constraint	$\text{cons} ::= \text{op} : P_{trg} \Rightarrow P_{req} \Downarrow \overline{R}$
predicate	$P ::= P_1 \wedge P_2 \mid P_1 \vee P_2 \mid P_1 \implies P_2 \mid R \mid \text{true} \mid \text{false}$
relation predicate	$R ::= \text{rel}(\bar{\alpha}) \mid \neg\text{rel}(\bar{\alpha})$
source instruction	$\text{instr} ::= x_{rslt} = x_{tgt}.m(\bar{x}) \mid x_{rslt} = \text{new}\,\tau(\bar{x}) \mid \text{eom} \mid \ldots$
instruction signature	$\text{op} ::= \tau_{tgt}.m(\bar{y} : \bar{\tau}) : \tau_{rslt} \mid \text{new}\,\tau(\bar{y} : \bar{\tau}) \mid \text{end-of-method} \mid \ldots$
meta variable	$\alpha ::= y \mid \ell$
ternary logic	$t ::= \text{True} \mid \text{False} \mid \text{Unknown}$
lattice elements	$E ::= \text{unknown} \mid \text{true} \mid \text{false} \mid \text{bot}$
flow lattice	$\rho ::= \text{rel}(\bar{\ell}) \mapsto E, \rho \mid \varnothing$
set of lattices	$\mathcal{P} ::= \{\rho\} \cup \mathcal{P} \mid \varnothing$
substitution	$\sigma ::= (y \mapsto \ell), \sigma \mid \varnothing$
set of substitutions	$\Sigma ::= \{\sigma\} \cup \Sigma \mid \varnothing$
alias lattice	$\mathcal{A} ::= < \Gamma_\ell ; \mathcal{L} >$
aliases	$\mathcal{L} ::= (x \mapsto \bar{\ell}), \mathcal{L} \mid \varnothing$
location types	$\Gamma_\ell ::= (\ell : \tau), \Gamma_\ell \mid \varnothing$
spec variable types	$\Gamma_y ::= (y : \tau), \Gamma_y \mid \varnothing$
relation type	$\mathcal{R} ::= \text{rel} \mapsto \bar{\tau}, \mathcal{R} \mid \varnothing$
constraints	$\mathcal{C} ::= \text{cons}, \mathcal{C} \mid \varnothing$
relation inference rules	$\mathcal{I} ::= P \Downarrow \overline{R}, \mathcal{I} \mid \varnothing$

x is a source variable
m is a method name
rel is a relation name
τ is a type
y is a spec variable, where the variables **target** and **result** have special meanings
ℓ is a label for a runtime object
$\perp_\mathcal{A}$ is a ρ where $\perp_\mathcal{A}$ is consistent with $\mathcal{A}$ and $\forall\, \text{rel}(\bar{\ell}) \mapsto E \in \perp_\mathcal{A} . E = \text{bot}$

Fig. 5. Abstract syntax

The lattice ρ has the usual operators of join ($\sqcup$) and comparison ($\sqsubseteq$), which work as expected for a tuple lattice. We also introduce three additional operators, defined in Fig. 6. Equivalence join ($\boxminus$) will resolve to unknown if the two sides are not equal. Overriding meet ($\leftharpoondown$) has the property that if the right side has a defined value (not bot), then it will use the right value, otherwise it will use the left value. The polarity operator ($\updownarrow$) will push all non-bottom values to the top of the lattice. Finally, we also define $\perp_\mathcal{A}$ as a tuple lattice which is consistent with the alias lattice $\mathcal{A}$ and which maps every relationship to bot.

4.1 Checking Predicate Truth

Before we show how constraint checking works, we must describe how the analysis tests the truth of a relationship predicate. The judgment for this is written as

$$\rho \vdash P\ t$$

$$\frac{}{\mathop{\updownarrow} \mathrm{bot} = \mathrm{bot}}\text{(POLAR-BOT)} \qquad \frac{E \neq \mathrm{bot}}{\mathop{\updownarrow} E = \mathrm{unknown}}\text{(POLAR-UNKNOWN)} \qquad \frac{}{E \mathbin{\sqcup\!\sqcup} E = E}\text{(EQJOIN-=)}$$

$$\frac{}{E \mathbin{\curlywedge} \mathrm{bot} = E}\text{(OVR-BOT)} \qquad \frac{E_r \neq \mathrm{bot}}{E_l \mathbin{\curlywedge} E_r = E_r}\text{(OVR-NOT-BOT)} \qquad \frac{E_l \neq E_r}{E_l \mathbin{\sqcup\!\sqcup} E_r = \mathrm{unknown}}\text{(EQJOIN-}\neq\text{)}$$

Fig. 6. Unusual lattice operations

$\boxed{\rho \vdash P\ t}$

$$\frac{\rho(\mathrm{rel}(\bar{\ell})) = \mathtt{true}}{\rho \vdash \mathrm{rel}(\bar{\ell})\ \mathsf{True}}\text{(REL-T)} \qquad \frac{\rho(\mathrm{rel}(\bar{\ell})) = \mathtt{false}}{\rho \vdash \mathrm{rel}(\bar{\ell})\ \mathsf{False}}\text{(REL-F)}$$

$$\frac{\rho(\mathrm{rel}(\bar{\ell})) = E \quad E \neq \mathtt{true} \quad E \neq \mathtt{false}}{\rho \vdash \mathrm{rel}(\bar{\ell})\ \mathsf{Unknown}}\text{(REL-U-SND/CMP)}$$

$$\frac{\begin{array}{c}\rho(\mathrm{rel}(\bar{\ell})) = E \quad E \neq \mathtt{true} \quad E \neq \mathtt{false} \\ \rho \text{ infers } \rho' \quad \rho \mathbin{\curlywedge} \rho' \vdash \mathrm{rel}(\bar{\ell})\ t \quad t \text{ is True or False}\end{array}}{\rho \vdash \mathrm{rel}(\bar{\ell})\ t}\text{(INFER-PRG)}$$

$$\frac{\begin{array}{c}\rho(\mathrm{rel}(\bar{\ell})) = E \quad E \neq \mathtt{true} \quad E \neq \mathtt{false} \\ \neg \exists\, \rho' .\ \rho \text{ infers } \rho' \ \wedge\ \rho \mathbin{\curlywedge} \rho' \vdash \mathrm{rel}(\bar{\ell})\ t \ \wedge\ t \text{ is True or False}\end{array}}{\rho \vdash \mathrm{rel}(\bar{\ell})\ \mathsf{Unknown}}\text{(REL-U-PRG)}$$

$\boxed{\rho \text{ infers } \rho'}$

$$\frac{P \mathbin{\Downarrow} \bar{R} \in \mathcal{I} \quad \rho \vdash P[\sigma]\ \mathsf{True} \quad \rho' = \mathrm{lattice}(\bar{R}[\sigma]) \quad \rho' \sqsubset \rho}{\rho \text{ infers } \rho'}\text{(DISCOVER)}$$

Fig. 7. Check predicate truth under a lattice. The remaining rules are as expected for ternary logic and can be found in [5].

and is read "the lattice ρ shows that predicate P is t", where t is either True, False, or Unknown. The rules for this judgment are similar to three-valued logic, and the interesting subset of them are in Fig. 7.

In the sound and complete variants, the rules are trivial. The analysis inspects the lattice to see what the value of the relationship is to determine whether it is True (REL-T), False (REL-F), or Unknown (REL-U-SND/CMP). If the lattice maps the relationship to either unknown or bot, then the predicate is considered Unknown. The rest of the predicate rules work as expected for a three-valued logic.

The interesting case is in the pragmatic variant when the relationship does not map to true or false. Instead of using the rule (REL-U-SND/CMP), the pragmatic variant admits the rules (REL-U-PRG) and (INFER-PRG). These rules attempt to use the inferred relationships, defined in Sect. 2.3, to retrieve the desired relationship. The rule for the inference judgement ρ infers ρ' is also defined in Fig. 7. This rule first checks to see if the trigger of an inferred relation is true, and if so, uses the function lattice to produce the inferred relationships described by $\bar{R}[\sigma]$. For all relationships not defined by $\bar{R}[\sigma]$, lattice defaults to bot to signal that there are no changes. There are two properties to note about the rules (REL-U-PRG), (INFER-PRG), and (DISCOVER):

1. The use of inferred relationships does not change the original lattice ρ. This allows the inferred relationships to disappear if the generator, P, is no longer true.
2. Any inferred values must be *strictly more precise* than the relationship's value in ρ, as enforced by $\rho' \sqsubseteq \rho$. This means that relationships can move from unknown to true, but they can not move from false to true. This property guarantees termination and gives declared effects precedence over inferred ones.

Inferred relationships can not be used in the sound and complete variants. This does not limit the expressiveness of the specifications, as inferred relations can always be written directly within the constraints. Doing so does make the specifications more difficult to write; the framework developer must add the inferred relations to any constraint which will also prove the trigger predicate. Since inferred relations do change the semantics, they are not syntactic sugar, but they are not necessary for reasons beyond the ease of writing specifications.

4.2   Matching on an Operator

In order to check a constraint, the analysis must determine whether a source instruction, called instr, matches the syntactic operation op defined by a constraint. This is realized in the judgment

$$\mathcal{A}; \Gamma_y \vdash \mathsf{instr} : \mathsf{op} \mapsto (\Sigma^t, \Sigma^u)$$

with rules defined in Fig. 8. Given the alias lattice $\mathcal{A}$ and a typing environment for the free variables in op, this judgment matches instr to op and produces two disjoint sets of substitutions that map specification variables in op to heap locations. The first set, Σ^t, represents possible substitutions where the locations are all known to be a subtype of the type required by the variables. The second set, Σ^u, are potential substitutions where the locations may or may not have the right type at runtime.

As an example, we will walk through the rule (INVOKE) in Fig. 8. The first premise checks that the free variables in op are in Γ_y, and the second premise builds the substitution set using the findLabels function. Each substitution in the set will map the specification variables in op (target, result, and $y_1 \ldots y_n$) to a location in the heap that is aliased by the appropriate source variables in instr (x_{tgt}, x_{rslt}, and $x_1 \ldots x_n$).

To produce the set Σ^t, the findLabels function must generate a substitution for each y_i in $\bar{y}$. It starts by verifying that the corresponding source variable x_i points to only one location ℓ, and it checks to see if the type of that location is a subtype of the type required for y_i. Every substitution σ which fits these requirements is in Σ^t.

Σ^u is a more interesting set. Unlike Σ^t, it checks all locations which x_i aliases and records a possible substitution for each. Additionally, when it checks the type, it allows the location if there is even a *possibility* of it being the right type. As an example, consider the class hierarchy and use of findLabels shown in Fig. 9. In the first row, ℓ

$$\mathcal{A}; \Gamma_y \vdash instr : op \mapsto (\Sigma^t, \Sigma^u)$$

$$FV(\tau_{tgt}.m(\overline{y} : \overline{\tau}) : \tau_{rslt}) \subseteq \Gamma_y$$
$$findLabels(\mathcal{A}; \Gamma_y; x_{rslt}, x_{tgt}, \overline{x}; result, target, \overline{y}) = (\Sigma^t, \Sigma^u)$$
$$\frac{}{\mathcal{A}; \Gamma_y \vdash x_{rslt} = x_{tgt}.m(\overline{x}) : \tau_{tgt}.m(\overline{y} : \overline{\tau}) : \tau_{rslt} \mapsto (\Sigma^t, \Sigma^u)} \text{(INVOKE)}$$

$$FV(\text{ new } \tau(\overline{y} : \overline{\tau})) \subseteq \Gamma_y$$
$$findLabels(\mathcal{A}; \Gamma_y; x_{rslt}, \overline{x}; target, \overline{y}) = (\Sigma^t, \Sigma^u)$$
$$\frac{}{\mathcal{A}; \Gamma_y \vdash x_{rslt} = \text{ new } m(\overline{x}) : \text{ new } \tau(\overline{y} : \overline{\tau}) \mapsto (\Sigma^t, \Sigma^u)} \text{(CONSTRUCTOR)}$$

$$\frac{}{\mathcal{A}; \Gamma_y \vdash eom : \text{end-of-method} \mapsto (\{\varnothing\}, \varnothing)} \text{(EOM)}$$

$$findLabels(\mathcal{A}, \Gamma_y, \overline{x}, \overline{y}) = (\Sigma^t, \Sigma^u)$$

$$|\overline{x}| = |\overline{y}| = n$$
$$\Sigma^t = \{(y_1 \mapsto \ell_1), \dots, (y_n \mapsto \ell_n) |$$
$$\forall i \in 1 \dots n . \mathcal{L}(x_i) = \{\ell_i\} \wedge \Gamma_\ell(\ell_i) <: \Gamma_y(y_i)\}$$
$$\Sigma^u = \{(y_1 \mapsto \ell_1), \dots, (y_n \mapsto \ell_n) |$$
$$\frac{\forall i \in 1 \dots n . \ell_i \in \mathcal{L}(x_i) \wedge \exists \tau' . \tau' <: \Gamma_\ell(\ell_i) \wedge \tau' <: \Gamma_y(y_i)\} - \Sigma^t}{findLabels(< \Gamma_\ell, \mathcal{L} >; \Gamma_y; \overline{x}; \overline{y}) = (\Sigma^t, \Sigma^u)} \text{(FINDLABELS)}$$

Fig. 8. Matching instructions to operations and type satisfaction

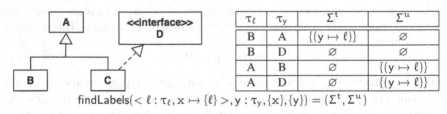

τ_ℓ	τ_y	Σ^t	Σ^u
B	A	$\{(y \mapsto \ell)\}$	$\varnothing$
B	D	$\varnothing$	$\varnothing$
A	B	$\varnothing$	$\{(y \mapsto \ell)\}$
A	D	$\varnothing$	$\{(y \mapsto \ell)\}$

$$findLabels(< \ell : \tau_\ell, x \mapsto \{\ell\} >, y : \tau_y, \{x\}, \{y\}) = (\Sigma^t, \Sigma^u)$$

Fig. 9. Examples of the difference between Σ^t and Σ^u

is definitely substitutable for y, so it is a substitution in Σ^t. In the second row, y can never be substituted by ℓ, so both sets are empty. In the third and fourth rows, ℓ may be substitutable for y (if ℓ has type B or C, respectively), so both substitutions are possibly, but not definitely, allowed and are therefore in Σ^u.

The need for Σ^u may seem surprising, but the rationale behind it is that framework constraints do not always adhere to behavioral subtyping [6]. Consider analyzing the DropDownList constraint on the code below:

```
1  ListControl list = ...;
2  ListItem item = list.getItems().findByValue("foo");
3  item.setSelected(true);
```

Since list is of type ListControl, the trigger clause of the first constraint in List. 7 will not be true, and the constraint will never trigger an error. However, we would like this to trigger a potential violation in the sound variant since list could be a

DropDownList. The root of the problem was that DropDownList is not following the principle of behavioral subtyping; it has added preconditions to methods that the base class did not require. Therefore, a DropDownList is not always substitutable where a ListControl is used! While frustrating for verification, this is common in frameworks; by trading off substitutability, the framework developers received code reuse internally. Other verification proposals have also recognized the need to support broken behavioral subtyping for this reason [7,8]. Inheritance was used here rather than composition because the type is structurally the same, and it is almost behaviorally the same. In fact, the methods on DropDownList itself do appear to be behaviorally substitutable. However, the subtype added a few constraints to *other* classes, like the ListItem class.

By keeping track of Σ^t and Σ^u separately, it will allow the variants of the analysis to use them differently. In particular, the sound variant will trigger errors from substitutions in Σ^u, while the complete and pragmatic variants will only use it to propagate lattice changes from the effect list.

4.3 Checking a Single Constraint

We will now show how the analysis checks an instruction for a single constraint. This is done with the judgment

$$\mathcal{A}; \rho; cons \vdash instr \hookrightarrow \rho^\Delta$$

shown in Fig. 10. This judgment takes the lattices and a constraint, and it determines what changes to make to the relation lattice for the given instruction. The lattice changes are represented in ρ^Δ, where a relationship mapped to bot signifies no changes.

The analysis starts by checking whether the instruction matches the constrained operation. If not, the instruction matching rules will return no substitutions and the rule (NO-MATCH) will apply. If there are substitutions, as shown in rule (MATCH), then the analysis must check this constraint for every aliasing configuration possible, as represented by Σ^t and Σ^u. This rule checks that for each substitution σ, the constraint passes and produces a change lattice ρ^Δ. If the substitution was from Σ^u, then the analysis must use the $\updownarrow$ operator on ρ^Δ. This is done because the analysis cannot be sure if the substitution is valid at runtime, so it can only make changes into unknown. Setting all changes to unknown could cause the analysis to lose precision when ρ^Δ prescribes a change that already exists in ρ. A possible solution is to let the polarizing operator return bot if the prescribed changes already exist in the lattice ρ, but we have not yet proven this extension is sound.

The last step the rule makes is to combine all the lattice changes, from all substitutions, using $\sqcup$. The use of $\sqcup$ means that a change is only made to true or false if all the aliasing configurations agree to it. Likewise, a signal to make no changes by way of bot must also show in all configurations. If any configurations disagree about a lattice change, then the lattice element changes to unknown.

Once the analysis has a syntactic match, it tries to find the aliasing configurations for a semantic match using

$$\mathcal{A}; \rho; \sigma \vdash_{part} cons \hookrightarrow \rho^\Delta$$

$$\boxed{\mathcal{A}; \rho; \mathsf{cons} \vdash \mathsf{instr} \hookrightarrow \rho^\Delta}$$

$$
\frac{
\begin{array}{c}
\mathsf{cons} = \mathsf{op} : \mathsf{P_{trg}} \Rightarrow \mathsf{P_{req}} \Downarrow \overline{\mathsf{R}} \qquad \mathcal{A}; \mathsf{FV(cons)} \vdash \mathsf{instr} : \mathsf{op} \mapsto (\Sigma^t, \Sigma^u) \\
\Sigma^t \cup \Sigma^u \neq \varnothing \qquad \mathcal{P}^t = \{\rho^\Delta \mid \sigma \in \Sigma^t \wedge \mathcal{A}; \rho; \sigma \vdash_{\mathsf{part}} \mathsf{cons} \hookrightarrow \rho^\Delta\} \\
\mathcal{P}^u = \{\Uparrow \rho^\Delta \mid \sigma \in \Sigma^u \wedge \mathcal{A}; \rho; \sigma \vdash_{\mathsf{part}} \mathsf{cons} \hookrightarrow \rho^\Delta\} \\
|\Sigma^t| = |\mathcal{P}^t| \qquad |\Sigma^u| = |\mathcal{P}^u| \qquad \mathcal{P}^\Delta = \mathcal{P}^t \cup \mathcal{P}^u
\end{array}
}{
\mathcal{A}; \rho; \mathsf{cons} \vdash \mathsf{instr} \hookrightarrow (\boxminus \mathcal{P}^\Delta)
}\text{(MATCH)}
$$

$$
\frac{
\mathsf{cons} = \mathsf{op} : \mathsf{P_{trg}} \Rightarrow \mathsf{P_{req}} \Downarrow \overline{\mathsf{R}} \qquad \mathcal{A}; \mathsf{FV(cons)} \vdash \mathsf{instr} : \mathsf{op} \mapsto (\varnothing, \varnothing)
}{
\mathcal{A}; \rho; \mathsf{cons} \vdash \mathsf{instr} \hookrightarrow \bot_\mathcal{A}
}\text{(NO-MATCH)}
$$

$$\boxed{\mathcal{A}; \rho; \sigma \vdash_{\mathsf{part}} \mathsf{cons} \hookrightarrow \rho^\Delta}$$

$$
\frac{
\begin{array}{c}
\mathsf{cons} = \mathsf{op} : \mathsf{P_{trg}} \Rightarrow \mathsf{P_{req}} \Downarrow \overline{\mathsf{R}} \\
\Gamma_y = \mathsf{FV(op)} \cup \mathsf{FV(P_{trg})} \cup \mathsf{FV(\overline{R})} \qquad \mathsf{allValidSubs}(\mathcal{A}; \sigma_{op}; \Gamma_y) = (\Sigma^t, \Sigma^u) \\
\Sigma^t \cup \Sigma^u \neq \varnothing \qquad \mathcal{P}^t = \{\rho^\Delta \mid \sigma \in \Sigma^t \wedge \mathcal{A}; \rho; \sigma \vdash_{\mathsf{full}} \mathsf{cons} \hookrightarrow \rho^\Delta\} \\
\mathcal{P}^u = \{\Uparrow \rho^\Delta \mid \sigma \in \Sigma^u \wedge \mathcal{A}; \rho; \sigma \vdash_{\mathsf{full}} \mathsf{cons} \hookrightarrow \rho^\Delta\} \\
|\Sigma^t| = |\mathcal{P}^t| \qquad |\Sigma^u| = |\mathcal{P}^u| \qquad \mathcal{P}^\Delta = \mathcal{P}^t \cup \mathcal{P}^u
\end{array}
}{
\mathcal{A}; \rho; \sigma_{op} \vdash_{\mathsf{part}} \mathsf{cons} \hookrightarrow (\boxminus \mathcal{P}^\Delta)
}\text{(BOUND)}
$$

$$
\frac{
\begin{array}{c}
\mathsf{cons} = \mathsf{op} : \mathsf{P_{trg}} \Rightarrow \mathsf{P_{req}} \Downarrow \overline{\mathsf{R}} \\
\Gamma_y = \mathsf{FV(op)} \cup \mathsf{FV(P_{trg})} \cup \mathsf{FV(\overline{R})} \qquad \mathsf{allValidSubs}(\mathcal{A}; \sigma_{op}; \Gamma_y) = (\varnothing, \varnothing)
\end{array}
}{
\mathcal{A}; \rho; \sigma_{op} \vdash_{\mathsf{part}} \mathsf{cons} \hookrightarrow \bot_\mathcal{A}
}\text{(CANT-BIND)}
$$

$$\boxed{\mathsf{allValidSubs}(\mathcal{A}; \sigma; \Gamma_y) = (\Sigma^t, \Sigma^u)}$$

$$
\frac{
\begin{array}{c}
\Sigma^t = \{\sigma' \mid \sigma' \supseteq \sigma \wedge \mathsf{dom}(\sigma') = \mathsf{dom}(\Gamma_y) \wedge \forall y \mapsto \ell \in \sigma' . \Gamma_\ell(\ell) <: \Gamma_y(y)\} \\
\Sigma^u = \{\sigma' \mid \sigma' \supseteq \sigma \wedge \mathsf{dom}(\sigma') = \mathsf{dom}(\Gamma_y) \wedge \\
\forall y \mapsto \ell \in \sigma' . \exists \tau' . \tau' <: \Gamma_\ell(\ell) \wedge \tau' <: \Gamma_y(y)\} - \Sigma^t
\end{array}
}{
\mathsf{allValidSubs}(< \Gamma_\ell; \mathcal{L} >; \sigma; \Gamma_y) = (\Sigma^t, \Sigma^u)
}\text{(VALIDSUBS)}
$$

Fig. 10. Checking a single constraint

The analysis must get all aliasing configurations that are consistent with the current aliases in σ and the types of the remaining free variables in cons. The substitutions are found by the allValidSubs function, shown in Fig. 10. The rule (BOUND) proceeds in a similar manner to the rule (MATCH), except it checks the constraint using the judgment

$$\mathcal{A}; \rho; \sigma \vdash_{\mathsf{full}} \mathsf{cons} \hookrightarrow \rho^\Delta$$

The rules for this judgment, shown in Fig. 11, are the primary point of difference between the variants of the analysis.

Sound Variant. The sound variant first checks $\mathsf{P_{trg}}[\sigma]$ under ρ. It uses this to determine which rule applies. If $\mathsf{P_{trg}}[\sigma]$ is True, as seen in rule (FULL-T-SND), then the analysis must check if $\mathsf{P_{req}}$ is True under ρ given any substitution. Since this is the sound variant, it

$\boxed{\mathcal{A}; \rho; \sigma \vdash_{\mathsf{full}} \mathsf{cons} \hookrightarrow \rho^{\Delta}, \text{ Sound Variant}}$

$$\frac{\begin{array}{c} \mathsf{cons} = \mathsf{op} : P_{\mathsf{trg}} \Rightarrow P_{\mathsf{req}} \Downarrow \overline{R} \qquad \rho \vdash P_{\mathsf{trg}}[\sigma] \text{ True} \\ \mathsf{allValidSubs}(\mathcal{A}; \sigma; \mathsf{FV}(\mathsf{cons})) = (\Sigma^{t}, \Sigma^{u}) \\ \exists \sigma' \in \Sigma^{t} . \rho \vdash P_{\mathsf{req}}[\sigma'] \text{ True} \end{array}}{\mathcal{A}; \rho; \sigma \vdash_{\mathsf{full}} \mathsf{cons} \hookrightarrow \mathsf{lattice}(\overline{R}[\sigma])} \text{(FULL-T-SND)}$$

$$\frac{\mathsf{cons} = \mathsf{op} : P_{\mathsf{trg}} \Rightarrow P_{\mathsf{req}} \Downarrow \overline{R} \qquad \rho \vdash P_{\mathsf{trg}}[\sigma] \text{ False}}{\mathcal{A}; \rho; \sigma \vdash_{\mathsf{full}} \mathsf{cons} \hookrightarrow \perp_{\mathcal{A}}} \text{(FULL-F-SND)}$$

$$\frac{\begin{array}{c} \mathsf{cons} = \mathsf{op} : P_{\mathsf{trg}} \Rightarrow P_{\mathsf{req}} \Downarrow \overline{R} \qquad \rho \vdash P_{\mathsf{trg}}[\sigma] \text{ Unknown} \\ \mathsf{allValidSubs}(\mathcal{A}; \sigma; \mathsf{FV}(\mathsf{cons})) = (\Sigma^{t}, \Sigma^{u}) \\ \exists \sigma' \in \Sigma^{t} . \rho \vdash P_{\mathsf{req}}[\sigma'] \text{ True} \qquad \rho^{\Delta} = \mathsf{lattice}(\overline{R}[\sigma]) \end{array}}{\mathcal{A}; \rho; \sigma \vdash_{\mathsf{full}} \mathsf{cons} \hookrightarrow\updownarrow \rho^{\Delta}} \text{(FULL-U-SND)}$$

$\boxed{\mathcal{A}; \rho; \sigma \vdash_{\mathsf{full}} \mathsf{cons} \hookrightarrow \rho^{\Delta}, \text{ Complete Variant}}$

$$\frac{\begin{array}{c} \mathsf{cons} = \mathsf{op} : P_{\mathsf{trg}} \Rightarrow P_{\mathsf{req}} \Downarrow \overline{R} \qquad \rho \vdash P_{\mathsf{trg}}[\sigma] \text{ True} \\ \mathsf{allValidSubs}(\mathcal{A}; \sigma; \mathsf{FV}(\mathsf{cons})) = (\Sigma^{t}, \Sigma^{u}) \\ \exists \sigma' \in \Sigma^{t} \cup \Sigma^{u} . \rho \vdash P_{\mathsf{req}}[\sigma'] \text{ True} \vee \rho \vdash P_{\mathsf{req}}[\sigma'] \text{ Unknown} \end{array}}{\mathcal{A}; \rho; \sigma \vdash_{\mathsf{full}} \mathsf{cons} \hookrightarrow \mathsf{lattice}(\overline{R}[\sigma])} \text{(FULL-T-CMP)}$$

$$\frac{\mathsf{cons} = \mathsf{op} : P_{\mathsf{trg}} \Rightarrow P_{\mathsf{req}} \Downarrow \overline{R} \qquad \rho \vdash P_{\mathsf{trg}}[\sigma] \text{ False}}{\mathcal{A}; \rho; \sigma \vdash_{\mathsf{full}} \mathsf{cons} \hookrightarrow \perp_{\mathcal{A}}} \text{(FULL-F-CMP)}$$

$$\frac{\begin{array}{c} \mathsf{cons} = \mathsf{op} : P_{\mathsf{trg}} \Rightarrow P_{\mathsf{req}} \Downarrow \overline{R} \qquad \rho \vdash P_{\mathsf{trg}}[\sigma] \text{ Unknown} \\ \rho^{\Delta} = \mathsf{lattice}(\overline{R}[\sigma]) \end{array}}{\mathcal{A}; \rho; \sigma \vdash_{\mathsf{full}} \mathsf{cons} \hookrightarrow\updownarrow \rho^{\Delta}} \text{(FULL-U-CMP)}$$

$\boxed{\mathcal{A}; \rho; \sigma \vdash_{\mathsf{full}} \mathsf{cons} \hookrightarrow \rho^{\Delta}, \text{ Pragmatic Variant}}$

$$\frac{\begin{array}{c} \mathsf{cons} = \mathsf{op} : P_{\mathsf{trg}} \Rightarrow P_{\mathsf{req}} \Downarrow \overline{R} \qquad \rho \vdash P_{\mathsf{trg}}[\sigma] \text{ True} \\ \mathsf{allValidSubs}(\mathcal{A}; \sigma; \mathsf{FV}(\mathsf{cons})) = (\Sigma^{t}, \Sigma^{u}) \\ \exists \sigma' \in \Sigma^{t} . \rho \vdash P_{\mathsf{req}}[\sigma'] \text{ True} \end{array}}{< \Gamma_{\ell}; \mathcal{L} >; \rho; \sigma \vdash_{\mathsf{full}} \mathsf{cons} \hookrightarrow \mathsf{lattice}(\overline{R}[\sigma])} \text{(FULL-T-PRG)}$$

$$\frac{\mathsf{cons} = \mathsf{op} : P_{\mathsf{trg}} \Rightarrow P_{\mathsf{req}} \Downarrow \overline{R} \qquad \rho \vdash P_{\mathsf{trg}}[\sigma] \text{ False}}{\mathcal{A}; \rho; \sigma \vdash_{\mathsf{full}} \mathsf{cons} \hookrightarrow \perp_{\mathcal{A}}} \text{(FULL-F-PRG)}$$

$$\frac{\begin{array}{c} \mathsf{cons} = \mathsf{op} : P_{\mathsf{trg}} \Rightarrow P_{\mathsf{req}} \Downarrow \overline{R} \qquad \rho \vdash P_{\mathsf{trg}}[\sigma] \text{ Unknown} \\ \rho^{\Delta} = \mathsf{lattice}(\overline{R}[\sigma]) \end{array}}{\mathcal{A}; \rho; \sigma \vdash_{\mathsf{full}} \mathsf{cons} \hookrightarrow\updownarrow \rho^{\Delta}} \text{(FULL-U-PRG)}$$

Fig. 11. Checking a fully bound constraint and producing effects. Shading highlights the differences between the three variants.

will only accept substitutions from Σ^t. If P_{req} is not True with a substitution from Σ^t, then the analysis produces an error. If there is no error, the rule produces the effects dictated by $\bar{R}[\sigma]$. The function $lattice$ simply converts this list to a lattice, where all unspecified relationships map to bot. If $P_{trg}[\sigma]$ is False, then the analysis uses rule (FULL-F-SND). In this situation the constraint does not trigger, so the requires predicate is not checked and the analysis returns no changes using $\bot_{\mathcal{A}}$.

In the case that $P_{trg}[\sigma]$ is Unknown, the sound variant proceeds in a similar manner to the case where $P_{trg}[\sigma]$ is True as it must consider the possibility that the trigger predicate is actually true. In fact the only difference in the rule (FULL-U-SND) is that the analysis must use the polarizing operator to be conservative with the effects it is producing in case the trigger predicate is actually false at runtime.

Complete Variant. Like the sound variant, the complete variant starts by checking $P_{trg}[\sigma]$ under ρ. If $P_{trg}[\sigma]$ is True, as seen in rule (FULL-T-CMP), then the analysis must check P_{req} under ρ given any substitution. As this is the complete variant, the analysis does not care whether the substitution came from Σ^t or Σ^u, and it does not matter whether P_{req} is True or Unknown. If no substitutions work, either because none exist or because they all show P_{req} to be false, then the analysis produces an error. Otherwise, the rule produces some effects. Since the constraint trigger was true, it will produce exactly the effects dictated by $\bar{R}[\sigma]$. If the analysis determines that $P_{trg}[\sigma]$ is False, then it uses the rule (FULL-F-CMP). Like the sound variant, the requires predicate is not checked and the analysis returns no changes.

Finally, if $P_{trg}[\sigma]$ is Unknown, the complete variant will not check P_{req} as it cannot be sure whether the constraint is actually triggered and it should not produce an error. However, it must still produce some conservative effects in case the constraint is triggered given a more concrete lattice. Like the sound rule in the case of an unknown trigger, the rule uses the polarizing operator $\updownarrow$ to produce only conservative effects.

Pragmatic Variant. The pragmatic variant is a combination of the sound and complete variants. It has the same rule for False as the other two variants, (FULL-F-PRG). The rule (FULL-T-PRG) is the same as the True rule for soundness, while the rule (FULL-U-PRG) is the same as the Unknown rule for completeness. This means that this variant can produce both false positives and false negatives. False negatives can occur when P_{trg} is Unknown under ρ, but a more precise lattice would have found P_{trg} to be True and eventually generated an error. False positives occur when P_{trg} is True under ρ and P_{req} is Unknown under ρ, but P_{req} would have been True under a more precise lattice.

4.4   The Flow Function

The flow function for the FUSION analysis checks all the individual constraints and produces the output lattice for the instruction. Using the judgments defined in the previous section, the flow function iterates through each constraint and receives a change lattice. As shown in below, these lattices are combined using the join operator. Once the analysis has the final change lattice ρ^{Δ}, it applies the changes using the overriding meet operation. This will preserve the old values of a relationship if the change lattice maps to bot, but it will override the old value otherwise. This provides us with the new relationship lattice ρ', which is used by the dataflow analysis to feed into the next instruction's flow function. This flow function is monotonic, and the lattice has a finite height, so the dataflow analysis will reach a fix point.

$$\frac{\forall \, cons_i \in \mathcal{C} \, . \, \mathcal{A}'; \rho; cons_i \vdash instr \hookrightarrow \rho_i^{\Delta} \qquad \rho^{\Delta} = \sqcup \{\rho_i^{\Delta}\} \qquad (i \in 1 \ldots n)}{f_{e;\mathcal{A}}(\rho, instr) = \rho \boxminus \rho^{\Delta}}$$

5 Implementation and Experience with the Pragmatic Variant

We implemented the pragmatic variant of the FUSION analysis in the Crystal dataflow analysis framework, an Eclipse plugin developed at Carnegie Mellon University for statically analyzing Java source [5]. The implementation interfaces to a boolean constant propagation analysis and a basic alias analysis; either of these could be replaced with more sophisticated implementation in order to improve the results.

We specified three sets of constraints, one for the ASP.NET framework[6] and two for the Eclipse JDT framework. These were all constraints which we had misused ourselves and were common problems that were posted on the help forums and mailing lists. These constraints exercised several different patterns, and the specifications were able to capture each of these patterns.

The specifications allowed us to easily describe structured relationships, such as the ListItems which are in a DropDownList and a tree of ASTNodes within the Eclipse JDT. In each of these cases, a relationship ties the "child" and "parent" objects together, and it is straightforward to check if two children have the same parent. Two of our constraints had a structured relationship where an operation required that some objects exist (or do not exist) in a structured relationship.

All three constraints had semantics which required operations to occur in a particular order. To define this pattern, we needed a relationship which binds relevant objects together. The operation which occurs first produces an effect which sets this relationship to true, and the operation which must occur second requires this relationship. An example of this was seen in the constraints on the DropDownList in List. 7. Additionally, relationships allowed us to specify partial orderings of operations. One of the Eclipse JDT constraints had this behavior, and in fact required three methods to be called before the constrained operation. Alternatively, the user could choose to call a fourth method that would replace all three method calls. We captured this constraint by having each of the four methods produce a relationship, and the constrained operation simply required either the three relationships produced from the group of three methods, or the single relationship produced from the fourth one.

Relationships also made it straightforward to associate any objects that were used in the same operation. For example, this allowed us to associate several fields of an object so that we could later check that they were only used together. We did this by annotating the constructor of the object with a relationship effect that tied the field parameters together. We could also associate objects that were linked by some secondary object, but had no direct connection, such as a DropDownList and the ListItems received from calls to the associated ListItemCollection.

---

[5] http://code.google.com/p/crystalsaf
[6] We translated the relevant parts of the API and the examples into Java.

After specifying the constraints, we ran the pragmatic variant on 20 examples based on real-world code. The examples we selected are based on our own misuses of these frameworks and on several postings on internet help forums and mailing lists. Of these, the pragmatic variant worked properly on 16, meaning that it either found an expected error or did not find an error on correct code. Most of these examples had little aliasing and used exact types, which reflected what we saw on the help forums.

These examples identified two sources of imprecision. The pragmatic variant failed on one example because the example used an unconstrained supertype, and it failed on the remaining three examples because the constraint required objects which were not in scope. The unconstrained supertype resulted in a false negative, and the three examples with objects out of scope resulted in false positives. In all four of these cases, the sound variant would have flagged an error, and the complete variant would not have.

Unconstrained supertypes, such as using a `ListControl` instead of a `Drop-DownList`, are the first potential source of imprecision for the pragmatic variant. While a sound analysis would have detected this type of error, in practice, using this superclass is not typical as it only exists for code reuse purposes. In fact, we never found code on the forum that used the superclass `ListControl`.

The more interesting, and more typical, source of imprecision occurs when a required object is not in scope. For example, one of the Eclipse JDT constraints required that an `ASTNode` have a relationship with an `AST` object. The plugin, however, did not have any `AST` objects in scope at all, even though this relationship did exist globally. Based on the examples we found, this does occur in practice, typically when the framework makes multiple callbacks in sequence, such as with a Visitor pattern.

Future revisions of the FUSION analysis could address the problem of out-of-scope objects with two changes. First, it should be possible for the framework to declare what relationships exist at the point where the callback occurs. This would have provided the correct relationships in the previous example, and it should be relatively straightforward to annotate the interface of the plugin with this information. Second, an inter-procedural analysis on only the plugin code could handle the case where the relationship goes out of scope for similar reasons, such as calls to a helper function. These changes would increase the precision of all three variants of the analysis.

The two sources of imprecision affect all three variants, though in different ways. While imprecision when checking a constraint can produce a false positive in the sound variant or a false negative in the complete variant, the location of the imprecision in the constraint directly changes how the pragmatic variant handles it. When the imprecision occurs in the trigger predicate, the pragmatic variant results in a false negative. When the trigger predicate is precise but the requires predicate is imprecise, the pragmatic variant results in a false positive. This reflects what we expect from the analysis; we only wish to see an error if there is reason to believe that the constraint applies to our plugin. If the trigger predicate is unknown, it is less likely that the constraint is relevant.

6   Related Work

Typestates [9] are traditionally used for specifying protocols on a single object by using a state machine, but there are several approaches to inter-object typestate. Lam et al.

manipulated the typestate of many objects together through their participation in data structures [10]. Nanda et al. take this a step further by allowing external objects to affect a particular object's state, but unlike relationships, it requires that the objects reference each other through a pre-defined path [11]. Bierhoff and Aldrich add permissions to typestates and allows objects to capture the permission of another object, thus binding the objects as needed for the protocol [12]. Relationships can combine multiple objects into a single state-like construct and are more general for this purpose than typestate; they can describe all of the examples used in multiple object typestate work.

With respect to the specifications, relationships are more incremental than typestate because the entire protocol does not need to be specified in order to specify a single constraint. Additionally, the plugin developer does not add any specifications, which she must do with some of the typestate approaches. However, because they require specifications on both sides, typestate analyses can soundly check that both the plugin and the framework meet the specification [9,10,12]. The relationship analysis assumes that the framework properly meets the specification and only analyzes the plugin.

Tracematches have also been used to enforce protocols [13]. Unlike typestate, which specifies the correct protocol, tracematches specify a temporal sequence of events which lead to an error state. This is done by defining a state machine for the protocol and then specifying the bad paths.

The tracematch specification approach is similar to that of relationships; the main difference is in how the techniques specify the path leading up to the error state. Tracematches must specify the entire good path leading up to the error state, which can lead to many specifications to define a single bad error state. In cases where multiple execution traces lead to the same error, such as the many ways to find an item in a DropDownList and select it incorrectly, a tracematch would have to specify each possibility. Instead of specifying the good path leading up to the error, relationships specify the context predicate, which is the same for all good paths. This difference affects how robust a specification is in the face of API changes. If the framework developer adds a new way to access ListItems in a ListControl, possibly through several methods calls, the existing tracematches will not cover that new sub-path. However, all the constraint specifications in the proposed technique will continue to work if the sub-path eventually results in the same relationships as other sub-paths.

Tracematches are enforced statically and dynamically using a global analysis [14]. The static analysis soundly determines possible violations, and it instruments the code to check them dynamically. Bodden et al. provide a static analysis which optimizes the dynamic analysis by verifying more errors statically [15], and Naeem and Lhoták specifically optimize with regard to tracematches that involve multiple objects [16]. While the FUSION analysis is static, it could be used in the same way by instrumenting all violations that are found by the sound variant but not by the complete variant.

Bierman and Wren formalized UML relationships as a first-class language construct [17]. The language extension they created gives relationships attributes and inheritance, and developers use the relationships by explicitly adding and removing them. Balzer et. al. expanded on this work by describing invariants on relations using discrete mathematics and support semantic invariants and invariants between several relations [18]. In contrast to previous work, the relationships presented in this paper are added and removed implicitly through use of framework operations, and if inferred relationships are used, they may be entirely hidden from the developer.

Like the proposed framework language, Contracts [19] also view relationships between objects as a key factor in specifying systems. A contract also declares the objects involved in the contract, an invariant, and a lifetime where the invariant is guaranteed to hold. Contracts allow all the power of first-order predicate logic and can express very complex invariants. Contracts do not check the conformance of plugins and the specifications are seemingly more complex to write.

The FUSION analysis is similar to a shape analysis, with the closest being TVLA [20]. TVLA allows developers to extend shape analysis using custom predicates that relate different objects. FUSION specifications could be written as custom TVLA predicates, but the lower level of abstraction would result in a more complex specification and would require greater expertise from the specifier.

7 Conclusion

Relationships capture the interaction between a plugin and framework by describing how abstract object associations change as the plugin makes calls to the framework. We can then use these relationships to describe constraints on framework operations. We have shown that FUSION's relationship-based constraints can describe many constraint paradigms found in real frameworks, capturing relationship structure, operation order, and object associations that may or may not derive from direct references. As the specifications are written entirely by framework developers, plugin developers only need to run the analysis on their code, so that investments by a few framework developers pay dividends to many plugin developers.

A currently intra-procedural static analysis can check that the plugin code meets framework constraints. This analysis is particularly interesting because it is adjustable. While many analyses strive to only be either sound or complete, the FUSION analysis can be run either soundly, completely, or as a pragmatic balance of the two, thereby allowing the plugin developer to choose the variant that provides the most useful results.

Acknowledgements. This work was supported in part by NSF grant CCF-0811592, NSF grant CCF-0546550, DARPA contract HR00110710019, the Department of Defense, and the Software Industry Center at CMU and its sponsors, especially the Alfred P. Sloan Foundation, and a fellowship from Los Alamos National Laboratory. The authors would also like to thank Donna Malayeri and Kevin Bierhoff for their feedback.

References

1. Johnson, R.E.: Frameworks = (components + patterns). Commun. ACM 40 (1997)
2. Jaspan, C., Aldrich, J.: Checking semantic usage of frameworks. In: Proc. of the symposium on Library Centric Software Design (2007)
3. Fowler, M.: Inversion of control containers and the dependency injection pattern (2004), http://www.martinfowler.com/articles/injection.html
4. Leavens, G.T., Baker, A.L., Ruby, C.: Preliminary design of JML: a behavioral interface specification language for Java. SIGSOFT Softw. Eng. Notes 31(3) (2006)

5. Jaspan, C., Aldrich, J.: Checking framework interactions with relationships: Extended. Technical Report CMU-ISR-140-08, Institute for Software Research, Carnegie Mellon University (December 2008)
6. Liskov, B.H., Wing, J.M.: A behavioral notion of subtyping. ACM Trans. Program. Lang. Syst. 16(6), 1811–1841 (1994)
7. Parkinson, M.J., Bierman, G.M.: Separation logic, abstraction and inheritance. In: Proc. of the symposium on Principles of Programming Languages (2008)
8. Dhara, K.K., Leavens, G.T.: Forcing behavioral subtyping through specification inheritance. In: Proc. of the International Conference on Software Engineering (1996)
9. DeLine, R., Fähndrich, M.: Typestates for objects. In: Odersky, M. (ed.) ECOOP 2004. LNCS, vol. 3086, pp. 465–490. Springer, Heidelberg (2004)
10. Kuncak, V., Lam, P., Zee, K., Rinard, M.: Modular Pluggable Analyses for Data Structure Consistency. IEEE Trans. Softw. Eng. 32(12) (2006)
11. Nanda, M.G., Grothoff, C., Chandra, S.: Deriving object typestates in the presence of inter-object references. In: Proc. of the Conference on Object Oriented Programming, Systems, Languages, and Applications (2005)
12. Bierhoff, K., Aldrich, J.: Modular typestate checking of aliased objects. In: Proc. of the Conference on Object Oriented Programming, Systems, Languages, and Applications (2007)
13. Walker, R.J., Viggers, K.: Implementing Protocols via Declarative Event Patterns. In: Proc. of the symposium on Foundations of Software Engineering (2004)
14. Bodden, E., Hendren, L., Lhoták, O.: A staged static program analysis to improve the performance of runtime monitoring. In: Ernst, E. (ed.) ECOOP 2007. LNCS, vol. 4609, pp. 525–549. Springer, Heidelberg (2007)
15. Bodden, E., Lam, P., Hendren, L.: Finding programming errors earlier by evaluating runtime monitors ahead-of-time. In: Proc. of the symposium on Foundations of Software Engineering (2008)
16. Naeem, N.A., Lhoták, O.: Typestate-like analysis of multiple interacting objects. In: Proc. of the Conference on Object Oriented Programming, Systems, Languages, and Applications (2008)
17. Bierman, G., Wren, A.: First-class relationships in an object-oriented language. In: Black, A.P. (ed.) ECOOP 2005. LNCS, vol. 3586, pp. 262–286. Springer, Heidelberg (2005)
18. Balzer, S., Gross, T., Eugster, P.: A relational model of object collaborations and its use in reasoning about relationships. In: Ernst, E. (ed.) ECOOP 2007. LNCS, vol. 4609, pp. 323–346. Springer, Heidelberg (2007)
19. Helm, R., Holland, I.M., Gangopadhyay, D.: Contracts: specifying behavioral compositions in object-oriented systems. In: Proc. of the Conference on Object Oriented Programming, Systems, Languages, and Applications (1990)
20. Sagiv, M., Reps, T., Wilhelm, R.: Parametric shape analysis via 3-valued logic. ACM Trans. Program. Lang. Syst. 24(3), 217–298 (2002)

COPE - Automating Coupled Evolution of Metamodels and Models

Markus Herrmannsdoerfer[1], Sebastian Benz[2], and Elmar Juergens[1]

[1] Institut für Informatik
Technische Universität München
Boltzmannstr. 3, 85748 Garching b. München, Germany
{herrmama,juergens}@in.tum.de
[2] BMW Car IT GmbH
Petuelring 116, 80809 München, Germany
sebastian.benz@bmw-carit.de

Abstract. Model-based development promises to increase productivity by offering modeling languages tailored to a specific domain. Such modeling languages are typically defined by a metamodel. In response to changing requirements and technological progress, the domains and thus the metamodels are subject to change. Manually migrating existing models to a new version of their metamodel is tedious and error-prone. Hence, adequate tool support is required to support the maintenance of modeling languages. This paper introduces COPE, an integrated approach to specify the coupled evolution of metamodels and models to reduce migration effort. With COPE, a language is evolved by incrementally composing modular coupled transformations that adapt the metamodel and specify the corresponding model migrations. This modular approach allows to combine the reuse of recurring transformations with the expressiveness to cater for complex transformations. We demonstrate the applicability of COPE in practice by modeling the coupled evolution of two existing modeling languages.

1 Introduction

Model-based development promises to increase productivity by offering modeling languages tailored to a specific domain. Consequently, a variety of metamodel-based approaches for the development of modeling languages, such as Model-Driven Architecture [1], Software Factories [2] and Domain-Specific Modeling [3] have been proposed in recent years. In response, modeling languages are receiving increased attention in industry. The AUTOSAR standard, for instance, defines a modeling language to specify automotive software architectures [4]. With the integration of modeling languages into industrial development practice, their maintenance is gaining importance. Although significant work in both academia and industry has been invested into tool support for the initial development of modeling languages, issues related to their maintenance are still largely disregarded.

S. Drossopoulou (Ed.): ECOOP 2009, LNCS 5653, pp. 52–76, 2009.

Even though often neglected, a language is subject to change like any other software artifact [5]. This holds for both general-purpose and domain-specific modeling languages. For instance, UML [6] – a general purpose modeling language – already has a rich evolution history, although it is relatively young. Domain-specific modeling languages like e. g. AUTOSAR are even more prone to change, as they have to be adapted whenever their domain changes due to technological progress or evolving requirements.

A modeling language is evolved by *adapting* its metamodel to the evolved requirements. Due to metamodel adaptation, existing models may no longer conform to the adapted metamodel. These models have to be *migrated* so that they can be used with the evolved modeling language. Throughout the paper, the combination of metamodel adaptation and reconciling model migration is referred to as *coupled evolution*. Manually migrating existing models to the adapted metamodel is tedious and error-prone. Consequently, in current practice two approaches are used to handle evolution of modeling languages.

The first approach advocates to perform language evolution in a downwards-compatible fashion. In other words, the metamodel is adapted in a way that the old models can still be used with the evolved modeling language without migration. However, downward compatibility heavily constrains the way in which a metamodel can be adapted. Furthermore, the preservation of old constructs can unnecessarily clutter and complicate a metamodel. This approach can be further refined by using deprecation to signal metamodel changes. More precisely, constructs are marked deprecated, before they are actually removed from the metamodel. Users of the modeling language are then informed about the deprecated constructs which should no longer be used. However, deprecation shifts the responsibility for model migration from the developer of the modeling language to its users. In addition, deprecation also clutters and complicates the metamodel, as it leads to non-orthogonal constructs being available at the same time. In a nutshell, both downwards compatibility and deprecation heavily threaten the simplicity and quality of the metamodel. As a lot of artifacts like language editors and interpreters depend on the metamodel, these approaches also affect their simplicity and quality.

The second approach is to adapt the metamodel in a breaking fashion and to later implement a migrator, i. e. when the new version of the modeling language is deployed. The migrator preserves the information of an existing model by transforming it into a new version that conforms to the adapted metamodel. This approach has the advantage that the metamodel can be adapted in a clean manner, because legacy constructs can be removed. However, implementation of a migrator after a number of metamodel adaptations is tedious, as the developers of the modeling language have to become clear about the intentions behind these metamodel adaptations. In addition, a migrator implemented as a model transformation does not allow for the reuse of recurring migration knowledge.

Hence, adequate tool support is required to further reduce the effort involved in migrator implementation. We have performed an empirical study on the histories of two industrial metamodels to determine the requirements for adequate tool support [7]. The study showed that there is a large fraction of recurring migration knowledge. Hence, effort can be saved by enabling the *reuse* of such recurring coupled evolution steps. However, it also revealed that there are a number of migrations that are specific to a certain domain and thus cannot be reused. In addition, the specification of these migrations requires an *expressive* language.

Currently, to our best knowledge, there is no approach that combines both the desired level of reuse and expressiveness. To alleviate this, we present COPE, an integrated approach to model the coupled evolution of metamodels and models. COPE is based on a language that provides means to combine metamodel adaptation and model migration into so-called *coupled transactions*. The stated requirements are fulfilled by two kinds of coupled transactions: reusable and custom coupled transactions. A *reusable coupled transaction* allows the reuse of recurring coupled transformations across metamodels. A *custom coupled transaction* can be manually defined by the metamodel developer for complex migrations that are specific to a metamodel. To ease the application of this language, COPE provides further abstraction by tool support. In order not to disturb the habits of the metamodel developer, we have integrated COPE into the metamodel editor. The user interface provides easy access to a number of reusable coupled transactions available through a *library*. A *language history* automatically keeps track of the consecutively performed coupled transactions.

Outline. In Section 2, we recapitulate the requirements derived from our empirical study. We analyze how these requirements are fulfilled by related work in Section 3. In Section 4, we introduce the language and show how its concepts directly fulfill the requirements from the study. The seamless integration of COPE into the Eclipse Modeling Framework (EMF) is presented in Section 5. In Section 6, we show the applicability of COPE in practice by performing the coupled evolution of existing metamodels and their models. We conclude and present directions for future work in Section 7.

2   Requirements for Automated Coupled Evolution

To better understand the nature of coupled evolution of metamodels and models in practice, we performed a study on the histories of two industrial metamodels [7]. The study's main goal was to determine substantiated requirements for tool support that is adequate for coupled evolution in practice. We investigated whether reuse of migration knowledge can significantly reduce migration effort. To this end, we developed a classification of metamodel changes with respect to the automatability of the corresponding model migration.

As is depicted in Figure 1(a), we introduced four main classes of language changes. *Metamodel-only* changes do not require the migration of models, e. g. metamodel extensions like the addition of an optional attribute, whereas *coupled changes* do. *Coupled changes* can be further subdivided into metamodel-independent, metamodel-specific and model-specific coupled changes. *Metamodel-independent* coupled changes do not depend on a specific metamodel, and thus can

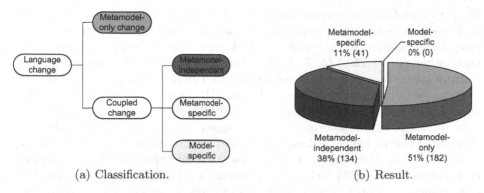

(a) Classification.   (b) Result.

Fig. 1. Empirical study

be reused across metamodels. Examples are well-known object-oriented refactorings [8] like e. g. rename or extract class. *Metamodel-specific* coupled changes are so specific to a certain metamodel that they cannot be reused across metamodels. An example is the removal of composite states from a statemachine metamodel which requires to flatten the state hierarchy in the models. *Model-specific* coupled changes require information from the developer of a model during migration, and thus the migration cannot be specified in a model-independent way. Examples are metamodel refinements which require to also refine the model.

For our study in [7], we deliberately chose two metamodel histories where the impact on the models was not taken into account during metamodel adaptation. The combined result of the study for both metamodel histories is shown in Figure 1(b) as a pie chart. The figure shows the fraction and the accumulated numbers of language changes that fall into each class. As only half of the changes were metamodel-only, a significant number of language changes required a migration of existing models. As we found no model-specific coupled changes, we would have been able to specify transformations to automate the migration of all models. To this end, we do not take model-specific coupled changes into account in the following. The proportion between metamodel-independent and metamodel-specific coupled changes leads to the following two central requirements for adequate tool support:

Reuse: More than three quarters of the coupled changes were metamodel-independent, thus indicating a high potential for reuse. To take advantage of these reuse opportunities, reuse of recurring migration knowledge is required.

Expressiveness: The remaining quarter of the coupled changes were metamodel-specific and therefore required a custom model migration. Tool support automating coupled evolution must thus be sufficiently expressive to cater for complex migrations involved in metamodel-specific coupled changes.

3   Related Work

When a specification is adapted, potentially all existing instances have to be migrated in order to reconcile them with the new version of the specification.

Since this problem of *coupled evolution* [9] affects all specification formalisms (e. g. database schemata, formats, grammars, metamodels) alike, numerous approaches for *coupled transformation* [10] of a specification and its instances have been proposed [11,12,13,14,15,16,17,18,19,20,21,22,23,24]. The idea of coupled transformation has even been generalized to a domain-independent approach that can be instantiated on different domains [25]. Apart from the target specification formalism, existing approaches mainly differ in their support for reuse and expressiveness. In this section, we outline approaches to coupled evolution from different domains, namely schema, grammar, format and metamodel evolution, focusing on how they fulfill the requirements rather than on idiosyncrasies of their target specification formalism. There are a number of other domains, like e. g. framework, workflow and ontology evolution, in which similar approaches are proposed.

Schema evolution denotes the migration of database instance data to an adapted version of the database schema. Schema evolution has been a field of study for several decades, yielding a substantial body of research [26,27]. For the ORION database system, Banerjee et al. propose a fixed set of change primitives that perform coupled evolution of the schema and data [11]. While reusing migration knowledge in case of these primitives, their approach is limited to local schema restructuring. To allow for non-local changes, Ferrandina et al. propose separate languages for schema and instance data migration for the O_2 database system [12]. While more expressive, their approach does not allow for reuse of coupled transformation knowledge. In order to reuse recurring coupled transformations, SERF – as proposed by Claypool et al. – offers a mechanism to define arbitrary new high-level primitives [13], providing both reuse and expressiveness. In a nutshell, the history of approaches for schema evolution exhibits a progression towards more expressiveness and reuse. In order to fulfill the requirements from [7], COPE transfers the concepts of SERF to the domain of metamodel evolution.

Grammar evolution denotes the migration of textual programs to adaptations of their underlying grammar. Grammar evolution has been studied in the context of grammar engineering [28]. Lämmel proposes a comprehensive suite of grammar transformation operations for the incremental adaptation of context free grammars [14]. The proposed operations are based on sound, formal preservation properties that allow reasoning about the relationship between grammars before and after transformation, thus helping developers to maintain consistency of their grammar. However, the proposed operations are not coupled since they do not take the migration of words into account. Building on Lämmel's work, Pizka and Juergens propose a tool for the evolutionary development of textual languages called Lever, which is also able to automate the migration of words [15]. Primitive grammar and word evolution operations can be invoked from within a general-purpose language to perform all kinds of coupled transformation. Similar to SERF, Lever provides a mechanism to define arbitrary new high-level primitives. COPE is not only strongly related to Lever because of its support for reuse and expressiveness, but also because it provides an explicit language history that allows to defer model migration to a later instant.

Format evolution denotes the migration of a class of documents to adaptations of their document schema. Lämmel and Lohmann suggest operators for format transformation, from which migrating transformations for documents are induced [16]. The suggested operators are based on Lämmel's work on grammar adaptation. Furthermore, Su et al. propose a complete, minimal and sound set of evolution primitives for formats and documents, and show that they preserve validity and well-formedness of both formats and documents [17]. Even though both approaches are able to automate document migration for a fixed set of format changes, they are not able to handle arbitrary, complex migrations.

Metamodel evolution denotes the migration of models in response to adaptations of their metamodel. In order to specify the model migration between two metamodel versions, Sprinkle introduces a visual graph-transformation-based language [18,19]. Compared to conventional languages for model transformation, this language allows to specify the differences between two metamodels rather than their similarities. However, Sprinkle's language does not provide a mechanism for reusing recurring migration knowledge.

There are a number of approaches to automatically derive a model migration from the difference between two metamodel versions. Gruschko et al. classify primitive metamodel changes into non-breaking, breaking resolvable and unresolvable changes [20,21]. Based on this classification, they propose to automatically derive a migration for non-breaking and resolvable changes, and envision to support the developer in specifying a migration for unresolvable changes. Cichetti et al. go even one step further and try to detect composite changes like e. g. extract class based on the difference between metamodel versions [22]. However, their approach is no longer automatic for composite changes which depend on each other. Although fully automated to some degree, the difference-based approaches have the disadvantage that the derived migration may not be the one intended by the developer. As a consequence, the developer has to manually modify and therefore understand the derived migration.

To avoid this problem, incremental transformation allows to capture the intention while performing metamodel adaptation. Several approaches to perform an incremental coupled transformation of metamodel and model have been proposed. Hößler and Soden present a number of high-level transformations which adapt the metamodel and migrate models [23]. These transformations are based upon a generic instance model for both metamodel and model which is required to support versioning. Wachsmuth adopts ideas from grammar engineering and proposes a classification of metamodel changes based on instance preservation properties [24]. Based on these preservation properties, the author defines a set of high-level coupled transformations. While both approaches enable the reuse of migration knowledge, they do not provide sufficient expressiveness to cater for complex coupled transformations.

In a nutshell, there is no approach for metamodel evolution that combines both the desired level of reuse and expressiveness. To alleviate this, we propose COPE, which integrates a number of features of existing approaches. Like Sprinkle's language, COPE also relieves the metamodel developer from specifying identity rules for metamodel elements which do not have changed. COPE achieves this by using a generic instance model during migration similar to the proposal of Hößler and Soden. Based on this generic instance model, COPE follows an incremental transformation approach which allows to capture the intention while performing the metamodel adaptation. In addition, the incremental approach allows to better modularize the coupled evolution into manageable transformations, and thus to easily combine reuse with expressiveness.

4   Coupled Evolution of Metamodels and Models

In this section, we present COPE's language to specify the coupled evolution of metamodels and models. This language provides concepts to fulfill both requirements presented in Section 2: reuse of recurring migration knowledge and expressiveness to cater for domain-specific migrations. Reuse is provided by an abstraction mechanism that allows to encapsulate both metamodel adaptation and model migration in a metamodel-independent way. Expressiveness is provided by embedding primitives for metamodel adaptation and model migration into a Turing-complete language. From our experience, developers prefer to use the metamodel editor over specifying the coupled evolution in this language. Consequently, COPE provides further abstraction from this language by a non-invasive integration into a metamodel editor. For simplicity of presentation, we outline the language here, and present the tool support in Section 5.

Running example. Throughout this section, we use a statemachine metamodel as a running example. Figure 2 shows the metamodel before and after adaptation as a UML class diagram. In version 0 of the metamodel, a State has a name and may be decomposed into sub states through its subclass CompositeState. A Transition belongs to its source state and refers to a target state, and is activated by a trigger. When a state is entered, a sequence of actions is performed as effect, and in case of a composite state, an initial state is entered. For version 1 of the metamodel, the following adaptations are performed[1]:

1. The statemachine is changed from a Moore to a Mealy machine. In Moore machines, the effect of the statemachine only depends on the current state. In contrast, the effect of the statemachine depends also on the trigger in Mealy machines. Therefore, we move the attribute effect from State to Transition.
2. Regions are introduced to support concurrency within states. Therefore, we insert the class Region. We further introduce the new composition region so that a composite state can define a number of concurrent regions. Finally, we move the composition state and the association initial to the new class Region, as regions are now composed of sub states.

In the following, we subsequently specify the coupled evolution in COPE's language in order to be able to migrate existing models.

---

[1] In Figure 1, the differences are indicated by numbered, dashed boxes.

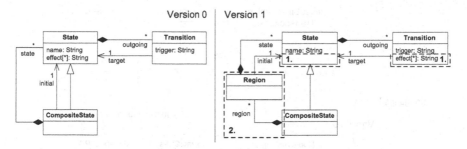

Fig. 2. Running example adaptation

4.1 Incremental Coupled Evolution

In practice, a modeling language is evolved by incremental adaptations to the metamodel. There are a number of primitive metamodel changes like create element, rename element, delete element, and so on. One or more such primitive changes compose a specific metamodel adaptation, like in our example the introduction of regions. COPE allows to attach information about how to migrate corresponding models in response to a metamodel adaptation. Consequently, the intended model migration can already be captured while adapting the metamodel, thus preventing the loss of intention. In COPE, such a combination of metamodel adaptation and model migration is called *coupled transaction*.

Coupled transactions can be easily composed by simply sequencing them. They are modular in the sense that the corresponding model migration can be specified independently of any neighboring coupled transaction. Due to their modularity, a comprehensive evolution can be decomposed into manageable coupled transactions, thus ensuring scalability. The notion of coupled transaction qualifies to fulfill the requirements of reuse and expressiveness. Certain coupled transactions can be reused resulting in *reusable coupled transactions*, while others have to be specified manually resulting in *custom coupled transactions*.

Figure 3 illustrates how coupled transactions can be used to compose the coupled evolution of our running example. The first coupled transaction changes the statemachine metamodel from a Moore to a Mealy machine. As the corresponding model migration is specific to the metamodel, it has to be performed by a custom coupled transaction. The last two coupled transactions introduce concurrent regions to the metamodel and are invocations of reusable coupled transactions. The invocation of ExtractClass extracts the sub states including the initial state of a composite state into the new class Region. The invocation of GeneralizeReference generalizes the multiplicity of the new reference from CompositeState to Region to enable concurrent regions.

Keeping track of the coupled transactions that lead from one metamodel version to the next results in a *language history*. The language history contains enough information to migrate a model from the metamodel version to which it conforms to any subsequent metamodel version. Hence, it is particularly suited to migrate models which are not accessible while performing the metamodel

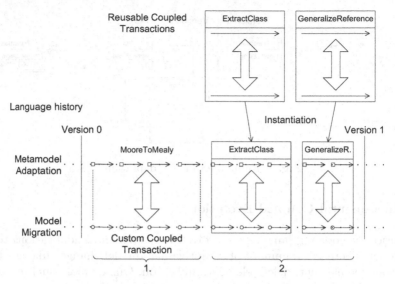

Fig. 3. Language history for the running example

adaptation. This is the case when the modeling language and the models are developed by different distributed parties. Figure 3 indicates the language history for our running example which consists of the sequence of coupled transactions together with markers for the different versions.

4.2 Coupled Transactions

Usually, the metamodel adaptation is manually performed in the metamodeling tool used for authoring the metamodel. The model migration can be manually encoded as a model transformation which transforms the old model to a new model conforming to the adapted metamodel. In general, we distinguish between *exogenous* and *endogenous* model transformation, depending on whether source and target metamodel of the transformation are different or not [29]. Exogenous model transformation requires to specify the mapping of all elements from the source to the target metamodel. As typically only a subset of metamodel elements are modified by the metamodel adaptation, a model migration specified as an exogenous transformation contains a high fraction of identity rules. Concerning this aspect, endogenous transformation is better suited to the nature of model migration, as it only has to address those metamodel elements for which the model needs to be modified. However, endogenous transformation requires the source and the target metamodel to be the same which is not the case for metamodel evolution. Hence, conventional languages for model transformation are not well suited to specify a model migration.

Instead, model migration is best served by a language that allows to directly combine the properties of both exogenous and endogenous model transformation: one needs to be able to specify the transformation from a source metamodel to a different target metamodel, but only for the metamodel elements for which a migration is required. In order to achieve this, we propose to soften the conformance between metamodel and its model during coupled evolution: the metamodel can first be adapted regardless of its models, and the model can then be migrated to the adapted metamodel. As a consequence, only the differences need to be specified for both metamodel adaptation and model migration. However, softening the conformance during model migration comes at the price that a model may not always conform to its metamodel. In order to ensure conformance after a certain change to metamodel and model, we require a coupled transaction to enforce the following properties:

Consistency preservation: The adapted metamodel is consistent, i.e. fulfills the constraints defined by the meta-metamodel, if the original one was.
Conformance preservation: The migrated model conforms to the adapted metamodel, if the original model conformed to the original metamodel.

Note that both consistency and conformance thus have to hold only at transaction boundaries, i.e. the metamodel may be inconsistent or the model may not conform to the metamodel during a transaction.

We have implemented COPE on top of the Eclipse Modeling Framework (EMF) [30] which is one of the most widely used metamodeling tools. In this implementation, the conformance is softened by a generic instance model which is only used during migration. To specify both metamodel adaptation and model migration, COPE provides a number of expressive primitives which operate on the generic instance model. These primitives can be invoked from within the general-purpose scripting language Groovy [31] in order to take advantage of its expressiveness. For more information about the generic instance model and a complete list of the primitives, we refer the reader to [32].

4.3 Custom Coupled Transactions

Expressiveness is provided by custom coupled transactions, which have to be specified manually by the metamodel developer. In doing so, the metamodel developer can apply a number of primitives for both metamodel adaptation and model migration. The primitives are complete in the sense that every possible metamodel adaptation as well as model migration can be specified with them. Completeness can be shown by first destroying the source metamodel or model, and then rebuilding the target metamodel or model from scratch as done in [11] for database schema evolution. As these primitives are embedded into the Turing-complete scripting language Groovy, the resulting language is expressive enough to even cater for very specific model migrations.

Example. Listing 1 shows the custom coupled transaction that was performed to change the statemachine from a Moore to a Mealy machine. More specifically, the depicted custom coupled transaction consists of a metamodel adaptation and a reconciling model migration. This example also shows that we only have to specify the differences for both metamodel and model in this language.

Listing 1. Custom coupled transaction MooreToMealy.

```
// metamodel adaptation
def effectAttribute = State.effect
Transition.eStructuralFeatures.add(effectAttribute)

// model migration
getEffect = { transition ->
  def effect = []
  def state = transition.target
  effect.addAll(state.get(effectAttribute))
  while(state.instanceOf(CompositeState)) {
    effect.addAll(state.initial.get(effectAttribute))
    state = state.initial
  }
  return effect
}

for(transition in Transition.allInstances) {
  def effect = getEffect(transition)
  transition.effect = effect
}

for(state in State.allInstances) {
  state.unset(effectAttribute)
}
```

The metamodel adaptation only moves the attribute effect from class State to class Transition. The attribute is assigned to the variable effectAttribute in order to be able to access its values for states, even though the attribute is no longer known to the class State. Note how metamodel elements can be accessed by means of fully qualified names (e. g. State.effect).

A Moore machine is migrated to a Mealy machine by moving the effect of each state to its incoming transitions. However, in the advent of composite states as well as initial states, the model migration is more involved. When a statemachine transitions to a composite state, it not only enters the composite state but also its initial state. Consequently, we also have to take the effect of the initial state into account when calculating the effect of the transition. Note that this may have to be applied recursively, as the initial state may again be a composite state, and so on. The model migration encoded in COPE's language is thus divided into two passes: First, we set the effect for each transition based on the states, and then we remove the effect from each state. The language provides the primitive allInstances to be able to iterate over all instances of a certain type. The effect of a transition is set by using transition.effect = effect which is a short form for transition.set(Transition.effect, effect). The effect of a transition is calculated by means of the helper method getEffect. As explained before, the effect consists of the effect of the transition's target state as well as the effects of the initial states. transition.target is the short form for transition.get(Transition.target). However, the short forms can only be used, in case a feature of that name is currently defined by the instance's type. As the attribute effect is no longer defined for class State, we thus have to use state.get(effectAttribute) to be able to access the effect of a state. Furthermore, the primitive instanceOf can be used to check whether a state is of type CompositeState. The effect of a state is removed by using a primitive to unset the effectAttribute.

4.4   Reusable Coupled Transactions

Reuse is provided by an abstraction mechanism to generalize coupled transactions into so-called reusable coupled transactions. Reusable coupled transactions are specified independently of the metamodel, and encapsulate both metamodel adaptation and reconciling model migration. They can be reused across metamodels, thus promising to significantly reduce effort associated with metamodel adaptation and model migration. COPE allows to declare new reusable coupled transactions and make them available through a *library*. The language employs the abstraction mechanism of procedures in Groovy in order to declare reusable coupled transactions. A reusable coupled transaction is declared independently of the specific metamodel by means of parameters. Reusable coupled transactions can be instantiated by invoking the procedure with parameters assigned to specific metamodel elements. The applicability of a reusable coupled transaction can be restricted by preconditions in the form of assertions.

Example. Listing 2 shows the invocation of the reusable coupled transactions ExtractClass and GeneralizeReference, which correspond to the second adaptation in our example history. ExtractClass is invoked to extract the references state and initial from CompositeState to the new class Region. The extracted region then is accessible from a composite state through the new single-valued containment reference named region. GeneralizeReference is invoked to increase the multiplicity of this new reference in order to enable multiple concurrent regions. Note that by invoking reusable coupled transactions, the metamodel developer does not have to specify neither metamodel adaptation nor model migration.

Listing 2. Instantiation of reusable coupled transactions.

```
extractClass([CompositeState.state, CompositeState.initial],
     "Region", "region")
generalizeReference(CompositeState.region, Region, 1, INF)
```

Listing 3 shows the declaration of the reusable coupled transaction Extract-Class which we just invoked to introduce regions into our example metamodel. This reusable coupled transaction extracts a number of features from a context class to a new class. The extracted class is accessible from the context class through a new single-valued containment reference. The reusable coupled transaction declares parameters for the attributes and references to be extracted (features), the name of the new class (className) and the name of the new reference (referenceName). Several preconditions in the form of assertions restrict

Listing 3. Declaration of reusable coupled transaction ExtractClass.

```
extractClass = {List<EStructuralFeature> features, String
className, String referenceName ->

  def EClass contextClass = features[0].eContainingClass

  // preconditions
  assert features.every{feature -> feature.eContainingClass ==
      contextClass} :
    "The features have to belong to the same class"
  assert contextClass.getEStructuralFeature(referenceName) ==
      null || features.contains(contextClass.
      getEStructuralFeature(referenceName)) :
    "A feature with the same name already exists"

  // metamodel adaptation
  def extractedClass = newEClass(className)
  def reference = contextClass.newEReference(referenceName,
      extractedClass, 1, 1, CONTAINMENT)
  extractedClass.eStructuralFeatures.addAll(features)

  // model migration
  for(contextInstance in contextClass.allInstances) {
    def extractedInstance = extractedClass.newInstance()
    contextInstance.set(reference, extractedInstance)
    for(feature in features) {
      extractedInstance.set(feature, contextInstance.unset(
          feature))
    }
  }
}
```

the applicability of the reusable coupled transaction, e. g. every feature has to belong to the same context class.

The metamodel adaptation creates the extracted class and the new single-valued containment reference from the context class to the extracted class. Then, the extracted features are moved from the context class to the extracted class. For the metamodel adaptation, we use the primitives of the meta-metamodel implementation together with some high-level primitives to create new metamodel elements (e. g. newEClass). The reusable coupled transaction is simplified in the sense that it leaves out the package in which the extracted class is created.

The model migration pretty much modifies the model accordingly. For each instance of the context class (contextInstance), a new instance of the extracted class is created and associated to the context instance through the new reference. Then, all the values of the extracted features are moved from the context instance to the new instance. Note that due to the generic instance model the context instance's value of a feature can still be accessed by the unset method, even though the feature has already been moved to the extracted class.

5   Tool Support

From our experience, metamodel developers do not want to script the coupled evolution, but rather prefer to adapt the metamodel directly in an editor. Consequently, COPE is implemented as a non-invasive integration into the existing EMF metamodel editor. Even though COPE is based on the language presented in Section 4, it shields the metamodel developer from this language as far as possible. COPE is open source and can be obtained from our website[2]. The web site also provides a screencast, documentation and several examples (including the running example from this paper). We first describe the workflow that is supported by COPE, before detailing on its integration into the user interface.

5.1   Tool Workflow

Figure 4 illustrates the tool workflow using the running example from Section 4.

COPE provides a *library* of reusable coupled transactions that can be invoked on a specific metamodel. Besides the transactions used in Section 4, the current library contains a number of other reusable coupled transactions like e. g. Rename

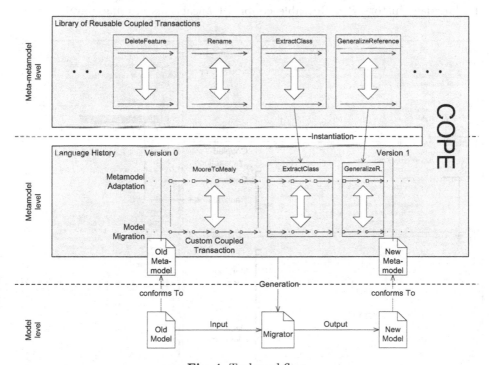

Fig. 4. Tool workflow

---

[2] http://cope.in.tum.de

or DeleteFeature. The library is extensible in the sense that new reusable coupled operations can be declared and registered. Reusable coupled transactions are declared independently of the specific metamodel, i.e. on the level of the meta-metamodel.

All changes performed to the metamodel are maintained in an explicit *language history*. The history keeps track of the coupled transactions which contain both metamodel adaptation and model migration. It is structured according to the major language versions, i.e. when the language was deployed. All previous versions of the metamodel can be easily reconstructed from the information available in the history. In Figure 4, the evolution from version 0 to version 1 is the sequence of coupled transactions we performed in Section 4.

A *migrator* can be generated from the language history that allows for the batch migration of models. The migrator can be invoked to automatically migrate existing models, i.e. no user interaction is required during migration.

5.2   User Interface

Figure 5 shows an annotated screen shot of COPE's user interface. COPE has been integrated into the existing structural metamodel editor provided by EMF (a). This metamodel editor has been extended so that it also provides access to the language history (b). Reusable coupled transactions are made available to

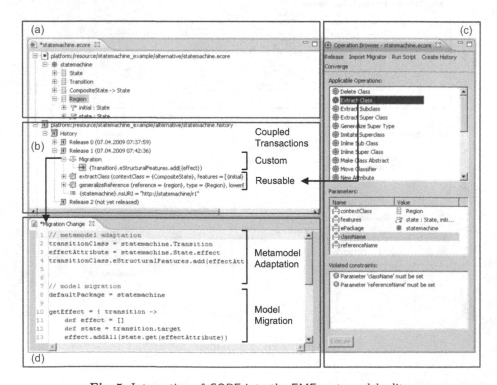

Fig. 5. Integration of COPE into the EMF metamodel editor

the metamodel developer through a special view called *operation browser* (c). An editor with syntax highlighting is provided for the specification of custom coupled transactions (d).

The metamodel developer can adapt the metamodel by invoking reusable coupled transactions through the *operation browser*. The browser is context-sensitive, i. e. offers only those reusable coupled transactions that are applicable to the elements currently selected in the metamodel editor. The operation browser allows to set the parameters of a reusable coupled transaction based on their type, and gives feedback on its applicability based on the preconditions. When a reusable coupled transaction is executed, its invocation is automatically tracked in the language history. Figure 5 shows the ExtractClass operation being available in the browser (c), and the reusable coupled transactions stored in the history (b). Note that the metamodel developer does not have to know about the coupled evolution language if she is only invoking reusable coupled transactions.

In case no reusable coupled transaction is available for the coupled evolution at hand, the metamodel developer can perform a custom coupled transaction. First, the metamodel is directly adapted in the metamodel editor, in response to which the changes are automatically tracked in the history. A migration can later be attached to the sequence of metamodel changes by encoding it in the language presented in Section 4. Note that the metamodel adaptation is automatically generated from the changes tracked in the history. In order to allow for different metamodeling habits, adapting the metamodel and attaching a model migration is temporally decoupled such that a model migration can be attached at any later instant. Figure 5 shows the model migration attached to the manual changes (b) in a separate editor with syntax highlighting (d).

The operation browser provides a release button to create a major version of the metamodel. After release, the metamodel developer can initiate the automatic generation of a migrator.

6   Case Study

In order to demonstrate its applicability in practice, we used COPE to model the coupled evolution of two existing metamodels. The detailed results of the case study in the form of the language histories as presented in Section 5 can be obtained from our website[3].

6.1   Goals

The study was performed to test the applicability of COPE to real-world coupled evolution and better understand the potential for reuse of recurring migration knowledge. More specifically, the study was performed to answer the following research questions:

---

[3] http://cope.in.tum.de

- Which fraction of the changes are simple metamodel extensions that do trivially not require a migration of models?
- Which fraction of the changes can be reused by means of reusable coupled transactions?
- Which fraction of the changes have to be implemented by means of custom coupled transactions?
- Can COPE be applied to specify the complete coupled evolution of real-world metamodels, i.e. including all intermediate versions?

6.2 Setup

As input to our study, we chose two EMF-based metamodels that already have an extensive evolution history. We deliberately chose metamodels from completely different backgrounds in order to achieve more representative results.

The first metamodel is developed as part of the open source project Graphical Modeling Framework[4] (GMF). It is used to define generator models from which code for a graphical editor is generated. For our case study, we modeled the coupled evolution from release 1.0 over 2.0 to release 2.1, which covers a period of 2 years. There exist a significant number of models conforming to this metamodel, most of which are not under control of the developers. In order to be able to migrate these models, the developers have handcrafted a migrator with test cases which can be used for validation.

The second metamodel is developed as part of the research project Palladio Component Model[5] (PCM), and is used for the specification and analysis of component-based software architectures. For our case study, we modeled the coupled evolution from release 2.0 over 3.0 to release 4.0, which covers a period of 1.5 years. As the metamodel developers control the few models, they were not forced to handcraft a migrator until now, but manually migrated the models instead. Since no migrator could be used for validation for this reason, the modeled coupled evolution was validated by the developers of PCM.

The evolution of the metamodels was only available in the form of snapshots that depict the state of the metamodel at a particular point in time. To this end, we had to infer both the metamodel adaptation as well as the corresponding model migration. We used the following systematic procedure to reverse engineer the coupled evolution:

1. *Extraction of metamodel versions*: We extracted versions of the metamodel from the version control system.
2. *Comparison of subsequent metamodel versions*: Since the version control systems of both projects are snapshot-based, they provide no information about the differences between the metamodel versions. Therefore, successive metamodel versions had to be compared to obtain a difference model. The difference model consists of a number of primitive changes between subsequent metamodel versions and was obtained by means of tool support[6].

---

[4] http://www.eclipse.org/modeling/gmf
[5] http://www.palladio-approach.net
[6] http://wiki.eclipse.org/index.php/EMF_Compare

3. *Generation of metamodel adaptation*: A first version of the history was obtained by generating a metamodel adaptation from the difference model between subsequent metamodel versions. For this purpose, a transformation was implemented that translates each of the primitive changes from the difference model to metamodel adaptation primitives specified in COPE.

4. *Detection of coupled transactions*: The generated metamodel adaptation was refined by combining adaptation primitives to coupled transactions based on the information on how corresponding models are migrated. In doing so, we always tried to map the compound changes to reusable coupled transactions already available in the library. If not possible, we tried to identify and develop new reusable coupled transactions. In case a certain model migration was too specific to be reused, it was realized as a custom coupled transaction.

5. *Validation of the history*: The validity of the obtained coupled evolution was tested on both levels. The metamodel adaptation is easy to validate, because the history can be executed and the result can be compared to the metamodel snapshots. Test models before and after model migration were used to validate whether the model migration performs as intended.

Steps 1 to 3 as well as 5 are fully automated, whereas step 4 had to be performed manually. In addition, there is an iteration over steps 4 and 5, as a failed validation leads to corrections of the history. It took roughly one person week for each studied metamodel to reach the fix point during the iteration. However, in this case study, the coupled evolution was obtained by reverse engineering, which requires a lot of effort for understanding the intended migration. We are convinced that the metamodel developers can model the coupled evolution with significantly less effort, when they use COPE for forward engineering.

6.3   Results

As the GMF developers do not have all the models under control, they employ a systematic change management process: the developers discuss metamodel adaptations and their impact on models thoroughly before actually carrying them out. Consequently, we found no destructive change at any instant in the history, that was reversed at a later instant. To this end, the obtained language history comprises all the intermediate versions. Figure 6(a) gives an impression of the size of the studied metamodel and its evolution over all the metamodel versions. In addition, the figure indicates the different releases of the metamodel. The metamodel is quite extensive, accumulating more than a hundred classes in the course of its history.

Figure 6(b) depicts the number of the different classes of metamodel adaptations that were used to model the coupled evolution using COPE. The metamodel extensions make up 64% of the adaptations, whereas reusable coupled transactions account for 34%. Table 1 refines this classification by listing the names and the number of occurrences of the different kinds of metamodel adaptations. The dashed line distinguishes the reusable coupled transactions known from the literature from those which have been implemented while conducting the case

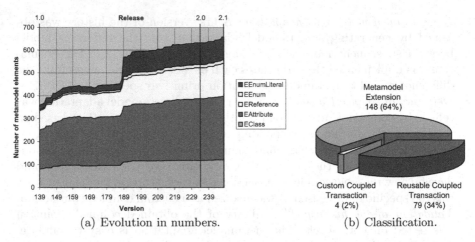

(a) Evolution in numbers.   (b) Classification.

Fig. 6. History of the GMF metamodel

study. For the GMF metamodel, these new reusable coupled transactions cover 15 out of 79 occurrences (19%). The remaining 2% of the metamodel adaptations consist of only 4 custom coupled transactions for which the model migration had to be implemented manually. The model migration code handcrafted for these custom coupled transactions amounts to 100 lines of code.

As the developers of the GMF metamodel do not have all the models under their control, they have manually implemented a migrator. This migrator constitutes a very technical solution, and is based on different mechanisms for the two stages. For the migration from release 1.0 to 2.0, the migrator patches the model while deserializing its XML representation. For the migration from release 2.0 to 2.1, a generic copy mechanism is used that first filters out non-conforming parts of the model, and later rebuilds them. Even though this migrator is very optimized, it is difficult to understand and maintain due the low abstraction level of its implementation.

As the developers of the PCM metamodel have all the models under their control, they apparently have not taken the impact on the models into account. Consequently, there were a lot of destructive changes between the intermediate versions, that were reversed at a later instant. To this end, the obtained language history comprises only the release versions. Figure 7(a) gives an impression of the size of the metamodel and its evolution over the studied releases. Similar to GMF, the PCM metamodel is quite extensive, being split up in a number of packages and defining more than a hundred classes throughout the history.

Figure 7(b) depicts the number of the different classes of metamodel adaptations that were used to model the coupled evolution. Here, the metamodel extensions account for only 25% of the metamodel adaptations, whereas reusable coupled transactions make up 74%. Again, Table 1 provides more detailed results. The reusable coupled transactions that were implemented while conducting the case study cover 12 out of 76 occurrences (16%). The remaining 1% of the metamodel adaptations consist of 1 custom coupled transaction for which

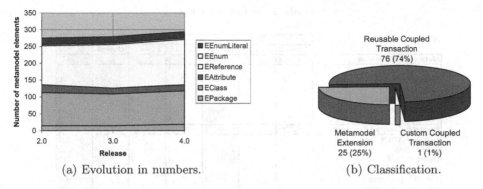

(a) Evolution in numbers.   (b) Classification.

Fig. 7. History of the PCM metamodel

the model migration had to be implemented manually. The model migration code handcrafted for this custom coupled transaction amounts to only 10 lines of code. As the developers have not yet provided tool support for model migration, our approach helped by providing an automatic migrator. However, they provided us with test models and helped to validate the obtained model migration.

6.4   Discussion

The fraction of metamodel extensions is very large for the GMF metamodel, whereas it is rather small for the PCM metamodel. A possible interpretation is that the GMF developers were as far as possible avoiding metamodel adaptations that required to enhance the migrator. The reason for the metamodel extensions could as well be the nature of the evolution: they were adding new generator features to the language which are orthogonal to existing ones.

For both metamodels, a large fraction of changes can be dealt with by reusable coupled transactions – aside from the metamodel extensions. This result strengthens the findings from the previous study as presented in Section 2 that a lot of migration effort can be saved by reuse in practice. Besides the reusable coupled transactions known from the literature, we have also identified a number of new reusable coupled transactions. It may seem odd that these new reusable coupled transactions could be used for one metamodel, but not for the other. However, two case studies may not suffice to show their usefulness in other scenarios. In addition, it may depend on the habits of the developer which reusable coupled transactions are often used and which not. The extension mechanism of COPE allows the developer to easily register new reusable coupled transactions which fit their habits.

For both metamodels, a very small fraction of changes were so specific that they had to be modeled as custom coupled transactions. Due to the expressiveness of the language, it was not difficult to manually implement these custom coupled transactions. This result also strengthens the findings from the previous study that a non-negligible number of changes are specific to the metamodel.

Table 1. Detailed results

	GMF			PCM			Overall
	1.0 - 2.0	2.0 - 2.1	Overall	2.0 - 3.0	3.0 - 4.0	Overall	
Metamodel Extension	136	12	148	9	16	25	173
Add Super Type				1	2	3	3
New Attribute	63	6	69		1	1	70
New Class	36	1	37	3	4	7	44
New Enumeration	12	1	13		4	4	17
New Package					4	4	4
New Reference	25	4	29	5	1	6	35
Reusable Coupled Transaction	76	3	79	44	32	76	155
Change Attribute Type				2	1	3	3
Delete Class				1		1	1
Delete Feature	14		14	4	2	6	20
Extract Class	1		1				1
Extract Super Class	5		5				5
Generalize Reference	5		5	2	2	4	9
Generalize Super Type				1	2	3	3
Inline Super Class	2		2				2
Move Classifier				1	4	5	5
Move Feature	2	1	3				3
Pull up Feature	3		3				3
Push down Feature	1		1				1
Rename	27	1	28	16	18	34	62
Replace Inheritance by Delegation	1	1	2	4		4	6
Specialize Super Type				3	1	4	4
Collect Feature	4		4				4
Combine Feature	1		1				1
Copy Feature	1		1				1
Extract and Group Attribute	1		1				1
Extract existing Class				2		2	2
Flatten Hierarchy	1		1				1
Propagate Feature	1		1				1
Remove Superfluous Super Type					1	1	1
Remove Super Type	1		1		1	1	2
Replace Class	2		2	7		7	9
Replace Enumeration	2		2				2
Replace Literal	1		1				1
Specialize Composition				1		1	1
Custom Coupled Transaction	2	2	4	1		1	5

The case studies further showed that COPE can be applied to specify the coupled evolution of real-world metamodels. In case of the GMF metamodel, we would even have been able to directly use COPE for its maintenance. As the GMF developers do not control the numerous existing models, they took also the impact on the models into account while adapting the metamodel. COPE can help here to perform more profound metamodel adaptations. In case of the PCM metamodel, we would not have been able to directly use COPE for its maintenance. For metamodel adaptation, the PCM developers preferred flexibility over preservation of existing models, as they have the few existing models under control. COPE can help here to perform the metamodel adaptations in a more systematic way by using reusable coupled transactions. Summing up, COPE provides a compromise between the two studied types of metamodel histories: its provides more flexibility for carrying out metamodel adaptations, and offers at the same time a more systematic approach for metamodel adaptation.

7   Conclusion

Just as other software artifacts, modeling languages and thus their metamodels have to be adapted. In order to reduce the effort for the resulting migration of models, adequate tool support is required. In previous work, we have performed a study on the histories of two industrial metamodels to determine requirements for adequate tool support. Adequate tool support needs to support the reuse of migration knowledge, while at the same time being expressive enough for complex migrations. To the best of our knowledge, existing approaches for model migration do not cater for both reuse and expressiveness. This paper presented COPE, an integrated approach fulfilling these requirements. Using COPE, the coupled evolution can be incrementally composed of coupled transactions that only require specification of the differences of metamodel and models in consecutive versions. The resulting modularity of coupled transactions ensures scalability, and is particularly suited to combine reuse with expressiveness. Reuse is provided by reusable coupled transactions that encapsulate recurring migration knowledge. Expressiveness is provided by a complete set of primitives embedded into a Turing-complete language, which can be used to specify custom coupled transactions. Tracking the performed coupled transactions in an explicit language history allows to migrate models at a later instant, and provides better traceability of metamodel adaptations. We implemented these language concepts based on the Eclipse Modeling Framework (EMF). To ease its application, COPE was seamlessly integrated into the metamodel editor, shielding the metamodel developer from technical details as far as possible. We demonstrated the applicability of COPE to real-world language evolution by reproducing the coupled evolution of two existing modeling languages over several years. These case studies strengthen the findings of our previous study [7]: while reuse saves a lot of effort, expressiveness is required for the rare, but important cases of complex migrations.

Future Work. During the case studies, we have validated the usefulness of well-known reusable coupled transactions, but also identified a number of new ones. Until now, we pretty much developed new reusable coupled transactions in a demand-driven way. However, we plan to compile a library of well-tested reusable coupled transactions that cover most scenarios of metamodel evolution. To this end, the existing ones may have to be refined, consolidated and aligned more orthogonally to each other. Building on [24], we intend to classify reusable coupled transactions according to instance preservation properties so that the metamodel developer can better assess their impact on models.

Currently, conformance preservation of a coupled transaction can only be verified while executing it on a certain model. To enable the verification of conformance preservation in a model-independent way, we intend to develop a static analysis. In contrast to the verification of properties, validation is more concerned with whether the migration performs as intended. In order to validate coupled transactions, we plan to develop a framework for the rigorous testing of model migrations. This may include specific coverage criteria as well as a method to derive new test models.

In this paper, we were only concerned with the migration of models in response to metamodel adaptation. However, there are also other artifacts like e. g. editors and generators which depend on the metamodel and which thus have to be migrated. We first focused on model migration, as the number of models of a successful modeling language typically outnumbers the number of other artifacts. To this end, we intend to extend COPE in a way that also the migration of other artifacts can be specified. Especially for reusable coupled transactions, we plan an extension mechanism to allow for the injection of migration code for other artifacts.

As we already mentioned, our approach is especially suited for the incremental development and maintenance of modeling languages. We claim that a good modeling language is hard to obtain by an upfront design, but rather has to be developed by an evolutionary process. A version of a modeling language is defined and deployed to obtain feedback from its users, which again may lead to a new version. We thus plan to define a systematic process in order to support the evolutionary development of modeling languages. This process should also cover the maintenance of existing modeling languages. To that end, it should also provide methods to identify bad metamodel designs and to replace them by better designs.

Acknowledgements. We are thankful to the PCM developers – especially Steffen Becker, Franz Brosch, and Klaus Krogmann – to grant us access to their metamodel history, and for the effort spent on migration validation. We also like to thank Steffen Becker, Antonio Cicchetti, Thomas Goldschmidt, Steven Kelly, Anneke Kleppe, Klaus Krogmann, Ed Merks, Alfonso Pierantonio, Juha-Pekka Tolvanen, Sander Vermolen, Markus Voelter, and Guido Wachsmuth for encouraging discussion, and for helpful suggestions. We are also grateful to anonymous reviewers for comments on earlier versions of this paper.

References

1. Kleppe, A.G., Warmer, J., Bast, W.: MDA Explained: The Model Driven Architecture: Practice and Promise. Addison-Wesley, Boston (2003)
2. Greenfield, J., Short, K., Cook, S., Kent, S.: Software Factories: Assembling Applications with Patterns, Models, Frameworks, and Tools. Wiley, Chichester (2004)
3. Kelly, S., Tolvanen, J.P.: Domain-Specific Modeling. John Wiley & Sons, Chichester (2007)
4. AUTOSAR Development Partnership: AUTOSAR Specification V3.1 (2008)
5. Favre, J.-M.: Languages evolve too! changing the software time scale. In: 8th International Workshop on Principles of Software Evolution (IWPSE), pp. 33–44. IEEE Computer Society Press, Los Alamitos (2005)
6. Object Management Group: Unified Modeling Language, Superstructure, v2.1.2 (2007)
7. Herrmannsdoerfer, M., Benz, S., Juergens, E.: Automatability of Coupled Evolution of Metamodels and Models in Practice. In: Czarnecki, K., Ober, I., Bruel, J.-M., Uhl, A., Völter, M. (eds.) MODELS 2008. LNCS, vol. 5301, pp. 645–659. Springer, Heidelberg (2008)

8. Fowler, M.: Refactoring: improving the design of existing code. Addison-Wesley Longman Publishing Co., Inc., Amsterdam (1999)
9. Mens, T., Wermelinger, M., Ducasse, S., Demeyer, S., Hirschfeld, R., Jazayeri, M.: Challenges in software evolution. In: 8th International Workshop on Principles of Software Evolution (IWPSE), pp. 13–22 (2005)
10. Lämmel, R.: Coupled Software Transformations (Extended Abstract). In: 1st International Workshop on Software Evolution Transformations (2004)
11. Banerjee, J., Kim, W., Kim, H.-J., Korth, H.F.: Semantics and implementation of schema evolution in object-oriented databases. In: SIGMOD Rec., vol. 16, pp. 311–322. ACM Press, New York (1987)
12. Ferrandina, F., Meyer, T., Zicari, R., Ferran, G., Madec, J.: Schema and database evolution in the O2 object database system. In: 21th International Conference on Very Large Data Bases (VLDB), pp. 170–181. Morgan Kaufmann, San Francisco (1995)
13. Claypool, K.T., Jin, J., Rundensteiner, E.A.: SERF: schema evolution through an extensible, re-usable and flexible framework. In: 7th International Conference on Information and Knowledge Management (CIKM), pp. 314–321. ACM Press, New York (1998)
14. Lämmel, R.: Grammar adaptation. In: Oliveira, J.N., Zave, P. (eds.) FME 2001. LNCS, vol. 2021, pp. 550–570. Springer, Heidelberg (2001)
15. Pizka, M., Juergens, E.: Automating language evolution. In: 1st Joint IEEE/IFIP Symposium on Theoretical Aspects of Software Engineering (TASE), pp. 305–315. IEEE Computer Society Press, Los Alamitos (2007)
16. Lämmel, R., Lohmann, W.: Format Evolution. In: 7th International Conference on Reverse Engineering for Information Systems (RETIS), vol. 155, pp. 113–134. OCG (2001)
17. Su, H., Kramer, D., Chen, L., Claypool, K., Rundensteiner, E.A.: XEM: Managing the Evolution of XML Documents. In: 11th International Workshop on research Issues in Data Engineering (RIDE), p. 103. IEEE Computer Society Press, Los Alamitos (2001)
18. Sprinkle, J.M.: Metamodel driven model migration. PhD thesis, Nashville, TN, USA (2003)
19. Sprinkle, J., Karsai, G.: A domain-specific visual language for domain model evolution. Journal of Visual Languages and Computing 15, 291–307 (2004)
20. Becker, S., Gruschko, B., Goldschmidt, T., Koziolek, H.: A Process Model and Classification Scheme for Semi-Automatic Meta-Model Evolution. In: 1st Workshop, MDD, SOA und IT-Management (MSI), GI, pp. 35–46. GiTO-Verlag (2007)
21. Gruschko, B., Kolovos, D., Paige, R.: Towards synchronizing models with evolving metamodels. In: International Workshop on Model-Driven Software Evolution (2007)
22. Cicchetti, A., Ruscio, D.D., Eramo, R., Pierantonio, A.: Automating co-evolution in model-driven engineering. In: Ceballos, S. (ed.) 12th International Enterprise Distributed Object Computing Conference (EDOC). IEEE Computer Society Press, Los Alamitos (2008)
23. Hößler, J., Soden, M., Eichler, H.: Coevolution of Models, Metamodels and Transformations. In: Models and Human Reasoning, pp. 129–154. Wissenschaft und Technik Verlag, Berlin (2005)
24. Wachsmuth, G.: Metamodel adaptation and model co-adaptation. In: Ernst, E. (ed.) ECOOP 2007. LNCS, vol. 4609, pp. 600–624. Springer, Heidelberg (2007)

25. Vermolen, S.D., Visser, E.: Heterogeneous coupled evolution of software languages. In: Czarnecki, K., Ober, I., Bruel, J.-M., Uhl, A., Völter, M. (eds.) MODELS 2008. LNCS, vol. 5301, pp. 630–644. Springer, Heidelberg (2008)
26. Li, X.: A survey of schema evolution in object-oriented databases. In: 31st International Conference on Technology of Object-Oriented Language and Systems (TOOLS), p. 362. IEEE Computer Society, Los Alamitos (1999)
27. Rahm, E., Bernstein, P.A.: An online bibliography on schema evolution. SIGMOD Rec. 35(4), 30–31 (2006)
28. Klint, P., Lämmel, R., Verhoef, C.: Toward an engineering discipline for grammarware. ACM Trans. Softw. Eng. Methodol. 14(3), 331–380 (2005)
29. Mens, T., Van Gorp, P.: A taxonomy of model transformation. Electronic Notes in Theoretical Computer Science 152, 125–142 (2006)
30. Budinsky, F., Brodsky, S.A., Merks, E.: Eclipse Modeling Framework. Pearson Education, London (2003)
31. Koenig, D., Glover, A., King, P., Laforge, G., Skeet, J.: Groovy in Action. Manning Publications Co., Greenwich (2007)
32. Herrmannsdoerfer, M., Benz, S., Juergens, E.: COPE: A Language for the Coupled Evolution of Metamodels and Models. In: 1st International Workshop on Model Co-Evolution and Consistency Management (2008)

Making Sense of Large Heaps

Nick Mitchell, Edith Schonberg, and Gary Sevitsky

IBM T.J. Watson Research Center
Hawthorne, NY, US 10532
{nickm,ediths,sevitsky}@us.ibm.com

Abstract. It is common for large-scale Java applications to suffer memory problems, whether inefficient designs that impede scalability, or lifetime bugs such as leaks. Making sense of heaps with many millions of objects is difficult given the extensive layering, framework reuse, and shared ownership in current applications. We present Yeti, a tool that summarizes memory usage to uncover the costs of design decisions, rather than of lower-level artifacts as in traditional tools, making it possible to quickly identify and remediate problems. Yeti employs three progressive abstractions and corresponding visualizations: it identifies costly groups of objects that collectively perform a function, recovers a logical data model for each, and summarizes the implementation of each model entity and relationship. Yeti is used by development and service teams within IBM, and has been effective in solving numerous problems. Through case studies we demonstrate how these abstractions help solve common categories of problems.

1 Introduction

Many Java applications suffer from excessive memory footprint [11]. Our group has diagnosed footprint problems in scores of large-scale commercial applications over the past eight years. For example, we commonly find server deployments that support only a thousand concurrent users per machine, thus missing desired targets by orders of magnitude. Poor memory usage impedes scalability, increases the burden on the garbage collector, results in increased power consumption when extra servers are needed to meet throughput requirements, and inhibits parallelism on architectures with limited memory bandwidth. It also impacts production schedules, as many problems are not uncovered until late in the cycle. In this paper, we present a memory analysis tool motivated by the realities of large-scale object-oriented development.

Developers construct applications by integrating many layers of separately developed libraries and frameworks, each designed to hide its implementation details. As a consequence, developers cannot easily understand the global cost implications of their local data modeling choices. The pile up of many small decisions can inadvertently lead to a large cost. For example, we worked with a team that implemented a data model for connections between users. While coding this, they followed standard software engineering practice of reusing existing

S. Drossopoulou (Ed.): ECOOP 2009, LNCS 5653, pp. 77–97, 2009.
© Springer-Verlag Berlin Heidelberg 2009

classes and favoring delegation over subclassing [6]. As a result, each connection consumed 27 instances from 17 distinct classes. This design incurred a surprisingly high memory overhead: pointers and Java object headers consumed 62% of a connection's memory footprint. The application did not scale beyond a few thousand simultaneous connections, despite needing to support a few million.

Developers also have difficulty managing long-lived structures. Applications developed in a layered and distributed fashion are prone to lifetime bugs such as memory leaks and memory drag [15], when objects remain live well beyond their last use. One common cause is *shared ownership* where, for example, two teams unknowingly disagree on who should clip the last reference to a structure. Beyond bugs, there is the complex task of configuring caches and resource pools. In order to establish size bounds that perform well, one must know the cost per cached element. Unfortunately, predicting unit costs is not easy, when so many disparate pieces of code participate in each structure. Further complicating matters, developers must manage the competing needs of multiple caches, while leaving headroom for temporary objects.

In this environment, finding the right abstractions for analysis and visualization presents a number of challenges. Heaps can have tens of millions of objects, so some form of aggregation is clearly necessary. Due to code reuse, the aggregations need to take context into account; e.g. `Strings`, `HashMaps`, and even higher level structures such as XML DOMs are used for many unrelated purposes in an application. However, understanding context is difficult because of the preponderance of cycles, recursive structures, and shared ownership [9]. It is also difficult because of the large number of layers. Classes are now the assembly language of memory; even low-level artifacts such as `Strings` and collections are implemented with multiple classes. Some existing tools employ very local context, often for special purposes such as memory leak detection [5,18], and leave it to the user to disambiguate the conflated uses of common classes. Other tools do maintain a great deal of context [3,17,2], but require the user to manually navigate through the many layers of raw references. In general, with existing tools, the user is left to piece together the larger picture from the details.

We present Yeti, a memory analysis tool that embodies three progressively finer abstractions, to help guide the user to problem areas. Each abstraction is geared towards the analysis needs of a given level of detail. Yeti takes as input one or more Java heap snapshots gathered from a running program, and produces an interactive report with the following elements.

The data structure and its sections. Most of the heap usually consists of a few large sections, each devoted to different area of functionality. For example, memory might be apportioned to session state, to user interface state, and to information cached from external sources. In Section 2, we show how Yeti infers an initial *costly data structures* breakdown, an approximation of the most important areas of functionality, based on an extended notion of ownership. Because of shared ownership, a data structure may consist of groups of objects that are simultaneously part of other data structures; we show how Yeti computes a graph of interconnected data structure *sections*.

A section's data model. The user can drill down from a section to view its *content schematic* [11], a concise approximation of its logical data model, annotated with costs. While a section can contain millions of objects, the schematics that Yeti infers typically contain only a handful of nodes. Each node represents either a logical entity, such as an employee or a chat server connection, or a collection used to glue the entities together. Section 3 shows how common modeling inefficiencies, such as using many small collections, can be easily spotted by simple inspection of a content schematic visualization.

A data model's implementation. Developers implement entities and collections by combining objects from multiple classes. Yeti employs a *focused type graph*, summarizing only the objects that implement a single entity or collection in a single section. In Section 4, we show how common implementation inefficiencies, such as unexpected base class baggage, or implementations with too much delegation, can be easily spotted in a focused type graph.

Given one heap snapshot, Yeti has been successfully used to find many memory footprint problems and large memory leaks. Given a second heap snapshot, Yeti aligns the corresponding components of each of the three primary visualizations, and augments them with differential information. Previously, differential analysis of memory state has only been used to find memory leaks [3,10,5]. In Section 5, we show differential analysis based on the Yeti abstractions is useful for more than diagnostic purposes.

The contributions of this paper are:

- A progressive, top-down, approach to making sense of very large heaps. We employ three abstractions to quickly guide the user to areas of excessive memory consumption. The abstractions capture the implications of the local decisions being made by developers across many layers of code. We term these the data structure, the content schematic, and the focused type graph.
- Strategies for finding memory leak or drag bugs, for predicting scalability, and for regression testing, by analyzing changes to memory consumption of the three abstractions.
- Yeti, a tool that automatically infers these abstractions analyzing the runtime state of an application's heap. Yeti includes novel visualizations that summarize memory footprint in those terms. Yeti is deployed within IBM, and has been used to solve dozens of problems in industrial applications.
- Examples of common architectural and coding choices that result in excessive memory consumption, with evidence showing how Yeti easily identifies them. These examples come from several large-scale applications that suffered from excessive memory consumption, and that Yeti helped to diagnose.

2   The Data Structure

Individual objects exist as parts of larger cohesive units. Each unit of functionality is likely to have been implemented by different groups, have different designs, change differently over time, and have defects that require different

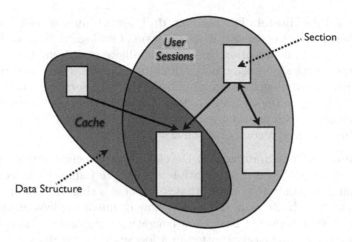

Fig. 1. Two data structures, Cache and User Sessions, consisting of four sections, one of which is shared between them

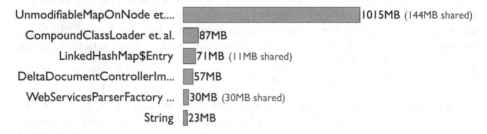

UnmodifiableMapOnNode et....	1015MB (144MB shared)
CompoundClassLoader et. al.	87MB
LinkedHashMap$Entry	71MB (11MB shared)
DeltaDocumentControllerIm...	57MB
WebServicesParserFactory ...	30MB (30MB shared)
String	23MB

Fig. 2. The Costly Data Structures from a snapshot with 20 million objects

remedies. We introduce the *data structure* abstraction to approximate these units of functionality.

To accommodate the fact that data structures overlap, we model a data structure as a graph of *sections*. Figure 1 illustrates two data structures, Cache and User Sessions, that share ownership of one section. Each section is a maximally sized subgraph of memory that contains objects with equivalent ownership. In Section 2.1 we show how to construct a graph of sections from a heap snapshot. From this, Yeti constructs a visualization that shows the most costly data structures, such as the one shown in Figure 2.

2.1 The Sections of a Data Structure

When one object dominates another [7], it acts as a gatekeeper; application code must follow references through the former to reach the latter. For this reason, the dominator relation is an important starting point for inferring the units of functionality in a heap. If we used the dominator relation in its textbook form, a unit of functionality would consist of those objects in a dominator tree, i.e. those objects dominated by the root of the tree.

There are three reasons why the dominator relation is insufficient for identifying data structures. First, there are many cases where one object artificially dominates another, because of the many systems-level mechanisms being implemented at the Java source level. Second, because of sharing, dominance does not preserve reachability. A dominator forest cannot represent shared ownership of an object when owners are located in different, disconnected trees. Third, a unit of functionality is often manifested by a *group* of dominator trees that are shared in an equivalent way. We now address these three issues.[1]

The Edge Pruning Heuristic. Artifacts of implementing systems functionality in the source language can result in too many or too few dominator trees. This is because some references in the heap artificially introduce sharing, and others artificially dominate. We give examples showing why, and present our solution, an edge pruning heuristic.

One example is the class loader, which often artificially dominates class objects. As a result, the class loader registry will indirectly (via static fields) dominate most of the objects in the heap. This can lead to the meaningless outcome of a single dominator tree that spans the entire heap, thus conflating unrelated areas of functionality. The class loader itself should also be treated as a separate unit of functionality.

The finalizer queue is an example of artificial sharing. In many JVMs, instances of a class with a `finalize` method are referenced by the finalizer queue throughout their lifetime. It is meaningful when finalizable objects are uniquely owned by the finalizer queue. These objects are now managed by the JVM, i.e. finalizable objects are part of the finalizer queue unit of functionality. It is less meaningful when non-finalizable objects are shared by the queue. This situation is a by-product of a choice made by the JVM developers: to implement an internal mechanism in the Java heap.

We maintain a catalog of common sources of artificial ownership, and Yeti prunes those edges from the object reference graph. Yeti computes two subsets of the objects: the *must-not-dominate* set D and the *must-not-share* set S. Figure 3 provides an example of both, and illustrates the effect of the following pruning heuristic. For every object in D that dominates an object not in D (or vice versa), we prune this dominating edge. This pruning results in a dominator forest with only those trees that contain objects in D, and those that don't (c.f. the classloader frontier in [9]). This rule avoids artificial dominance. For every object in S that references, but does not dominate, some other object, we prune that edge, so as to avoid artificial sharing.

The must-not-dominate and must-not-share sets are crafted from experience with common frameworks. The must-not-dominate set consists of instances of known classloader data types, such as `java.lang.ClassLoader`. In some cases, applications use data modeling frameworks (such as the Eclipse Modeling Framework [16]), that include application-level analogs to class and package mechanisms; we include these in D. The must-not-share set consists of instances of, or

---

[1] A fourth issue, diamond structures, is not addressed in this paper.

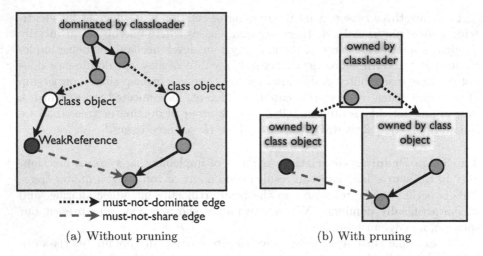

(a) Without pruning   (b) With pruning

Fig. 3. Pruning artificial ownership, to create sections that more meaningfully capture the domains of functionality

any instances dominated by: weak and finalizer references, any local variables, iterators, thread local storage, and any tracing or logging facilities. By also including those objects dominated by such instances, we are able to cope with must-not-share properties that are distant; e.g. if object a is weakly referenced and eventually references b which shares ownership of c, then the edge from b to c is also a must-not-share edge.

The Ownership Graph. To reintroduce reachability to the dominator forest, we adopt the *ownership graph* [9]. The ownership graph has a node for each dominator tree. If any object in dominator tree A references the head of dominator tree B, then we form an edge from one ownership graph node to the other.

The Same-Type-Same-Context Heuristic. When a group of sections are shared, the dominator forest will contain a separate dominator tree for each, even if they are shared in the same way. Consider Figure 4(a), which illustrates a situation with five subgraphs dominated by an object of type T. Each of the five subgraphs is simultaneously owned by two higher-level structures. A common example that appears when using many application server frameworks is session state, each instance of which is simultaneously stored in two larger structures. Large-scale applications can support tens of thousands of active sessions. In this situation, the dominator relation would separate this single pattern into many thousands of trees. We apply a simple yet powerful heuristic that resolves this problem: merge dominator trees that are each dominated by an object of a common type, and shared by dominator trees headed by nodes of the same type (c.f. [13]). The result is such as shown in In our example, as illustrated in Figure 4(b), this heuristic would merge the six nodes down to one.

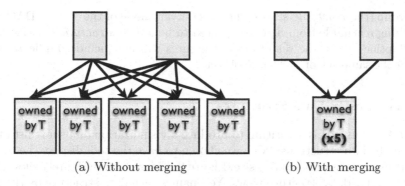

(a) Without merging   (b) With merging

Fig. 4. Merging sections based on the same-type-same-context heuristic

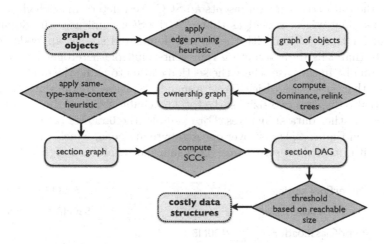

Fig. 5. The algorithm to construct the data structure sections and the costly data structures visualization that Yeti shows

2.2   Data Structure Inference Algorithm

We now show how to construct a section graph, such as the one conceptualized in Figure 1. The algorithm proceeds as shown in Figure 5. Given an object reference graph, first apply the edge pruning heuristic to remove sources of artificial ownership. Compute the dominator relation over the resulting pruned graph of objects. Relink the dominator trees into an ownership graph; this produces a graph where each node is a dominator tree. Collapse nodes of this graph based on the same-type-same-context heuristic. This results in a graph where each node is a *section*.

The remaining steps produce a set of data structures. Compute the strongly-connected components (SCCs) of the section graph, and collapse every SCC down to a single node. This produces a directed acyclic graph (DAG) where each node is either a section, or a group of sections. Every "group" node of this section DAG has the property that the number of objects reachable from members of that group (the *reachable size*) is the same. Every node of the section DAG, and everything reachable from it, is considered to be a *data structure*. Observe that, by collapsing SCCs, the set of data structures will not include duplicates that explain the same set of reachable objects.

2.3   The Costly Data Structures

The Yeti tool uses this algorithm to produce a visualization of a short list of the most costly data structures. We have chosen to have the tool display the top six structures in terms of reachable size. Figure 2, Figure 6, and Figure 7 show three example costly data structure views. Yeti names each data structure by the type of the nodes at the root of the dominator tree for that structure's sections. In the case that the data structure represents an SCC, Yeti determines which sections have no outgoing edges, i.e. edges that exit the SCC, and uses the dominator root name for that section with the largest dominated size; it appends "et al" to indicate that this data structure represents multiple heterogeneously typed sections. Finally, in the case where the section chosen to name the data structure has a root that is a class object, Yeti appends "statics" to the data structure name. Yeti also displays two sizings: the total reachable size, and the amount that overlaps with other data structures. For example, the `UnmodifiableMapOnNode` structure from Figure 2, is just over one gigabyte in size, of which 144 megabytes is shared with other data structures. This snapshot contains roughly 20 million

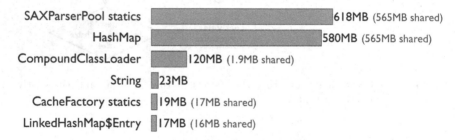

Fig. 6. The Costly Data Structures from a snapshot with 19 million objects

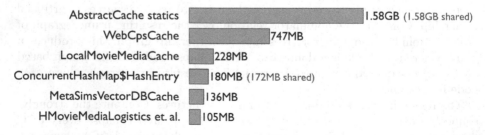

Fig. 7. The Costly Data Structures from a snapshot with 36 million objects

live objects that consume 1.46 gigabytes of heap; most of this space is concisely summarized by the top six costly data structures.

This list provides a jumping off point for further exploration. The Yeti user can drill down from a costly data structure to a list of the largest reachable sections, and from there to a more detailed view of a section's design.

3   The Data Model

Each data structure section can contain millions of objects. In Yeti, we summarize a data structure section, by recovering an organization that reveals its underlying design. We approximate this logical data model by grouping objects based on context and on the role they serve – as entities or the implementation of relationships – in the design. Yeti infers this distinction by automatically recognizing the backbones of collections [9]. These groups are arranged into a DAG called the *content schematic*. The content schematic was introduced in [11]. We show here how it is used to diagnose problems.

3.1   The Content Schematic Visualization

The content schematic shows the containment of collections and entities (i.e. non-collection data). This view intentionally differs from the traditional visualization of data models which draws entities as nodes and the relationships between them as edges. In our recovered data model, nodes represent either entities or collection infrastructure. Each node may represent instances from multiple classes; e.g. a `Vector` and its underlying array. Content schematic edges represent containment. Edge labels show the average number of dominating references from the source to the target; for collections, this represents the average number of entries.

Differentiating collections from entities is a natural way to model heap storage. First, in Java, collections are used to implement relationships. Memory footprint problems are often caused by poor use of collections, including too many empty collections, sparse collections, or wrong collection choice. Second, the nature of collection problems are different from entity implementation problems. Fixing a collection problem typically involves making a new selection from the standard library and configuring it. Fixing a problem with entity implementation typically involves refactoring classes.

The algorithm for building a content schematic is primarily based on structural information, and does not use specific knowledge about specific libraries. Therefore, the analysis recognizes collections that are not defined in the standard library. However, there are several cases when specific knowledge is needed. For example, to recognize hash sets with no collisions, we recognize objects with the substring `$Entry` in their names.

3.2   Examples

Figure 8 shows a content schematic for the data structure section `GatewaySession`, taken from the Yeti tool. This section belongs to a server framework layer of a social-network application. From 36 megabytes of objects in the `GatewaySession`, Yeti

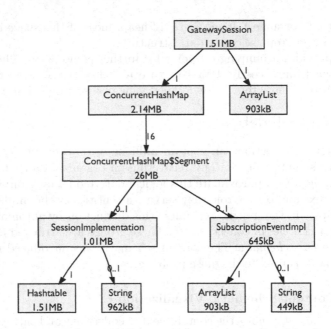

Fig. 8. The content schematic of a `GatewaySession`, rendered by the Yeti tool

has recovered a data model with just ten nodes that explain the bulk of the cost. Observe that the largest contributor is `ConcurrentHashMap$Segment`, which consumes 26 megabytes. The standard concurrent hash map in Java is implemented using a two-level collection, so it appears as two distinct nodes in the content schematic: `ConcurrentHashMap` and `ConcurrentHashMap$Segment`. Both of these nodes represent pure overhead cost, since they represent collection infrastructure. The question is whether this cost is justified, that is, is the use of a concurrent hash map appropriate here.

Looking deeper (via tooltip, as shown in Figure 9), one can discover that there are 16505 `ConcurrentHashMaps` and 264080 `ConcurrentHashMap$Segments`); these figures show up as the "count" fields in the tooltips. We also observe that the GatewaySession section itself is nested in a `ConcurrentHashMap`, since there is another section called `ConcurrentHashMap` that owns it (shown in the Yeti tool, but not in this figure). The developers confirmed that the granularity of these nested concurrency structures is too fine, and the inner concurrent hash map is not needed to assure concurrent access; typically there are a large number of concurrent `GatewaySessions`, but only a few subscribers per session. This allowed them to replace the inner concurrent hash map with a `Hashtable`, which provides thread safety, but no concurrency. This reduced the storage cost of the `GatewaySession` section by over 90%, and the cost of the whole heap by 10-20%. This type of problem, using the wrong collection for a given task, is a common pattern.

Figure 10 shows a different content schematic from the same application, for the section `ClientConnectionImpl`. One visible potential problem is that the 6.88 megabytes `ArrayList` has an average fanout of 1.33. In general, if there

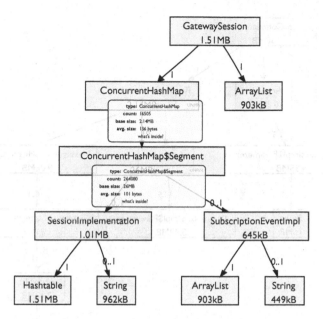

Fig. 9. A portion of the `GatewaySession` content schematic from Figure 8, showing two tooltips rendered by Yeti

are many small collections, the overhead cost of the collections is not justified by the small number of entries they contain. The two largest cost contributors are `RequestImpl` and `ClientConnectionImpl`. However, we cannot determine whether this cost can be reduced from just the content schematic. The next section shows how to obtain more detailed information.

4   The Model's Implementation

In the previous example, the content schematic focused our attention on the `RequestImpl` and `ClientConnectionImpl`, responsible for a significant portion of the data structure's cost. We would now like to understand the implementation of these entities, to see if they can be optimized. We introduce a *type graph* view to show the implementation of a given entity or collection. We show its application to some common types of storage inefficiencies.

Figure 11 shows the type graph view of the `ClientConnectionImpl` entity from Figure 10. This graph shows the actual objects that implement a single entity or collection, aggregated into nodes according to type. An edge summarizes all references between instances of two types. Edges are labeled with the average fanout, i.e. the average, per instance of source type, of the number of references to the target type. Flying over each node yields additional detail, such as the number of instances and the average instance size.

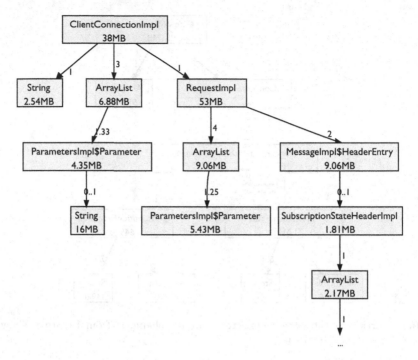

Fig. 10. The content schematic of a `ClientConnectionImpl`, rendered by Yeti

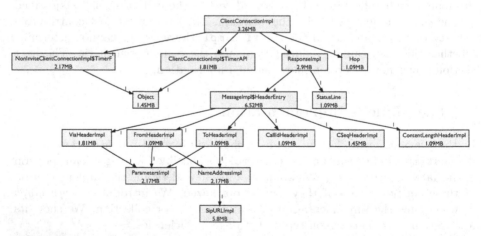

Fig. 11. Type graph showing the highly delegated implementation of a ClientConnectionImpl entity

4.1 Highly Delegated Entities

It is common for entities to be represented by more than one object type. One reason is that Java has limited data modeling mechanisms, lacking such features as composition (i.e. an object may only point to, but not contain another object), union types, and multiple inheritance. As a result, even a primitive string in Java must be implemented using two classes (`String` and `char[]`) connected by a reference. In addition, our software engineering culture favors loosely coupled design patterns, as well as reuse of existing assets.

From the view we learn that `ClientConnectionImpl` has a highly delegated design, with each connection requiring on average 27 instances (from 17 distinct classes). Each connection object points to a response object which in turn contains six header entries. Each type of header entry (e.g. `ViaHeaderImpl`, `ToHeaderImpl`, `FromHeaderImpl`) is modeled by delegating to a separate object rather than by extending `MessageImpl$HeaderEntry`. Low-level attributes such as a web address employ multiple levels of delegation to make use of existing framework functionality. The memory costs of such designs are high due to object header, object alignment, and pointer costs [11]. In this example these costs alone are responsible for 62% of the storage of each `ClientConnectionImpl`. Unfortunately current JITs do nothing to optimize the storage of these designs. In the type graph of `RequestImpl` (not shown) we find a similar, delegated design.

Limiting the type graph to a particular entity or collection has many benefits. In this example, the content schematic and the focused type graph together let us see whether the `ClientConnectionImpl`'s *design is appropriate for its context*. This is an important issue in framework-based systems, where developers cannot predict the uses of their designs, and thus can easily misjudge their space budget. The focused type graph also separates out unrelated uses of common types, such as `Object` in this example.

4.2   Expensive Classes and Base Classes

Highly delegated entity designs can also magnify other expensive patterns in the modeling of individual Java classes. The type graph can be useful for uncovering these problems. A customer relationship management (CRM) application where Yeti was successfully employed exhibited a few of these common patterns. The content schematic showed that the customer profile entity was a large consumer of storage, and its type graph view showed that each customer profile was modeled as 30 instances. Low-level attributes such as email address, phone number, and physical address were modeled as separate classes, each in turn with additional side objects. Yeti provides the ability to drill down from each node in the type graph to show type hierarchy, field, and instance size information.[2] Figure 12 shows that the base class of each piece of contact information costs 40 bytes. Seeing the cost in context lets the developer decide if it is worth modeling at this fine granularity, or if it would be better to move information, such as when contact information was changed, up to the customer profile.

The field information revealed another problem. Many of the classes and base classes implementing this entity had a similar coding pattern, one of storing both a scalar and a formatted string version of the same value (e.g. `countryCodeId`

---

[2] In this example, class hierarchy information was available from the heap snapshot, but not exact type information for reference types.

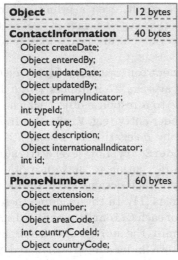

(a) Phone number.   (b) Electronic address.

Fig. 12. Detailed class information from two CRM application entities, as rendered by Yeti

and `countryCode`). The type graph led us to find the unnecessary fields (the formatted versions) in each class and also explained related String objects that appeared in the content schematic.

4.3 Collection Implementations

Collections in Java are implemented using multiple classes; the type graph can provide a concise summary of the structure and costs of these implementation. This view can show why a particular use of collections is expensive. For example, the type graph view can be used to determine if a collection has been misconfigured. In the example of small `ArrayLists` from Section 3.2, drilling down to the type graph view (not shown) reveals a graph with two types, `ArrayList` and `Object[]`. Looking at the average size of each `Object[]` shows if the developers made a common error, sizing the collections too large relative to the small number of entries they contain. The type graph can also yield insight into the scaling properties of a collection. In a document processing application with a scalability problem diagnosed with Yeti, a large `TreeMap` was the largest element of a large section. The type graph view showed that its size was almost entirely due to the instance size of the `TreeMap$Entry` class, a cost that will not be amortized at a larger scale.

5 Differential Analysis

In the previous sections, we have shown how problems of excessive memory footprint can be identified with a single heap snapshot. In many cases, problems can

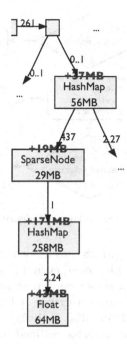

Fig. 13. A content schematic, with each note annotated with its change in size

be resolved by inspecting the content schematics and type graphs of the biggest data structure sections. This strategy works, but in a relatively limited scope: the problematic abstraction must be big (e.g. for memory leaks, when the leak has had time to accrue). It also requires a human to impose a judgment that big is bad. A differential analysis avoids these problems, and opens up the possibility for several new analyses. We show how the same abstractions used for footprint analysis serve as useful units for summarizing change. For example, even a simple inspection of Figure 13, a content schematic annotated with changes to the *byte size* of entities and collection infrastructure, is enlightening.

We first present an algorithm to compute a model of how content schematics change. We then present a family of differential analyses, both intra-run and cross-build, that utilize this differential model.

5.1 The Differential Algorithm

A single data structure, and even a single data structure section, may participate in multiple independent changes over time. For example, we may have one snapshot taken with 500 users logged on, and another, from a different build that introduces a memory footprint optimization, with 1000 users logged on. Comparing these snapshots should show that this data structure has, simultaneously, both shrinkage (due to optimizations) and growth (due to an increase in the number of users). For this reason alone, it is important to compute a

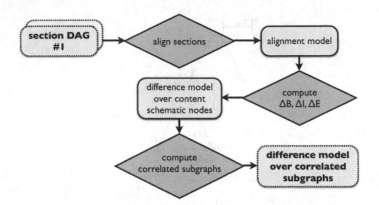

Fig. 14. The differential algorithm

differential model that includes context; to do otherwise would show only that there is some change occurring. Moreover, even if a data structure exhibits only a single kind of change, a data structure almost always has some parts that remain stable. Knowing that a data structure, or large portions of it, have not changed is itself an important differential analysis.[3]

The differential algorithm proceeds as outlined in Figure 14. The algorithm takes as input the section DAGs from two heap snapshots; recall the section inference algorithm from Section 2.2, and outlined in Figure 5. It then aligns the sections, and produces an *alignment model*. This model is a mapping that corresponds each section in the first snapshot to zero or one snapshots in the second snapshot; for a section not in the domain of this mapping, we say it is *nascent*, and for a section not in the range of this mapping, we say that it has *disappeared*. One section aligns with another if they satisfy the same-type-same-context heuristic, as described in Section 2.1. Within aligned sections, it further aligns the content schematic nodes using a straightforward tree matching based on the type of each node. Nodes, as with sections, can be nascent or disappear. In this way, the alignment model does not require any notion of persistent object identities that span heap snapshots.[4]

Next, the differential algorithm sizes each content schematic node, and computes deltas of these sizes based on the alignment model. The algorithm relies on three node sizings: byte size B, the number of nodes in the type graph I, and element count E. For example, in the content schematic shown in Figure 13, the upper `HashMap` collection infrastructure consumes 56 megabytes using five data types; this data structure currently contains 2153 such HashMaps.[5] To compute

---

[3] We discuss lack of change in more depth in Section 5.2.

[4] This algorithm would not align in the presence of certain changes, such as refactorings that affect class names.

[5] The latter two numbers aren't shown in the figure. When using Yeti, the count of types can been seen by drilling down from that content schematic node to the corresponding type graph; the number of HashMaps can be seen in a tooltip over the content schematic node, as in Figure 9.

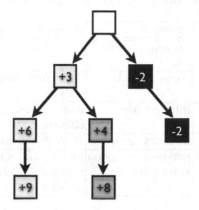

Fig. 15. A content schematic with three subgraphs of correlated growth; e.g. the two nodes with a change in element count of -2

the change in byte size ΔB of each content schematic node, use the alignment model: $\Delta B = B_2 - B_1$, where B_1 or B_2 is defined to have the value of zero when that respective region or the entire section is not present. The same goes for the other two sizings. This yields a difference model over the content schematic nodes, which provides a Δ for each sizing, for each node.

Finally, the algorithm accounts for lock-step changes in element count. Consider a HashSet of Vectors of Strings. When the application adds one more Vector to the outer set, it is likely that this data structure will also contain more Strings. If the change in the element count (ΔE) of the latter is a multiple of the ΔE of the former, the algorithm interprets this to mean that these two changes are likely to be part of a single, encompassing, trend in the program. We define a *correlated subgraph* of a content schematic as a maximally sized connected subgraph over which the ΔE of each node is a multiple of its parent. Figure 15 shows a content schematic with three correlated subgraphs, e.g. where one exhibits a growth trend with three nodes $\{+3, +6, +9\}$. From this, the algorithm refines the difference model over content schematic nodes to one over correlated subgraphs in the obvious way.

5.2   Changes within a Run

By comparing multiple snapshots taken from a single run of an application, we can spot and quantify trends in memory consumption. While much related work has focused on memory leaks, a wide array of issues can benefit for this style of analysis. Table 1 shows five categories of intra-run differential analysis; we describe two of them in detail.

Developers of server applications are faced with the important task of quantifying the size of session state, normalized per user. Without intimate knowledge of which node in which content schematic corresponds to session state, this task is quite difficult. A very similar task is that of discovering which runtime memory

Table 1. Yeti infers trends within a run by observing changes to a content schematic

Trend Analysis	Example	A correlated subgraph where ...
One-off	broken round-trip	E of the root increases by n, once
Growth	memory leak	ibid, but increases monotonically
Cache-like	infer caches	ibid, but plateaus, and then oscillates
Steady State	memory drag	B, I, E unchanged
Incremental Unit Cost	per-user session state size	root's ΔE equals added users; compute $\sum_i B_i/n$ for subgraph nodes i

structures correspond to certain configuration parameters (e.g. one that determines the capacity of a cache). In both cases, one can tweak the external property (by adding more users, or changing the configuration option) by a known value of k, and searching for a correlated subgraph with $\Delta E = k$. In addition to the program understanding benefits, this technique further allows one to present normalized figures: divide the sum of the byte sizes B by n, for all nodes in the correlated subgraph. We have used this analysis with many IBM internal and customer applications; we find many applications where the per-user session costs are over 100 kilobytes. At this rate, the application would require 1 gigabyte of memory, just for session state, to support only ten thousand simultaneous users. This normalized figure quickly focused development effort.

We can also use the differential algorithm to identify portions of memory that are possibly "dragging" [15]. Applications often contain large sections of memory that are either rarely used, or only used during application startup. This combination, of being large and infrequently accessed, present opportunities for tuning. To approximately find portions of data structures that have memory drag, Yeti presents correlated subgraphs in which all three sizing criteria remain unchanged ($\Delta B = \Delta I = \Delta E = 0$), for all nodes in the subgraph; we have found that unchanging structures are often the unused ones. We have used this analysis to find several large dragging sections in IBM products.

5.3   Changes Across Builds

The second style of differential analysis is used by development teams to track changes across builds of their application. This can be used to quantify the benefits of a code optimization, or to pinpoint and quantify the negative effects of a newly introduced feature. Table 2 provides three examples of this style of cross-build differential analysis. To infer that developers have changed the field structure of application data types, one can look for correlated subgraphs where $\Delta I = 0$ and $\Delta E = 0$ (no change in number of types required to implement model elements, and no change in the number of entities or collections), but

Table 2. The Yeti differential analysis can also detect cross-build changes

Cross-build Analysis	Example	Any correlated subgraph where ...
Type Optimization	remove fields	B decreases, but I, E unchanged
Entity Optimization	lower use of delegation	B, I decreases, but E unchanged
Change in Data Model	switch from `TreeMap` to parallel arrays	E become zero, while another subgraph's E become nonzero

where $\Delta B < 0$. A common example of this kind of type optimization is when developers change a data type to make some fields computed, rather than stored, attributes.

6   Related Work

Earlier work introduces summarization according to ownership structure and inference of collection infrastructure, to enable characterization of heaps [9]. Work on memory health introduces the content schematic and shows how it can be used to enable design health and scalability assessments [11]. Our present work combines and extends these abstractions, embodying them in a visual tool for diagnosing storage inefficiencies and lifetime management bugs, in point-in-time and differential analyses.

Most work on memory analysis is focused on leak detection and problems of memory drag. A number of these works use dominance relations to aggregate objects with the same type and ownership context. Tools such as LeakBot [10], YourKit [17] and MAT [2] use dominance to compute measures of uniquely owned storage and give users a starting point for more detailed exploration. None of these tools provides explicit support for shared ownership. In [14], ownership information is combined with trace information, enabling object usage and access information to be aggregated according to ownership structure. Many tools aggregate objects according to type and immediate references. In Jinsight [3] and many commercial tools, such as Yourkit, this aggregation supports navigation to neighboring groups of objects. Cork employs a *type points-from graph* over the whole heap and annotates it with volume information gathered with the garbage collector [5]. Changes in volume along paths in the graph are used to pinpoint growing structures. Container profiling uses a priori knowledge of collection classes to track usage of collections in order to rank leak suspects [18].

Shape analysis aims at summarizing the structure of connected groups of objects [1,8]. Recent characterization work identifies and summarizes temporary data structures using lifetime and connectivity information [4].

7   Yeti in Practice

Yeti runs as a web-based service. Users submit snapshots and receive interactive reports that can be saved and distributed. It accepts standard heap snapshots, and does not require a collection agent. Yeti has been available within IBM for well over a year, and is in active use by at least five development, testing, and services organizations. It has enabled more than twenty critical problems to be solved in over a dozen products and customer applications, problems of both scalability and lifetime management.

8   Conclusions

That systems are built by assembling parts from so many sources has made it nearly impossible to assess the global impact of local design choices. Yeti's abstractions for the first time enable visibility across all the layers, via concise cost summaries from a design perspective. Yeti's approximations, while not perfect, have proven in practice to enable users to quickly and easily solve problems. For example, Yeti may sometimes combine what the user thinks of as two logical entities into a single one, or segregate two very similar sections only because some instances happen to be shared at a moment in time. The consequence of this imprecision has been that users will examine a few extra sections or entities — still a relatively small effort compared with exploring thousands of links in detail-oriented tools. The difficulties of current techniques have led developers to postpone memory analysis until there is a serious problem. It is encouraging that Yeti's views are simple enough that it is now being used earlier in the lifecycle by development and testing groups.

Meaningful cost summaries are a first step toward mitigating memory-related risks across the development cycle. First, Yeti's summarizations have made evident to us many common patterns of data design. We have been compiling a catalog of costly patterns, from real-world Yeti case studies, and have made it available as a tutorial [12] aimed at preventing problems. Work is in progress to automatically recognize these patterns and suggest solutions. Another area of opportunity is scalability prediction, where developers' inability to measure unit costs of their own or others' code makes it difficult to predict how designs will scale, or to configure parameters. We are exploring how Yeti's analyses can enable understanding of scalability, in the context of development and testing tools. Finally, Yeti's differential analysis can be of value for project tracking, by spotting trends in design scalability as a project progresses, and pinpointing functional areas that are to blame.

References

1. Berdine, J., Calcagno, C., Cook, B., Distefano, D., O'Hearn, P.W., Wies, T., Yang, H.: Shape analysis for composite data structures. In: Damm, W., Hermanns, H. (eds.) CAV 2007. LNCS, vol. 4590, pp. 178–192. Springer, Heidelberg (2007)

2. Buchen, A., Tsvetkov, K.: Automated heap dump analysis for developers, testers, and support employees. JavaOne (2008)
3. De Pauw, W., Sevitsky, G.: Visualizing reference patterns for solving memory leaks in Java. Concurrency: Practice and Experience 12, 1431–1454 (2000)
4. Dufour, B., Ryder, B., Sevitsky, G.: A scalable technique for characterizing the usage of temporaries in framework-intensive java applications. In: Foundations of Software Engineering (2008)
5. Jump, M., McKinley, K.S.: Cork: dynamic memory leak detection for garbage-collected languages. In: Symposium on Principles of Programming Languages (2007)
6. Kegel, H., Steimann, F.: Systematically refactoring inheritance to delegation in a class-based object-oriented programming language. In: International Conference on Software Engineering (2008)
7. Lengauer, T., Tarjan, R.E.: A fast algorithm for finding dominators in a flow graph. ACM Transactions on Programming Languages and Systems 1(1), 121–141 (1979)
8. Marron, M., Hermenegildo, D.S.M., Kapur, D.: Heap analysis in the presence of collection libraries. In: Workshop on Program Analysis For Software Tools and Engineering (2007)
9. Mitchell, N.: The runtime structure of object ownership. In: Thomas, D. (ed.) ECOOP 2006. LNCS, vol. 4067, pp. 74–98. Springer, Heidelberg (2006)
10. Mitchell, N., Sevitsky, G.: Leakbot: An automated and lightweight tool for diagnosing memory leaks in large Java applications. In: Cardelli, L. (ed.) ECOOP 2003, vol. 2743. Springer, Heidelberg (2003)
11. Mitchell, N., Sevitsky, G.: The causes of bloat, the limits of health. In: Object-oriented Programming, Systems, Languages, and Applications (2007)
12. Mitchell, N., Sevitsky, G.: Building memory-efficient java applications. In: International Conference on Software Engineering (2008)
13. Potanin, A., Noble, J., Biddle, R.: Checking ownership and confinement. Concurrency and Computation: Practice and Experience 16(7), 671–687 (2004)
14. Rayside, D., Mendel, L.: Object ownership profiling: a technique for finding and fixing memory leaks. In: Automated Software Engineering (2007)
15. Rojemo, N., Runciman, C.: Lag, drag, void and use — heap profiling and space-efficient compilation revisited. In: International Conference on Functional Programming (1996)
16. Steinberg, D., Budinsky, F., Paternostro, M., Merks, E.: EMF: Eclipse Modeling Framework. Addison-Wesley, Reading (2003)
17. Yourkit LLC. Yourkit profiler, http://www.yourkit.com
18. Xu, G., Rountev, A.: Precise memory leak detection for java software using container profiling. In: International Conference on Software Engineering (2008)

Scaling CFL-Reachability-Based Points-To Analysis Using Context-Sensitive Must-Not-Alias Analysis

Guoqing Xu[1], Atanas Rountev[1], and Manu Sridharan[2]

[1] Ohio State University, Columbus, OH, USA
[2] IBM T.J. Watson Research Center, Hawthorne, NY, USA

Abstract. Pointer analyses derived from a Context-Free-Language (CFL) reachability formulation achieve very high precision, but they do not scale well to compute the points-to solution for an entire large program. Our goal is to increase significantly the scalability of the currently most precise points-to analysis for Java. This CFL-reachability analysis depends on determining whether two program variables may be aliases. We propose an efficient but less precise pre-analysis that computes context-sensitive *must-not-alias* information for all pairs of variables. Later, these results can be used to quickly filter out infeasible CFL-paths during the more precise points-to analysis. Several novel techniques are employed to achieve precision and efficiency, including a new approximate CFL-reachability formulation of alias analysis, as well as a carefully-chosen trade-off in context sensitivity. The approach effectively reduces the search space of the points-to analysis: the modified points-to analysis is more than three times faster than the original analysis.

1 Introduction

Pointer analysis is used pervasively in static analysis tools. There are dozens (or maybe even hundreds) of analyses and transformations that need information about pointer values and the corresponding memory locations. Many of these tools — e.g., software verifiers [1,2], data race detectors [3,4], and static slicers [5] — require both precision and scalability from the underlying pointer analysis. The quality of the results generated by such tools is highly sensitive to the precision of the pointer information. On the other hand, it is highly desirable for the pointer analysis to scale to large programs and to quickly provide points-to/aliasing relationships for a large number of variables. To date, existing pointer analysis algorithms have to sacrifice one of these two factors for the sake of the other, depending on the kind of client analysis they target.

Of existing pointer analysis algorithms, the family of the refinement-based analyses [6,7] derived from the Context-Free-Language (CFL) reachability formulation [8] are some of the most precise ones. They achieve precision by simultaneously approximating CFL-reachability on two axes: method calls and heap accesses. Method calls are handled context sensitively: a method's entry and exit

S. Drossopoulou (Ed.): ECOOP 2009, LNCS 5653, pp. 98–122, 2009.

are treated as balanced parentheses and are matched in order to avoid propagation along unrealizable paths (with the appropriate approximations needed to handle recursive calls). Heap accesses are handled to precisely capture the flow of pointer values through the heap: the read (load) and write (store) of a field of the same object are treated as balanced parentheses. These analyses answer particular points-to/alias queries raised from a client analysis, starting with an approximate solution and refining it until the desired precision is achieved.

Refinement-based pointer analyses may not scale well if a client analysis requires highly-refined information for a large number of variables [9]. For example, the Sridharan-Bodik analysis from [6], when using its default configuration, spent more than 1000 seconds on computing the whole-program points-to solution for a simple Java program and the large number of library classes transitively used by it. This solution was required by our static slicer to compute a program slice for a particular slicing criterion. It is important to note that the slicer requires points-to information not only for variables in the application code (i.e., the program we wrote), but also for variables in all reachable library methods; this is needed in order to compute appropriate dependence summary edges [5] at call sites. Less-refined (i.e., more approximate) points-to information, even though it can be produced quite efficiently, could introduce much more imprecision in the generated slice. For example, the generated slice contained the entire program (i.e., it was very imprecise) if we imposed a 500-second time constraint on the pointer analysis. In fact, this scalability problem prevents many similar *whole-program* analyses from obtaining highly-precise points-to information with acceptable running time. The goal of the analysis proposed in this paper is to help the analysis from [6] to generate highly-refined points-to information in a more efficient way.

Insight. The work performed by the Sridharan-Bodik analysis can be coarsely decomposed into core work that is performed to find the true points-to relationships, and auxiliary work performed to filter out infeasible points-to relationships. As analysis precision increases, *so does the ratio of auxiliary work to core work*. In fact, the increase of the amount of auxiliary work is usually much more noticeable than the expected precision improvement, which is detrimental to algorithm scalability. In order to obtain high precision while maintaining scalability, staged analysis algorithms [2,10] have been proposed. A staged analysis consists of several independent analyses. A precise but expensive analysis that occurs at a later stage takes advantage of the results of an earlier inexpensive but relatively imprecise analysis. This can reduce significantly the amount of auxiliary work that dominates the running time of the precise analysis. Our technique is inspired by this idea. We propose an analysis which efficiently pre-computes relatively imprecise results. Later, these results can be used to quickly filter out infeasible graph paths during the more precise Sridharan-Bodik analysis.

Targeted inefficiency. At the heart of the CFL-reachability formulation proposed in [6] is a context-free language that models heap accesses and method calls/returns. Given a graph representation of the program (described in Section 2), a variable v can point to an object o if there exists a path from o to v labeled with a string from this language. Specifically, v can point to o if there exists a pair of statements $v = a.f$ and $b.f = o$ such that a and b are aliases. Deciding if a and b are aliases requires finding an object o' that may flow to both a and b. This check may trigger further recursive field access checks and context sensitivity checks (essentially, checks for matched parentheses) that can span many methods and classes. All checks transitively triggered need to be performed every time the analysis tries to verify whether a and b may be aliases, because the results may be different under different calling contexts (i.e., a method may be analyzed under different sequences of call sites starting from main). There could be a large number of calling contexts for a method and it may be expensive to repeat the check for each one of them.

Recent work [11,12] has identified that there exists a large number of *equivalent* calling contexts. The points-to sets of a variable under the equivalent contexts are the same; thus, distinguishing these contexts from each other is unnecessary. This observation also applies to aliasing. Suppose variables a and b may point to the same object o under two sets of equivalent contexts C_1 and C_2, respectively. Clearly, a and b may be aliases under $C_1 \cap C_2$. It is desirable for the analysis from [6] to remember the aliasing relationship of a and b for this entire set of contexts, so that this relationship needs to be computed only once for all contexts in the set. However, because in [6] the context-sensitivity check is performed along with the field access check, the context equivalence classes are not yet known when the aliasing relationship of a and b is computed. Ideally, a separate analysis can be performed to pre-compute context equivalence class information for all pairs of variables in the program. This information can be provided to the points-to analysis from [6], which will then be able to reuse the aliasing relationships under their corresponding equivalent calling contexts. In addition, this pre-analysis has to be sufficiently inexpensive so that its cost can be justified from the time saving of the subsequent points-to analysis.

Proposed approach. Since the number of calling contexts (i.e., sequences of call graph edges) in a Java program is usually extremely large even when treating recursion approximately, the proposed analysis adopts the following approach: instead of computing context equivalence classes for every pair of variables, it focuses on pairs that are not aliases *under any possible calling contexts*. This information is useful for early elimination of infeasible paths. The analysis from [6] does not have to check whether a and b are aliases if this pre-analysis has already concluded that they cannot possibly be aliases under any calling context. The pre-analysis will thus be referred to as a *must-not-alias analysis*.

The key to the success of the proposed approach is to make the must-not-alias analysis sufficiently inexpensive while maintaining relatively high precision. Several novel techniques are employed to achieve this goal:

- Aliases are obtained *directly* by performing a new form of CFL-reachability, instead of obtaining them by intersecting points-to sets [7].
- The *heap access* check of the analysis is formulated as an all-pairs CFL-reachability problem over a simplified balanced-parentheses language [13],

which leads to an efficient algorithm that has lower complexity than solving the Sridharan-Bodik CFL-reachability. The simplification of the language is achieved by computing CFL-reachability over a program representation referred to as an *interprocedural symbolic points-to graph*, which introduces approximations for heap loads and stores.

- The *context sensitivity* check is performed by combining bottom-up inlining of methods with 1-level object cloning (i.e., replicating each object for each call graph edge that enters the object-creating method). Hence, the analysis is fully-context-sensitive for pointer variables (with an approximation for recursion), but only 1-level context-sensitive for pointer targets. This approach appears to achieve the desired balance between cost and precision.

The must-not-alias analysis was implemented in Soot [14,15] and was used to pre-compute alias information for use by the subsequent Sridharan-Bodik points-to analysis. As shown experimentally, the approach effectively reduces the search space of the points-to analysis and eliminates unnecessary auxiliary work. On average over 19 Java programs, the modified points-to analysis (including the alias pre-analysis) is *more than three times faster* than the original analysis.

2   Background

This section provides a brief description of the CFL-reachability formulation of context-sensitive points-to analysis for Java [6]. It also illustrates the key idea of our approach through an example.

2.1   CFL-Reachability Formulation

The CFL-reachability problem is an extension of standard graph reachability that allows for filtering of uninteresting paths. Given a directed graph with labeled edges, a relation R over graph nodes can be formulated as a CFL-reachability problem by defining a context-free grammar such that a pair of nodes $(n, n') \in R$ if and only if there exists a path from n to n' for which the sequence of edge labels along the path is a word belonging to the language L defined by the grammar. Such a path will be referred to as an L-path. If there exists an L-path from n to n', then n' is L-reachable from n (denoted by $n \ L \ n'$). For any non-terminal S in L's grammar, S-paths and $n \ S \ n'$ are defined similarly.

A variety of program analyses can be stated as CFL-reachability problems [8]. Recent developments in points-to analysis for Java [16,6] extend this formulation to model (1) context sensitivity via method entries and exits, and (2) heap accesses via object field reads and writes. A demand-driven analysis is formulated as a single-source L-reachability problem which determines all nodes n' such that $n \ L \ n'$ for a given source node n. The analysis can be expressed by CFL-reachability for language $L_F \cap R_C$. Language L_F, where F stands for "flows-to", ensures precise handling of field accesses. Regular language R_C ensures a degree of calling context sensitivity. Both languages encode balanced-parentheses properties.

Graph representation. L_F-reachability is performed on a graph representation G of a Java program, such that if a heap object represented by the abstract location o can flow to variable v during the execution of the program, there exists an L_F path in G from o to v. Graph G is constructed by creating edges for the following canonical statements:

- Allocation $x =$ new O: edge $o \xrightarrow{\text{new}} x \in G$
- Assignment $x = y$: edge $y \xrightarrow{\text{assign}} x \in G$
- Field write $x.f = y$: edge $y \xrightarrow{\text{store}(f)} x \in G$
- Field read $x = y.f$: edge $y \xrightarrow{\text{load}(f)} x \in G$

Parameter passing is represented as assignments from actuals to formals; method return values are treated similarly. Writes and reads of array elements are handled by collapsing all elements into an artificial field arr_elm.

Language L_F. First, consider a simplified graph G with only new and assign edges. In this case the language is regular and its grammar can be written simply as $flowsTo \rightarrow$ new (assign)*, which shows the transitive flow due to assign edges. Clearly, o $flowsTo$ v in G means that o belongs to the points-to set of v.

For field accesses, inverse edges are introduced to allow a CFL-reachability formulation. For each graph edge $x \rightarrow y$ labeled with t, an edge $y \rightarrow x$ labeled with $\bar{t}$ is introduced. For any path p, an inverse path $\bar{p}$ can be constructed by reversing the order of edges in p and replacing each edge with its inverse. In the grammar this is captured by a new non-terminal $\overline{flowsTo}$ used to represent the inverse paths for $flowsTo$ paths. For example, if there exists a $flowsTo$ path from object o to variable v, there also exists a $\overline{flowsTo}$ path from v to o.

May-alias relationships can be modeled by defining a non-terminal $alias$ such that $alias \rightarrow \overline{flowsTo}\, flowsTo$. Two variables a and b may alias if there exists an object o such that o can flow to both a and b. The field-sensitive points-to relationships can be modeled by $flowsTo \rightarrow$ new (assign | store(f) $alias$ load(f))*. This production checks for balanced pairs of store(f) and load(f) operations, taking into account the potential aliasing between the variables through which the store and the load occur.

Language R_C. The context sensitivity of the analysis ensures that method entries and exits are balanced parentheses: $C \rightarrow$ entry(i) C exit(i) | C C | ϵ. Here entry(i) and exit(i) correspond to the i-th call site in the program. This production describes only a subset of the language, where all parentheses are fully balanced. Since a realizable path does not need to start and end in the same method, the full definition of R_C also allows a prefix with unbalanced closed parentheses and a suffix with unbalanced open parentheses [6]. In the absence of recursion, the balanced-parentheses language is a finite regular language (thus the notation R_C instead of L_C); approximations are introduced as necessary to handle recursive calls. Context sensitivity is achieved by considering entries and exits along a L_F path and ensuring that the resulting string is in R_C.

2.2 CFL-Reachability Example

Figure 1 shows an example with an implementation of a List class, which is instantiated twice to hold two objects of class A. One of the List instances is wrapped in a ListClient object, which declares a method retrieve to obtain an object contained in its list. We will use t_i to denote the variable t whose first occurrence is at line i, and o_i to denote the abstract object for the allocation site at line i. For example, s_{31} and o_{26} represent variable s declared at line 31 and the A object created at line 26, respectively. Literal "abc" is used to denote the corresponding string object. Class A has a string-typed field f, initialized to some default value in A's constructor; the actual code for A is not shown.

The program representation for this example is shown in Figure 2; for simplicity, the inverse edges are not shown. Each entry and exit edge is also treated as an assign edge for L_F, in order to represent parameter passing and method returns. To simplify the figure, edges due to the call at line 32 are not shown. The context-insensitive points-to pairs are defined by $flowsTo$ paths. For example, there exists such a path from o_{26} to s_{31}. To see this, consider that $this_{17}$ $alias$ $this_{19}$ (due to o_{27}) and therefore l_{17} $flowsTo$ t_{19} due to the matching store and load of field list. Based on this, $this_5$ $alias$ $this_{11}$ due to o_{25} (note that because of the call at line 32, they are also aliases due to o_{28}). Since $this_5$ $alias$ $this_7$ (due to o_{25} or due to o_{28}), it can be concluded that t_7 $alias$ t_{11} (due to o_4). This leads to the $flowsTo$ path $o_{26} \rightarrow t_{26} \rightarrow m_6 \rightarrow t_7 \rightarrow \ldots \rightarrow t_{11} \rightarrow p_{12} \rightarrow r_{20} \rightarrow s_{31}$.

Since the precise computation of $flowsTo$ path can be expensive, the analysis from [6] employs an approximation by introducing artificial *match edges*. If, due to aliasing, there may be a path from the source of a store(f) edge to the target of a load(f) edge, a match edge is added between the two nodes. Such edges are added before the balanced-parentheses checks for heap accesses are performed. An initial approximate solution is computed using the match edges. All encountered match edges are then removed, and the paths between their endpoints are explored. These new paths themselves may contain new match edges. In the next iteration of refinement, these newly-discovered match edges

```
1  class List{                        18      Object retrieve(){
2      Object[] elems;                 19          t = this.list;
3      int count;                      20          Object r = t.get(0);
4      List(){ t = new Object[10];     21          return r;
5              this.elems = t; }       22      }
6      void add(Object m){             23  }
7          t = this.elems;             24  static void main(String[] args){
8          t[count++] = m;             25      List l1 = new List();
9      }                               26      A t = new A(); l1.add(t);
10     Object get(int ind){            27      ListClient client = new ListClient(l1);
11         t = this.elems;             28      List l2 = new List();
12         p = t[ind]; return p;       29      A i = new A(); i.f = "abc";
13     }                               30      l2.add(i);
14  }                                  31      A s = (A)client.retrieve();
15  class ListClient{                  32      A j = (A)l2.get(0);
16     List list;                      33      String str = s.f;
17     ListClient(List l){ this.list = l; }   34  }}
```

Fig. 1. Code example

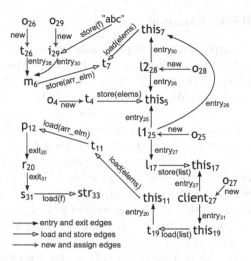

Fig. 2. Illustration of CFL-reachability

are removed, etc. Since we are interested in a highly-refined solution, the example and the rest of the paper will assume complete refinement of match edges.

Not every *flowsTo* path is feasible. Consider, for example, path $o_{29} \rightarrow i_{29} \rightarrow m_6 \rightarrow t_7 \rightarrow \ldots \rightarrow t_{11} \rightarrow p_{12} \rightarrow r_{20} \rightarrow s_{31}$. Even though this is a valid *flowsTo* path, the entry and exit edges along the path are not properly matched. To see this, consider the following subpaths. First, for the path from $this_5$ to s_{31}, the sequence of entry/exit edges is $\overline{entry(25)}, entry(27), \overline{entry(27)}, entry(31), entry(20), \overline{exit(20)}, \overline{exit(31)}$. Here the inverse of an entry edge can be thought of as an exit edge and vice versa. All edges except for the first one are properly matched. Second, consider the two paths from o_{29} to $this_5$: the first one goes through $\underline{o_{28}}$ and the second one goes through o_{25}. The first path contains edges $entry(30), \overline{entry(30)}$, $entry(28)$ and the second path contains edges $entry(30), \overline{entry(26)}, entry(25)$. Neither path can be combined with the path having the unmatched $\overline{entry(25)}$ to form a valid string in R_C. On the other hand, there exists a path from o_{26} to $this_5$ with edges $entry(26), \overline{entry(26)}, entry(25)$, which can be correctly combined.

In the example, suppose that an analysis client queries the points-to set of s_{31}. The analysis starts from the variable and reaches p_{12} after traversing back through the two exit edges. It then finds the matched arr_elm edges from m_6 to t_7 and from t_{11} to p_{12}. At this point, the analysis does not know whether t_7 and t_{11} can alias, and hence, it queries the points-to sets of t_7 and t_{11}. For t_7, due to the matched load and store edges for elems, the analysis tries to determine whether $this_5$ and $this_7$ can be aliases. Since o_{25} can flow to both variables, they indeed are aliases. (Note that o_{28} also flows to both variables, but its inclusion in the full path starting at s_{31} leads to unbalanced entry/exit edges.) Eventually, the conclusion is that t_7 and t_{11} can alias because there exists an *alias* path between them with balanced entry and exit edges. From this point, the analysis can continue with a backward traversal from m_6, which encounters o_{26} and o_{29}.

Only the path from o_{26} to s_{31} has the balanced entry/exit property, and the analysis reports that the points-to set of s_{31} is $\{o_{26}\}$.

2.3 Using Must-Not-Alias Information

The proposed must-not-alias analysis is based on a program representation we refer to as the interprocedural symbolic points-to graph (ISPG). The definition and the construction algorithm for the ISPG are presented Section 3. Using this representation, it is possible to conclude that certain variables are definitely not aliases. The description of this analysis algorithm is presented in Section 4 and Section 5. For the example in Figure 2, the analysis can conclude that i_{29} and s_{31} cannot be aliases under any calling context. This information is pre-computed before the CFL-reachability-based points-to analysis from [6] starts.

Consider a match edge — that is, the edge from z to w for a pair of matching $z \xrightarrow{\text{store}(f)} x$ and $y \xrightarrow{\text{load}(f)} w$. When the points-to analysis removes this edge, it normally would have to explore the paths from x to y to decide whether x *alias* y. Instead, it queries our must-not-alias analysis to determine whether x and y may be aliases. If they cannot be aliases, further exploration is unnecessary. For illustration, consider an example where a client asks for the points-to set of str_{33}. The store(f) edge entering i_{29} and the load(f) edge exiting s_{31} mean that the points-to analysis needs to determine whether i_{29} *alias* s_{31}. However, our must-not-alias information has already concluded that under no calling context these two variables can be aliases. Hence, the points-to analysis can quickly skip the check and conclude that "abc" does not belong to the points-to set of str_{33}. In contrast, without the must-not-alias information, the points-to analysis would have to explore further for an *alias* path between s_{31} and i_{26}, which involves traversal of almost the entire graph.

3 Program Representation for Must-Not-Alias Analysis

The must-not-alias analysis runs on the interprocedural symbolic points-to graph. This section describes the approach for ISPG construction. Section 3.1 shows the first phase of the approach, in which an SPG is constructed separately for each method. Section 3.2 discusses the second phase which produces the final ISPG. To simplify the presentation, the algorithm is described under the assumption of an input program with no static fields and no dynamic dispatch.

3.1 Symbolic Points-to Graph for a Method

The SPG for a method is an extension of a standard points-to graph, with the following types of nodes and edges:

- $\mathcal{V}$ is the domain of variable nodes (i.e., local variables and formal parameters)
- $\mathcal{O}$ is the domain of allocation nodes for **new** expressions
- $\mathcal{S}$ is the domain of symbolic nodes, which are created to represent objects that are not visible in the method

- Edge $v \rightarrow o_i \in \mathcal{V} \times \mathcal{O}$ shows that variable v points to object o_i

- Edge $v \rightarrow s_i \in \mathcal{V} \times \mathcal{S}$ shows that (1) the allocation node that v may point to is defined outside the method, and (2) symbolic node s_i is used as a placeholder for this allocation node

- Edge $o_i \xrightarrow{f} o_j \in (\mathcal{O} \cup \mathcal{S}) \times \textit{Fields} \times (\mathcal{O} \cup \mathcal{S})$ shows that field f of allocation or symbolic node o_i points to allocation or symbolic node o_j

In order to introduce symbolic nodes as placeholders for outside objects, the CFL-reachability graph representation of a method is augmented with the following types of edges. An edge $s \xrightarrow{\text{new}} fp$ is added for each formal parameter fp of the method. Here s is a symbolic node, created to represent the objects that fp points to upon entry into the method. A separate symbolic node is created for each formal parameter. Similarly, for each call site $v = m()$, an edge $s \xrightarrow{\text{new}} v$ is created to represent the objects returned by the call. A separate symbolic node is introduced for each call site. For each field dereference expression $v.f$ whose value is read at least once, edges $s \xrightarrow{\text{new}} t$ and $t \xrightarrow{\text{store(f)}} v$ are created. Here symbolic node s denotes the heap location represented by $v.f$ before the method is invoked, and t is a temporary variable created to connect s and $v.f$.

The SPG for a method m can be constructed by computing intraprocedural $flowsTo$ paths for all $v \in \mathcal{V}$. A points-to edge $v \rightarrow o \in \mathcal{V} \times (\mathcal{O} \cup \mathcal{S})$ is added to the SPG if o $flowsTo$ v. A points-to edge $o_i \xrightarrow{f} o_j$ is added if there exists $x \xrightarrow{\text{store(f)}} y$ in m's representation such that o_i $flowsTo$ y and o_j $flowsTo$ x.

Both symbolic nodes and allocation nodes represent abstract heap locations. A variable that points to a symbolic node n_1 and another variable that points to an allocation/symbolic node n_2 may be aliases if it is eventually decided that n_1 and n_2 could represent the same abstract location. The relationships among allocation/symbolic nodes in an SPG are ambiguous. A symbolic node, even though it is intended to represent outside objects, may sometimes also represent inside objects (e.g., when the return value at a call site is a reference to some object created in the caller). Furthermore, two distinct symbolic nodes could represent the same object — e.g., due to aliasing of two actual parameters at some call site invoking the method under analysis. Such relationships are accounted for later, when the ISPG is constructed.

The introduction of symbolic nodes is similar to pointer analyses from [17,18,19,20,12]. These analysis algorithms use symbolic nodes to compute a summary for a caller from the summaries of its callees during a bottom-up traversal of the DAG of strongly connected components (SCC-DAG) in the call graph. Unlike previous analyses that create symbolic nodes to compute the actual points-to solution, we do so to approximate the flow of heap objects in order to perform a subsequent CFL-reachability analysis on the ISPG. This reachability analysis, described in Section 4 and Section 5, identifies alias relationships among allocation and symbolic nodes, and ignores the points-to relationships involving variables. These results are used to reduce the cost of the *alias* path exploration for the points-to analysis outlined in Section 2.

$$\text{actual } a_i \in \mathcal{V}_p, \text{formal } f_i \in \mathcal{V}_m$$

$$\frac{a_i \rightarrow n \in SPG_p, f_i \rightarrow s \in SPG_m}{n \xrightarrow{\text{entry(e)}} s \in ISPG}$$

$$\frac{ret \in \mathcal{V}_m, r \in \mathcal{V}_p, ret \rightarrow n \in SPG_m, r \rightarrow s \in SPG_p}{n \xrightarrow{\text{exit(e)}} s \in ISPG}$$

Fig. 3. Connecting method-level SPGs

3.2   Interprocedural Symbolic Points-To Graph

In order to perform interprocedural analysis, the SPGs of individual methods are connected to build the ISPG for the entire program. The ISPG is not a completely resolved points-to graph, but rather a graph where SPGs are trivially connected. Figure 3 shows the rules for ISPG construction at a call site $r = a_0.m(a_1, \ldots, a_i, \ldots)$. Suppose the call site is contained in method p.

In the figure, e denotes the call graph edge that goes from p to m through this particular call site. The callee m is assumed to have an artificial local variable ret in which the return value of the method is stored. For a formal-actual pair (f_i, a_i), an entry edge is added between each object/symbolic node n that a_i points to in caller and the symbolic node s created for f_i in the callee. The second rule creates an exit edge to connect the returned object/symbolic nodes n_1 from the callee and the symbolic node s created for r at the call site. Similarly to the entry and exit edges in the CFL-reachability formulation from Section 2, the entry and exit edges in the ISPG are added to represent parameter passing and value return. The annotations with call graph edge e for these ISPG edges will be used later to achieve context sensitivity in the must-not-alias analysis.

Figure 4 shows part of the ISPG built for the running example, which connects SPGs for methods `main`, `retrieve`, `add`, and `get`. Symbolic nodes are represented by shaded boxes, and named globally (instead of using code line numbers). For example, in method `add`, S_1 is the symbolic object created for `this`, S_2 is created due to the read of `this.elems`, and the ISPG contains an edge from S_1 to S_2. Name S_3 represents the object to which formal `m` points; due to `t[count++]=m`, the SPG contains an edge from S_2 to S_3 labeled with arr_elm. Due to the calls to `add` at lines 26 and 30, entry edges connect O_{25} and O_{28} with S_1, and O_{26} and O_{29} with S_3.

The *backbone* of an ISPG is the subgraph induced by the set of all allocation nodes and symbolic nodes. Edges in the backbone are either field points-to edges $o_i \xrightarrow{f} o_j$ computed by the intraprocedural construction described in Section 3.1, or entry/exit edges created at call sites, as defined above. Variable points-to edges (e.g., $this_7 \rightarrow S_1$ from above) are not included in the backbone. Section 4 and Section 5 show how to perform CFL-reachability on the backbone of an ISPG to compute the must-not-alias information.

Why use the ISPG? The benefits of performing the alias analysis using the ISPG backbone are two-fold. First, this graph abstracts away variable nodes, and partitions the heap using symbolic and allocation nodes (essentially, by defining

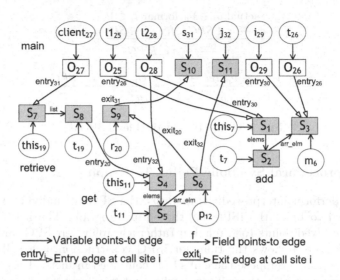

Fig. 4. Illustration of the ISPG for the running example

equivalence classes for these nodes). Hence, the backbone of an ISPG contains fewer nodes and edges than the graph representation for CFL-reachability points-to analysis from Section 2. Second, the ISPG allows simple modeling of the alias computation — the CFL-reachability used to formulate the context-insensitive version of the problem, as described in the next section, is restricted to a language *memAlias* which is simpler to handle than the more general CFL-reachability for context-insensitive points-to analysis [6,7].

4   Context-Insensitive Memory Alias Formulation

This section defines a CFL-reachability formulation of a context-insensitive version of the must-not-alias analysis. The context sensitivity aspects are described in the next section. Hereafter, the term "node" will be used as shorthand for "allocation or symbolic node in the ISPG", unless specified otherwise.

Two nodes o_1 and o_2 are memory aliases if they may denote the same heap memory location. We describe the memory aliases using relation *memAlias* $\subseteq$ $(\mathcal{O} \cup \mathcal{S}) \times (\mathcal{O} \cup \mathcal{S})$. This relation is reflexive, symmetric, and transitive, and therefore is an equivalence relation. The computation of *memAlias* is formulated as a CFL-reachability problem over the backbone of the ISPG. The relation has the following key property: for any pair of variables v_1 and v_2 in relation *alias* computed by the points-to analysis from Section 2, there must exist ISPG edges $v_1 \rightarrow o_1$ and $v_2 \rightarrow o_2$ such that the ISPG backbone contains a *memAlias* path from node o_1 to node o_2 (and also from o_2 to o_1). For a variable pair (v_1, v_2) for which such a pair (o_1, o_2) does *not* exist, the points-to analysis from Section 2 does not need to explore *alias* paths between v_1 and v_2, since all such work is guaranteed to be wasted. This section presents an efficient algorithm for solving

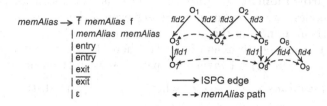

Fig. 5. Language *memAlias*

the all-pairs *memAlias*-path problem. We first assume that the backbone of the ISPG is free of recursive data structures. The approximation for recursive data structures is addressed later in the section.

Figure 5 shows the grammar for language *memAlias* and an example illustrating several such paths. An edge label f shows the field name for an ISPG edge $o_i \xrightarrow{f} o_j$. As before, $\bar{f}$ denotes the inverse of the edge labeled with f. The existence of a *memAlias* path from o_1 to o_2 also means that there is a *memAlias* path from o_1 to o_2. For this reason, the figure uses double-headed arrows to show such paths. In this example, o_7 *memAlias* o_9 because of path $o_7 \overline{fld1}\ o_3\ \overline{fld2}\ o_1\ fld2\ o_4\ \overline{fld3}\ o_2\ fld3\ o_5\ \overline{fld1}\ o_8\ \overline{fld4}\ o_6\ fld4\ o_9$.

Example. For illustration, consider the ISPG shown in Figure 4. Some of the *memAlias* pairs in this graph are (S_7, O_{27}), (S_1, S_4), (S_2, S_5), (S_3, S_6), (S_6, O_{29}), (S_{11}, O_{29}), (S_9, O_{29}), and (S_{10}, O_{29}).

Production *memAlias* $\rightarrow$ *memAlias memAlias* encodes the transitivity of the relation. The productions for entry/exit edges and their inverses allow arbitrary occurrences of such edges along a *memAlias* path; this is due to the context insensitivity of this version of the analysis. Production *memAlias* $\rightarrow \bar{f}$ *memAlias* f says that if x and y are reachable from the same node z through two paths, and the sequences of fields along the paths are the same, x and y may denote the same memory location. This is an over-approximation that is less precise than the alias information computed by the analysis from Section 2.

Consider the sources of this imprecision. Suppose x, y, z and w are nodes in the ISPG and variables v_x, v_y, v_z and v_w point to them. If w and z are memory aliases, and there exist two points-to edges $x \xleftarrow{f} z$ and $w \xrightarrow{f} y$ in the ISPG, x and y are memory aliases based on our definition. The existence of these two edges can be due to four combinations of loads and stores in the program:

- $v_x = v_z.f$ and $v_y = v_w.f$: in this case, x and y are true memory aliases
- $v_x = v_z.f$ and $v_w.f = v_y$: x and y are true memory aliases because there exists a *flowsTo* path from v_y to v_x.
- $v_z.f = v_x$ and $v_y = v_w.f$: again, x and y are true memory aliases
- $v_z.f = v_x$ and $v_w.f = v_y$: this case is handled imprecisely, since x and y do not need to be aliases. Our approach allows this one source of imprecision in order to achieve low analysis cost.

Precision improvement. It is important to note that two allocation nodes (i.e., non-symbolic nodes) are never memory aliases even if there exists a *memAlias* path between them. Hence, in the final solution computed by the analysis, node x is considered to not be an alias of y if (1) there does not exist a *memAlias* path between them, or (2) all *memAlias* paths between them are of the form $x \xrightarrow{\overline{f_i...f_0}} o_i$ *memAlias* $o_j \xrightarrow{f_0...f_i} y$, where o_i and o_j are distinct allocation nodes.

Soundness. The formulation presented above defines a sound must-not-alias analysis. Consider any two variables v_1 and v_2 such that v_1 *alias* v_2 in the approach from Section 2. It is always the case that there exist ISPG edges $v_1 \rightarrow o_1$ and $v_2 \rightarrow o_2$ such that o_1 and o_2 are declared to be memory aliases by our analysis. Here one of these nodes is a symbolic node, and the other one is either a symbolic node or an allocation node. The proof of this property is not presented in the paper due to space limitations.

4.1 Solving All-Pairs *memAlias*-Reachability

Solving CFL-reachability on the mutually-recursive languages *alias* and *flowsTo* from [6] yields $O(m^3 k^3)$ running time, where m is the number of nodes in the program representation and k is the size of L_F. As observed in existing work [21,22,13], the generic bound of $O(m^3 k^3)$ can be improved substantially in specific cases, by taking advantage of certain properties of the underlying grammar. This is exactly the basis for our approach: the algorithm for *memAlias*-reachability runs in $O(n^4)$ where n is the number of nodes in the ISPG backbone. The value of n is smaller than m, because variable nodes are abstracted away in the ISPG; Section 6 quantifies this observation. This algorithm speeds up the computation by taking advantage of the symmetric property of *memAlias* paths. This subsection assumes that the ISPG is an acyclic graph; the extension to handle recursive types is presented in the next subsection.

The pseudocode of the analysis is shown in Algorithm 1. The first phase considers production *memAlias* $\rightarrow$ $\bar{f}$ *memAlias* f. Strings in the corresponding language are palindromes (e.g., *abcddcba*). Once a *memAlias* path is found between nodes a and b, pair (a, b) is added to set *memAlias* (line 9). The *memAlias* set for this particular language can be computed through depth-first traversal of the ISPG, starting from each node n (line 4-13). The graph traversal (line 5) is implemented by function COMPUTEREACHABLENODES, which finds all nodes n' that are reachable from n, and their respective sequences $l_{n,n'}$ of labels along the paths from which they are reached (n' could be n). Sequence $l_{n,n'}$ will be referred to as the *reachability string* for a path between n and n'. Due to space limitations, we omit the detailed description of this function. Also, for simplicity of presentation, we assume that there exists only one path between n and n'. Multiple paths and their reachability strings can be handled in a similar manner. The function returns a map which maps each pair (n, n') to its reachability string $l_{n,n'}$. A similar map *cache* accumulates the reachability information for all nodes (line 7). For any pair of nodes (a, b) reachable from n such that $l_{n,a} = l_{n,b}$, there exists a *memAlias*

Algorithm 1. Pseudocode for solving all-pairs $memAlias$-reachability.

SolveMemAliasReachability (ISPG backbone IG)

1:   Map $cache$ // a cache map that maps a pair of nodes (n, a) to their reachability string $l_{n,a}$
2:   List $endNodes$ // a worklist containing pairs of nodes that are two ends of a sequence of edges
        that forms a $memAlias$ path
3:   /* phase 1: consider only production $memAlias \rightarrow \bar{f}\ memAlias\ f$ */
4:   **for** each node n in IG **do**
5:      Map $m \longleftarrow$ ComputeReachableNodes(n)
6:      **for** each pair of entries $[(n, a), l_{n,a}]$ and $[(n, b), l_{n,b}]$ in m **do**
7:         $cache \longleftarrow cache \cup [(n, a), l_{n,a}] \cup [(n, b), l_{n,b}]$ // remember the reachability information
8:         **if** $l_{n,a} = l_{n,b}$ **then**
9:            $memAlias \longleftarrow memAlias \cup (a, b)$ // a $memAlias$ path exists between a and b
10:           $endNodes \longleftarrow endNodes \cup (a, b)$
11:         **end if**
12:      **end for**
13:   **end for**
14:   /* phase 2: consider production $memAlias \rightarrow memAlias\ memAlias$ */
15:   /* a worklist-based algorithm */
16:   **while** $endNodes \neq \emptyset$ **do**
17:      remove a pair (a, b) from $endNodes$
18:      **if** (a, b) has been processed **then**
19:         **continue**
20:      **else**
21:         mark (a, b) as processed
22:      **end if**
23:      **for** each (c, a) in $memAlias$ **do**
24:         **for** each (b, d) in $memAlias$ **do**
25:            $memAlias \longleftarrow memAlias \cup (c, d)$
26:            $endNodes \longleftarrow endNodes \cup (c, d)$
27:         **end for**
28:      **end for**
29:      **for** each $[(a, c), l_{a,c}]$ in $cache$ **do**
30:         **for** each $[(b, d), l_{b,d}]$ in $cache$ **do**
31:            **if** $l_{a,c} = l_{b,d}$ **then**
32:               /* add to the worklist all pairs of nodes with a $memAlias$ path between them */
33:               $memAlias \longleftarrow memAlias \cup (c, d)$
34:               $endNodes \longleftarrow endNodes \cup (c, d)$
35:            **end if**
36:         **end for**
37:      **end for**
38:   **end while**

---

path between them (line 9). This pair is added to relation $memAlias$ and to a list $endNodes$ for further processing.

Phase 1 complexity. Each graph traversal at line 5 takes time $O(m)$, where m is the number of edges in the ISPG backbone. The *for* loop at lines 6-12 takes $O(m^2)$. Note that when a reachability string is generated, the hashcode of the string is computed and remembered. Hence, line 8 essentially compares two integers, which takes constant time. Since there are $O(m)$ nodes in the program, the complexity of computing all $memAlias$ paths in this phase is $O(m^3)$.

The second phase employs a worklist-based iteration which considers the entire $memAlias$ language. As usual, the phase computes a closure by continuously processing pairs of nodes between which there exists a $memAlias$ path. Such pairs of nodes are contained in list $endNodes$, and are removed from the list upon processing. Lines 23-28 update the transitive closure of $memAlias$. Next, all nodes reachable from a or from b are retrieved from $cache$, together with their reachability strings (line 29 and 30). Due to the caching of reachability information, graph traversal is no longer needed. If reachability strings $l_{a,c}$ and $l_{b,d}$ match, a memAlias path exists between c and d. Hence, pair (c, d) is added to memAlias and to worklist endNodes.

Phase 2 complexity. Each *while* iteration (lines 17-37) takes $O(m^2)$ time. The worst case is that all possible pairs of nodes (a, b) in the ISPG backbone have been added to endNodes and processed. There are $O(m^2)$ such pairs; hence, the worst-case time complexity for the entire algorithm is $O(m^4)$.

Although a slightly modified algorithm is used in the actual context-sensitive version of the analysis (presented in the next section), the description from above illustrates the key to computing memAlias-reachability. It is important to note again that the design of this efficient algorithm is due to the specific structure of the grammar of language memAlias. Since the grammar is symmetric and self-recursive (instead of being mutually-recursive), the finite number of open field parentheses can be computed a priori (i.e., stored in the cache). Thus, at the expense of the single source of imprecision discussed earlier, this approach avoids the cost of the more general and expensive CFL-reachability computation described in Section 2.

4.2   Approximation for Recursive Data Structures

Existing analysis algorithms have to introduce *regularity* into the context-free language and approximate either recursive calls [16,6], or recursive data structures [23] over the regularized language. Because memAlias-reachability is performed over the backbone of an ISPG, we focus on the handling of cycles consisting of field points-to edges caused by recursive data structures.

The key to the handling of a recursive type is to collapse an ISPG SCC caused by the recursion. For any path going through a SCC, a *wildcard* (*) is used to replace the substring of the path that includes the SCC nodes. The wildcard can represent an arbitrary string. During the string comparison performed by Algorithm 1, two paths match as long as the regular expressions representing them have non-empty intersection. Figure 6 shows an example of reachability checking in the presence of recursive types. In this example, it is necessary to check whether the two regular expressions $fld1 * fld2\, fld3\, fld6$ and $fld1 * fld6$ have non-empty intersection.

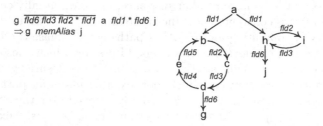

Fig. 6. Handling of recursive data structures

The handling of recursive types requires modifications to the comparison of reachability strings. If neither string contains wildcards, no changes are needed. If at least one string contains wildcards, it is necessary to consider the corresponding finite automata and to check if there exists a common sequence of state transitions that can lead both automata to accepting states. Although deciding whether two general-form regular expressions have non-empty intersection is a non-trivial problem, the alias analysis needs to handle a significantly simplified version of the problem in which the regular expressions do not contain general closure. In practice, the cost of this processing is insignificant.

Formulation of points-to analysis from *memAlias*. Although we use language *memAlias* to formulate an alias analysis, a points-to relation *pointsTo* can be easily derived from the following production: *pointsTo* $\rightarrow$ var_pts *memAlias*. Here var_pts is the label on an ISPG edge from a variable node to a (symbolic or allocation) node. The set of all such edges forms the complement of the backbone edge set. All var_pts edges are constructed in the intraprocedural phase of ISPG construction, as described in Section 3.1. For example, in Figure 4, j_{32} *pointsTo* O_{29} because j_{32} var_pts S_{11} and S_{11} *memAlias* O_{29} hold.

Due to the approximations described earlier and the limited context sensitivity (discussed shortly), the points-to information derived from *memAlias* is less precise than the solution computed by the analysis from Section 2. However, as shown in our experimental results, a large number of infeasible alias pairs can be eliminated early, leading to considerable overall performance improvement.

5   Context-Sensitive Must-Not-Alias Analysis

A context-sensitivity check can be performed along with the heap access check to guarantee that a *memAlias* path contains balanced entry and exit edges. Previous work [24,11] has shown that heap cloning (i.e., context-sensitive treatment not only of pointer variables, but also of pointer targets) is one of the most important factors that contribute to the precision of the analysis. Existing analysis algorithms achieve heap cloning primarily in two ways: (1) they maintain a push-down automaton to solve CFL-reachability over language R_C described in Section 2, or (2) they explicitly clone pointer variables and pointer targets (i.e., allocation nodes) for each distinct calling context [11,25,12], so that the cloned nodes are automatically distinguished. In order to achieve both efficiency and precision, we develop a hybrid algorithm that combines both approaches.

5.1   Analysis Overview

This subsection gives a high-level overview of the proposed approach; the detailed definitions are presented in the next subsection. The analysis uses bottom-up propagation on the call graph to ensure context sensitivity for pointer variables, with appropriate approximations for recursion. This enables a summary-based approach to propagate reachability strings from callees to callers, which yields efficiency. By composing summary functions (i.e., reachability strings for nodes that parameters and return variables point to in the ISPG) at call sites, reachability strings for nodes in callees are concatenated with reachability strings for nodes in callers. At each call graph edge e, if the analysis enters the callee through edge $\overline{\text{entry}(e)}$, it has to exit through edge $\overline{\text{entry}(e)}$ or $\text{exit}(e)$. This type of context sensitivity corresponds to the classical *functional* approach [26]. However, functional context sensitivity does not automatically enforce heap cloning. A (symbolic or allocation) node in a method may represent different objects if the method is inlined to a caller through different call chains. If these objects are not differentiated, imprecise *memAlias* paths may be derived.

Our proposal is to perform lightweight cloning for (symbolic and allocation) nodes when composing summary function at a call site. In this cloning, there may be several "clones" (copies) of an ISPG node, each annotated with a different calling context. The level of cloning, of course, has an impact on the analysis precision. Since the primary concern is efficiency, the level of cloning is restricted to 1, and thus, each symbolic or allocation node in the analysis has only one call graph edge associated with it. In fact, for some programs in our benchmark set, increasing the level of cloning to 2 (i.e., a chain of two call graph edges) makes the alias analysis too expensive compared to the cost reduction for the subsequent points-to analysis.

5.2   Analysis Details

This subsection defines the context-sensitive alias analysis using the rules shown in Figure 7. The analysis state is represented by cache map *cache*, worklist *endNodes*, and relation *memAlias*, whose functions are similar to those defined in Algorithm 1. In the rules, ϵ denotes the empty string and operator $\circ$ represents string concatenation.

The first rule describes the intraprocedural analysis with a rule of the form *endNodes, cache, memAlias* $\Rightarrow$ *endNodes', cache', memAlias'* with unprimed and primed symbols representing the state before and after an SPG field points-to edge $p \xrightarrow{f} o$ is traversed. The intraprocedural analysis performs backward traversal of the SPG for the method being processed, and updates the state as described above. When edge $p \xrightarrow{f} o$ is traversed backwards, the reachability from p to n is established for any n already reachable from o: that is, for any $[(o, n), l_{o,n}] \in cache$ where $l_{o,n}$ is a reachability string. Given the updated *cache*, it is necessary to consider the set of pairs (a, b) of nodes reachable from p such that the corresponding reachability strings $l_{p,a}$ and $l_{p,b}$ have non-empty intersection (represented by predicate OVERLAP); this processing is similar to the functionality of lines 6-12 in Algorithm 1.

The second rule describes the processing of an entry edge from o to s, corresponding to a call graph edge e. In this rule, p^e denotes the clone of node p for e. Here o represents a symbolic or allocation node to which an actual parameter points, s represents a symbolic node created for the corresponding formal parameter in the callee, and p^c is a node reachable from s. Node p^c may represent a node in the callee itself (i.e., when c is the empty string ϵ), or a node in a method deeper in the call graph that is cloned to the callee due to a previously-processed call. When

[Intraprocedural state update]

$[(o, n), l_{o,n}] \in cache$

$cache' = cache \cup [(p, n), f \circ l_{o,n}] \cup [(p, p), \epsilon]$

$pairs = \{ (a, b) \mid [(p, a), l_{p,a}], [(p, b), l_{p,b}] \in cache' \wedge \text{OVERLAP}(l_{p,a}, l_{p,b}) \}$

$memAlias' = memAlias \cup pairs$

$endNodes' = endNodes \cup pairs$

$$\overline{endNodes, cache, memAlias \Rightarrow^p \xrightarrow{f} {}^\circ endNodes', cache', memAlias'}$$

[Method call]

$[(s, p^c), l_{s,p}] \in cache$

$p^x = p^e$ if $c = \epsilon$ and $p^x = p^c$ otherwise

$triples = \{ [(o, p^x), l_{s,p}] \} \cup \{ [(o, s^e), \epsilon] \} \cup$

$\qquad \{ [(o, q), l_{s,p} \circ l_{n,q}] \mid (p^c \xrightarrow{\text{exit}(e)} n \vee p^c \xrightarrow{\overline{\text{entry}(e)}} n) \wedge [(n, q), l_{n,q}] \in cache \}$

$cache' = cache \cup triples$

$pairs = \{ (a, b) \mid [(p, a), l_{p,a}], [(p, b), l_{p,b}] \in cache' \wedge \text{OVERLAP}(l_{p,a}, l_{p,b}) \}$

$memAlias' = memAlias \cup pairs$

$endNodes' = endNodes \cup pairs$

$$\overline{endNodes, cache, memAlias \Rightarrow^\circ \xrightarrow{\text{entry}(e)} {}^s endNodes', cache', memAlias'}$$

Fig. 7. Inference rules defining the context-sensitive alias analysis algorithm

a call site is handled, all nodes that are reachable from a symbolic node created for a formal parameter, and all nodes that can reach a node pointed-to by a return variable, are cloned from the callee to the caller. All edges connecting them are cloned as well. The algorithm uses only 1-level cloning. If the existing context c of node p is empty, it is updated with the current call graph edge e; otherwise, the new context x remains c. Note that multiple-level cloning can be easily defined by modifying the definition of p^x.

In addition to updating the cache with (o, p^x) and (o, s^e), it is also necessary to consider any node n in the caller's SPG that is connected with p^c either through an exit(e) edge (i.e., p^c is a symbolic node pointed-to by the return variable), or through an entry(e) edge (i.e., p^c is a symbolic node created for another formal parameter). The analysis retrieves all nodes q in the caller that are reachable from n, together with their corresponding reachability strings $l_{n,q}$, and updates the state accordingly. Now q becomes reachable from o, and the reachability string $l_{o,q}$ is thus the concatenation of $l_{s,p}$ and $l_{n,q}$.

After all edges in the caller are processed, the transitive closure computation shown at lines 16-38 of Algorithm 1 is invoked to find all *memAlias* pairs in the caller as well as all its (direct and transitive) callees. This processing is applied at each call graph edge e, during a bottom-up traversal of the call graph.

Termination. To ensure termination, the following approximation is adopted: when a call-graph-SCC method m is processed, edge $a \xrightarrow{f} b$ (which is reachable from m's formal parameter) is not cloned in its caller n if an edge $a^e \xrightarrow{f} b^e$ (where e is the call graph edge for the call from n to m) already exists in n.

Table 1. Java benchmarks

Benchmark	#Methods	#Statements	#SB/ISPG Nodes	#SB/ISPG Edges
compress	2344	43938	18778/10977	18374/3214
db	2352	44187	19062/11138	18621/3219
jack	2606	53375	22185/12605	21523/15560
javac	3520	66971	23858/14119	23258/3939
jess	2772	51021	22773/13421	21769/4754
mpegaudio	2528	55166	22446/12774	21749/4538
mtrt	2485	46969	20344/11878	19674/3453
soot-c	4583	71406	31054/18863	29971/5010
sablecc-j	8789	125538	44134/26512	42114/9365
jflex	4008	25150	31331/18248	30301/4971
muffin	4326	80370	33211/19659	32497/5282
jb	2393	43722	19179/11275	18881/3146
jlex	2423	49100	21482/11787	20643/3846
java_cup	2605	50315	22636/13214	21933/3438
polyglot	2322	42620	18739/10950	18337/3128
antlr	2998	57197	25505/15068	24462/4116
bloat	4994	79784	38002/23192	35861/5428
jython	4136	80067	34143/19969	33970/5179
ps	5278	84540	39627/23601	38746/5646

The processing of a SCC method stops as soon as the analysis determines that no more nodes need to be cloned to this method during the interprocedural propagation.

6 Experimental Evaluation

The proposed approach was implemented using the Soot 2.2.4 analysis framework [14,15]. The analyses included the Sun JDK 1.3.1_20 libraries, to allow comparison with previous work [11,6]. All experiments were performed on a machine with an Intel Xeon 2.8GHz CPU, and run with 2GB heap size. The experimental benchmarks, used in previous work [12], are shown in Table 1. Columns *Methods* and *Statements* show the number of methods in the original context-insensitive call graph computed by Soot's Spark component [27], and the number of statements in these methods. The ISPG was constructed using this call graph. Columns *#SB/ISPG Nodes (Edges)* shows the comparison between the number of nodes (edges) in the Sridharan-Bodik (SB) graph representation of the program, and the number of nodes (edges) in the corresponding ISPG backbone. On average, the numbers of ISPG backbone nodes and edges are 1.7× and 5.6× smaller than the numbers of SB nodes and edges, respectively.

The rest of this section presents an experimental comparison between the optimized version and the original version of the Sridharan-Bodik analysis. Specifically, queries were raised for the points-to set of each variable in the program.

6.1 Running Time Reduction

Table 2 compares the running times of the two analysis versions. Since the analysis cannot scale to compute fully-refined results, it allows users to specify a

Table 2. Analysis time (in seconds) and precision comparison

Benchmark	Original	Optimized				Speedup	Precision				
	SB	ISPG	Alias	SB'	Total		Casts	Ins	mA	1H	SB
compress	1101	59	20	203	282	3.9	6	0	0	0	2
db	1180	62	10	198	270	4.4	24	0	6	6	19
jack	1447	223	37	241	501	2.9	148	14	40	42	49
javac	1727	86	20	339	445	3.9	317	0	38	40	55
jess	1872	92	51	228	371	5.0	66	6	8	8	38
mpegaudio	866	56	20	185	261	3.3	13	1	4	4	4
mtrt	873	67	16	192	275	3.2	10	0	4	4	4
soot-c	3043	159	64	672	895	3.4	797	7	72	89	142
sablecc-j	4338	445	59	2350	2854	1.5	327	6	35	30	62
jflex	3181	151	43	1148	1342	2.4	580	1	12	2	43
muffin	3378	232	50	599	891	3.8	148	2	20	21	69
jb	802	58	9	287	354	2.3	38	0	3	2	24
jlex	833	54	14	237	305	2.7	47	1	4	3	14
java_cup	1231	73	10	342	425	2.9	460	24	24	24	372
polyglot	707	48	15	208	271	2.6	9	0	2	1	4
antlr	1211	87	13	453	553	2.2	77	7	4	3	28
bloat	3121	139	80	1655	1874	1.7	1298	80	91	80	148
jython	1576	83	64	415	562	2.8	458	11	29	30	167
ps	2676	236	73	1226	1535	1.7	667	17	41	189	49

threshold value to bound the total number of refinement passes (or nodes visited) — once the number of passes (or nodes visited) exceeds this value, the analysis gives up refinement and returns a safe approximate solution.

We inserted a guard in the points-to analysis code that returns immediately after the size of a points-to set becomes 1. If the points-to set contains multiple objects, the refinement continues until the maximum number of passes (10) or nodes (75000) is reached. Because the same constraint (i.e., #passes and #nodes) is used for both the original version and the optimized version, the optimized version does not lose any precision — in fact, it could have higher precision because it explores more paths (in our experiments, this affects only **ps**, in which two additional downcasts are proven to be safe).

The running time reduction is described in Table 2. Column *SB* shows the running time of the original version of the Sridharan-Bodik analysis. Columns *ISPG*, *Alias*, and *SB'* show the times to build the ISPG, run the must-not-alias analysis, and compute the points-to solution. Column *Speedup* shows the value of *Refine/Total*. On average, using the must-not-alias information provided by our analysis, the points-to analysis ran more than 3 times faster, and in some case the speedup was as large as five-fold.

The smallest performance improvement ($1.6\times$) is for **sablecc-j**. We inspected the program and found the reason to be a large SCC (containing 2103 methods) in Spark's call graph. The fixed-point iteration merged a large number of symbolic/object nodes in the SCC methods, resulting in a large reachability map and limited filtering of un-aliased variables. In general, large SCCs (containing thousands of methods) are well known to degrade the precision and performance of context-sensitive analysis. Large cycles may sometimes be formed due to the existence of a very small number of spurious call graph edges. Based on this observation, we employ an optimization that uses the original (un-optimized) version of the points-to analysis to compute precise points-to sets for the receiver variables at call sites that have too many call graph edges in Spark's call graph. This is done if the number of outgoing call graph edges at a call site exceeds a threshold value (e.g., the current value is 10). Hence, the approach pays the price of the increased ISPG construction time to reduce the cost and imprecision of the *memAlias* computation.

Note that our analysis does not impose heavy memory burden — once the must-not-alias analysis finishes and relation *memAlias* is computed, all reachability maps are released. The only additional needed memory is to hold the relation and the ISPG nodes. Both the reachability analysis and the subsequent points-to analysis ran successfully within the 2GB heap limit. We also performed experiments with 2-level-heap cloning (defined in Section 5). Due to space limitations, these results are not included in the paper. For some programs in the benchmark set, the analysis ran out of memory; for others, the *memAlias* computation became very slow. Thus, 1-level heap cloning appears to strike the right balance between cost and precision.

6.2   Analysis Precision

Column *Precision* in Table 2 shows a precision comparison between a points-to solution derived from relation *memAlias* (as described at the end of Section 4) and those computed by other analyses. The table gives the number of downcasts that can be proven safe by context-insensitive points-to analysis (*Ins*), our analysis (*mA*), object-sensitive analysis with 1-level heap cloning (*1H*), and the Sridharan-Bodik analysis (*SB*). From existing work, it is not surprising that *Ins* and *SB* have the lowest and highest precision, respectively. Analyses *1H* and *mA* have comparable precision. Although *mA* is fully context-sensitive for pointer variables, this does not have a significant effect on precision. The reason is that heap cloning is more important than context-sensitive treatment of pointer variables [24,11,6]. Even though *mA* can prove a much smaller number of safe casts than *SB*, it does prune out a large number of spurious aliasing relationships. For example, the points-to set of a variable computed by *mA* can be much smaller than the one computed by *Ins*. Thus, the analysis proposed in this paper could either be used as a pre-analysis for the Sridharan-Bodik points-to analysis (in which case it significantly reduces the overall cost without any loss of precision), or as a stand-alone analysis which trades some precision for higher efficiency (e.g., since it is significantly less expensive than *1H*).

7   Related Work

There is a very large body of work on precise and scalable points-to analysis [28,11]. The discussion in this section is restricted to the analysis algorithms that are most closely related to our technique.

CFL-reachability. Early work by Reps et al. [8,29,30,31,32] proposes to model realizable paths using a context-free language that treats method calls and returns as pairs of balanced parentheses. Based on this framework, Sridharan et al. defined a CFL-reachability formulation to precisely model heap accesses, which results in demand-driven points-to analyses for Java [16,6]. Combining the CFL-reachability formulations of both heap accesses and interprocedural realizable paths, [6] proposes a context-sensitive analysis that achieves high precision by continuously refining points-to relationships. The analysis is the most precise one among a set of context-sensitive, field-sensitive, subset-based points-to analysis algorithms, and can therefore satisfy the need of highly-precise points-to information. However, the high cost associated with this precision is an obstacle for the practical real-world use of the analysis, which motivates our work on reducing the cost while maintaining the precision.

Zheng and Rugina [7] present a CFL-reachability formulation of alias analysis and implement a context-insensitive demand-driven analysis for C programs. The key insight is that aliasing information can be directly computed without having to compute points-to information first. Similarly to computing a points-to solution, this analysis also needs to make recursive queries regarding the aliasing relationships among variables. Hence, our pre-computed must-not-alias information could potentially be useful to improve the performance of this analysis.

Must-not-alias analysis. Naik and Aiken [33] present a conditional must-not-alias analysis and use it to prove that a Java program is free of data races. The analysis is conditional, because it is used to show that two objects can not alias under the assumption that two other objects can not alias. If it can be proven that any two memory locations protected by their respective locks must not alias as long as the two lock objects are distinct, the program cannot contain potential data races. Our analysis uses the must-not-alias relationship of two memory locations to disprove the existence of *alias* paths between two variables. These two analyses are related, because both use must-not-alias information to disprove the existence of certain properties (data race versus *alias* path).

Improving the scalability of points-to analysis. Similarly to our technique, there is body of work on scaling of points-to analysis. Rountev and Chandra [34] present a technique that detects equivalence classes of variables that have the same points-to set. The technique is performed before the points-to analysis starts and can speed up context-insensitive subset-based points-to analysis by a factor of two. Work from [35] observes that such equivalence classes still exist as points-to sets are propagated, and proposes an online approach to merge equivalent nodes to achieve efficiency. A number of other approaches have employed binary decision diagrams and Datalog-based techniques (e.g., [36,37,38,39,40]) to achieve high performance and precision. Our previous work [12] identifies equivalence classes of calling contexts and proposes merging of equivalent contexts. This analysis has strong context sensitivity — it builds a symbolic points-to graph for each individual method, and clones all non-escaping SPG nodes from callees to callers. Although the technique proposed in this paper uses a variation of this ISPG as program representation, it is fundamentally different from this previous analysis. In this older work, which is not based on CFL-reachability, both variable and field points-to edges are cloned

120   G. Xu, A. Rountev, and M. Sridharan

to compute a complete points-to solution. The technique in this paper formulates a
new alias analysis as a CFL-reachability problem, uses a completely different analysis algorithm, employs a different form of context sensitivity, and aims to reduce
the cost of a subsequent points-to analysis that is based on a more general and expensive CFL-reachability algorithm.

8 Conclusions

The high precision provided by CFL-reachability-based pointer analysis usually comes with great cost. If relatively precise alias information is available
at the time heap loads and stores are matched, many irrelevant paths can be
eliminated early during the computation of CFL-reachability. Based on this observation, this paper proposes a must-not-alias analysis that operates on the
ISPG of the program and efficiently produces context-sensitive aliasing information. This information is then used in the Sridharan-Bodik points-to analysis.
An experimental evaluation shows that the points-to analysis is able to run 3×
faster without any precision loss. This technique is orthogonal to existing CFL-
reachability-based points-to analysis algorithms — it does not aim to compute
precise points-to information directly, but rather uses easily computed aliasing
information to help the points-to analyses quickly produce a highly-precise solution. These scalability results could directly benefit a large number of program
analyses and transformations that require high-quality points-to information at
a practical cost, for use on large programs in real-world software tools.

Acknowledgments. We would like to thank the ECOOP reviewers for their
valuable and thorough comments and suggestions. This research was supported
in part by the National Science Foundation under CAREER grant CCF-0546040.

References

1. Das, M., Lerner, S., Seigle, M.: ESP: Path-sensitive program verification in poly-
   nomial time. In: ACM SIGPLAN Conference on Programming Language Design
   and Implementation, pp. 57–68 (2002)
2. Fink, S., Yahav, E., Dor, N., Ramalingam, G., Geay, E.: Effective typestate verification in the presence of aliasing. In: ACM SIGSOFT International Symposium
   on Software Testing and Analysis, pp. 133–144 (2006)
3. Naik, M., Aiken, A., Whaley, J.: Effective static race detection for Java. In: ACM
   SIGPLAN Conference on Programming Language Design and Implementation, pp.
   308–319 (2006)
4. Voung, J.W., Jhala, R., Lerner, S.: RELAY: Static race detection on millions of
   lines of code. In: ACM SIGSOFT International Symposium on the Foundations of
   Software Engineering, pp. 205–214 (2007)
5. Horwitz, S., Reps, T., Binkley, D.: Interprocedural slicing using dependence graphs.
   ACM Transactions on Programming Languages and Systems 12(1), 26–60 (1990)
6. Sridharan, M., Bodik, R.: Refinement-based context-sensitive points-to analysis
   for Java. In: ACM SIGPLAN Conference on Programming Language Design and
   Implementation, pp. 387–400 (2006)

7. Zheng, X., Rugina, R.: Demand-driven alias analysis for C. In: ACM SIGPLAN-SIGACT Symposium on Principles of Programming Languages, pp. 197–208 (2008)
8. Reps, T.: Program analysis via graph reachability. Information and Software Technology 40(11-12), 701–726 (1998)
9. Sridharan, M. (2006), http://www.sable.mcgill.ca/pipermail/soot-list/2006-January/000477.html
10. Kahlon, V.: Bootstrapping: A technique for scalable flow and context-sensitive pointer alias analysis. In: ACM SIGPLAN Conference on Programming Language Design and Implementation, pp. 249–259 (2008)
11. Lhoták, O., Hendren, L.: Context-sensitive points-to analysis: Is it worth it? In: International Conference on Compiler Construction, pp. 47–64 (2006)
12. Xu, G., Rountev, A.: Merging equivalent contexts for scalable heap-cloning-based context-sensitive points-to analysis. In: ACM SIGSOFT International Symposium on Software Testing and Analysis, pp. 225–235 (2008)
13. Kodumal, J., Aiken, A.: The set constraint/CFL reachability connection in practice. In: ACM SIGPLAN Conference on Programming Language Design and Implementation, pp. 207–218 (2004)
14. Soot Framework, http://www.sable.mcgill.ca/soot
15. Vallée-Rai, R., Gagnon, E., Hendren, L., Lam, P., Pominville, P., Sundaresan, V.: Optimizing Java bytecode using the Soot framework: Is it feasible? In: International Conference on Compiler Construction, pp. 18–34 (2000)
16. Sridharan, M., Gopan, D., Shan, L., Bodik, R.: Demand-driven points-to analysis for Java. In: ACM SIGPLAN Conference on Object-Oriented Programming, Systems, Languages, and Applications, pp. 59–76 (2005)
17. Chatterjee, R., Ryder, B.G., Landi, W.: Relevant context inference. In: ACM SIGPLAN-SIGACT Symposium on Principles of Programming Languages, pp. 133–146 (1999)
18. Wilson, R., Lam, M.: Efficient context-sensitive pointer analysis for C programs. In: ACM SIGPLAN Conference on Programming Language Design and Implementation, pp. 1–12 (1995)
19. Cheng, B., Hwu, W.: Modular interprocedural pointer analysis using access paths. In: ACM SIGPLAN Conference on Programming Language Design and Implementation, pp. 57–69 (2000)
20. Whaley, J., Rinard, M.: Compositional pointer and escape analysis for Java programs. In: ACM SIGPLAN Conference on Object-Oriented Programming, Systems, Languages, and Applications, pp. 187–206 (1999)
21. Melski, D., Reps, T.: Interconvertibility of a class of set constraints and context-free-language reachability. Theoretical Computer Science 248, 29–98 (2000)
22. Rehof, J., Fähndrich, M.: Type-based flow analysis: From polymorphic subtyping to CFL-reachability. In: ACM SIGPLAN-SIGACT Symposium on Principles of Programming Languages, pp. 54–66 (2001)
23. Kodumal, J., Aiken, A.: Regularly annotated set constraints. In: ACM SIGPLAN Conference on Programming Language Design and Implementation, pp. 331–341 (2007)
24. Nystrom, E., Kim, H., Hwu, W.: Importance of heap specialization in pointer analysis. In: PASTE, pp. 43–48 (2004)
25. Lattner, C., Lenharth, A., Adve, V.: Making context-sensitive points-to analysis with heap cloning practical for the real world. In: ACM SIGPLAN Conference on Programming Language Design and Implementation, pp. 278–289 (2007)

26. Sharir, M., Pnueli, A.: Two approaches to interprocedural data flow analysis. In: Muchnick, S., Jones, N. (eds.) Program Flow Analysis: Theory and Applications, pp. 189–234. Prentice-Hall, Englewood Cliffs (1981)
27. Lhoták, O., Hendren, L.: Scaling java points-to analysis using SPARK. In: Hedin, G. (ed.) CC 2003. LNCS, vol. 2622, pp. 153–169. Springer, Heidelberg (2003)
28. Hind, M.: Pointer analysis: Haven't we solved this problem yet? In: PASTE, pp. 54–61 (2001)
29. Reps, T., Horwitz, S., Sagiv, M.: Precise interprocedural dataflow analysis via graph reachability. In: ACM SIGPLAN-SIGACT Symposium on Principles of Programming Languages, pp. 49–61 (1995)
30. Horwitz, S., Reps, T., Sagiv, M.: Demand interprocedural dataflow analysis. In: ACM SIGSOFT International Symposium on the Foundations of Software Engineering, pp. 104–115 (1995)
31. Reps, T.: Solving demand versions of interprocedural analysis problems. In: Fritzson, P.A. (ed.) CC 1994. LNCS, vol. 786, pp. 389–403. Springer, Heidelberg (1994)
32. Reps, T., Horwitz, S., Sagiv, M., Rosay, G.: Speeding up slicing. In: ACM SIGSOFT International Symposium on the Foundations of Software Engineering, pp. 11–20 (1994)
33. Naik, M., Aiken, A.: Conditional must not aliasing for static race detection. In: ACM SIGPLAN-SIGACT Symposium on Principles of Programming Languages, pp. 327–338 (2007)
34. Rountev, A., Chandra, S.: Off-line variable substitution for scaling points-to analysis. In: ACM SIGPLAN Conference on Programming Language Design and Implementation, pp. 47–56 (2000)
35. Hardekopf, B., Lin, C.: The ant and the grasshopper: Fast and accurate pointer analysis for millions of lines of code. In: ACM SIGPLAN Conference on Programming Language Design and Implementation, pp. 290–299 (2007)
36. Berndl, M., Lhoták, O., Qian, F., Hendren, L., Umanee, N.: Points-to analysis using BDDs. In: ACM SIGPLAN Conference on Programming Language Design and Implementation, pp. 103–114 (2003)
37. Lhoták, O., Hendren, L.: Jedd: A BDD-based relational extension of Java. In: ACM SIGPLAN Conference on Programming Language Design and Implementation, pp. 158–169 (2004)
38. Whaley, J., Lam, M.: Cloning-based context-sensitive pointer alias analysis using binary decision diagrams. In: ACM SIGPLAN Conference on Programming Language Design and Implementation, pp. 131–144 (2004)
39. Zhu, J., Calman, S.: Symbolic pointer analysis revisited. In: ACM SIGPLAN Conference on Programming Language Design and Implementation, pp. 145–157 (2004)
40. Bravenboer, M., Smaragdakis, Y.: Doop framework for Java pointer analysis (2009), doop.program-analysis.org

NePaLTM: Design and Implementation of Nested Parallelism for Transactional Memory Systems

Haris Volos[1], Adam Welc[2], Ali-Reza Adl-Tabatabai[2], Tatiana Shpeisman[2],
Xinmin Tian[2], and Ravi Narayanaswamy[2]

[1] University of Wisconsin Madison, WI 53706
hvolos@cs.wisc.edu
[2] Intel Corporation Santa Clara, CA 95054
{adam.welc,ali-reza.adl-tabatabai,tatiana.shpeisman,
xinmin.tian,ravi.naraynaswamy}@intel.com

Abstract. Transactional memory (TM) promises to simplify construction of parallel applications by allowing programmers to reason about interactions between concurrently executing code fragments in terms of high-level properties they should possess. However, all currently existing TM systems deliver on this promise only partially by disallowing parallel execution of computations performed inside transactions. This paper fills in that gap by introducing NePaLTM (Nested **PA**ralle**L**ism for **T**ransactional **M**emory), the first TM system supporting nested parallelism inside transactions. We describe a programming model where TM constructs (atomic blocks) are integrated with OpenMP constructs enabling nested parallelism. We also discuss the design and implementation of a working prototype where atomic blocks can be used for concurrency control at an arbitrary level of nested parallelism. Finally, we present a performance evaluation of our system by comparing transactions-based concurrency control mechanism for nested parallel computations with a mechanism already provided by OpenMP based on mutual exclusion.

1 Introduction

As the microprocessor industry transitions to multithreaded and multicore chips, programmers must use multiple threads to obtain the full performance of the underlying platform [24]. Transactional memory (TM), first proposed by Herlihy and Moss [13], has recently regained interest in both industry and academia [9,10,11,18,19] as a mechanism that seeks to simplify multithreaded programming by removing the need for explicit locks. Instead, a programmer can declare a section of code *atomic* which the TM system executes as a transaction; its operations execute atomically (i.e. all or nothing) and in isolation with respect to operations executed inside other transactions. While transactions appear to execute in some sequential order, their actual execution may overlap increasing the degree of available parallelism.

S. Drossopoulou (Ed.): ECOOP 2009, LNCS 5653, pp. 123–147, 2009.

However as the number of processors increases, by Amdahl's law [3], the single transaction may become the sequential bottleneck hindering speedup achieved via parallelism. *Transactional nested parallelism*, that is the ability to use multiple threads inside a transaction, proves to be useful in removing this bottleneck. For example, resizing of a concurrent data structure constitutes a relatively long-lasting and heavyweight operation which nevertheless must be executed transactionally to prevent interference with other transactions concurrently accessing the same data structure. By parallelizing the resize operation within a transaction, we can still guarantee non-interference but without letting sequential resize operation adversely affect overall performance.

Transactions are also meant to compose better than locks. Programmers should be able to integrate arbitrary library code into their own concurrent applications without fear of deadlock or unpredictable performance loss, regardless of how concurrency is managed inside the library. The existing TM systems deliver on this composability promise only partially as they do not support nested parallelism inside transactions and thus transactional code cannot take advantage of efficient parallel implementations of common algorithms, even if they are readily available in a packaged library form.

At the same time, dynamic (implicit) multithreading provided by languages such as Cilk [23] or libraries such as OpenMP [22] is becoming a widely used and efficient method of introducing parallelism into applications. An application programmer expresses the parallelism by identifying elements that can safely execute in parallel, and letting the runtime system decide dynamically how to distribute work among threads. Most of the systems supporting dynamic multithreading is based on the *fork-join* concurrency model which is simple to reason with and yet has great expressive power. For example, an important class of problems can be solved using the divide-and-conquer technique which maps well to the fork-join model: a problem is broken into sub-problems, and then these sub-problems can be solved independently by multiple threads whose partial computation results are ultimately combined into a complete problem solution. The parallel computation of the sub-problems can often proceed with little or no internal synchronization.

Despite the growing significance of dynamic multithreading, only few researchers have previously explored issues related to integration of TM constructs into the fork-join concurrency model. In particular, Agrawal et al. describe a high-level design for supporting nested parallelism inside transactions in the context of Cilk [2]. However, similarly to the first published design of a system supporting transactional nested parallelism (in a context of persistent programming languages) by Wing et al. [28], they provide neither implementation nor performance evaluation of their design. Integration of TM constructs into OpenMP has been explored by Baek et al. [4] and Milovanović et al. [16] but neither of these solutions allows nested parallelism inside transactions.

Our paper makes the following contributions:

1. We describe a programming model for a system where OpenMP's constructs enabling nested parallelism can be nested inside TM constructs used for

concurrency control (atomic blocks) (Section 3). Our programming model defines an execution model which is a logical extension of an existing transactional execution model to the case of nested parallelism.

2. We describe the design (Section 4) and implementation (Section 5) of the first TM system, NePaLTM (Nested **PA**ralle**L**ism for **T**ransactional **M**emory), where atomic blocks can be used for concurrency control at an arbitrary level of nested parallelism. We discuss in detail extensions and modifications to the existing TM mechanisms required to support atomic blocks in presence of nested parallelism.

3. We evaluate performance of our system by comparing transactions-based concurrency control mechanism for nested parallel computations with a mechanism already provided by OpenMP based on mutual exclusion, and demonstrate that the performance of the former is in many cases superior to the latter. (Section 6).

2   Background

Before diving into details of our programming model and describing NePaLTM's design and implementation, we would like to provide some relevant background information on both TM-style concurrency control and OpenMP-style fork-join programming model.

2.1   C/C++ Software Transactional Memory

Intel's Software Transactional Memory (STM) system, extending C/C++ with a set of TM constructs, forms our base TM system [19]. The __tm_atomic statement is used to define an *atomic block* which executes as a transaction; its operations execute atomically (i.e. all or nothing) and in isolation with respect to operations executed inside other transactions. The __tm_abort statement (user abort) allows a programmer to explicitly abort an atomic block. This statement can only appear in the lexical scope of an atomic block. When a user abort is triggered, the TM system rolls back all side effects of the atomic block and transfers control to the statement immediately following the block.

The TM system provides SLA (Single Lock Atomicity) [14] semantics; atomic blocks behave as if they were protected by a single global lock. This guarantees that programs that are race free under a single global lock will execute correctly when executed transactionally. Providing no guarantees for programs containing data races[1] is consistent with the emerging C/C++ memory model specification [7]. We next give an overview of the base system's structure [19].

The base system performs updates in-place with strict two-phase locking for writes, and supports both optimistic and pessimistic concurrency control for reads. The system keeps a *descriptor* structure per transaction which encapsulates the transaction's *context* (i.e. meta-data such as transactional logs). The

---

[1] A data race occurs when multiple threads access the same piece of memory, and at least one of those accesses is a write.

system also keeps a table of *transaction records* called the *ownership table*. Every memory address is hashed to a unique transaction record in this table but multiple addresses may be hashed to the same record. A transaction record contains information used by the concurrency control algorithm to control access to memory addresses mapped to this record. When a transaction record is write-locked, it contains information about the single lock owner. When a transaction record is read-locked, it contains information about all transactions holding read-locks for a given location. Additionally, when a transaction record is not write-locked, it contains a version timestamp used by optimistic readers as explained below.

Transactional memory accesses are performed through three types of transactional barriers: *write, optimistic read* and *pessimistic read* barriers. On a transactional store, the write barrier tries to exclusively write-lock the transaction record. If the record is locked by another transaction, the runtime resolves the conflict before continuing, which may abort the current transaction. If it is unlocked, the barrier write-locks the record, records the old value and the address in its *undo log*, adds the record to its *write log* (which keeps the transaction's *write set*), and then updates the memory location. On a transactional load, the optimistic read barrier checks if the transaction record is locked, but does not try to lock it. In contrast, the pessimistic read barrier tries to read-lock it. In both cases, if the record is write-locked by another transaction, the conflict is handled. If it is unlocked or read-locked, both optimistic and pessimistic read barriers return the value of the location and add the record to the *read log* (which keeps the *read set*). The optimistic read barrier also records the transaction record's timestamp, used to keep track of when the memory location is being updated.

On commit, an optimistic transaction uses the recorded timestamps to validate that no transaction record in its read set has been updated after the transaction read them. If validation succeeds, the transaction unlocks all transaction records in its write set; otherwise it aborts. A pessimistic transaction does not need to validate its read set but does need to unlock all transaction records in both its read and write set. On abort, in addition to all locks being released, the old values recorded in the undo log are written back to the corresponding addresses. On both commit and abort, the runtime modifies the timestamps of the updated locations – subsequent timestamp values are obtained by incrementing a global counter.

To provide SLA semantics correctly, the runtime guarantees several important safety properties, namely granular safety, privatization safety and observable consistency [15]. For granular safety, the runtime records transactional data accesses into the undo log at an appropriate granularity level – when accessing N (= 1, 2, 4 or 8) bytes of data, the runtime must be careful to record and restore only these N bytes without affecting memory adjacent to the location where the data is stored. Privatization safety and observable consistency are an issue only with optimistic transactions. Privatization [21] is a common programming idiom where a thread privatizes a shared object inside a critical section, then continues accessing the object outside the critical section. Privatization, if not supported correctly, can cause incorrect behavior in the following way: a committing privatizer may implicitly abort a conflicting optimistic transaction due to an update resulting from its privatization action, and subsequent non-transactional code may read locations that were speculatively modified by the conflicting transaction, which has yet to abort and roll back. The system provides privatization safety through a quiescence algorithm [26]. Under this algorithm a committing transaction waits until all other optimistic transactions verify that their read set does not overlap with the committing transaction's write set. Observable consistency guarantees that a transaction observes side effects only if it is based upon a consistent view of memory. In other words, a transactional operation (a read or a write) is valid in the sense of observable consistency if it is executed under some consistent memory snapshot, even if that operation needs to be subsequently undone. The runtime provides this by having each transaction validate its read set before accessing any location written by a transaction that has committed since the previous validation of the read set.

2.2 OpenMP API

The OpenMP API is a collection of compiler directives, runtime library routines, and environment variables that can be used to explicitly control shared-memory parallelism in C/C++ [22]. We next give an overview of the features of version 2.5 of the OpenMP specification [5] which are relevant to this work. At the point of writing this paper we had no access to an implementation supporting the new features available in version 3.0 [6] such as OpenMP tasks so we defer exploration of these new features to future work.

Parallel regions. OpenMP's fundamental construct for specifying parallel computation is the `parallel` pragma. OpenMP uses the *fork-join* model of parallel execution. An OpenMP program begins as a single thread of execution, called the *initial thread*. When a thread encounters the `parallel` pragma, it creates a *thread team* that consists of itself and zero or more additional threads, and becomes the *master* of the new team. Then each thread of the team executes the parallel region specified by this pragma. Upon exiting the parallel construct, all the threads in the team join the master at an implicit barrier, after which only the master thread continues execution. The `parallel` pragma supports two types of variables within the parallel region: shared and private. Variables default to *shared* which means shared among all threads in a parallel region. A *private* variable has a separate copy for every thread.

Work-sharing. All of a team's threads replicate the execution of the same code unless a work-sharing directive is specified within the parallel region. The specification defines constructs for both iterative (`for`) and non-iterative (`sections`, `single`) code patterns. The `for` pragma may be used to distribute iterations of a for loop among a team's threads. The `sections` pragma specifies a work-sharing construct that contains a set of structured blocks defined using the `section` pragma that are to be divided among and executed by the threads in a team. Each structured block is executed once by one of the threads in the team. The `single` pragma specifies that the associated code block is executed by only one thread in the team. The rest of the threads in the team do not execute the block but wait at an implicit barrier at the end of the single construct unless a `no wait` clause is specified.

Synchronization. Synchronization constructs control how the execution of each thread proceeds relative to other team threads. The `atomic` pragma is used to guarantee that a specific memory location is updated atomically. A more general synchronization mechanism is provided by the `critical` pragma used to specify a block of code called a *critical region*. A critical region may be associated with a name, and all anonymous critical regions are assumed to have the same unspecified name. Only one thread at a time is allowed to execute any of the critical regions with the same name. In addition to the implicit barriers required by the OpenMP specification at certain points (such as the end of a parallel region), OpenMP provides the `barrier` pragma which can be used to introduce explicit barriers at the point the pragma appears; team threads cannot proceed beyond the barrier until all of the team's members arrive at the barrier. The specification does not allow nesting of `barrier` pragma inside a critical region.

3   Programming Model

The programming model we present in this section allows atomic blocks to benefit from OpenMP and vice versa. Transactions can use OpenMP's parallel regions to reduce their completion time and OpenMP can use transactions to synchronize access to shared data. We chose OpenMP because of its industry-wide acceptance as a method for programming shared memory, as well as because of the simplicity and expressive power of the fork-join execution model that OpenMP is based on. However, nothing prevents transactional nested parallelism to be supported in an alternative setting, exemplified by systems using explicit threading models.

3.1   Constructs

Our programming model adds TM's atomic block construct to the existing, more traditional, synchronization constructs specified by OpenMP (e.g. critical regions). Simultaneous use of these constructs is legal as long as they are used to synchronize accesses to disjoint sets of data. Previous work, exploring composition of the traditional synchronization constructs with atomic blocks, has shown that such composition is non-trivial [25,27,29], and, as such, is beyond the scope of this paper. Our programming model also supports OpenMP's `barrier` pragma for declaring synchronization barriers, but like the original OpenMP specification which does not allow the use of this pragma inside critical regions, we do not allow its use inside atomic blocks.

An atomic block is orthogonal to an OpenMP's parallel region. Thus an atomic block may be nested inside a parallel region and vice versa. When an atomic block is nested inside a parallel region, each dynamic instance of the atomic

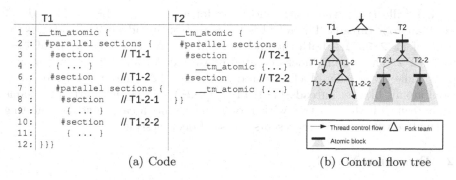

	T1	T2
1 :	__tm_atomic {	__tm_atomic {
2 :	#parallel sections {	#parallel sections {
3 :	#section // T1-1	#section // T2-1
4 :	{ ... }	__tm_atomic {...}
6 :	#section // T1-2	#section // T2-2
7 :	#parallel sections {	__tm_atomic {...}
8 :	#section // T1-2-1	}}
9 :	{ ... }	
10:	#section // T1-2-2	
11:	{ ... }	
12:	}}}	

(a) Code   (b) Control flow tree

Fig. 1. Shallow (T1) and deep (T2) nesting

block is executed by a single thread of that region. In the opposite case when a parallel region is nested inside an atomic block, a team of threads is created and all the threads execute under the same atomic block on behalf of the same transaction. We refer to the transitive closure of the threads created under the same atomic block as *atomic thread team* (or *atomic team* for short). When a user abort is triggered by a member of an atomic team using the __tm_abort construct, all the team's threads abort their computation and the entire transaction aborts.

An atomic block is also orthogonal to OpenMP work sharing constructs, with only one exception. While an atomic block can be nested inside a **single** construct, the opposite is not true. Recall from Section 2.2 that all team threads but the one executing the **single** region wait at an implicit barrier at the end of the region. If a **single** pragma was allowed to be nested inside an atomic block then it would be possible for the threads waiting at the barrier to transactionally hold resources needed by the thread executing the **single** region resulting in a deadlock. To prevent such a case, we disallow **single** from being nested inside of an atomic block. Note that this is not different from the original OpenMP specification which prevents nesting of a **single** pragma inside a critical region.

Before moving on with the description of the execution model, we need to introduce some more terminology. We call a thread that begins an outermost atomic block a *root thread*. We reason about the hierarchy between threads in terms of a parent-child relation; a thread spawning some threads becomes the *parent* of these threads (and the *ancestor* of these and all other transitively created threads), the spawned threads become its *children* and one another's *siblings*. Conceptually, execution of the parent thread is suspended at the spawn point and resumed when all children complete their execution. The *transactional parent* of a child thread is its ancestor thread that created an atomic block immediately enclosing the point of the child thread's creation. Atomic blocks form a nesting hierarchy. We refer to the atomic block of a root thread as a *root atomic block*, and to an atomic block created by a nested thread as a *parallel-nested atomic block*. When the threads spawned under a root atomic block do not use any additional atomic blocks, we have *shallow nesting*. If however these threads do use additional atomic blocks then we have *deep nesting*. For example,

Figure 1 [2] illustrates the control flow tree for a given code block. Threads T1 and T2 are root threads. Thread T1 is the parent of thread T1-2 and T1-2 is the parent of T1-2-2. T1 is both the ancestor and the transactional parent of T1-2 and T1-2-2. The atomic blocks created by threads T1 and T2 are root atomic blocks while the atomic blocks created by threads T2-1 and T2-2 are parallel-nested atomic blocks. Threads T1-1, T1-2, T1-2-1, T1-2-2 are part of the same atomic team. Finally, the tree with root T1 represents a case of shallow nesting and the tree with root T2 represents a case of deep nesting.

3.2 Execution Model

Recall from section 2.1 that our base TM model provides the SLA (Single Lock Atomicity) semantics for race free programs; atomic blocks behave as if they were protected by a single global abstract [3] lock. However in the presence of nested parallelism this model is insufficient. To see why, consider again Figure 1; if a single abstract lock was used by all atomic blocks, then threads T2-1 and T2-2 would block-wait for their parent, thread T2, to release the abstract lock protecting its atomic block resulting in a deadlock.

Our programming model logically extends the SLA execution model into the *HLA (Hierarchical Lock Atomicity)* model to account for nested parallelism. Like SLA, HLA defines semantics for race free programs. HLA is similar to the model used by Moore and Grossman in their formal definition of small-step operational semantics for transactions [17]. In HLA, abstract locks protecting atomic blocks form a hierarchy; a "fresh" abstract lock is used whenever a child thread starts a new atomic block, and it is used for synchronizing data accesses between this thread and threads that have the same transactional parent. Note how in the case of shallow nesting HLA degrades to SLA; only a single abstract lock is required to maintain concurrency control between all atomic blocks.

HLA semantics differs from the semantics of OpenMP's critical regions in that critical regions with the same name are not re-entrant. This implies that if we hierarchically nest critical regions in the same fashion as atomic blocks, we end up with a non-recoverable deadlock.

To better understand HLA consider the example given in Figure 2 which extends the example in Figure 1. In contrast to the previous example, threads T1-2-1 and T1-2-2 create new atomic blocks which are nested under the atomic block of thread *T1*. Let's first consider how abstract locks are assigned to the atomic blocks according to HLA. The root atomic blocks of threads T1 and T2 are assigned abstract lock *AL*, atomic blocks of threads T1-2-1 and T1-2-2 are assigned lock *AL-1*, and atomic blocks of threads T2-1 and T2-2 are assigned lock *AL-2*. Too see how these abstract locks are used to synchronize data accesses consider the accesses of threads T2-1 and T2-2. Accesses to x and w by T2-1 and T2-2 respectively are isolated from the accesses of T1-2-1 and T1-2-2 using

---

[2] For readability we abbreviate OpenMP pragmas in all figures by omitting the initial pragma omp.

[3] We call this and other locks abstract because locks do not have to be used to enforce a semantics, even if this semantics is expressed in terms of locks.

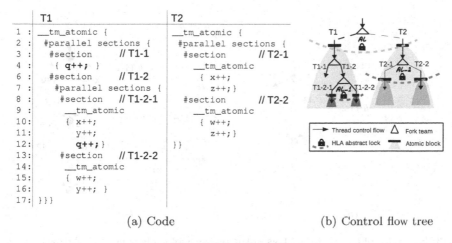

	T1	T2
1 :	__tm_atomic {	__tm_atomic {
2 :	#parallel sections {	#parallel sections {
3 :	#section // T1-1	#section // T2-1
4 :	{ q++; }	__tm_atomic
6 :	#section // T1-2	{ x++;
7 :	#parallel sections {	z++; }
8 :	#section // T1-2-1	#section // T2-2
9 :	__tm_atomic	__tm_atomic
10:	{ x++;	{ w++;
11:	y++;	z++; }
12:	q++; }	} }
13:	#section // T1-2-2	
14:	__tm_atomic	
15:	{ w++;	
16:	y++; }	
17:	} } }	

(a) Code   (b) Control flow tree

Fig. 2. HLA Example

lock *AL*. Accesses to z by T2-1 and T2-2 are isolated from each other using lock *AL-2*. Similarly, accesses to y by T1-2-1 and T1-2-2 are isolated from each other using lock *AL-1*. Finally consider the accesses to q by threads T1-1 and T1-2-1. Since the two threads do not synchronize their accesses to q through the same lock, these accesses are not correctly synchronized and therefore they are racy.

4   Design

The HLA semantics can be supported through two different types of concurrency mechanisms: transactions and mutual exclusion locks. Our design choice is to use transactions for concurrency control between root atomic blocks and mutual exclusion locks for parallel-nested atomic blocks. This choice is motivated by the following three observations. First, it has been demonstrated that transactions scale competitively to locks or better [1,11,12,19]. Thus our system offers root atomic blocks that can execute efficiently as transactions and which can use transactional nested parallelism to further accelerate their execution in case shallow nesting is used. Second, by supporting deep nesting through locks, our system provides composability, which is a very important property for the adoption of the model. Third, while we considered supporting parallel-nested atomic blocks using transactions, previous work by Agrawal et al. [2] has shown that such a design is complex and its efficient implementation appears to be questionable. As we discuss at the end of this section, our personal experience on the subject is very similar.

4.1   Shallow Nesting

In the case of shallow nesting no transactional synchronization is enforced between the members of an atomic team. Nevertheless, because operations of all the team members are executed on behalf of a single transaction, they must

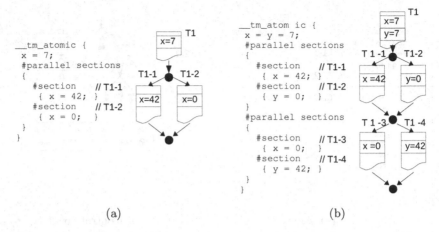

Fig. 3. Examples of transactional logs in the presence of shallow nesting. Arrows depict ordering constraints.

appear to be executed as a single atomic unit and in isolation from other concurrent root transactions. To achieve this, atomic team members inherit the transactional context of their transactional parent and perform all transactional operations using that context. Having multiple threads working on behalf of a single transaction has several important implications on how the runtime manages transactional logs and how it guarantees transactional safety properties. Below we describe these implications in detail:

Logging. Recall that there are three types of logs associated with a transactional context: read, write, and undo log. The read and write logs track transaction's read and write sets, respectively, and the undo log keeps the old values of the locations written by the transaction. Conceptually members of an atomic team and their parent share the same log, so a simple solution would be to have threads use a single log instance and synchronize access to that log. However this would require excessive synchronization making this solution impractical. Instead of using a single log and paying the cost of synchronizing log accesses, we leverage several properties described below so as to allow each atomic team member to maintain its own private instances of transactional logs.

Write log. A transaction's write log is used to release write locks when the transaction completes. Because locks can be released in any order, they can be freely distributed between multiple logs. A potential problem of using multiple logs is double-releasing of a write lock if the same lock appears in more than one log. However, since children acquire locks on behalf of their parent, at most one child will find the lock not held and bring it into its log.

Read log. In the pessimistic case, a transaction's read log is used to release read locks, and therefore the correctness reasoning is the same as in the write log above. In the optimistic case, the read log is used for validation, but the ordering with which validation is done is not important either. Moreover, since no locks are released, the read log can tolerate multiple entries per location.

Undo log. In contrast to read and write logs, ordering of undo log entries matters because side effects must be rolled back in the opposite order to that in which they happened. While undo entries do not need to be totally ordered, undo entries for the same memory location must be partially ordered. There are two cases of writes to the same memory location that we need to consider. First, simultaneous writes by multiple threads of the same atomic team may generate multiple undo entries. Since these writes constitute a race, and according to our programming model racy programs have undefined behavior, their undo entries need not be ordered. Figure 3(a) shows an example where two threads of the same atomic team both write x; ordering of the undo entries is not important because the writes are racy. In the second case, writes of a memory location by threads in different atomic teams may also generate multiple undo entries. However, if the writes are performed in different parallel regions executed one after the other then they are ordered and therefore they are not racy. For example in Figure 3(b) writes to x and y by threads T1-1, T1-3 and T1-2, T1-4 respectively are partially ordered. In order for undo entries distributed between multiple logs to be recorded correctly, atomic team members merge their logs with that of their parent at join points, and the parent records the ordering.

Safety Properties. NePaLTM must guarantee the three safety properties discussed in Section 2, namely granular safety, privatization safety, and observable consistency. For granular safety no additional support is necessary because granular safety depends only on undo logging granularity which is not affected by having multiple threads working on behalf of a single transaction. However, having multiple threads does have implications on the mechanisms used to provide observable consistency and privatization safety. For observable consistency, children must not only validate their private read sets but they must also validate the read set of their (suspended) parent. This is because their computations depend on their parent's computation and therefore they must have a view of memory which is consistent with that of their parent. For privatization safety, a committing transaction waits separately for the atomic team members to validate and become stable rather than waiting for validation of the root thread's transaction as a whole which can only happen after execution of all the team members is completed and could thus be sub-optimal.

4.2 Deep Nesting

NePaLTM supports deeply nested atomic blocks using mutual exclusion locks. As defined by the HLA semantics presented in Section 3.2, a fresh mutual exclusion lock is allocated per atomic team and used for concurrency control between atomic blocks created by the atomic team's threads.

Despite using mutual exclusion for concurrency control in case of deep nesting, all the code executed by deeply nested atomic blocks must be *transactionalized*,

134   H. Volos et al.

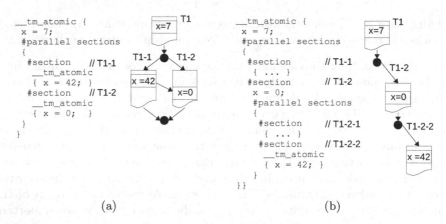

(a)   (b)

Fig. 4. Examples transactional logs in the presence of deep nesting. Arrows depict ordering constraints.

that is instrumented to support transactional execution. First, transactional instrumentation of memory accesses is necessary to be able to roll back side effects in case the atomic block needs to abort. Second, transactional concurrency control must still be used for synchronizing memory accesses performed by threads inside a root atomic block with memory accesses done by threads executing inside other root atomic blocks. We now present a discussion of how deep nesting impacts logging and safety properties.

Logging. In Section 4.1 we reasoned about the correctness of our design decision to let children use private instances of transactional logs. Deep nesting, however, adds the additional ordering constraint that logs must respect the order enforced by parallel-nested atomic blocks. This is particularly important in case of undo logs since undo operations must be executed in order opposite to that of transaction commits. A child committing an atomic block, in order to correctly capture the commit order of this atomic block with respect to other atomic blocks executed under the same parent, must merge its current private log with the log of its transactional parent before releasing the mutual exclusion lock guarding its atomic block. If "intermediate" threads have been forked between a child's transactional parent and the child itself then log merging must respect the order implied by the fork operations in case these intermediate threads performed data accesses on their own. To accomplish this a child must transitively merge logs up the parent/child hierarchy until it reaches its transactional parent.

Figure 4 shows two examples of deeply nested transactional logs. In the example presented in Figure 4(a), thread T1-2 commits its atomic block after T1-1 does so. Log merging must respect the commit ordering of the two atomic blocks as shown by the arrow connecting the two logs. In the example presented in Figure 4(b), thread T1-2-2 commits a deeply nested atomic block with an intermediate thread T1-2 forked between the time when thread T1-2-2 has been created and the time when thread T1-2-2's transactional parent T1 has started its transaction. To capture the fork order shown by the arrows, T1-2-2's log must be first merged with T1-2's log and then the resulted log must be merged together with T1's log.

Safety Properties. Since parallel-nested atomic blocks use mutual-exclusion locks to handle synchronization, no additional support is necessary to guarantee the safety properties for these atomic blocks.

4.3 Discussion

We initially considered an alternative design where transactional concurrency control is used at all nesting levels. However we eventually abandoned it in favor of the one we described above for the reasons we discuss here. When using transactions at all nesting levels, as described by Agrawal et al. [2], the parent/child relation plays a very important role in ensuring correctness of data access operations. Maintenance and querying of the structure representing this relation is likely to significantly complicate the implementation and decrease its efficiency. Moreover, supporting optimistic transactions further complicates the algorithms used for guaranteeing privatization safety and observable consistency between atomic blocks at all nesting levels.

5 Implementation

Our prototype implementation follows our design guidelines and supports HLA via transactions for root atomic blocks and via mutual-exclusion locks for deeper nesting levels. As a base for our implementation we used Intel's STM runtime library and Intel's TM C/C++ compiler [19], as well as Intel's implementation of the OpenMP library supporting version 2.5 of the OpenMP specification. Despite a somewhat simplified design for deep nesting, significant extensions and modifications to the algorithms of the base TM runtime were required. Additionally we needed to modify the compiler and the OpenMP runtime library to correctly compile and execute OpenMP constructs that are nested inside atomic blocks.

In the remainder of this section we describe the data structures used in NePaLTM as well as the mechanisms that implement concurrency control in the presence of nested parallelism, with emphasis on the implementation of the abort procedure and the transactional logs. We finally discuss the required modifications to the TM compiler to support nested parallelism.

5.1 Concurrency Control

Execution Modes and Descriptor. We introduce two new execution modes to the base TM system, namely *omp_optimistic* and *omp_pessimistic* which are used by atomic team members working on behalf of an optimistic or pessimistic transaction respectively. The base TM system supports multiple execution modes through a layer of indirection similar to a vtable. Each execution mode defines its own dispatch table of pointers to functions that implement the transactional read/write barriers and transaction begin/commit/abort routines specific to that mode. At runtime, the dispatch table of the current execution mode is used to indirectly call that mode's routines. This mechanism allows us to incrementally pay the overheads associated with nested parallelism. A transaction always starts at a base execution mode (e.g. optimistic) where it uses the original barrier implementations. Then, when it spawns an atomic team, its children transition into one of the two new execution modes where they use the nested-parallelism-aware barriers and begin/commit/abort routines.

In NePaLTM, similarly to the base system, every thread in the system (both root and child threads) is associated with a *descriptor* which is stored in the thread's local storage and encapsulates the thread's transactional context. We have extended the descriptor structure to keep some additional state related to nested parallelism. In particular: information to reconstruct the parent/child hierarchy such as pointers to the descriptor of the parent and the transactional parent, state used by the recursive abort mechanism described later, and a mutual exclusion lock for use by parallel-nested atomic blocks under this transaction.

To correctly switch execution mode and construct the parent/child hierarchy we extended the OpenMP runtime library functions responsible for spawning and collecting team threads with callbacks to the TM runtime.

Transactional Barriers. We have implemented new transactional read and write barriers for instrumenting memory accesses performed by team members that run at one of the two new execution modes (*omp_optimistic* and *omp_pessimistic*). Our new barriers are based on the original ones which we have extended to support nested-parallelism.

On transactional store, the write barrier executed by transactional thread tries to exclusively lock the transaction record associated with the memory location. If it is already locked by this thread's root transaction then the thread proceeds without acquiring the lock. However the barrier must still record the old value and the address in its own private undo log[4]. If the record is locked by another root transaction, the runtime resolves the conflict before continuing, which may abort the current transaction. If the transaction record is unlocked then the barrier locks it using the current thread's root transaction descriptor, adds the record to its own private write log, records the old value and address in its private undo log, and then updates the memory location.

On an optimistic transactional load, the optimistic read barrier checks if the transaction record is already locked but does not try to lock it. If the record is write-locked by another root transaction, the conflict is handled. If it is unlocked, locked by the current thread's root transaction or read-locked by another root transaction, the barrier returns the value of the location, adds the record into its read log and records the transaction record's timestamp.

---

[4] This is necessary because the ownership table is implemented as a hash table where multiple memory locations may be hashed on the same transaction record.

On a pessimistic transactional load, the pessimistic read barrier tries to read-lock the transaction record. If the record is write-locked by another root transaction, the conflict is handled. If it is already read-locked or write-locked by the current thread's root transaction then the barrier returns the value of the location without acquiring the lock. If it is unlocked or read-locked by another root transaction then the barrier read-locks the transaction record using the current thread's root transaction descriptor, adds the lock into its own private read log, and returns the value of the location.

Observable Consistency and Privatization Safety. For observable consistency, a thread executing inside of an optimistic transaction validates the read sets of all of its ancestors, up to and including the root transaction, in addition to its own read set. As an optimization, when a thread validates the read set of an ancestor, it updates the last validation timestamp of that ancestor so that other threads with the same ancestor do not need to re-validate that read set. For privatization safety, we modified the base quiescence algorithm so that a parent thread temporarily removes itself from the list of in-flight transactions until its child threads complete execution. By removing itself from that list, other committing transactions do not have to wait for that thread. This is safe because those other committing transactions will wait for that thread's children instead.

Transaction Commit and Abort. Transaction begin, commit and abort procedures executed by atomic team members are also different than those executed by root threads. Since deep nesting is implemented using locks, the routines do not implement a full-fledged begin and commit. Instead they simply acquire and release the mutual exclusion lock of the transactional parent at entry and exit to a parallel-nested atomic block. Additionally, since parents must access transactional logs of its children, as described in Section 4, children must pass their logs to their parents at commit. The implementation details of this procedure are described in Section 5.2.

NePaLTM supports a *recursive abort* mechanism, which can be used by any active thread in the parent/child hierarchy to trigger an abort of the whole computation executing under a transaction. Our extension to the OpenMP library implementing this mechanism keeps some additional state: a per atomic team *abort flag* stored in the transactional descriptor of every parent, and *internal checkpoint* of the stack/register context for each atomic team's thread, taken before the thread starts its computation. Please not that in presence of transactional nested parallelism it is no longer sufficient to record a checkpoint only at transaction begin – restoration of a child thread's state to the checkpoint taken by the parent would be incorrect.

An atomic team member triggers an abort of the entire transaction by setting the its parent's abort flag and then aborting its current computation. An atomic team member detects abort requests by recursively checking the abort flag of all of its ancestors up to the root thread. All these checks happen either in the slow path of the transactional barriers or when a thread waits behind the lock protecting a parallel-nested atomic block. When a team member detects an abort request, it aborts its current computation by marking its state as completed and then restoring its internal checkpoint. After restoring its checkpoint, the thread appears to OpenMP as completed, and OpenMP can safely shutdown and recycle that thread. When execution of all the child threads is completed, execution of their parent thread is resumed. When the parent thread resumes, it checks for a pending abort request; if the thread itself is a child then the abort is propagated up the parent/child hierarchy.

We support aborts requested both implicitly through a TM conflict and explicitly through the __tm_abort statement (user-level abort). The abort flag carries the reason for the abort giving priority to conflict aborts. The __tm_abort statement in our system is required to be lexically scoped within an atomic block and, when executed, it aborts this atomic block only. As a result, abort propagation stops upon reaching the atomic block lexically enclosing the __tm_abort statement.

Admittedly, there exists alternative implementations of the abort mechanism, but we believe that our implementation achieves a good balance between efficiency and required modifications to an already complex and carefully tuned OpenMP runtime library.

5.2   Transactional Logs

As explained in the design section, each child thread uses private transactional logs and whenever ordering information needs to be captured, a child merges its private log together with the log of its parent. We have implemented log merging using a hybrid algorithm that combines two methods: *concatenation* and *copy-back*. Whenever we need to merge two logs together, our hybrid algorithm calculates the log size of the source log to be merged. If the log size is above what we call a *concatenation threshold*, the log is concatenated; otherwise, the log is copied-back. We next describe *concatenation* and *copy-back* separately.

Concatenation. In this method, a transactional log is composed of several log fragments linked together to form a list. Similarly to logs in the base TM

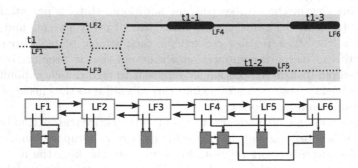

Fig. 5. Representation of the log as a list of log fragments

system, log fragments keep pointers to potentially multiple log buffers. A source log is merged with a target log by connecting the log fragment list of the former at the tail of the list of the latter. For example, in Figure 5, log fragment **LF1** (log fragments are represented by empty grey rectangles) associated with the root thread executing transaction **t1** has all the log fragments that belong to its children linked to it.

A log is split into log fragments only when necessary. Thus if nested parallelism is not used inside atomic blocks, a log is represented by a single log fragment. However, when nested parallelism is used, we only utilize log fragments at points where we need to establish correct log ordering as previously described. There are two cases in which this may happen. First, in the case when a child thread reaches its join point, its parent connects the log fragment currently used by the child to its own list of log fragments. Then the child is assigned a fresh log with a new buffer. A fresh log is necessary because the child thread may be recycled by OpenMP and used by another parent. In Figure 5, **LF2** and **LF3** represent log fragments passed from children to their parent at the join point.

Second, in the case when a child commits a nested atomic block, it splits its log and then connects the produced log fragment to the parent's log fragment list. If ancestor threads exist between the child and the root thread, the child splits the log fragments of all ancestor threads and connects them recursively until reaching the root thread. Since only one child can acquire an atomic team's lock at any given time, this child can safely access and modify logs of all its ancestors. Returning to our example in Figure 5 (atomic blocks created by children are represented by narrow rounded black rectangles), the child thread at the top of the figure splits its log when committing its first atomic block (**t1-1**) to create log fragment **LF4**. Then the child thread at the bottom of the figure splits when committing its own atomic block (**t1-2**) to create log fragment **LF5**. Finally the last log fragment, **LF6**, is created when the child thread at the top of the figure commits its second atomic block (**t1-3**). In contrast to thread join where we assign new buffers to children because they complete their execution, the committing child is still active so it keeps using its assigned buffers continuing from the last buffer entries used by its log fragments. As a result, a buffer can be shared between multiple log fragments as in the case of log fragments **LF4** and **LF6** in Figure 5 (log buffers are represented as solid grey rectangles). Naturally, a transaction using a given log fragment may fill up a buffer initially associated with this log fragment and attach a new buffer (e.g. log fragments **LF1** and **LF4** in Figure 5).

Copy-back. In this method two transactional logs are merged together by simply copying every single entry of the source log to the target log at appropriate points, the same in fact as the points when the logs are concatenated as described above. It is the parent that copies entries from the child's log into its own when the child has already reached the join point. It is the child that copies entries from its own log to that of the parent whenever that child commits a nested atomic block.

5.3 TM Compiler

The most important compiler-related issue was to ensure that the code generated for OpenMP's parallel region executed inside transactions is appropriately transactionalized, as described in Section 4.2. The TM compiler automatically transactionalizes function calls (direct and indirect) that are annotated with a special tm_callable attribute. However, OpenMP's parallel region is specified as a code block at the source level and packaged into a form of a function internally by the compiler. As a result it could not be transactionalized automatically and the compiler needed to be modified to do it explicitly. Also, certain OpenMP functions are called as part of setting up the execution environment of a parallel region. The TM compiler had to be modified to treat these functions as transactional intrinsics (similarly to calls to the TM runtime library) otherwise they would be treated as non-transactional functions of unknown origin. For safety reasons, a transaction encountering a call to a non-transactional function transitions to the so called *serial mode* which allows only a single transaction to execute in the system. Clearly this would defeat the purpose of introducing nested parallelism in the first place.

6 Performance Evaluation

Our performance evaluation focuses on evaluating our design decisions of using transactions at the outermost level and locks at the deep nested levels. Because benchmarks exercising nested parallelism are not easily available, we evaluate performance of our prototype implementation using an in-house implementation of the multi-threaded OO7 benchmark [8]. This benchmark is highly configurable so it allows us to study the behavior of our system under different scenarios.

   We seek to answer the following two questions:

1. Can transactions retain their performance advantage over locks in presence of nested parallelism?
2. How does performance of parallel-nested atomic blocks compare with performance of the atomic blocks executing the same workloads sequentially?

6.1 Benchmark Description

OO7 is a highly configurable benchmark that has been previously used in several TM-related studies [1,27,29]. The benchmark is also easy to port and modify, which was an important factor since the previous TM-enabled version of this benchmark was written in Java, was not OpenMP-enabled and did not support nested parallelism.

   The OO7 benchmark operates on a synthetic design database consisting of a set of composite parts. Each composite part consists of a graph of atomic parts. Composite parts are arranged in a multi-level assembly hierarchy, called a module. Assemblies are divided into two classes: base assemblies (containing composite parts) and complex assemblies (containing other assemblies).

The multi-threaded workload consists of multiple *client threads* running a set of parameterized traversals composed of primitive operations. A traversal chooses a single path through the assembly hierarchy and at the base assembly level randomly chooses a fixed number of composite parts to visit. When the traversal reaches the composite part, it has two choices: (a) it may access atomic parts in the read-only mode; or, (b) it may swap certain scalar fields in each atomic part visited. To foster some degree of interesting interleaving and contention, the benchmark defines a parameter that allows additional work to be added to read operations to increase the time spent performing traversals.

Unlike the previous implementations of the OO7 benchmark used for TM-related studies, ours has been written in C++ and uses OpenMP pragmas for thread creation and coordination. Similarly to these previous implementations, while the structure of the design database used by the benchmark conforms to the standard OO7 database specification, the database traversals differ from the original OO7 traversals. In our implementation we allow placement of synchronization constructs (either atomic blocks or mutual exclusion locks provided by OpenMP) at various levels of the database hierarchy, and also allow multiple composite parts to be visited during a single traversal rather than just one as in the original specification. We introduce nested parallelism by allowing the work of visiting multiple composite parts to be split among multiple *worker threads*. Naturally, in order to remain compliant with the original workload executed

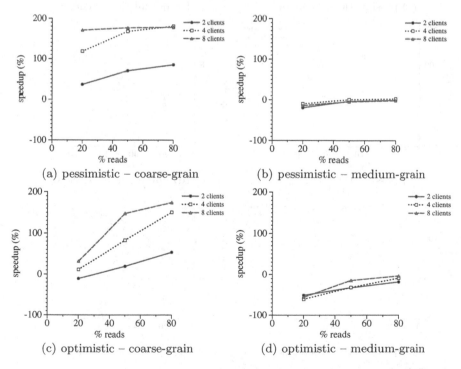

(a) pessimistic – coarse-grain   (b) pessimistic – medium-grain

(c) optimistic – coarse-grain   (d) optimistic – medium-grain

Fig. 6. Performance of transactions vs. locks – no nested parallelism

during benchmark traversals performing database updates, the worker threads have to be synchronized using appropriate synchronization constructs (atomic blocks or locks, depending on a specific configuration).

6.2 Setup

We performed our experiments on a 4 x six-core (24 CPUs total) Intel Xeon 7400 (Dunnington) machine and running Redhat Enterprise Edition 4 at 2.66GHz.

In our experiments with the OO7 benchmark, we compare configurations where mutual exclusion locks (provided by OpenMP implementation) are used for synchronization with configurations where transactional atomic blocks are used for

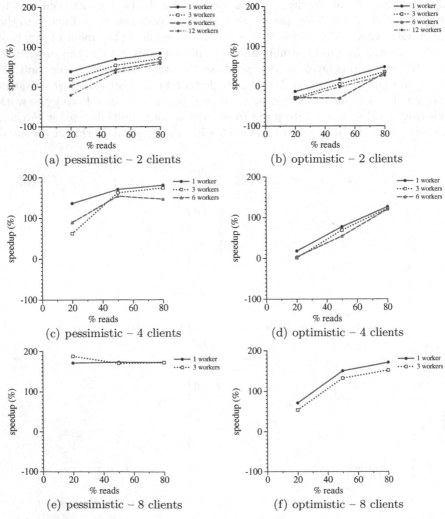

Fig. 7. Performance of transactions vs. locks – coarse-grain + nested parallelism

synchronization. We use the standard medium-size OO7 design database. Each client thread performs 1000 traversals and visits 240 (so that it is divisible by 1, 3, 6, 12 and 24 threads) random composite parts at the base assembly level. Since worker threads are created at the base assembly level, which represents level 8 of the database hierarchy (where level is the module), synchronization constructs must be placed at the same level to guard accesses to parts located at the lower levels of the hierarchy.

We vary the following parameters of the OO7 benchmark to achieve good coverage of possible nested parallel workloads:

- number of clients: 2, 4 and 8
- number of workers: between 1 and 24 (to complement number of clients up to 24 total parallel threads)
- percentage of reads vs. writes: 80-20, 50-50 and 20-80
- synchronization level: 1 and 4 for the clients (to simulate coarse-grain and medium-grain synchronization strategy) and 8 for the workers (to guarantee correctness)

We have also experimentally established the value of the concatenation threshold to be 224 log entries, based on the results obtained from a simple single-threaded microbenchmark executing a sequence of memory accesses triggering a series of log operations.

6.3   Evaluation

When attempting to answer questions we have raised at the beginning of this section, we report performance numbers for both optimistic and pessimistic concurrency protocol as they exhibit different characteristics for a given workload, which may or may not change upon introduction of nested parallelism.

Can transactions retain their performance advantage over locks in presence of nested parallelism? Our hypothesis is that introduction of nested parallelism into a TM system should not change the relative performance characteristics between transactions and locks, regardless of the type of concurrency protocol (optimistic or pessimistic) being used.

Figure 6 depicts the relative performance of transactions over locks for pessimistic and optimistic concurrency. In this and the rest of the performance charts, unless noted otherwise, Y axis is speedup of transactions over locks (100% speedup indicates that a transactional configuration was 2x faster) and X axis represents the percentage of reads executed during OO7's database traversals. As we can see, this particular benchmark favors pessimistic protocols. Even though both optimistic and pessimistic transactions perform better than coarse-grain locks, only pessimistic transactions are competitive with medium-grain locks – optimistic transactions can perform up to 50% worse. It is important to note that this is a characteristic of a specific workload executed by OO7 benchmark. Several studies [12,19,20] report that optimistic protocols may in fact perform

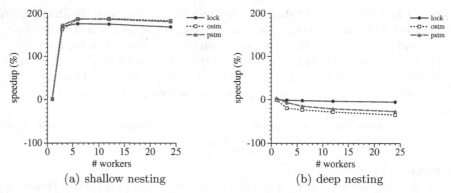

(a) shallow nesting　　　　　　　(b) deep nesting

Fig. 8. Performance of a multi-threaded transaction vs. a single-threaded transaction

better than the pessimistic ones. It is therefore important to support both types of protocols in a TM system.

In Figure 7 we plot results for configurations utilizing nested parallelism, varying the number of worker threads and comparing the performance of transactions over coarse-grain locks. The number of worker threads gets lower as we increase the number of clients to sum up to 24 threads, which is equal to the number of CPUs available on the machine we use for running all the experiments.

By comparing Figure 7 to Figure 6 we observe that transactional memory with support for nested parallelism preserves the performance benefits that transactions provide over locks. While the parallel nested transactions do not maintain the exact same relative performance difference with respect to a lock-based solution, significant performance improvements can still be expected (up to approximately 200% speedup) especially in cases when contention between client threads is significant, as is the case even with just 4 or 8 client threads. The same performance trend holds for configurations using medium-grain synchronization style (we do not report numbers of medium-grain configurations due to space constraints).

How does performance of parallel-nested atomic blocks compare with performance of the atomic blocks executing the same workloads sequentially? Because of our decision to use locks for synchronization at deeper nesting levels, our expectation is that introduction of transactional nested parallelism should provide the largest performance advantage over sequential execution of code inside transactions when nested parallel threads do not need to be synchronized, that is in the case of shallow nesting. However, the only OO7 workload that can be safely executed without having worker threads synchronized within the same transaction is the read only workload. Nevertheless, we decided to present numbers for some selected configurations of this somewhat trivial workload as they serve as an indication of the performance improvement achievable by applications exercising shallow nesting. In Figure 8(a) we plot results for a single client executing a read-only workload, when varying the number of worker threads between 1 and 24. The worker threads execute unsynchronized but the client thread executes synchronization operation (at level 1), even though it is not necessary for correctness, to account for the cost incurred by transactional execution of the workload (i.e. transaction begin and commit and the cost of read barriers). We report numbers for both optimistic and pessimistic transactional modes, as well as for a configuration that uses an OpenMP's mutual exclusion lock to implement client's synchronization operation and that does not include any transactional overheads. Every data point in Figure 8(a) is normalized with respect to the equivalent configuration (optimistic, pessimistic or lock-based) that does not use nested parallelism and executes the entire workload sequentially. As we can observe, in case of shallow nesting, nested parallelism helps to improve performance of the workload over its sequential execution. However, while it improves performance quite dramatically when increasing the number of worker threads from 1 to 6, it remains constant or even degrades slightly when further increasing the number of worker threads. We attribute this effect to the cost of worker thread maintenance incurred by the OpenMP library that starts playing a more important role as the amount of work executed by a single worker thread gets smaller. This observation is indirectly confirmed by the fact that the configurations using OpenMP locks exhibit similar characteristics.

The remaining question is then how sequential execution of transactional code compares performance-wise with configurations exercising deep nesting. In Figure 8(b) we plot results for a single client executing a workload where the percentage of writes is equal to the percentage of reads [5] and where the worker threads require synchronization in addition to synchronization operations executed by the client. The numbers are normalized similarly to the numbers presented in Figure 8(a). As we can observe, in case of OO7 benchmark the performance of parallel-nested transactional configurations is actually worse than that of configurations executing transactional code sequentially. This result is not surprising, considering that the majority of useful work in the OO7 benchmark is performed by the worker threads. As a result, if the execution of these threads is serialized then, especially after adding inherent overhead incurred by the STM implementation, no performance improvement over the sequential configurations should be expected. However, please note that lock-based parallel-nested configurations provide no performance benefit over their sequential counterpart either.

To summarize, our performance evaluation indicates that with nested parallelism inside transactions enabled, performance of transaction-based concurrency control mechanisms can still be better than of those based on mutual exclusion. However the serialization imposed by the lock used to implement parallel-nested atomic blocks might detrimentally affect performance of transactions exercising deep nesting.

7 Conclusions

In this paper we have presented the design and implementation of the first STM system supporting nested parallelism inside of transactions, along with a

---

[5] Configurations with other read-write percentages exhibit similar characteristics.

programming model where OpenMP's constructs enabling nested parallelism can be nested inside of TM constructs used for concurrency control (atomic blocks). We expect our system to benefit more applications that use nested parallelism inside transactions with no or low synchronization between nested threads.

References

1. Adl-Tabatabai, A.-R., Lewis, B.T., Menon, V.S., Murphy, B.R., Saha, B., Shpeisman, T.: Compiler and runtime support for efficient software transactional memory. In: PLDI 2006 (2006)
2. Agrawal, K., Fineman, J.T., Sukha, J.: Nested parallelism in transactional memory. In: PPoPP 2007 (2007)
3. Amdahl, G.M.: Validity of the single-processor approach to achieving large scale computing capabilities. In: AFIPS (1967)
4. Baek, W., Minh, C.C., Trautmann, M., Kozyrakis, C., Olukotun, K.: The OpenTM transactional application programming interface. In: PACT (2007)
5. OpenMP Architecture Review Board. OpenMP Application Programming Interface, Version 2.5
6. OpenMP Architecture Review Board. OpenMP Application Programming Interface, Version 3.0
7. Boehm, H.J., Adve, S.: Foundations of the C++ concurrency memory model. In: PLDI 2008 (2008)
8. Carey, M.J., DeWitt, D.J., Kant, C., Naughton, J.F.: A status report on the OO7 OODBMS benchmarking effort. In: OOPSLA 1994 (1994)
9. Dice, D., Shalev, O., Shavit, N.: Transactional locking II. In: Dolev, S. (ed.) DISC 2006. LNCS, vol. 4167, pp. 194–208. Springer, Heidelberg (2006)
10. Hammond, L., Wong, V., Chen, M., Carlstrom, B.D., Davis, J.D., Hertzberg, B., Prabhu, M.K., Wijaya, H., Kozyrakis, C., Olukotun, K.: Transactional memory coherence and consistency. In: ISCA 2004 (2004)
11. Harris, T., Fraser, K.: Language support for lightweight transactions. In: OOPSLA 2003 (2003)
12. Harris, T., Plesko, M., Shinnar, A., Tarditi, D.: Optimizing memory transactions. In: PLDI 2006 (2006)
13. Herlihy, M., Moss, J.E.B.: Transactional memory: architectural support for lock-free data structures. In: ISCA 1993 (1993)
14. Larus, J., Rajwar, R.: Transactional Memory. Morgan & Claypool Publishers (2006)
15. Menon, V.S., Balensiefer, S., Shpeisman, T., Adl-Tabatabai, A.-R., Hudson, R.L., Saha, B., Welc, A.: Practical weak-atomicity semantics for Java STM. In: SPAA 2008 (2008)
16. Milovanović, M., Ferrer, R., Gajinov, V., Unsal, O.S., Cristal, A., Ayguadé, E., Valero, M.: Multithreaded software transactional memory and OpenMP. In: MEDEA 2007 (2007)
17. Moore, K.F., Grossman, D.: High-level small-step operational semantics for transactions. In: POPL 2008 (2008)
18. Moore, K.E., Bobba, J., Moravan, M.J., Hill, M.D., Wood, D.A.: LogTM: Log-based transactional memory. In: HPCA 2006 (2006)

19. Ni, Y., Welc, A., Adl-Tabatabai, A.-R., Bach, M., Berkowits, S., Cownie, J., Geva, R., Kozhukow, S., Narayanaswamy, R., Olivier, J., Preis, S., Saha, B., Tal, A., Tian, X.: Design and implementation of transactional constructs for C/C++. In: OOPSLA 2008 (2008)
20. Saha, B., Adl-Tabatabai, A.-R., Hudson, R., Minh, C.C., Hertzberg, B.: McRT-STM: A high performance software transactional memory system for a multi-core runtime. In: PPoPP 2006 (2006)
21. Spear, M.F., Marathe, V.J., Dalessandro, L., Scott, M.L.: Brief announcement: Privatization techniques for software transactional memory. In: PODC 2007 (2007)
22. The OpenMP API specification for parallel programming. OpenMP application programming interface
23. Supercomputing Technologies Group, Massachusetts Institute of Technology Laboratory for Computer Science. Cilk 5.4.6 Reference Manual
24. Sutter, H., Larus, J.: Software and the concurrency revolution. ACM Queue 7 (September 2005)
25. Volos, H., Goyal, N., Swift, M.: Pathological interaction of locks with transactional memory. In: TRANSACT 2008 (2008)
26. Wang, C., Chen, W.-Y., Wu, Y., Saha, B., Adl-Tabatabai, A.-R.: Code generation and optimization for transactional memory constructs in an unmanaged language. In: CGO 2007 (2007)
27. Welc, A., Hosking, A.L., Jagannathan, S.: Transparently reconciling transactions with locking for java synchronization. In: Thomas, D. (ed.) ECOOP 2006. LNCS, vol. 4067, pp. 148–173. Springer, Heidelberg (2006)
28. Wing, J.M., Fähndrich, M., Morrisett, J.G., Nettles, S.M.: Extensions to standard ml to support transactions. Technical report, Carnegie Mellon University (1992)
29. Ziarek, L., Welc, A., Adl-Tabatabai, A.-R., Menon, V.S., Shpeisman, T., Jagannathan, S.: A uniform transactional execution environment for java. In: Vitek, J. (ed.) ECOOP 2008. LNCS, vol. 5142, pp. 129–154. Springer, Heidelberg (2008)

Implicit Dynamic Frames: Combining Dynamic Frames and Separation Logic

Jan Smans, Bart Jacobs, and Frank Piessens

Katholieke Universiteit Leuven, Belgium

Abstract. The dynamic frames approach has proven to be a powerful formalism for specifying and verifying object-oriented programs. However, it requires writing and checking many frame annotations. In this paper, we propose a variant of the dynamic frames approach that eliminates the need to explicitly write and check frame annotations. Reminiscent of separation logic's frame rule, programmers write access assertions inside pre- and postconditions instead of writing frame annotations. From the precondition, one can then infer an upper bound on the set of locations writable or readable by the corresponding method. We implemented our approach in a tool, and used it to automatically verify several challenging programs, including subject-observer, iterator and linked list.

1 Introduction

Last year's distinguished paper at ECOOP, Regional Logic for Local Reasoning about Global Invariants [1], proposed Hoare-style proof rules for reasoning about dynamic frames in a Java-like language. In the dynamic frames approach [1,2,3,4,5,6], the programmer specifies upper bounds on the locations that can be read or written by a method in terms of expressions denoting sets of locations. To preserve information hiding, these expressions can involve dynamic frames, pure methods or ghost fields that denote sets of locations. A disadvantage of this approach is that frame annotations must be provided for each method, and that they must be checked explicitly at verification time.

This paper improves upon regional logic and other dynamic frames-based approaches in two ways: (1) method contracts are more concise and (2) fewer proof obligations must be discharged by the verifier. More specifically, we propose a variant of the dynamic frames approach inspired by separation logic that eliminates the need to explicitly write and check frame annotations. Instead, frame information is inferred from access assertions in pre- and postconditions. We have proven the soundness of our approach, implemented it in a verifier prototype and demonstrated its expressiveness by verifying several challenging examples from related work.

The remainder of this paper is structured as follows. In Section 2, we show how our approach solves the frame problem. Section 3 extends this solution with support for data abstraction. In Section 4, we sketch the soundness argument (for the complete proof, see [7]). Subclassing and inheritance are discussed in Section 5 . Finally, we discuss our experience with the verifier prototype, compare with related work, and conclude in Sections 6, 7 and 8.

S. Drossopoulou (Ed.): ECOOP 2009, LNCS 5653, pp. 148–172, 2009.

2 Framing

To reason modularly about a method invocation, one should not rely on the callee's implementation, but only on its specification. For example, consider the code in Figure 1(b). To prove that the assertion at the end of the code snippet holds in every execution, one should only take into account $Cell$'s method contracts. However, the given contracts are too weak to prove the assertion. Indeed, $setX$'s implementation is allowed to change the state arbitrarily, as long as it ensures that **this**.x equals v on exit. In particular, the contract does not prevent $c_2.setX(10)$ from modifying $c_1.x$.

```
class Cell {
    int x;

    Cell()                          Cell c1 := new Cell();
        ensures this.x = 0;         c1.setX(5); //A
        { this.x := 0; }
                                    Cell c2 := new Cell();
                                    c2.setX(10);
    void setX(int v)
        ensures this.x = v;         assert c1.x = 5;
        { this.x := v; }                   (b)
}
            (a)
```

Fig. 1. A class $Cell$ and some client code

To prove the assertion at the end of Figure 1(b), we must strengthen $Cell$'s method contracts. More specifically, the contracts should additionally specify an upper bound on the set of memory locations modifiable by the corresponding method. This problem is called the *frame problem*.

Various solutions to the frame problem have been proposed in the literature (see Section 7 for a detailed comparison). The solution proposed in this paper is as follows. A method may only access a memory location $o.f$ if it has permission to do so. More specifically, writing to or reading from a memory location $o.f$ requires $o.f$ to be *accessible*. Accessibility of $o.f$ is denoted $\mathbf{acc}(o.f)$. Method implementations are not allowed to mention $\mathbf{acc}(o.f)$. In particular, they are not permitted to branch over accessibility of a memory location. As a consequence, a location $o.f$ that was allocated before execution of a method m is only known to be accessible during execution of m if m's precondition requires accessibility of $o.f$. In other words, a method's precondition provides an upper bound on the set of memory locations modifiable by the corresponding method: a method can only modify an existing location $o.f$ if that location is required to be accessible by its precondition. As an example, consider the revised version of the class $Cell$ of Figure 2. $setX$ can only modify **this**.x, since its precondition only requires accessibility of **this**.x. Similarly, $Cell$'s constructor does not require access to any location, and can therefore only assign to fields of the new object.

```
class Cell {
  int x;

  Cell()
    ensures acc(this.x) ∧ this.x = 0;
  { this.x := 0; }

  void setX (int v)
    requires acc(this.x);
    ensures acc(this.x) ∧ this.x = v;
  { this.x := v; }
}
```

Fig. 2. A revised version of the class *Cell* from Figure 1(a)

The accessibility of a memory location can change over time. For example, when a new object is created, the fields of the new object become accessible. How does a method invocation affect the set of accessible memory locations? Since Java does not provide a mechanism for explicit deallocation and assertions can only mention allocated locations, it would be safe to assume that the set of accessible locations only grows across a method invocation. However, this assumption would rule out interesting specification patterns, where a method "captures" accessibility of a location. Furthermore, this assumption would break in the presence of concurrency, where accessibility of memory locations is passed on to other threads (cfr. [8,9]). Therefore, we use the following rule instead: a memory location $o.f$ that is known to be accessible before a method invocation is still accessible after the invocation, if $o.f$ was not required to be accessible by the callee's precondition. On the other hand, a location $o.f$ that was required to be accessible by the callee's precondition is still accessible after the call only if the callee's postcondition ensures accessibility of $o.f$. In other words, $\mathbf{acc}(o.f)$ in a precondition transfers permission to access $o.f$ from the caller to the callee, and vice versa $\mathbf{acc}(o.f)$ in a postcondition returns that permission to the caller.

Given the new method contracts for *Cell* of Figure 2 together with the rules for framing outlined above, we can now prove the assertion at the end of Figure 1(b). Informally, the reasoning is as follows. At program location A, the postcondition of $c_1.setX(5)$ holds: $c_1.x$ is accessible and its value is 5. Since c_2's constructor does not require access to any location, it can modify neither the accessibility nor the value of any existing location. In particular, $c_1.x$ is still accessible and still holds 5. Similarly, the call $c_2.setX(10)$ only requires $c_2.x$ to be accessible, and hence $c_1.x$ is not affected. We may conclude that the assertion, $c_1.x = 5$, holds in any execution.

2.1   Formal Details

In the remainder of this section, we describe a small Java-like language with contracts. Secondly, we define the notion of valid program. Informally, a program

π is valid if each method successfully verifies, i.e. if the verification conditions of π's methods are valid.

Language. We describe the details of our verification approach with respect to the small Java-like language of Figure 3. A program consists of a number of classes and a main routine $\bar{s}$. Each class declares a number of fields and methods. For now, we consider only mutator methods. Each mutator method has a corresponding method body, consisting of a sequence of statements. A statement is either a field update, a variable declaration, a variable update, an object construction, a mutator invocation or an assert statement. In addition, a mutator method declares a method contract, consisting of two assertions: a precondition and a postcondition. An assertion is either **true**, an access assertion, a conjunction, a separating conjunction, an equality or a conditional assertion. A separating conjunction holds only if both conjuncts hold and the left and right-hand side demand access to disjoint parts of the heap. Both statements and assertions contain expressions. An expression is either a variable, a field read, or a constant (**null** or an integer constant).

$$
\begin{array}{lll}
program & ::= & \overline{class}\ \bar{s} \\
class & ::= & \textbf{class}\ C\ \{\ \overline{field}\ \overline{method}\ \} \\
field & ::= & t\ f; \\
method & ::= & mutator \\
mutator & ::= & \textbf{void}\ m(\overline{t\ x})\ contract\ \{\ \bar{s}\ \} \\
contract & ::= & \textbf{requires}\ \phi;\ \textbf{ensures}\ \phi; \\
t & ::= & \textbf{int}\ |\ C \\
s & ::= & e.f := e;\ |\ t\ x;\ |\ x := e;\ |\ x := \textbf{new}\ C;\ |\ e.m(\bar{e});\ |\ \textbf{assert}\ e = e; \\
\phi & ::= & \textbf{true}\ |\ \textbf{acc}(e.f)\ |\ \phi \wedge \phi\ |\ \phi * \phi\ |\ e = e\ |\ e = e\ ?\ \phi : \phi \\
e & ::= & x\ |\ e.f\ |\ c
\end{array}
$$

Fig. 3. Syntax of a Java-like language with contracts

We assume the usual syntactic sugar. In particular, a constructor

$$C(t_1\ x_1, \ldots, t_n\ x_n)\ \textbf{requires}\ \phi_1;\ \textbf{ensures}\ \phi_2;\ \{\ \bar{s}\ \}$$

is a shorthand for the mutator method

$$
\begin{array}{l}
\textbf{void}\ init_C(t_1\ x_1, \ldots, t_n\ x_n) \\
\quad \textbf{requires}\ \textbf{acc}(f_1) * \ldots * \textbf{acc}(f_n) * \phi_1;\ \textbf{ensures}\ \phi_2; \\
\{\ \bar{s}\ \}
\end{array}
$$

where $f_1, \ldots, f_n$ are the fields of C. Accordingly, a constructor invocation $x :=$ **new** $C(e_1, \ldots, e_n)$; abbreviates $x :=$ **new** $C;\ x.init_C(e_1, \ldots, e_n);$.

Verification. We check the correctness of a program by generating verification conditions. The verification conditions are first-order formulas whose validity implies the correctness of the program. In our implementation, we rely on an SMT solver [10] to discharge the verification conditions automatically.

Logic. We target a multi-sorted, first-order logic with equality. That is, a term τ is either a variable or a function application. A formula ψ is either *true*, *false*, a conjunction, a disjunction, an implication, a negation, an equality among terms or a quantification. The formula $\mathsf{ite}(\tau_1 = \tau_2, \psi_1, \psi_2)$ is a shorthand for $(\tau_1 = \tau_2 \Rightarrow \psi_1) \wedge (\tau_1 \neq \tau_2 \Rightarrow \psi_2)$. An application of a function g with arity 0 is denoted g instead of $g()$. Functions with arity 0 are called constants.

Each term in the logic has a corresponding sort. The sorts are the following: the sort of values, *val*, the sort of object references, *ref*, the sort of integers, *int*, the sort of heaps, *heap*, the sort of booleans, *bool*, the sort of sets of memory locations, *set*, the sort of field names, *fname*, and finally the sort of class names, *cname*. We omit sorts whenever they are clear from the context.

The signature of the logic consists of *built-in functions* and a number of *program-specific functions*. The built-in functions include the following:

function	sort
null	*ref*
emptyset	*set*
singleton	*ref* × *fname* → *set*
intersect	*set* × *set* → *set*
union	*set* × *set* → *set*
contains	*ref* × *fname* × *set* → *bool*
select	*heap* × *ref* × *fname* → *val*
store	*heap* × *ref* × *fname* × *val* → *heap*
allocated	*ref* × *heap* → *bool*
allocate	*ref* × *heap* → *heap*
ok	*heap* × *set* → *bool*
succ	*heap* × *set* × *heap* × *set* → *bool*

In addition to the built-in functions, the logic contains a number of program-specific functions. In particular, the logic includes a constant C with sort *cname* for each class C and a constant f with sort *fname* for each field f in the program text. In Section 3, we will introduce additional program-specific functions.

Interpretation. We interpret the functions using the interpretation $\mathfrak{I}$. The interpretation of the built-in functions is as expected. More specifically, *null* is interpreted as the constant **null**. The functions *emptyset*, *singleton*, *union*, *intersect*, and *contains* are interpreted as their mathematical counterpart. We abbreviate applications of these functions by their mathematical notation. The function $select(h, o, f)$ corresponds to applying h to (o, f). Accordingly, $store(h, o, f, v)$ corresponds to an update of the function h at location (o, f) with v. We abbreviate $select(h, o, f)$ as $h(o, f)$ and $store(h, o, f, v)$ as $h[(o, f) \mapsto v]$. $ok(h, a)$ denotes that the state with heap h and access set a is well-formed. Well-formedness implies that both the access set a and the range of the heap h contain only allocated objects. $succ(h, a, h', a')$ states that the state with heap h' and access set a' is a successor of the state with heap h and access set a. Successors of well-formed states are well-formed. Furthermore, a successor state has more allocated locations than its predecessor. We interpret the built-in constant f as the field name f and the constant C as the class name C.

Theory. We assume that the theory $\Sigma_{prelude}$ (incompletely) axiomatizes the built-in functions. That is, $\Im$ is a model for $\Sigma_{prelude}$: $\Im \models \Sigma_{prelude}$. $\Sigma_{prelude}$ may for instance contain a subtheory which axiomatizes the set functions. For example, in our verifier prototype the prelude includes an axiom that encodes that the empty set contains no locations:

$$\forall o, f \bullet (o, f) \notin emptyset$$

For now, we assume that Σ_π, the theory for verifying mutator methods and the main routine, equals $\Sigma_{prelude}$.

statements	verification condition
$e_1.f := e_2;\ \overline{s}$	$\mathsf{Df}(e_1) \wedge \mathsf{Df}(e_2) \wedge (\mathsf{Tr}(e_1), f) \in a \wedge$
	$\mathsf{vc}(\overline{s}, \psi)[h[(\mathsf{Tr}(e_1), f) \mapsto \mathsf{Tr}(e_2)]/h]$
$t\ x;\ \overline{s}$	$\forall x \bullet \mathsf{vc}(\overline{s}, \psi)$
$x := e;\ \overline{s}$	$\mathsf{Df}(e) \wedge \mathsf{vc}(\overline{s}, \psi)[\mathsf{Tr}(e)/x]$
$x := \mathbf{new}\ C;\ \overline{s}$	$\forall y \bullet y \neq null \wedge \neg allocated(y, h) \Rightarrow$
	$\mathsf{vc}(\overline{s}, \psi)[y/x, (a \cup \{(y, f_1), \ldots, (y, f_n)\})/a, allocate(y, h)/h]$
	where $f_1, \ldots, f_n$ are the fields of C
$e_0.m(e_1, \ldots, e_n);\ \overline{s}$	$\mathsf{Df}(e_0) \wedge \ldots \wedge \mathsf{Df}(e_n) \wedge \mathsf{Tr}(e_0) \neq null \wedge \mathsf{Tr}(P) \wedge$
	$(\forall h', a' \bullet$
	$\quad succ(h, a, h', a') \wedge$
	$\quad \mathsf{Tr}(Q)[h'/h, a'/a] \wedge$
	$\quad (\forall o, f \bullet (o, f) \in a \setminus \mathsf{R}(P) \Rightarrow (o, f) \in a' \wedge h(o, f) = h'(o, f)) \wedge$
	$\quad (\forall o, f \bullet (o, f) \in \mathsf{R}(Q)[h'/h, a'/a] \setminus \mathsf{R}(P) \Rightarrow (o, f) \notin a)$
	$\quad \Rightarrow$
	$\quad \mathsf{vc}(\overline{s}, \psi)[h'/h, a'/a])$
	where C is the type of e_0,
	$x_1, \ldots, x_n$ are the parameters of $C.m$,
	P is $\mathsf{mpre}(C, m)[e_0/\mathbf{this}, e_1/x_1, \ldots, e_n/x_n]$ and
	Q is $\mathsf{mpost}(C, m)[e_0/\mathbf{this}, e_1/x_1, \ldots, e_n/x_n]$
$\mathbf{assert}\ e_1 = e_2;\ \overline{s}$	$\mathsf{Df}(e_1 = e_2) \wedge \mathsf{Tr}(e_1 = e_2) \wedge \mathsf{vc}(\overline{s}, \psi)$
nil	ψ

Fig. 4. Verification conditions (vc) of statements with respect to postcondition ψ

Verification Conditions. We check the correctness of a program by generating verification conditions. The verification conditions for each statement are shown in Figure 4. The free variables of $\mathsf{vc}(\overline{s}, \psi)$ are h, a, and the free variables of ψ and $\overline{s}$. The variable h denotes the heap, while the variable a denotes the set of accessible locations. Tr and Df denote the translation and respectively the definedness of expressions and assertions (shown in Figure 5). $\mathsf{mpre}(C, m)$ and $\mathsf{mpost}(C, m)$ respectively denote the pre- and postcondition of the method $C.m$.

The first core ingredient of our approach is that a method can only access a memory location if it has permission to do so. To enforce this restriction, the verification condition for field update checks that the assignee is in the access set a. Similarly, a field read $o.f$ is only well-defined if $o.f$ is an element of a.

expression	Tr	Df
x	x	*true*
$e.f$	$h(\mathsf{Tr}(e), f)$	$\mathsf{Df}(e) \wedge (\mathsf{Tr}(e), f) \in a$
c	c	*true*
true	*true*	*true*
$\mathbf{acc}(e.f)$	$(\mathsf{Tr}(e), f) \in a$	$\mathsf{Df}(e) \wedge \mathsf{Tr}(e) \neq null$
$\phi_1 \wedge \phi_2$	$\mathsf{Tr}(\phi_1) \wedge \mathsf{Tr}(\phi_2)$	$\mathsf{Df}(\phi_1) \wedge (\mathsf{Tr}(\phi_1) \Rightarrow \mathsf{Df}(\phi_2))$
$\phi_1 * \phi_2$	$\mathsf{Tr}(\phi_1 \wedge \phi_2) \wedge (\mathsf{R}(\phi_1) \cap \mathsf{R}(\phi_2) = \emptyset)$	$\mathsf{Df}(\phi_1 \wedge \phi_2)$
$e_1 = e_2$	$\mathsf{Tr}(e_1) = \mathsf{Tr}(e_2)$	$\mathsf{Df}(e_1) \wedge \mathsf{Df}(e_2)$
$e_1 = e_2 \ ? \ \phi_1 : \phi_2$	$\mathsf{ite}(\mathsf{Tr}(e_1 = e_2), \mathsf{Tr}(\phi_1), \mathsf{Tr}(\phi_2))$	$\mathsf{ite}(\mathsf{Tr}(e_1 = e_2), \mathsf{Df}(\phi_1), \mathsf{Df}(\phi_2))$

Fig. 5. Translation (Tr) and definedness (Df) of expressions and assertions

assertion	R
true	$\emptyset$
$\mathbf{acc}(e.f)$	$\{(\mathsf{Tr}(e), f)\}$
$\phi_1 \wedge \phi_2$	$\mathsf{R}(\phi_1) \cup \mathsf{R}(\phi_2)$
$\phi_1 * \phi_2$	$\mathsf{R}(\phi_1 \wedge \phi_2)$
$e_1 = e_2$	$\emptyset$
$e_1 = e_2 \ ? \ \phi_1 : \phi_2$	$\mathsf{ite}(\mathsf{Tr}(e_1 = e_2), \mathsf{R}(\phi_1), \mathsf{R}(\phi_2))$

Fig. 6. Required access set (R) of assertions

The second core ingredient of our approach is that we deduce frame information from a callee's precondition. More specifically, a callee can only read or modify an existing location $o.f$ if its precondition demands access to $o.f$. A naive, literal encoding of this property does not lead to good performance with automatic theorem provers. In particular, the combination of the literal encoding and our approach for data abstraction of Section 3 yields verification conditions that are too hard for those provers. Therefore, we propose a slightly different encoding. More specifically, we syntactically infer from the callee's precondition a *required access set*, i.e. a term denoting the set of memory locations required to be accessible by the precondition. The definition of required access set (R) of an assertion is shown in Figure 6. The subformula

$$\forall o, f \bullet (o, f) \in a \setminus \mathsf{R}(P) \Rightarrow (o, f) \in a' \wedge h(o, f) = h'(o, f)$$

in the verification condition of method invocation encodes the property that all locations $o.f$ that are accessible to the callee and that were not in the required access set of the precondition remain accessible and retain their value. Note that this is a *free* postcondition: callers can assume the postcondition holds, but it is not necessary to explicitly prove the postcondition when verifying the method's implementation (see Definition 1). In addition to the "free modifies" clause, callers may assume a second free postcondition, the swinging pivot property:

$$\forall o, f \bullet (o, f) \in \mathsf{R}(Q)[h'/h, a'/a] \setminus \mathsf{R}(P) \Rightarrow (o, f) \notin a$$

The swinging pivot property states that all locations required to be accessible by the postcondition are either required to be accessible by the precondition or are not accessible to the callee. In Section 3, this property will be crucial to ensure disjointness.

A program is *valid* (Definition 3) if it successfully verifies. More specifically, a valid program only contains valid methods and has a valid main routine. A mutator is valid (Definition 1) if both its pre- and postcondition are well-defined assertions and if its body satisfies the method contract. A method body $\bar{s}$ satisfies the contract if the postcondition holds after executing $\bar{s}$, whenever execution starts in a state satisfying the precondition. The main routine is valid (Definition 2) if it satisfies the contract **requires true; ensures true;**. Executions of valid programs never deference null and assert statements never fail. We outline a proof of this property in Section 4.

Definition 1. *A mutator method*

$$\textbf{void } m(t_1 \ x_1, \dots, t_k \ x_k) \textbf{ requires } \phi_1; \textbf{ ensures } \phi_2; \ \{ \ \bar{s} \ \}$$

is valid *if all of the following hold:*

- *The precondition is well-defined and the postcondition is well-defined, provided the precondition holds.*

$$\Sigma_\pi \vdash \forall h, a, h', a', this, x_1, \dots, x_k \bullet ok(h, a) \wedge succ(h, a, h', a') \wedge this \neq null \wedge$$
$$\Downarrow$$
$$\mathsf{Df}(\phi_1) \wedge (\mathsf{Tr}(\phi_1) \Rightarrow \mathsf{Df}(\phi_2)[h'/h, a'/a])$$

- *The method body satisfies the method contract.*

$$\Sigma_\pi \vdash \forall h, a, this, x_1, \dots, x_k \bullet ok(h, a) \wedge this \neq null \wedge \mathsf{Tr}(\phi_1) \Rightarrow \mathsf{vc}(\bar{s}, \mathsf{Tr}(\phi_2))$$

Definition 2. *The main routine $\bar{s}$ is* valid *if the following holds:*

$$\Sigma_\pi \vdash \forall h, a \bullet ok(h, a) \Rightarrow \mathsf{vc}(\bar{s}, true).$$

Definition 3. *A program π is* valid *(denoted* valid(π)*) if all mutator methods and the main routine are valid.*

3   Data Abstraction

Data abstraction is crucial in the construction of modular programs, since it ensures that internal changes in one module do not propagate to other modules. However, the class *Cell* of Figure 2 and its specifications were not written with data abstraction in mind. More specifically, (1) client code must directly access the field x to query a *Cell* object's internal state and (2) *Cell*'s method contracts are not implementation-independent as they mention the internal field x. Any change to *Cell*'s implementation, such as renaming x to y, would break or at least oblige us to reconsider the correctness of client code.

Developers typically solve issue (1) by adding "getters" to their classes. For example, the class *Cell* of Figure 7(a) defines a method *getX* to query a *Cell*'s internal state. The method is marked **pure** to indicate it does not have side-effects.

```
class Cell {
  int x;

  Cell()
    ensures valid() ∧ getX() = 0;
  { this.x := 0; }

  void setX(int v)
    requires valid();
    ensures valid() ∧ getX() = v;
  { this.x := v; }

  predicate bool valid()
  { return acc(this.x); }

  pure int getX()
    requires valid();
  { return this.x; }

  void swap(Cell c)
    requires valid() * c ≠ null ∧ c.valid();
    ensures valid() * c.valid();
    ensures getX() = old(c.getX());
    ensures c.getX() = old(getX());
  { int i := x; x := c.getX(); c.setX(i); }
}
```

(a)

```
Cell c₁ := new Cell();
c₁.setX(5); //A

Cell c₂ := new Cell();
c₂.setX(10);

assert c₁.getX() = 5;
```
(b)

Fig. 7. A revised version of class *Cell* with data abstraction

As shown in Figure 7(b), the assertion of Figure 1(b) can now be rephrased in terms of *getX*.

To complete the decoupling between *Cell*'s implementation and client code, we should also solve issue (2) and make *Cell*'s method contracts implementation-independent. In this paper, we solve the latter issue by allowing getters to be used inside specifications. That is, we allow the effect of one method to be specified in terms of other methods. For example, the behavior of *setX* in Figure 7(a) is described in terms of its effect on *getX*.

In this paper, methods used within contracts are called *pure methods*. We distinguish two kinds of pure methods: normal pure methods (annotated with **pure**) and predicates (annotated with **predicate**). A pure method's body consists of a single return statement, returning either an expression (in case of a normal pure method) or an assertion (in case of a predicate). That is, a normal pure method abstracts over an expression, while a predicate abstracts an assertion. Since assertions and expressions are side-effect free, execution of a pure method never modifies the state. Since we disallow mentioning assertions inside method bodies, predicates can only be called from contracts and from the bodies of predicates. Furthermore, predicates are not allowed to have preconditions. In our running example, both *getX* and *valid* are pure methods. The former is a normal pure method, while the latter is a predicate. Predicates are typically used to represent invariants and to abstract over accessibility of memory locations.

To prove the assertion at the end of Figure 7(b), one must show that c_2's constructor and $c_2.setX(10)$ do not affect the return value of $c_1.getX()$. In other words, it suffices to show that the locations modified by those statements is disjoint from the set of locations that $c_1.getX()$ depends on. But how can we determine which locations influence the return value of *getX*? The answer is simple.

We can deduce from the precondition of a normal pure method an upper bound on the set of locations readable by that method: a pure method p can only read $o.f$ if p's precondition requires $o.f$ to be accessible. In other words, the return value of a normal pure method only depends on locations required to be accessible by its precondition. A predicate does not have a precondition, so what locations does its return value depend on? We say a predicate is *self-framing*. That is, the return value of a predicate q only depends on locations that q itself requires to be accessible.

Given these properties of pure methods, we can now prove the assertion at the end of Figure 7(b). Informally, the reasoning is as follows. At program location A, the postcondition of $c_1.setX(5)$ holds: $c_1.valid()$ is true and $c_1.getX()$ returns 5. Because c_2's constructor does not require access to any existing location, it can only modify fresh locations (i.e. c_2's fields and fields of objects allocated within the constructor itself). Since $c_1.valid()$ only requires access to non-fresh locations, both its own return value and the return value of $c_1.getX()$ are not affected by c_2's constructor. In addition, the set of memory locations required to be accessible by $c_1.valid()$ is disjoint from the set of locations required to be accessible by $c_2.valid()$, since the latter set only contains fresh locations (follows from the swinging pivot property). $c_2.setX()$ can only modify locations covered by $c_2.valid()$. The latter set of locations is disjoint from $c_1.valid()$, hence the return values of $c_1.valid()$ and $c_1.getX()$ are not affected by $c_2.setX(10)$. We may conclude that the assertion, $c_1.getX() = 5$, holds in any execution.

To illustrate the use of the separating conjunction, consider the method *swap* of Figure 7(a). *swap*'s precondition requires that the receiver and c are "separately" valid, i.e. that both **this**.*valid*() and $c.valid()$ hold and that the set of locations required to be accessible by **this**.*valid*() is disjoint from the set of locations required to be accessible by $c.valid()$. If we would have used a normal conjunction instead of a separating conjunction, we would not be able to prove $c.valid()$ holds after the assignment to x. In particular, the separating conjunction ensures that $c.valid()$ does not depend on **this**.x.

3.1 Formal Details

Language. We extend the language of Figure 3 with normal pure methods (typically denoted as p) and predicates (typically denoted as q) as shown in Figure 8. Accordingly, we add predicate invocations to the assertion language and normal pure method invocations to the expression language.

$$
\begin{array}{ll}
method & ::= \ldots \mid predicate \mid pure \\
predicate & ::= \textbf{predicate bool } q(\overline{t\ x})\ \{\ \textbf{return } \phi;\ \} \\
pure & ::= \textbf{pure } t\ p(\overline{t\ x})\ contract\ \{\ \textbf{return } e;\ \} \\
\phi & ::= \ldots \mid e.q(\overline{e}) \\
e & ::= \ldots \mid e.p(\overline{e})
\end{array}
$$

Fig. 8. An extension of the language of Figure 3 with pure methods

To ensure consistency of the encoding of pure methods, we enforce that pure methods terminate by syntactically checking that a pure method p only calls pure methods defined before p in the program text. We discuss this restriction together with more liberal solutions for ensuring consistency in Section 4.

Verification

Logic. A standard technique in verification is to represent pure methods as functions in the verification logic [11,12]. More specifically, for a normal pure method $C.p$ with parameters $t_1\ x_1, \ldots, t_n\ x_n$ and return type t, the verification logic includes a function $C.p$ with sort $heap \times set \times ref \times \text{sort}(t_1) \times \ldots \times \text{sort}(t_n) \rightarrow \text{sort}(t)$, where sort maps a type to its corresponding sort. Similarly, for each predicate $C.q$ with parameters $t_1\ x_1, \ldots, t_n\ x_n$, the logic includes a function $C.q$ with sort $heap \times set \times ref \times \text{sort}(t_1) \times \ldots \times \text{sort}(t_n) \rightarrow bool$ and a function $C.q_{\text{FP}}$ with sort $heap \times set \times ref \times \text{sort}(t_1) \times \ldots \times \text{sort}(t_n) \rightarrow set$. The latter function, $C.q_{\text{FP}}$, is called q's footprint function.

An invocation of a pure method is encoded in the verification logic as an application of the corresponding function. For example, the postcondition of $setX$ of Figure 7(a) is encoded as $Cell.valid(h, a, this) \wedge Cell.getX(h, a, this) = v$.

Interpretation. We extend $\mathfrak{I}$ to these new program-specific functions as follows. For each normal pure method $C.p$ and for all heaps H, access sets A and values $v_0, \ldots, v_n$, $\mathfrak{I}(C.p)(H, A, v_0, \ldots, v_n)$ equals v, if evaluation of $v_0.p(v_1, \ldots, v_n)$ terminates and yields value v. Otherwise, $\mathfrak{I}(C.p)(H, A, v_0, \ldots, v_n)$ equals the default value of the method's return type. The interpretation of predicates and footprint functions is similar (see [7]).

Theory. The behavior of a pure method is encoded via several axioms. Each normal pure method p has a corresponding axiomatization Σ_p, consisting of an implementation and a frame axiom. More specifically, the axioms corresponding to the normal pure method

$$\textbf{pure } t\ p(t_1\ x_1, \ldots, t_k\ x_k)\ \textbf{requires } \phi_1;\ \textbf{ensures } \phi_2;\ \{\ \textbf{return } e;\ \}$$

are the following:

- **Implementation axiom.** The implementation axiom relates the function symbol $C.p$ to the pure method's implementation: applying the function equals evaluating the method body, provided the precondition holds.

$$\forall h, a, this, x_1, \ldots, x_k \bullet ok(h, a) \wedge this \neq null \wedge \mathsf{Tr}(\phi_1)$$
$$\Downarrow$$
$$C.p(h, a, this, x_1, \ldots, x_k) = \mathsf{Tr}(e)$$

– **Frame axiom.** The frame axiom encodes the property that a pure method only depends on locations in the required access set of its precondition. That is, the return value of p is the same in two states, if locations in the required access set of the precondition have the same value in both heaps.

$$\forall h_1, a_1, h_2, a_2, this, x_1, \ldots, x_k \bullet$$
$$ok(h_1, a_1) \wedge ok(h_2, a_2) \wedge this \neq null \wedge$$
$$\mathsf{Tr}(\phi_1)[h_1/h, a_1/a] \wedge \mathsf{Tr}(\phi_1)[h_2/h, a_2/a] \wedge$$
$$(\forall o, f \bullet (o, f) \in \mathsf{R}(\phi_1)[h_1/h, a_1/a] \Rightarrow (o, f) \in a_2 \wedge h_1(o, f) = h_2(o, f))$$
$$\Downarrow$$
$$C.p(h_1, a_1, this, x_1, \ldots, x_k) = C.p(h_2, a_2, this, x_1, \ldots, x_k)$$

Each predicate q has a corresponding axiomatization Σ_q, consisting of an implementation axiom, frame axiom, footprint implementation axiom, footprint frame axiom and a footprint allocated axiom. More specifically, the axioms corresponding to the predicate

predicate bool $q(t_1\ x_1, \ldots, t_k\ x_k)$ { **return** ϕ; }

are the following:

– **Implementation axiom.** The implementation axiom relates q's function symbol to its implementation.

$$\forall h, a, this, x_1, \ldots, x_k \bullet ok(h, a) \wedge this \neq null$$
$$\Downarrow$$
$$C.q(h, a, this, x_1, \ldots, x_k) = \mathsf{Tr}(\phi)$$

– **Frame axiom.** The frame axiom encodes the property that a predicate is self-framing.

$$\forall h_1, a_1, h_2, a_2, this, x_1, \ldots, x_k \bullet$$
$$ok(h_1, a_1) \wedge ok(h_2, a_2) \wedge this \neq null \wedge$$
$$C.q(h_1, a_1, this, x_1, \ldots, x_k) \wedge$$
$$(\forall o, f \bullet (o, f) \in C.q_{\mathsf{FP}}(h_1, a_1, this, x_1, \ldots, x_k) \Rightarrow (o, f) \in a_2 \wedge h_1(o, f) = h_2(o, f))$$
$$\Downarrow$$
$$C.q(h_2, a_2, this, x_1, \ldots, x_k)$$

– **Footprint implementation axiom.** The footprint implementation axiom relates the function symbol $C.q_{\mathsf{FP}}$ to the required access set of the body of the predicate.

$$\forall h, a, this, x_1, \ldots, x_k \bullet ok(h, a) \wedge this \neq null \wedge C.q(h, a, this, x_1, \ldots, x_k)$$
$$\Downarrow$$
$$C.q_{\mathsf{FP}}(h, a, this, x_1, \ldots, x_k) = \mathsf{R}(\phi)$$

- **Footprint frame axiom**. The footprint frame axiom encodes the property that a footprint function frames itself, provided the corresponding predicate holds.

$$\forall h_1, a_1, h_2, a_2, this, x_1, \ldots, x_k \bullet$$
$$ok(h_1, a_1) \wedge ok(h_2, a_2) \wedge this \neq null \wedge$$
$$C.q(h_1, a_1, this, x_1, \ldots, x_k) \wedge C.q(h_2, a_2, this, x_1, \ldots, x_k) \wedge$$
$$(\forall o, f \bullet (o, f) \in C.q\mathsf{FP}(h_1, a_1, this, x_1, \ldots, x_k) \Rightarrow (o, f) \in a_2 \wedge h_1(o, f) = h_2(o, f))$$
$$\Downarrow$$
$$C.q\mathsf{FP}(h_1, a_1, this, x_1, \ldots, x_k) = C.q\mathsf{FP}(h_2, a_2, this, x_1, \ldots, x_k)$$

- **Footprint accessible axiom**. The footprint accessible axiom states that a predicate footprint only contains accessible locations, provided the predicate itself holds.

$$\forall h, a, this, x_1, \ldots, x_k \bullet$$
$$ok(h, a) \wedge this \neq null \wedge C.q(h, a, this, x_1, \ldots, x_k)$$
$$\Downarrow$$
$$C.q\mathsf{FP}(h, a, this, x_1, \ldots, x_k) \subseteq a$$

We redefine Σ_π as $\Sigma_{prelude} \cup \bigcup_{p \in \pi} \Sigma_p$. That is, Σ_π is the union of the axioms for the built-in functions and the axioms of each pure method in π. Moreover, we define Σ_{p*} as the axiomatization of all pure methods defined before p in the program text. Note that Σ_{p*} does not include Σ_p.

Verification Conditions. To support data abstraction, we added pure methods and pure method invocation to our language. Figure 9 extends the table of Figure 5 with invocations of pure methods. In particular, pure methods are encoded as functions in the verification logic. An invocation of a pure method is well-defined if the arguments are well-defined and the receiver is not null. In addition, the precondition must hold for a normal pure method invocation to be well-defined.

expression	Tr	Df
$e_0.p(e_1, \ldots, e_n)$	$C.p(h, a, \mathsf{Tr}(e_0), \ldots, \mathsf{Tr}(e_n))$	$\mathsf{Df}(e_0) \wedge \ldots \wedge \mathsf{Df}(e_n) \wedge \mathsf{Tr}(e_0) \neq null \wedge$
		$\mathsf{Tr}(mpre(C, p)[e_0/\mathbf{this}, e_1/x_1, \ldots, e_n/x_n])$
$e_0.q(e_1, \ldots, e_n)$	$C.q(h, a, \mathsf{Tr}(e_0), \ldots, \mathsf{Tr}(e_n))$	$\mathsf{Df}(e_0) \wedge \ldots \wedge \mathsf{Df}(e_n) \wedge \mathsf{Tr}(e_0) \neq null$

Fig. 9. Translation (Tr) and definedness (Df) of pure method invocations

In this section, we added a new kind of assertion, namely predicate method invocation. What is the required access set of such an assertion? One solution would be to define the required access set of a predicate invocation as the required access set of the predicate's body. However, such a definition would expose implementation details to client code. For example, the required access set of the precondition of *getX* of Figure 7(a) would be the singleton $\{(this, x)\}$. Yet, this is just a detail of the current implementation, and client code should not rely on

assertion	R
$e_0.q(e_1, \ldots, e_n)$	$C.q_{\mathsf{FP}}(h, a, \mathsf{Tr}(e_0), \ldots, \mathsf{Tr}(e_n))$

Fig. 10. Required access set (R) of predicate instances

it. Instead, we propose introducing an extra layer of indirection. More specifically, as shown in Figure 10 the required access set of a predicate invocation is an application of the footprint function.

We redefine the notion of valid program. More specifically, for a program to be valid, we now additionally require that all pure methods are valid (Definition 6). Informally, a pure method is valid if its body and contract are well-defined (Definitions 4 and 5). Note that a pure method p is not verified with respect to the theory Σ_π but with respect to $\Sigma_{prelude} \cup \Sigma_{p*}$. That is, during verification of a pure method, one can only assume that the prelude axioms and axioms of pure methods defined before p in the program text hold.

Definition 4. *A predicate*

$$\textbf{predicate bool } q(t_1\ x_1, \ldots, t_k\ x_k)\ \{\ \textbf{return }\phi;\ \}$$

is valid if its body is a well-defined assertion:

$$\Sigma_{prelude} \cup \Sigma_{q*} \vdash \forall h, a, this, x_1, \ldots, x_k \bullet ok(h, a) \wedge this \neq null \Rightarrow \mathsf{Df}(\phi)$$

Definition 5. *A pure method*

$$\textbf{pure } t\ p(t_1\ x_1, \ldots, t_k\ x_k)\ \textbf{requires }\phi_1;\ \{\ \textbf{return }e;\ \}$$

is valid if its precondition is well-defined and its body is well-defined, provided the precondition holds:

$$\Sigma_{prelude} \cup \Sigma_{p*} \vdash \forall h, a, this, x_1, \ldots, x_k \bullet$$
$$ok(h, a) \wedge this \neq null \Rightarrow \mathsf{Df}(\phi_1) \wedge (\mathsf{Tr}(\phi_1) \Rightarrow \mathsf{Df}(e))$$

Definition 6. *A program π is valid (denoted $\mathsf{valid}(\pi)$) if all methods (both pure and mutator) and the main routine are valid.*

4   Soundness

The structure of the soundness proof is as follows. We define a run-time checking execution semantics for the language of Figure 8. Execution gets stuck at null dereferences and assertion violations. We then define the notion of valid configuration. We show that valid programs do not get stuck by proving progress and preservation for valid configurations in valid programs. In the remainder of this section, we elaborate all the steps described above. For the full proof, we refer the reader to a technical report [7].

We start by defining an execution semantics for programs written in the language of Figure 8. More specifically, a configuration (H, S) consists of a heap

H and a stack S. The former component is a partial function from object references to objects states. An object state is a partial function from field names to values. The stack consists of a list of activation records. Each activation record $(\Gamma, A, G, B, \overline{s})$ is a 5-tuple consisting of an environment Γ that maps variables to values, a set of accessible locations, an old heap G, an old access set B, and finally a sequence of statements. The old heap holds the value of the heap at the time the activation record was put onto the call stack, while the old access stores a copy of the callee's access set. A configuration can perform a step and get to a successor configuration as defined by the small-step relation $\rightarrow$. As an example, consider the definition of $\rightarrow$ for field update.

$$\frac{H, \Gamma, A \vdash e_1 \Downarrow v_1 \qquad (v_1, f) \in A \qquad H' = H[(v_1, f) \mapsto v_2]}{(H, (\Gamma, A, G, B, e_1.f := e_2;\ \overline{s}) \cdot S) \rightarrow (H', (\Gamma, A, G, B, \overline{s}) \cdot S)}$$

In this definition, $H, \Gamma, A \vdash e_1 \Downarrow v_1$ denotes that the expression e_1 evaluates to value v_1. $H[(v_1, f) \mapsto v_2]$ denotes the update of the function H at location (v_1, f) with value v_2. Note that $\rightarrow$ defines a *run-time checking* semantics. For example, a field update is stuck if the location being assigned to is not in the activation record's access set. In general, $\rightarrow$ gets stuck at a null deference, precondition violation, postcondition violation, when a non-accessible location is read or written or when the condition of an assert statement evaluates to false.

$\rightarrow$ preserves certain well-formedness properties. In particular, it preserves the fact that (1) access sets of different activation records are disjoint and (2) that the access set of each activation record (except for the top of the stack) frames part of the heap with respect to the old heap. More specifically, for each activation record $(\Gamma_i, A_i, G_i, B_i, \overline{s_i})$, property (2) states that for all locations $o.f$ in A_i, the value of $o.f$ in the current heap H equals the value of $o.f$ in G_{i-1}. In other words, each location that is accessible to the callee but that is not required to be accessible by the caller cannot be changed during the callee's execution.

A configuration σ is *valid* if each activation record is valid. The top activation record $(\Gamma_1, A_1, G_1, B_1, \overline{s_1})$ is valid if $\mathfrak{J}, H, \Gamma_1, A \models \mathsf{vc}(\overline{s_1}, \psi_1)$, where ψ_1 is the postcondition of the method being executed. That is, the verification condition of the remaining statements satisfies the postcondition, when interpreting functions as defined in $\mathfrak{J}$, h as the heap H, a as the access set A and all variables by their value in Γ. Similarly, any other activation record $(\Gamma_i, A_i, G_i, B_i, \overline{s_i})$ is valid if $\mathfrak{J}, G_{i-1}, \Gamma_i, B_{i-1} \models \mathsf{vc}(\overline{s}, \psi_i)$.

Finally, we prove that for valid programs (i.e. for programs that successfully verify according to Definition 6) $\rightarrow$ preserves validity of configurations and that valid configurations are never stuck. In particular, we prove preservation for the return step by relying on the well-formedness properties described above. It follows that executions of valid programs do not violate assertions and never dereference null. Moreover, it is safe to *erase* the ghost state (e.g. access set per activation record) and the corresponding checks (e.g. that any location being assigned to is in the activation record's access set is accessible) in executions of valid programs.

Consistency. For verification to be sound, the theory Σ_π must be consistent. To show consistency, it suffices to prove that $\mathfrak{I} \models \Sigma_\pi$ if π is a valid program. Since $\mathfrak{I} \models \Sigma_{prelude}$, it is sufficient to demonstrate that $\mathfrak{I}$ is a model for the axiomatization of each pure method. We prove the latter property by constructing a set of pure methods S, such that if a pure method p is in S, then all pure methods defined before p in the program text are also in S. We define Σ_S as the union of the axioms of all pure methods in S. We proceed by induction on the size of S. If S is empty, then trivially $\mathfrak{I} \models \Sigma_S$. If S is not empty, select the pure method p from S that appears last in the program text. It follows from the induction hypothesis that $\mathfrak{I} \models \Sigma_{p*}$. We have to show that $\mathfrak{I}$ is a model for each of p's axiom. The fact that $\mathfrak{I}$ models the implementation axiom follows from the fact that pure methods must terminate (i.e. a pure method can only call pure methods defined earlier in the program text) and the definition of $\mathfrak{I}$ for normal pure methods. The complete proof for all the axioms can be found in [7].

The main goal of our soundness proof is to show that the rules for framing are sound. We consider ensuring consistency of the logic in the presence of pure methods as an orthogonal issue. For that reason, we choose to ensure consistency in the proof by a very simple, but restrictive rule: a pure method p can only call pure methods defined before p in the program text. However, more flexible solutions exist [11,13]. For example in our verifier prototype, we allow cycles in the call graph, provided the size of the precondition's required access set decreases along the call chain. Furthermore, a predicate may call any other predicate, provided the call occurs in a positive position.

5   Inheritance

Inheritance is a key component of the object-oriented programming paradigm that allows a class to be defined in terms of one or more existing classes. For example, the class *BackupCell* of Figure 11 extends its superclass *Cell* with a method *undo*. Dealing with inheritance in verification is challenging. In particular, for verification to be modular, the addition of a new subclass should not break or oblige us to reconsider the correctness of existing code. In this section, we informally describe how our approach can be extended to cope with Java-like inheritance in a modular way. Our approach for dealing with inheritance is based on earlier proposals by Leavens *et al.* [14], Parkinson *et al.* [15] and Jacobs *et al.* [12].

Methods can both be statically and dynamically bound, depending on the method and the calling context. For example, *getX* is dynamically bound in the client code of Figure 7(b), while it is statically bound in the body of *setX* in Figure 11. To distinguish statically bound invocations of pure methods from dynamically bound ones, we introduce additional function symbols in the verification logic. That is, for a pure method p defined in a class C with parameters $x_1, \ldots, x_n$, the logic not only includes a function symbol $C.p$ but also a function $C.p_D$. The former function symbol is used for statically bound calls, while the latter is used for dynamically bound calls.

```
class BackupCell extends Cell {
  int backup;

  BackupCell()
    ensures valid() ∧ getX() = 0;
  { super(); }

  void setX(int v)
    requires valid();
    ensures valid();
    ensures getX() = v ∧ getBackup() = old(getX());
  { backup := super.getX(); super.setX(v); }

  void undo()
    requires valid();
    ensures valid() ∧ getX() = old(getBackup());
  { super.setX(backup); }

  predicate bool valid()
  { return acc(backup) * super.valid(); }

  pure int getBackup()
    requires valid();
  { return backup; }
}
```

Fig. 11. A class *BackupCell* (similar to *Recell* from [15]) which extends *Cell* with *undo*

The relationship between $C.p$ and $C.p_D$ is encoded via a number of axioms. More specifically, $C.p$ equals $C.p_D$ whenever the dynamic type of the receiver (denoted as $typeof(this)$) equals C.

$$\forall h, a, this, x_1, \ldots x_n \bullet ok(h, a) \land typeof(this) = C \Rightarrow$$
$$C.p(h, a, this, x_1, \ldots, x_n) = C.p_D(h, a, this, x_1, \ldots, x_n)$$

Furthermore, whenever a method $D.p$ overrides $C.p$, we include the following axiom:

$$\forall h, a, this, x_1, \ldots x_n \bullet ok(h, a) \land typeof(this) <: D \Rightarrow$$
$$C.p_D(h, a, this, x_1, \ldots, x_n) = D.p_D(h, a, this, x_1, \ldots, x_n)$$

That is, if the dynamic type of the receiver is a subtype (denoted as $<:$) of D, then dynamically bound invocations of both $C.p$ and $D.p$ yield the same result. For the footprint function of a predicate, we use a similar encoding.

Calls with receiver **this** are treated differently in code and in contracts. If a method invocation is statically bound, then invocations of pure methods with receiver **this** in the callee's contract are also considered to be statically bound; otherwise, such invocations are considered to be dynamically bound. Methods themselves are verified under the assumption they are called statically, i.e. calls with receiver **this** in the contract are statically bound. Doing so is sound, provided each subclass overrides each method. Indeed, if a method is called statically, then the caller and callee agree on the method contract. If a method is called dynamically, then the dynamic type of the receiver equals the static type, and therefore it follows that the static contract equals the dynamic contract.

To ensure the implementation of a subclass D does not break the contracts of a superclass C, we check that the contract of each method in C is satisfied by a method body that satisfies the contract of D. More specifically, for each method m in C, we check that a method body that calls $D.m$ satisfies the contract of $C.m$, assuming that the dynamic type of the receiver is D. The latter proof obligation ensures that no existing code is broken by the addition of the subclass C.

Note that *BackupCell* is just another client of *Cell* that is oblivious to *Cell*'s implementation. If we were to change *Cell*'s implementation (within the boundaries set by its method contracts), then the correctness of *BackupCell* would not be endangered.

6 Experience

To demonstrate the approach described in this paper is amenable to automatic, static verification, we implemented it in a verifier prototype. The prototype was used to verify several (variations of) programs used in related work.

The time taken to verify each program and a reference to the paper(s) containing the program is shown in Table 1. The experiments were executed on a desktop machine with a Pentium Core Duo 2.66 GHz processor and 4 GB of memory running Windows Vista. To discharge the verification conditions, we used the Z3 [10] theorem prover. The verifier itself and the programs shown in Table 1 can be downloaded from http://www.cs.kuleuven.be/~jans/vericool2.

Table 1. Table showing the time taken (in seconds) to verify each program

program	time taken	source
Cell	0.1	[16,17,12]
ArrayList and Iterator	0.8	[2,18]
LinkedList	43	[19,2]
Resource Pool	2.1	[17]
Marriage	0.2	[20]
MasterClock	0.2	[21]
Subject-Observer	11	[1,22]
Recell, TCell, DCell	0.5	[15]
Visitor (framing only)	127	[17]

To ensure a method's correctness proof does not depend on internal details of other modules, our verifier prototype makes a pure method's implementation axioms available only to other methods implemented in the same module.

Iterated Star. In many programs, it is useful to specify that an assertion holds for a statically unknown number of objects. For example in the Subject-Observer pattern, the invariant of the subject typically states that all registered observers are valid. In our tool, there are two ways two write such invariants. First of all, one can define the invariant in terms of a recursive predicate. However, reasoning about recursive predicates in first-order provers is tricky, since this often involves proving inductive lemmas. To avoid reasoning about recursive predicates, our tool provides another way of quantifying over an unknown number of objects, namely iterated star. An iterated star assertion has the form $(\forall^* x \in (min : max) \bullet \phi)$, where min and max are integer expressions. Informally, the latter assertion states that ϕ holds for all integers between min (inclusive) and max (exclusive) and that for any two different integers in that range, the locations required to be accessible by ϕ are disjoint. For example, the invariant of the subject can be written as follows. Note that obs is a field of type $List < Observer >$.

> **predicate bool** $subobs()$ {
> **return** $\mathbf{acc}(value) * \mathbf{acc}(obs) * obs \neq \mathbf{null} \wedge obs.valid()*$
> $(\forall^* i \in (0 : obs.size())\bullet$
> $obs.get(i) \neq \mathbf{null} \wedge obs.get(i).valid() \wedge$
> $obs.get(i).getSubject() = \mathbf{this} \wedge obs.get(i).upToDate()); \}$

We translate iterated star as follows (i and j are fresh variables).

$$(\forall x \bullet \mathsf{Tr}(min) \leq x < \mathsf{Tr}(max) \Rightarrow \mathsf{Tr}(\phi)) \wedge$$
$$(\forall i, j \bullet \mathsf{Tr}(min) \leq i < \mathsf{Tr}(max) \wedge \mathsf{Tr}(min) \leq j < \mathsf{Tr}(max) \wedge i \neq j \Rightarrow$$
$$\mathsf{R}(\phi[i/x]) \cap \mathsf{R}(\phi[j/x]) = \emptyset)$$

The first quantification states that ϕ holds for all integers between min and max, while the second one states that the required access set is disjoint at different indices. An iterated star is well-defined only if the bounds are well-defined and the assertion is well-defined for all integers within those bounds. That is, the definedness of an iterated star is as follows.

$$\mathsf{Df}(min) \wedge \mathsf{Df}(max) \wedge (\forall x \bullet \mathsf{Tr}(min) \leq x < \mathsf{Tr}(max) \Rightarrow \mathsf{Df}(\phi))$$

What is the required access set of an iterated star? Informally, the required access is the union of the required access sets of ϕ for all indices in the range: $\bigcup_{\mathsf{Tr}(min) \leq x < \mathsf{Tr}(max)} \mathsf{R}(\phi)$. However, $\bigcup$ is not a first-order concept. Therefore, we encode the required access set of an iterated star as follows (inspired by [23]). For each iterated star in the program text, we generate a function in the verification logic $union_i$ (where i is unique for each iterated star) with sort $heap \times set \times int \times int \rightarrow set$. This function represents the required access set of the corresponding iterated star. Several axioms describe the behavior of $union_i$. For example, we add an axiom that states a set is disjoint from a union only if it is disjoint from all the elements.

$$\forall h, a, min, max, s \bullet s \cap union_i(h, a, min, max) = \emptyset \Leftrightarrow$$
$$(\forall x \bullet \mathsf{Tr}(min) \leq x < \mathsf{Tr}(max) \Rightarrow s \cap \mathsf{R}(\phi) = \emptyset)$$

Whenever two different iterated stars are sufficiently similar, we generate only one union function instead of two. Two iterated stars are sufficiently similar if they differ only in the name of the quantified variable or in their range. Such similar iterated stars typically occur in loop invariants and postconditions.

Partial Permissions

In this paper, we do not distinguish full access permissions (permission to read and write a location) from partial access permissions (permission to read). That is, a method either has permission to both read and write a location or it cannot access the location at all. Therefore, even if a mutator only reads an existing location, it still has to demand full access to that location in its precondition. This problem can be solved in many ways. For instance, Boyland [24] proposes using fractional permissions. We could extend our solution with support for fractions by tracking an access map, which maps each location to a fraction, instead of an access set.

In our implementation, we use a different solution. A mutator should indicate it only reads a location $o.f$ by ensuring in its postcondition that $o.f$'s value is

```
class ArrayList {
  int n; Object[] items;

  ArrayList()
    ensures valid() ∧ size() = 0;

  void add(Object o)
    requires valid();
    ensures valid();
    ensures size() = old(size() + 1);
    ensures (∀*i ∈ (0 : size() − 1)•
      get(i) = old(get(i)));
    ensures get(size() − 1) = o;

  predicate bool valid()
  { return acc(n) * acc(items)*
    items ≠ null * acc_Elems(items)*
    0 ≤ n ≤ items.length; }

  pure int size()
    requires valid();
  { return n; }

  pure Object get(int index)
    requires valid();
    requires 0 ≤ index < size();
  { return items[index]; }
}
```

```
class Iterator {
  ArrayList list; int index;

  Iterator(List l)
    requires l ≠ null ∧ l.valid();
    ensures valid() ∧ getList() = l;
    ensures untouched(getList().valid());

  Object next()
    requires valid() ∧ hasNext();
    ensures valid();
    ensures getList() = old(getList());
    ensures untouched(getList().valid());

  predicate bool valid()
  { return acc(list) * acc(index)*
    list ≠ null ∧ list.valid()*
    0 ≤ index ≤ list.size(); }

  pure bool hasNext()
    requires valid();
  { return index < list.size(); }

  pure bool getList()
    requires valid();
  { return list; }
}
```

Fig. 12. The iterator design pattern

not modified. However, a mutator's precondition can include predicates that its implementation relies on to call pure methods. In other words, the mutator might require a predicate to be true only to read locations protected by the predicate. Since the predicate's body may not be visible to the mutator, the mutator's postcondition may not be able to enumerate all those locations to ensure their value did not change. Therefore, our implementation includes a special assertion: **untouched**(ϕ). The assertion states that (1) all locations in ϕ's required access set have the same value in the old and the new heap, (2) those locations are still accessible in the new state and (3) the swinging pivot property holds for $R(\phi)$.

As an example, consider the classes *ArrayList* and *Iterator* from Figure 12. The last postcondition of the method *next* allows the verifier to deduce that other iterators of the same list remain valid. The conjunct **acc**$_{Elems}(items)$ in *ArrayList*'s invariant is a special access assertion that gives permission to access the elements of the array. Also, note that it is ok for the invariant to read *items.length* without demanding access since *length* is immutable.

7   Related Work

The dynamic frames approach [1,2,3,4,5,6] solves the frame problem by explicitly annotating methods with effect annotations. More specifically, the contract of a mutator consists of a modifies clause and a "swinging pivot postcondition", while a pure method's contract includes a reads clause. The expressiveness of the dynamic frames approach stems from the fact that these effect annotations can mention arbitrary sets of memory locations. To support data abstraction, these location sets may be specified in terms of dynamic frames, i.e. pure methods or ghost fields that denote sets of locations. As an example, consider the dynamic frames version of the class *Cell* from Figure 7(a) (method *swap* not included) shown in Figure 13. *setX*'s contract includes a modifies clause indicating that all locations in the dynamic frame *footprint* can potentially be changed by the method. In addition, *setX*'s last postcondition encodes the swinging pivot property. The contract of each pure method includes a reads clause indicating that its return value only depends on locations in *footprint*(). All the latter effect annotations (indicated with the grey background) need to be provided by the developer, and must be checked explicitly by the verifier. In our approach on the other hand, none of the annotations in grey need to be provided or checked explicitly (they are free postconditions!). Instead, we only check at each field access that the corresponding location is accessible, which allows us to deduce an upper bound on the set of readable and writable locations. Since access assertions can typically be piggy-backed onto invariants, as shown in the predicate *valid* of class *ArrayList* of Figure 12, contracts do not need to include additional effect annotations. Moreover, as callers typically already have to establish a callee's invariant and the invariant is opaque to the caller, checking the access assertions inside the callee's precondition incurs no additional cost.

Our approach was heavily inspired by separation logic [16,15,25]. In particular, the access assertion **acc**$(e.f)$ is similar to separation logic points-to predicate

```
class Cell {
  int x;

  Cell()
    modifies ∅;
    ensures valid() ∧ getX() = 0;
    ensures fresh(footprint());
  { x := 0; }

  void setX(int v)
    requires valid();
    modifies footprint();
    ensures valid() ∧ getX() = v;
    ensures fresh(footprint()
      \old(footprint()));
  { x := v; }
```

```
  pure bool valid()
    reads footprint();
  { return true; }

  pure set footprint()
    reads footprint();
  { return { (this, x) }; }

  pure int getX()
    requires valid();
    reads footprint();
  { return x; }
}
```

Fig. 13. The class *Cell* with traditional dynamic frames annotations

$e.f \mapsto \_$ and Parkinson and Bierman's abstract predicates inspired our predicate pure methods. To the best of our knowledge, this is the first approach based on verification condition generation and automatic, first-order theorem proving that encodes separation logic's idea of deducing frame information from preconditions. One difference between separation logic and implicit dynamic frames is that we allow using heap-dependent expressions, in particular field reads and pure method invocations, inside assertions. Distefano and Parkinson [17] recently implemented a verifier for Java based on separation logic, called jStar. jStar relies on symbolic execution, while we use the more traditional combination of verification condition generation and automated theorem proving. The access set used in our verification conditions resembles the coloring of objects used in SLICK [26] for runtime checking of separation logic assertions.

In [27], the authors propose using data groups to specify side-effects. To ensure soundness, their approach imposes two methodological restrictions: the pivot uniqueness and owner exclusion restriction. Our approach imposes no such restrictions, and as a consequence it can handle programs that [27] cannot. For example, the former restriction rules out sharing of representation objects, as is the case in the iterator pattern.

In the universe type system [28] and the Boogie methodology [29], abstractions (pure methods, invariants or model fields) can depend on the fields of owned objects and the fields of peers (i.e. objects with the same owner as the receiver), provided the abstraction is visible to the peer. For example, the method *hasNext* of an iterator would have to be visible to the list class. Our approach has no such restriction.

The use of pure methods in specifications has been discussed extensively in the literature [11,12,13]. In particular, encoding pure methods as functions in the logic is a standard technique in verification. To the best of our knowledge, this is the first approach that derives an upper bound on the set of readable locations from preconditions of pure methods. Some authors propose broadening the range of admissible pure methods by allowing certain side-effects. We believe our approach can be extended to support such weakly pure methods.

Verification of Java-programs with JML-like [30] annotations has received considerable attention in the research community [30,31,32]. To the best of our knowledge, all the JML tools rely on explicit effect annotations for framing. We believe those tools might benefit from our approach to reduce the number of effect annotations.

Zee *et al.* [19] focus on verification of linked data structures. Their technique for dealing with such data structures inspired our specification of linked list. In particular, they use a ghost field to represent the set of all nodes in a list and rely on quantification over that set in the invariant to appropriately constrain the values and next pointers of the list.

A preliminary version of this work was presented at the 2008 FTFJP workshop [33]. This preliminary version already sparked the interest of other authors [34]. In particular, Leino and Müller combine implicit dynamic frames with fractional permissions and concurrency. However, they encode accessibility differently and do not show how to deal with data abstraction or inheritance in their encoding. Moreover, they provide no formal soundness proof.

8   Conclusion

In this paper, we improve upon the classical dynamic frames approach in two ways: (1) method contracts are more concise and (2) fewer proof obligations must be discharged by the verifier. We have proven soundness, implemented the approach in a verifier prototype and demonstrated its expressiveness by verifying several challenging examples from related work.

In the future, we plan to extend our approach to concurrent programs.

Acknowledgments

Jan Smans is a research assistant of the Fund for Scientific Research - Flanders (FWO). Bart Jacobs is a postdoctoral fellow of the Fund for Scientific Research - Flanders (FWO). This research is partially funded by the Interuniversity Attraction Poles Programme Belgian State, Belgian Science Policy.

References

1. Banerjee, A., Naumann, D.A., Rosenberg, S.: Regional logic for local reasoning about global invariants. In: Vitek, J. (ed.) ECOOP 2008. LNCS, vol. 5142, pp. 387–411. Springer, Heidelberg (2008)

2. Kassios, I.T.: Dynamic frames: Support for framing, dependencies and sharing without restrictions. In: Misra, J., Nipkow, T., Sekerinski, E. (eds.) FM 2006. LNCS, vol. 4085, pp. 268–283. Springer, Heidelberg (2006)
3. Banerjee, A., Barnett, M., Naumann, D.A.: Boogie meets regions: a verification experience report. In: Shankar, N., Woodcock, J. (eds.) VSTTE 2008. LNCS, vol. 5295, pp. 177–191. Springer, Heidelberg (2008)
4. Rustan, K., Leino, M.: Specification and verification of object-oriented software. In: Marktoberdorf International Summer School (2008)
5. Schoeller, B.: Making Classes Provable through Contracts, Models and Frames. PhD thesis, Departement Informatik ETH Zurich (2007)
6. Smans, J., Jacobs, B., Piessens, F., Schulte, W.: An automatic verifier for java-like programs based on dynamic frames. In: Fiadeiro, J.L., Inverardi, P. (eds.) FASE 2008. LNCS, vol. 4961, pp. 261–275. Springer, Heidelberg (2008)
7. Smans, J., Jacobs, B., Piessens, F.: Implicit dynamic frames: Combining dynamic frames and separation logic (soundness proof). Technical Report CW542, Katholieke Universiteit Leuven (2009)
8. Gotsman, A., Berdine, J., Cook, B., Rinetzky, N., Sagiv, M.: Local reasoning for storable locks and threads. In: Shao, Z. (ed.) APLAS 2007. LNCS, vol. 4807, pp. 19–37. Springer, Heidelberg (2007)
9. Haack, C., Hurlin, C.: Separation logic contracts for a java-like language with fork/join. In: Meseguer, J., Roşu, G. (eds.) AMAST 2008. LNCS, vol. 5140, pp. 199–215. Springer, Heidelberg (2008)
10. de Moura, L., Bjørner, N.: Z3: An efficient SMT solver. In: Ramakrishnan, C.R., Rehof, J. (eds.) TACAS 2008. LNCS, vol. 4963, pp. 337–340. Springer, Heidelberg (2008)
11. Rudich, A., Darvas, Á., Müller, P.: Checking well-formedness of pure-method specifications. In: Cuellar, J., Maibaum, T., Sere, K. (eds.) FM 2008. LNCS, vol. 5014, pp. 68–83. Springer, Heidelberg (2008)
12. Jacobs, B., Piessens, F.: Inspector methods for state abstraction. Journal of Object Technology 6(5) (2007)
13. Leino, K.R.M., Middelkoop, R.: Proving consistency of pure methods and model fields. In: FASE (2009)
14. Leavens, G.T.: JML's rich, inherited specifications for behavioral subtypes. In: Liu, Z., He, J. (eds.) ICFEM 2006. LNCS, vol. 4260, pp. 2–34. Springer, Heidelberg (2006)
15. Parkinson, M., Bierman, G.: Separation logic, abstraction and inheritance. In: POPL (2008)
16. Parkinson, M., Bierman, G.: Separation logic and abstraction. In: POPL (2005)
17. Distefano, D., Parkinson, M.: jStar: Towards Practical Verification for Java. In: OOPSLA (2008)
18. Parkinson, M.: Local Reasoning for Java. PhD thesis, University of Cambridge (2005)
19. Zee, K., Kuncak, V., Rinard, M.C.: Full functional verification of linked data structures. In: PLDI (2008)
20. Leino, K.R.M., Müller, P.: Object invariants in dynamic contexts. In: Odersky, M. (ed.) ECOOP 2004. LNCS, vol. 3086, pp. 491–515. Springer, Heidelberg (2004)
21. Barnett, M., Naumann, D.A.: Friends need a bit more: Maintaining invariants over shared state. In: Kozen, D. (ed.) MPC 2004. LNCS, vol. 3125, pp. 54–84. Springer, Heidelberg (2004)
22. Parkinson, M.: Class invariants: The end of the road? In: IWACO (2007)

23. Leino, K.R.M., Monahan, R.: Automatic verification of textbook programs that use comprehensions. In: FTFJP (2007)
24. Boyland, J.: Checking interference with fractional permissions. In: Cousot, R. (ed.) SAS 2003. LNCS, vol. 2694. Springer, Heidelberg (2003)
25. Reynolds, J.C.: Separation logic: A logic for shared mutable data structures. In: LICS (2002)
26. Nguyen, H.H., Kuncak, V., Chin, W.-N.: Runtime checking for separation logic. In: Logozzo, F., Peled, D.A., Zuck, L.D. (eds.) VMCAI 2008. LNCS, vol. 4905, pp. 203–217. Springer, Heidelberg (2008)
27. Leino, K.R.M., Poetzsch-Heffter, A., Zhou, Y.: Using data groups to specify and check side effects. In: PLDI (2002)
28. Müller, P.: Modular Specification and Verification of Object-Oriented Programs. PhD thesis, FernUniversität Hagen (2001)
29. Barnett, M., DeLine, R., Fähndrich, M., Leino, K.R.M., Schulte, W.: Verification of object-oriented programs with invariants. Journal of Object Technology 3(6) (2003)
30. Leavens, G.T., Baker, A.L., Ruby, C.: JML: A notation for detailed design (1999)
31. Beckert, B., Hähnle, R., Schmitt, P.H. (eds.): Verification of Object-Oriented Software. LNCS, vol. 4334. Springer, Heidelberg (2007)
32. Flanagan, C., Leino, K.R.M., Lillibridge, M., Nelson, G., Saxe, J.B., Stata, R.: Extended static checking for java. In: PLDI (2002)
33. Smans, J., Jacobs, B., Piessens, F.: Implicit dynamic frames. In: FTFJP (2008)
34. Leino, K.R.M., Müller, P.: A basis for verifying multi-threaded programs. In: Castagna, G. (ed.) ESOP 2009. LNCS, vol. 5502, pp. 378–393. Springer, Heidelberg (2009)

Fine-Grained Access Control with Object-Sensitive Roles*

Jeffrey Fischer, Daniel Marino, Rupak Majumdar, and Todd Millstein

Computer Science Department
University of California, Los Angeles
{fischer,dlmarino,rupak,todd}@cs.ucla.edu

Abstract. Role-based access control (RBAC) is a common paradigm to ensure that users have sufficient rights to perform various system operations. In many cases though, traditional RBAC does not easily express application-level security requirements. For instance, in a medical records system it is difficult to express that doctors should only update the records of *their own* patients. Further, traditional RBAC frameworks like Java's Enterprise Edition rely solely on dynamic checks, which makes application code fragile and difficult to ensure correct.

We introduce Object-sensitive RBAC (ORBAC), a generalized RBAC model for object-oriented languages. ORBAC resolves the expressiveness limitations of RBAC by allowing roles to be parameterized by properties of the business objects being manipulated. We formalize and prove sound a dependent type system that statically validates a program's conformance to an ORBAC policy. We have implemented our type system for Java and have used it to validate fine-grained access control in the OpenMRS medical records system.

1 Introduction

Controlled access to data and operations is a key ingredient of system security. *Role-based access control* (RBAC) [9] is an elegant and frequently-used access control mechanism in which a layer of *roles* interposes between users and access privileges. Roles represent responsibilities within a given organization. Authorizations for resource access are granted to roles rather than to individual users and users are given roles according to their functions in the organization. Users acquire all privileges associated with their roles. The intuition behind RBAC is that roles change infrequently within organizations relative to users, and so associating roles with access privileges ensures a stable and reliable access control policy.

As a concrete scenario, consider a hospital in which users can be doctors or patients. Doctors should be able to view and update their patients' records, and patients should be able to view (but not update) their own records. The RBAC way to represent this policy is to introduce two roles *Doctor* and *Patient*, where the *Doctor* role is allowed to both look up and modify patient records and the *Patient* role is allowed only to look up a medical record. Users are then classified as having the *Doctor* or *Patient* roles and

---

* This material is based upon work supported in part by the National Science Foundation under grants CCF-0545850 and CCF-0546170.

S. Drossopoulou (Ed.): ECOOP 2009, LNCS 5653, pp. 173–194, 2009.
© Springer-Verlag Berlin Heidelberg 2009

inherit the corresponding access privileges. RBAC is available in standard enterprise software development environments such as Java's Enterprise Edition (Java EE) [16], which insert runtime role checks whenever a privileged operation is invoked.

This simple example highlights two key limitations of the RBAC model and its usage today:

Lack of expressiveness. The role-based implementation described above does not capture all the constraints of our desired policy. The role-based implementation allows doctors to access and modify *any* patient's record, rather than only their own patients. Similarly, the role-based implementation allows patients to access any other patient's record. One way to solve the problem is to give each user his or her own role, but that would remove the advantages of using roles altogether! Simply put, the RBAC model is not fine-grained enough to express common access control requirements.

As a result of this limitation, programmers may be forced to insert manual access checks that augment the ones provided by systems like Java EE. This manual process is error prone, and it is difficult to ensure that the inserted checks properly enforce the desired policy. Alternatively, a system may only enforce a coarse-grained access control policy but additionally maintain a log of accesses to allow system administrators to detect finer-grained violations *a posteriori*.[1]

Lack of static checking. The reliance solely on dynamic checks in today's RBAC-based systems leads to several problems. First, it is difficult for programmers to ensure that their code properly respects the access control policy. Programmers must manually keep track of what roles must be held when each function is invoked, which depends on the set of privileged operations that can potentially be reached during the function's execution. If a function is ever executed in the wrong environment, the only feedback will be a runtime role failure when a privileged operation is invoked, making the problem difficult to diagnose and fix.

Further, because of the cost of runtime role checks, the checks are often hoisted from the privileged operations themselves to the "entry points" of an application. For example, after user authentication, a single role check could be used to determine which web page to display (e.g., one for doctors and another for patients). However, in this case the programmer must manually ensure the sufficiency of this check for all potentially reachable privileged operations downstream, or else the intended access policy can be subverted.

In this paper we address both of these limitations of the traditional RBAC model and associated frameworks. First, we extend the RBAC model to support fine-grained policies like that of our medical records example above. The basic idea is to allow roles and privileged operations to be *parameterized* by a set of *index* values, which intuitively are used to distinguish users of the same role from one another. A privileged operation can only be invoked if both the appropriate role is held and the role's index values matches the operation's index value.

---

[1] This was the case in two recent security breaches in the news: unauthorized access to Britney Spears' medical records by employees at UCLA medical center and to Barack Obama's cell phone records by employees at Verizon Wireless.

Our parameterized form of RBAC, which we call *Object-sensitive* RBAC (ORBAC), has a natural interpretation and design in the context of an object-oriented language (Sect. 2). Traditional RBAC policies control access at the level of a class. For example, with Java EE a method `getHistory` in a `Patient` class can be declared to require the caller to hold the *Patient* role. In other words, a user with the *Patient* role can invoke the `getHistory` method on *any* instance of `Patient`. In contrast, ORBAC supports access control at the level of an individual object. For example, `getHistory` can now be declared to require the caller to hold the *Patient<this.patientId>* role, where the `patientId` field of `Patient` stores a patient's unique identifier.

Second, we provide a type system that *statically* ensures that a program meets a specified ORBAC policy, providing early feedback on potential access control violations. We formalize our static checker for a core Java-like language (Sect. 3). Since types and roles are parameterized by program values (e.g., `this.patientId`), our static checker is a form of *dependent type system*.

We have implemented our static type system for ORBAC as a pluggable type system for Java in the JavaCOP framework [2]. As with frameworks like Java EE, we leverage Java's annotation syntax to specify the role requirements on method calls, but the Java-COP rules statically ensure the correctness and sufficiency of these annotations. We have augmented the OpenMRS medical records application [21] with a fine-grained access control policy using ORBAC and have used our JavaCOP checker to statically ensure the absence of authorization errors (Sect. 4).

2 Object-Sensitive RBAC

We now overview Object-sensitive RBAC and its associated static type system through a simple medical records example in Java, comparing an implementation using standard RBAC in Java EE with one using ORBAC.

2.1 Role-Based Access Control

An RBAC policy can be described as a tuple (U, R, P, PA, UA) consisting of a set of users U, a set of roles R, and a set of permissions P, together with relations $PA \subseteq P \times R$ giving permissions to roles and $UA \subseteq U \times R$ giving (sets of) roles to users [9]. An access of permission p by user u is *safe* if there exists a role $r \in R$ such that $(u, r) \in UA$ (user u has role r) and $(p, r) \in PA$ (role r has permission p).

Figure 1 shows how this model applies to a `Patient` class for which we wish to protect access. Our simplified class provides a factory method `getPatient`, which retrieves the specified patient from the database, and two instance methods: `getHistory` to return a history of the patient's visits and `addPrescription` to associate a new prescription with the patient.

We can group the users of our application into two groups: doctors and patients. In a typical medical records application, doctors can access the data of their patients and patients can access their own data (e.g., through a web self-service feature). In a standard RBAC model, we can represent these two groups with *Doctor* and *Patient* roles. Java EE supports the specification of an RBAC policy through the `@RolesAllowed` annotation [16]. This annotation is placed on a method definition to indicate the set of roles

```
public class Patient {
    private int patientId;

    /* factory method to retrieve a patient */
    @RolesAllowed({"Doctor", "Patient"})
    public static Patient getPatient(int pid) { ... }

    @RolesAllowed({"Doctor", "Patient"})
    public List<String> getHistory() { ... }

    @RolesAllowed({"Doctor"})
    public void addPrescription(String prescription) { ... }
    ...
}

public class PatientServlet {
    void displayHistory(int pid, Request req, Response resp) {
        if (req.isUserInRole("Patient")) {
            if (req.userId != pid) {
                throw new AccessError("Cannot access this patient");
            }
        }
        Patient p = Patient.getPatient(pid);
        List<String> hist = p.getHistory();
        ... code to write html representation of hist to resp ...
    }
}
```

Fig. 1. Standard RBAC version of doctor-patient example

that have permission to invoke the method. In Fig. 1 we have annotated the getPatient and getHistory methods to permit users with either the *Doctor* or *Patient* role to call these methods. On the other hand, the addPrescription method has been annotated to ensure that only doctors can add a prescription to a medical record.

The Java EE tools, and other application frameworks, enforce an RBAC policy dynamically by inserting runtime checks to verify that the user indeed has at least one of the specified roles when an annotated method is invoked. These checks are supported by standard infrastructure that performs user authentication and queries a database or configuration files to determine role membership.

For example, one might maintain a database of users and the roles granted to each user in an external LDAP server, where it can be managed by an administrator. The first time a user attempts to access a protected application resource (e.g., a web page), he is redirected to a login page. The user is *authenticated* by comparing his credentials against those stored in the LDAP server. The user's identity and roles are then stored in memory (e.g., in a session context) for use by dynamic access control checks.

Limitations of the RBAC model. Consider the PatientServlet class of Fig. 1, which accesses a patient's medical record. The displayHistory method writes an HTML representation of the patient history to a response stream. To do this, it obtains a `Patient` object using `Patient.getPatient` and then calls its `getHistory` method. Due to the annotations on these methods, the Java EE framework will insert dynamic checks on these calls to ensure that the user has either the *Doctor* or *Patient* role.

Unfortunately, these checks are not sufficient to enforce the desired access control policy. For example, the checks allow any patient to access any other patient's medical record! Therefore, programmers must manually insert additional checks, as shown at the beginning of the `displayHistory` method. A similar check may also be necessary to ensure that a doctor only accesses the records of her own patients. These kinds of checks are very fragile and error-prone — one can easily forget or improperly implement the check on some code path that leads to an invocation of a protected method, resulting in a serious security vulnerability.

Another limitation of traditional RBAC frameworks like Java EE is the reliance solely on dynamic checks, which makes it difficult to statically ensure that application code in fact respects the access policy of a protected class. For example, the programmer must ensure that the `displayHistory` method is never invoked by a user who does not have either the *Doctor* or *Patient* roles. This requirement is completely implicit and can only be understood by examining the implementation of `displayHistory` (and in general the implementations of methods transitively called by `displayHistory`). If a program disobeys the requirement, the programmer will receive no warning about the error, which will instead result in a dynamic access check failure. Such dynamic errors can be difficult to diagnose and fix. Further, if the error is not expected by the calling code, it may result in very unfriendly behavior from the user's perspective (e.g., a Java uncaught exception).

2.2   Object-Sensitive RBAC

ORBAC is a natural generalization of the formal model for RBAC defined above. With ORBAC, we define $UA \subseteq U \times R \times I$ to be a ternary relation, in which $UA(u,r,i)$ gives a user u an *indexed role* $(r,i) \in R \times I$, where I is a set of *index values*. Permissions are also indexed, and an access by user u to the *indexed permission* $(p,i) \in P \times I$ is *safe* if there exists a role $r \in R$ such that $(u,r,i) \in UA$ (user u has indexed role (r,i)) and $(p,r) \in PA$ (role r has permission p).

In Fig. 2, we reimplement our example using an ORBAC policy. We use two roles: *Patient* and *DoctorOf*, both of which are parameterized by a patient identifier (a Java integer). A patient is given the *Patient* role for his own identifier, allowing him to access his own record but not those of other patients. A doctor is given a *DoctorOf* role for each of her patients, allowing access to those patients but no others.

Conceptually, classes are now parameterized by a set of role indices, which are part of the class's static type, analogous with ordinary type parameters in Java. These role indices may then be used in role annotations within the class. While our formalism explicitly parameterizes classes in this way, as shown later, our implementation employs additional annotations to achieve the same effect without modifying Java's syntax. Class role parameters are modeled as public final fields of the class that are declared with the `@RoleParam` annotation. For example, the `@RoleParam` annotation on the `patientId` field of `Patient` indicates that this field will be used as an index in role annotations

```
public class Patient {
    @RoleParam public final int patientId;

    /* factory method to retrieve a patient */
    @Requires(roles={"DoctorOf", "Patient"}, params={"pid", "pid"})
    @Returns(roleparams="patientId", vals="pid")
    public static Patient getPatient(@RoleParam final int pid) { ... }


    @Requires(roles={"DoctorOf", "Patient"},
              params={"this.patientId", "this.patientId"})
    public List<String> getHistory() { ... }

    @Requires(roles="DoctorOf", params="this.patientId")
    public void addPrescription(String prescription) { ... }
    ...
}

public class PatientServlet {
    @Requires(roles={"DoctorOf", "Patient"},
              params={"pid", "pid"})
    void displayHistory(@RoleParam final int pid,
                        Request req, Response resp) {
        Patient p = Patient.getPatient(pid);
        List<String> hist = p.getHistory();
        ... code to write html representation of hist to resp ...
    }
}
```

Fig. 2. ORBAC version of doctor-patient example

within the class. The @RoleParam annotation can also be used on final formal parameters to achieve the effect of method parameterization, as seen on the pid parameter of the getPatient method.

Our @Requires annotation is analogous to Java EE's @RolesAllowed annotation, indicating the set of roles that have permission to invoke the annotated method. To stay within Java's metadata syntax we use two parallel arrays, roles and params, to specify the roles. For example, the @Requires annotation on getPatient in Fig. 2 allows only users with either the DoctorOf<pid> or Patient<pid> role to invoke the method, where pid is the patient identifier passed to the method. The @Requires annotations on the other methods are similar but they use the patientId field of the receiver as the role index to appropriately restrict access to that Patient object. Unlike the @RolesAllowed annotation, @Requires does not introduce a dynamic check. Instead, all calling code is statically checked to ensure at least one of the required roles is held.

The @Requires annotation is a form of method precondition for access control, while our @Returns annotation is a form of postcondition. For example, the @Returns annotation on getPatient asserts that the returned Patient object has a patientId role parameter field which is equal in value to the patient identifier passed to the method. Our static type system checks the body of the method to ensure the equality between the role parameters holds. The type system can then assume that this equality holds after a call to getPatient. In this way, we support modular typechecking for access control.

Resolving the limitations of the RBAC model. The PatientServlet class of Fig.2 illustrates how ORBAC resolves the limitations identified earlier of the RBAC model. Unlike the version in Fig. 1, no manual access checks are required. These checks are now part of the access control policy and are reflected in the @Requires annotations on the methods of Patient. Therefore, it is easy for both humans and tools to reason about a program's access control policy just based on program annotations, without examining the bodies of methods.

Further, access control is now statically checked, providing early feedback on possible violations. The displayHistory method is annotated with @Requires, restricting the method to users of the DoctorOf<pid> and Patient<pid> roles. With this annotation, the method's body can be statically guaranteed to obey the access control policy of Patient. The call to getPatient satisfies that method's @Requires clause, so the call typechecks. The getPatient method's @Returns clause indicates that the returned patient object's patientId parameter is equal to pid, which then allows the call to getHistory to typecheck successfully.

Subtle errors are now caught statically rather than dynamically. For example, if the call to getPatient in displayHistory passed a patient identifier other than pid, the call would correctly fail to typecheck, since a patient could be accessing the record of a patient other than himself. Also, the annotation on displayHistory in turn allows *its* callers to be modularly checked at compile time, ensuring that they have the necessary roles for the eventual access to Patient.

Incorporating dynamic checks. Our static type system makes explicit (via the @Requires annotation) the precondition that must be satisfied on entry to a method m to ensure that the access control policies of all methods transitively called by m will be obeyed. We insist that top-level methods (e.g., main for a standalone application or service for a servlet-based web application) have no @Requires annotation. That is, the application's external interface must have no precondition and thus can assume nothing about the roles that the current user holds. In order to allow an unprotected method to call a method protected by a @Requires annotation, our type system provides a flexible mechanism for interfacing with the program's authorization and authentication logic through the definition of *role predicate methods*. These methods are identified by the @RolePredicate annotation, which also indicates the role that the method tests for. Our static type system incorporates a simple form of flow sensitivity to ensure that method calls whose role requirements are not met by the current method's @Requires annotation occur only after appropriate dynamic checks succeed.

As a simple example, Fig. 3 contains a new version of PatientServlet's displayHistory method that performs the necessary role checks dynamically. The method no longer has a @Requires clause, but our static type system recognizes that the method is safe: the dynamic role checks ensure that the calls on the Patient class are only reached when the user has the appropriate *Patient* or *DoctorOf* role. Unlike the

```
public class Request {
    @RolePredicate(roles="Patient", params="pid")
    public boolean hasPatientRole(@RoleParam final int pid) { ... }

    @RolePredicate(roles="DoctorOf", params="pid")
    public boolean hasDoctorOfRole(@RoleParam final int pid) { ... }
}

public class PatientServlet {
    void displayHistory(@RoleParam final int pid,
                        Request req, Response resp) {
        if (!(req.hasPatientRole(pid) ||
              req.hasDoctorOfRole(pid)))
        {
            throw AccessError("Cannot access this patient");
        }
        Patient p = Patient.getPatient(pid);
        List<String> hist = p.getHistory();
        ... code to write html representation of hist to response ...
    }
}
```

Fig. 3. Use of role predicate methods in `displayHistory`

manual dynamic checks in the standard RBAC example shown earlier, these checks are statically ensured to be sufficient. Any errors in the dynamic checks in Fig. 3 (e.g., accidentally using a patient identifier other than `pid`) will be caught at compile time. Further, the dynamic checks can be placed as early as possible in the execution of an application without the risk that a check will be forgotten on some code path to a protected method.

The role predicate methods are treated as black boxes by our type system. They are free to consult a framework's security infrastructure or to implement authentication and authorization however the application designer sees fit. In fact, a particular predicate method could always return true and be used to achieve an effect similar to J2EE's `@RunAs` annotation, which allows components to be invoked with a security identity other than that of the currently authenticated user. In short, predicate methods provide a flexible mechanism for incorporating the runtime checks that are necessary to ascertain security credentials, and our type system ensures that their use is sufficient to satisfy declared method preconditions.

3   Formal Semantics

We have formalized the static and dynamic semantics of a small Java-like language in which ORBAC policies can be expressed and statically checked, and we have proven a type soundness theorem. Figure 4 shows the syntax of our language, a variant of Featherweight Java [14]. Our language models only the core features necessary to study the ORBAC model and its static type system formally. For this reason we have omitted inheritance, although our implementation handles it in the standard way, as described in Sect. 4.1.

ClassDecl	K	$::=$	class $C\langle\bar{r}\rangle\{\overline{T\,f};\overline{M}\}$
MethodDecl	M	$::=$	$\langle\bar{r}\rangle T\ m(\overline{T\ x})$ requires $\Phi\{e\}$
Exprs	e	$::=$	$x \mid e.f \mid e.m\langle\bar{\rho}\rangle(\bar{e}) \mid$ new $T(\bar{e}) \mid e \square e \mid$ use Φ in e
			$\mid$ pack $\rho, e \mid$ unpack e as r, x in e
Vals	v	$::=$	new $C\langle\bar{i}\rangle(\bar{v}) \mid$ pack i, v
Types	T	$::=$	$C\langle\bar{\rho}\rangle \mid \exists r.T$
RoleContext	Φ	$::=$	propositional formula over atoms in Q
Roles	Q	$::=$	$R\langle\rho\rangle$
Indices	ρ	$::=$	$r \mid i$
IndexVarContext	Δ	$::=$	$\cdot \mid \Delta, r$
VariableContext	Γ	$::=$	$\cdot \mid \Gamma, x : T$

Fig. 4. Grammar for the ORBAC language and type system. Metavariable C ranges over class names, m over method names, f over field names, R over role names, r and q over index variables, i and j over index constants, and x over program variables.

In our Java implementation of ORBAC described in the previous section, index variables are specially designated fields and method parameters. In our formal language, we explicitly parameterize classes, methods, and roles using the syntax of Java generics. For greater expressiveness, we include a form of existential types to classify expressions whose role indices are not statically known. This models, for example, the situation in our Java implementation where a method's return type is parameterized by an index, but no information about this index's value is provided (e.g., via a @Returns annotation). Expressions of existential type are introduced in our core language by a *pack* expression and eliminated by an *unpack* expression, in the usual way [24]. Our core language includes a use expression for dynamically changing the set of held roles, which is a simplified form of the role predicate methods in our Java implementation.[2] Finally, we include a non-deterministic choice construct ($e_1 \square e_2$) as a simple form of conditional.

Access protection is expressed in our Java implementation using a @Requires annotation indicating the set of roles that may invoke a method. This set can be viewed as a *disjunctive* predicate to be satisfied on entry to the method. We provide a more general mechanism in our formal language; methods include a requires clause which can specify an arbitrary propositional formula over roles as a precondition for invocation.

The typing rules for our formal language are shown in Fig. 5. Expressions are type-checked under three contexts: Φ is the role context represented as a propositional formula over roles, Δ keeps track of the index variables that are in scope, and Γ is the usual free-variable typing context. The rules depend on a set of simple well-formedness judgments, which ensure that all referenced index variables are in scope. For example, $\Delta \vdash T$ in the premise of T-NEW ensures that the type being constructed does not refer to any undefined index variables.

The most interesting rule is T-INVK which includes a logical entailment check in the premise that guarantees that the current role context Φ satisfies the callee's requires

---

[2] The use expression can be viewed as a role predicate method that always succeeds. The possibility of a predicate method returning false can be modeled by combining use with non-deterministic choice. For example, the expression (use Φ in e_1) $\square\ e_2$ models the situation where e_1 is executed if a dynamic check for predicate Φ succeeds, and otherwise e_2 is executed.

$\boxed{K \text{ ok}}$

$$\frac{\bar{r} \vdash \bar{T} \qquad \overline{M} \text{ ok in } C\langle\bar{r}\rangle}{\text{class } C\langle\bar{r}\rangle \{\overline{T f}; \overline{M}\} \text{ ok}} \qquad \text{(C-OK)}$$

$\boxed{M \text{ ok in } T}$

$$\frac{\bar{r},\bar{q} \vdash \bar{T} \qquad \bar{r},\bar{q} \vdash \bar{T} \qquad \bar{r},\bar{q} \vdash \Phi \qquad \Phi; \bar{r},\bar{q}; \bar{x} : \bar{T}, \text{this} : C\langle\bar{r}\rangle \vdash e : T}{\langle\bar{q}\rangle T \ m(\overline{T} \ \bar{x}) \text{ requires } \Phi\{e\} \text{ ok in } C\langle\bar{r}\rangle} \qquad \text{(M-OK)}$$

$\boxed{\Phi; \Delta; \Gamma \vdash e : T}$

$$\Phi; \Delta; \Gamma \vdash x : \Gamma(x) \qquad \text{(T-VAR)}$$

$$\frac{\Phi; \Delta; \Gamma \vdash e : T \qquad \text{fields}(T) = \overline{T} \ \bar{f}}{\Phi; \Delta; \Gamma \vdash e.f_i : T_i} \qquad \text{(T-FIELD)}$$

$$\frac{\text{fields}(T) = \overline{T} \ \bar{f} \qquad \Phi; \Delta; \Gamma \vdash \bar{e} : \overline{T} \qquad \Delta \vdash T}{\Phi; \Delta; \Gamma \vdash \text{new } T(\bar{e}) : T} \qquad \text{(T-NEW)}$$

$$\frac{\Phi; \Delta; \Gamma \vdash e_1 : T \qquad \Phi; \Delta; \Gamma \vdash e_2 : T}{\Phi; \Delta; \Gamma \vdash e_1 \ \square \ e_2 : T} \qquad \text{(T-CHOOSE)}$$

$$\frac{\Delta \vdash \rho \qquad \Phi; \Delta; \Gamma \vdash e : [r \mapsto \rho]T}{\Phi; \Delta; \Gamma \vdash \text{pack } \rho, e : \exists r.T} \qquad \text{(T-PACK)}$$

$$\frac{r \notin \Delta \qquad \Gamma(x) \text{ undefined}}{\Phi; \Delta; \Gamma \vdash e_1 : \exists q.S \qquad \Delta \vdash T \qquad \Phi; \Delta, r; \Gamma, x : [q \mapsto r]S \vdash e_2 : T}{\Phi; \Delta; \Gamma \vdash \text{unpack } e_1 \text{ as } r, x \text{ in } e_2 : T} \qquad \text{(T-UNPACK)}$$

$$\frac{\Delta \vdash \Phi' \qquad \Phi'; \Delta; \Gamma \vdash e : T}{\Phi; \Delta; \Gamma \vdash \text{use } \Phi' \text{ in } e : T} \qquad \text{(T-USE)}$$

$$\frac{\Phi; \Delta; \Gamma \vdash e : S \qquad \Delta \vdash \bar{\rho} \qquad \text{msig}(S, m) = \langle\bar{r}\rangle\overline{T} \xrightarrow{\Phi'} T}{\Phi; \Delta; \Gamma \vdash \bar{e} : [\bar{r} \mapsto \bar{\rho}]\overline{T} \qquad \Phi \Rightarrow [\bar{r} \mapsto \bar{\rho}]\Phi'}{\Phi; \Delta; \Gamma \vdash e.m\langle\bar{\rho}\rangle(\bar{e}) : [\bar{r} \mapsto \bar{\rho}]T} \qquad \text{(T-INVK)}$$

$\boxed{\text{fields}(T) = \overline{T} \ \bar{f}}$

$$\frac{\text{class } C\langle\bar{r}\rangle\{\overline{T f}; \overline{M}\} \in \text{ClassDecls}}{\text{fields}(C\langle\bar{\rho}\rangle) = \overline{[\bar{r} \mapsto \bar{\rho}]T} \ \bar{f}} \qquad \text{(FIELDS)}$$

$\boxed{\text{msig}(T, m) = \langle\bar{r}\rangle\overline{T} \xrightarrow{\Phi} T}$

$$\frac{\text{class } C\langle\bar{r}\rangle\{\overline{T f}; \overline{M}\} \in \text{ClassDecls} \qquad \langle\bar{q}\rangle S \ m(\overline{S} \ \bar{x}) \text{ requires } \Phi\{e\} \in \overline{M}}{\text{msig}(C\langle\bar{\rho}\rangle, m) = \langle\bar{q}\rangle[\bar{r} \mapsto \bar{\rho}]\overline{S} \xrightarrow{[\bar{r} \mapsto \bar{\rho}]\Phi} [\bar{r} \mapsto \bar{\rho}]S} \qquad \text{(M-SIG)}$$

Fig. 5. Typing rules for our formal language

precondition after appropriate substitution of actual indices for index parameters. Methods are typechecked modularly by rule M-OK which uses the Φ specified in a method's `requires` clause as the role context when checking the body.

Rules T-PACK and T-UNPACK are standard for existential type systems. The role variable r in rule T-UNPACK is required to be fresh, which matches the intuition that existential types classify objects with unknown index values. An unpacked role variable r can only be employed to satisfy role checks within a use statement that grants roles involving r. This is analogous to performing a dynamic role predicate check on an object with an unknown index in our Java implementation. Rules FIELDS and M-SIG only apply to class types, so an existential package must be unpacked before its fields and methods are accessed and values of existential type cannot be directly instantiated.

Evaluation Contexts E $::=$ $[\,]\mid E.f\mid E.m\langle\overline{\rho}\rangle(\overline{e})\mid v.m\langle\overline{\rho}\rangle(v,\dots,E,e,\dots,e)$
$\mid$ new $T(v,\dots,E,e,\dots,e)\mid$ pack $\rho,E\mid$ unpack E as r,x in e

$$\boxed{\Phi\vdash e\longrightarrow e}$$

$$\frac{\Phi\vdash e\longrightarrow e'}{\Phi\vdash E[e]\longrightarrow E[e']}\qquad\text{(E-CONGRUENCE)}$$

$$\frac{\text{fields}(T)=\overline{T}\ \overline{f}}{\Phi\vdash\text{new }T(\overline{v}).f_i\longrightarrow v_i}\qquad\text{(E-FIELD)}$$

$$\frac{\text{mbody}(T,m\langle\overline{\rho}\rangle)=(\overline{x},e)\qquad\text{msig}(T,m)=\langle\overline{\sigma}\rangle\overline{S}\xrightarrow{\Phi'}S\qquad\Phi\Rightarrow[\overline{\sigma}\mapsto\overline{\rho}]\Phi'}{\Phi\vdash\text{new }T(\overline{v}).m\langle\overline{\rho}\rangle(\overline{v'})\longrightarrow[\overline{x}\mapsto\overline{v'}][\text{this}\mapsto\text{new }T(\overline{v})]e}\qquad\text{(E-INVK)}$$

$$\Phi\vdash\text{unpack (pack }i,v\text{) as }r,x\text{ in }e\longrightarrow[x\mapsto v][r\mapsto i]e\qquad\text{(E-UNPACK)}$$

$$\Phi\vdash e_1\,\square\,e_2\longrightarrow e_1\qquad\text{(E-CHOOSE1)}$$

$$\Phi\vdash e_1\,\square\,e_2\longrightarrow e_2\qquad\text{(E-CHOOSE2)}$$

$$\frac{\Phi'\vdash e\longrightarrow e'}{\Phi\vdash\text{use }\Phi'\text{ in }e\longrightarrow\text{use }\Phi'\text{ in }e'}\qquad\text{(E-USE1)}$$

$$\Phi\vdash\text{use }\Phi'\text{ in }v\longrightarrow v\qquad\text{(E-USE2)}$$

$$\boxed{\text{mbody}(T,m\langle\overline{\rho}\rangle)=(\overline{x},e)}$$

$$\frac{\text{class }C\langle\overline{r}\rangle\{\overline{T}\,\overline{f};\overline{M}\}\in ClassDecls\qquad\langle\overline{q}\rangle S\ m(\overline{S}\ \overline{x})\text{ requires }\Phi\{e\}\in\overline{M}}{\text{mbody}(C\langle\overline{\rho}\rangle,m\langle\overline{\sigma}\rangle)=(\overline{x},[\overline{q}\mapsto\overline{\sigma}][\overline{r}\mapsto\overline{\rho}]e)}\qquad\text{(M-BODY)}$$

Fig. 6. Evaluation for our formal language

The dynamic semantics for our formal language is shown in Fig. 6. These evaluation rules perform role checks that model the dynamic checks on privileged operations used in most existing RBAC systems. Our type soundness result, however, establishes that such dynamic role checking is unnecessary for well-typed programs. Like the typing judgment, the evaluation judgment includes a role context. This context is used in rule E-INVK, which performs a dynamic entailment check that the current role context is sufficient to satisfy the method's declared precondition. Rule E-CONGRUENCE steps subexpressions according to the evaluation order established by the evaluation contexts, leaving the role context unchanged. Rule E-USE1 ignores the current role context and dynamically evaluates its subexpression under the specified context.

We have proven a type soundness theorem, which ensures that well-typed programs cannot fail dynamic role entailment checks. The theorem is proven using the standard progress and preservation style [30]. Full details are given in the accompanying technical report [10]; we provide statements of the key results here:

Lemma 1 (Progress). *If* $\Phi; \cdot; \cdot \vdash e : T$, *then either e is a value or there is an expression e' such that* $\Phi' \vdash e \longrightarrow e'$ *for any Φ' where* $\Phi' \Rightarrow \Phi$.

Lemma 2 (Preservation). *If* $\Phi; \Delta; \Gamma \vdash e : T$ *and* $\Phi \vdash e \longrightarrow e'$, *then* $\Phi; \Delta; \Gamma \vdash e' : T$.

These lemmas imply a type soundness theorem as well as the key corollary about role checking:

Theorem 1 (Type Soundness). *If* $\Phi; \cdot; \cdot \vdash e : T$, *then e will not get stuck when evaluated under any role context Φ' such that* $\Phi' \Rightarrow \Phi$.

Corollary 1 (Dynamic Entailment Checks Unnecessary). *Well-typed programs cannot fail dynamic role entailment checks.*

4   Experience: The OpenMRS Case Study

We implemented our ORBAC checker as an extension to Java in the JavaCOP pluggable types framework [2]. To evaluate our approach, we took OpenMRS [21], an existing open source medical records application, and retrofitted it to use an ORBAC policy to protect access to patient data. OpenMRS is implemented in Java using the Spring application framework [28], which is a commonly used alternative to Java EE. Spring provides several useful modules, including an *inversion of control* container, an aspect-oriented programming framework, and integration with the Hibernate framework for persistence [13]. Spring's access control framework supports standard RBAC policies, which can be configured by an administrator.

4.1   Implementation of ORBAC Using JavaCOP

Our checker implementation makes use of the annotations @Requires, @Returns, and @RolePredicate that were introduced in Sect. 2.2.

Several practical issues that are not modeled in the formalism are addressed in our implementation. Class inheritance is supported. The checker enforces the standard requirements on method overriding: an overriding method must have a compatible, possibly weaker precondition (@Requires annotation) and a compatible, possibly stronger postcondition (@Returns clause). Methods without a @Requires annotation are considered to have the precondition true, so they can be invoked in any context. Hence, methods that override such methods are required to not have a @Requires annotation.

While our formalism uses arbitrary propositional formulas for requires clauses, our Java implementation restricts @Requires and @RolePredicate annotations to be disjunctions of roles. This means that role contexts are formulas in conjunctive normal form (CNF); the @Requires clause of a method provides the first conjunct and dynamic role predicate checks add conjuncts to the context. This simplifies typechecking by allowing us to perform a series of subset checks rather than checking arbitrary logical implication.

We make use of JavaCOP's support for flow-sensitive reasoning [17] to implement the static updating of the role context based on role predicate method invocations. Java-COP's flow framework properly handles Java's complex control flow, including exceptional control flow. As a result, our checker can statically validate the style of dynamic checks used in Fig. 3, as well as many other styles.

The implementation of the checker was fairly straightforward. It contains 174 lines of code in the declarative JavaCOP language and about 450 lines of Java code defining the flow analysis and some supporting functions and data structures.

4.2 OpenMRS Architecture

The OpenMRS source contains over 160,000 lines of code, spread over 633 files, not including the frameworks and other infrastructure that it depends upon. Figure 7 shows a simplified UML diagram of some key patient-related classes defined by OpenMRS. Patients are represented by the Patient class. Each patient has a number of associated *encounters*, each representing a visit to the hospital or clinic. Each encounter may contain multiple *observations* (represented by the Obs class) which are used for recording test results and patient vitals.

The OpenMRS application interacts with the client via Java servlets. In Fig. 7, we show the two primary servlets for patients, PatientDashBoardController, which renders to HTML a summary of a patient's data, and PatientFormController, which accepts a new or updated patient and saves it to the database. These servlets obtain patient records from the database via classes implementing the PatientService interface, which defines methods for creating, querying, updating, and voiding patients (as well as many others not shown here). The implementation of PatientService is provided by PatientServiceImpl, which in turn uses a class implementing PatientDAO (DAO stands for "Data Access Object"). The implementation of PatientDAO is provided by HibernatePatientDAO, which interacts with the Hibernate framework and isolates Hibernate-specific code.

The patient service implementation PatientServiceImpl is made available to servlets via the Context class. This class provides static methods for accessing global

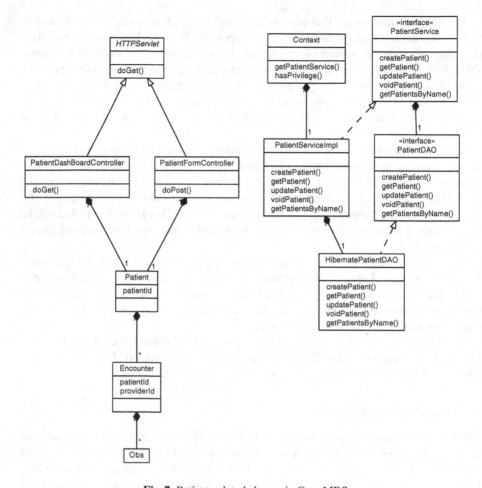

Fig. 7. Patient-related classes in OpenMRS

system state (e.g., mappings between "service" interfaces and their configured implementations) as well as state specific to a given user (e.g., a user id and permissions).

OpenMRS access control framework. The implementation of RBAC in OpenMRS adds a level of indirection to the standard RBAC model: methods are protected by assigning required *privileges* through annotations in the code, *roles* are defined as mappings from role names to sets of privileges, and *users* are assigned sets of roles. The role-privilege mapping and the user-role mapping are maintained in the database, permitting them to be changed by an administrator at runtime.

Access policies are configurable in OpenMRS, but the limitations of the RBAC model make it impossible to configure a policy that permits access to a specific object while preventing access to other objects of the same class. In other words, only coarse-grained policies, which restrict access at the level of classes rather than objects, are supported. For example, in one reasonable policy within these restrictions, patients would have no access to the system at all and every healthcare provider would have read-write access to all patients.

Access control requirements are defined using method annotations representing the set of privileges needed to access the method. These annotations are converted to dynamic checks by Spring's aspect-oriented programming framework. For patient data, these annotations are made on the `PatientService` class. There are separate privileges defined for viewing, creating, updating, and deleting patients. The administrator must then assign these privileges to RBAC roles.

Each servlet in OpenMRS may (indirectly) invoke many dynamic privilege checks inserted by Spring. Unfortunately, there is no easy way to tell which privileges are required by a servlet. Changes to the implementation of a servlet may inadvertently change the set of privileges checked in a given situation, leading to runtime errors, which are displayed as an HTML rendering of a Java stack trace.

Privileges may be explicitly checked in the code by calling the `hasPrivilege` method on the `Context` class. These explicit checks are used in situations where authorization occurs in a conditionally executed block or where an implementation needs additional authorization requirements beyond those specified for an interface.

4.3   An ORBAC Policy for OpenMRS

With ORBAC we were able to create a new fine-grained access control policy for patient objects, with three roles:

1. Users with the *Supervisor* role have read and write access to all patients. This role is unparameterized — it behaves as a standard RBAC role.
2. Users with the *ProviderFor* role (e.g., doctors) have read and write access to their patients, but not to other patients. This role is parameterized by the patient's id.
3. Users with the *Patient* role have read access to their own patient record, but not to those of other patients. This role is parameterized by the patient's id.

We only changed the access policies for objects related to patients; other objects in the system are protected by OpenMRS's original RBAC policy.

Example 1. Figure 8 shows an example set of user-to-role assignments and the resulting access rights of these users. There are three patients in the system: Britney, Carol, and

User	Assigned roles	Patients allowed read-only access	Patients allowed read-write access	Patients denied access
Alice	Supervisor		Britney, Carol, Dave	
Bob	ProviderFor<Carol>		Carol	Britney, Dave
Britney	Patient<Britney>	Britney		Carol, Dave
Carol	Patient<Carol>, ProviderFor<Britney>	Carol	Britney	Dave
Dave	Patient<Dave>	Dave		Britney, Carol

Fig. 8. Example of access rights for OpenMRS extended with ORBAC

Dave. All three have a *Patient* role parameterized by their own id and can thus see, but not modify, their own patient records. Alice holds the unparameterized *Supervisor* role and has read-write access to the three patients. Bob is a provider for Carol, and thus has read-write access to her record, but no access to the other patients. Carol is both a provider for Britney and a patient herself. She does not have read-write access to her own record.   □

The mechanism for assigning the *ProviderFor* role turned out to be an interesting design consideration. The OpenMRS database schema and object model implement a one-to-many doctor-patient relationship, so one might consider using the presence of this relationship to grant *ProviderFor* status. However, in a real healthcare environment, multiple doctors and nurses might need to interact with a patient and thus see the patient's record. We chose to base the granting of the *ProviderFor* role on whether there is an encounter record associated with the patient and the provider. This can be determined by an SQL query against the `Encounter` table, the results of which can then be cached to speed up future checks.

The presumed workflow for granting access rights to a patient's data are as follows:

1. When a patient enters the clinic, a user with *Supervisor* access looks up the patient's record, or creates it if necessary.
2. The *Supervisor* selects a doctor to see the patient and then creates an encounter record referencing the patient and the doctor.
3. The doctor now has the *ProviderFor* role for this patient and can update the patient record.

Thus, all the providers who have participated in a patient's care can access the patient record. Other approaches to granting access rights to patient data are possible and enforceable with our pluggable type system.

Implementing the ORBAC policy. To implement our fine-grained access control policy in OpenMRS, we first made the `patientId` field of the `Patient` class a role parameter via the `@RoleParam` annotation. We then replaced the original privilege annotations on the `PatientService` interface with `@Requires` annotations. For example, the declaration of the `getPatient` method is now:

```
@Requires(roles={"ProviderFor", "Patient", "Supervisor"},
          params={"patientId", "patientId", ""})
public Patient getPatient(@RoleParam final Integer patientId)
    throws APIException;
```

This method fetches the patient identified by `patientId` from the database. To call it, the caller must possess either the *ProviderFor*, *Patient*, or *Supervisor* roles. These first two roles are parameterized by the specific `patientId`, while *Supervisor* is unparameterized.

To provide dynamic role checks, we first created three new privileges in Open-MRS, corresponding to our three roles: ORBAC_PATIENT, ORBAC_PROVIDER, and ORBAC_SUPERVISOR. Each of these privileges has an associated OpenMRS role, which can then be assigned to users. We added role predicate methods for each of our ORBAC roles to the Context class. For example, the role predicate for the *Patient* role is defined as follows:

```
@RolePredicate(roles="Patient", params="patientId") public static
boolean hasPatientRole(
    @RoleParam final Integer patientId) {
    User user = Context.getAuthenticatedUser();
    if (user==null || !Context.hasPrivilege("ORBAC_PATIENT"))
        return false;
    else return user.getUserId().equals(patientId);
}
```

The method checks if the user has the OpenMRS privilege ORBAC_PATIENT and if so it compares the user's identifier to the specified patient identifier.

Checking the OpenMRS source code. To ensure that the required roles for accessing patients were enforced, we ran our pluggable type system on the entire OpenMRS code base (a total of 633 Java files). The checking takes 11 seconds on a MacBook Pro with a 2.4 GHz Intel Core 2 Duo processor and 2 GB of memory.

We used our type checker in an iterative manner in order to add necessary annotations and dynamic checks until all type errors were resolved. In general we used @Requires annotations on methods to remove static type errors. As mentioned in Sect. 2.2, we cannot place a @Requires annotation on the top-level methods in servlets through which all user requests must pass. This is the natural place to use predicate methods that perform dynamic security credential checks to satisfy the type checker.

In total, we made changes to 81 (13%) of the files. A total of 298 @Requires annotations and 151 dynamic checks were added. Since the pluggable type system successfully checks the code, the dynamic role checks that occur within servlet code are guaranteed to be sufficient on all paths to the protected methods of PatientServiceImpl.

The count of dynamic checks represents individual role predicate calls (hasPatientRole, hasProviderRole, or hasSupervisorRole). In many cases, these predicates are used together in a single if statement. In general, dynamic checks for patient reads use a disjunction of all three predicates, checks for patient writes use a disjunction of the provider and supervisor predicates, and checks for servlets that generate reports (which access many patients) use the supervisor predicate alone.

4.4 Limitations and Tradeoffs

Final fields and role parameters In the ORBAC example of Sect. 2, role parameter fields are declared as final. Our type system requires that role parameters do not change. If role parameters can change, the type system becomes unsound, potentially allowing prohibited calls.

Unfortunately, Hibernate requires that persisted objects have default constructors and non-final id fields. These id fields are frequently the same fields used as role parameters (e.g., the patientId of class Patient). To address this, we permit role parameter fields to be non-final but include checks in our pluggable type system to ensure that role parameter fields are not assigned outside of constructors. We also use the JavaCOP flow framework to ensure that every constructor initializes all role parameter fields.

ProviderFor vs. Provider roles. In our case study, we chose to define for doctors a *ProviderFor* role which is parameterized by a patient id. This approach is straightforward and easily handles the case where a patient has multiple providers. However, it is problematic when representing collections. For example, the getPatientsByName method of PatientService takes a partial patient name and returns a Collection<Patient> of matching patients. The names of these patients are then displayed to the user, who can drill down to a specific patient record. We changed this method to return only those patients accessible to the user. Unfortunately, there is no way to represent the precise element type of this collection in our type system, since each patient has a different id. Therefore, we use a collection object with no role parameter. This lack of static validation cannot cause a security violation, but it does necessitate the use of dynamic role predicate checks in order to fetch the actual Patient object when the provider "drills down."

An alternative would be to instead use a *Provider* role, which is parameterized by the doctor's user id. Thus, the patients returned by getPatientsByName would all be parameterized by the same value, allowing easier representation in our type system.

This alternative approach is not without disadvantages. In the most obvious implementation of this policy, the Patient object would be parameterized by two fields: patientId and providerId. However, this does not work well if a patient can have multiple providers. One work-around is to change the getPatient method for PatientServiceImpl to populate the providerId with the current user's id, if the user is in the set of providers for the patient.

Access control for encounters and observations. In our current implementation, accesses to objects logically contained within patients, such as encounters and observations, are not protected by @Requires annotations. In theory, this could lead to an unsoundness in the security policy, although, in practice, the OpenMRS navigation design prevents users from accessing these sub-objects without first accessing the parent Patient instance. To be sure there is no violation, we could add @Requires annotations to encounters and observations. Alternatively, we could use a form of *object ownership* [7] to verify that these objects are in fact logically contained within their associated patient objects.

5   Related Work

Role-based access control [9] has been used successfully in many systems and is now a NIST standard. Several approaches have been explored by researchers to extend declarative access control models like RBAC to represent and enforce instance-level policies. However, these approaches have employed only dynamic enforcement of such policies.

The emphasis in some prior work [1,15,4] is on clarifying the formal semantics of a parameterized access control model. For example, Abdallah and Khayat [1] provide a set-theoretic semantics in a formal specification language, and Barth *et al.* [4] briefly mentions a parameterized role extension to a temporal logic for reasoning about privacy. We adapt a variant of these generalized RBAC models to an object-oriented language, provide a static type system for enforcing access control, and have implemented and validated the approach in Java.

The Resource Access Decision facility (RAD) [3] extends RBAC-based access control policies with access checks based on user relationships. Policies may be configured to require certain relationship predicates to be true when an activated role is used to access an object. For example, a rule might state that doctors can only access the records of patients to which they have an *attending* relationship. However, these relationship predicates are not defined in a declarative manner — a CORBA interface must be implemented in the application to evaluate each predicate. This precludes any use of a static analysis based on the relationships required by a policy.

The database community has also addressed the enforcement of instance-level access control policies (e.g., [12,26,20,22]). In particular, [12] extends RBAC with parameterized *role templates*, where the parameters of a template refer to database columns or constants and serve a similar function as our role parameters. Implementing fine-grained access control policies at the database level has two key advantages: one can define policies directly on the data to be protected and the filtering of records can be integrated with query optimization. However, database-level access control also has several disadvantages. First, it would be very difficult to statically determine the code paths in an application which lead to a given dynamically-generated SQL statement, which would be necessary to statically detect access violations. Second, developers may also want to enforce restrictions on function invocations in the application, which would require a separate mechanism from the database-level access control policies. Third, most modern application deployments store the mapping of users to roles in an external repository (e.g., an LDAP server). Information stored in such a repository might not be available to the database query engine.

Instance-level access control policies can also be defined using domain-specific languages. For example, the XAML standard [8] permits the definition of access policies for web services which reference data in individual request messages. Cassandra [6,5] extends Datalog to express constraint rules referencing parameterized RBAC-style roles. These approaches are appropriate for enforcing access control *between* applications but are not so easily applied *within* an application. To (dynamically) enforce such policies within an application, one would need to map the entities referenced by the policy to actual object instances. In addition, the more expressive semantics of these policies would complicate static analysis.

We enforce access control policies through explicit dynamic and static checks added to the codebase through annotations. One could also write policies in a separate language outside the codebase and automatically insert them into the code at compile time or runtime (via bytecode manipulation). This approach has been explored [23], with policies expressed as *access constraint* rules — boolean expressions over an object and its relationships. Our ORBAC annotations could be translated to access constraint rules.

Our approach is orthogonal to *Hierarchical RBAC* [27], where a partial order is defined on roles. If a role R_1 is greater than a role R_2 in this hierarchy, then any user holding R_1 also holds the permissions associated with R_2. This hierarchy is statically defined and not dependent on individual object instances, so it still only supports coarse-grained policies. For example, if a *Physician* role dominates a *Healthcare-Provider* role in the hierarchy, assigning two users to *Physician* roles gives them the exact same permissions, which are a superset of the permissions granted to users assigned the

Healthcare-Provider role. One could extend our ORBAC model to support hierarchies by including a partial order on (parameterized) roles.

There has also been work on static analysis for RBAC systems. Closest to our work is that of Pistoia *et al.* on static analysis of security policies in Java EE [25]. They employ an interprocedural analysis to identify RBAC policies that are *insufficient* (i.e., can lead to runtime authorization failures), *redundant* (i.e., grants more roles than necessary), and *subversive* (i.e., allows bypassing access control requirements). Our static type system prevents the first and third of these errors, but for the more expressive ORBAC model. Using a type system as opposed to an interprocedural analysis allows us to provide modular guarantees about proper access control on each function in a scalable manner, at the expense of requiring user annotations.

Researchers have explored many forms of dependent type systems [18], whereby types depend on program values. The closest to our work is the notion of *constrained types* in the X10 programming language [19]. In X10, classes are explicitly parameterized by a set of *properties*, which are treated within the class as public final fields. Our design is similar but uses annotations to implicitly parameterize a class by a designated set of fields without modifying Java's syntax. Similarly, an X10 type has the form C{e}, where C is a class name and e is a constraint on the class's properties, while we use annotations to specify constraints. In our type system, these constraints are always simple equality constraints. The X10 compiler has built-in support for checking equality constraints, but it also allows users to plug in solvers for other constraints.

The static checking of roles in our type system has no analogue in X10's constrained types. This part of our type system is most closely related to *type-and-effect* systems [11], which statically track a set of computational effects. The computational effects we track are the privileged operations that a function may invoke, which determine the roles that are allowed to invoke the function. Roles are also similar to *capabilities* [29], which are a dual to effects. However, roles are disjunctive rather than conjunctive: it is sufficient for an execution to hold *any* of a function's roles, while capability systems require all capabilities to be held to ensure proper execution.

6   Conclusions

We have presented the design, implementation, formalization, and practical validation of Object-sensitive RBAC (ORBAC), a generalization of the widely used RBAC model for access control. ORBAC allows different instances of the same class to be distinguished by a designated set of object properties. These properties can then be used to parameterize roles thereby supporting fine-grained access policies that are useful in common scenarios but hard to implement in traditional RBAC. We have implemented a novel static type system that employs forms of dependent types and flow sensitivity to provide sound yet precise reasoning about an application's adherence to an ORBAC policy. Our OpenMRS case study illustrates the practical utility of the ORBAC model and our type system in a realistic setting.

We have focused on a useful but restricted version of ORBAC. This model can be naturally extended to support a more expressive policy language. Our current JavaCop-based implementation could be enhanced to support role predicates as arbitrary propositional formulas as well as multiple parameters per role, both of which are in our formalization. Useful extensions to the type system presented here include the addition of a partial order on roles, a richer constraint language for index values, and static tracking of the temporal order of privileged operations. Finally, we would like to investigate both local and global type inference of object-sensitive roles.

References

1. Abdallah, A.E., Khayat, E.J.: A formal model for parameterized role-based access control. In: Dimitrakos, T., Martinelli, F. (eds.) Formal Aspects in Security and Trust, pp. 233–246. Springer, Heidelberg (2004)
2. Andreae, C., Noble, J., Markstrum, S., Millstein, T.: A framework for implementing pluggable type systems. In: OOPSLA 2006: Proceedings of the 21st annual ACM SIGPLAN Conference on Object-Oriented Programming Systems, Languages, and Applications, pp. 57–74. ACM Press, New York (2006)
3. Barkley, J., Beznosov, K., Uppal, J.: Supporting relationships in access control using role based access control. In: RBAC 1999: Proceedings of the fourth ACM workshop on Role-based access control, pp. 55–65. ACM, New York (1999)
4. Barth, A., Mitchell, J., Datta, A., Sundaram, S.: Privacy and utility in business processes. In: CSF 2007, pp. 279–294. IEEE Computer Society Press, Los Alamitos (2007)
5. Becker, M.: Information governance in nhs's npfit: A case for policy specification. International Journal of Medical Informatics (IJMI) 76(5-6) (2007)
6. Becker, M., Sewell, P.: Cassandra: Distributed access control policies with tunable expressiveness. In: POLICY 2004, pp. 159–168 (2004)
7. Clarke, D.G., Potter, J.M., Noble, J.: Ownership types for flexible alias protection. In: Proceedings of the 13th ACM SIGPLAN conference on Object-oriented programming, systems, languages, and applications, pp. 48–64. ACM Press, New York (1998)
8. eXtensible Access Control Markup Language (XACML) Version 2.03. OASIS Standard (February 2005)
9. Ferraiolo, D., Kuhn, R.: Role-based access control. In: 15th National Computer Security Conference (1992)
10. Fischer, J., Marino, D., Majumdar, R., Millstein, T.: Fine-grained access control with object-sensitive roles. Technical Report CSD-TR-090010, UCLA Comp. Sci. Dept. (2009)
11. Gifford, D.K., Lucassen, J.M.: Integrating functional and imperative programming. In: LFP 1986: Proceedings of the 1986 ACM Conference on LISP and Functional Programming, pp. 28–38. ACM Press, New York (1986)
12. Giuri, L., Iglio, P.: Role templates for content-based access control. In: RBAC 1997: Proceedings of the second ACM workshop on Role-based access control, pp. 153–159. ACM Press, New York (1997)
13. Hibernate home page, http://www.hibernate.org
14. Igarashi, A., Pierce, B.C., Wadler, P.: Featherweight Java: a minimal core calculus for Java and GJ. ACM Transactions on Programming Languages and Systems 23(3), 396–450 (2001)
15. Jaeger, T., Michailidis, T., Rada, R.: Access control in a virtual university. In: WETICE 1999: Proceedings of the 8th Workshop on Enabling Technologies on Infrastructure for Collaborative Enterprises, Washington, DC, USA, pp. 135–140. IEEE Computer Society Press, Los Alamitos (1999)
16. Java Platform, Enterprise Edition home page, http://java.sun.com/javaee
17. Markstrum, S., Marino, D., Esquivel, M., Millstein, T.: Practical enforcement and testing of pluggable type systems. Technical Report CSD-TR-080013, UCLA Comp. Sci. Dept. (2008)

194   J. Fischer et al.

18. Martin-Löf, P.: Constructive mathematics and computer programming. In: Sixth International Congress for Logic, Methodology, and Philosophy of Science, pp. 153–175. North-Holland, Amsterdam (1982)
19. Nystrom, N., Saraswat, V., Palsberg, J., Grothoff, C.: Constrained types for object-oriented languages. In: OOPSLA 2008: Proceedings of the 23rd ACM SIGPLAN Conference on Object Oriented Programming Systems Languages and Applications, pp. 457–474. ACM Press, New York (2008)
20. Olson, L., Gunter, C., Madhusudan, P.: A formal framework for reflective database access control policies. In: CCS 2008: Proceedings of the 15th ACM conference on Computer and communications security, pp. 289–298. ACM Press, New York (2008)
21. OpenMRS home page, http://openmrs.org
22. Oracle 11ᵍ Virtual Private Database (2009), http://www.oracle.com/technology/deploy/security/database-security/virtual-private-database/index.html
23. Pandey, R., Hashii, B.: Providing fine-grained access control for Java programs. In: Guerraoui, R. (ed.) ECOOP 1999. LNCS, vol. 1628, pp. 668–692. Springer, Heidelberg (1999)
24. Pierce, B.C.: Types and Programming Languages. The MIT Press, Cambridge (2002)
25. Pistoia, M., Fink, S., Flynn, R., Yahav, E.: When role models have flaws: Static validation of enterprise security policies. In: ICSE 2007, pp. 478–488. IEEE, Los Alamitos (2007)
26. Rizvi, S., Mendelzon, A., Sudarshan, S., Roy, P.: Extending query rewriting techniques for fine-grained access control. In: SIGMOD 2004: Proceedings of the 2004 ACM SIGMOD international conference on Management of data, pp. 551–562. ACM Press, New York (2004)
27. Sandhu, R., Coyne, E., Feinstein, H., Youman, C.: Role-based access control models. IEEE Computer 29(2), 38–47 (1996)
28. Spring Application Framework home page, http://www.springsource.org
29. Walker, D., Crary, K., Morrisett, G.: Typed memory management via static capabilities. ACM Trans. Program. Lang. Syst. 22(4), 701–771 (2000)
30. Wright, A.K., Felleisen, M.: A syntactic approach to type soundness. Information and Computation 115(1), 38–94 (1994)

Practical API Protocol Checking
with Access Permissions

Kevin Bierhoff, Nels E. Beckman, and Jonathan Aldrich

Institute for Software Research, Carnegie Mellon University
5000 Forbes Avenue, Pittsburgh, PA 15213, USA
{kevin.bierhoff,nbeckman,jonathan.aldrich}@cs.cmu.edu

Abstract. Reusable APIs often define usage protocols. We previously
developed a sound modular type system that checks compliance with
typestate-based protocols while affording a great deal of aliasing flexibility. We also developed Plural, a prototype tool that embodies our approach as an automated static analysis and includes several extensions
we found useful in practice. This paper evaluates our approach along the
following dimensions: (1) We report on experience in specifying relevant
usage rules for a large Java standard API with our approach. We also
specify several other Java APIs and identify recurring patterns. (2) We
summarize two case studies in verifying third-party open-source code
bases with few false positives using our tool. We discuss how tool shortcomings can be addressed either with code refactorings or extensions to
the tool itself. These results indicate that our approach can be used to
specify and enforce real API protocols in practice.

1   Introduction

Reusable APIs often define usage protocols. Loosely speaking, usage protocols
are constraints on the order in which events are allowed to occur. For example,
a database connection can only be used to execute SQL commands until it is
closed. It has been a long-standing research challenge to ensure *statically* (before
a program ever runs) that API protocols are followed in client programs using
an API. An often overlooked but related problem is ensuring that the protocol
being checked is consistent with the actual implementation of that protocol. Both
of these challenges are complicated by object *aliasing* (objects being referenced
and possibly updated from multiple places)—the hallmark feature of imperative
languages like C and Java.

We previously developed a *sound* (no false negatives) and *modular* (each
method checked separately) type system that checks compliance with typestate-
based protocols while affording a great deal of aliasing flexibility [7,3]. *Typestates* [33] allow specifying usage protocols as finite-state machines. Our approach
tracks *access permissions*, which combine typestate and aliasing information,
and was proven sound for core single-threaded [7] and multi-threaded [3] object-
oriented calculi. Unlike previous approaches, access permissions do *not* require

S. Drossopoulou (Ed.): ECOOP 2009, LNCS 5653, pp. 195–219, 2009.

precise tracking of all object aliases (e.g. [15,17]) or impose an ownership discipline on the heap (e.g. [2]).

We have implemented Plural, a tool that embodies our approach as an automated static analysis [9] and includes several extensions found to be useful in practice (section 2.2).[1] Plural requires developer-provided annotations on methods and classes, specifically on the APIs to be checked, although others may be necessary.

While previous modular protocol checking approaches have been proven sound and shown to work on well-known examples such as file access protocols, these approaches generally have not been evaluated on real APIs or third-party code bases. (Notable exceptions include Vault [15] and Fugue [17,16]). The general lack of evaluation begs important questions: Can these approaches accurately specify protocols that occur in practice? Can they verify their use and implementation without an unreasonable number of false-positives? And can they do so at a low computational cost and without imposing too great of an annotation burden?

In this paper we attempt to answer these questions. Contributions of this paper include the following:

- **Specification.** We report on experience in specifying relevant usage rules for 440 methods defined in the Java Database Connectivity (JDBC) API for relational database access with our approach (section 3).[2] To our knowledge, this is the largest case study available in the literature that evaluates the applicability of a usage protocol specification method for real APIs. Several other Java APIs were specified and are also discussed.
- **Checking.** We summarize two case studies in using Plural on third-party open-source code bases.
  - We checked about 2,000 lines taken from the Apache Beehive project against the specified APIs (section 4).
  - We also checked PMD, a program of about 40KLOC, for compliance to a simple iterator protocol (section 5).

  We find that the code can be checked with few false positives and report the annotation overhead of using our tool. We also discuss how tool shortcomings can be addressed (section 6). To our knowledge, precision and annotation overhead measurements are not available for previous modular protocol checking approaches.
- **API Patterns.** We comment on several recurring patterns that we found to be interesting. These patterns represent challenges that any practical protocol enforcement technique should be able to handle. Moreover, several of these patterns are handled elegantly by the novel technical features of our system. For example:
  - It is crucial to track what we refer to as "dynamic state tests," methods that can query the abstract state of an object at run-time. For example, the hasNext method of the Iterator interface.

---

[1] Plural is open-source: http://code.google.com/p/pluralism/

[2] API specifications are available at http://www.cs.cmu.edu/~kbierhof/

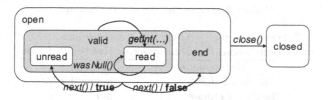

Fig. 1. Simplified JDBC `ResultSet` protocol. Rounded rectangles denote states refining another state. Arches represent method calls, optionally with return values.

- State guarantees, which allow multiple references to modify an object while all depending on the fact that it will not leave a particular state, were similarly quite useful.
- Inter-object dependencies, where the state of one object depends on the state of another, are common but can be precisely checked with our approach.

We first describe permissions and the Plural tool in section 2, and then we discuss our case studies in the subsequent sections. Section 7 summarizes related work and section 8 concludes.

2   Typestate Protocols with Access Permissions

This section summarizes our previous work on access permissions [7] for enforcing typestate protocols and our work on Plural, an automated tool for checking permission-based typestate protocols in Java [9]. Plural is described in more detail in the first author's dissertation [5].

2.1   Access Permissions

Our static, modular approach to checking API protocols is based on access permissions, predicates associated with program references descring the abstract state of that reference and the ways in which is may be aliased.

In our approach, developpers start by specifying their protocol. Figure 1 shows a simplified protocol for the JDBC `ResultSet` interface as a Statechart [22]. `ResultSet`s represent SQL query results, and we will use their protocol as a running example in this and the following section.

We allow developers to associate objects with a *hierarchy* of typestates, similar to Statecharts [22]. For example, while a result set is *open*, it is convenient to distinguish whether it currently points to a *valid* row or reached the *end* (figure 1).

Methods correspond to state transitions and are specified with *access permissions* that describe not only the state required and ensured by a method but also how the method will access the references passed into the method. We distinguish exclusive (unique), exclusive modifying (full), read-only (pure), immutable, and shared access (table 1). Furthermore, permissions include a *state guarantee*,

Table 1. Access permission taxonomy

Access through other permissions	Current permission has ...	
	Read/write access	Read-only access
None	unique	unique
Read-only	full	immutable
Read/write	share	pure

a state that the method promises not to leave [7]. For example, next can promise not to leave *open* (figure 1).

Permissions are associated with object references and govern how objects can be accessed through a given reference [7]. They can be seen as rely-guarantee contracts between the current reference and all other references to the same object: they provide guarantees about other references and restrict the current reference to not violate others' assumptions. Permissions capture three kinds of information:

1. *What kinds of references exist?* We distinguish read-only and modifying references, leading to the five different kinds of permissions shown in table 1.
2. *What state is guaranteed?* A guaranteed state cannot be left by any reference. References can rely on the guaranteed state even if the referenced object was modified by other modifying references.
3. *What do we know about the current state of the object?* Every operation performed on the referenced object can change the object's state. In order to enforce protocols, we ultimately need to keep track of what state the referenced object is currently in.

Permissions can only co-exist if they do not violate each other's assumptions. Thus, the following aliasing situations can occur for a given object: a single reference (unique), a distinguished writer reference (full) with many readers (pure), many writers (share) and many readers (pure), and no writers and only readers (immutable and pure).

Permissions are linear in order to preserve this invariant. But unlike linear type systems [34], they allow aliasing. This is because permissions can be *split* when aliases are introduced. For example, we can split a unique permission into a full and a pure permission, written unique $\Rightarrow$ full $\otimes$ pure to introduce a read-only alias. Using *fractions* [11] we can also *merge* previously split permissions when aliases disappear (e.g., when a method returns). This allows recovering a more powerful permission. For example, full $\Rightarrow \frac{1}{2} \cdot$ share $\otimes \frac{1}{2} \cdot$ share $\Rightarrow$ full.

2.2   Plural: Access Permissions for Java

Our tool, Plural, is a plug-in to the Eclipse IDE that implements the previously developed type system [7,3] as a static dataflow analysis for Java [9].

```
@Param(name = "stmt", releasedFrom("open"))
  public interface ResultSet {
    @Full(guarantee = "open")
    @TrueIndicates("unread")
    @FalseIndicates("end")
    boolean next();

    @Full(guarantee = "valid", ensures = "read")
    int getInt(int column);

    @Pure(guarantee = "valid", requires = "read")
    boolean wasNull();

    @Full(ensures = "closed")
    @Release("stmt")
    void close();
}
```

Fig. 2. Simplified `ResultSet` specification in Plural (using the typestates shown in figure 1)

In the remainder of this section we show example annotations and explain how permissions are tracked and API implementations are verified. Then we discuss tool features we found useful in practice.

Developer annotations. Developers use Java 5 annotations to specify method pre- and post-conditions with access permissions (figure 2). Figure 2 shows a simplified `ResultSet` specification with Plural's annotations (compare to figure 1). Annotations on methods specify *borrowed* permissions for the receiver, while annotations on method parameters do the same for the associated parameter. Borrowed permissions are returned to the caller when the method returns. The attribute "guarantee" specifies a state that cannot be left while the method executes. For example, `next` advances to the next row in the query result, guaranteeing the result set to remain *open*. Cell values can be read with `getInt` (and similar but omitted methods) if the result points to a *valid* row. Conversely, a required (or ensured) state only has to hold when the method is called (or returns). For instance, only after calling `getInt` is it legal to call `wasNull`. Additional annotations will be explained below.

Permission tracking and local permission inference. Our goal is to avoid annotations inside method bodies completely: based on the declared protocols, Plural infers how permissions flow through method bodies. Since Plural is based on a dataflow analysis, it automatically infers loop invariants as well.

However, Plural does require additional annotations on method parameters that have a declared protocol, such as the `ResultSet` parameter in figure 3. Notice that we use the same annotations for annotating parameters in client code that we use for declaring API protocols. While protocol annotations on the

```
public static int getFirstInt(@Full(guarantee = "open") ResultSet rs)
{
    Integer result = null;
    if(rs.next()) {
        result = rs.getInt(1);
        if(rs.wasNull())
            result = null;
        return result;
    }
    else {
        return rs.getInt(1); // ERROR: rs in "end" instead of "valid"
    }
}
```

Fig. 3. Simple `ResultSet` client with error in *else* branch that is detected by Plural

API itself (e.g., figure 2) can conceivably be provided by the API designer and amortize over the many uses of that API, the annotation shown in figure 3 is specific to this client program. In section 6 we discuss the overhead of providing these additional annotations for two open-source code bases.

Annotations make the analysis modular: Plural checks each method separately, temporarily trusting annotations on called methods and checking their bodies separately. For checking a given method or constructor, Plural assumes the permissions required by the method's annotations, i.e., it assumes the declared pre-condition. At each call site, Plural makes sure that permissions required for the call are available, splits them off (these permissions are "consumed" by the called method or constructor), and merges permissions ensured by the called method or constructor back into the current context. Notice that most methods "borrow" permissions (cf. figure 2), which means that they are both required and ensured. At method exit points, Plural checks that permissions ensured by its annotations are available, i.e., it checks the declared post-condition.

Thus, permissions are handled by Plural akin to conventional Java typing information: Permissions are provided with annotations on method parameters and then tracked automatically through the method body, like conventional types for method parameters. Unlike with Java types, local variables do not need to be annotated with permissions; instead, their permissions are inferred by Plural. Permission annotations can be seen as augmenting method signatures. They do not affect the conventional Java execution semantics; instead, they provide a static guarantee of protocol compliance without any runtime overhead.

Figure 3 shows a simple client method that retrieves an integer value from the first column in the first row of the given result set. Plural can be used to check whether this code respects the protocol declared for the `ResultSet` interface in figure 2. (It does not!)

API implementation checking. Our approach not only allows checking whether a client of an API follows the protocol required by that API, it can also check that the implementation of the protocol is consistent with its specification. The key abstraction for this is the *state invariant*, which we adapted from Fugue [17]. A state invariant associates a typestate of a class with a predicate over the fields of that class. In our approach, this predicate usually consists of access permissions for fields. An example can be found in figure 7, and details on the semantics of state invariants can be found in previous work [7].

Method cases. The idea of method cases goes back to behavioral specification methods, e.g., in the JML [27]. Method cases amount to specifying the same method with multiple pre-/post-condition pairs, allowing methods to behave differently in different situations. We early on recognized their relevance for specifying API protocols [6,4], but we are not aware of any other protocol checking approaches that support method cases. In order to support method cases, Plural supports tracking disjunctions of possible permissions.

Branch sensitivity. APIs often include methods whose return value indicates the current state of an object, which we call *dynamic state tests*. For example, next in figure 2 is specified to return **true** if the cursor was advanced to a *valid* row and **false** otherwise.

In order to take such tests into account, Plural performs a *branch-sensitive* flow analysis: if the code tests the state of an object, for instance with an **if** statement, then the analysis updates the state of the object being tested *according to the test's result*. For example, Plural updates the result set's state to *unread* at the beginning of the outer *if* branch in figure 3. Likewise, Plural updates the result set's state to *end* in the *else* branch and, consequently, signals an error on the call to getInt.

Notice that this approach does not make Plural path-sensitive; analysis information is still joined at control-flow merge points. Thus, at the end of figure 3, Plural no longer remembers that there was a path through the method on which the result set was *valid*. We believe that Plural could be extended to retain this information, but then we would have to deal with the usual complications of path sensitivity, i.e., large or infinite numbers of paths even through small methods.

When checking the implementation of a state test method, Plural checks at every method exit that, assuming **true** (or **false**) is returned, the receiver is in the state indicated by **true** (resp. **false**). This approach can be extended to other return types, although reasoning about predicates such as integer ranges may require using a theorem prover [8].

Dependent objects. Another feature of many APIs is that objects can become invalid if other, related objects are manipulated in certain ways. For example, SQL query results become invalid when the originating database connection is closed. (A similar problem, called concurrent modification, exists with iterators [4].) There are no automated modular protocol checkers that we know of that can handle these protocols, although recent global protocol checking approaches can [10,30].

Our solution is to "capture" a permission in the dependent object (the result set in the example) which prevents the problematic operation (closing the connection in the example) from happening. The dependent object has to be invalidated before "releasing" the captured permission and re-enabling the previously forbidden operation.

Captured permissions are typically required by a method but not returned. We use @Perm annotations for these situations, which allow declaring permissions required and ensured by a method separately (unlike @Full and similar annotations, which borrow a permission). Additionally, @Capture tells Plural to keep tracking the captured permission as a dependent of the capturing object, i.e., the method or constructor result. That allows explicitly releasing captured permissions with @Release. Additionally, such permissions will be implicitly released when the capturing object is no longer used. Released permissions become available to the client program again. For instance, executeQuery in figure 5 captures a receiver permission in the returned result set instance, which is explicitly released with close (figure 2) or implicitly when the result set is no longer used.

Others have modeled dependent objects with linear implications [12,25,21] but it is unclear how well those approaches can be automated. Our solution is to use a live variable analysis to detect *dead objects*, i.e., dead references to objects with unique permissions, and implicitly release any captured permissions from these dead objects.[3]

3   JDBC: Specifying a Java API

The Java Database Connectivity (JDBC) API defines a set of interfaces that Java programs can use to access relational databases with SQL commands. Database vendors provide *drivers* for their databases that are essentially implementations of the JDBC interfaces. Database client applications access databases primarily through Connection, Statement, and ResultSet objects. Clients first acquire a Connection which typically requires credentials such as a username and password. Then clients can create an arbitrary number of Statements on a given connection. Statements are used to send SQL commands through the connection. Query results are returned as ResultSet objects to the client. Conventionally, only one result set can be open for a given statement; sending another SQL command "implicitly closes" or invalidates any existing result sets for that statement.

This section discusses the specification of these major interfaces (including subtypes) using Plural annotations. The specified interfaces are massive: they define over 400 methods, each of which is associated with about 20 lines of informal documentation in the source files themselves, for a total of almost 10,000 lines including documentation (see table 2).

---

[3] We could delete these objects (in C or C++) or mark them as available for garbage collection (in Java or C#), but we are not exploring this optimization possibility here.

Table 2. Specified JDBC interfaces with total lines, size increase due to annotations, methods, annotation counts (on methods, for defining state spaces, and total), and the use of multiple method cases in each file. Note that each file's length is almost entirely due to extensive informal documentation

JDBC interface	Lines (Increase)	Methods	On methods	State space	Total	Mult. cases
Connection	1259 (9.8%)	47	84	4	88	2
Statement	936 (9.4%)	40	64	2	66	0
PreparedStatement	1193 (5.5%)	55	58	0	58	0
CallableStatement	2421 (5.0%)	111	134	1	135	0
ResultSet	4057 (15.4%)	187	483	8	491	82
Total	9866 (10.4%)	440	823	15	838	84

```
@States({"open", "closed"})
public interface Connection {

@Capture(param = "conn")
@Perm(requires = "share(this, open)", ensures = "unique(result) in open")
Statement createStatement() throws SQLException;

@Full(ensures = "closed")
void close() throws SQLException;

@Pure
@TrueIndicates("closed")
boolean isClosed() throws SQLException; }
```

Fig. 4. Simplified JDBC Connection interface specification

Connections. The Connection interface primarily consists of methods to create statements, to control transactional boundaries, and a close method to disconnect from the database (figure 4). Closing a connection invalidates all statements created with it, which will lead to runtime errors when using an invalidated statement. Due to space limits, we do not discuss our specification of transaction-related features here, but they are included in table 2.

Our goal was to specify JDBC in such a way that statements and result sets are invalidated when their connections are closed. Our solution is a variant on our previous work with iterators [4,7]: we capture a share connection permission each time a statement is created on it. The captured permission has the *open* state guarantee, which guarantees that the connection cannot be closed while the statement is active. Plural releases the captured connection permission from a statement that is no longer used or when the statement is closed, as explained in section 2.2. When all statements are closed then a full permission for the connection can be re-established, allowing close to be called.

Statements. Statements are used to execute SQL commands. Statements define methods for running queries, updates, and arbitrary SQL commands (figure 5).

```
@Refine({
  @States({"open", "closed"}),
  @States(refined="open", value={"hasResultSet","noResultSet"}, dim="rs") })
@Param(name = "conn", releasedFrom = "open")
public interface Statement {

@Capture(param = "stmt")
@Perm(requires = "full(this, open)", ensures = "unique(result) in scrolling")
ResultSet executeQuery(String sql) throws SQLException;

@Share("open")
int executeUpdate(String sql) throws SQLException;

@Full("open")
@TrueIndicates("hasResultSet")
@FalseIndicates("noResultSet")
boolean execute(String sql) throws SQLException;

@Capture(param = "stmt")
@Perm(requires = "full(this, open) in hasResultSet",
        ensures = "unique(result) in scrolling")
ResultSet getResultSet() throws SQLException;

@Full(value = "open")
@TrueIndicates("hasResultSet")
@FalseIndicates("noResultSet")
boolean getMoreResults() throws SQLException;

@Full(ensures = "closed")
@Release("conn")
void close(); }
```

Fig. 5. JDBC `Statement` interface specification (fragment)

We specify `executeQuery` similarly to how statements are created on connections. The resulting `ResultSet` object captures a full permission to the statement, which enforces the requirement that only one result set per statement exists. Conversely, `executeUpdate` borrows a share statement permission and returns the number of updated rows. Since share and full permissions cannot exist at the same time, result sets have to be closed before calling `executeUpdate`. The `Statement` documentation implies that result sets should be closed before an update command is run, and our specification makes this point precise.

The method `execute` can run any SQL command. If it returns `true` then the executed command was a query, which we indicate with the state *hasResultSet*. `getResultSet` requires this state and returns the actual query result.

In rare cases a command can have multiple results, and `getMoreResults` advances to the next result. Again, `true` indicates the presence of a result set.

```
@Refine({
  @States({"open", "closed"}),
  @States(refined = "open", value = {"scrolling", "inserting"}),
  @States(refined = "scrolling", value = {"begin", "valid", "end"}, dim = "row"),
  @States(refined = "valid", value = {"read", "unread"}, dim = "access"),
  @States(refined = "valid", value = {"noUpdates", "pending"}, dim = "update")
  /*...*/ })
@Param(name = "stmt", releasedFrom = "open")
public interface ResultSet {

// changes from figure 2

@Full(guarantee = "scrolling", requires = "noUpdates")
@TrueIndicates("valid")
boolean next() throws SQLException;

@Full(guarantee = "scrolling", requires = "valid", ensures = "read")
int getInt(int columnIndex) throws SQLException;

@Pure(guarantee = "scrolling", requires = "read", ensures = "read")
boolean wasNull() throws SQLException;

// scrolling and updating result sets

@Pure("open")
@TrueIndicates("begin")
boolean isBeforeFirst() throws SQLException;

@Full(guarantee = "open", requires = "updatable")
@Cases({
  @Perm(requires = "this in valid", ensures = "this in pending"),
  @Perm(requires = "this in insert", ensures = "this in insert")
})
void updateInt(int columnIndex, int x) throws SQLException;

@Full(guarantee = "scrolling", requires = "pending", ensures = "noUpdates")
void updateRow() throws SQLException;

@Full(guarantee = "open", ensures = "insert")
void moveToInsertRow() throws SQLException; }
```

Fig. 6. JDBC `ResultSet` interface specification (fragment)

We use a full permission because, like `execute` methods, `getMoreResults` closes any active result sets, as stated in that method's documentation: "Moves to this `Statement` object's next result, returns `true` if it is a `ResultSet` object, and implicitly closes any current `ResultSet` object(s) obtained with the method `getResultSet`."

Besides a plain `Statement` interface for sending SQL strings to the database, JDBC defines two other flavors of statements, prepared and callable statements. The former correspond to pattern into which parameters can be inserted, such as search strings. The latter correspond to stored procedures.

Since these interfaces are subtypes of `Statement` they inherit the states defined for `Statement`. The additional methods for prepared statements are straightforward to define with these states, while callable statements need an additional state distinction for detecting NULL cell values.

Overall, we were surprised at how well our approach can capture the design of the `Statement` interface.

Result sets. `ResultSet` is the most complex interface we encountered. We already discussed its most commonly used features in section 2. In addition, result sets allow for random access of their rows, a feature that is known as "scrolling". Scrolling caused us to add a *begin* state in addition to the *valid* and *end* states. Furthermore, the cell values of the current row can be updated, which caused us to add orthogonal substates inside *valid* to keep track of *pending* updates (in parallel to *read* and *unread*, see figure 2).

Finally, result sets have a buffer, the "insert row", for constructing a new row. The problem is that, quoting from the `ResultSet` documentation for `moveToInsertRow`, "[o]nly the updater, getter, and `insertRow` methods may be called when the cursor is on the insert row." Thus, scrolling methods are not available while on the insert row, *although the documentation for these methods does not hint at this problem.*

Our interpretation is to give result sets two modes (i.e., states), *scrolling* and *inserting*, where the former contains the states for scrolling (shaded in figure 1) as substates. `moveToInsertRow` and `moveToCurrentRow` switch between these modes. In order to make the methods for updating cells applicable in both modes we use method cases which account for all 82 methods with multiple cases in `ResultSet` (see table 2).

Figure 6 shows a fragment of the `ResultSet` interface with our actual protocol annotations. Notice how the two modes affect the methods previously shown in figure 2. The figure also shows selected methods for scrolling, updating (including method cases), and inserting.[4]

4   Beehive: Verifying an Intermediary Library

This section summarizes a case study in using Plural for checking API compliance in a third-party open source code base, Apache Beehive. In the process we specified protocols for several other APIs besides JDBC (see section 3) including a simple protocol for Beehive itself.

---

[4] `updateInt` defines two cases, which are both based on a borrowed full permission. One case requires that permission in the *valid* state and ensures *pending*, while the other case requires and ensures *insert*.

Beehive[5] is an open-source library for declarative resource access. We have focused on the part of Beehive that accesses relational databases using JDBC. Beehive clients define Java interfaces and, using Java annotations, choose which SQL commands should be executed when a method in those interfaces is called. Notice that this design is highly generic: the client-specified SQL commands can include parameters that are filled with the parameters passed to the associated method. Beehive then generates code implementing the client-defined interfaces that simply calls a generically written SQL execution engine, `JdbcControl`, whose implementation we discuss below.

We first describe the APIs used by Beehive before discussing the challenges in checking that Beehive correctly implements a standard Java and its own API.

4.1   Checked Java standard APIs

We specified four Java standard APIs used by Beehive, highlighting Plural's ability to treat APIs orthogonally.

JDBC. We described the JDBC specification in section 3. Since Beehive has no apriori knowledge of the SQL commands being executed (they are provided by a client), it uses the facilities for running "any" SQL command described in section 3. Its use of result sets is limited to reading cell values, and a new statement is created for every command. We speculate that the Beehive developers chose this strategy in order to ensure that result sets are never rendered invalid from executing another SQL command, which ends up helping our analysis confirm just that.

Beehive is tricky to reason about because it aliases result sets through fields of various objects. Plural's modular approach nonetheless allowed us to move outwards from methods calling into JDBC to callers of those methods. In other words, we followed a process of running Plural "out of the box" on a given Beehive class first. Places where Plural issued warnings usually required annotations on method parameters (or for state invariants). Running Plural again would possibly result in warnings on the methods calling the previously annotated methods. Providing annotations for these methods would move the warnings again until a calling method was able to provide the required permissions by itself because it created the needed API object.

Collections API. Beehive generically represents a query result row as a map from column names to values. One such map is created for each row in a result set and added to a list which is finally returned to the client.

The Java Collections API defines common containers such as lists and maps. *Iterators* are available for retrieving all elements in a container one by one. Maps provide *views* of their keys, values, and key-value pairs as sets. Lists support sublist views that contain a subsequence of the list's elements. Views are "backed" by the underlying container, i.e., changes to the view affect the underlying container.

---

[5] http://beehive.apache.org/

We specified the Collections API following our previous work [7]. Iterators are challenging because they do not tolerate "concurrent modification" of the underlying collection. We address this problem by capturing a immutable collection permission in the iterator [4,7]. Views can be similarly handled by capturing a permission from the underlying collection when creating the view.

Regular expressions. Regular expressions are only used once in Beehive. The pattern being matched is a static field in one of Beehive's classes, which we annotate with @Imm.

The API includes two classes. A `Pattern` is created based on a given regular expression string. Then, clients call `find` or `match` to match the pattern in a given string. The `Matcher` resulting from these operations can be used to retrieve details about the current match and to find the next matching substring.

We easily specified this protocol in Plural. As with iterators, we capture a immutable `Pattern` permission in each `Matcher`. We use a typestate *matched* to express a successful match and require it in methods that provide details about the last match.

Exceptions. When creating an exception, a "cause" (another exception) can be set *once*, either using an appropriate constructor or, to our surprise, using the method `initCause`. The latter is useful when using exceptions defined before causes were introduced in Java 1.4. Beehive uses `initCause` to initialize a cause for such a legacy exception, `NoSuchElementException`. This protocol is trivial to specify in Plural, but it was fascinating that even something as simple as exceptions has a protocol.

Recurring patterns. There were at least three common challenges that we found across several of the APIs we specified.

1. We were surprised how prevalent *dynamic state test* methods are, and how important they are in practice. We found dynamic state test methods in JDBC, Collections, and regular expressions, and a large number of them in JDBC alone. For example, the method `hasNext` in the Java `Iterator` interface tests whether another element is *available* ([4], cf. section 4.2), and `isEmpty` tests whether a collection is *empty*. It was crucial for handling the Beehive code that our approach can express and benefit from the tests that are part of JDBC's facilities for executing arbitrary SQL commands.

2. We also found protocols involving multiple *interdependent objects* in these APIs (and very prevalent in JDBC). We could model these protocols by capturing and later releasing permissions.

3. We used *method cases* in JDBC and the Collections API. As previously shown, method cases can be used to specify full Java iterators, which may modify the underlying collection [4].

We believe that these are crucial to address in any practical protocol checking approach; our approach was expressive enough to handle these challenges for all the examples in our case study (see section 3).

4.2 Protocol Implementations

This section summarizes challenges in checking that Beehive implements the Java iterator API and that Beehive's main class is implemented correctly assuming clients follow Beehive's API protocol.

Implementing an iterator. Beehive implements an **Iterator** over the rows of a result set. Figure 7 shows most of the relevant code. We use state invariants, i.e., predicates over the underlying result set (see section 2.2), to specify iterator states. Notice that *alive* is our default state that all objects are always in. Thus its state invariant is a conventional class invariant [27,2] that is established in the constructor and preserved afterwards.

When checking the code as shown, Plural issues 3 warnings in **hasNext** (see table 3). This is because our vanilla iterator specification [7] assumes **hasNext**, which tests if an element can be retrieved, to be pure. Beehive's **hasNext**, however, is not pure because it calls **next** on the **ResultSet**!

The way to fix this problem depends on whether or not you believe the **hasNext** method is supposed to be pure in all cases. If you believe it should be pure, you could modify Beehive's implementation of the iterator interface so that all effects are performed in the **next** method. Alternatively, you can specify the **hasNext** method as requiring a full permission, which we have done, and which causes the warnings to disappear.

Note that **next**'s specification requires *available*, which guarantees that _primed is true (see figure 7), making the initial check in **next** superfluous (if all iterator clients were checked with Plural as well).

Formalizing Beehive client obligations. Beehive is an intermediary library for handling resource access in applications: it uses various APIs to access these resources and defines its own API through which applications can take advantage of Beehive. We believe that this is a very common situation in modern software engineering: application code is arranged in layers, and Beehive represents one such layer. The resource APIs, such as JDBC, reside in the layer below, while the application-specific code resides in the layer above, making applications using Beehive appear like an hourglass.

Beehive's API is defined in the **JdbcControl** interface, which **JdbcControlImpl** implements. **JdbcControlImpl** in turn is a client to the JDBC API. **JdbcControlImpl** provides three methods **onAcquire**, **invoke**, and **onRelease** to clients. The first one creates a database connection, which the third one closes. **invoke** executes an SQL command and, in the case of a query, maps the result set into one of several possible representations. One representation is the iterator mentioned above; another one is a conventional **List**. Each row in the result is individually mapped into a map of key-value pairs (one entry for each cell in the row) or a Java object whose fields are populated with values from cells with matching names.

Notice that some of these representations, notably the iterator representation, of a result require the underlying result set to remain open. The challenge now is

```
@ClassStates({
  @State(name="alive",
    inv="full(_rs,scrolling) && full(_rowMapper) in init &&
      _primed == true => _rs in valid"),
  @State(name="available", inv="_primed == true") })
@NonReentrant
public class ResultSetIterator implements java.util.Iterator {
  private final ResultSet _rs;
  private final RowMapper _rowMapper;
  private boolean _primed = false;

  @Pure(guarantee = "next", fieldAccess = true)
  @TrueIndicates("available")
  public boolean hasNext() {
    if (_primed) { return true; }

    try {
      _primed = _rs.next();
    } catch (SQLException sqle) { return false; }
    return _primed;
  }

  @Full(requires = "available", ensures = "hasCurrent", fieldAccess = true)
  public Object next() {
    try {
      if (!_primed) {
        _primed = _rs.next();
        if (!_primed) {
          throw new NoSuchElementException();
        }
      }
      // reset upon consumption
      _primed = false;
      return _rowMapper.mapRowToReturnType(/* analysis-only */ _rs);
    } catch (SQLException e) {
      // Since Iterator interface is locked, all we can do
      // is put the real exception inside an expected one.
      NoSuchElementException xNoSuch = new NoSuchElementException("
          ResultSet exception: " + e);
      xNoSuch.initCause(e);
      throw xNoSuch;
    }
  }
}
```

Fig. 7. Beehive's iterator over the rows of a result set (constructor omitted). Plural issues warnings because **hasNext** is impure.

to ensure that `onRelease` is not called while these are still in use because closing the connection would invalidate the results. This requirement is identical to the one we described for immediate clients of `Connection`, and thus we should be able to specify it in the same way.

However, the connection is in this case a field of a surrounding Beehive `JdbcControlImpl` object, and Plural has currently no facility for letting `Jdbc-ControlImpl` clients keep track of the permission for one of its fields. Therefore, we currently work with a simplified `JdbcControlImpl` that always closes result sets at the end of `invoke`. Its specification, as desired, enforces that `onAcquire` is called before `onRelease` and `invoke` is only called "in between" the other two. This, however, means that our simplified `JdbcControlImpl` does not support returning iterators over result sets to clients, since they would keep result sets open. Overcoming this problem is discussed in the next section.

As mentioned, Beehive generates code that calls `invoke`. The generated code would presumably have to impose usage rules similar to the ones for `invoke` on *its* clients. Plural could then be used to verify that the generated code follows `JdbcControlImpl`'s protocol.

5   PMD: Scalability

We used the version of PMD included in the DaCapo 2006-10-MR2 benchmarks[6] to investigate how Plural can be used to check existing large code bases. In the next section this case study is used for direct comparison with state-of-the-art global protocol analyses [10,30], which typically focus on simple protocols such as the well-known iterator protocol. Iterators are widely used in PMD, and most iterations in PMD are over Java Collections (see section 4.1), but PMD implements a few iterator classes over its own data structures as well.

Iterator protocol. We decided to focus on the simple and well-known iterator protocol (see section 4.1). It took one of the authors 75 minutes to examine and specify PMD, a specification that ultimately consisted of just 15 annotations. This then enabled Plural to check that this protocol is followed all across PMD, which includes 170 distinct calls to the `next` method defined in the `Iterator` interface. Most iterator usages could be verified by Plural without any additional annotations because they are entirely local to a method. Annotations were needed where iterators were returned from a method call inside PMD and then used elsewhere. In one place an iterator is passed to a helper method *after* checking `hasNext`, and we could express the contract of this helper method with a suitable annotation.

Iterator implementations. PMD implements three iterators of its own. In one of them, `TreeIterator`, the implementation of `hasNext` is not only impure, like Beehive's iterator, but advances the iterator every time it is called. Thus, failure to call `next` after `hasNext` results in lost elements. The other iterators exhibit

---
[6] http://dacapobench.org/

behavior compatible with the conceptual purity of hasNext: next is used to pre-fetch the element to be returned the *next* time it is called before returning the current element. hasNext then simply checks the pre-fetched element is valid, which is typically a pure operation.

In light of these and the iterator implementation in Beehive (figure 7), it appears legitimate to ask whether hasNext is really a pure operation. This would have significant consequences for behavioral specification approaches like the JML [27] or Spec# [2] because they use pure methods in specifications. Conventionally, the specification of next in the JML would be "requires hasNext()", but that would be illegal if hasNext was not pure. In contrast, our specifications are more robust to the non-purity of hasNext. In fact, Plural can verify iterator usage in PMD with a full permission for hasNext with the same precision.

6   Evaluation

This section summarizes overhead and precision of applying Plural to Beehive and discusses improvements to the tool to address remaining challenges.

Annotation overhead: The price of modularity. The overhead for specifying *Beehive* is summarized in table 3. We used about 1 annotation per method and 5 per Beehive class, for a total of 66 annotations in more than 2,000 lines, or about one annotation every 30 lines. Running Plural on the 12 specified Beehive source files takes about 34 seconds on a 800 Mhz laptop with 1GB of heap space for Eclipse including Plural.

For *PMD* we mentioned in section 5 that we only needed 15 annotations in total, which one of the authors provided in approximately 75 minutes. Thus,

Table 3. Beehive classes checked with Plural. The middle part of the table shows annotations (on methods, invariants, and total) added to the code. The last 2 columns indicate Plural warnings and false positives.

Beehive class	Lines / Methods	Annotations Meths.	Invs.	Total	Plural warnings	False pos.
DefaultIteratorResultSetMapper	37 / 2	1	0	1	0	0
DefaultObjectResultSetMapper	127 / 2	2	0	2	0	0
JdbcControlImpl	521 / 13	13	1	14	2	1
ResultSetHashMap	85 / 9	9	0	9	0	0
ResultSetIterator	106 / 4	4	3	7	3	0
ResultSetMapper	32 / 2	2	0	2	0	0
RowMapper	260 / 5	9	1	10	0	0
RowMapperFactory	156 / 7	3	0	3	4	4
RowToHashMapMapper	57 / 2	4	1	5	0	0
RowToMapMapper	49 / 2	4	1	5	0	0
RowToObjectMapper	236 / 3	4	0	4	0	0
SqlStatement	511 / 14	4	0	4	0	0
Total	2158 / 65	59	7	66	9	5

checking the iterator protocol was straightforward and imposed almost no over-head. Running Plural on PMD's entire codebase of 40KLOC in 446 files (with the same configuration as for Beehive) takes about 15 minutes.

Precision: A benefit of modularity. Plural reports 9 problems in *Beehive*. Three of them are due to the impure `hasNext` method in `ResultSetIterator` (see section 4.2). Letting `hasNext` use a full permission removes these warnings. Another warning in `JdbcControlImpl` is caused by an assertion on a field that arguably happens in the wrong method: `invoke` asserts that the database connection is open before delegating the actual query execution to another, "protected" method that uses the connection. Plural issues a warning because a subclass could override one, but not the other, of these two methods, and then the state invariants may no longer be consistent. The warning disappears when moving the assertion into the protected method. Furthermore we note our state invariants guarantee that the offending runtime assertion succeeds.

The remaining warnings issued by Plural are false positives. This means that our false positive rate is is around 1 per 400 lines of code. We consider this to be quite impressive for a behavioral verification tool applied to complicated APIs (JDBC and others) and a very challenging case study subject (Beehive).

The false positive rate in *PMD* is extremely low. Warnings remained only in three places where PMD checks that a set is non-empty before creating an iterator and immediately calling `next` to get its first element. This is also mentioned as a source of imprecision in the most recent global protocol compliance checkers, which check for the same iterator protocol in PMD with 6 [10] and 2 [30] remaining warnings, respectively.

Future improvements. The remaining warnings in Beehive fall into the following categories:

- *Reflection (1).* Plural currently cannot assign permissions to objects created using reflection in
  `RowMapperFactory`.
- *Static fields (3).* `RowMapperFactory` manipulates a static map object, which we specified to require full permissions. For soundness, we only allow duplicable permissions, i.e., share, pure, and immutable, on static fields.
- *Complex invariant (1).* `JdbcControlImpl` opens a new database connection in `onAcquire` only if one does not already exist. We currently cannot express the invariant that a non-`null` field implies a permission for that field, which would allow Plural to verify the code.

These are common sources of imprecision in static analyses. We are considering tracking fields as implicit parameters in method calls, as discussed in section 4.2, and static fields could be handled in this way as well. Related to this issue is also a place in Beehive where a result set that was assigned to a field in the constructor is implicitly passed in a subsequent method call. We turned it into an explicit method parameter for now (the call to `mapRowToReturnType` in figure 7). Java(X) has demonstrated that fields can be tracked individually [14], although we would like to track permissions for "abstract" fields that do not necessarily correspond to actual fields in the code. We are also working on a strategy for handling object construction through reflection, and on generalizing the state invariants expressible in Plural.

We also simplified the Beehive code in a few places where our approach for tracking local aliases leads to analysis imprecisions. Since local alias tracking is orthogonal to tracking permissions we used the simplest available, sound solution in Plural, which is insufficient in some cases. We plan to evaluate other options.

Problems occur when the same variable is assigned different values on different code paths, usually depending on a condition. When these code paths rejoin, Plural assumes that the variable could point to one of several locations, which forbids strong updates. We are investigating using more sophisticated approaches that avoid this problem. Alternatively, Plural will work fine when the part of the code that initializes a variable on different paths is refactored into a separate method. Notice, however, that tracking local aliasing is a lot more tractable than tracking aliasing globally. Permissions reduce the problem of tracking aliasing globally to a local problem.

Finally, we assumed one class to be non-reentrant, but we believe a more complicated specification would allow the class to be analyzed assuming re-entrancy. Our approach conservatively assumes that all classes are re-entrant [7]—meaning that within the dynamic scope of a method, another method of the same class may be invoked with the same receiver object—but in practice that is not always the developer's intention. Therefore, we use the (currently unchecked) annotation shown in figure 7 to mark a class as non-reentrant, which causes Plural to omit certain checks during API implementation checking. We are planning on checking this annotation with Plural in the future.

Refactoring option. Notice that besides improving the tool there is usually the option of refactoring the problematic code. We believe that this is an indicator for the viability of our approach in practice, independent of the features supported by our tool: developers can often circumvent tool shortcomings with (fairly local) code changes. On the other hand, we have not seen many examples that fundamentally could not be handled by our approach.

Iterative process. We noticed that Plural has several characteristics that seem to facilitate its retroactive use with existing code. First, running Plural on un-annotated API client code will result in warnings on some of the calls into the API. Removing these warnings requires annotating the client methods in question, which will "move" the warnings to where these methods are invoked. This process continues until it reaches code where API objects are created. In the case of iterators, that is often the method where they are also used, in which case no developer intervention is required. Second, our experience also suggests that checking protocols for different APIs is largely orthogonal. Finally, annotations allow making assumptions about parts of the codebase that one wants to ignore for the time being, for instance because that part of the code is known not to interfere with the API protocol at hand.

7   Related Work

We previously proposed access permissions for sound, modular typestate protocol enforcement in the presence of aliasing, first for single-threaded [7] and recently for multi-threaded programs [3]. We showed on paper that the proposed type systems can handle interesting protocols, including iterators. We also developed Plural, an automated tool that embodies our permission-based approach as a static dataflow analysis for Java [9]. A comprehensive description of the Plural tool is part of the first author's dissertation [5]. This paper evaluates our approach for specifying and checking compliance to API protocols using Plural.

A plethora of approaches was proposed in the literature for checking protocol compliance and program behavior in general. These approaches differ significantly in the way protocols are specified, including typestates [33,15,26,19,17,7], type qualifiers [20], size properties [13], direct constraints on ordering [24,10,30], type refinements [29,14], first-order [27,2] or separation logic [32], and various temporal logics [23]. In these approaches, like in ours, usage rules of the API(s) of interest have to be codified by a developer. Once usage protocols are codified, violations can be detected statically (like in our and most of the above approaches) or dynamically (while the program is executing, e.g. [6,18]).

Many of the proposed static approaches, including ours, are modular and require developer-provided annotations in the analyzed code in addition to codifying API usage rules (e.g. [17,14]) but there are also global approaches that require no or minimal developer intervention (e.g. [20,23]). Unlike previous modular approaches, our approach does not require precise tracking of all object aliases (e.g. [15,17]) or impose an ownership discipline on the heap (e.g. [2]) in order to be modular.

Ours is one of the few approaches that can reason about correctly *implementing* APIs independent from their clients. (Interestingly, all of these approaches that we are aware of are modular typestate analyses [17,26,7].) Ours is the only approach (that we are aware of) that can verify correct usage *and implementation* of dynamic state test methods. Several other approaches can verify their correct usage (e.g., [29,13]), but not their implementation.

Previous modular approaches are often proven sound and shown to work for well-known examples such as file access protocols. But automated checkers are rare, and case studies with real APIs and third-party code hard to find. Notable exceptions include Vault [15] and Fugue [17,16], which are working automated checkers that were used to check compliance to Windows kernel and .NET standard library protocols, respectively (although Vault requires rewriting the code into its own C-like language).

This paper shows that our approach can be used in practical development tools for enforcing real API protocols. As far as we know, this paper is the first one that reports on challenges and recurring patterns in specifying typestate protocols of large, real APIs. We also report overhead (in terms of annotations) and precision (in terms of false positives) in checking open-source code bases with our tool.

We suspect that empirical results are sparse because APIs such as the ones discussed in this paper would be difficult to handle with existing modular approaches due to their limitations in reasoning about aliased objects. These limitations make it difficult to specify the object dependencies we found in the JDBC, Collections, and Regular Expressions APIs in the Java standard library. Fugue, for instance, was used for checking compliance with the .NET equivalent of JDBC, but the published specification does not seem to enforce that connections remain open while "commands" (the .NET equivalent of JDBC "statements") are in use [16]. Existing work on permissions recognized these challenges [11,12] but only supports unique and immutable permissions directly and does not track behavioral properties (such as typestates) with permissions.

In contrast to modular checkers, many global analyses have been implemented and empirically evaluated. While model checkers [23] typically have severe limitations in scaling to larger programs, approaches based on abstract interpretations have been shown to scale quite well in practice. "Sound" (see below) approaches rely on a global aliasing analysis [1,19,10,30] and become imprecise when alias information becomes imprecise.

This paper shows that our approach at least matches the most recently proposed global analyses that we are aware of in precision when verifying iterator usage in PMD [10,30] with extremely low developer overhead. Another previous global typestate analysis has also been used—with varying precision—to check simple iterator protocols, but in a different corpus of client programs [19].

These global typestate-based analyses have been used to make sure that dynamic state test methods are *called*, but not that the test actually indicated the needed state [19,10,30]. For example, the protocols being checked require calling `hasNext` before calling `next` in iterators, but they do not check whether `hasNext` returned `true`, which with our approach is expressed and ensured easily. Tracematch-based analyses [10,30] currently lack the expressiveness to capture these protocols more precisely, while approaches based on must-alias information (e.g. [19]) should be able to, but do not in their published case studies, encode these protocols. This is arguably an omission in these approaches that, given the importance of dynamic state tests in practice, we believe should be addressed.

Note that our approach, unlike global analyses, can reason about API implementations separately from clients and handles dynamic state tests soundly, as discussed above. Reasoning about API implementations separately from clients is critical for libraries such as Beehive that may have many clients. Our approach also seems to match the precision of global analysis for checking a simple iterator protocol. Additional empirical comparisons with global analyses can be found elsewhere [5].

Lastly, work has been done on inferring API usage protocols [31] and flagging deviations from commonly followed rules using statistical methods [28]. These approaches are complimentary to ours as the inferred protocols could be specified and checked with our approach.

8   Conclusions

This paper evaluates access permissions for enforcing API protocols using our prototype tool, Plural. It reports on our experience in specifying JDBC and several other important Java standard APIs, identifying common challenges for any practical API protocol enforcement technique. The paper also summarizes case studies in checking third-party open source applications *after the fact*, i.e., by using Plural on the existing code base, injecting annotations, and performing small refactorings. In future work we plan to evaluate Plural *during* software development.

Intermediary libraries, such as the one we consider in this paper, represent a compelling use case for Plural. Because Plural is modular *and* can verify implementations of protocols it can be used to verify the library by itself, assuming the specification of underlying APIs and imposing rules on potential clients but *without* depending on the specifics of a sample client or a concrete implementation of the underlying APIs. Thus, the effort for verifying a library can amortize across the users of the library *and* the possible combinations of underlying API implementations (such as the drivers for various databases).

To our knowledge, this is the first comprehensive evaluation of a modular protocol checking approach in terms of its ability to specify large, real APIs. We also report annotation overhead and precision in checking open-source code bases with our tool. We find that our approach imposes moderate developer overhead in the form of annotations on classes and methods and produces few false positives. These results indicate that our approach can be used to specify and enforce API protocols in practice. From specifying APIs we notice several recurring patterns including the importance of dynamic state tests, method cases, and the dependency of API objects on each other. The extremely small overhead of enforcing a simple protocol (iterators) in a large code base (PMD) also suggests that our approach can be introduced gracefully into existing projects, with increasing effort for increasingly interesting protocols.

Acknowledgments. We thank Ciera Jaspan, Joshua Sunshine, and the anonymous reviewers for feedback on drafts of this paper. This work was supported in part by a University of Coimbra Joint Research Collaboration Initiative, DARPA grant #HR0011-0710019, and NSF grant CCF-0811592. Nels Beckman is supported by a National Science Foundation Graduate Research Fellowship (DGE-0234630).

References

1. Ball, T., Rajamani, S.K.: Automatically validating temporal safety properties of interfaces. In: Dwyer, M.B. (ed.) SPIN 2001. LNCS, vol. 2057, pp. 101–122. Springer, Heidelberg (2001)

2. Barnett, M., DeLine, R., Fähndrich, M., Leino, K.R.M., Schulte, W.: Verification of object-oriented programs with invariants. Journal of Object Technology 3(6), 27–56 (2004)
3. Beckman, N.E., Bierhoff, K., Aldrich, J.: Verifying correct usage of Atomic blocks and typestate. In: ACM Conference on Object-Oriented Programming, Systems, Languages & Applications, October 2008, pp. 227–244 (2008)
4. Bierhoff, K.: Iterator specification with typestates. In: 5th International Workshop on Specification and Verification of Component-Based Systems, pp. 79–82. ACM Press, New York (2006)
5. Bierhoff, K.: API Protocol Compliance in Object-Oriented Software. PhD thesis, Carnegie Mellon University, School of Computer Science (April 2009)
6. Bierhoff, K., Aldrich, J.: Lightweight object specification with typestates. In: Joint European Software Engineering Conference and ACM Symposium on the Foundations of Software Engineering, september 2005, pp. 217–226 (2005)
7. Bierhoff, K., Aldrich, J.: Modular typestate checking of aliased objects. In: ACM Conference on Object-Oriented Programming, Systems, Languages & Applications, October 2007, pp. 301–320 (2007)
8. Bierhoff, K., Aldrich, J.: Permissions to specify the composite design pattern. In: 7th International Workshop on Specification and Verification of Component-Based Systems (November 2008)
9. Bierhoff, K., Aldrich, J.: PLURAL: Checking protocol compliance under aliasing. In: Companion of the 30th International Conference on Software Engineering, pp. 971–972. ACM Press, New York (2008)
10. Bodden, E., Lam, P., Hendren, L.: Finding programming errors earlier by evaluating runtime monitors ahead-of-time. In: ACM Symposium on the Foundations of Software Engineering, November 2008, pp. 36–47 (2008)
11. Boyland, J.: Checking interference with fractional permissions. In: Cousot, R. (ed.) SAS 2003. LNCS, vol. 2694, pp. 55–72. Springer, Heidelberg (2003)
12. Boyland, J.T., Retert, W.: Connecting effects and uniqueness with adoption. In: ACM Symposium on Principles of Programming Languages, January 2005, pp. 283–295 (2005)
13. Chin, W.-N., Khoo, S.-C., Qin, S., Popeea, C., Nguyen, H.H.: Verifying safety policies with size properties and alias controls. In: International Conference on Software Engineering, May 2005, pp. 186–195 (2005)
14. Degen, M., Thiemann, P., Wehr, S.: Tracking linear and affine resources with Java(X). In: Ernst, E. (ed.) ECOOP 2007. LNCS, vol. 4609, pp. 550–574. Springer, Heidelberg (2007)
15. DeLine, R., Fähndrich, M.: Enforcing high-level protocols in low-level software. In: ACM Conference on Programming Language Design and Implementation, pp. 59–69 (2001)
16. DeLine, R., Fähndrich, M.: The Fugue protocol checker: Is your software baroque? Technical Report MSR-TR-2004-07, Microsoft Research (2004)
17. DeLine, R., Fähndrich, M.: Typestates for objects. In: Odersky, M. (ed.) ECOOP 2004. LNCS, vol. 3086, pp. 465–490. Springer, Heidelberg (2004)
18. Dwyer, M.B., Kinneer, A., Elbaum, S.: Adaptive online program analysis. In: International Conference on Software Engineering, pp. 220–229. IEEE Computer Society Press, Los Alamitos (2007)
19. Fink, S., Yahav, E., Dor, N., Ramalingam, G., Geay, E.: Effective typestate verification in the presence of aliasing. In: ACM International Symposium on Software Testing and Analysis, July 2006, pp. 133–144 (2006)

20. Foster, J.S., Terauchi, T., Aiken, A.: Flow-sensitive type qualifiers. In: ACM Conference on Programming Language Design and Implementation, pp. 1–12 (2002)
21. Haack, C., Hurlin, C.: Resource usage protocols for iterators. In: International Workshop on Aliasing, Confinement and Ownership (July 2008)
22. Harel, D.: Statecharts: A visual formalism for complex systems. Science of Computer Programming 8, 231–274 (1987)
23. Henzinger, T.A., Jhala, R., Majumdar, R., Sutre, G.: Lazy abstraction. In: ACM Symposium on Principles of Programming Languages, pp. 58–70 (2002)
24. Igarashi, A., Kobayashi, N.: Resource usage analysis. In: ACM Symposium on Principles of Programming Languages, January 2002, pp. 331–342 (2002)
25. Krishnaswami, N.: Reasoning about iterators with separation logic. In: 5th International Workshop on Specification and Verification of Component-Based Systems, pp. 83–86. ACM Press, New York (2006)
26. Kuncak, V., Lam, P., Zee, K., Rinard, M.: Modular pluggable analyses for data structure consistency. IEEE Transactions on Software Engineering 32(12), 988–1005 (2006)
27. Leavens, G.T., Baker, A.L., Ruby, C.: JML: A notation for detailed design. In: Kilov, H., Rumpe, B., Simmonds, I. (eds.) Behavioral Specifications of Businesses and Systems, pp. 175–188. Kluwer Academic Publishers, Boston (1999)
28. Livshits, B., Zimmermann, T.: DynaMine: Finding common error patterns by mining software revision histories. In: Joint European Software Engineering Conference and ACM Symposium on the Foundations of Software Engineering, September 2005, pp. 296–305 (2005)
29. Mandelbaum, Y., Walker, D., Harper, R.: An effective theory of type refinements. In: ACM International Conference on Functional Programming, pp. 213–225 (2003)
30. Naeem, N., Lhoták, O.: Typestate-like analysis of multiple interacting objects. In: ACM Conference on Object-Oriented Programming, Systems, Languages & Applications, October 2008, pp. 347–366 (2008)
31. Nanda, M.G., Grothoff, C., Chandra, S.: Deriving object typestates in the presence of inter-object references. In: ACM Conference on Object-Oriented Programming, Systems, Languages & Applications, October 2005, pp. 77–96 (2005)
32. Parkinson, M.J., Bierman, G.M.: Separation logic, abstraction and inheritance. In: ACM Symposium on Principles of Programming Languages, January 2008, pp. 75–86 (2008)
33. Strom, R.E., Yemini, S.: Typestate: A programming language concept for enhancing software reliability. IEEE Transactions on Software Engineering 12, 157–171 (1986)
34. Wadler, P.: Linear types can change the world? In: Working Conference on Programming Concepts and Methods, pp. 347–359. North-Holland, Amsterdam (1990)

Adding State and Visibility Control
to Traits Using Lexical Nesting*

Tom Van Cutsem[1,**], Alexandre Bergel[2], Stéphane Ducasse[2],
and Wolfgang De Meuter[1]

[1] Programming Technology Lab, Vrije Universiteit Brussel, Belgium
[2] RMoD research group, INRIA Lille, France

Abstract. Traits are reusable building blocks that can be composed to share methods across unrelated class hierarchies. Original traits are stateless and cannot express visibility control for methods. Two extensions, stateful traits and freezable traits, have been proposed to overcome these limitations. However, these extensions introduce complexity and have not yet been combined to simultaneously add both state *and* visibility control to traits.

This paper revisits the addition of state and visibility control to traits. Rather than extending the original traits model with additional operations, we allow traits to be lexically nested within other modules. Traits can then have (shared) state and visibility control by hiding variables or methods in their lexical scope. Although the Traits' "flattening property" has to be revisited, the combination of traits with lexical nesting results in a simple and expressive trait model. We discuss an implementation of the model in AmbientTalk and specify its operational semantics.

1 Introduction

Traits have been proposed as a mechanism to compose and share behavioral units between distinct class hierarchies. They are an alternative to multiple inheritance, the most significant difference being that name conflicts must be explicitly resolved by the trait composer. Traits are recognized for their potential in supporting better composition and reuse. They have been integrated into a significant number of languages, such as Perl 6, Slate [1], Squeak [2], DrScheme OO [3] and Fortress [4]. Although originally designed in a dynamically typed setting, several type systems have been built for Traits [5,6,7,8].

Several extensions of the original traits have been proposed to fix their limitations. Stateful traits present a solution to include state in traits [9]. In addition to defining methods, a trait may define state. This state is private by default and may be accessed within the composing entity. Freezable traits [10] provide a visibility control mechanism for methods defined in a trait: a method may either be (i) public and late bound or (ii) private and early bound. This enables the composer to change a trait method's visibility at composition time to deal with unanticipated name conflicts.

Although these extensions have been formally described and implementations were proposed, their main drawback is that the resulting language has too many operators

---

* Funded by the Interuniversity Attraction Poles Program, Belgian State, Belgian Science Policy.
** Postdoctoral Fellow of the Research Foundation - Flanders (FWO).

S. Drossopoulou (Ed.): ECOOP 2009, LNCS 5653, pp. 220–243, 2009.

and may introduce complex interactions with the host language. For example, freezable traits introduce early bound message dispatch semantics to support method privacy which may conflict with the host language's late bound semantics. Stateful traits introduce private state that may conflict with the host language's visibility rules. Finally, stateful traits must extend the host language's memory layout with a "copy down" technique [11] when linearizing variables whose offset in the memory layout is not constant among different composition locations.

This paper proposes a unique and simpler extension to traits to achieve both state and visibility control (to distinguish public from private state and behavior). We first revisit previous extensions to traits (as defined by among others this paper's second and third author). Subsequently, instead of providing two different visibility control mechanisms – one for state and another one for methods – we use lexical scoping as the sole visibility control mechanism for both state and methods.

Our approach is validated in AmbientTalk, a classless object-based language. In AmbientTalk, traits are plain, first-class objects that can be lexically nested (within other objects or methods). Traits can have private or public state. Unanticipated name conflicts can be reduced because a trait can make methods private by hiding them in its lexical scope. However, there is no mechanism to fully support unanticipated name conflicts, since the composer cannot rename or hide conflicting methods.

The contribution of this paper is a trait model that supports both state and visibility control without the introduction of any new composition operators, in contrast to stateful or freezable traits. Instead, our model relies on the introduction of one feature: lexical nesting. Our simpler model does require more support from its host language than the original one and is therefore not as straightforward to add to existing languages as is the original. Our contribution is validated as follows:

- we describe an existing implementation of our model in the AmbientTalk language.
- we demonstrate the effectiveness of our trait model by using it to structure a non-trivial Morphic-like UI framework.
- we provide an operational semantics to model lexical nesting of objects and the composition of lexically nested traits.

The paper is organized as follows. We first give a brief review of traits and point out some limitations related to state and visibility (Section 2). We then show how lexical nesting may be combined with traits (Section 3). To illustrate the implication of this combination in practice, we discuss a small case study (Section 4). We then formalize our approach by giving an operational semantics (Section 5), the properties of which are subsequently discussed (Section 6). A related work section (Section 7) and a conclusion end this paper (Section 8).

2   Traits and Their Limitations

This section provides a brief description of the original Traits model. Readers already familiar with Traits may safely skip Section 2.1 and jump directly to Section 2.2.

2.1   Traits in a Nutshell

An exhaustive description of Traits may be found in previous work [12]. This section highlights the most relevant aspects of Traits for the purpose of this paper.

Reusable groups of methods. A trait is a set of methods that serves as the behavioral building block of classes and is a primitive unit of code reuse. Traits cannot define state but may manipulate state via accessor methods.

Explicit composition. A class is built by reference to its superclass, uses a set of traits, defines state (variables) and behavior (methods) that glue the traits together; a class implements the required trait methods and resolves any method conflicts. Trait composition respects the following three rules:

- Methods defined in the composer (*i.e.*, class or trait) using a trait take precedence over trait methods. This allows methods defined in a composer to override methods with the same name provided by used traits; we call these methods *glue methods*.
- Traits may be flattened. In any class composer the traits can be in-lined to yield an equivalent class definition that does not use traits. This helps to understand classes that are composed of a large number of traits.
- Composition order is irrelevant. All the traits have the same precedence, and hence conflicting trait methods must be explicitly disambiguated by the composer.

Conflict resolution. While composing traits, method conflicts may arise. A *conflict* arises if two or more traits are combined that provide identically named methods not originating from the same trait. The composer can resolve a conflict in two ways: by defining a (glue) method that *overrides* the conflicting methods, or by *excluding* a method from all but one trait. Traits allow method *aliasing* to introduce an additional name for a method provided by a trait. The new name is used to obtain access to a method that would otherwise be unreachable because it has been overridden.

2.2   Issues with Freezable Traits and Stateful Traits

Since the original paper *Traits: Composable Units of Behavior* was published at ECOOP 2003 [13], several communities expressed their interest in Traits. In spite of its acceptance, the trait model suffers from several drawbacks.

State. First, state is not modeled: a trait is made of a set of method definitions, required method declarations and a composition expression. At that time, allowing traits to define variables was not considered and was intentionally left as future work. The follow-up work, stateful traits [9], addressed this very issue. It introduces state and a visibility mechanism for variable privacy. Trait variables are private. Variable sharing is obtained with a new composition operation (called @ @). Variables defined in different traits may be merged when those traits are composed with each other. This model raises several questions regarding encapsulation since a trait may be proposed as a black box and the composer has means to "open" it up. Since a linear object memory layout is employed in most efficient object-oriented language implementation, a trait variable may have a different offset in the object layout at different composer locations. To be able to keep using a linear object layout, a technique known as "copy down" has to be employed [11].

Visibility. Second, no visibility control was proposed in the original version of traits. Reppy and Turon [14] proposed a visibility mechanism *à la* Java with public and private keywords. These access modifiers determine the visibility the members will have after they are inlined into a class but cannot be changed by the trait composer. Although having these visibilities for classes seems to be widely accepted, having the very same visibilities for traits seems not appropriate since the range of composition operators is far greater than the one for classes. Van Limberghen and Mens [15] showed that adding public/private/protected properties to attributes in mixins does not offer an adequate encapsulation mechanism. Traits can be composed in more ways than classes or mixins.

Freezable Traits [10] introduced visibility control to fully support unanticipated name conflicts. The composer may change the visibility of trait methods at composition time using two new operators freeze and defrost: the first operator turns a public late-bound method into a private early-bound method while the second reverts a private method into a public one. The problem of Freezable Traits is that it is complex to grasp the consequence of a change. More importantly Freezable Traits are based on the use of early-bound method dispatch. Such a mechanism may not be available in the host language implementation and adding it may radically change the resulting language.

Analysis. The two extensions to traits described above were designed in separation. Combining them into a unique language leads to a complex situation where two different visibility mechanisms coexist. Although doable, this would significantly raise the complexity of the trait model since 3 new operators (@ @, freeze, defrost) and two visibility mechanisms would need to be added, which clearly goes against the simplicity of the original model.

In the following Section, we extend traits with both state and visibility control solely by combining them with lexical nesting of objects in the host language. Our model does not introduce any additional composition operators with respect to the original model.

3 Lexically Nested Object-Based Traits

In this Section, we discuss how state and visibility control can be added to traits. Our first change to the model is that we no longer represent traits as distinct, declarative program entities, but rather as plain runtime objects (as in Self [16]). More specifically, traits will be represented as objects that close over their lexical environment *i.e.,* as closures. In languages that support closures, such as Scheme, function bodies close over their defining lexical environment. By doing so, the lexical environment may outlive the activation record in which it was created. Thus, a lexically free variable will retain its value and is said to have an indefinite extent. This property enables closures to hide (mutable) variables and auxiliary functions in their lexically enclosing scope.

In the following section we discuss how lexical scoping can and has been reconciled with object-oriented programming. We then introduce lexically nested traits in Section 3.2. Section 3.3 discusses how to compose such traits.

3.1 Objects as Closures

It has long been known that closures can be used to implement objects [17, 18, 19]. While closures successfully capture the essence of OOP, the expression of objects as functions and message passing as function calls models objects only as a "second class" abstraction. There do exist a number of object-oriented languages that have introduced first-class support for objects and message passing without losing the benefits of representing objects as closures. Examples of such languages include Emerald [20], ECMAScript (a.k.a. Javascript) [21], Beta [22], E [23] and Newspeak [24].

We introduce traits as closures in the AmbientTalk language [25,26], an object-based distributed programming language that is closest in style to Miller's E language.

Objects as closures in AmbientTalk. AmbientTalk is a classless, object-based language. Listing 1 defines a simple counter abstraction with operations to access, increment and decrement its value. In languages that support (either first or second class) objects as closures, the role of classes as object generators is often replaced by functions that return a new object whenever they are called (cf. E [23], Emerald [20], Scheme [18]). We will name such functions, like the `makeCounter` function defined above, "constructor functions". To create a new counter, one calls the `makeCounter` constructor function.

```
def makeCounter(val) {
  object: {
    def count() { val };
    def inc() { val := val + 1 };
    def dec() { val := val - 1 };
  }
}
```

Listing 1. Constructor function for counter objects.

AmbientTalk fully exploits lexical scoping and allows object definitions to be nested within other object definitions or within the scope of a function or method body. In the above listing, the object construction expression `object: {...}` is lexically nested within the function `makeCounter`. The object expression groups the methods and fields of an object and evaluates to a new, independent object. Within the expression one can refer to lexically free variables, such as `val`. Objects close over their lexical environment, such that these variables have an indefinite extent. This allows the counter to keep track of its state using `val`, while keeping this variable completely hidden within its lexical scope. Executing `makeCounter(0).val` will raise an exception.

This simple object model removes the need for special language constructs for object creation (replaced by calling a constructor function), visibility control (hiding names using lexical scoping), special constructor methods (replaced by constructor functions), static fields or methods (which are free variables of the constructor function) and singletons (by not nesting an object definition within a constructor function).

Lexical nesting and inheritance. AmbientTalk, like Self [27], supports *object-based inheritance* which is a relationship between two objects, a *delegator* and a *delegate*, rather than between a class and a superclass. Object-based inheritance implies that if the delegator receives a message it does not understand, it will delegate this message to its delegate object. Delegating a message to an object is different from sending a message to an object. *Delegation*, as first proposed by Henry Lieberman [28], implies that if a matching method is found in the delegate, in the subsequent method invocation the **self** pseudovariable will refer to the delegator (that is: the object that originally received the message). This property ensures that object-based inheritance properly supports method overriding.

In AmbientTalk, every object has a field named **super** which refers to an object's delegate. There is only one such field in each object; multiple inheritance is not supported. Objects by default delegate to an object named **nil**. Listing 2 exemplifies object-based inheritance. It shows the abstraction of a counter that cannot be decremented below zero. The delegate of such a "positive" counter object is a regular counter object. Any message for which a positive counter does not implement a method will be delegated to a regular counter object. The positive counter overrides the dec method and, if the counter has not reached zero yet, explicitly delegates the dec message to its delegate by means of the syntax **super**^dec().

```
def isStrictlyPositive(x) { x > 0 };

def makePositiveCounter(val) {
  extend: makeCounter(val) with: {
    def dec() {
      if: isStrictlyPositive(self.count()) then: {
        super^dec()
      }
    }
  }
}
```

Listing 2. Object-based inheritance.

Because AmbientTalk allows both lexical nesting and (object-based) inheritance, we must clarify the semantics of looking up identifiers, as there are now two hierarchies of names: the lexical scope (starting with the object itself, ending in the top-level scope via lexical nesting) and the object's inheritance chain (starting with **self**, ending in **nil** via each object's **super** field). An unqualified identifier, such as val, is *always* looked up in the object's lexical scope. A qualified identifier, such as inc in c.inc() or count in **self**.count(), is looked up in the receiver's inheritance chain. The major difference with mainstream object-oriented languages is that m() is *not* equivalent to **self**.m(). This is similar to method lookup in Newspeak [24], except that in Newspeak the inheritance chain is still considered if the method is not lexically visible.

The example given above shows how the positive counter abstraction can unambiguously make use of both lexically visible as well as inherited methods. The call to isStrictlyPositive is guaranteed to refer to the lexically visible definition. The invocation **self**.count() will find the method defined in the delegate object.

3.2 Lexically Nested Traits

AmbientTalk supports trait-based composition between objects. An object can import zero or more traits when it is defined. This causes the object to acquire all of the methods defined by its imported traits, as if it had defined those methods itself. If an imported method name clashes with another imported name, or with a name explicitly defined by the importing object, an exception is raised when the object is created to signal this conflict. Conflicts should be dealt with by the programmer by either aliasing an imported method name or by excluding it.

In AmbientTalk, traits are regular objects rather than distinct runtime values or static program declarations. Any object can play the role of a trait. Hence, like all objects, traits can make use of lexical nesting to hide private state or auxiliary functions. To the best of our knowledge, this combination hasn't been achieved before: it is a novel property that is not available in other languages with explicit support for trait composition.

Listing 3 defines a trait that provides a reusable abstraction for animating arbitrary objects. The example is taken from the implementation of a Morphic-like graphical kernel for AmbientTalk which is discussed in more detail in Section 4. The animation trait is parameterized with the refresh rate between animation calls (in milliseconds). It provides two methods, start and stop, to start and stop the animation loop. The start method triggers the animation loop by sending the message every:do: to its timer, passing as the second argument an anonymous zero-argument closure to be executed every refreshRate milliseconds. Note that the timer variable is hidden within the lexical environment of the animation trait object. As such, the variable is private to the trait and will not be visible to the composing clients. This example illustrates that traits can be stateful in AmbientTalk.

```
def makeAnimationTrait(refreshRate) {
  def timer := makeTimer();
  object: {
    def start() { timer.every: refreshRate do: { self.animate() } };
    def stop() { timer.reset() };
  }
}
```

Listing 3. A trait as a regular object.

To actually perform the animation, the animation trait requires the composite (*i.e.,* the object using the trait) to define a method named animate. The set of methods required by a trait is implicit in the source code. A method is required by a trait if the trait does not implement the method, yet it is invoked in the code (e.g. by means of a self-send).

Listing 4 shows the implementation of a particle morph that uses the above animation trait to move within a given direction at a constant rate (see Section 4 for a more in-depth explanation of a "morph"). We assume that makeCircleMorph creates an object that is graphically represented as a circle. The particle morph implements the animate method as required by the animation trait. At each step of the animation, the particle morph moves itself at the given moveRate.

Composition of traits is performed by means of the **import** statement. Because the animation trait is stateful, the particle morph first generates a new instance of this trait (by invoking the makeAnimationTrait constructor function) and then imports this new instance. The operational effect of the **import** statement is that the particle morph acquires its own, local definitions for the methods start and stop. How exactly this acquisition of methods takes place is the topic of the following section. For now, it suffices to

```
def makeParticleMorph(radius, moveRate, dx, dy) {
  extend: makeCircleMorph(radius) with: {
    import makeAnimationTrait(moveRate);
    def animate() {
      self.move(dx, dy);
    };
  }
}
```

Listing 4. Composing an object with a trait.

understand that when `start` is sent to a particle morph, the implementation of the animation trait is invoked and a `self.animate()` call will invoke the particle morph's `animate` method, as expected.

Conflict resolution. When the composite object is created, the `import` statement raises an exception if the composite and the trait define slots with the same name. It is up to the composite to explicitly resolve name conflicts between imported traits, or between an imported trait and itself. The composite can do so by aliasing or excluding imported methods[1]. For example, the particle morph can import the animation trait as follows:

```
import makeAnimationTrait(moveRate) alias start := startMoving
exclude stop;
```

In this case, the particle morph will acquire a method named `startMoving` rather than `start`. Because the `stop` method is excluded, the particle morph will not acquire this method such that it cannot be stopped by client code.

Initialization. As discussed previously, AmbientTalk objects are constructed by calling ordinary functions. All code executed when calling such constructor functions is regarded as initialization code. When objects are used as traits (*i.e.*, constructed as part of an `import` statement), their initialization code is ran in the order in which the `import` statements occur in the code. If more control over the composition of initialization code is required, such code can be transferred to a dedicated trait method that can then be composed, aliased or excluded at will by the composing object.

3.3   Flattening Lexically Nested Traits

We now discuss how exactly a composite object acquires the method definitions of its imported traits. In the original version of the traits model, trait composition enjoys the so-called *flattening property*, which states that the semantics of a class defined using traits is exactly the same as that of a class constructed directly from all of the non-overridden methods of the traits [13]. The intuitive explanation is that trait composition can be understood in terms of copy-pasting the method definitions of the trait into the class definition.

---

[1] Note that aliasing solves name conflicts, but does not guarantee that the intentional behavior of the composed traits is preserved. This issue has previously been addressed [10] and is not further discussed here.

When traits can be lexically nested, trait composition no longer adheres to the flattening property. The reason is that each imported trait method has its own distinct lexical environment upon which it may depend. If the method body of an imported trait method were copy-pasted verbatim into the composing object, lexically free variables of the method may become unbound or accidentally rebound to a variable with the same name in the lexical environment of the composing object. An imported trait method should retain its own lexical environment, which implies that it is not equivalent to a method defined by the composing object with the same method body.

In this Section, we explore an alternative semantics for trait composition based on delegation to avoid the obvious problems related to the flattening property when traits are closures. More specifically, we make use of a language feature of AmbientTalk that has not been explained thus far, which is the explicit delegation of messages between objects. In what follows, we first discuss this language feature. Subsequently, we apply it to implement trait composition.

Explicit delegation. As discussed in Section 3.1, an AmbientTalk object delegates any message it does not understand to the delegate object stored in its **super** field. This mechanism is known as object-based inheritance. In this case, delegation of the message happens *implicitly*. However, AmbientTalk also provides a delegation operator ^ that allows objects to *explicitly* delegate messages to objects other than the object stored in their **super** field. This enables objects to reuse code from different objects without resorting to multiple inheritance. Listing 5 exemplifies such reuse by extracting the reusable behavior of enumerable collections into a separate object (modeled after Ruby's Enumerable mixin module [2]). All reusable methods depend on a required method named each:. A collection representing an interval of integers $[min, max[$ reuses this behavior by providing an implementation for each:.

```
def Enumerable := object: {
    def collect: function {
        def sequence := makeSequence();
        self.each: { |elt| sequence.append(function(elt)) };
        sequence
    };
    def detect: predicate {...};
    ...
}
def makeInterval(min, max) {
    extend: Collection with: {
        // delegate messages to Enumerable to acquire its behavior
        def collect: function { Enumerable^collect: function };
        def detect: predicate { Enumerable^detect: predicate };
        ...
        def each: function { // the method needed by Enumerable
            // apply function to all Integer objects between min and max
            min.to: max do: function
        };
    }
}
```

Listing 5. Composition of a reusable object via explicit delegation.

[2] http://www.ruby-doc.org/core/classes/Enumerable.html

In order to reuse the functionality provided by `Enumerable`, the interval object defines a number of *delegating methods*. The sole purpose of such methods is to explicitly delegate a message to another object. The expression `obj^m()` denotes the delegation of a message `m` to an object `obj`. Recall from Section 3.1 that the difference between a delegation and a regular message send (*i.e.,* `obj.m()`) is that the former leaves the **self** pseudovariable unchanged during the invocation of `m()` (*i.e.,* **self** is not rebound to refer to `obj`). This property is crucial to enable the kind of reuse exemplified above: the implementation of `Enumerable`'s methods is only partial. It depends on a method call to `each:` (shown underlined) that should generate a sequence of the collection's elements by feeding them to a single-argument function. This method is therefore implemented by the interval object. Because the interval uses explicit delegation to forward the `collect:` and `detect:` messages to `Enumerable`, any occurrence of `self.each:` in these methods will refer to the implementation provided by the interval object.

The above example shows that explicit delegation allows objects to reuse partially implemented methods via object composition rather than via (object-based) inheritance. The advantage of composition over (multiple) inheritance is that it enables the reuse of methods from multiple objects without introducing ambiguity. Its disadvantage is that the composing object needs to define explicit delegating methods for each method it wants to reuse as part of its interface. Below, we discuss how the definition of these delegating methods can be automated, by defining trait composition in terms of generating delegating methods.

Trait composition by delegating method generation. Even though traits cannot be flattened in a language that models traits as closures (as discussed previously), we can attribute a simple semantics to trait composition in terms of explicit delegation. To acquire a method defined in an imported trait object, the composite object can generate a delegating method for it. This has the following desirable properties:

– Because the composite explicitly delegates to the trait object, the trait method is invoked in its proper lexical environment. The lexical environment of the trait's methods is unaffected by the trait composition.
– Because delegation does not alter the binding of **self**, this pseudovariable can be used by the trait to invoke its required methods, implemented by the composite.

Given this semantics, if we regard the `Enumerable` object as a trait, the interval object's definitions for the delegating methods can be replaced by a single **import** `Enumerable` statement to achieve the same operational effect. Listing 6 shows the definition of the particle morph from Section 3.2 where the trait import has been transformed into a set of delegating methods. In this example, we assume `t_` to be a fresh variable name. Note that the animation trait's methods retain their proper lexical environment. Furthermore, this semantics respects the ability of nested traits to close over their lexical environment to encapsulate state and private behavior. For example, the particle morph cannot access the `timer` variable associated with its imported trait.

Given the semantics of trait composition by means of explicit delegation, aliasing a method by means of **alias** `oldName := newName` generates the delegating method **def** `newName() { t_^oldName() }` and the semantics of **exclude** `name` is simply that no delegating method for `name` is defined in the importing scope.

```
def makeParticleMorph(radius, moveRate, dx, dy) {
  def t_ := makeAnimationTrait(moveRate);
  extend: makeCircleMorph(radius) with: {
    // import is transformed into a set of delegating method definitions
    def start() { t_^start() };
    def stop() { t_^stop() };
    def animate() {
      self.move(dx, dy);
    };
  }
}
```

Listing 6. Trait composition is transformed into delegation.

Dealing with state. The example objects that we have shown up to now have private state because the fields holding this state are hidden in their lexical environment. It is also possible for objects to declare fields directly as part of their public interface. Since traits are ordinary objects, they may also declare fields in addition to methods. As previously described, when a trait is imported a delegate method is defined for each of its provided methods. In addition, for each field provided by the trait, a field with the same name is defined in the object that imports the trait. Each object that imports a trait with public state will thus have its own copy of that state. As is the case with methods, an exception is raised if the names of imported fields conflict with those defined in the importing object.

3.4 Summary

Objects can be augmented with private state and visibility control by allowing them to close over their environment of definition. We added these properties to traits by similarly representing them as plain objects that close over their environment of definition. However, when representing traits in this way, the traditional way of composing traits by flattening them must be reconsidered. If we were to copy the method bodies of a trait's provided methods directly in the importing scope, their lexical scope would be ill-defined. One way to reconcile trait composition with lexical nesting is by expressing the composition in terms of *delegating methods* that delegate a message to a trait. The composite acquires the delegating method, rather than the method's implementation. The use of delegation allows the trait to execute the method in its proper lexical scope yet access any required methods provided by the composite via self-sends.

Contrary to Stateful and Freezable traits, our model does not introduce any new trait composition operators, thus preserving the simplicity of the original model. The drawback is that our model cannot express certain compositions that can be expressed using Stateful or Freezable traits. For example, contrary to Freezable Traits we provide no operators to deal with unanticipated name conflicts since the composer cannot change the visibility of a trait's provided fields or methods.

4 Case Study: AmbientMorphic

We demonstrate the applicability of lexically nested traits by means of a concrete case study. AmbientMorphic is a minimal implementation of the Morphic user-interface construction framework [29] in AmbientTalk[3]. In Morphic, the basic unit of abstraction is called a *morph*. A morph is an object with a graphical manifestation on the screen. Morphs can be composed into typical user interface widgets, but they can equally be used for rendering more lively applications such as e.g. a simulation of atoms in a gas tank [30]. The goal of the morphic framework is to create the illusion that the graphical "objects" which can be seen on the screen really *are* the objects that the programmer manipulates in the code.

Morphic is an ideal case study for traits because morphs can be decomposed into many different yet interdependent concerns. Typical concerns include drawing and re-drawing, resizing, keeping track of which morph has the current focus, determining what morph is currently under the cursor (which is represented by the "hand morph" in Morphic), etc. In our framework, a Morph is composed of many small traits that each en-code such a concern. Figure 1 depicts a subset of the framework. The entire framework totals 18 traits (13 of which are stateful) and 12 morphs.

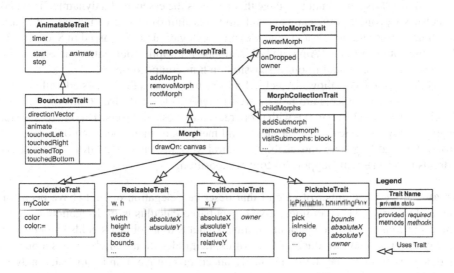

Fig. 1. A selection of the traits used in the AmbientMorphic framework

Decomposing a morph into separate traits leads to separation of concerns (*i.e.,* increased modularity) and also enables programmers to reuse traits to build other kinds of morphs (*i.e.,* increased reuse). Because our trait model additionally enables state and visibility control, we gain the following benefits:

1. Since traits can be stateful, the Morph object does not need to be polluted with the fields, accessors and mutators that would otherwise be required by the traits.
2. State remains well encapsulated within each trait. If one of the traits modifies the representation of its state, this will not impact the Morph.

---

[3] The framework is included in the open-source AmbientTalk distribution available online at http://prog.vub.ac.be/amop.

These benefits would not have been achieved using the original traits model. The first benefit can be achieved with stateful traits and the second with freezable traits. However, these extensions have not before been combined into a single model.

5 Operational Semantics

We now formalize the features presented in Section 3 by providing an operational semantics for three increasingly descriptive calculi: PROTOLITE, LEXLITE, and AMBIENTTALKLITE. PROTOLITE is a core calculus that is gradually extended with the features required for lexically nested traits. The goal of this formalization is to provide the necessary technical description required when one would want to reproduce our implementation of lexically nested traits. This section does not provide any hint on how to make this implementation fast (this is not the focus of this paper), but it conveys the necessary details to realize one.

PROTOLITE is a minimal language that captures the essence of a dynamically typed, object-based programming language. It features ex-nihilo object creation, message passing, field access and update and finally explicit delegation (as discussed in Section 3.3). We chose not to formalize AmbientTalk's support for implicit delegation via **super** fields because it is not essential to our discussion on trait composition.

While PROTOLITE allows object definitions to be syntactically nested within other object definitions, objects are not allowed to refer to lexically free fields or methods. LEXLITE extends PROTOLITE with proper lexically nested objects. This enables nested objects to access lexically visible fields and methods of their enclosing objects, a key property for adding state and visibility control to traits. Finally, AMBIENTTALKLITE extends LEXLITE with support for trait composition.

Related work. A number of calculi that describe delegation or traits have been formulated so far. δ [31] is an imperative object based calculus with delegation. δ allows objects to change their behavior at runtime. Updates to an object's fields can be either lazy or eager. δ also introduces a form of explicit delegation. An object has a number of delegates (which may be dynamically added or removed) and a message may be explicitly directed at a delegate. We chose not to use δ as our starting point because dynamic addition and removal of delegates and methods is not required for our purpose and because it does not support lexical nesting.

Incomplete Featherweight Java [32] is an extension of Featherweight Java with incomplete objects *i.e.*, objects that require some missing methods which can be provided at run-time by composition with another complete object. The mechanism for method invocation is based on delegation and it is disciplined by static typing. The authors extend the class-based inheritance paradigm to make it more flexible.

Bono and Fisher [33] have designed an imperative object calculus to support class-based programming via a combination of extensible objects and encapsulation. Two pillars of their calculus are an explicit type hierarchy and an automatic propagation of changes. Their focus is thus rather different from ours.

5.1 PROTOLITE

Figure 2 presents the syntax of PROTOLITE. This syntax is reduced to the minimum set of syntactic constructions that models object creation, message sending, and message delegation. We use the meta-variable e for expressions, m for method names, f for field names and x for variable names.

$$
\begin{aligned}
e = \ &\textbf{object}\{\textit{field}^*\ \textit{meth}^*\} \\
&|\ e.f\ |\ e.f := e\ |\ e.m(e^*)\ |\ e^{\smallfrown}m(e^*)\ |\ \underline{e\langle oid\rangle^{\smallfrown}m(e^*)} \\
&|\ e\,;\,e\ |\ x\ |\ \textbf{self}\ |\ \text{nil}\ |\ \underline{oid} \\
\textit{meth} = \ &m(x^*) = e \\
\textit{field} = \ &f := e
\end{aligned}
$$

Fig. 2. PROTOLITE expressions (run-time expressions are shown underlined)

Objects are created by means of the object creation expression **object**$\{\ldots\}$. An object consists of a set of fields and methods. We assume that all object expressions are valid, *i.e.,* field and method names are unique within an object creation expression. Each field declaration is associated with an initialization expression, which is evaluated when the object is created. Messages may be sent to the result of an expression using an arbitrary number of arguments ($e.m(e^*)$). Messages may also be delegated ($e^{\smallfrown}m(e^*)$). The figure shows run-time expressions, which are underlined, following the notation of Flatt *et. al* [34]. These expressions cannot be formulated in source code. They exist at runtime and may contain annotations to store additional information about the expression (shown using $\langle\rangle$).

Figure 3 shows the evaluation contexts using the notation of Felleisen and Hieb [35]. Evaluation contexts specify the evaluation order on expressions. For example, the receiver expression of a message send must be evaluated before its arguments. The notation $v^*\ E\ e^*$ indicates the evaluation of expressions from left to right. The names v, o and o' are meta-variables that designate object references.

$$
\begin{aligned}
E = \ &[\,]\ |\ E.f\ |\ E.f := e\ |\ E.m(e^*)\ |\ E\langle o\rangle^{\smallfrown}m(e^*) \\
&|\ o.f := E\ |\ o.m(v^*\ E\ e^*)\ |\ o\langle o'\rangle^{\smallfrown}m(v^*\ E\ e^*)\ |\ E\,;\,e \\
v, o, o' = \ &\text{nil}\ |\ oid
\end{aligned}
$$

Fig. 3. PROTOLITE Evaluation contexts

Figure 4 describes the generation of PROTOLITE run-time expressions. Such expressions are generated to annotate objects and replace **self**. This annotation and replacement occurs before evaluating a field initialization expression contained in an object definition and before evaluating a method body.

Message sending and delegation require a mechanism to bind the **self** pseudo-variable to an arbitrary value (the receiver). The $[\![e]\!]_o$ operator recursively replaces all references to **self** by o in the expression e. References to **self** within a nested object creation expression in e are not substituted because **self** references within this expression should refer to the nested object itself. Delegated message sends need to keep a

$$[\![x]\!]_o = x$$
$$[\![\textbf{self}]\!]_o = o$$
$$[\![\textbf{nil}]\!]_o = \textsf{nil}$$
$$[\![e \,;\, e']\!]_o = [\![e]\!]_o \,;\, [\![e']\!]_o$$

$$[\![e.f]\!]_o = [\![e]\!]_o.f$$
$$[\![e.f := e']\!]_o = [\![e]\!]_o.f := [\![e']\!]_o$$
$$[\![e.m(e_i^*)]\!]_o = [\![e]\!]_o.m([\![e_i]\!]_o^*)$$
$$[\![e\hat{\;}m(e_i^*)]\!]_o = [\![e]\!]_o\langle o\rangle\hat{\;}m([\![e_i]\!]_o^*)$$
$$[\![\textbf{object}\{\mathit{field}^* \ \mathit{meth}^*\}]\!]_o = \textbf{object}\{\mathit{field}^* \ \mathit{meth}^*\}$$

Fig. 4. Annotating PROTOLITE expressions

reference to the object that performs the delegation. To this end, they are replaced by a run-time expression that is annotated with the value of **self**. This reference is used to replace the **self** variable when the delegated send is executed.

Figure 5 shows the reduction rules of PROTOLITE. Each of these is an elementary reduction, mapping an evaluation context E and a store S onto a reduced evaluation context and an updated store. Objects are represented as tuples $\langle \mathcal{F}, \mathcal{M} \rangle$ of a map of fields $\mathcal{F}$ and methods $\mathcal{M}$. In the [*object*] reduction rule, fields are initialized to nil when the object is created. Their initial values are subsequently assigned by evaluating the initialization expressions before the object is returned. References to **self** within a field initialization expression are first substituted for the new object.

In the [*delegate*] reduction rule, note that o' (the delegator) rather than o (the receiver) substitutes **self** in the invoked method. In the [*send*] and [*delegate*] rules, before evaluating a method body $e[v^*/x^*]$ substitutes parameters x^* for the argument values v^*. In the method body, a field f of the enclosing object is accessible via **self**.f.

$$\langle E[\textbf{object}\{\mathit{field}^* \ \mathit{meth}^*\}], S \rangle \hookrightarrow \langle E[(o.f := [\![e]\!]_o)^*; o], S[o \mapsto \langle \mathcal{F}, \mathcal{M} \rangle] \rangle \qquad [object]$$
where $o \notin \mathrm{dom}(S)$ and $\mathcal{F} = \{ f \mapsto \textsf{nil} \mid \forall f := e \in \mathit{field}^* \}$
and $\mathcal{M} = \{ m \mapsto \langle x^*, e' \rangle \mid \forall m(x^*) = e' \in \mathit{meth}^* \}$

$$\langle E[o.f], S \rangle \hookrightarrow \langle E[v], S \rangle \qquad [get]$$
where $S(o) = \langle \mathcal{F}, \mathcal{M} \rangle$ and $\mathcal{F}(f) = v$

$$\langle E[o.f := v], S \rangle \hookrightarrow \langle E[v], S[o \mapsto \langle \mathcal{F}[f \mapsto v], \mathcal{M} \rangle] \rangle \qquad [set]$$
where $S(o) = \langle \mathcal{F}, \mathcal{M} \rangle$ and $f \in \mathrm{dom}(\mathcal{F})$

$$\langle E[o.m(v^*)], S \rangle \hookrightarrow \langle E[[\![e[v^*/x^*]]\!]_o], S \rangle \qquad [send]$$
where $S(o) = \langle \mathcal{F}, \mathcal{M} \rangle$ and $m \mapsto \langle x^*, e \rangle \in \mathcal{M}$

$$\langle E[o\langle o'\rangle\hat{\;}m(v^*)], S \rangle \hookrightarrow \langle E[[\![e[v^*/x^*]]\!]_{o'}], S \rangle \qquad [delegate]$$
where $S(o) = \langle \mathcal{F}, \mathcal{M} \rangle$ and $m \mapsto \langle x^*, e \rangle \in \mathcal{M}$

$$\langle E[o \,;\, e], S \rangle \hookrightarrow \langle E[e], S \rangle \qquad [seq]$$

Fig. 5. Reductions for PROTOLITE

5.2 LEXLITE

PROTOLITE does not allow objects to access fields and methods of their enclosing objects. LEXLITE extends PROTOLITE with a new syntax and semantics that allows objects to access lexically visible fields and methods. Figure 6 shows the syntax extensions of LEXLITE with respect to PROTOLITE. The new expressions denote the invocation of a lexically visible method m and the access to a lexically visible field f. LEXLITE

$$e = \ldots \mid m(e^*) \mid f \mid \mathbf{object}\{\textit{field}^* \ \textit{meth}^*\}\langle L \rangle$$

Fig. 6. LEXLITE syntax extensions to PROTOLITE

supports an additional run-time expression that annotates an object creation expression with a lexical environment L. This annotation is generated when closing over the lexical environment. This is explained in more detail below.

In LEXLITE, receiverless (*i.e.*, lexically resolved) method invocation and field access are interpreted as if the method or field was invoked on the lexically visible object in which the method or field is defined. Also, object definitions must now close over their lexical environment, such that expressions contained in their methods may correctly refer to methods and fields defined in an enclosing lexical environment. We represent the lexical environment as a function $L(n) = o$ mapping a method or field name n to the object o in which that name is defined. Figure 7 shows how each expression e closes over a lexical environment L by means of the transformation $\mathcal{C}_L[\![e]\!]$. Following the convention previously introduced, code generated by this transformation is underlined.

$$
\begin{aligned}
\mathcal{C}_L[\![x]\!] &= x & \mathcal{C}_L[\![e.f := e']\!] &= \mathcal{C}_L[\![e]\!].f := \mathcal{C}_L[\![e']\!] \\
\mathcal{C}_L[\![\mathbf{self}]\!] &= \mathbf{self} & \mathcal{C}_L[\![e.m(e_i^*)]\!] &= \mathcal{C}_L[\![e]\!].m(\mathcal{C}_L[\![e_i]\!]^*) \\
\mathcal{C}_L[\![\mathbf{nil}]\!] &= \mathbf{nil} & \mathcal{C}_L[\![e\hat{}m(e_i^*)]\!] &= \mathcal{C}_L[\![e]\!]\hat{}m(\mathcal{C}_L[\![e_i]\!]^*) \\
\mathcal{C}_L[\![e\ ;\ e']\!] &= \mathcal{C}_L[\![e]\!]\ ;\ \mathcal{C}_L[\![e']\!] & \mathcal{C}_L[\![f]\!] &= \underline{l.f} \text{ where } l = L(f) \\
\mathcal{C}_L[\![e.f]\!] &= \mathcal{C}_L[\![e]\!].f & \mathcal{C}_L[\![m(e_i^*)]\!] &= \underline{l}.m(\mathcal{C}_L[\![e_i]\!]^*) \text{ where } l = L(m)
\end{aligned}
$$
$$\mathcal{C}_L[\![\mathbf{object}\{\textit{field}^* \ \textit{meth}^*\}]\!] = \mathbf{object}\{\textit{field}^* \ \textit{meth}^*\}\underline{\langle L \rangle}$$

Fig. 7. LEXLITE expressions closing over a lexical scope L

Because lexically scoped method invocations and field accesses are transformed into regular method invocations and field accesses when expressions close over their defining lexical environment, no special reduction semantics must be added for these expressions. However, the reduction semantics for [*object*] must be refined such that method bodies now close over the lexical environment in which the object has been defined. This new reduction rule is shown in Figure 8. The other reduction rules for LEXLITE are the same as those defined in Figure 5.

Note that a lexical closure is not defined as a "snapshot" of the lexical environment at the time the object is created. This would work for a functional language, but since LEXLITE is stateful, the closure must refer to the actual enclosing objects such that state changes in those objects remain visible to the nested object. Finally, note that by transforming a receiverless method invocation $m()$ into a receiverful method invocation $l.m()$ on the enclosing object l, within m the binding of **self** will correctly refer to the enclosing object (*i.e.*, l) rather than to the nested object that performed the invocation.

In LEXLITE, lexical lookup proceeds via a chain of L functions. In order to be well-defined, this lookup must eventually end. Therefore, the top-level expression of a LEXLITE program must close over an empty top-level environment $T(n) = \bot$ before it can be reduced. If one wants to bootstrap the lexical environment with top-level methods and fields, these can be encoded as follows. If e is the top-level expression encoding a

$$\langle E[\textbf{object}\{\textit{field}^*\textit{meth}^*\}\langle L\rangle], S\rangle \hookrightarrow \langle E[(o.f:=C_{L'}\,[\![[e]\!]_o]\!])^*; o], S[o \mapsto \langle \mathcal{F}, \mathcal{M}\rangle]\rangle \quad [\textit{object}]$$
where $o \notin \text{dom}(S)$ and $\mathcal{F} = \{\,f \mapsto \text{nil} \mid \forall f := e \in \textit{field}^*\}$
and $\mathcal{M} = \{\,m \mapsto \langle x^*, C_{L'}[\![e']\!]\rangle \mid \forall\, m(x^*) = e' \in \textit{meth}^*\}$
and $L'(n) = \begin{cases} o & \text{if } n \in \text{dom}(\mathcal{F}) \cup \text{dom}(\mathcal{M}) \\ L(n) & \text{otherwise} \end{cases}$

Fig. 8. Redefined reduction rule for LEXLITE

program and m is a fresh name then the expression **object**$\{...m() = e...\}.m()$ introduces an explicit top-level environment. All fields and methods declared in this outer object expression can be regarded as top-level in e.

5.3 AMBIENTTALKLITE

AMBIENTTALKLITE extends LEXLITE with explicit support for trait composition. It exhibits the properties of AmbientTalk regarding state and visibility control (cf. Section 3.2) and describes trait composition in terms of generating delegate methods (cf. Section 3.3). Figure 9 shows the syntax extensions of AMBIENTTALKLITE with respect to LEXLITE. An object creation expression may contain **import** declarations to acquire the fields and methods of trait objects. The expression e in the **import** declaration is eagerly reduced to the trait object. A run-time **import** declaration is introduced which is annotated with a mapping $\mathcal{A}$ that maps names to their aliases and a set $\mathcal{E}$ of field or method names to be excluded. Figure 10 shows how these annotations are generated based on the **alias** and **exclude** clauses of the original **import** declaration.

$$e = \ldots \mid \textbf{object}\{\textit{field}^*\ \textit{meth}^*\ \textit{import}^*\}$$
$$\textit{import} = \textbf{import}\ e\ \textbf{alias}\ \textit{alias}^*\ \textbf{exclude}\ n^*$$
$$\mid\ \textbf{import}\ e\ \langle \mathcal{A}, \mathcal{E}\rangle$$
$$\textit{alias} = n \leftarrow n$$
$$n = \text{a method or field name}$$

$$E = \ldots \mid \textbf{object}\{\textit{field}^*\ \textit{meth}^*\ \textbf{import}\ v\ \langle \mathcal{A}, \mathcal{E}\rangle^*\ \textbf{import}\ E\ \langle \mathcal{A}, \mathcal{E}\rangle\ \textbf{import}\ e\ \langle \mathcal{A}, \mathcal{E}\rangle^*\}$$

Fig. 9. AMBIENTTALKLITE syntax and evaluation context extensions to LEXLITE

$$[\![\textbf{object}\{\textit{field}^*\ \textit{meth}^*\ \textit{import}^*\}]\!]_o = \textbf{object}\{\textit{field}^*\ \textit{meth}^*\ [\![\textit{import}^*]\!]_o\}$$
$$[\![\textbf{import}\ e\ \textbf{alias}\ \textit{alias}^*\ \textbf{exclude}\ n^*]\!]_o = \textbf{import}\ [\![e]\!]_o\langle \mathcal{A}, \mathcal{E}\rangle$$
$$\text{where } \mathcal{A}(n) = \begin{cases} n' & \text{if } n' \leftarrow n \in \textit{alias}^* \\ n & \text{otherwise} \end{cases}$$
$$\text{and } \mathcal{E} = \{n \mid n \in n^*\}$$

Fig. 10. Annotating AMBIENTTALKLITE expressions

The [*import*] reduction rule in Figure 11 shows how the **import** declarations are expanded into a set of generated fields and delegating methods. Field definitions present in the value being imported, t_i, are copied (as explained in Section 3.3). For each imported method m, a delegating method n is generated which delegates m to t_i. Note that the use of $\mathcal{A}_i$ ensures a field or method renaming if specified. The last two lines indicate the constraint that duplicate field or method names are disallowed. Once the **import** declarations are reduced, a regular LEXLITE object creation expression remains.

$$\langle E[\textbf{object}\{\textit{field}^*\ \textit{meth}^*\ \textbf{import}\ t_i\langle\mathcal{A}_i,\mathcal{E}_i\rangle^*\}\langle L\rangle], \mathcal{S}\rangle \qquad\qquad [\textit{import}]$$
$$\hookrightarrow\ \langle E[\textbf{object}\{\textit{field}^*\ \underline{\textit{ifield}^*}\ \textit{meth}^*\ \underline{\textit{imeth}^*}\}\langle L\rangle], \mathcal{S}\rangle$$
$$\text{where } \mathcal{S}(t_i) = \langle\mathcal{F}_i,\mathcal{M}_i\rangle$$
$$\text{and } \textit{ifields}_i = \{\ \underline{n := v}\ |\ f \mapsto v \in \mathcal{F}_i,\ f \notin \mathcal{E}_i,\ n = \mathcal{A}_i(f)\}$$
$$\text{and } \textit{imeths}_i = \{\ \underline{n(x^*) = t_i\hat{\ }m(x^*)}\ |\ m \mapsto \langle x^*, e\rangle \in \mathcal{M}_i,\ m \notin \mathcal{E}_i,\ n = \mathcal{A}_i(m)\}$$
$$\text{and } \textit{ifields}_1 \cap \cdots \cap \textit{ifields}_n \cap \textit{field}^* = \emptyset$$
$$\text{and } \textit{imeths}_1 \cap \cdots \cap \textit{imeths}_n \cap \textit{meth}^* = \emptyset$$

Fig. 11. Additional reduction rule for AMBIENTTALKLITE

The following example illustrates how trait composition is expressed in terms of delegation. The code on the left summarizes the essence of the animation trait example from Section 3.2. The resulting store is depicted on the right. Note the generated startMoving method of the *morph* object.

```
animationtrait := object {
    start()  = STARTCODE
    stop()   = STOPCODE
}

morph := object {
    animate() = ANIMATECODE
    import animationtrait
    alias startMoving<-start exclude stop
}
```

$$\mathcal{S} = \{$$
$$animationtrait \mapsto \langle\emptyset, \{$$
$$start \mapsto \langle[], \text{STARTCODE}\rangle,$$
$$stop \mapsto \langle[], \text{STOPCODE}\rangle\}\rangle$$
$$morph \mapsto \langle\emptyset, \{$$
$$animate \mapsto \langle[], \text{ANIMATECODE}\rangle$$
$$startMoving \mapsto$$
$$\langle[], animationtrait\hat{\ }start()\rangle\}\rangle\}$$

This concludes our description of the operational semantics of trait composition in AmbientTalk. In the following Section, we discuss how state and visibility control for traits are expressed using this operational semantics.

6 Properties and Discussion

State and visibility control. From the operational semantics of AMBIENTTALKLITE we can derive how state and visibility control are expressed through lexical nesting:

- *Public state.* Trait objects can be stateful by declaring public fields which are explicitly copied into the composing object (cf. Figure 11).
- *Lexically hidden state.* Trait objects can depend upon a field of an object in which they are nested. These fields are not copied into the composing object. Rather, the field remains accessible from the original trait method by lexically referring to it (cf. the syntax extension presented in Figure 6). This is possible because all trait methods close over their lexical scope when created (cf. Figure 8).

- *Lexical visibility control.* An object creation expression that is lexically nested within another object creation expression can refer to the fields and methods of the outer expression. However, an object that has a reference to the nested object cannot access these outer fields or methods via that nested object. As expressed in the [*get*] and [*send*] rules (Figure 5), the lexical scope of an object is not involved in external field access or method invocation. As a consequence, outer fields and methods are inaccessible to clients of the inner object.
- *Shared visibility.* When two object creation expressions are lexically nested within the same outer object creation expression, the two inner objects may refer to the same outer field and method declaration. This allows for sharing state and behavior while keeping it private to external clients. In the operational semantics, sharing is expressed in terms of two lexical environments L_1 and L_2 that may both forward to the same lexical environment L_3 when a name n is not found locally (cf. Figure 8).

Limitations. Traits do not by themselves support advanced resolution strategies required to resolve any unanticipated name conflicts. If two traits are composed that intentionally (rather than accidentally) provide a method with the same name, neither exclusion nor aliasing is an appropriate solution to resolve this conflict. One possible solution would be to completely rename one of the two methods (which, unlike aliasing, requires changing the calls to that method in the method bodies of one of the traits). Another solution would be to change the visibility of one of the two methods, such that it effectively becomes private to its trait. Lexically nested traits by themselves support neither renaming nor changing the visibility of imported methods. Hence, dealing with unanticipated conflicts remains an open issue even with lexically nested traits.

Because lexically nested traits can be stateful, they reintroduce the problem of duplicated state in the case of "diamond inheritance". For example, an object may import two traits A and B, and these two traits both import a third trait C which is stateful. The composite object will then acquire C's state twice. To avoid such issues, one must revert to stateless traits that use accessor and mutator methods to manipulate their state, which is deferred to the composite, as in the original Traits model [13].

Cost. In AmbientTalk, a delegated method invocation has the same runtime cost as a normal method invocation. Without additional optimizations, invoking an imported "delegate method" on a composite is about twice as expensive as a normal method call, because of the additional delegation to the trait. Caching techniques can be used to reduce this overhead, by storing the imported method rather than the delegating method in the composite object's method cache. Improving the performance of our implementation is an area of future work.

Summary. The Trait model supported by AmbientTalk adds both state and visibility control to traits via lexical nesting. Trait composition is made independent of lexical nesting by introducing delegate methods in the composite. Such methods explicitly delegate messages to the imported trait, leaving the lexical environment of the trait's methods intact. Our model does not introduce any additional composition operators.

7 Related Work

Traits in Self. The term *traits* was introduced in the prototype-based language Self to refer to objects that factor out behavior common to objects of the same type [16]. Self traits are not a special kind of object: any object can be a trait and objects "use" a trait by delegating to it using Self's support for object-based inheritance. Like AmbientTalk traits, Self traits exploit delegation to access the "composite" (e.g. for accessing state or invoking an overridden method) by means of late-bound self-sends. Self traits can be stateful, but state is *shared* by all objects using the trait (like class variables shared between all instances).

When multiple inheritance was added to Self, an object was able to specify multiple parent objects, and could thus use traits as mixins. However, since Self relies on object-based (multiple) inheritance to enable the use of (multiple) traits, naming conflicts are not explicitly resolved by the composite object. Resolving such conflicts is instead done by the method lookup algorithm. Self later abandoned multiple inheritance due to its complexity in favor of a simpler "copy-down" approach [30].

AmbientTalk combines the properties of Self traits and Squeak traits. This is illustrated in Figure 12 by means of the example presented in Section 3.1. An `Enumerable` trait defines a `collect:` method and requires an `each:` method which is defined by the composite, in this case a `Range` object that represents an interval.

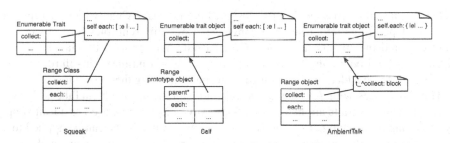

Fig. 12. Comparing trait composition in Squeak, Self and AmbientTalk

Like Self traits, AmbientTalk traits are object-based: any object can be a trait and both languages use the mechanism of delegation to allow the trait to access the composite. Note that in Self the composite delegates to the trait by means of object-based inheritance (via a so-called "parent slot") while in AmbientTalk delegation to the trait happens by means of the ^ operator in the delegating method.

Like Squeak traits, AmbientTalk traits require an explicit composition operation (`import`) during which naming conflicts must be explicitly resolved by the composite. Note how trait composition is compiled away in Squeak by means of the flattening property: the `collect:` method is added to class `Range`. Similarly, in AmbientTalk the trait composition is transformed by adding a delegate method to the composite object. Note that contrary to Self, the trait is not directly accessible from the composite object. Rather, it is referred to by means of a variable private to the delegating method.

Neither Self nor Smalltalk exploit lexical nesting of objects or classes. Similarly, neither language provides a means to hide the visibility of certain methods. Thus, traits defined in these languages have no standard means of controlling visibility. Ambient-Talk exploits an object's lexical scope to restrict the visibility of state and behavior. Since a trait is a regular AmbientTalk object, it can continue to use this technique to restrict the visibility of the state or behavior that it needs, but does not want to provide to its clients.

Jigsaw. In his PhD work, Bracha [36] defined Jigsaw as a minimal programming language in which packages and classes are unified under the notion of a module. A module in Jigsaw is a self-referential scope that binds names to values (*i.e.,* constants and functions). By being an object generator, a module acts as a class and as a coarse-grained structural software unit. Modules can be nested, therefore a module can define a set of classes. A number of operators are provided to compose modules.

In Jigsaw, modules may refer to each other, and functions defined in one are invokable by others according to some visibility rules. Behavior may be shared by merging two modules, or making one override another one. Using these operators, a mixin and its application are nicely modeled. It appears that the same set of operators is used to express both module specialization and mixin uses.

Traits require a different composition operator than inheritance. Traits cannot be expressed in Jigsaw directly because it imposes an ordering on mixins, while one of the design principles of traits states that the composition order of traits is irrelevant.

CHAI. Smith and Drossopoulou [6] designed the language Chai, which incorporates statically typed traits into a Java-like language. Three different roles for traits in Chai were explored in separate languages: $Chai_1$ (traits may be used by classes), $Chai_2$ (a trait may be a type), and $Chai_3$ (traits play a role at runtime). This third language allows traits to be added to objects at runtime, thus changing their behavior.

The differences with AmbientTalk's traits are significant. AmbientTalk is dynamically typed and its traits are first class values. Any object can be used as a trait simply by importing it into another object. In $Chai_3$ only a trait subtype can be applied to an object. Consequently, a more restricted set of traits may be applied to a given object but type safety is upheld.

8   Conclusion

Traits have originally been presented as groups of reusable methods, without state and a mechanism to control the visibility of provided methods. Extensions have been proposed to add these properties (stateful and freezable traits, respectively) but these models introduce many ad hoc operators that have not before been combined into a unified model supporting both properties. This paper demonstrates that state and visibility control can be added to traits by means of just one linguistic mechanism: lexical nesting.

We have shown that introducing trait composition in a host language that supports lexical nesting requires special attention. Whereas in the original model the flattening property allows trait composition to be implemented by almost literally copying the methods provided by the trait into the composite, this approach fails to hold when traits can be lexically nested, because their methods may refer to lexically free variables.

Our approach to solving this problem is based upon delegation of messages. Trait composition is described in terms of generating delegating methods, whose purpose is to delegate a received message to the imported trait object. The actual method invocation is then performed in the proper lexical environment (*i.e.,* that of the trait), but delegation ensures that the trait can still access its required methods via **self** sends. Because methods are generated in the composite, trait composition remains explicit. Name clashes must still be resolved by the composing object, staying true to the original design principles behind traits. Our proposed model has been validated by implementing it in a concrete host language, AmbientTalk, and by describing in detail its operational semantics for a calculus, AMBIENTTALKLITE.

This work started out as an investigation of how traits, a composition mechanism that has been very successfully applied to class-based languages, could be applied to our object-based AmbientTalk language. It became apparent that AmbientTalk's ability to lexically nest objects lead to a simpler trait model since state and visibility control are supported without introducing any additional composition operators. We did need delegation as an additional mechanism to ensure that trait methods can both refer to names in their lexical scope as well as to names provided by the composite. However, our experience tells us that the basic model only relies on lexical nesting, not on the fact that our language is object-based. We think that our model of lexically nested traits can thus be applied more generally to class-based languages as well, provided that they allow classes to be nested and that they provide a solution to the problem of flattening traits in the presence of lexical nesting.

Acknowledgements

We would like to thank Yves Vandriessche who designed and implemented the Ambient-Morphic framework. We also like to thank all reviewers and Erik Ernst in particular, for his valuable improvements to the formal semantics.

References

1. Slate, http://slate.tunes.org
2. Ingalls, D., Kaehler, T., Maloney, J., Wallace, S., Kay, A.: Back to the future: The story of Squeak, a practical Smalltalk written in itself. In: Proceedings of the 12th ACM SIGPLAN conference on Object-oriented programming, systems, languages, and applications, pp. 318–326. ACM Press, New York (1997)
3. Flatt, M., Finder, R.B., Felleisen, M.: Scheme with classes, mixins and traits. In: AAPLAS 2006 (2006)
4. The Fortress language specification, http://research.sun.com/projects/plrg/fortress0866.pdf
5. Fisher, K., Reppy, J.: Statically typed traits. Technical Report TR-2003-13, University of Chicago, Department of Computer Science (December 2003)
6. Smith, C., Drossopoulou, S.: *chai*: Traits for java-like languages. In: Black, A.P. (ed.) ECOOP 2005. LNCS, vol. 3586, pp. 453–478. Springer, Heidelberg (2005)
7. Liquori, L., Spiwack, A.: FeatherTrait: A modest extension of Featherweight Java. ACM Transactions on Programming Languages and Systems (TOPLAS) 30(2), 1–32 (2008)

8. Reppy, J., Turon, A.: Metaprogramming with traits. In: Ernst, E. (ed.) ECOOP 2007. LNCS, vol. 4609, pp. 373–398. Springer, Heidelberg (2007)

9. Bergel, A., Ducasse, S., Nierstrasz, O., Wuyts, R.: Stateful traits and their formalization. Journal of Computer Languages, Systems and Structures 34(2-3), 83–108 (2007)

10. Ducasse, S., Wuyts, R., Bergel, A., Nierstrasz, O.: User-changeable visibility: Resolving unanticipated name clashes in traits. In: Proceedings of 22nd International Conference on Object-Oriented Programming, Systems, Languages, and Applications, pp. 171–190. ACM Press, New York (2007)

11. Bak, L., Bracha, G., Grarup, S., Griesemer, R., Griswold, D., Hölzle, U.: Mixins in Strongtalk. In: ECOOP 2002 Workshop on Inheritance (2002)

12. Ducasse, S., Nierstrasz, O., Schärli, N., Wuyts, R., Black, A.: Traits: A mechanism for fine-grained reuse. ACM Transactions on Programming Languages and Systems (TOPLAS) 28(2), 331–388 (2006)

13. Schärli, N., Ducasse, S., Nierstrasz, O., Black, A.: Traits: Composable units of behavior. In: Cardelli, L. (ed.) ECOOP 2003. LNCS, vol. 2743, pp. 248–274. Springer, Heidelberg (2003)

14. Reppy, J., Turon, A.: A foundation for trait-based metaprogramming. In: International Workshop on Foundations and Developments of Object-Oriented Languages (2006)

15. Mens, T., van Limberghen, M.: Encapsulation and composition as orthogonal operators on mixins: A solution to multiple inheritance problems. Object Oriented Systems 3(1), 1–30 (1996)

16. Ungar, D., Chambers, C., Chang, B.W., Hölzle, U.: Organizing programs without classes. LISP and Symbolic Computation 4(3) (1991)

17. Reddy, U.: Objects as closures: abstract semantics of object-oriented languages. In: LFP 1988: Proceedings of the ACM conference on LISP and functional programming, pp. 289–297. ACM, New York (1988)

18. Abelson, H., Sussman, G.J., Sussman, J.: Structure and interpretation of computer programs. MIT electrical engineering and computer science series. McGraw-Hill, New York (1991)

19. Dickey, K.: Scheming with objects. AI Expert 7(10), 24–33 (1992)

20. Black, A., Hutchinson, N., Jul, E., Levy, H.: Object structure in the Emerald system. In: Proceedings OOPSLA 1986, ACM SIGPLAN Notices, vol. 21, pp. 78–86 (November 1986)

21. International, E.C.M.A.: ECMA-262: ECMAScript Language Specification, 3rd edn. ECMA (European Association for Standardizing Information and Communication Systems), Geneva, Switzerland (December 1999)

22. Madsen, O.L., Moller-Pedersen, B., Nygaard, K.: Object-Oriented Programming in the Beta Programming Language. Addison Wesley, Reading (1993)

23. Miller, M.S.: Robust Composition: Towards a Unified Approach to Access Control and Concurrency Control. PhD thesis, Johns Hopkins University, Baltimore, Maryland, USA (May 2006)

24. Bracha, G.: On the interaction of method lookup and scope with inheritance and nesting. In: 3rd ECOOP Workshop on Dynamic Languages and Applications (2007)

25. Dedecker, J., Cutsem, T.V., Mostinckx, S., Theo D'Hondt, W.D.M.: Ambient-oriented programming in ambienttalk. In: Thomas, D. (ed.) ECOOP 2006. LNCS, vol. 4067, pp. 230–254. Springer, Heidelberg (2006)

26. Van Cutsem, T., Mostinckx, S., Boix, E., Dedecker, J., De Meuter, W.: Ambienttalk: Object-oriented event-driven programming in mobile ad hoc networks. In: XXVI International Conference of the Chilean Society of Computer Science, 2007. SCCC 2007, pp. 3–12 (November 2007)

27. Ungar, D., Smith, R.B.: Self: The power of simplicity. In: Proceedings OOPSLA 1987, ACM SIGPLAN Notices, vol. 22, pp. 227–242 (December 1987)

28. Lieberman, H.: Using prototypical objects to implement shared behavior in object oriented systems. In: Proceedings OOPSLA 1986, ACM SIGPLAN Notices, vol. 21, pp. 214–223 (December 1986)
29. Maloney, J.H., Smith, R.B.: Directness and liveness in the morphic user interface construction environment. In: UIST 1995: Proceedings of the 8th annual ACM symposium on User interface and software technology, pp. 21–28. ACM, New York (1995)
30. Smith, R.B., Ungar, D.: Programming as an experience: The inspiration for self. In: Olthoff, W. (ed.) ECOOP 1995. LNCS, vol. 952, pp. 303–330. Springer, Heidelberg (1995)
31. Anderson, C., Drossopoulou, S.: delta an imperative object based calculus. In: Proceedings of USE 2002 (2002)
32. Bettini, L., Bono, V.: Type Safe Dynamic Object Delegation in Class-based Languages. In: Proc. of PPPJ, Principles and Practice of Programming in Java. ACM Press, New York (2008)
33. Bono, V., Fisher, K.: An imperative, first-order calculus with object extension. In: Proceedings of the 12th European Conference on Object-Oriented Programming, London, UK, pp. 462–497. Springer, Heidelberg (1998)
34. Flatt, M., Krishnamurthi, S., Felleisen, M.: Classes and mixins. In: Proceedings of the 25th ACM SIGPLAN-SIGACT Symposium on Principles of Programming Languages, pp. 171–183. ACM Press, New York (1998)
35. Felleisen, M., Hieb, R.: The revised report on the syntactic theories of sequential control and state. Theor. Comput. Sci. 103(2), 235–271 (1992)
36. Bracha, G.: The Programming Language Jigsaw: Mixins, Modularity and Multiple Inheritance. PhD thesis, Dept. of Computer Science, University of Utah (1992)

Featherweight Jigsaw:
A Minimal Core Calculus
for Modular Composition of Classes*

Giovanni Lagorio, Marco Servetto, and Elena Zucca

DISI, Univ. of Genova, v. Dodecaneso 35, 16146 Genova, Italy
{lagorio,servetto,zucca}@disi.unige.it

Abstract. We present FJIG, a simple calculus where basic building blocks are classes in the style of Featherweight Java, declaring fields, methods and one constructor. However, inheritance has been generalized to the much more flexible notion originally proposed in Bracha's Jigsaw framework. That is, classes play also the role of modules, that can be composed by a rich set of operators, all of which can be expressed by a minimal core.

We keep the nominal approach of Java-like languages, that is, types are class names. However, a class is not necessarily a structural subtype of any class used in its defining expression.

The calculus allows the encoding of a large variety of different mechanisms for software composition in class-based languages, including standard inheritance, mixin classes, traits and hiding. Hence, FJIG can be used as a unifying framework for analyzing existing mechanisms and proposing new extensions.

We provide two different semantics of an FJIG program: *flattening* and *direct* semantics. The difference is analogous to that between two intuitive models to understand inheritance: the former where inherited methods are copied into heir classes, and the latter where member lookup is performed by ascending the inheritance chain. Here we address equivalence of these two views for a more sophisticated composition mechanism.

Introduction

Jigsaw is a framework for modular composition largely independent of the underlying language, designed by Gilad Bracha in his seminal thesis [8], and then formalized by a minimal set of operators in module calculi such as [21,3]. In this paper, we define an instantiation of Jigsaw, called Featherweight Jigsaw (FJIG for short), where basic building blocks are classes in the style of Java-like languages. That is, classes are collections of fields, methods and constructors, that can be instantiated to create objects; also, class names are used as types (nominal typing).

---

* This work has been partially supported by MIUR EOS DUE - Extensible Object Systems for Dynamic and Unpredictable Environments.

S. Drossopoulou (Ed.): ECOOP 2009, LNCS 5653, pp. 244–268, 2009.

The motivation for this work is that, even though Jigsaw has been proposed a long time ago and since then it has been greatly influential[1], its design has been never fully exploited in the context of Java-like languages, as recently pointed out as an open question in [4]. Here, we provide a foundational answer to this question, by defining a core language which, however, embodies the key features of Java-like languages, in the same spirit of Featherweight Java [15] (FJ for short). Indeed, formally, a basic class of FJIG looks very much as a class in FJ. However, standard inheritance has been replaced by the much more flexible (module) composition, that is, by the rich set of operators of the Jigsaw framework.

Instantiating Jigsaw on Java-like languages poses some non trivial design problems. Just to mention one (others are discussed in Sect. 1), we keep the nominal approach of Java-like languages, that is, types are class names. However, a class is not necessarily a structural subtype of any class used in its defining expression. While this allows a more flexible reuse, it may prevent the (generalized) inheritance relation to be a subtyping relation. So, the required subtyping relations among classes are declared by the programmer and checked by the type system.

Another challenging issue is the generalization to FJIG of two intuitive models to understand inheritance: one where inherited methods are copied into heir classes, and the other one where member lookup is performed by ascending the inheritance chain. We address the equivalence of these two views for a much more sophisticated composition mechanism. Formally, we provide two different semantics for an FJIG program: *flattening* semantics, that is, by translation into a program where all composition operators have been performed, and *direct* semantics, that is, by formalizing a dynamic look-up procedure.

The paper is organized as follows. Sect. 1 provides an informal introduction to FJIG by using a sugared surface syntax. Sect. 2 introduces a lower level syntax and defines flattening semantics. Sect. 3 defines the type system and states its soundness. Sect. 4 defines direct semantics of FJIG and states the equivalence between the two semantics. In the Conclusion, we summarize the contribution of the paper and briefly discuss related and further work.

A preliminary version of this paper, focused on the equivalence between flattening and direct semantics, and not including the type system, is [17]. An extended version including proofs of results is [16].

1   An Informal Introduction

In this section we illustrate the main features of FJIG by using a sugared surface syntax, given in Fig. 1. We assume infinite sets of *class names* C, *(member) names* N, and *variables* x. We use the bar notation for sequences, e.g., $\bar{\mu}$ is a metavariable for sequences $\mu_1 \ldots \mu_n$.

---

[1] Just to mention two different research areas, Jigsaw principles are present in work on extending the ML module system with mutually recursive modules [9,13,14], and Jigsaw operators already included those later used in mixin classes and traits [11,1,20,10,19].

p	$::= \overline{cd}\ \overline{leq}$	program
cd	$::= cmod\ \textbf{class}\ C\ CE$	class declaration
leq	$::= C <= C'$	subtype declaration
$cmod$	$::= \textbf{abstract} \mid \epsilon$	class modifier
CE	$::=$	class expression
	B	basic class
	$\mid C$	class name
	$\mid \textbf{merge}\ CE_1, CE_2$	merge
	$\mid CE_1\ \textbf{override}\ CE_2$	override
	$\mid \textbf{rename}\ N\ \textbf{to}\ N'\ \textbf{in}\ CE$	rename
	$\mid \textbf{restrict}\ N\ \textbf{in}\ CE$	restrict
	$\mid \textbf{hide}\ N\ \textbf{in}\ CE$	hide
	$\mid \ldots$	
	$\mid CE[\tau]$	**ThisType** wrapper
	$\mid CE[kh\{\textbf{super}(\overline{e})\}]$	constructor wrapper
N	$::= F \mid M$	member name
kh	$::= \textbf{constructor}(\overline{C\ x})$	constructor header
B	$::= \{\tau\ \overline{\varphi}\ \kappa\ \overline{\mu}\}$	basic class
τ	$::= \textbf{ThisType} <= C$	**ThisType** constraint
φ	$::= mod\ C\ F;$	field
κ	$::= kh\{\overline{F=e}\}$	constructor
μ	$::= mod\ C\ M\ (\overline{C\ x})\{\textbf{return}\ e;\}$	
	$\mid \textbf{abstract}\ C\ M(\overline{C\ x});$	method
mod	$::= \textbf{abstract} \mid \textbf{virtual} \mid \textbf{frozen} \mid \textbf{local}$	member modifier
e	$::=$	expression
	x	variable
	$\mid e.F$	client field access
	$\mid e.M(\overline{e})$	client method invocation
	$\mid F$	internal field access
	$\mid M(\overline{e})$	internal method invocation
	$\mid \textbf{new}\ C(\overline{e})$	object creation

Fig. 1. FJig (surface) syntax

This syntax is designed to keep a Java-like flavour as much as possible. In the next section we will use a lower-level representation, which allows to formalize the semantics in a simpler and natural way.

We will first revise Jigsaw features in the context of FJig, then discuss some issues that are specific to the instantiation on Java-like languages.

Basic classes. Jigsaw is a programming paradigm based on (module) composition, where a basic module (in our case, a class) is a collection of components (in our case, members), which can be of four different kinds, indicated by a modifier: **abstract**, **virtual**, **frozen**, and **local**. A method has no body if and only if its modifier is **abstract**. The meaning of modifiers is as follows:

– An **abstract** member has no definition, and is expected to be defined later when composing the class with others.

- A `virtual` or `frozen` member has a definition, which can be changed by using the composition operators. However, the redefinition of a `frozen` member does not affect the other members, which still refer to its original definition.
- Finally, as the name suggests, a `local` member cannot be selected by a client[2], and is not affected by composition operators, hence its definition cannot be changed.

We assume by default the modifier `frozen` for fields and `virtual` for methods. A class having at least one `abstract` member must be declared `abstract`.
The following example shows two abstract basic classes.[3]

```
abstract class A {
  abstract int M1();
  int M2() { return M1() + M3(); }
  local int M3() { return 1; }
} abstract class B {
  abstract int M2();
  frozen int M1() { return 1 + M2(); }
}
```

Merge and override operators. A concrete class can be obtained by applying the `merge` operator as follows:

```
class C merge A, B
```

This declaration is equivalent to the following:

```
class C {
  frozen int M1() { return 1 + M2(); }
  int M2() { return M1() + M3(); }
  local int M3() { return 1; }
}
```

Conflicting definitions for the same non-local member are not permitted, whereas `abstract` members with the same name are shared. Members can be selected by client code unless they are `local`, that is, we can write, e.g., `new C().M2()` but not `new C().M3()`. To show the difference between `virtual` and `frozen` members, in the next examples we use the `override` operator, a variant of `merge` where conflicts are allowed and the left argument has the precedence.

```
class D1
  { int M2() { return 2; } } override C
```

An invocation `new D1().M2()` will evaluate to 2, and an invocation `new D1().M1()` to 3. On the other hand, in this case:

```
class D2
  { int M1() { return 3; } } override C
```

---

[2] Note the difference with `private` modifier in Java, which allows client selection when clients are of the same class, see more details in the sequel.

[3] To write more readable examples, we assume that the primitive type `int` and its operations are available.

an invocation `new D2().M1()` will evaluate to 3, *but* an invocation `new D2().M2()` will not terminate, since the internal invocation `M1()` in the body of `M2()` still refers to the old definition.

Client and internal member selection. In a programming paradigm based on module composition, a module component can be either selected by a client, or used by other components inside the module itself. Correspondingly, in FJIG we distinguish between *client* field accesses and method invocations, which specify a receiver, and *internal* field accesses and method invocations, whose implicit receiver is the current object. Note that $e.M(\ldots)$ behaves differently from $M(\ldots)$ even in the case e denotes an object of the same class (that is, internal selection *does not* correspond to selection of `private` members as in, e.g., Java). For instance, consider the following class, where we use the operator `rename`, which changes the name of a member.

```
class E merge
  (rename M1 to M4 in {
    int M1() { return 1; }
    int M2() { return M1(); }
    int M3() { return new E().M1(); }
}), { int M1() { return 3; } }
```

An invocation `new E().M2()` returns 1, since the internal invocation in the body of M2 refers to the method now called M4. However, an invocation `new E().M3()` returns 3, since the client invocation in the body of M3 refers to method M1 in E. Note that this does not even coincide with privateness on a "per object" basis as, e.g., in Smalltalk, since this would be the case even with a client invocation `e.M1()`, where e denotes, as special case, the current object.

Other operators of the Jigsaw framework, besides the ones mentioned above, are `restrict`, which eliminates the definition for a member[4], and `hide`, which makes a member no longer selectable from the outside. We refer to [8] and [3] for more details. All these operators and many others can be easily encoded (see [3]) by using a minimal set of *primitive* operators: *sum*, *reduct*, and *freeze*, which will be formally defined in next section.

We discuss now the issues specific to the instantiation on Java-like classes.

Fields and constructors. It turns out that the above modifiers can be smoothly applied to fields as well, with analogous meaning, as shown by the following example which also illustrates how constructors work.

```
class A1 {
  abstract int F1; virtual int F2; int F3;
  constructor(int x) { F2 = x; F3 = x; }
  int M() { return F2 + F3; }
} class C1 {
  int F1; int F2; int F3;
  constructor(int x) { F1 = x+1; F2 = x+1; F3 = x+1; }
} override A1
```

---

[4] Indeed, CE_1 `override` CE_2 = `merge` CE_1, `restrict` N_1 `in` ... `restrict` N_k `in` CE_2 where $N_1, \ldots N_k$ are the common members.

A basic class defines one[5] constructor which specifies a sequence of parameters and a sequence of initialization expressions, one for each non-abstract field. We assume a default constructor with no parameters for classes having no fields. Note the difference with FJ, where the class constructor has a canonical form (parameters exactly correspond to fields). This would be inadequate in our framework since object layout must be hidden to clients. In order to be composed by merge/overriding, two classes should provide a constructor with the same parameter list (if it is not the case, a *constructor wrapper* can be inserted, see the last example of this section), and the effect is that the resulting class provides a constructor with the same parameter list, that executes both the original constructors. An instance of class C1 has five fields (A1.F2, A1.F3, C1.F1, C1.F2, C1.F3), and an invocation **new** C1(5).M() will return 11, since F2 in the body of M refers to the field declared in C1 (initialized with 5+1), while F3 refers to the field declared in A1 (initialized with 5).[6]

Classes composed by merge/overriding can share the same field, provided it is abstract in all except (at most) one. Note that this corresponds to *sharing* fields as in, e.g., [5]; however, in our framework we do not need an ad-hoc notion.

Inheritance and subtyping. Since our aim is to instantiate the Jigsaw framework on a Java-like language, we keep a nominal approach, that is, types are class names. However, subtyping *does not* coincide with the generalized inheritance relation, since some of the composition operators (e.g., renaming) do not preserve structural subtyping. Hence, we assume that a program includes a sequence of subtyping relations among classes explicitly declared by the programmer, and the type system checks, for each $C <= C'$ subtype declaration, that the relation can be safely assumed since C is a structural subtype of C'.

Type of the current object. The following code

```
{ C M() { return this; } }
```

can be safely inherited only by classes which are a subtype of C. To ensure this, basic classes can declare a **ThisType** constraint:

```
{ ThisType <= C;
  C M() { return this; }
}
```

This constraint is used to typecheck the occurrences of **this** inside method bodies. Moreover, the constraint is checked when inheriting the code:

```
class C {
   ThisType <= C;
   C M() {return this;}
} class D   ... C ... //ok only if D <= C
```

---

[5] Since overloading is not allowed.

[6] Note that an overriden member, such as A1.F2, could still be selected, as usual, by a **super** mechanism, which can be encoded in Jigsaw, notably by renaming [2].

The ThisType constraint can be strengthened by the ThisType wrapping operator

```
C [ThisType <= D] //ok only if D <= C
```

We assume a default constraint ThisType <= Object, where Object is a pre-defined class with no members.

To conclude this section, we show a more significant example, where we also assume to have the type void and some statements in the syntax.

The following class DBSerializable, an example of the pattern *template method* [12], contains the method saveToDB, which writes the object serialized representation onto a database. While the behaviour of saveToDB is fixed, the details on how to open the connection are left unspecified, and the implementation of the method serialize can be changed.[7] This is reflected by the method modifiers. Class DBConnection is a given library class.

```
abstract class DBSerializable {
  abstract DBConnection openConnection ();
  virtual void serialize(DBConnection c) {}
  frozen void saveToDB() {
    DBConnection connection = openConnection ();
    // ...
    serialize (connection);
    connection.close ();
  }
}
```

Suppose we want to specialize the class DBSerializable for the DB server MySQL. We can create this specialization, called MySQLSerializable, in two steps: first, we provide an implementation of method openConnection with the specific code for MySQL, then we *hide* it, since clients of MySQLSerializable should never invoke this method directly. We start by defining an auxiliary class _MySQLSerializable, merging DBSerializable with an anonymous basic class:

```
class _MySQLSerializable
  merge
    DBSerializable[ constructor(String cs) {
                      super()
                    } ],
    { local String connectionString;
      constructor(String cs) { connectionString = cs; }
      virtual DBConnection openConnection () {
        /* ... use connectionString ... */}
    }
```

Note the use of the constructor wrapper: the constructor of the anonymous basic class has a String parameter, whereas that of the class DBSerializable, which has no fields, is the default (parameterless) constructor. Hence, a constructor wrapper is inserted, so that the classes we are merging have both a constructor with the same parameters. This allows to create objects of the new class with expressions like new _MySQLSerializable("someConnectionString..."). As

---

[7] This method could be declared abstract as well.

mentioned before, the class _MySQLSerializable provides, along the method saveToDB, the method openConnection that we can hide as follows:

```
class MySQLSerializable
  hide openConnection in _MySQLSerializable
```

Consider now the following class Person, providing a method, named **write**, to serialize its objects to a database:

```
class Person {  // ...
  frozen void write(DBConnection c) {
    /* serializes the data on c*/}
}
```

Notwithstanding the inherited method DBSerializable.saveToDB writes the data by invoking the method serialize and not write, using the class Person with MySQLSerializable is not a problem, since we can rename the method before merging the two classes:

```
class MySQLSerializablePerson
  hide serialize in
    (rename write to serialize in Person)
      [constructor(String cs){super()}]
    override MySQLSerializable
```

2   FJIG Calculus

In this section we formally define the (flattening) semantics of FJIG. To this aim, we use a different representation for basic classes w.r.t. the surface syntax given in Fig. 1. That is, instead of having explicit modifiers, their semantics is encoded by distinguishing between *external* and *internal* member names. Internal names are used to refer to members inside code (method bodies), whereas external names are used in class composition via operators and in selection of members by clients. Correspondingly, basic classes include, besides previous components which are collected in the *local part*, an *input map* from internal to external names, and an *output map* from external to internal names. Intuitively, the input map translates required internal names to external names which are actually required from other classes, and the output map translates provided external names to internal names which actually provide their definitions. We could have alternatively expressed the semantics directly on the surface language, getting a more FJ-like flavour. However, the representation with i/o maps has some advantages: a clean distinction between internal names, which can be α-renamed, and external names, as in the tradition of module calculi [21,3]; renaming (reduct operator) can be modeled without changing (occurrences of names in) code; in general, operators can be modeled in a uniform way, whereas the other representation would require a case analysis on the four kinds of members.

The syntax of the calculus is given in Fig. 2. Besides class names, (external) names and variables, we assume an infinite set of *internal (member) names* n. A program consists of two components: a sequence of *class declarations* (class name and class expression), as in FJ, and a sequence of *subtype declarations*. We assume that no class is declared twice and order is immaterial, hence we can write $p(C)$ for the class expression associated with C. Class expressions CE are basic classes B, class names C, or are inductively constructed by a set of composition operators. Let us say that C "inherits from" C' if the class expression associated with C contains a subterm C', or, transitively, C'' which inherits from C'. In a well-formed program, we require this generalized inheritance relation to be acyclic, exactly as for standard inheritance. Input and output maps are represented as sequences of pairs where the first element has a type annotation. In an input map, internal names which are mapped to the same external name are required to have the same annotation, whereas this is not required in output names, that is, the same member can be exported under different names with different types, see the type system in next section. Renamings σ are maps from (annotated) external names into (annotated) external names, represented as sequences of pairs; pairs of form $\_ \mapsto N{:}T$ are used to represent non-surjective maps. We use some shorter keywords w.r.t. the surface syntax, and expressions include *runtime expressions*, that is, (pre-)objects and blocks.

We denote by *dom* and *img* the domain and image of a map, respectively. Given a basic class $[\iota\,|\,o\,|\,\rho]$, with $\rho = \{\tau\,\overline{\varphi}\,\kappa\,\overline{\mu}\}$, we denote by $dom(\overline{\mu})$ and $dom(\overline{\varphi})$ the sets of internal names declared in $\overline{\mu}$ and $\overline{\varphi}$, respectively, which are assumed to be disjoint. The union of these two sets, denoted by $dom(\rho)$, is the set of *local* names. An internal name n is, instead, *abstract* if $n \in dom(\iota)$, $\iota(n) \notin dom(o)$, and *virtual* if $\iota(n) \in dom(o)$. An external name N is *abstract* if $N \in img(\iota)\backslash dom(o)$, *virtual* if $N \in img(\iota) \cap dom(o)$, *frozen* if $N \in dom(o)\backslash img(\iota)$. In a well-formed basic class, local names must be distinct from abstract/virtual internal names, that is, $dom(\iota) \cap dom(\rho) = \emptyset$. Moreover, $img(o) \subseteq dom(\rho)$, and, denoting by $names(e)$ the set of internal names in an expression e, $names(e) \subseteq dom(\iota) \cup dom(\rho)$ for each method body e.

A basic class of the surface language can be easily encoded in the calculus as follows. For each member name N we assume (at most) a corresponding external name N and (at most) two internal names n, n', depending on the member kind, as detailed below. Client references to N are unaffected, whereas internal references are translated according to the member kind:

- if N is abstract, then there is an association $n \mapsto N$ in the input map, and internal references are translated by n,
- if N is virtual, then there is an association $n \mapsto N$ in the input map, an association $N \mapsto n'$ in the output map, a definition for n' in ρ, and internal references are translated by n,
- if N is frozen, then there is an association $N \mapsto n'$ in the output map, a definition for n' in ρ, and internal references are translated by n'.
- if N is local, then there is a definition for n' in ρ, and internal references are translated by n'.

Inside constructor bodies, a field name F on the left-hand side is always translated by f' (and internal member selection is forbidden).

For instance, the class C shown in the previous section is translated by

p	$::= \overline{cd}\ leq$	program
cd	$::= C \mapsto CE$	class declaration
leq	$::= C \le C'$	subtype declaration
CE	$::= B \mid C \mid$	class expression
	$CE_1 + CE_2$	sum
	$\mid {}_{\sigma^\iota \mid} CE_{\mid \sigma^o}$	reduct
	$\mid freeze_N CE$	freeze
	$\mid CE[\mathtt{K}(\overline{C\ x})\{\overline{e}\}] \mid CE[\mathtt{TT} \le C]$	constructor and **ThisType** wrappers
σ	$::= \overline{N{:}T \mapsto N'{:}T'},\ \_\mapsto N{:}T$	renaming
N	$::= F \mid M$	external member name
T	$::= C \mid MT$	member type
MT	$::= \overline{C} \to C$	method type
B	$::= [\iota \mid o \mid \rho]$	basic class
ι	$::= \overline{n{:}T \mapsto N}$	input map
o	$::= \overline{N{:}T \mapsto n}$	output map
n	$::= f \mid m$	internal member name
ρ	$::= \{\tau\ \overline{\varphi}\ \kappa\ \overline{\mu}\}$	local part
τ	$::= \mathtt{TT} \le C$	**ThisType** constraint
φ	$::= C\ f;$	field
κ	$::= \mathtt{K}(\overline{C\ x})\{\overline{f=e}\}$	constructor
μ	$::= C\ m(\overline{C\ x})\{\mathtt{return}\ e;\}$	method
e	$::= x \mid e.F \mid e.M(\overline{e}) \mid f \mid m(\overline{e}) \mid \mathtt{new}\ C(\overline{e})$	expression
	$\mid [\overline{\mu}; v \mid e]$	block
	$\mid C(\overline{f=e})$	(pre-)object
v, v^C	$::= C(\overline{f=e})$	value (object)

Fig. 2. Syntax

$$[m_2{:}() \to \mathtt{int} \mapsto M_2 \mid M_1{:}() \to \mathtt{int} \mapsto m_1', M_2{:}() \to \mathtt{int} \mapsto m_2', \mid \rho]$$

```
ρ = {
    TT≤Object      K(){}
    int m₁'(){return 1 + m₂();}
    int m₂'(){return m₁'() + m₃'();}
    int m₃'(){return 1;}
}
```

We describe now the two kinds of runtime expressions introduced in the calculus.

Expressions of form $C(\overline{f=e})$ denote a *pre-object* of class C, where for each field f there is a corresponding initialization expression. Note the difference with the form $\mathtt{new}\ C(\overline{e})$, which denotes a constructor invocation, whereas in FJ objects can be identified with object creation expressions where arguments are values. As already noted, in FJ it is possible, and convenient, to take this simple and nice solution, since the structure of the instances of a class is globally visible to the whole program. In FJIG, instead, object layout must be hidden to clients, hence constructor parameters have no a priori relation with fields.

Values of the calculus are *objects*, that is, pre-objects where all initialization expressions are (in turn) values. We use both v^C and v as metavariables for values of class C, the latter when the class is not relevant.

Moreover, runtime expressions also include *block* expressions of the form $[\overline{\mu}; v \mid e]$, which model the execution of e where method internal names are bound in $\overline{\mu}$ and field internal names in the current object v. Hence, denoting by $dom(v)$ the set $\{f_1, \ldots, f_n\}$ if $v = C(f_1 = v_1 \ldots f_n = e_n)$, a block expression is well-formed only if $names(e) \subseteq dom(\overline{\mu}) \cup dom(v)$ (hence $names([\overline{\mu}; v \mid e]) = \emptyset$) and these two sets are disjoint.

The semantics of an expression e in the context of a program p can be defined in two different ways. The former, which we call *flattening semantics* and illustrate in this section, is given in two steps. First, p is reduced to a *flat* program p', that is, a program where every class is basic. To this end, operators are performed and the occurrences of class names are replaced by their defining expressions. Then, e is reduced in the context of p'. Note that in this case dynamic look-up is always trivial, that is, a class member (e.g., a method) can be always found in the class of the receiver. In next section, we define an alternative *direct* semantics, where expressions are reduced in the context of non flat programs, hence where dynamic look-up is non trivial.

Flattening rules are defined in the top section of Fig. 3. We omit subtype declarations for simplicity since they do not affect semantics.

The first two rules define reduction steps of programs, which can be obtained either by reducing one of the class expressions, or, if some class C has already been reduced to a basic class B, by replacing by B all occurrences of C as class expression.

The remaining rules define reduction steps of class expressions. Rules for sum, reduct and freeze operators are essentially those given in [3], to which we refer for more details. We omit standard contextual closure for brevity.

The expression o_1, o_2 is well-formed only if the two maps have disjoint domains, and analogously for other maps. Hence, rule (SUM) can only be applied (implicit side conditions) when the two sets of internal names are disjoint, as are the sets of output names. The former condition can be always satisfied by an appropriate α-conversion, whereas the latter corresponds to a conflict that the programmer can only solve by an explicitly renaming (reduct operator). Note that `ThisType` constraints and constructor parameters are required to be the same, in order both to get a commutative operator and to keep the calculus minimal; indeed, this can be always achieved by using wrapping operators.

In rule (REDUCT), new input and output names are chosen, modeled by $img(\sigma^\iota)$ and $dom(\sigma^o)$, respectively. Old input names are mapped in new input names by σ^ι, whereas new output names are mapped into old output names by σ^o. Input names can be shared or added, whereas output names can be duplicated or removed. The symbol $\circ$ denotes composition of maps, which is

(CDEC1) $\dfrac{CE \longrightarrow CE'}{(p, C \mapsto CE) \longrightarrow (p, C \mapsto CE')}$

(CDEC2) $\dfrac{}{(p, C \mapsto B) \longrightarrow (p[B/C], C \mapsto B)}$

(SUM) $\dfrac{}{[\iota_1 \,|\, o_1 \,|\, \rho_1] + [\iota_2 \,|\, o_2 \,|\, \rho_2] \longrightarrow [\iota_1, \iota_2 \,|\, o_1, o_2 \,|\, \rho]}$ $\begin{array}{l} \rho_i = \{\tau \;\overline{\varphi}_i \; \mathrm{K}(\overline{C\ x})\{(\overline{f=e})_i\} \;\overline{\mu}_i\}, \\ \qquad\qquad\qquad\qquad\qquad\quad i \in \{1,2\} \\ \rho = \{\tau \;\overline{\varphi}_1, \overline{\varphi}_2 \\ \quad \mathrm{K}(\overline{C\ x})\{(\overline{f=e})_1, (\overline{f=e})_2\} \;\overline{\mu}_1, \overline{\mu}_2\} \end{array}$

(REDUCT) $\dfrac{}{\sigma^\iota [\![\iota \,|\, o \,|\, \rho]\!]_{|\sigma^o} \longrightarrow [\sigma^\iota \circ \iota \,|\, o \circ \sigma^o \,|\, \rho]}$

(FREEZE) $\dfrac{}{\begin{array}{c} freeze_N[\iota, n_1 : T \mapsto N \ldots n_k : T \mapsto N \,|\, o \,|\, \rho] \longrightarrow \\ [\iota \,|\, o \,|\, \rho[n'/n_1] \ldots [n'/n_k]] \end{array}}$ $\begin{array}{l} n' = o(N) \\ N \notin img(\iota) \end{array}$

(TT WRAP) $\dfrac{}{[\iota \,|\, o \,|\, \{\mathrm{TT} \leq C' \; \overline{\varphi} \; \kappa \; \overline{\mu}\}][\mathrm{TT} \leq C] \longrightarrow [\iota \,|\, o \,|\, \{\mathrm{TT} \leq C \; \overline{\varphi} \; \kappa \; \overline{\mu}\}]}$

(K WRAP) $\dfrac{}{[\iota \,|\, o \,|\, \rho][\mathrm{K}(\overline{\mathrm{D}\ y})\{\overline{e}\}] \longrightarrow [\iota \,|\, o \,|\, \rho']}$ $\begin{array}{l} \overline{x} = x_1 \ldots x_n \\ \rho = \{\tau \;\overline{\varphi} \; \mathrm{K}(C_1 \, x_1 \ldots C_n \, x_n)\{\overline{f=e}\} \;\overline{\mu}\} \\ \rho' = \{\tau \;\overline{\varphi} \; \mathrm{K}(\overline{\mathrm{D}\ y})\{\overline{f=e[\overline{e}/\overline{x}]}\} \;\overline{\mu}\} \end{array}$

(CTX) $\dfrac{e \longrightarrow_p e'}{\mathcal{E}\{e\} \longrightarrow_p \mathcal{E}\{e'\}}$ (CLIENT-FIELD) $\dfrac{}{v^C.F \longrightarrow_p [\overline{\mu}; v^C \,|\, f]}$ $\begin{array}{l} p(C) = [\iota \,|\, o \,|\, \{\tau \;\overline{\varphi} \; \kappa \; \overline{\mu}\}] \\ o(F) = f \end{array}$

(CLIENT-INVK) $\dfrac{}{v^C.M(\overline{v}) \longrightarrow_p [\overline{\mu}; v^C \,|\, m(\overline{v})]}$ $\begin{array}{l} p(C) = [\iota \,|\, o \,|\, \{\tau \;\overline{\varphi} \; \kappa \; \overline{\mu}\}] \\ o(M) = m \end{array}$

(INT-FIELD) $\dfrac{}{[\overline{\mu}; v \,|\, \mathcal{E}\{f\}] \longrightarrow_p [\overline{\mu}; v \,|\, \mathcal{E}\{v_i\}]}$ $\begin{array}{l} f \notin HB(\mathcal{E}) \\ v = C(f_1 = v_1 \ldots f_n = v_n) \\ f = f_i \end{array}$

(INT-INVK) $\dfrac{}{[\overline{\mu}; v^C \,|\, \mathcal{E}\{m(\overline{v})\}] \longrightarrow_p [\overline{\mu}; v^C \,|\, \mathcal{E}\{e[\overline{v}/\overline{x}][v^C/\mathbf{this}]\}]}$ $\begin{array}{l} m \notin HB(\mathcal{E}) \\ \overline{\mu}(m) = \langle \overline{x}, e \rangle \end{array}$

(OBJ-CREATION) $\dfrac{}{\mathbf{new}\ C(\overline{v}) \longrightarrow_p C(\overline{f = e[\overline{v}/\overline{x}]})}$ $\begin{array}{l} p(C) = [\emptyset \,|\, o \,|\, \rho] \\ \rho = \{\tau \;\overline{\varphi} \; \mathrm{K}(C_1 \, x_1 \ldots C_n \, x_n)\{\overline{f=e}\} \;\overline{\mu}\} \\ \overline{x} = x_1 \ldots x_n \end{array}$

(EXIT-BLOCK) $\dfrac{}{[\overline{\mu}; v \,|\, e] \longrightarrow_p e}$ $names(e) = \emptyset$

Fig. 3. Flattening semantics

well-formed only if type annotations are the same and the annotation of the new name is kept in the resulting map.

In rule (FREEZE), association from internal names into N are removed from the input map, and occurrences of these names in method bodies are replaced by the local name of the corresponding definition, thus eliminating any dependency on N. The second side condition ensures that we actually take *all* such names.

Rules for constructor and ThisType wrapping just correspond to changing the constructor and the ThisType constraint for a class, respectively. In (K WRAP), n is the arity of the old constructor, and the body of the new constructor has n initialization expressions, as implicitly imposed by the well-formedness of multiple substitution $\overline{e}$ for $\overline{x}$. We chose a permissive semantics for ThisType wrapping, alternatively we could perform a runtime check on the relation between C and C'.

Reduction rules are given in the second section of Fig. 3.

The first rule is the standard contextual closure, where $\mathcal{E}$ denotes a one-hole context and $\mathcal{E}\{e\}$ denotes the expression obtained by filling the hole by e.

Client field accesses and method invocations are reduced in two steps. First, they are reduced to a block where the current object is the receiver and the expression to be executed is the corresponding internal member selection on the name found in the receiver's class; moreover, methods found in the receiver's class are copied into the block and used for resolving further internal method invocations.[8] Then, the following two rules can be applied.

An internal field access can only be reduced if it appears inside a block. In this case, it is replaced by the corresponding field of the current object. The first side condition says that the occurrence of f or m in the position denoted by the hole of the context $\mathcal{E}$ is free (that is, not captured by any binder around the hole), hence ensures that it is correctly bound to the current object in the first enclosing block. The standard formal definition of HB is omitted. For instance, in the expression $[\overline{\mu}; v \mid m(f, [\overline{\mu}'; v' \mid f])]$, the first occurrence of f denotes a field of the object v, whereas the second occurrence denotes a field of the object v'. Analogously, an internal method invocation is replaced by the corresponding body, found in $\overline{\mu}$, where parameters are replaced by arguments and this by the current object. We denote by $\overline{\mu}(m)$ the pair $\langle x_1 \ldots x_n, e \rangle$ if $\overline{\mu}$ contains a (unique) method $C\ m(C_1\ x_1\ \ldots\ C_n\ x_n)\{\text{return } e;\}$.

Note that there are two kinds of references to the current object in a method body: through the keyword this (in client member selection, or in a non-receiver position, e.g. return this), and through internal names. Whereas the former can be substituted at invocation time, as in FJ, the latter are modeled by a block, otherwise we would not be able to distinguish, among the objects of form v^C, those which actually refer to the original receiver of the invocation.

In rule (OBJ-CREATION), note that only classes where all members are frozen can be instantiated. This is a simplification: the execution model could be easily

---

[8] Alternatively, the method body corresponding to an internal name could be again found in the basic class of the receiver; we choose this model because it can be better generalized to direct semantics, see the following.

generalized to handle internal member selection on a virtual internal name by retrieving the input map as well in blocks (in rules (CLIENT-FIELD) and (CLIENT-INVK)) and adding two reduction rules which, roughly, reduce such an internal field access/method invocation into the corresponding client member selection. We preferred to stick to an equivalent simpler model which, assuming that all classes have been frozen before being instantiated, avoids these redundant lookup steps.

Finally, in (EXIT-BLOCK), a block can be eliminated when the enclosed expression does no longer contain internal member selections, hence in particular when a value is obtained.

Examples illustrating flattening semantics (in comparison with direct semantics) will be provided in Sect. 4.

3   Type System

The type system uses four kinds of type environments, shown in Fig. 4.

Δ	$:: = \overline{C{:}CT}\ \overline{leq}$	class type environment
CT	$:: = [\Sigma^\iota; \Sigma^o; \overline{C}; C]$	class type
Γ	$:: = \overline{n{:}T}$	internal type environment
Π	$:: = \overline{x{:}C}$	parameter type environment
Σ	$:: = \overline{N{:}T}$	signature
Δ^r	$:: = \overline{C{:}\Gamma}$	runtime class type environment

Fig. 4. Type environments

A class type environment is a pair consisting of a map from class names into class types and a sequence of subtype declarations. A class type is a 4-tuple consisting of input and output signatures, constructor type and type of this. We use the abbreviated notations $C \le C' \in \Delta$ and $\Delta(C) = CT$.

Signatures are maps from external names into types.

We denote by $mtype(\Delta, C, N)$ the type of member named N in $\Delta(C)$, which is the output type[9] for a defined member, the input type for an abstract member.

Internal type environments map internal names to types. Parameter type environments map variables (parameters) into class names. Finally, runtime class type environments map class names to internal type environments.

Typing rules in Fig. 5 define judgments $\vdash p{:}\Delta$ for programs and $\Delta \vdash CE{:}CT$ for class expressions.

In (PROG-T), a program has type Δ if each declared class C has type $\Delta(C)$ w.r.t. Δ, ThisType constraints are satisfied, and declared subtyping relations are safe. The judgment $\Delta \vdash C \le C'$ checks whether C and C' are in the reflexive and transitive closure of subtyping declarations in Δ. The judgment $\Delta \vdash C \le C'$ OK

---

[9] To provide a richer interface to clients.

$$\text{(PROG-T)} \quad \dfrac{\begin{array}{l} \Delta \vdash CE_i\!:\!CT_i \ \ \forall i \in 1..n \\[2pt] \Delta \vdash C_i \le C_i^\tau \ \forall i \in 1..n \\[2pt] \Delta \vdash C_i' \le C_i'' \ \text{OK} \ \forall i \in 1..k \end{array}}{\vdash C_1 \mapsto CE_1 \ldots C_n \mapsto CE_n \ \overline{leq}\!:\!\Delta} \quad \begin{array}{l} \overline{leq} = C_1' \le C_1'' \ldots C_k' \le C_k'' \\[2pt] \Delta = C_1\!:\!CT_1 \ldots C_n\!:\!CT_n \ \overline{leq} \\[2pt] CT_i = [\_;\_;\_; C_i^\tau] \end{array}$$

$$\text{(CNAME-T)} \quad \dfrac{}{\Delta \vdash C\!:\!CT} \quad \Delta(C) = CT$$

$$\text{(BASIC-T)} \quad \dfrac{\begin{array}{c} \Delta; \Gamma^\iota, \Gamma^{\overline{\mu}}, \Gamma^{\overline{\varphi}}; C \vdash \overline{\mu}\!:\!\Gamma^{\overline{\mu}} \\[3pt] \Delta; \Gamma^{\overline{\varphi}} \vdash \kappa\!:\!\overline{C} \end{array}}{\Delta \vdash [\iota \,|\, o \,|\, \{\text{TT} \le C \ \overline{\varphi} \ \kappa \ \overline{\mu}\}]\!:\![\Sigma^\iota; \Sigma^o; \overline{C}; C]} \quad \begin{array}{l} \Delta \vdash \Sigma^o(N) \le \Sigma^\iota(N) \\[2pt] \qquad \forall N \in img(\iota) \cap dom(o) \\[2pt] \Delta \vdash (\Gamma^{\overline{\varphi}}, \Gamma^{\overline{\mu}})(o(N)) \le \Sigma^o(N) \\[2pt] \qquad \forall N \in dom(o) \end{array}$$

$$\text{(METHODS-T)} \quad \dfrac{\Delta; \Gamma; C \vdash \mu_i\!:\!MT_i \ \forall \ i \in 1..n}{\Delta; \Gamma; C \vdash \overline{\mu}\!:\!\Gamma^{\overline{\mu}}} \quad \begin{array}{l} \overline{\mu} = \mu_1 \ldots \mu_n \\[2pt] \Gamma^{\overline{\mu}} = m_1\!:\!MT_1 \ldots m_n\!:\!MT_n \end{array}$$

$$\text{(METHOD-T)} \quad \dfrac{\Delta; \Gamma; \text{this}\!:\!C, x_1\!:\!C_1 \ldots x_n\!:\!C_n \vdash e\!:\!C'}{\begin{array}{c} \Delta; \Gamma; C \vdash \ C_0 \ m(C_1 \ x_1 \ldots C_n \ x_n)\{\text{return } e;\}\!: \\[3pt] C_1 \ldots C_n \to C_0 \end{array}} \quad \Delta \vdash C' \le C_0$$

$$\text{(K-T)} \quad \dfrac{\Delta; \emptyset; x_1\!:\!C_1 \ldots x_n\!:\!C_n \vdash e_i\!:\!C_i'' \ \forall i \in 1..k}{\Delta; f_1\!:\!C_1' \ldots f_k\!:\!C_k' \vdash \kappa\!:\!C_1 \ldots C_n} \quad \begin{array}{l} \kappa = \text{K}(C_1 \ x_1 \ldots C_n \ x_n)\{f_1 = e_1 \ldots f_k = e_k\} \\[2pt] \Delta \vdash C_i'' \le C_i' \ \forall i \in 1..k \end{array}$$

$$\text{(SUM-T)} \quad \dfrac{\begin{array}{c} \Delta \vdash CE_1\!:\![\Sigma_1^\iota; \Sigma_1^o; \overline{C}; C] \\[2pt] \Delta \vdash CE_2\!:\![\Sigma_2^\iota; \Sigma_2^o; \overline{C}; C] \end{array}}{\Delta \vdash CE_1 + CE_2\!:\![\Sigma_1^\iota, \Sigma_2^\iota; \Sigma_1^o, \Sigma_2^o; \overline{C}; C]} \quad dom(\Sigma_1^o) \cap dom(\Sigma_2^o) = \emptyset$$

$$\text{(REDUCT-T)} \quad \dfrac{\Delta \vdash CE\!:\![\Sigma_1^\iota; \Sigma^o; \overline{C}; C]}{\Delta \vdash \ _{\sigma^\iota}|CE_{|\sigma^o}\!:\![\Sigma^\iota; \Sigma^o; \overline{C}; C]} \quad \begin{array}{l} \Delta \vdash \sigma^\iota\!:\!\Sigma_1^\iota \to \Sigma^\iota \\[2pt] \Delta \vdash \sigma^o\!:\!\Sigma^o \to \Sigma_1^o \end{array}$$

$$\text{(FREEZE-T)} \quad \dfrac{\Delta \vdash CE\!:\![\Sigma^\iota, N\!:\!T; \Sigma^o; \overline{C}; C]}{\Delta \vdash freeze_N CE\!:\![\Sigma^\iota; \Sigma^o; \overline{C}; C]} \quad N \in dom(\Sigma^o)$$

$$\text{(TT-WRAP-T)} \quad \dfrac{\Delta \vdash CE\!:\![\Sigma^\iota; \Sigma^o; \overline{C}; C']}{\Delta \vdash CE[\text{TT} \le C]\!:\![\Sigma^\iota; \Sigma^o; \overline{C}; C]} \quad \Delta \vdash C \le C'$$

$$\text{(K-WRAP-T)} \quad \dfrac{\begin{array}{c} \Delta; \emptyset; x_1\!:\!C_1 \ldots x_n\!:\!C_n \vdash e_i\!:\!C_i'' \ \forall i \in 1..k \\[2pt] \Delta \vdash CE\!:\![\Sigma^\iota; \Sigma^o; C_1' \ldots C_k'; C] \end{array}}{\begin{array}{c} \Delta \vdash \ CE[\text{K}(C_1 \ x_1 \ldots C_n \ x_n)\{e_1 \ldots e_k\}]\!: \\[3pt] [\Sigma^\iota; \Sigma^o; C_1 \ldots C_n; C] \end{array}} \quad \begin{array}{l} \Delta \vdash C_i'' \le C_i' \\[2pt] \forall i \in 1..k \end{array}$$

Fig. 5. Typing rules for programs and class expressions

checks whether C is a structural subtype of C. The straightforward definition of these judgments is omitted (see [16]).

In (BASIC-T), we denote by Σ^ι and Σ^o the signatures extracted from ι and o, respectively; analogously, we denote by $\Gamma^\iota, \Gamma^{\overline{\mu}}$ and $\Gamma^{\overline{\varphi}}$ the internal type environments extracted from ι, $\overline{\mu}$ and $\overline{\varphi}$, respectively.

A basic class is well-typed w.r.t. Δ under three conditions. First, methods have their declared types w.r.t. Δ, the internal type environment assigning to member internal names their annotations, and the type in the ThisType constraint (assumed as type for this). Second, the constructor has its declared type w.r.t. Δ and the internal type environment assigning to internal field names their annotations. Finally, type annotations in input signature, output signature and local part must be consistent, that is, a virtual member can be used inside the class with a supertype of its exported type (first side condition), and a member can be exported with a supertype of its internal type (second side condition).

Typing rules for sum, reduct and freeze are based on those in [3]. Rule (SUM-T) imposes the same constructor type and ThisType constraint, and disjoint output signatures. In (REDUCT-T), the judgment $\Delta \vdash \sigma : \Sigma \to \Sigma'$ means that, if σ maps $N : T$ into $N' : T'$, then $\Delta \vdash T' \leq T$ holds. Hence, the side condition allows a member to be imported with a more specific type, and exported with a more general type. Analogously, rule (THIS-TYPE-T) allows the type of this to become more specific.

Typing rules in Fig. 6 define the judgment $\Delta ; \Gamma ; \Pi \vdash e : C$ for well-typed expressions. They are analogous to FJ rules. However, note that member type is found in receiver's class for client member selection, whereas it is found in the internal type environment for internal member selection. Also, note that (NEW-T) requires a class to have an empty input signature in order to be instantiated (see comment to rule (OBJ-CREATION) in previous section).

Finally, typing rules in Fig. 7 define the judgment $\Delta ; \Delta^r ; \Gamma ; \Pi \vdash e : C$ for well-typed runtime expressions. These expressions are typed using an additional type environment Δ^r, which gives for each class the types of its internal field names.

Rule (BLOCK-T) checks that the current object is well-typed and, moreover, that the enclosed method declarations and expression are well-typed in the internal type environment corresponding to the current object's class in Δ^r. In this case, the type of the block is that of the enclosed expression. Rule (PRE-OBJ-T) checks that each initialization expressions has a subtype of the type of the corresponding field internal name, found in the internal type environment associated to the (pre)object's class in Δ^r. Rules for other forms of expressions are analogous to those in Fig. 6, plus propagation of the runtime class type environment.

Soundness of the type system is expressed by the following theorems.

Theorem 1 (Soundness w.r.t. flattening relation). *If $\vdash p : \Delta$, then $p \xrightarrow{*} p'$ for some p' flat program, and $\vdash p' : \Delta$.*

Let us denote by Δ_p^r the runtime class type environment extracted from a flat program p. That is, for each basic class declaration of form $C \mapsto [\emptyset \,|\, o \,|\, \{ \tau \ \overline{\varphi} \ \kappa \ \overline{\mu} \}]$ in p, $\Delta_p^r(C) = \Gamma^{\overline{\varphi}}$.

$$(\text{VAR-T}) \quad \frac{}{\Delta; \Gamma; \Pi \vdash x : C} \quad \Pi(x) = C \qquad (\text{CLIENT-FIELD-T}) \quad \frac{\Delta; \Gamma; \Pi \vdash e_0 : C_0}{\Delta; \Gamma; \Pi \vdash e_0.F : C} \quad mtype(\Delta, C_0, F) = C$$

$$(\text{CLIENT-INVK-T}) \quad \frac{\Delta; \Gamma; \Pi \vdash e_0 : C_0 \quad \Delta; \Gamma; \Pi \vdash e_i : C_i' \; \forall i \in 1..n}{\Delta; \Gamma; \Pi \vdash e_0.M(e_1 \ldots e_n) : C} \quad \begin{array}{l} mtype(\Delta, C_0, M) = C_1 \ldots C_n \to C \\ \Delta \vdash C_i' \le C_i \; \forall i \in 1..n \end{array}$$

$$(\text{INT-FIELD-T}) \quad \frac{}{\Delta; \Gamma; \Pi \vdash f : C} \quad \Gamma(f) = C$$

$$(\text{INT-INVK-T}) \quad \frac{\Delta; \Gamma; \Pi \vdash e_i : C_i' \; \forall i \in 1..n}{\Delta; \Gamma; \Pi \vdash m(e_1 \ldots e_n) : C} \quad \begin{array}{l} \Gamma(m) = C_1 \ldots C_n \to C \\ \Delta \vdash C_i' \le C_i \; \forall i \in 1..n \end{array}$$

$$(\text{NEW-T}) \quad \frac{\Delta; \Gamma; \Pi \vdash e_i : C_i' \; \forall i \in 1..n}{\Delta; \Gamma; \Pi \vdash \mathbf{new}\; C(e_1 \ldots e_n) : C} \quad \begin{array}{l} \Delta(C) = [\emptyset; \_; C_1 \ldots C_n; \_] \\ \Delta \vdash C_i' \le C_i \; \forall i \in 1..n \end{array}$$

Fig. 6. Typing rules for expressions

$$(\text{BLOCK-T}) \quad \frac{\begin{array}{l} \Delta; \Delta^r; \Gamma; \Pi \vdash v : C' \\ \Delta; \Delta^r; \Gamma; C' \vdash \overline{\mu} : \Gamma^{\overline{\mu}} \\ \Delta; \Delta^r; \Gamma'; \Pi \vdash e : C \end{array}}{\Delta; \Delta^r; \Gamma; \Pi \vdash [\overline{\mu}; v \,|\, e] : C} \quad \Gamma' = \Gamma, \Delta^r(C'), \Gamma^{\overline{\mu}}$$

$$(\text{PRE-OBJ-T}) \quad \frac{\Delta; \Delta^r; \Gamma; \Pi \vdash e_i : C_i' \; \forall i \in 1..n}{\Delta; \Delta^r; \Gamma; \Pi \vdash C(f_1 = e_1; \ldots f_n = e_n;) : C} \quad \begin{array}{l} \Delta^r(C) = f_1 : C_1 \ldots f_n : C_n \\ \Delta \vdash C_i' \le C_i \; \forall i \in 1..n \end{array}$$

Fig. 7. Typing rules for runtime expressions

Theorem 2 (Progress). *If $\vdash p : \Delta$, then $\Delta; \Delta_p^r; \emptyset; \emptyset \vdash e : C$ implies that either e is a value or $e \longrightarrow_p e'$ for some e'.*

Theorem 3 (Subject reduction). *If $\vdash p : \Delta$, then $\Delta; \Delta_p^r; \Gamma; \Pi \vdash e : C$ and $e \longrightarrow_p e'$ imply that $\Delta; \Delta_p^r; \Gamma; \Pi \vdash e' : C'$, and $\Delta \vdash C' \le C$.*

Proof of Th. 1 is is a simple adaptation from [3], others can be found in [16].

4   Direct Semantics

Direct semantics allows a modular approach where each class (module) can be analyzed (notably, compiled) in isolation, since references to other classes do not need to be resolved before runtime. In this case, look-up is a non trivial procedure where a class member (e.g., method) is retrieved from other classes and possibly modified as effect of the module operators. Since FJIG subsumes a variety of mechanisms for class composition, including standard inheritance, mixins, traits, and hiding, the definition of direct semantics for FJIG provides a guideline which can be emulated by real extensions of class-based languages, and also a hint to implementation.

In order to give this definition, block expressions are generalized as shown in the top section of Fig. 8. That is, besides the previous components, a block contains a *path map* $\hat{\iota}$ which maps internal names to *paths* π, which denote a subterm in the class expression defining the class C of the current object (an implementation could use a pointer). More precisely, a path π always denotes a subterm of the form $freeze_N CE$, and is used as a permanent reference to the definition of member N in CE. Indeed, the external name N can be changed or removed by effect of outer reduct operators; however, references via π are not affected. Hence, when a reference π is encountered during current method execution, lookup of N in CE is triggered (see more explanations below). In flattening semantics, C is always a basic class, hence this case never happens.

The center section of the figure contains the new rules for expression reduction.

When a member reference (external name or path) $\hat{N}$ needs to be resolved, the lookup procedure starts the search of $\hat{N}$ from receiver's class C and, if successful, returns a corresponding internal name inside a block expression, as shown in rules (CLIENT-FIELD) and (CLIENT-INVK). In flattening semantics, C is always a basic class, hence lookup is trivial and the side condition can be equivalently expressed as in the analogous rules in Fig. 3.

When an internal name n is encountered, it is either directly mapped to a definition, or to a path. The former case happens when n was a local name in the basic class containing the definition of the method which is currently being executed. In this case, the corresponding definition is taken, as shown in rules (INT-FIELD) and (INT-INVK). The latter case happens when n was an abstract or virtual name inside the basic class containing the definition of the method which is currently executed, and n has been permanently bound to some definition by an outer freeze operator (recall that only classes where all members are frozen can be instantiated). In this case, lookup of this definition is started from receiver's class via the path π, and, if successful, the internal name n is replaced by the name n' found by lookup; moreover, the corresponding path map and methods are merged with the original ones (α-renaming can be used to avoid conflicts among internal names in this phase). This is shown in rule (PATH). In flattening semantics, the latter case never happens, hence only the first two rules are needed.

Creation of an instance of class, say, C, also involves a *constructor lookup* procedure, which returns, starting from class C, the appropriate constructor, by retrieving and possibly modifying constructors of other classes (this generalizes what happens in standard Java-like languages, where the superclass constructor is always invoked). In flattening semantics, C is always a basic class, hence

$$\pi ::= i_1 \ldots i_k \qquad \textbf{path } (i \in \{1,2\})$$
$$\hat{N} ::= N \mid \pi \qquad \textbf{member reference (external name or path)}$$
$$\hat{\iota} ::= n_1 \mapsto \pi_1 \ldots n_k \mapsto \pi_k \quad \textbf{path map}$$
$$e ::= \ldots \mid [\hat{\iota}; \overline{\mu}; v \mid e] \qquad \textbf{(generalized) block}$$

(CLIENT-FIELD) $$\dfrac{}{v^C.F \longrightarrow_p [\hat{\iota}; \overline{\mu}; v^C \mid f]} \quad lookup_p\langle F, C \rangle = [\hat{\iota}; \overline{\mu} \mid f]$$

(CLIENT-INVK) $$\dfrac{}{v^C.M(\overline{v}) \longrightarrow_p [\hat{\iota}; \overline{\mu}; v^C \mid m(\overline{v})]} \quad lookup_p\langle M, C \rangle = [\hat{\iota}; \overline{\mu} \mid m]$$

(INT-FIELD) $$\dfrac{}{[\hat{\iota}; \overline{\mu}; v \mid \mathcal{E}\{f\}] \longrightarrow_p [\hat{\iota}; \overline{\mu}; v \mid \mathcal{E}\{v_i\}]} \quad \begin{array}{l} f \notin HB(\mathcal{E}) \\ v = C(f_1=v_1 \ldots f_n=v_n) \\ f=f_i \end{array}$$

(INT-INVK) $$\dfrac{}{[\hat{\iota}; \overline{\mu}; v \mid \mathcal{E}\{m(\overline{v})\}] \longrightarrow_p [\hat{\iota}; \overline{\mu}; v \mid \mathcal{E}\{e[\overline{v}/\overline{x}][v^C/\texttt{this}]\}]} \quad \begin{array}{l} m \notin HB(\mathcal{E}) \\ \overline{\mu}(m) = \langle \overline{x}, e \rangle \end{array}$$

(PATH) $$\dfrac{}{[\hat{\iota}, n \mapsto \pi; \overline{\mu}; v^C \mid e] \longrightarrow_p [\hat{\iota}, \hat{\iota}'; \overline{\mu}[n'/n], \overline{\mu}'; v^C \mid e[n'/n]]} \quad \begin{array}{l} n \in names(e) \\ lookup_p\langle \pi, C \rangle = \\ [\hat{\iota}'; \overline{\mu}' \mid n'] \end{array}$$

(OBJ-CREATION) $$\dfrac{}{\texttt{new } C(\overline{v}) \longrightarrow_p C(\overline{f=e[\overline{v}/\overline{x}]})} \quad \begin{array}{l} \textit{k-lookup}_p(C) = K(C_1 \ x_1 \ldots C_n \ x_n)\{\overline{f=e}\} \\ \overline{x}=x_1 \ldots x_n \end{array}$$

(EXIT-BLOCK) $$\dfrac{}{[\hat{\iota}; \overline{\mu}; v \mid e] \longrightarrow_p e} \quad names(e)=\emptyset$$

$$lookup_p\langle \hat{N}, \pi, C \rangle = lookup_p\langle \hat{N}, \pi, CE \rangle$$
$$\quad \text{if } p(C) = CE$$
$$lookup_p\langle N, \pi, [\iota \mid o, N \mapsto n \mid \{\tau \ \overline{\varphi} \ \kappa \ \overline{\mu}\}]\rangle = [\iota; \emptyset; \overline{\mu} \mid n]$$
$$lookup_p\langle \hat{N}, \pi, CE_1 + CE_2 \rangle = \alpha_i([\iota; \hat{\iota}; \overline{\mu} \mid n])$$
$$\quad \text{if } lookup_p\langle \hat{N}, \pi.i, CE_i \rangle = [\iota; \hat{\iota}; \overline{\mu} \mid n], i \in \{1,2\}$$
$$lookup_p\langle \hat{N}, \pi, \sigma^\iota | CE_{|\sigma^o} \rangle = [\sigma^\iota \circ \iota; \hat{\iota}; \overline{\mu} \mid n]$$
$$\quad \text{if } lookup_p\langle \hat{N}', \pi.1, CE \rangle = [\iota; \hat{\iota}; \overline{\mu} \mid n],$$
$$\quad \hat{N}' = \sigma^o(N) \text{ if } \hat{N} = N, \hat{N}' = \hat{N} \textbf{ otherwise}$$
$$lookup_p\langle \hat{N}, \pi, freeze_N CE \rangle = [\iota; \hat{\iota}, n_1 \mapsto \pi \ldots n_k \mapsto \pi; \overline{\mu} \mid n]$$
$$\quad \text{if } \hat{N} \neq \pi, N \notin img(\iota),$$
$$\quad lookup_p\langle \hat{N}, \pi.1, CE \rangle = [\iota, n_1 \mapsto N \ldots n_k \mapsto N; \hat{\iota}; \overline{\mu} \mid n]$$
$$lookup_p\langle \pi, \pi, freeze_N CE \rangle = [\iota; \hat{\iota}, n_1 \mapsto \pi \ldots n_k \mapsto \pi; \overline{\mu} \mid n]$$
$$\quad \text{if } N \notin img(\iota),$$
$$\quad lookup_p\langle N, \pi.1, CE \rangle = [\iota, n_1 \mapsto N \ldots n_k \mapsto N; \hat{\iota}; \overline{\mu} \mid n]$$
$$lookup_p\langle \hat{N}, \pi, CE[\texttt{TT}{\leq}C] \rangle = lookup_p\langle \hat{N}, \pi.1, CE \rangle$$
$$lookup_p\langle \hat{N}, \pi, CE[K(\overline{C \ x})\{\overline{e}\}] \rangle = lookup_p\langle \hat{N}, \pi.1, CE \rangle$$

$$\textit{k-lookup}_p(C) = \textit{k-lookup}_p(CE)$$
$$\quad \text{if } p(C) = CE$$
$$\textit{k-lookup}_p([\emptyset \mid o \mid \{\tau \ \overline{\varphi} \ \kappa \ \overline{\mu}\}]) = \kappa$$
$$\textit{k-lookup}_p(CE_1 + CE_2) = K(\overline{C \ x})\{\alpha_1(\overline{f=e}), \alpha_2(\overline{f'=e'})\}$$
$$\quad \text{if } \textit{k-lookup}_p(CE_1) = K(\overline{C \ x})\{\overline{f=e}\},$$
$$\quad \textit{k-lookup}_p(CE_2) = K(\overline{C \ x})\{\overline{f'=e'}\}$$
$$\textit{k-lookup}_p(\sigma^\iota | CE_{|\sigma^o}) = \textit{k-lookup}_p(CE)$$
$$\textit{k-lookup}_p(freeze_N CE) = \textit{k-lookup}_p(CE)$$
$$\textit{k-lookup}_p(CE[\texttt{TT}{\leq}C]) = \textit{k-lookup}_p(CE)$$
$$\textit{k-lookup}_p(CE[K(\overline{D \ y})\{\overline{e}\}]) = K(\overline{D \ y})\{\overline{f=e[\overline{e}/\overline{x}]}\}$$
$$\quad \text{if } \overline{x} = x_1 \ldots x_n,$$
$$\quad \textit{k-lookup}_p(CE) = K(C_1 \ x_1 \ldots C_n \ x_n)\{\overline{f=e}\}$$

Fig. 8. Direct semantics

constructor lookup is trivial and the side condition can be equivalently expressed as in the corresponding rule in Fig. 3.

Lookup and constructor lookup are defined in the bottom section of the figure.

The lookup procedure is modeled by a function which, given a program p, takes three more arguments: a member reference (external name or path) $\hat{N}$, a path π, which acts as an accumulator and keeps track of the current subterm of the class expression which is examined, and a class name C. When lookup is started, π is always the empty path Λ, and $lookup_p\langle \hat{N}, \Lambda, C\rangle$ is abbreviated by $lookup_p\langle \hat{N}, C\rangle$.

The lookup function returns a triple consisting of input map, path map, methods and an internal name, written $[\iota; \hat{\iota}; \overline{\mu} \mid n]$. However, the final result of lookup (that is, the result returned for the initial call) is expected to be always of form $[\emptyset; \hat{\iota}; \overline{\mu} \mid n]$, abbreviated by $[\hat{\iota}; \overline{\mu} \mid n]$, since all abstract/virtual internal names are expected to be eventually bound to a path as effect of some freeze operator.

The first two clauses defining lookup are trivial and state that looking for a member reference starting from a class name C means looking in the definition of C, and that looking for an external name N in a basic class only succeeds if the name is present in the class, and returns the corresponding input map, methods and internal name. Note that the case where we look for a path π in a basic class is expected to never happen.

The third clause defines lookup on a sum expression. In this case, lookup is propagated to both arguments. This definition is a priori non-deterministic, but is expected to be deterministic on class expressions which can be safely flattened, since in this case an external name cannot be found on both sides. For member references which are paths, instead, determinism is guaranteed by construction since the path exactly corresponds to a subterm. In case lookup succeeds on one of the two arguments, the result is modified by renaming field local names in a way which keeps track of this argument. For instance, if lookup succeeded on the first argument, then every field internal name f is renamed to $f.1$. This renaming is denoted by α_i. We choose this canonical α-renaming for concreteness, but any other could be chosen, provided that it is consistent with that in constructor lookup.

For instance, let us consider the following program[10]:

$$C \mapsto C_1 + C_2$$
$$C_1 \mapsto [\emptyset \mid \ldots \mid \{ \text{ int } f; \text{ K}()\{f = 3\} \ldots \}]$$
$$C_2 \mapsto [\emptyset \mid \ldots, M \mapsto m \mid \{ \text{ int } f; \text{ K}()\{f = 5\} \text{ int } m()\{\text{return } f + 1;\}\}]$$

and the expression new $C().M()$. An instance of class C has two fields, inherited from C_1 and C_2, and initialized to 3 and 5, respectively. They are both named f in the original classes; however, they are renamed during constructor lookup (see the clause for sum), hence the above expression reduces to $C(f.1\mapsto 3, f.2\mapsto 5).M()$. Now, M is invoked, starting the lookup from C, and the search is propagated to both C_1 and C_2. Only the lookup in C_2 is successful and returns the result

---

[10] In order to write more readable examples, we assume integer values and operations, and omit default constructor and ThisType constraint.

$[; ; \texttt{int } m()\{\texttt{return } f + 1;\} \, | \, m]$

which is modified in $[; ; \texttt{int } m()\{\texttt{return } f.2+1;\} \, | \, m]$ to take into account that the method has been found in the second argument. Hence, this method invocation reduces to $[; \texttt{int } m()\{\texttt{return } f.2 + 1;\}; \, C(f.1 \mapsto 3, f.2 \mapsto 5) \, | \, m]$ where the body of m correctly refers to the second field.

In flattening semantics, C reduces to the following basic class:

$[\emptyset \, | \dots, M \mapsto m \, | \{ \texttt{ int } f.1; \texttt{ int } f.2; \, \kappa \texttt{ int } m()\{\texttt{return } f.2 + 1;\} \dots \}]$
$\kappa = \texttt{K}()\{f.1 = 3, f.2 = 5\}$

Note that here the clash between the two fields is resolved during flattening (hence before runtime), by α-renaming. We have chosen as α-renaming the same used in direct semantics as an help for the reader, but of course in this case any other arbitrary α-renaming would work as well.

The fourth clause defines lookup on a reduct expression. In this case, lookup of an external name is propagated under the name the member has in the argument, given by the output renaming σ^o. Instead, lookup of a path is simply propagated, since paths are permanent references which are not affected by renamings. Moreover, the result of lookup on the argument must be modified to ensure that internal names refer to the appropriate external names obtained via the input renaming σ^ι.

For instance, consider a program including

$C \mapsto {}_{M_1 \mapsto M_1'} C'_{|M \mapsto M'}$
$C' \mapsto [m' \mapsto M_1 \, | \, M' \mapsto m \, | \{ \; \dots \; \texttt{int } m()\{\texttt{return } m'();\}\}]$

and assume that some method invocation triggers the lookup for M in C. Then, the lookup is propagated under the name M' to C'. The lookup of M' in C' is successful and returns the result $[m' \mapsto M_1; ; \texttt{int } m()\{\texttt{return } m'();\} \, | \, m]$ which is modified in $[m' \mapsto M_1'; ; \texttt{int } m()\{\texttt{return } m'();\} \, | \, m]$ as an effect of the input renaming.

In flattening semantics, C reduces to the following basic class:

$[m' \mapsto M_1' \, | \, M \mapsto m \, | \{ \; \dots \; \texttt{int } m()\{\texttt{return } m'();\}\}]$

There are two clauses defining lookup on a freeze expression. The former handles most cases, except the special situation in which we are exactly looking for the member that has been frozen in the current subterm π, which has the form $freeze_N CE$. In this special case (second clause) the lookup of N in CE is triggered. Moreover, the result is modified, since internal names referring to N must now refer to the permanent reference π. Otherwise (first clause), the lookup is propagated, and the result of the lookup on the argument is modified as in the previous case.

Consider the program

$C \mapsto freeze_F C'$
$C' \mapsto [f \mapsto F \, | \, F \mapsto f', M \mapsto m \, | \{ \texttt{ int } f'; \texttt{K}()\{f' = 42\} \texttt{ int } m()\{\texttt{return } f + 1;\}\}]$

and the expression $\texttt{new } C().M()$.

An instance of class C has one field, inherited from C' and initialized to 42. Hence, the above expression reduces to $C(f' \mapsto 42).M()$. Now, M is invoked, starting the lookup from C, and the search is propagated to C'. The lookup in C' is successful and returns the result $[f \mapsto F;; \texttt{int } m()\{\texttt{return } f + 1;\} \mid m]$,

---

$$\mu_A \equiv C\ m()\{\texttt{return } m'();\}$$
$$\overline{\mu}_{sum} \equiv \mu_A\ C\ m''()\{\texttt{return } f;\}$$
$$\overline{\mu}_C \equiv C\ m()\{\texttt{return } m''();\}\ C\ m''()\{\texttt{return } f;\}$$
$$\overline{\mu}_D \equiv \overline{\mu}_C\ C\ m'()\{\texttt{return } 8;\}$$
$$\mu'' \equiv C\ m''()\{\texttt{return } f.2.1;\}$$

$$p \equiv A = [m' \mapsto M' \mid M \mapsto m \mid \{\mu_A\}]$$
$$B = [\emptyset \mid M' \mapsto m' \mid \{\ C\ f;\ \texttt{K}()\{f = 0\}\ C\ m'()\{\texttt{return } f;\}\}]$$
$$C = freeze_{M'}(A + B)$$
$$D = {}_{\emptyset \mid} C_{\mid \_ \mapsto M', M \mapsto M} + [\emptyset \mid M' \mapsto m' \mid \{C\ m'()\{\texttt{return } 8;\}\}]\}$$

$$freeze_{M'}(A + B) \longrightarrow$$
$$freeze_{M'}[m' \mapsto M' \mid M \mapsto m, M' \mapsto m'' \mid \{\ C\ f;\ \texttt{K}()\{f = 0\}\ \overline{\mu}_{sum}\}] \longrightarrow$$
$$[\emptyset \mid M \mapsto m, M' \mapsto m'' \mid \{\ C\ f;\ \texttt{K}()\{f = 0\}\ \overline{\mu}_C\}]$$

$$D \overset{*}{\longrightarrow}$$
$$[\emptyset \mid M \mapsto m \mid \{\ C\ f;\ \texttt{K}()\{f = 0\}\ \overline{\mu}_C\}] + [\emptyset \mid M' \mapsto m' \mid \{C\ m'()\{\texttt{return } 8;\}\}]\} \longrightarrow$$
$$[\emptyset \mid M \mapsto m, M' \mapsto m' \mid \{\ C\ f;\ \texttt{K}()\{f = 0\}\ \overline{\mu}_D\}]$$

$$p' \equiv A = [m' \mapsto M' \mid M \mapsto m \mid \{\mu_A\}]$$
$$B = [\emptyset \mid M' \mapsto m' \mid \{\ C\ f;\ \texttt{K}()\{f = 0\}\ C\ m'()\{\texttt{return } f;\}\}]$$
$$C = [\emptyset \mid M \mapsto m, M' \mapsto m'' \mid \{\ C\ f;\ \texttt{K}()\{f = 0\}\ \overline{\mu}_C\}]$$
$$D = [\emptyset \mid M \mapsto m, M' \mapsto m' \mid \{\ C\ f;\ \texttt{K}()\{f = 0\}\ \overline{\mu}_D\}]$$

$$\textbf{new } D().M() \longrightarrow_{p'} D(f = 0).M() \longrightarrow_{p'} [\overline{\mu}_D; D(f = 0) \mid m()] \longrightarrow_{p'}$$
$$[\overline{\mu}_D; D(f = 0) \mid m''()] \longrightarrow_{p'} [\overline{\mu}_D; D(f = 0) \mid f] \longrightarrow_{p'} [\overline{\mu}_D; D(f = 0) \mid 0] \longrightarrow_{p'} 0$$

$$\textbf{new } D().M() \longrightarrow_p \qquad\qquad k\text{-}lookup_p(D) = \texttt{K}()\{f.2.1 = 0\}$$
$$D(f.2.1 = 0).M() \longrightarrow_p \qquad\qquad lookup_p\langle M, \Lambda, D\rangle = [\Lambda; m' \mapsto 1.1; \mu_A \mid m]$$
$$[m' \mapsto 1.1; \mu_A; D(f.2.1 = 0) \mid m()] \longrightarrow_p$$
$$[m' \mapsto 1.1; \mu_A; D(f.2.1 = 0) \mid m'()] \longrightarrow_p$$
$$[m' \mapsto 1.1; \mu_A, \mu''; D(f.2.1 = 0) \mid m''()] \longrightarrow_p \qquad lookup_p\langle 1.1, \Lambda, D\rangle = [\Lambda; \Lambda; \mu'' \mid m'']$$
$$[m' \mapsto 1.1; \mu_A, \mu''; D(f.2.1 = 0) \mid f.2.1] \longrightarrow_p$$
$$[m' \mapsto 1.1; \mu_A, \mu''; D(f.2.1 = 0) \mid 0] \longrightarrow_p$$
$$0$$

Fig. 9. Example

which is modified in $[; f \mapsto \varLambda; \texttt{int } m()\{\texttt{return } f + 1;\} \mid m]$, where $\varLambda$ denotes the empty path, to take into account that F has been frozen. Hence, the method invocation reduces to $[f \mapsto \varLambda; \texttt{int } m()\{\texttt{return } f + 1;\}; C(f \mapsto 42) \mid m]$, where the body of m correctly refers to F frozen in the top level freeze.

In flattening semantics, C reduces to the following basic class:

$$[\emptyset \mid F \mapsto f', M \mapsto m \mid \{ \texttt{ int } f'; \texttt{K}()\{f' = 42\} \texttt{ int } m()\{\texttt{return } f' + 1;\}\}]$$

Fig. 9 shows a more involved example comparing flattening and direct semantics.

The top section of the figure lists some abbreviations, the second shows the four classes composing program p. Class A defines a method M whose body invokes the abstract method M'. Class B has a local field f initialized to 0 and defines a method M' which returns this field. Class C is obtained by summing A and B, and then freezing method M'. Finally, class D is obtained by hiding method M' in C (in the reduct, the input renaming is empty since there are no input names, and the output renaming maps "no new name" into M' and is the identity on M) and then summing a new definition for M'. The following three sections of the figure shows how the class expressions for C and D are reduced, the resulting flat program p' and the reduction of expression new $D().M()$ in the context of p'. Finally, the last section shows direct semantics of the same expression in the context of p.

The example shows how the method originally called M' in B is correctly invoked via the path 1.1, even though M' has been hidden and then replaced by an homonymous method.

The following theorem states that flattening is equivalent to direct semantics. We denote by $\overset{*}{\longrightarrow}$ the reflexive and transitive closure of the flattening relation, and analogously for the reduction relation. The proof can be found in [17].

Theorem 4. *If* $p \overset{*}{\longrightarrow} p'$, *and* e *is an expression with no paths, then* $e \overset{*}{\longrightarrow}_p v$ *iff* $e \overset{*}{\longrightarrow}_{p'} v$.

5   Conclusion

We have presented F JIG, a core calculus which formalizes the Bracha's Jigsaw framework [8] in a Java-like setting. The design of F JIG comes out naturally, yet not trivially, by taking Featherweight Java [15] as starting point and replacing inheritance by the more general composition operators of Jigsaw.

We believe that such a core calculus can be useful for many research directions. First, it provides a simple unifying formalism for encoding and comparing a large variety of different mechanisms for software composition in class-based languages, including standard inheritance, mixin classes, traits and hiding. Then, it can serve as the basis for the design of a real language based on Jigsaw principles. Moreover, it could be enriched by behavioural types, leading to a class-based specification language, in the spirit of, e.g., JML [18], allowing modular development and composition of class specifications.

We have also defined two different execution models for the calculus, flattening and direct semantics, and proved their equivalence. That is, we have shown the equivalence of two different views on inheritance in a formal setting with a more sophisticated composition mechanism, where, e.g., mixin classes and traits can be subsumed. This can also greatly help in integrating such features, or other modularity mechanisms, in standard class-based languages, since it gives practical hints on implementation.

Apart from the two key references mentioned above, this work has been directly influenced by work on traits [20,10], mostly by the recent developments [19,6,7]. In particular, we share with [6,7] the objective of replacing inheritance by more flexible operators. Concerning flattening and direct semantics, the most direct source of inspiration for our work has been [19], which defines a direct semantics for traits. Essentially, their dynamic look-up algorithm can be seen as a simplified version, handling sum and output reduct only, of ours.

The focus of this paper is on providing a simple and compact model for a language based on the Jigsaw framework in a Java-like setting, hence we have only outlined in Sect. 1 a simple surface language. As mentioned above, we leave to further work a deeper investigation of a realistic language design, and a more precise analysis on how different mechanisms such as standard inheritance, mixin classes, traits can be encoded into FJIG. We also plan to develop a prototype; a very preliminary interpreter of flattening semantics, assigned as master thesis, can be found at http://www.disi.unige.it/person/LagorioG/FJig/. We also plan to investigate smart implementation techniques of direct semantics in the prototype interpreter.

References

1. Ancona, D., Lagorio, G., Zucca, E.: Jam—designing a Java extension with mixins. ACM Transactions on Programming Languages and Systems 25(5), 641–712 (2003)
2. Ancona, D., Zucca, E.: Overriding operators in a mixin-based framework. In: Hartel, P.H., Kuchen, H. (eds.) PLILP 1997. LNCS, vol. 1292. Springer, Heidelberg (1997)
3. Ancona, D., Zucca, E.: A calculus of module systems. Journ. of Functional Programming 12(2), 91–132 (2002)
4. Bergel, A., Ducasse, S., Nierstrasz, O., Wuyts, R.: Stateful traits. In: De Meuter, W. (ed.) ISC 2006. LNCS, vol. 4406, pp. 66–90. Springer, Heidelberg (2007)
5. Bergel, A., Ducasse, S., Nierstrasz, O., Wuyts, R.: Stateful traits and their formalization. Comput. Lang. Syst. Struct. 34(2-3), 83–108 (2008)
6. Bono, V., Damiani, F., Giachino, E.: Separating type, behavior, and state to achieve very fine-grained reuse. In: 9th Intl. Workshop on Formal Techniques for Java-like Programs (2007)
7. Bono, V., Damiani, F., Giachino, E.: On traits and types in a Java-like setting. In: TCS 2008 - IFIP Int. Conf. on Theoretical Computer Science. Springer, Heidelberg (2008)
8. Bracha, G.: The Programming Language JIGSAW: Mixins, Modularity and Multiple Inheritance. PhD thesis, Department of Comp. Sci., Univ. of Utah (1992)

9. Duggan, D., Sourelis, C.: Mixin modules. In: Intl. Conf. on Functional Programming 1996. ACM Press, New York (1996)
10. Fisher, K., Reppy, J.: A typed calculus of traits. In: FOOL 2004 - Intl. Workshop on Foundations of Object Oriented Languages (2004)
11. Flatt, M., Krishnamurthi, S., Felleisen, M.: Classes and mixins. In: ACM Symp. on Principles of Programming Languages 1998. ACM Press, New York (1998)
12. Gamma, E., Helm, R., Johnson, R.E., Vlissides, J.M.: Design Patterns: Elements of Reusable Object-Oriented Software. Addison-Wesley Professional Computing Series. Addison-Wesley, Reading (1995)
13. Hirschowitz, T., Leroy, X.: Mixin modules in a call-by-value setting. In: Le Métayer, D. (ed.) ESOP 2002. LNCS, vol. 2305, pp. 6–20. Springer, Heidelberg (2002)
14. Hirschowitz, T., Leroy, X., Wells, J.B.: Call-by-value mixin modules. In: Schmidt, D. (ed.) ESOP 2004. LNCS, vol. 2986, pp. 64–78. Springer, Heidelberg (2004)
15. Igarashi, A., Pierce, B.C., Wadler, P.: Featherweight Java: a minimal core calculus for Java and GJ. ACM Transactions on Programming Languages and Systems 23(3), 396–450 (2001)
16. Lagorio, G., Servetto, M., Zucca, E.: Featherweight Jigsaw - a minimal core calculus for modular composition of classes. Technical report, Dipartimento di Informatica e Scienze dell'Informazione, Università di Genova (December 2008) (Full version)
17. Lagorio, G., Servetto, M., Zucca, E.: Flattening versus direct semantics for Featherweight Jigsaw. In: FOOL 2009 - Intl. Workshop on Foundations of Object Oriented Languages (2009)
18. Leavens, G.T.: Tutorial on JML, the Java modeling language. In: Automated Software Engineering (ASE 2007). ACM Press, New York (2007)
19. Liquori, L., Spiwack, A.: FeatherTrait: A modest extension of Featherweight Java. ACM Transactions on Programming Languages and Systems 30(2) (2008)
20. Schärli, N., Ducasse, S., Nierstrasz, O., Black, A.P.: Traits: Composable units of behaviour. In: Cardelli, L. (ed.) ECOOP 2003. LNCS, vol. 2743. Springer, Heidelberg (2003)
21. Wells, J.B., Vestergaard, R.: Confluent equational reasoning for linking with first-class primitive modules. In: Smolka, G. (ed.) ESOP 2000. LNCS, vol. 1782, p. 412. Springer, Heidelberg (2000)

Modular Visitor Components
A Practical Solution to the Expression Families Problem

Bruno C.d.S. Oliveira

Oxford University Computing Laboratory
Wolfson Building, Parks Road, Oxford OX1 3QD, UK
bruno@comlab.ox.ac.uk

Abstract. The *expression families problem* can be defined as the problem of achieving *reusability and composability* across the components involved in a *family* of related datatypes and corresponding operations over those datatypes. Like the traditional *expression problem*, adding new components (either variants or operations) should be possible while preserving *modular and static type-safety*. Moreover, different combinations of components should have different type identities and the subtyping relationships between components should be preserved. By generalizing previous work exploring the connection between type-theoretic encodings of datatypes and visitors, we propose two solutions for this problem in Scala using *modular visitor components*. These components can be grouped into *features* that can be easily composed in a *feature-oriented programming* style to obtain customized datatypes and operations.

1 Introduction

Component-oriented programming (COP) [1], a programming style in which software is assembled from independent components has, for a long time, been advocated as a solution to the so-called *software crisis* [2]. However, the truth is that to date the COP vision has not been fully realised, largely due to limitations of current programming languages. A particular problem is that most languages have a bias towards one kind of decomposition of software systems, which imposes a corresponding bias on the kinds of *extensibility* available [3,4]: in same languages adding new datatype variants is easy, while in others adding new operations is easy. Providing software systems that support both kinds of extensibility at the same time has proved itself quite elusive to achieve in existing languages and leads to what Wadler calls the *expression problem* [5].

In this paper we will look at a variation of the expression problem (EP) that we call the *expression families problem* (EFP). The EFP can be defined as the problem of achieving *reusability and composability* across the components involved in a *family* of related expression datatypes and corresponding operations over those datatypes. Like with the traditional EP, adding new components (either variants or operations) should be possible while preserving *modular and static type-safety* (that is, no modification or duplication and no re-compilation and re-typechecking of existing code should be needed). Furthermore, it should

S. Drossopoulou (Ed.): ECOOP 2009, LNCS 5653, pp. 269–293, 2009.

also be possible to combine independently developed extensions [6]. Additionally, a solution to the EFP should: allow different combinations of components to have *different type identities*; *preserve the subtyping relationships* between the different components (whether in the same family or a different one); and *provide a high degree of composability and decoupling of components*.

By generalizing previous work [7,8] exploring the connection between type-theoretic encodings of datatypes [9,10] and the VISITOR pattern [11], we propose two solutions for this problem in Scala[1] using *modular visitor components*. These components can be grouped into *features* that can be easily composed in a *feature-oriented programming* style. The solutions presented in this paper do not require any extensions to Scala and rely only on features that, although not yet widely available in mainstream OO languages, have been shown to be independently useful in the past. In particular, we make use of the following features: *higher-order type parameters* [12,13], *traits and mixin composition* [14,15], *self-types* [16] and *variance annotations* [17]. Of these, self-types are only required by one of the solutions and could potentially be completely eliminated using a technique devised by Torgersen [18]. The other three features are needed to address all the requirements of the EFP. However we should remark that variance annotations are only required to ensure that the subtyping relations between different datatypes are preserved, but otherwise they would not be necessary (in particular, they would not be needed to solve the traditional EP).

In Section 2 we motivate and formulate the expression families problem. The technical contributions follow:

- Section 3 shows how to adapt type-theoretic encodings of datatypes to support extensibility of variants as well as extensibility of operations.
- Section 4 shows a simple solution for the EFP inspired by Church encodings of datatypes. It is also shown how the subtyping relations between components of different families can be helpful for scalability and reuse.
- Section 5 shows another solution for the EFP inspired by Parigot encodings of datatypes. This solution is more expressive than the one in Section 4, but it is also slightly more complex to use.
- Section 6 shows how we can group the modular visitor components into features that can be easily combined by clients to obtain customized datatypes and operations.

A comparison between our work and solutions to the expression problem is presented in the Section 7. Conclusions are presented in Section 8.

2   The Expression Families Problem

In the expression families problem we are interested in modularizing and reusing the common parts of a family of expression datatypes and corresponding family

---

[1] Source code available at: http://web.comlab.ox.ac.uk/people/Bruno.Oliveira/ EFP.tgz

of operations. For example, in some context, we may have a system composed of a datatype of expressions Exp_1 that supports numeric, addition and subtraction variants together with a corresponding evaluation function:

data $Exp_1 = Num_1\ Int\ |\ Add_1\ Exp_1\ Exp_1\ |\ Minus_1\ Exp_1\ Exp_1$

$eval_1 :: Exp_1 \to Int$
$eval_1\ (Num_1\ x) \qquad = x$
$eval_1\ (Add_1\ e1\ e2) \quad = eval_1\ e1 + eval_1\ e2$
$eval_1\ (Minus_1\ e1\ e2) = eval_1\ e1 - eval_1\ e2$

In a different context we may have a system composed of a datatype Exp_2 that also supports negation and provides both an evaluation operation and an operation that narrows Exp_2 expressions into Exp_1 expressions:

data $Exp_2 = Num_2\ Int\ |\ Add_2\ Exp_2\ Exp_2\ |\ Minus_2\ Exp_2\ Exp_2\ |\ Neg_2\ Exp_2$

$eval_2 :: Exp_2 \to Int$
$eval_2\ (Num_2\ x) \qquad = x$
$eval_2\ (Add_2\ e1\ e2) \quad = eval_2\ e1 + eval_2\ e2$
$eval_2\ (Minus_2\ e1\ e2) = eval_2\ e1 - eval_2\ e2$
$eval_2\ (Neg_2\ e) \qquad = - (eval_2\ e)$

$narrow_{21} :: Exp_2 \to Exp_1$
$narrow_{21}\ (Num_2\ x) \qquad = Num_1\ x$
$narrow_{21}\ (Add_2\ e1\ e2) \quad = Add_1\ (narrow_{21}\ e1)\ (narrow_{21}\ e2)$
$narrow_{21}\ (Minus_2\ e1\ e2) = Minus_1\ (narrow_{21}\ e1)\ (narrow_{21}\ e2)$
$narrow_{21}\ (Neg_2\ e) \qquad = Minus_1\ (Num_1\ 0)\ (narrow_{21}\ e)$

The two systems are clearly related and share a lot of code, but there is not any reuse of code (in a software engineering sense) between them. In current programming languages, achieving reusability between these two systems is not easy because datatypes and operations are evolving at the same time. This is, after all, the EP — we suggest [6] for a good introduction to the original EP for readers unfamiliar with it. However, there is something more about this example that is not normally emphasized in the context of the EP. The $narrow_{21}$ operation takes a value of Exp_2 and converts it to a value of Exp_1. Among other things, it is *statically* known that the result of $narrow_{21}$ will not contain any negation variant. Solutions for the EP are only required to allow extensibility, but there is no explicit requirement about the interaction between *distinct* types of expressions. In particular, this allows for solutions where there is only a single, global expression datatype [19,20,21]. However, with these approaches it is not possible to accurately express the type of $narrow_{21}$. Consequently these solutions fail to solve the EFP because they do not meet the following requirement:

Different kinds of expressions should have different type identities.

Another aspect about this example that is not normally emphasized in the context of the EP — although both Wadler [5] and Zenger and Odersky [20] do mention it — is that there are interesting subtyping relationships between some of the components *in different families*. In particular $Exp_1 <: Exp_2$ and $eval_2 <: eval_1$. More generally, the extension of a datatype becomes a *supertype* of the original datatype; while the extension of an operation becomes a *subtype* of the original operation [22]. These relations are important for legacy and performance reasons since it means that, for example, a value of type Exp_1 can be *automatically* and *safely* coerced (at no run-time cost) into a value of type Exp_2, allowing some interoperability between new functionality and legacy code. This leads us to the following requirement for the EFP:

> *Subtyping relationships between components should be preserved.*

In our example we can identify a number of different features: on the one hand we have the set of operations $\{eval, narrow\}$ and, on the other hand, we have set of variants $\{Num, Add, Neg, Minus\}$. The two systems above are just two possible combinations of those features, but there are many other valid possibilities. Ideally, we would like to allow any possible combination of features, since in general it is not possible to know which of these features are relevant to the different clients. We expect the EFP to be particularly relevant in the context of component-based frameworks and software product-lines. In fact, the EFP is closely related to the *expression product lines* of Herrejon et al. [23]. Therefore, the final requirement for the EFP is that:

> *A solution should allow a high degree of composability and decoupling of components so that no valid combinations of features are ruled out.*

3   Extensible Encodings of Datatypes

In this section, we discuss the relationship between visitors and encodings of datatypes, and show how to make these encodings extensible. This will provide the foundations for the two Scala solutions presented in Sections 4 and 5.

3.1   Encodings of Datatypes and the Visitor Pattern

The VISITOR design pattern [11] shows how to separate the structure of an object hierarchy from the behaviour of traversals over that hierarchy; it can be used in object-oriented languages to provide a functional decomposition style. Buchlovsky and Thielecke [7] formalized the relation between two variants of the VISITOR pattern and encodings of datatypes in a minor variant of System F_ω with products. They observed that *external visitors* (visitors where the traversal of the object structure is explicitly controlled by the programmer) are related to Parigot encodings of datatypes [10], while internal visitors (visitors where the traversal is automatically performed by the object structure) are related to Church encodings of datatypes [9]. The basic idea behind the relationship between visitors and encodings of datatypes is briefly illustrated next (the reader wishing to know more details may look at [7,8]):

$$Expr \equiv \forall X. \ \overbrace{(Int \Rightarrow X)}^{num} \Rightarrow \overbrace{(X \Rightarrow X \Rightarrow X)}^{add} \Rightarrow X$$

$$\overbrace{}^{ExprVisitor}$$

$ExprVisitor\ X \equiv \{\,num \in Int \Rightarrow X, add \in X \Rightarrow X \Rightarrow X\,\}$

$Expr \qquad\quad \equiv \{\,accept \in \forall X.\ ExprVisitor\ X \Rightarrow X\,\}$

$Num \qquad\quad \in Int \Rightarrow Expr$

$Num\ x \qquad \equiv \{\,accept\ v \equiv v.num\ x\,\}$

$Add \qquad\quad \in Expr \Rightarrow Expr \Rightarrow Expr$

$Add\ e1\ e2 \quad \equiv \{\,accept\ v \equiv v.add\ (e1.accept\ v)\ (e2.accept\ v)\,\}$

Fig. 1. Church encoding for numeric expressions using records

$ExprVisitor\ X \equiv \{\,num \in Int \Rightarrow X, add \in Expr \Rightarrow Expr \Rightarrow X\,\}$

$Expr \qquad\quad \equiv \{\,accept \in \forall X.\ ExprVisitor\ X \Rightarrow X\,\}$

$Num \qquad\quad \in Int \Rightarrow Expr$

$Num\ x \qquad \equiv \{\,accept\ v \equiv v.num\ x\,\}$

$Add \qquad\quad \in Expr \Rightarrow Expr \Rightarrow Expr$

$Add\ e1\ e2 \qquad \equiv \{\,accept\ v \equiv v.add\ e1\ e2\,\}$

Fig. 2. Parigot encoding for numeric expressions using records

This example is based on the type of a Church encoding for a simple datatype of expressions. What the reader should note is that the two functional arguments *num* and *add* can be seen as, what in the VISITOR pattern are called, the *visit* methods for the type *Expr*. In order to make the connection to OO languages more clear we will assume, in what follows, a calculus much like the one presented by Buchlovsky and Thielecke, but also featuring subtyping [24] and using records [25] instead of products.

In Figure 1, instead of defining *Expr* as a higher-order function type, we use a record *ExprVisitor* to capture the visitor type and *visit* methods explicitly. We also use a record for *Expr* and name the functional type as *accept*. The two functions *Num* and *Add* are the two constructors (or concrete elements) for the *Expr* datatype. This is essentially an instance of the VISITOR pattern and can be easily translated into any OO language with support for generics.

A very similar construction can be done using Parigot encodings instead (but we need to additionally extend the calculus with both value and type level recursion). We show the code for Parigot encodings in Figure 2. The essential difference to Church encodings is that, for constructors with recursive occurrences of expressions such as *Add*, the expressions are not traversed by the constructor but are instead passed to the *add* visit method, delegating the responsibility of traversal to the client implementing the *add* operation.

Buchlovsky and Thielecke show that we can provide a *shape generic* version of the encodings that can be instantiated with different visitor shapes, by parametrizing over the visitor type — in this context "shape" essentially means the set of visit methods in a visitor. We need two versions of the shape generic encodings for internal and external visitors.

$$Expr\ V \qquad\qquad \equiv \{\, accept \in \forall X.\,V\ X \Rightarrow X \,\}$$
$$num\ X \qquad\qquad \equiv \{\, num \in Int \Rightarrow X \,\}$$
$$add\ \ X \qquad\qquad \equiv \{\, add\ \in X \Rightarrow X \Rightarrow X \,\}$$
$$Expr_{Num}\ (V <: num) \equiv Expr\ V$$
$$Expr_{Add}\ (V <: add) \equiv Expr\ V$$
$$Num \qquad\qquad\quad \in \forall(V <: num).\ Int \Rightarrow Expr_{Num}\ V$$
$$Num\ x \qquad\qquad\ \equiv \{\, accept\ v \equiv v.num\ x \,\}$$
$$Add \qquad\qquad\quad\ \in \forall(V <: add).\ Expr\ V \Rightarrow Expr\ V \Rightarrow Expr_{Add}\ V$$
$$Add\ e1\ e2 \qquad\quad \equiv \{\, accept\ v \equiv v.add\ (e1.accept\ v)\ (e2.accept\ v) \,\}$$

Fig. 3. Extensible Church encoding using record subtyping

$$Internal\ V \equiv \{\, accept \in \forall X.\,V\ X \Rightarrow X \,\}$$
$$External\ V \equiv \{\, accept \in \forall X.\,V\ (External\ V)\ X \Rightarrow X \,\}$$

In each case, V is a *type constructor* (that is, a type that is itself parametrized by other types) and abstracts over the concrete visitor components. In the case of *Internal*, the visitor only needs to be parametrized by the result type. For *External*, the visitor also requires a second argument for abstracting over the recursive occurrences of *External*. Although type constructors are native to calculi of the System F_ω family, they are not normally found in mainstream OO languages with generics, since only first-order type parameters are allowed. So, these generic versions of visitors cannot be encoded in those languages. However, Scala has recently been extended with support for type constructors [13] and there have been proposals for supporting them in Java too [26].

3.2   Extensible Encodings of Datatypes Using Record Subtyping

A major problem with the encodings of datatypes presented in Section 3.1 is that they are not extensible: we cannot easily add new variants to a datatype. With a standard encoding like the one presented in Figure 1, the datatype (or composite) type needs to know in advance about all the variants because of the fixed *shape* imposed by *ExprVisitor*. Interestingly, in the generic version of the encodings, the visitor shape is abstracted and the composite types *Internal* and *External* are not tied to any particular variants. Inspired by this observation, we can define an expression type that does not commit to a particular shape:

$$Expr\ V \equiv \{\, accept \in \forall X.\,V\ X \Rightarrow X \,\}$$

(This is basically the same type as *Internal*). We could easily obtain the type for expressions presented in Figure 1, by simply parametrizing *Expr* with *ExprVisitor*. However, we want to be able to define the constructors for numeric and addition expressions in a way that does not commit to a particular shape.

Clearly, we seek a solution that provides just enough information to define the constructor, but no more. In fact, all we need to know is that, for the constructor that we are defining, the visitor provides a corresponding visit method. This *minimal shape information* can be easily captured using standard record subtyping bounds as we can see in Figure 3. The type *Expr V* is, as we have already discussed, just the type for expressions with a parametrized visitor shape. The types *num X* and *add X* define two atomic visitor components that provide, respectively, *num* and *add* visit methods. Here, we use the convention that these atomic visitor types have names spelled in exactly the same way than the visit methods they contain. The idea is that when we see a bound like $V <: num$ we can read it as "the visitor V contains the visit method *num*". The types $Expr_{Num} V$ and $Expr_{Add} V$ define refinements of *Expr V* that specify some extra information about the shape. These types are used to provide constructors with more accurate types; but we should note that they are orthogonal to the extensibility problem and a slightly simpler extensible encoding can be achieved by just using *Expr V* instead. Finally, the constructors *Num* and *Add* are defined almost in the same way as with traditional Church encodings. The only difference is that the types of our extensible encodings only assume minimal shape information by using subtyping bounds to specify which visitor component provides the respective visit method.

With this encoding the expression type is parametrized by a shape instead of having a hard reference to a particular shape, which decouples the expression type from the visitor. Furthermore, the constructors only need minimal shape information, which allows them to be developed independently of other variants. This means that adding new variants and new functions is possible and, consequently, achieves a solution to the expression problem. A very similar construction can be done for Parigot encodings. We will now switch to Scala and explore solutions to the expression (families) problem using both generic Church encodings (in Section 4) and generic Parigot encodings (in Section 5).

4   Modular Internal Visitor Components

In this section we explore a solution to the expression families problem using modular internal visitors, inspired by Church encodings of datatypes.

4.1   Modular Internal Visitors in Scala

In Figure 4 we show a translation of the code in Figure 3 into Scala. Apart from fairly obvious idiomatic conversions (like, for example, encodings types as *traits* and *classes*) the Scala code is surprisingly faithful to the original code in Figure 3. Even though there is a significant gap between a calculus like System $F_{\omega}^{<:}$ and Scala, the fact is that Scala supports the essential features that are required by the encodings. In particular, the encoding requires *type parametrization* (or *parametric polymorphism*) in both the first-order and higher-order forms, the latter of which has been recently added to Scala [13]. The most significant difference between the Scala version and the System $F_{\omega}^{<:}$ version is the use of a *contravariance* annotation (the "-" preceding V) for the visitor type parameter.

```
trait Expr [− V [_]] {
  def accept [a] (vis : V [a]) : a
}
trait num [A] {
  def num (x : Int) : A
}
case class Num [− V [X] <: num [X]] (x : Int) extends Expr [V] {
  def accept [a] (vis : V [a]) : a = vis.num (x)
}
trait add [A] {
  def add (e1 : A, e2 : A) : A
}
case class Add [− V [X] <: add [X]] (e1 : Expr [V], e2 : Expr [V]) extends Expr [V] {
  def accept [a] (vis : V [a]) : a = vis.add (e1.accept (vis), e2.accept (vis))
}
```

Fig. 4. Extensible expressions in Scala

This annotation is not strictly necessary, but without it this solution would not preserve the following subtyping relationship

$Expr [V] <: Expr [U]$ if $U <: V$

which is one of the requirements for a solution for the EFP. There are a few other minor points that are worthwhile noting. Firstly, the Scala version combines the definitions of the constructors with the refined types for those constructors. For example, in the extensible Church encoding, we define a type $Expr_{Num}$ which captures the more refined type for the result type of the constructor Num. In Scala, a class declaration together with the **extends** clause captures these two constructions. Secondly, in Scala type constructor declarations are provided together with their corresponding arity and bounds. For example, $V [X] <: num [X]$ declares a type constructor variable V that has one type argument X and is bounded by $num [X]$. In the definition $Expr [− V [_]]$, naming the type constructor argument is not necessary, so we use the anonymous variable "_" to declare the existence of one type argument. Finally, we use a *case class* [27] instead of a standard class for syntactical brevity when constructing new values (since it allows us to avoid uses of **new**).

4.2 Adding New Operations

An operation that evaluates expressions can be defined, using a visitor, with the following trait:

```
trait BaseEval extends num [Int] with add [Int] {
  def num (x : Int)         = x
  def add (e1 : Int, e2 : Int) = e1 + e2
}
```

This trait extends the numeric and addition visitors, using mixin composition [14] of traits, and provides the definition for the corresponding visit methods.

Because we use an internal visitor, all the traversal code is handled in the constructors, so in the *add* visit method, the only thing that is left to be done is to add the two results together.

We can write some simple testing code that demonstrates a possible way to use *BaseEval* from a client perspective.

type *numadd* [*A*] = *num* [*A*] **with** *add* [*A*]
type *NumAdd*   = *Expr* [*numadd*]

def *exp* : *NumAdd* =
    Add [*numadd*] (*Num* [*numadd*] (3), *Num* [*numadd*] (4))

def *evalNumAdd* (*e* : *NumAdd*) : *Int* = *e.accept* (**new** *BaseEval* () {})

val *test₁* : *Int* = *evalNumAdd* (*exp*)

For the sake of clarity and brevity, we define *numadd* and *NumAdd* type synonyms, which correspond, respectively, to the visitor and composite types instantiated with a more concrete shape. We create a basic test expression *exp* that encodes the expression $3 + 4$ and test it by calling the *evalNumAdd* on that expression. There are a couple of inconveniences about this client code that we should note. Firstly, we need to parametrize the constructors with the visitor type, which makes the use of constructors significantly verbose (we would like to write *Add* (*Num* (3), *Num* (4)) instead). Secondly, we are providing *evalNumAdd* in the client code. It would be preferable to have a "generic" *eval* definition that would be provided in the library code instead. We shall address these convenience issues in Section 6.

4.3   Adding New Variants and Extending Existing Operations

Suppose that we want to add a new constructor that negates expressions. With our approach, this is also very easy: all we need to do is to introduce the visitor and corresponding constructor.

trait *neg* [*A*] {
    def *neg* (*e* : *A*) : *A*
}

case class *Neg* [− *V* [*X*] <: *neg* [*X*]] (*e* : *Expr* [*V*]) **extends** *Expr* [*V*] {
    def *accept* [*a*] (*vis* : *V* [*a*]) : *a* = *vis.neg* (*e.accept* (*vis*))
}

The trait *neg* is the visitor type and defines the *neg* visit method and the case class *Neg* defines a constructor taking a single expression as argument.

We can provide a definition for *eval* independently of the definitions for *num* and *add*

trait *NegEval₁* **extends** *neg* [*Int*] {
    def *neg* (*e* : *Int*) = − *e*
}

and later mix it in with those definitions:

trait *NumAddNegEval* **extends** *BaseEval* **with** *NegEval₁*

Alternatively, we could directly extend *BaseEval*:

```
trait NegEval₂ extends BaseEval with neg [Int] {
    def neg (e : Int) = −e
}
```

4.4 Subtyping between Components for Scalability and Reuse

Interestingly, while we may think that the trait *NegEval₁* is more reusable than *NegEval₂* (since it has no references to *BaseEval*) *this is, in fact, not the case*! Indeed the two variants are equally reusable and there is no advantage of one against the other in that respect. Because visitor extension usually follows the standard subtyping relation (although there are some exceptions, as shown in Section 4.5), a concrete visitor supporting *num*, *add* and *neg* can be passed when a visitor just supporting *num* and *add* is expected. For example, we could have alternatively defined *evalNumAdd* in the client code as:

def *evalNumAdd* (*e* : *Expr* [*numadd*]) : *Int* = *e.accept* (**new** *NegEval₂* () { })

The point here is that we do not need to carefully design visitor components for operations like this one independently of each other, which is helpful for scalability: we can pack many cases together (like in the trait *BaseEval*) and avoid code scattering and redundancy.

Another interesting point that is worthwhile noting is that, because of the subtyping relationships between different types of expressions we can apply operations defined over some type of expressions to expressions with strictly fewer variants. For example,

def *evalNumAddNeg* (*e* : *Expr* [*numaddneg*]) = *e.accept* (**new** *NegEval₂* () { })

val *test₂* = *evalNumAddNeg* (*exp*)

the function *evalNumAddNeg* takes an expression that supports numeric, addition and negation variants, but *exp* (defined above) is a *different* type of expressions that supports numeric and addition variants only. However, because *Expr* [*numadd*] <: *Expr* [*numaddneg*] we can pass *exp* to *evalNumAddNeg*.

4.5 Narrowing Operation

As we pointed out in Section 2 a solution to the EFP should allow the incremental definition of a narrow operation, so that it can be reused by any pair of expression types. With our solution we can achieve this by creating a visitor component that is itself parametrized by the type of another visitor component (which is the shape of the target expression type). We show the code for the narrow components in Figure 5. We expect that, for the most part, the majority of the variants are shared between the two expression types involved in the narrow operation and that the conversion between those variants will essentially be a matter of decomposing the variant of the input expression, narrowing recursively and rebuilding the same variant on the output expression. The visitors *NumNarrow*, *AddNarrow* and *NegArrow* do exactly this. However, when the target type of the expression does not have the variant that we are interested in, we need to convert the expression using some other variants. The *NMNarrow*

```
trait NumNarrow [V [X] <: num [X]] extends num [Expr [V]] {
    def num (x : Int)                    = Num [V] (x)
}

trait AddNarrow [V [X] <: add [X]] extends add [Expr [V]] {
    def add (e1 : Expr [V], e2 : Expr [V]) = Add [V] (e1, e2)
}

trait NegNarrow [V [X] <: neg [X]] extends neg [Expr [V]] {
    def neg (e : Expr [V])               = Neg [V] (e)
}

trait NMNarrow [V [X] <: num [X] with minus [X]] extends neg [Expr [V]] {
    def neg (e : Expr [V])               = Minus [V] (Num [V] (0), e)
}
```

Fig. 5. Components for the narrow operation

visitor shows how we could provide an alternative translation from an expression with negation into an expression without that variant, by using numeric and subtraction variants (we assume the existence of the visitor *minus* and the *Minus* variant here). Note that the following definition for *neg*

   def *neg* (*e* : *Expr* [*V*]) = *Neg* [*V*] (*e*)

would be a static type error in the *NMNarrow* trait. By using mixin composition, we are free to assemble a narrow operation in very flexible ways and there may be multiple alternatives to pick from for the same case. For example, the object

   object *myNarrow* **extends** *NumNarrow* [*num*] **with** *NMNarrow* [*numminus*]

provides a concrete narrow visitor that converts between expressions with *Num* and *Neg* variants into expressions with *Num* and *Minus* variants. Unlike the visitor for evaluation, with the narrow operation visitors we need to be careful when grouping the different cases together since we can create dependencies on variants because of the constraints imposed by the visitor type argument.

5   Modular External Visitor Components

In this section we explore a solution to the expression families problem using modular external visitors, inspired by Parigot encodings of datatypes.

5.1   Modular External Visitors in Scala

In Figure 6 we show the Scala code necessary to implement a small library of expression components using modular external visitors. The trait *Expr* defines the base component for our expression families; all constructors extend this trait. Like with the internal visitor solution, we need a contravariance annotation for the visitor type parameter $V [-\_, \_]$. However, we also need an extra contravariance annotation for the first type argument of V. As before, these variance annotations are required to ensure that the following subtyping relation holds:

```
object Components {
    // The base component for expression families
    trait Expr [− V [−_, _]] {
        def accept [a] (vis : V [Expr [V ], a]) : a
    }
    // The components for the Num variant
    trait num [−R, A] {
        def num (x : Int) : A
    }
    case class Num [V [−R, A] <: num [R, A]] (x : Int) extends Expr [V ] {
        def accept [a] (vis : V [Expr [V ], a]) : a = vis.num (x)
    }
    // The components for the Add variant
    trait add [−R, A] {
        def add (e1 : R, e2 : R) : A
    }
    case class Add [V [−R, A] <: add [R, A]] (e1 : Expr [V ], e2 : Expr [V ])
        extends Expr [V ] {
        def accept [a] (vis : V [Expr [V ], a]) : a = vis.add (e1, e2)
    }
    // The components for the Neg variant
    trait neg [−R, A] {
        def neg (e : R) : A
    }
    case class Neg [− V [−R, A] <: neg [R, A]] (e : Expr [V ]) extends Expr [V ] {
        def accept [a] (vis : V [Expr [V ], a]) : a = vis.neg (e)
    }
    // An evaluation component
    trait EvalVisitor [V [−R, A]] extends
        num [Expr [V ], Int] with add [Expr [V ], Int] with neg [Expr [V ], Int] {
        self : V [Expr [V ], Int] ⇒

        def num (x : Int)                          = x
        def add (e1 : Expr [V ], e2 : Expr [V ]) = e1.accept (this) + e2.accept (this)
        def neg (e : Expr [V ])                    = −e.accept (this)
    }
    // Some components for the narrow operation
    trait NumNarrow [V1 [−_, _], V2 [−R, X ] <: num [R, X ]]
        extends num [Expr [V1 ], Expr [V2 ]] {
        def num (x : Int)                          = Num [V2 ] (x)
    }
    trait AddNarrow [V1 [−_, _], V2 [−R, X ] <: add [R, X ]]
        extends add [Expr [V1 ], Expr [V2 ]] {self : V1 [Expr [V1 ], Expr [V2 ]] ⇒
        def add (e1 : Expr [V1 ], e2 : Expr [V1 ]) =
            Add [V2 ] (e1.accept (this), e2.accept (this))
    }
}
```

Fig. 6. The library code for expression components

$Expr\,[\,V\,] <: Expr\,[\,U\,]$ **if** $U <: V$

but, if we did not want to preserve this relation, then the contravariance annotation would not be required. Visitors take two type arguments instead of a single one (when compared to the internal visitor solution) because we need to distinguish the types of the recursive arguments from the result type.

We provide three variants in the library for numeric, addition and negation expressions. The constructors define *accept* methods that do not recur on the expressions, delegating that responsibility to the visitors, and following the Parigot encoding of datatypes presented in Figure 2. Two sets of components for operations are provided: the first one evaluates expressions; and the second one provides some definitions for the narrow operation. For operations with recursive calls we need a self-type annotation because, without the annotation, it would not be safe to assume that all the cases present in the expressions being recursively traversed would be handled. This is the same issue that was encountered, for example, by Torgersen [18] in his second solution for the expression problem.

In this section, we do not provide a step-by-step explanation of how independent extensibility of components can be achieved, because this can be done in essentially the same way as the solution presented in Section 4. We focus instead on discussing some practical concerns when assembling components and also on the extra expressiveness provided by external visitors over internal visitors.

5.2   Ad-Hoc Assembling of Components

The code presented in Figure 6 captures the code involved in a family of expressions, but it does not define any member of that family in particular. We need to *combine* (some of the) expression components if we want to obtain a particular type of expressions. The combination of components is not a responsibility of the library writer, because he cannot predict which combinations are interesting. Obviously, he cannot enumerate all possible combinations too, since the number of combinations rises very fast in respect to the number of components. So, *the assembling of components should be delegated to the clients of the library.*

In Figure 7 we present the code for a client of the component library, which supports expressions with numeric and addition variants and evaluation. The value C is used as a shortcut to the *Components* object (note that, in Scala, objects also play the role of modules). The type *ExprShape* defines a concrete visitor shape that combines several smaller visitors using mixin composition; and then we use that shape to define the type of expressions *Expr*. We also define an *ExprVisitor* trait that can be used to easily create new visitors for our expressions. Next we define some useful shorthands for the constructors, which avoid parametrization over the visitor type. Finally, operations like *eval* are defined by calling the *accept* method on the corresponding visitor.

The nice thing about this client is that it provides an abstraction on top of the component library. This is important because the components of the library use some advanced Scala features and extra parametrization that would not normally be needed if the program had been defined conventionally. If those components had been used directly, then some familiarity with the Scala features used in

```
trait Client {
  protected val C = Components
  // Defining the members of the datatype
  protected type ExprShape [−R, A] = C.num [R, A] with C.add [R, A]
  type Expr                        = C.Expr [ExprShape]
  // Shorthand for Expression Visitors
  trait ExprVisitor [A] extends C.num [Expr, A] with C.add [Expr, A]
  // Shorthands for the constructors
  def Num (x : Int)              = C.Num [ExprShape] (x)
  def Add (e1 : Expr, e2 : Expr) = C.Add [ExprShape] (e1, e2)
  // The operations
  def eval (e : Expr) : Int =
    e.accept [Int] (new C.EvalVisitor [ExprShape] () {})
}
```

Fig. 7. Ad-hoc assemblage of components for expressions

the library would probably be needed and difficult to interpret error messages arising from the misuse of these features would almost certainly occur. Happily, any code that uses *Client* does not need to be aware of the components in the expression library: all that is visible is a fairly *conventional* interface. However, the definition of clients like this one is somewhat ad-hoc, and similar preparation code is needed for other clients. In Section 6, we show how we can define these client interfaces in a more compositional and less ad-hoc way.

5.3   Extensible Modular Components with Multiple Dispatching

As the reader may notice, external visitors are more complicated to use than internal visitors because they require extra typing and the responsibility of traversal is delegated to the programmer. So, an obvious question is why should we bother with external visitors in the first place. Ignoring the extensibility issue for a moment, the main reason to use external visitors is when the recursion pattern of the operations we are defining does not follow a simple *structural recursion*, which is what internal visitors excel at. External visitors are essentially equivalent to *case analysis* [8] and, in a language like Scala, they can be used to define operations that do not follow standard recursion patterns. In particular, with external visitors it is possible to define operations that *dynamically dispatch over multiple arguments* or perform *nested case analysis* over some of the arguments.

The interesting question to ask is whether the ability to define these non-standard recursive schemes translates into our modular external visitors. This would imply a modular and statically type-safe solution for *extensible* multiple dispatching, without the need for any special purpose language extensions. As we shall see, this is indeed possible, but it is not simple. The good news is that there is a fairly mechanical scheme that can be used to define operations with such recursion patterns, which hints at a possible higher-level notation similar to multi-methods [28,19] or pattern matching as a language extension.

We use structural equality between expressions (which is a binary method) as our working example. When working with non-extensible visitors, the trick to achieve multiple dispatching is to use a series of visitors to handle each dispatching (the reader may look at [8] for an example of *equality* defined in this way). The strategy that we will use to define extensible equality is similar. It is helpful to look at a definition of equality by pattern matching to understand what happens when we define the modular components for structural equality:

$$eq :: (Expr, Expr) \rightarrow Expr$$
$$eq\ (Num\ n1, Num\ n2)\quad = n1.equals\ (n2)$$
$$eq\ (Add\ e1\ e2, Add\ e3\ e4) = eq\ (e1, e3) \wedge eq\ (e2, e4)$$
$$eq\ (Neg\ e1, Neg\ e2)\quad\ = eq\ (e1, e2)$$
$$eq\ (\_, \_)\quad\quad\quad\quad = false$$

There is some modularity in a definition like this. In order to add a new clause, we do not need to touch the code of other clauses. We explore exactly the same form of modularity in our components for equality shown in Figure 8. The *BaseHandleDefault* visitor, handles the default cases that return false. This can be seen as the code corresponding to the last clause in the definition of *eq*. In order to handle one of the other clauses we need three visitors: one for extending the default visitor with the new case, another for handling the first matched pattern and a third one to handle the second matched pattern. For the *eq (Num n1, Num n2)* clause, the *NumHandleDefault* visitor extends the default visitor with a *num* visit case. The *NumEquals* visitor defines the case for the first matched pattern and calls an instance of the visitor than handles the second match, which is handled by the third visitor *HandleNum*. Providing code for other clauses proceeds in a similar fashion. We show the code that handles the *eq (Neg e1, Neg e2)*, but skip the code for *eq (Add e1 e2, Add e3 e4)* for space reasons.

6 Feature-Oriented Programming

In this section, inspired by ideas from *feature-oriented programming* (FOP) [29], we show how to organize components into features that can be used to easily and *compositionally* assemble customized expressions datatypes and operations.

6.1 Organizing Components into Features

In Section 5.2 we have already seen how we can fairly easily assemble visitor components in an ad-hoc, non-compositional way. However, some overhead is still required. Ideally, assembling a final system should be as easy as composing a few smaller subsystems together. The comments in Figure 6 identify what components are needed for *numeric*, *addition* and *negation* variants and which components are needed for *evaluation* and *narrowing*. Each of these groups of components can be seen as what in FOP is called a *feature*.

In Scala it is possible to more precisely capture these features by grouping the required functionality for each feature in a trait. We illustrate this in Figure 9.

```
object ExtendedComponents {
    // Default case for equality : eq (_, _) = false
    trait BaseHandleDefault [V [−_, _], A] {
        self : V [Expr [V], A ⇒ Boolean] ⇒
        // recursive call reference
        def eqVis : V [Expr [V], Expr [V] ⇒ Boolean]
        // default value
        val default = (_ : A) ⇒ false
    }
    // Components for handling : eq (Num n1, Num n2) = n1.equals (n2)
    trait NumHandleDefault [V [−_, _], A] extends BaseHandleDefault [V, A]
        with num [Expr [V], A ⇒ Boolean] {
        self : V [Expr [V], A ⇒ Boolean] ⇒
        def num (n2 : Int) = default
    }
    trait NumEquals [V [−_, _]] extends num [Expr [V], Expr [V] ⇒ Boolean] {
        self : V [Expr [V], Expr [V] ⇒ Boolean] ⇒
        def eqNum : V [Expr [V], Int ⇒ Boolean]
        def num (n : Int) = e ⇒ e.accept (eqNum) (n)
    }
    trait HandleNum [V [−R, A]] extends NumHandleDefault [V, Int] {
        self : V [Expr [V], Int ⇒ Boolean] ⇒
        override def num (n2 : Int) = n1 ⇒ n1.equals (n2)
    }
    // Components for handling : eq (Neg e1, Neg e2) = eq (e1, e2)
    trait NegHandleDefault [V [−_, _], A] extends BaseHandleDefault [V, A]
        with neg [Expr [V], A ⇒ Boolean] {
        self : V [Expr [V], A ⇒ Boolean] ⇒
        def neg (e : Expr [V]) = default
    }
    trait NegEquals [V [−R, A]] extends neg [Expr [V], Expr [V] ⇒ Boolean] {
        self : V [Expr [V], Expr [V] ⇒ Boolean] ⇒
        val eqNeg : V [Expr [V], Expr [V] ⇒ Boolean]
        def neg (e2 : Expr [V]) = e1 ⇒ e1.accept (eqNeg) (e2)
    }
    trait HandleNeg [V [−R, A]] extends NegHandleDefault [V, Expr [V]] {
        self : V [Expr [V], Expr [V] ⇒ Boolean] ⇒
        override def neg (e2 : Expr [V]) = e1 ⇒ e1.accept (eqVis) (e2)
    }
}
```

Fig. 8. Extensible components for equality

```
trait Base {//Base feature
  protected val C = Components
  protected type ExprVisitor [−R, A]
  type Expr = C.Expr [ExprVisitor]
}
trait Numeric extends Base {//Numeric Feature
  type ExprVisitor [−R, A] <: C.num [R, A]//feature constraints
  def Num (x : Int) = C.Num [ExprVisitor] (x)
}
trait Addition extends Base {//Addition Feature
  type ExprVisitor [−R, A] <: C.add [R, A]//feature constraints
  def Add (e1 : Expr, e2 : Expr) = C.Add [ExprVisitor] (e1, e2)
}
trait Negation extends Base {//Negation Feature
  type ExprVisitor [−R, A] <: C.neg [R, A]//feature constraints
  def Neg (e : Expr) = C.Neg [ExprVisitor] (e)
}
trait Eval extends Base {//Evaluation Feature
  protected type BaseEval   = C.BaseEval [ExprVisitor]
  protected type EvalVisitor = BaseEval with ExprVisitor [Expr, Int]
  protected val evalVisitor : EvalVisitor//abstract
  def eval (e : Expr) : Int = e.accept [Int] (evalVisitor)
}
trait Narrow extends Base {//Narrowing Feature
  type TExpr = C.Expr [TExprVisitor]
  protected type TExprVisitor [−R, A]
  protected type NarrowVisitor = ExprVisitor [Expr, TExpr]
  protected val narrowVisitor : NarrowVisitor//abstract
  def narrow (e : Expr) : TExpr = e.accept [TExpr] (narrowVisitor)
}
trait NumNarrow extends Numeric with Narrow {//Narrowing for numbers
  protected type TExprVisitor [−R, A] <: C.num [R, A]
  protected type NumNarrow = C.NumNarrow [ExprVisitor, TExprVisitor]
}
trait NegNarrow extends Negation with Narrow {//Narrowing for negation
  protected type TExprVisitor [−R, A] <: C.num [R, A] with C.minus [R, A]
  protected type NMNarrow = C.NMNarrow [ExprVisitor, TExprVisitor]
}
```

Fig. 9. Expression features

```
object Client extends NumNarrow with NegNarrow with Eval {
    type TExprVisitor [−R, A]    = C.num [R, A] with C.minus [R, A]
    type ExprVisitor [−R, A]     = C.num [R, A] with C.neg [R, A]

    protected val evalVisitor    = new BaseEval { }
    protected val narrowVisitor = new NumNarrow with NMNarrow
}
```

Fig. 10. A client with numeric, negation, narrowing and evaluation features

The *Base* feature (on which all other features depend) abstracts over the concrete visitor shape using a virtual type *ExprVisitor*, and a type *Expr* defines the type of expressions with that shape. Note that we could also have parametrized *Base* by the visitor instead of using an abstract type, but we feel that an abstract type captures the nature of the abstraction better here. The *Numeric* feature imposes a constraint on the shape in order to support the *num* visit method, and defines a method *Num* that can be used to construct numeric expressions with the particular shape required by *ExprVisitor*. The features for *Addition* and *Negation* are defined in a similar way to *Numeric*, imposing corresponding constraints on the visitor shape and defining a constructor method. The *Eval* feature defines a type *EvalVisitor* that specifies the expected type for evaluation visitors for the particular *ExprVisitor* shape. A method *eval* that supports evaluation of expressions is also specified in the trait by using an instance of *EvalVisitor*. However, this instance reference is abstract (because it cannot be created without knowing the final shape) and is expected to be provided in the object implementing the trait. The narrowing feature requires a second abstract visitor, which defines the shape of the output expression type for the narrowing operation. The *NumNarrow* and *NegNarrow* traits are examples of *composite features* (that is, they are built on top of more basic features). Each of these two features constrains the output visitor type of the narrowing operation.

Figure 10 shows how we could assemble a client by combining some of the features using mixin composition. The first line of the object declaration for *Client* expresses what we may expect from a FOP language, defining a client to be the composition of three features that will provide support for numeric and subtraction variants together with evaluation and a narrowing operation. In Scala we still need to do a little bit more work because we need to instantiate the visitor shapes and the visitors required for the operations, but this is fairly trivial code and certainly shorter than the code that needs to be provided for a client like the one in Figure 7.

7   Related Work

In this section we discuss related work. We also assess existing solutions to the extensibility problem against the requirements of the EFP.

7.1   Extensible Visitors and Algebraic Datatypes

There have been several proposals to make visitors more flexible and extensible in the past [30,31,32]. Like our solution, an important motivation for most of these approaches is to remove the dependencies between visitors and concrete subclasses of the object structure. As Vlissides [32] observes, the VISITOR pattern (in its classic form) is unsuitable to be used in frameworks because of the references to concrete subclasses, violating the dependency inversion principle [33] and endangering modularity. However, the flexibility and extensibility in those approaches comes at a price: the solutions are not statically type-safe; casts or reflection are used and run-time type errors can occur if a visitor (or *visit* method) is called on a variant it does not handle. Both Krishnamurthi et al. [30] and Vlissides [32] describe variations of the VISITOR pattern that follow a structure similar to ours. The former solution can avoid run-time errors if all existing visitors are subclassed and some factory methods are overriden when a new variant is added; while the later solution can use catch-all cases for the same purpose. In both approaches the correct usage of the pattern (so that it does not incur of run-time type errors) is quite complex and error-prone.

Zenger and Odersky [20] propose *extensible algebraic datatypes with defaults* (EADDs) as a possible solution for the expression problem. They observe that the subtyping relationship between a datatype and its extension is inverted (the extension is a supertype of the original datatype), which leads to the idea of adding a default variant to every algebraic datatype. This has the effect of subsuming all variants defined in future extensions. Unlike our datatypes, in their approach *the extension is a subtype* of the original datatype. Because of this static type-safety is guaranteed even when a new, unforeseen, variant is added. However, this solution is subject to single inheritance and only linear extensions are possible. Moreover, it assumes that sensible default cases exist for all functions, which may not necessarily be the case. *Case classes* in Scala [27] and the *open datatypes and functions* proposal for Haskell [21] can be seen as close relatives of EADDs as they allow easy introduction of new variants and it is possible to provide a default case in a function, which ensures that the function will not fail with a run-time type error. Still, the use of a default case is not enforced, which provides some extra flexibility but also means that run-time type errors can occur.

One important requirement of the expression families problem (but not of the expression problem) is that *expressions used in different domains should have distinct types*. While most of the solutions above do solve the extensibility problem (even if at the cost of static type-safety), they do not easily allow us to have distinct types with reuse because we normally have single, simple types like *Expr*, *Num* or *Add* which are impossible to distinguish when used in different domains. Our solution allows the two distinct numeric expressions to have distinct types, while reusing most of the common, domain-independent functionality because we have types parametrized by visitors: $Expr[V]$, $Num[V]$ or $Add[V]$. In a sense, the visitor parameter can be seen as the different domain of expressions. So, by using two different visitor types we can distinguish between expressions used in different domains while achieving reuse.

7.2 Multiple Dispatch and Open Classes

Mainstream object-oriented languages, like C++, C# and Java, all use a *single dispatching* mechanism, where a single argument (the **self** object) is *dynamically* dispatched and all other dispatching is static. A problem arises, however, when a method requires dynamic dispatching on two or more arguments. The VISITOR pattern can be seen as a way to emulate double-dispatching in a single dispatching language [34,11]. By using nested visitors, we can also emulate a limited, non-extensible form of multiple dispatching. Modular visitors overcome the extensibility limitation and can be used to develop extensible and modular operations that dynamically dispatch over more than one argument. However, the use of visitors to emulate multiple dispatching is not trivial and, admittedly, it is much less practical to use than programming language extensions like multi-methods [28,19,35].

In a language with multiple dispatching the need for the classic VISITOR pattern is greatly reduced as most multiple dispatching languages support the notion of *open classes* [19], since multi-methods are normally defined independently of the classes. Consequently, we can use multi-methods to add a new operation to an object structure modularly. However, this does not solve the problem of reuse across similar object structures while allowing distinct type identities (see the discussion at the end of Section 7.1). We believe that the two lines of work are essentially complementary. On the one hand, modular visitors could benefit from a mechanism similar to multi-methods or pattern matching to better express reusable, extensible and modular operations that dynamically dispatch over multiple arguments. There is an extensive amount of work around multi-methods covering syntax, type checking and ambiguities between different clauses; this could be very useful for such a hypothetical extension. On the other hand, our work could potentially provide an alternative compilation model for multi-methods targeting conventional single dispatching languages without using any form of run-time type analysis and while supporting modularity and extensibility. It would be interesting to explore this in the future.

7.3 Generics

Wadler proposed a solution using generics to solve the expression problem [5], but he later found a subtle typing problem. Kim Bruce [36] proposed a solution to the expression problem using generics and self-types. He also made an attempt to solve the expression problem using an instance of the VISITOR pattern (again with generics and self-types). However, he failed to obtain a fully statically type-safe visitor solution. Nevertheless, he observed that type constructors (that we use in our solution) could be useful. Torgersen's second and third solutions to the expression problem [18] addressed the typing problems of Bruce's solution and showed fully statically type-safe solutions just using conventional generics and an instance of the VISITOR pattern. The idea is simple: use imperative instead of functional style visitors. Consequently, visitors do not need to be parametrized types and type constructors can be avoided. Self-types are also avoided by parametrizing the *visit* methods with an extra visitor parameter provided by the concrete elements. These solutions are a close relative to the modular external visitors presented in Section 5. However, by avoiding type-constructors some expressiveness is lost. For example, it is no longer possible to apply the same technique to datatypes that are themselves parametrized by types (that is, types like *Vector*⟨*A*⟩) as this would require visitors themselves to be parametrized by types. Furthermore, these solutions only work in languages with mutable-state, while functional-style visitors do not have such requirement. Torgersen also presented two other solutions for the problem: the first one works in both Java and C#, while the fourth relies on dynamic reification of type parameters that is only present in C#.

All of the generics solutions have an important characteristic in common with our solution: they are parametrized by the family of expressions or the family of visitors (or both). This means that, like our solution, it is possible to distinguish between different types of expressions. The third solution by Torgerson has another thing in common with our solution: the subtyping relationships between different expressions are preserved. An important limitation of these techniques is their lack of support for independent extensibility [6].

7.4   Type Classes and Polymorphic Variants

Oliveira et al. [37] addressed the problem of *extensible generic functions* in Haskell using records in the form of constructor type classes (that is, type classes parametrized by a type constructor) and noted the connection to the expression problem. This solution is essentially an instance of internal visitors in disguise [38] and inspired the solution presented in Section 4. Swierstra [39] proposed a solution to the expression problem using extensible sums (or variants) that has some close similarities to Oliveira's et. all technique and the solution proposed here. However, this approach relies on variant subtyping, which needs to be encoded in Haskell. From an OO perspective, Swierstra's technique seems less appealing than a solution that uses records because while nearly all OO languages natively support some form of record subtyping, most (if not all) do not support variant subtyping and a manual implementation of the subtyping machinery for variants would also be required.

Garrigue [40] shows how *polymorphic variants* can be used to solve the expression problem. With polymorphic variants, different datatypes can share the same constructor. When a definition using pattern matching is written every usage of a polymorphic variant will raise a type constraint which ensures that only a datatypes containing all of those constraints will be used in the definition. An important drawback of this approach is that functions are not extensible and open recursion has to be used manually to emulate extensible functions.

Both the Haskell solutions and polymorphic variants have very good support for type inference. This can be seen as an advantage because it allows us to program without ever closing extensions. In our approach this is also possible but, because support for type inference in Scala is weaker, this becomes more cumbersome (see, for example, the client code in Section 4.2). However, by programming in this open style, the client will also be exposed to the complexity of the advanced language features to achieve extensibility, which can lead, for example, to difficult error messages to interpret. With our solution we can provide an abstraction on top of the reusable infrastructure that hides that complexity away. We believe that in practice having this abstraction is preferable as this keeps the interfaces very simple and familiar to most programmers. Also, in all these approaches there are important limitations when the functions we want to write do not follow a simple structurally recursive scheme.

7.5   Virtual Types

Odersky and Zenger [6] present two solutions for the expression problem using a combination of virtual types and nested classes. In the top-level classes, some operations and variants are initially added and the hard references that would preclude extensibility are replaced with virtual types. In the subclasses, new operations and/or variants can be added by suitably extending the top-level class and refining the virtual types. Their solution has, somehow, the flavour of *virtual classes*, which provide a more direct way to solve the problem as Ernst demonstrates in GBeta [41]. Ernst's solution also benefits from a special form of composition that can compose two classes and all of their inner classes automatically. In Scala we have to perform this operation manually. Nystrom et al. propose Java extensions similar to virtual classes that support *nested inheritance* [42] and *nested intersection* [43]; and present a solution for the EP that is very similar to the virtual classes solution by Ernst. More recently, Qi and Myers [44] have proposed *class sharing* as a new language mechanism that aims at allowing objects of one family to be used as members of another family. Our use of variance annotations to allow subtyping relations across components of different families also achieves this kind of interchange of objects in different families. Nonetheless, class sharing does not induce subtyping relations and can be used to make adaptations that are not possible with our approach. However, class sharing requires significant annotations, which places an additional burden on the programmer.

Solutions that use some form of virtual types (or classes) are generally very readable and easy to understand because the reusable code is very similar to the code that would be written if we would not be aiming at extensibility. In solutions like ours, or the ones discussed in Sections 7.3 and 7.4, the reusable code has to be written in a slightly different style and genericity becomes explicitly visible due to some extra typing effort involved. We believe that virtual types provide a particularly good solution to problems where a relatively small amount of customization is expected and a small, interesting set of composable functionality is identified. However, we think that when the expected degree of customization is higher and potentially all valid combination of features should be allowed, then virtual types do have some drawbacks. If we want to use virtual types to allow the degree of compositionality and decoupling required by the EFP, we basically need to have a class with the corresponding nested virtual types for each feature. Furthermore, we need to scatter the reusable code for the operations very finely across those classes so that entanglement between features is not created. Therefore, although it would be possible to achieve a similar degree of customization and compositionality, the readability advantage would be lost and a considerable amount of boilerplate code to set up each feature would be required. Moreover, if the language that we use supports virtual types, but not nested inheritance (like, for example, Scala) then the amount of effort to compose features can be quite overwhelming. Our solution on the other hand, allows small features to be created with very little boilerplate code and, for most operations, we do not need to scatter code around since, as we have discussed in Section 4.4, we can exploit the subtyping relationship between visitors to group many cases together without entangling features.

8 Conclusions

We have shown how to solve the EFP using two alternative variations of modular visitors. One very simple and practical alternative is to use internal visitors. Another alternative is to use external visitors, which are slighty more complex to use but allow additional expressiveness. Inspired by some ideas of FOP, we have also shown how to organize the visitor components into features that can be easily composed to provide customized systems of datatypes and operations. We believe that our techniques can be very helpful for the development of software in a FOP style without requiring any special tool or language extension and using only generic language constructs.

While in most situations internal visitors are preferable, there are a few situations where external visitors may be more suitable, which seems to force us into a design decision. In earlier work [8] we have presented a reusable, generic and type-safe visitor library (VisLib) that is parametrizable over the traversal strategy. Internal and External visitors can be recovered by suitably parametrizing the concrete visitors with the corresponding traversal strategy. As it happens, *extensibility is orthogonal to VisLib* and we can in fact easily use the original VisLib to develop extensible visitor components using techniques similar to the ones in this paper, without having to commit to internal or external visitors in advance. Although we have not presented such solution here, in the companion code for this paper a solution using VisLib is also presented and documented.

Acknowledgements

We are very thankful to the anonymous reviewers for their excellent reviews, which have greatly helped to improve the presentation of this paper. Jeremy Gibbons provided valuable feedback on an earlier draft. This work is supported by the EPSRC grant *Generic and Indexed Programming* (EP/E02128X).

References

1. McIlroy, D.: Mass produced software components. In: [2], pp. 138–155
2. Naur, P., Randell, B. (eds.): Software Engineering: Report of a Conference Sponsored by the NATO Science Committee, Garmisch, Germany (1969)
3. Reynolds, J.C.: User-defined types and procedural data structures as complementary approaches to type abstraction. In: Schuman, S.A. (ed.) New Directions in Algorithmic Languages, Rocquencourt, pp. 157–168 (1975)
4. Cook, W.R.: Object-oriented programming versus abstract data types. In: Stein, J. (ed.) REX Workshop/School on the Foundations of Object-Oriented Languages. LNCS, vol. 173, pp. 151–178. Springer, Heidelberg (1990)
5. Wadler, P.: The expression problem. Java Genericity Mailing list (November 1998)
6. Odersky, M., Zenger, M.: Independently extensible solutions to the expression problem. In: FOOL 2005 (2005)
7. Buchlovsky, P., Thielecke, H.: A type-theoretic reconstruction of the visitor pattern. In: MFPS XXI. Electronic Notes in Theoretical Computer Science (ENTCS) (2005)
8. Oliveira, B.C.d.S., Wang, M., Gibbons, J.: The visitor pattern as a reusable, generic, type-safe component. In: OOPSLA 2008 (2008)
9. Böhm, C., Berarducci, A.: Automatic synthesis of typed lambda-programs on term algebras. Theoretical Computer Science 39, 135–153 (1985)
10. Parigot, M.: Recursive programming with proofs. Theor. Comput. Sci. 94(2), 335–356 (1992)
11. Gamma, E., Helm, R., Johnson, R., Vlissides, J.: Design Patterns: Elements of Reusable Object-Oriented Software. Addison-Wesley, Reading (1995)
12. Girard, J.Y., Taylor, P., Lafont, Y.: Proofs and types. Cambridge University Press, Cambridge (1989)
13. Moors, A., Piessens, F., Odersky, M.: Generics of a higher kind. In: OOPSLA 2008 (2008)
14. Bracha, G., Cook, W.: Mixin-based inheritance. In: OOPSLA 1990, pp. 303–311. ACM Press, New York (1990)
15. Schärli, N., Ducasse, S., Nierstrasz, O., Black, A.: Traits: Composable units of behavior. In: Cardelli, L. (ed.) ECOOP 2003. LNCS, vol. 2743, pp. 248–274. Springer, Heidelberg (2003)
16. Bruce, K., Schuett, A., van Gent, R., Fiech, A.: Polytoil: A type-safe polymorphic object-oriented language. ACM Trans. Program. Lang. Syst. 25(2), 225–290 (2003)
17. Igarashi, A., Viroli, M.: Variant parametric types: A flexible subtyping scheme for generics. ACM Trans. Program. Lang. Syst. 28(5), 795–847 (2006)
18. Torgersen, M.: The expression problem revisited. In: Odersky, M. (ed.) ECOOP 2004. LNCS, vol. 3086, pp. 123–146. Springer, Heidelberg (2004)
19. Clifton, C., Leavens, G.T., Chambers, C., Millstein, T.: MultiJava: Modular open classes and symmetric multiple dispatch for Java. In: OOPSLA 2000, pp. 130–145 (2000)
20. Zenger, M., Odersky, M.: Extensible algebraic datatypes with defaults. In: ICFP 2001, pp. 241–252 (2001)
21. Löh, A., Hinze, R.: Open data types and open functions. In: PPDP 2006, pp. 133–144 (2006)
22. Poll, E.: Subtyping and inheritance for inductive types. In: Informal proceedings of the 1994 TYPES Workshop (1997)
23. Lopez-Herrejon, R.E., Batory, D.S., Cook, W.R.: Evaluating support for features in advanced modularization technologies. In: Black, A.P. (ed.) ECOOP 2005. LNCS, vol. 3586, pp. 169–194. Springer, Heidelberg (2005)

24. Pierce, B.C.: Types and Programming Languages. MIT Press, Cambridge (2002)
25. Cardelli, L.: Extensible records in a pure calculus of subtyping. In: Theoretical Aspects of Object-Oriented Programming, pp. 373–425. MIT Press, Cambridge (1994)
26. Cremet, V., Altherr, P.: Adding type constructor parameterization to Java. Journal of Object Technology 7(5), 25–65 (2008)
27. Odersky, M., et al.: An overview of the Scala programming language (2 nd edn.). Technical Report IC/2006/001, EPFL Lausanne, Switzerland (2006)
28. Chambers, C., Leavens, G.T.: Typechecking and modules for multimethods. ACM Transactions on Programming Languages and Systems 17(6), 805–843 (1995)
29. Prehofer, C.: Feature-oriented programming: A fresh look at objects. In: Aksit, M., Matsuoka, S. (eds.) ECOOP 1997. LNCS, vol. 1241, pp. 419–443. Springer, Heidelberg (1997)
30. Krishnamurthi, S., Felleisen, M., Friedman, D.P.: Synthesizing object-oriented and functional design to promote re-use. In: Jul, E. (ed.) ECOOP 1998. LNCS, vol. 1445, pp. 91–113. Springer, Heidelberg (1998)
31. Palsberg, J., Jay, C.B.: The essence of the visitor pattern. In: Proc. 22nd IEEE Int. Computer Software and Applications Conf., COMPSAC, pp. 9–15 (19-21 1998)
32. Vlissides, J.: Pattern hatching - visitor in frameworks (1999)
33. Martin, R.C.: The Dependency Inversion Principle. The C++ Report (May 1996)
34. Ingalls, D.H.H.: A simple technique for handling multiple polymorphism. In: OOPSLA 1986, pp. 347–349 (1986)
35. Ernst, M., Kaplan, C., Chambers, C.: Predicate dispatching: A unified theory of dispatch. In: Jul, E. (ed.) ECOOP 1998. LNCS, vol. 1445, pp. 186–211. Springer, Heidelberg (1998)
36. Bruce, K.B.: Some challenging typing issues in object-oriented languages. Electr. Notes Theor. Comput. Sci. 82(7) (2003)
37. Oliveira, B.C.d.S., Hinze, R., Löh, A.: Extensible and modular generics for the masses. In: TFP 2006, pp. 109–138 (2006)
38. Oliveira, B.C.d.S.: Genericity, Extensibility and Type-Safety in the VISITOR Pattern. PhD thesis, University of Oxford (2007)
39. Swierstra, W.: Data types à la carte. Journal of Functional Programming 18(4), 423–436 (2008)
40. Garrigue, J.: Code reuse through polymorphic variants. In: Workshop on Foundations of Software Engineering, pp. 93–100 (2000)
41. Ernst, E.: The expression problem, Scandinavian style. In: Lahire, P., et al. (eds.) MASPEGHI 2004 (2004)
42. Nystrom, N., Chong, S., Myers, A.C.: Scalable extensibility via nested inheritance. In: OOPSLA 2004, pp. 99–115. ACM Press, New York (2004)
43. Nystrom, N., Qi, X., Myers, A.C.: J&: nested intersection for scalable software composition. In: OOPSLA 2006, pp. 21–36. ACM Press, New York (2006)
44. Qi, X., Myers, A.C.: Sharing classes between families. In: PLDI 2009 (June 2009)

Debugging Method Names

Einar W. Høst and Bjarte M. Østvold

Norwegian Computing Center
{einarwh,bjarte}@nr.no

Abstract. Meaningful method names are crucial for the readability and maintainability of software. Existing naming conventions focus on syntactic details, leaving programmers with little or no support in assuring meaningful names. In this paper, we show that naming conventions can go much further: we can mechanically check whether or not a method name and implementation are likely to be good matches for each other. The vast amount of software written in Java defines an implicit convention for pairing names and implementations. We exploit this to extract rules for method names, which are used to identify "naming bugs" in well-known Java applications. We also present an approach for automatic suggestion of more suitable names in the presence of mismatch between name and implementation.

1 Introduction

It is well-known that maintenance costs dominate — if not the budget — then the true cost of software [7]. It is also known that code readability is a vital factor for maintenance [5]: unintelligible software is necessarily hard to modify and extend. Finally, it has been demonstrated that the quality of identifiers has a profound effect on program comprehension [14]. We conclude that identifier quality affects the cost of software! Hence, we would expect programmers to have powerful analyses and tools available to help assure that identifier quality is high.

The reality is quite different. While the importance of good names is undisputed among leading voices in the industry [2, 18, 19], the analyses and tools are lacking. Programmer guidance is limited to naming convention documents such as those provided by Sun Microsystems for Java. The following quote is typical for the kind of advice given by such documents: "Except for variables, all instance, class, and class constants are in mixed case with a lowercase first letter"[1]. In other words, the documents mandate a certain uniformity of lexical syntax. Since such uniformity is easily checked mechanically, there are tools available to check for violations against these rules. While this is certainly useful, it does little to ensure meaningful identifiers. (Arguably, syntactic uniformity helps reduce the cost of "human parsing" of identifiers, but not the interpretation.) Since identifiers clearly must be meaningful to be of high quality, current tool-support must be considered unsatisfactory.

---

[1] http://java.sun.com/docs/codeconv/html/CodeConventions.doc8.html

S. Drossopoulou (Ed.): ECOOP 2009, LNCS 5653, pp. 294–317, 2009.

This begs the question what meaningful identifiers really are. Consider what an identifier is used for: it represents some program entity, and allows us to refer to that entity by means of the identifier alone. In other words, the identifier is an abstraction, and the meaning relates to the program entity it represents. The identifier is meaningful if the programmer can interpret it to gain an understanding of the program entity without looking at the entity itself. Intuitively, we also demand that the abstraction be sound: we must agree that the identifier is a suitable replacement for the entity. Hence, what we really require are identifiers that are both *meaningful* and *appropriate*.

In this work, we consider only method names. Methods are the smallest named units of aggregated behaviour in most conventional programming languages, and hence a cornerstone of abstraction. A method name is meaningful and appropriate if it adequately describes the implementation of the method. Naming is non-trivial because there is a potential for conflict between names and implementations: we might choose an inappropriate name for an implementation, or provide an inappropriate implementation for a name. The label *appropriate* is not really a binary decision: there is a sliding scale from the highly appropriate to the utterly inappropriate. Inappropriate or even meaningless identifiers are obviously bad, but subtle mistakes in naming can be as confusing or worse. Since the programmer is less likely to note the subtle mistake, a misconception of the code's behaviour can be carried for a long time.

Consider the following example, taken from AspectJ 1.5.3, where the method name has been replaced by underscores:

```
/**
 * @return field object with given name, or null
 */
public Field ___(String name) {
  for (Iterator e = this.field_vec.iterator(); e.hasNext();) {
    Field f = (Field) e.next();
    if (f.getName().equals(name))
      return f;
  }
  return null;
}
```

Most Java programmers will find it easy to come up with a name for this method: clearly, this is a *find* method! More precisely, we would probably name this method findField; a suitable description for a method that indeed tries to find a Field. The name used in AspectJ, however, is containsField. We consider this to be a *naming bug*, since the name indicates a question to the object warranting a boolean reply ("Do you contain a field with this name?") rather than an instruction to return an object ("Find me the field with this name!"). In this paper, we show how to derive rules for implementations of *contains* methods, *find* methods and other methods with common names, allowing us to identify this naming bug and many others. We also present an approach for automatic correction of faulty names that successfully suggests using the verb *find* rather than *contains* for the code above.

It is useful to speak of method names in slightly abstract terms; for instance, we speak of *find* methods, encompassing concrete method names like `findField` and `findElementByID`. We have previously introduced the term *method phrase* for this perspective [12]. Typically, the rules uncovered by our analysis will refer to method phrases rather than concrete method names. This is because method phrases allow us to focus on essential similarities between method names, while ignoring arbitrary differences.

The main contributions of this paper are as follows:

- A formal definition of a naming bug (Sect. 3.1).
- An approach for encoding the semantics of methods (Sect. 3.3), building on our previous work [12, 11].
- An approach for extracting name-specific implementation rules for methods (Sect. 3.4).
- An automatically generated "rule book" containing implementation rules for the most common method names used in Java programming (Sect. 3.4).
- An approach for automatic suggestion of a more suitable name in the case of mismatch between the name and implementation of a method (Sect. 3.6).

We demonstrate the usefulness of our analysis by finding genuine naming bugs in well-known Java applications (Sect. 5.2).

2   Motivation

Our goal is to exploit the vast amount of software written in Java to derive name-specific implementation rules for methods. Our approach is to compare the names and implementations of methods in a large corpus of well-known open-source Java applications. In this section, we motivate our approach, based on philosophical considerations about the meaning of natural language expressions.

2.1   The Java Language Game

We have previously argued that method identifiers act as hosts for expressions in a natural language we named *Programmer English* [12]. Inspired by Wittgenstein and Frege, we take a pragmatic view of how meaning is constructed in natural language. According to Wittgenstein, "the meaning of a word is its use in the language" [27]. In other words, the meaning is simply the sum of all the uses we find of the word — there is no "objective" definition apart from this sum. It follows that meaning is not static, since new examples of use will skew the meaning in their own direction. Also, any attempt at providing a definition for a word (for instance in a dictionary, or our own phrase book for Java [12]) is necessarily an imperfect approximation of the meaning.

Wittgenstein used the term *language game* (Sprachspiel) to designate simple forms of language, "consisting of language and the actions into which it is

woven" [27]. Intuitively, a language game should be understood as interplay between natural language expressions and behaviours. Hence, our object of inquiry
is really the Java language game, where the language expressions are encoded in
method identifiers and the actions are encoded in method bodies.

In discussing the meaning of symbolic language expressions, Frege [9] introduces the terms *sign*, *reference* and *sense*. The sign is the name itself, or a
combination of words. The reference is the object to which the sign refers. The
sense is our collective understanding of the reference. In the context of Java
programming, we take the sign to be the method phrase, the reference to be
the "true meaning" indicated by that phrase (that Wittgenstein would claim is
illusory), and the sense to be the Java community's collective understanding of
what the phrase means. Of course, the collective understanding is really unavailable to us: we are left with our own subjective and imperfect understanding of
the sign. This is what Frege refers to as the individual's *idea*. Depending on our
level of insight, that idea may be in various degrees of harmony or conflict with
the actual sense.

Interestingly, when analysing Java methods, we *do* have direct access to a
manifestation of the programmer's idea of the method name's sense: the method
body. By collecting and analysing a large number of such ideas, we can approximate the sense of the name. This, in turn, allows us to identify naming bugs:
ideas that are in conflict with the approximated sense.

3 Analysis of Methods

We turn our understanding of how meaning is constructed into a practical approach for approximating the meaning of method names in Java. This approximation is then used to create rules for method implementations. Finally, these
rules help us identify naming bugs. Fig. 1 provides an overview of the approach.
The analysis consists of three major phases: data preparation, mining of implementation rules, and identification of naming bugs.

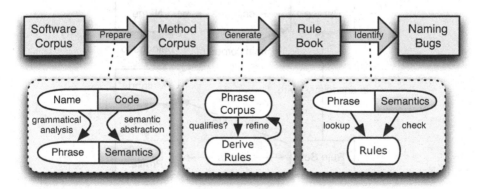

Fig. 1. Overview of the approach

298   E.W. Høst and B.M. Østvold

In the data preparation phase, we transform our corpus of Java applications into an idealised corpus of methods. The transformation entails analysing each Java method in two ways. On the one hand, we perform a natural language analysis on the method name (Sect. 3.2). This involves decomposing the name into individual words and performing part-of-speech tagging of those words. The tags allow us to form abstract phrases from the concrete method names. On the other hand, we analyse the signature and Java bytecode of the method implementation, deriving a semantic profile for each implementation (Sect. 3.3).

This sets us up to investigate the semantics of methods that share the same abstract phrase. We start with very abstract phrases that we gradually refine into more concrete phrases, more closely matching the actual method names. If a given phrase fulfils certain criteria pertaining to prevalence, we derive a corresponding set of implementation rules (Sect. 3.4) that all methods whose names match the phrase must obey. Failure to obey an implementation rule is considered a naming bug (Sects. 3.5 and 3.6).

3.1 Definitions

In the following, please refer to Fig. 2 for an overview of the relationships between the introduced terms.

We define a *method* m as a tuple consisting of a unique *fingerprint* u, a *name* n, and a *semantic profile* $[\![m]\!]$. The unique fingerprints prevent set elements from collapsing into one; hence, a set made from arbitrary methods $m_1, \ldots, m_k$ will always have k elements. The name n is a non-empty list of *fragments* f. Each fragment is annotated with a *tag* t.

The semantic profile $[\![m]\!]$ for a method m is defined in terms of *attributes*. We define a set $\mathcal{A}$ of attributes $\{a_1, \ldots, a_k\}$, and let a denote an attribute from $\mathcal{A}$. Given a method m and an attribute a, the expression $check(m, a)$ is a binary value $b \in \{0, 1\}$. Intuitively, *check* determines whether or not m fulfils the predicate

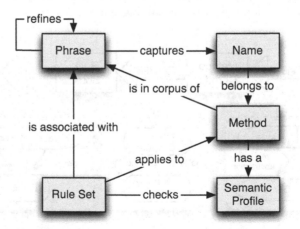

Fig. 2. Conceptual model of phrase terms

defined by a. We then define $[\![m]\!]$ as the list $[check(m, a_1), \ldots, check(m, a_k)]$. It follows that there are at most $2^{|\mathcal{A}|}$ distinct semantic profiles. The *rank* of a semantic profile in a corpus is the proportion of methods that have that semantic profile.

A *phrase* p is a non-empty list of *parts* ρ; its purpose is to abstract over method names. A part ρ may be a fragment f, a tag t, or a special wildcard symbol $*$. The wildcard symbol may only appear as the last part of a phrase. A phrase that consists solely of fragments is *concrete*; all other phrases are *abstract*.

A phrase *captures* a name if each individual part of the phrase captures each fragment of the name, in order from first to last. A fragment part captures a fragment if they are equal. A tag part captures a fragment if it is equal to the fragment's tag. A wildcard part captures any remaining fragments in a name, including zero fragments. A concrete phrase can only capture a single name, whereas an abstract phrase can capture multiple names. For instance, the abstract phrase **is-⟨adjective⟩-*** captures names like **is-empty**, **is-valid-signature** and so forth.

A *corpus* $\mathcal{C}$ is a set of methods. Implicitly, $\mathcal{C}$ defines a set $\mathcal{N}$, consisting of the names of the methods $m \in \mathcal{C}$. A *name corpus* $\mathcal{C}_n$ is the subset of $\mathcal{C}$ with the name n. Similarly, a *phrase corpus* $\mathcal{C}_p$ is the subset of $\mathcal{C}$ whose names are captured by the phrase p. The *frequency value* $\xi_a(\mathcal{C})$ for an attribute a given a corpus $\mathcal{C}$ is defined as:

$$\xi_a(\mathcal{C}) \stackrel{\text{def}}{=} \frac{\sum_{m \in \mathcal{C}} check(m, a)}{|\mathcal{C}|}$$

The semantics of a corpus $\mathcal{C}$ is defined as the list $[\xi_{a_1}(\mathcal{C}), \ldots, \xi_{a_k}(\mathcal{C})]$. We write $[\![p]\!]_{\mathcal{C}}$ for the semantics of a phrase in corpus $\mathcal{C}$, and define it as the semantics of the corresponding phrase corpus. The subscript will be omitted when there can be no confusion as to which corpus we refer to.

We introduce a subset $\mathcal{A}_o \subset \mathcal{A}$ of *orthogonal attributes*. Two attributes a_1 and a_2 are considered orthogonal if $check(m, a_1)$ does not determine $check(m, a_2)$ or vice versa for any method m. We define the *semantic distance* $d(p_1, p_2)$ between two phrases p_1 and p_2 as the vector distance

$$d(p_1, p_2) \stackrel{\text{def}}{=} \sum_{a \in \mathcal{A}_o} \left(\xi_a(\mathcal{C}_{p_1}) - \xi_a(\mathcal{C}_{p_2}) \right)^2$$

A *rule* r is a tuple consisting of an attribute a, a *trigger condition* c and a *severity* s. The trigger condition c is a binary value, indicating whether the rule is triggered when the function *check* evaluates to 0 or to 1. The severity s is defined as $s \in \{forbidden, inappropriate, reconsider\}$. For example, the rule $r = (a_{reads\_field}, 1, inappropriate)$ indicates that it is considered *inappropriate* for the **reads field** attribute to evaluate to 1. Applied to a method implementation, the rule states that the implementation should not read field values. In practice, rules are relevant for specific phrases. Hence, we associate with each phrase p a set of rules $\mathcal{R}_p$ that apply to the methods $m \in \mathcal{C}_p$.

Finally, we define a boolean function $bug(r, m) \stackrel{\text{def}}{=} check(m, a) = c$ that evaluates to true when the rule $r = (a, c, s)$ is triggered by method m.

3.2 Analysing Method Names

Far from being arbitrary labels, method names act as hosts for meaningful phrases. This is the premise we rely on when we state that it is possible to define name-specific rules for the implementation of methods. According to Liblit [15], "[method] names exhibit regularities derived from the grammars of natural languages, allowing them to combine together to form larger pseudo-grammatical phrases that convey additional meaning about the code". To reconstruct these phrases, we decompose the method names into individual fragments, and apply a natural language processing technique called part-of-speech tagging [17] to identify their grammatical structure.

Decomposition. By convention, Java programmers use "camel case" when forming method names that consist of multiple fragments ("words"). A camel case method name uses capitalised fragments to compensate for the lack of whitespace in identifiers. For instance, instead of writing `create new instance` (which would be illegal), Java programmers write `createNewInstance`. To recover the individual fragments, we reverse the process, using capital characters as an indicator to split the name, with special treatment of uppercase acronyms. For instance, we decompose `parseXMLNode` into `parse XML node` as one would expect. Some programmers use underscore as delimiter instead of case-switching; however, we have previously noted that this is quite rare [12]. For simplicity, we therefore choose to omit such methods from the analysis.

Part-of-speech Tagging. Informally, part-of-speech tagging refers to the process of tagging each word in a natural language expression with information about its the grammatical role in the expression. In our scenario, this translates to tagging each fragment in the decomposed method name. We consider a decomposed method name to be an untagged method phrase.

An overview of the tagging process is shown in Fig. 3. First, we use the tags **verb, noun, adjective, adverb, pronoun, preposition, conjunction, article, number, type** and **unknown** to tag each fragment in the phrase. In other words, apart from the special tags **number, type** and **unknown**, we use the basic word classes. The **number** tag is used for numeric fragments like **1**. The **type** tag is used when we identify a fragment as the name of a type in scope of the method. Fragments that we fail to tag default to the **unknown** tag.

We make three attempts at finding suitable tags for a fragment. First, we use WordNet [8], a large lexical database of English, to find verbs, nouns, adjectives and adverbs. We augment the results given by WordNet with lists of pronouns, prepositions, conjunctions and articles. If we fail to find any tags, we use a mechanism for identifying invented words. Programmers sometimes derive nouns and adjectives from verbs (for instance, **handler** from **handle** and **foldable** from **fold**), or verbs from nouns (for instance, **tokenize** from **token**). If we can

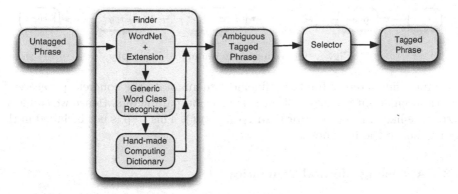

Fig. 3. Part-of-speech tagging for method phrases

discover such derivations, we tag the fragment accordingly. Finally, we resort to a manual list of tags for commonly used programming terms.

Since a fragment may receive multiple tags (for instance, WordNet considers **object** to be both a noun and a verb), the initial tagging leads to an ambiguously tagged phrase. We then perform a selection of tags that takes into account both the fragment's position in the phrase, and the tags of surrounding fragments. This yields an unambiguously tagged phrase. We have previously estimated the accuracy of the part-of-speech tagger to be approximately 97% [12].

Method Phrases and Refinement. The decomposed, tagged method names are concrete method phrases. The tags allow us to form abstract phrases as well; phrases where concrete fragments have been replaced by tags. Phrases are written like this: **get-⟨noun⟩-***, where the individual parts are separated by hyphens, fragments are written straightforwardly: **get**, tags are written in angle brackets: ⟨**noun**⟩, and the * symbol indicates that the phrase can be further refined.

Refinement involves reducing the corresponding phrase corpus to a subset. In general, there are three kinds of refinement:

1. Introduce tag: **p-*** ⇒ **p-⟨t⟩-***.
   For instance, the phrase **is-*** may be refined to **is-⟨adjective⟩-***. The former phrase would capture a name like `isObject`, the latter would not.
2. Remove wildcard: **p-*** ⇒ **p**.
   For instance, the phrase **is-⟨adjective⟩-*** may be refined to **is-⟨adjective⟩**. The former phrase would capture a name like `isValidSignature`, the latter would not.
3. Replace tag with fragment: **p-⟨t⟩-*** ⇒ **p-f-***.
   For instance, the phrase **is-⟨adjective⟩-*** may be refined to **is-empty-***. The former phrase would capture a name like `isValid`, the latter would not.

Fig. 4 shows the refinement steps leading from the completely abstract phrase *****, to the concrete phrase **is-empty**. When we reach a concrete phrase, we

Fig. 4. The refinements leading to **is-empty**

attempt a final step of further refinement to annotate the concrete phrase with information about the types of return value and parameters. Hence we can form signature-like phrases like **boolean is-empty()**. This step is not included in the figure, nor in the list above.

3.3   Analysing Method Semantics

In any data mining task, the outcome of the analysis depends on the domain knowledge of the analyst [26]. Hence, we must rely on our knowledge of Java programming when modelling the semantics of methods. In particular, we consider some aspects of the implementation to be important clues as to the behaviour of methods, whereas others are considered insignificant.

A method m has some basic behaviours pertaining to data flow and control flow that we would like to capture: 1) read or write fields, 2) create new objects, 3) return a value to the caller, 4) call methods, 5) branch and/or repeat iteration, and 6) catch and/or throw exceptions. We concretise the basic behaviours by means of a list of machine-traceable *attributes*, formally defined as predicates on Java bytecode. In addition to the attributes stemming from the basic behaviours, called *instruction attributes*, we define a list of *signature attributes*. Table 1 lists all the attributes, coarsely sorted in groups. Note that some attributes, such as **returns created object** really belong to more than one group. Attributes marked with an asterisk belong to the subset of orthogonal attributes.

Most of the attributes should be fairly self-explanatory; however, the attributes pertaining to object creation warrant further explanation. A regular object is an object that does not inherit from the type `java.lang.Throwable`, a string object is an instance of the type `java.lang.String`, and a custom object is one that does not belong to either of the namespaces `java.*` and `javax.*`. Finally, the attribute **creates own type objects** indicates that the method creates an instance of the class on which the method is defined.

3.4   Deriving Phrase-Specific Implementation Rules

We derive a set of implementation rules for method phrases that are *prevalent* in a large corpus of Java applications. A phrase is considered prevalent if it fulfils a simple heuristic: it must occur in at least half of the applications in the corpus, and it must cover at least 100 method instances. While somewhat arbitrary, this heuristic guards against idiosyncratic naming in any single application, and ensures a fairly broad basis for the semantics of the phrase. Each prevalent phrase is included in a conceptual "rule book" derived from the corpus, along with a corresponding set of rules. Intuitively, all methods captured by a certain phrase must obey its implementation rules.

Table 1. Attributes. Orthogonal attributes marked with an asterisk.

Signature	
Returns void*	Returns reference
Returns int	Returns boolean
Returns string	No parameters*
Return type in name	Parameter type in name

Data Flow	
Reads field*	Writes field*
Writes parameter value to field	Returns field value
Returns created object	Runtime type check*

Object Creation	
Creates regular objects*	Creates string objects
Creates custom objects	Creates own type objects

Control Flow	
Contains loop*	Contains branch
Multiple return points*	

Exception Handling	
Throws exceptions*	Catches exceptions*
Exposes checked exceptions	

Method Call	
Recursive call*	Same name call*
Same verb call*	Method call on field value
Method call on parameter value	Parameter value passed to method call on field value

We define the implementation rules on the level of individual attributes. To do so, we consider the frequency values of the attributes for different phrase corpora. The intuition is that for a given phrase corpus, the frequency value for an attribute indicates the probability for the attribute's predicate to be fulfilled for methods in that corpus. For each attribute $a \in \mathcal{A}$, we find that the the frequency value $\xi_a(\mathcal{C}_n)$ is distributed within the boundaries $0 \leq \xi_a(\mathcal{C}_n) \leq 1$. We assume that method names therefore can be used to predict whether or not an attribute will evaluate to 1: different names lead to different frequency values. Fig. 5 shows example distributions for the attributes **reads field** and **returns void** for some corpus. We see that the two distributions are quite different. Both attributes distinguish between names, but **returns void** is clearly the most polarising of the two for the corpus in question.

A frequency value close to 0 indicates that it is rare for methods in the corresponding corpus to fulfil the predicate defined by the attribute; a value close to 1 indicates the opposite. We exploit this to define rules. Any method that deviates from the norm set by the phrase corpus to which it belongs is suspect. If the norm is polarised (close to 0 or 1), we induce a rule stating that the attribute should indeed evaluate to only the most common value. Breaking a rule constitutes a naming bug. Note that there are two kinds of naming bugs, that we call *inclusion bugs* and *omission bugs*. The former refers to methods that fulfil

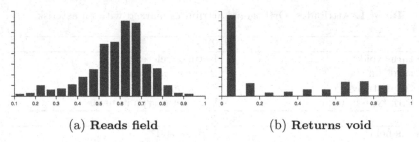

(a) **Reads field**   (b) **Returns void**

Fig. 5. Distribution of frequency values for two attributes

the predicate of an attribute it should not, the latter to methods that fail to
fulfil a predicate it should. We expect inclusion bugs to be more common (and
arguably more severe) than omission bugs. For instance, it might be reasonable
to refrain from doing anything at all (an empty method) regardless of name,
whereas throwing an exception from a seemingly innocent `hasChildren` method
is more dubious.

Specifically, we induce rules by defining percentiles on the distribution of frequency values for each attribute $a \in \mathcal{A}$. The percentiles are 0.0%, 2.5%, 5.0%,
95.0%, 97.5% and 100.0%, and are associated to a degree of severity when the corresponding rules are violated (see Table 2). The intuition is that the percentiles
classify the frequency values of different phrases relative to each other. Assume,
for instance, that we have a corpus $\mathcal{C}$ and a phrase p with a corresponding cor-
pus $\mathcal{C}_p \subset \mathcal{C}$ of methods yielding a frequency value $\xi_a(\mathcal{C}_p)$ for a certain attribute
$a \in \mathcal{A}$. Now assume that the frequency value belongs to the lower 2.5% when
compared to that of other phrases in $\mathcal{C}$. Then we deem it *inappropriate* for a
method $m \in \mathcal{C}_p$ to fulfil the predicate defined by a.

Table 2. Percentile groups for frequency values

Percentiles (%)	Severity
0.0	Forbidden (if included)
0.0 − 2.5	Inappropriate (if included)
2.5 − 5.0	Reconsider (if included)
5.0 − 95.0	No violation
95.0 − 97.5	Reconsider (if omitted)
97.5 − 100.0	Inappropriate (if omitted)
100.0	Forbidden (if omitted)

3.5   Finding Naming Bugs

Once a set of rules has been obtained for each prevalent phrase in the corpus,
finding naming bugs is trivial. For each of the methods we want to check, we
attempt to find the rule set for the most concrete capturing phrase (see Fig. 2).
In a few cases, the capturing phrase may be fully concrete, so that it perfectly

matches the method name. This is likely to be the case for certain ubiquitous method names and signatures such as `String toString()` and `int size()`, for instance. In most other cases, we expect the phrase to be more abstract. For instance, for the method name `Element findElement()`, the most concrete capturing phrase might be something like **ref find-⟨type⟩**. Failure to find any capturing phrase at all could be considered a special kind of naming bug; that the name itself is rather odd.

When we have found the most concrete capturing phrase p, we obtain the corresponding rule set $\mathcal{R}_p$ that applies to the method. For each rule in the rule set, we pass the rule and the method to the function *bug*. Whenever *bug* returns true, we have a rule violation, and hence a naming bug. Note that a single method might violate several implementation rules, yielding multiple naming bugs.

3.6   Fixing Naming Bugs

Naming bugs manifest themselves as violations of phrase-specific implementation rules. A rule violation indicates a conflict between the name and the implementation of a method. There are two ways to resolve the conflict: either we assume that the name is correct and the implementation is broken, or vice versa. The former must be fixed by removing offending or adding missing behaviour. While it is certainly possible to attempt to automate this procedure, it is likely to yield unsatisfactory or even wrong results. The programmer should therefore attend to this manually, based on warnings from the analysis.

We are more likely to succeed, at least partially, in automating the latter. We propose the following approach to find a suitable replacement name for an implementation that is assumed to be correct. The implementation is represented by a certain semantic profile. Every prevalent phrase that has been used for that profile is considered a *relevant* phrase for replacement. Some of the relevant phrases may be unsuitable, however, because they have rules that are in conflict with the semantic profile. We therefore filter the relevant phrases for rule violations against the semantic profile. The resulting list of phrases are *candidates* for replacement. Note that, in some cases, the list may be empty. If so, we deem the semantic profile to be *unnameable*.

Finding the best candidate for replacement is a matter of sorting the candidate list according to some criterion. We consider three relevant factors: 1) the rank of the semantic profile in the candidate phrase corpus, 2) the semantic distance from the inappropriate phrase to the candidate phrase, and 3) the number of syntactic changes we must apply to the inappropriate phrase to reach the candidate phrase. We assume that the optimal sorting function would take all three factors — and possibly others — into consideration. As a first approximation to solving the problem, however, we suggest simply sorting the list according to profile rank and semantic distances separately, and letting the programmer choose the most appropriate of the two.

4   The Corpus

The main requirements for the corpus are as follows:

- It must be representative of real-world Java programming.
- It must cover a variety of applications and domains.
- It must include most well-known and influential applications.
- It must be large enough to be credible as establishing "canonical" use of method names.

Table 3 lists the 100 Java applications, frameworks and libraries that constitute our corpus. Building and cleaning a large corpus is time-consuming labour; hence we use the same corpus that we have used in our previous work [12, 11]. The corpus was constructed to cover a wide range of application domains and has been carefully pruned for duplicate code. The only alteration we have made in retrospect is to remove a large number of near-identical code-generated `parse` methods from XBeans and Geronimo. The code clones resulted in visibly skewed results for the **parse-*** phrase, and proves that code generation is a real problem for corpus-based data mining.

Some basic numbers about the pruned corpus are listed in Table 4. We omit methods flagged as synthetic (generated by the compiler) as well as methods with "non-standard names". We consider a standard name be at least two characters long, start with a lowercase letter, and not contain any dollar signs or underscores.

5   Results

Here we present results from applying the extracted implementation rules on the corpus, as well as a small set of additional Java applications. In general, the rules can be applied to any Java application or library. For reasons of practicality and scale, however, we focus primarily on bugs in the corpus itself. We explain in detail how the analysis automatically identifies and reports a naming bug, and proceeds to suggest a replacement phrase to use for the method. We then investigate four rather different kinds of naming bugs revealed by the analysis. Finally, we present some overall naming bug statistics, and discuss the validity of the results.

5.1   Name Debugging in Practice

We revisit the example method from the introduction, and explain how the analysis helps us debug it.

```
public Field containsField(String name) {
  for (Iterator e = this.field_vec.iterator(); e.hasNext();) {
    Field f = (Field) e.next();
    if (f.getName().equals(name))
      return f;
  }
  return null;
}
```

Table 3. The corpus of Java applications and libraries

Desktop applications			
ArgoUML 0.24	Azureus 2.5.0	BlueJ 2.1.3	Eclipse 3.2.1
JEdit 4.3	LimeWire 4.12.11	NetBeans 5.5	Poseidon CE 5.0.1
Programmer tools			
Ant 1.7.0	Cactus 1.7.2	Checkstyle 4.3	Cobertura 1.8
CruiseControl 2.6	Emma 2.0.5312	FitNesse	JUnit 4.2
Javassist 3.4	Maven 2.0.4	Velocity 1.4	
Languages and language tools			
ANTLR 2.7.6	ASM 2.2.3	AspectJ 1.5.3	BSF 2.4.0
BeanShell 2.0b	Groovy 1.0	JRuby 0.9.2	JavaCC 4.0
Jython 2.2b1	Kawa 1.9.1	MJC 1.3.2	Polyglot 2.1.0
Rhino 1.6r5			
Middleware, frameworks and toolkits			
AXIS 1.4	Avalon 4.1.5	Google Web Toolkit 1.3.3	JXTA 2.4.1
JacORB 2.3.0	Java 5 EE SDK	Java 6 SDK	Jini 2.1
Mule 1.3.3	OpenJMS 0.7.7a	PicoContainer 1.3	Spring 2.0.2
Sun WTK 2.5	Struts 2.0.1	Tapestry 4.0.2	WSDL4J 1.6.2
Servers and databases			
DB Derby 10.2.2.0	Geronimo 1.1.1	HSQLDB	JBoss 4.0.5
JOnAS 4.8.4	James 2.3.0	Jetty 6.1.1	Tomcat 6.0.7b
XML tools			
Castor 1.1	Dom4J 1.6.1	JDOM 1.0	Piccolo 1.04
Saxon 8.8	XBean 2.0.0	XOM 1.1	XPP 1.1.3.4
XStream 1.2.1	Xalan-J 2.7.0	Xerces-J 2.9.0	
Utilities and libraries			
Batik 1.6	BluePrints UI 1.4	c3p0 0.9.1	CGLib 2.1.03
Ganymed ssh b209	Genericra	HOWL 1.0.2	Hibernate 3.2.1
JGroups 2.2.8	JarJar Links 0.7	Log4J 1.2.14	MOF
MX4J 3.0.2	OGNL 2.6.9	OpenSAML 1.0.1	Shale Remoting
TranQL 1.3	Trove	XML Security 1.3.0	
Jakarta commons utilities			
Codec 1.3	Collections 3.2	DBCP 1.2.1	Digester 1.8
Discovery 0.4	EL 1.0	FileUpload 1.2	HttpClient 3.0.1
IO 1.3.1	Lang 2.3	Modeler 2.0	Net 1.4.1
Pool 1.3	Validator 1.3.1		

Recall that we manually identified this as a *naming bug*, since we expect **contains-*** methods to return boolean values. Intuition tells us that *find* would be a more appropriate verb to use.

Finding the Bug. The analysis successfully identifies this as a naming bug, in the following way. First, we analyse the method. The name is decomposed into the fragments "contains" and "Field", which are tagged as **verb** and **type**, respectively. From the implementation, we extract a semantic profile that has the following attributes from Table 1 evaluated to 1, denoting presence: **return type**

Table 4. Basic numbers about the corpus

JAR files	1003
Class files	189941
Candidate methods	1226611
Included methods	1090982

Table 5. Rules for **contains-*** methods

Attribute	*Condition*	*Severity*	*Violation*
Returns void	1	Forbidden	No
Returns boolean	0	Inappropriate	Yes
Returns string	1	Inappropriate	No
Returns reference	1	Reconsider	Yes
Return type in name	1	Inappropriate	Yes
Parameter type in name	1	Reconsider	No
Writes field	1	Reconsider	No
Returns created object	1	Forbidden	No
Creates own class objects	1	Inappropriate	No

in name, reads field, runtime type-check, contains loop, has branches, multiple returns, method call on field. The rest of the attributes are evaluated to 0, denoting absence. We see that the attributes conspire to form an abstract description of the salient features of the implementation.

The most suitable phrase in our automatically generated rule book corresponding to the concrete phrase **contains-Field** is the abstract phrase **contains-***. The rule set for **contains-*** is listed in Table 5, along with the violations for the semantic profile. The mismatch between the name and implementation in this case manifests itself as three naming bugs. A **contains-*** should not return a reference type (much less echo the name of that type in the name of the method); rather, it should return a boolean value.

Fixing the Bug. There are two ways to fix a naming bug; either by changing the implementation, i.e., by returning a boolean value if the `Field` is found (rather than the `Field` itself), or by changing the name. In Sect. 3.6 we describe the approach for automatic suggestion of bug-free method names, to assist in the latter scenario.

Consider the top ten candidate replacement phrases listed in Table 6. An immediate reaction is that the candidates are fairly similar, and that *all* of them seem more appropriate than the original. Here we have sorted the list according to the sum of the orders given by the two ordering metrics *semantic distance* and *profile rank*; in cases of equal sum, we have arbitrarily given precedence to the phrase with the highest rank. In this particular example, we see that a rank ordering gives the better result, by choosing **ref find-⟨type⟩** over the more generic **find-⟨noun⟩-***.

Table 6. Candidate replacement phrases

Phrase	Distance	Rank	Sum
find-⟨type⟩	4	3	7
find-*	2	5	7
ref find-⟨type⟩	7	1	8
find-⟨type⟩-*	5	4	9
find-⟨adjective⟩-*	3	6	9
ref find-⟨type⟩-*	8	2	10
find-⟨noun⟩-*	1	9	10
get-⟨type⟩-*(String...)	6	8	14
ref get-⟨type⟩-*(String...)	9	7	16
ref get-⟨type⟩-*	10	10	20

5.2 Notable Naming Bugs

To illustrate the diversity of naming bugs the phrase-specific implementation rules help us find, we explore a few additional examples of naming bugs found in the corpus. The four methods shown in Fig. 6 exhibit rather different naming bugs. Note that since both strategies for choosing replacement phrases yield similar results, we have included only the top candidate according to profile rank in the figure.

The first example, taken from Ant 1.7.0, is representative of a fairly common naming bug: the inappropriately named "boolean setter". While both Java convention and the JavaBean specification[2] indicate that the verb *set* should be used for all methods for writing properties (including boolean ones), programmers sometimes use an inappropriate **is-*** form instead. This mirrors convention in some other languages such as Objective-C, but yields the wrong expectation when programming Java. The problem is, of course, that isCaching reads like a question: "is it true that you are caching?". We expect the question to be answered. The analysis indicates three rule violations for the method, and suggests using the phrase **set-⟨adjective⟩-*** instead.

The second example, taken from the class Value in JXTA 2.4.1, shows a broken implementation of an equals method. According to Sun's documentation, "The equals method implements an equivalence relation on non-null object references"[3]: it should be reflexive, symmetric, transitive and consistent. It turns out that this is notoriously hard to implement correctly. An influential book on Java devotes much attention to the details of fulfilling this contract [3]. The problem with the implementation from JXTA is that it is *not* symmetric, and the symptom is the creation of an instance of the type that defines the method. Assume that we have a Value instance v. The last instruction returns true whenever the parameter can be serialised to a String that in turn is used to create a Value object that is equal to v. For instance, we can get a true return value if we pass in a suitable String object s. However, if we pass v to the equals method of s,

---

[2] http://java.sun.com/javase/technologies/desktop/javabeans/docs/spec.html
[3] http://java.sun.com/j2se/1.4.2/docs/api/java/lang/Object.html

	Semantic Profile: Returns void, Writes field, Parameter to field

`// Ant 1.7.0`
`public void isCaching(boolean value) {`
`   this.caching = value;`
`}`
	Violated rules for 'is-<adjective>-'*
	Returns void: Reconsider if included
	Returns boolean: Inappropriate if missing
	Parameter to field: Inappropriate if included

	Replacement phrase: 'set-<adjective>-*'

`// JXTA 2.4.1`
`public boolean equals(Object obj) {`
`   if (this == obj)`
`      return true;`
`   if (obj instanceof Value)`
`      return equals((Value)obj);`
`   return equals(new Value(obj.toString()));`
`}`
	Semantic Profile:
	Returns boolean, Runtime type-check, Has branches, Multiple returns, Creates regular objects, Creates custom objects, Creates own class objects, Same name call, Method call on parameter

	Violated rules for 'boolean equals(Object...) Creates own class objects: Reconsider if included
	Replacement phrase: --- None ---

`// Java 5 EE SDK`
`public Iterator iterator()`
`throws DomainRegistryException {`
`   return new RegistryIterator(this, this);`
`}`
	Semantic Profile:
	Returns reference, No parameters, Return type in name, Returns created object, Creates regular objects, Creates custom objects, Exposes checked exceptions

	Violated rules for 'ref iterator()' Exposes checked exceptions: Notify if included
	Replacement phrase: 'create-<adjective>-<noun>'

`// DB Derby 10.2.2.0`
`public OutputStream setBinaryStream(long val)`
`throws SQLException {`
`   checkValidity();`
`   synchronized (this.agent_.connection_) {`
`      // Logging code removed.`
`      BlobOutputStream result = new`
`         BlobOutputStream(this, val);`
`      // Logging code removed.`
`      return result;`
`   }`
`}`
	Semantic Profile:
	Returns reference, Reads field, Returns created object, Has branches, Creates regular objects, Exposes checked exceptions, Method call on field

	Violated rules for 'set-<adjective>-'* Returns created object: Inappropriate if included
	Replacement phrase: 'open-*'

Fig. 6. Four notable naming bugs from the corpus

we will get `false`. Interestingly, we find no appropriate replacement phrase for this method. This is good news, since it makes little sense to rename a broken `equals` method.

The third example, an `iterator` method from the class `Registry` in Java 5 Enterprise Edition, illustrates the problem of overloading and redefining a well-established method name. The heavily implemented `Iterable<T>` interface defines a method signature `Iterator<T> iterator()`. Since the signature does not include any checked exceptions, the expectation naturally becomes that `iterator` methods in general do not expose any checked exceptions — indeed, the compiler will stop implementors of `Iterable<T>` if they try. However, `Registry` does not implement `Iterable<T>`, it simply uses a similar signature. But it is a bad idea to do so, since violating expectations is bound to cause confusion. It is particularly troublesome that the implementation exposes a checked exception, since this is something *iterator* methods practically never do. Note that the replacement phrase makes perfect sense since the method acts as a *factory* that creates new objects.

The final example is a bizarrely named method from DB Derby 10.2.2.0: clearly this is no *setter*! The semantic profile of the method is complicated a bit by the synchronisation and logging code, but for all intents and purposes, this is a factory method of sorts. The essential behaviour is that an object is created and returned to the caller. Creating and returning objects is inappropriate behaviour for methods that match the phrase **set-⟨adjective⟩-***; hence we get a rule violation. The suggested replacement phrase, **open-***, is not completely unreasonable, and certainly better than the original.

5.3 Naming Bug Statistics

We now consider the more general prevalence of naming bugs. Table 7 presents naming bug statistics for all the applications in the corpus, as well as a small number of additional applications. The additional applications are placed beneath a horizontal line near the bottom of the table. For each application, we list the number of methods, the percentage of those methods covered by implementation rules, and the percentage of covered methods violating an implementation rule. We see that the naming bug rates are fairly similar for applications in and outside the corpus, suggesting that the rules can meaningfully be applied to any Java application. It is worth noting that the largest applications (for instance, Java, Eclipse and NetBeans) to some extent have the power to dictate what is common usage. At the same time, such applications are developed by many different programmers over a long period of time, making diversity more likely.

It is important to remember that the numbers really indicate how canonical the method implementations are with respect to the names used. Herein lies an element of conformity as well. The downside is that some applications might be punished for being too "opinionated" about naming. For instance, JUnit 4.2 is written by programmers who are known to care about naming, yet the reported naming bug rate, 3.50%, is fairly high. We believe this is due to the tension between maintaining the status quo and trying to improve it.

Where to draw the line between appropriate and inappropriate usage of names is a pragmatic choice, and a trade-off between false positives and false negatives. A narrow range for appropriate usage increases the number of false positives, a broad range increases the number of false negatives. We are not too concerned with false negatives, since our focus is on demonstrating the existence of naming bugs, rather than finding them all. False positives, on the other hand, could pose a threat to the usefulness of our results.

False positives, i.e., that the analysis reports a naming bug that we intuitively disagree with, might occur for the following reasons:

- The corpus may contain noise that leads to rules that are not in harmony with the intuitions of Java programmers.
- Some legitimate sub-use of a commonly used phrase may be deemed inappropriate because the sub-use is drowned by the majority. (Arguably a new phrase should be invented to cover the sub-use.)

Table 7. Naming bug statistics

Application	Methods	Covered	Buggy	Application	Methods	Covered	Buggy
ANTLR 2.7.6	1641	61.66%	1.18%	ASM 2.2.3	724	45.30%	0.30%
AXIS 1.4	4290	91.35%	1.65%	Ant 1.7.0	7562	89.35%	0.85%
ArgoUML 0.24	13312	81.17%	0.85%	AspectJ 1.5.3	24976	74.41%	1.24%
Avalon 4.1.5	280	82.14%	2.17%	Azureus 2.5.0	14276	78.32%	1.30%
Batik 1.6	9304	85.90%	0.76%	BSF 2.4.0	274	77.37%	0.00%
BeanShell 2.0 Beta	907	74.97%	0.73%	BlueJ 2.1.3	3369	82.13%	1.48%
BluePrints UI 1.4	662	89.57%	0.67%	C3P0 0.9.1	2374	83.06%	1.52%
CGLib 2.1.03	675	80.29%	1.66%	Cactus 1.7.2	3004	87.61%	1.36%
Castor 1.1	5094	91.44%	0.88%	Checkstyle 4.3	1350	76.07%	0.09%
Cobertura 1.8	328	82.92%	1.47%	Commons Codec 1.3	153	79.08%	0.00%
Commons Collections 3.2	2914	77.93%	1.14%	Commons DBCP 1.2.1	823	88.69%	1.09%
Commons Digester 1.8	371	79.24%	0.34%	Commons Discovery 0.4	195	92.30%	0.00%
Commons EL 1.0	277	59.20%	4.87%	Commons FileUpload 1.2	123	91.86%	0.88%
Commons HttpClient 3.0.1	1071	88.98%	1.46%	Commons IO 1.3.1	357	81.23%	5.17%
Commons Lang 2.3	1627	82.72%	1.93%	Commons Modeler 2.0	376	93.35%	1.42%
Commons Net 1.4.1	726	69.69%	1.58%	Commons Pool 1.3	218	71.55%	0.00%
Commons Validator 1.3.1	443	88.03%	1.02%	CruiseControl 2.6	5479	87.18%	0.85%
DB Derby 10.2.2.0	15470	80.08%	2.09%	Dom4J 1.6.1	1645	92.15%	0.39%
Eclipse 3.2.1	110904	81.65%	1.03%	Emma 2.0.5312	1105	82.62%	0.65%
FitNesse	2819	74.49%	2.14%	Ganymed ssh build 209	424	76.65%	1.23%
Genericra	454	86.78%	0.50%	Geronimo 1.1.1	26753	85.28%	0.71%
Google WT 1.3.3	4129	73.40%	1.78%	Groovy 1.0	10237	76.14%	1.01%
HOWL 1.0.2	173	81.50%	1.41%	HSQLDB	3267	86.16%	2.98%
Hibernate 3.2.1	11354	80.47%	2.00%	J5EE SDK	148701	83.56%	1.17%
JBoss 4.0.5	34965	84.69%	0.95%	JDOM 1.0	144	80.55%	0.86%
JEdit 4.3	3330	80.36%	1.30%	JGroups 2.2.8	4165	77.52%	2.04%
JOnAS 4.8.4	30405	81.88%	1.16%	JRuby 0.9.2	7748	76.69%	1.27%
JUnit 4.2	365	62.46%	3.50%	JXTA 2.4.1	5210	86.96%	1.30%
JacORB 2.3.0	8007	71.01%	1.16%	James 2.3.0	2382	79.21%	1.85%
Jar Jar Links 0.7	442	53.84%	0.42%	Java 6 SDK	80292	81.03%	1.16%
JavaCC 4.0	370	77.02%	2.80%	Javassist 3.4	1842	84.03%	1.42%
Jetty 6.1.1	15177	73.54%	1.06%	Jini 2.1	8835	80.00%	1.38%
Jython 2.2b1	3612	72.09%	1.65%	Kawa 1.9.1	6309	65.36%	2.01%
Livewire 4.12.11	12212	81.96%	1.15%	Log4J 1.2.14	1138	83.39%	0.63%
MJC 1.3.2	4957	73.77%	1.72%	MOF	28	100.00%	0.00%
MX4J 3.0.2	1671	85.33%	1.26%	Maven 2.0.4	3686	84.69%	0.86%
Mule 1.3.3	4725	86.79%	1.09%	NetBeans 5.5	113355	87.60%	0.85%
OGNL 2.6.9	502	88.24%	0.45%	OpenJMS 0.7.7 Alpha	3624	85.89%	0.70%
OpenSAML 1.0.1	306	92.48%	1.76%	Piccolo 1.04	559	77.10%	0.46%
PicoContainer 1.3	435	67.81%	1.35%	Polyglot 2.1.0	3521	67.33%	1.64%
Poseidon CE 5.0.1	25739	77.73%	1.19%	Rhino 1.6r5	2238	77.56%	1.67%
Saxon 8.8	6596	73.12%	1.22%	Shale Remoting 1.0.3	96	72.91%	0.00%
Spring 2.0.2	8349	88.05%	1.52%	Struts 2.0.1	6106	88.97%	1.06%
Sun Wireless Toolkit 2.5	20538	80.37%	1.59%	Tapestry 4.0.2	3481	78.71%	0.87%
Tomcat 6.0.7 Beta	5726	88.31%	0.90%	TranQL 1.3	1639	77.85%	1.17%
Trove 1.1b4	3164	82.01%	0.23%	Velocity 1.4	3635	81.62%	0.67%
WSDL4J 1.6.2	651	94.16%	0.00%	XBean 2.0.0	7000	81.10%	1.33%
XML Security 1.3.0	819	86.56%	1.55%	XOM 1.1	1399	77.05%	1.85%
XPP 1.1.3.4	426	84.50%	1.38%	XStream 1.2.1	916	77.83%	0.84%
Xalan-J 2.7.0	14643	81.38%	1.21%	Xerces-J 2.9.0	590	89.15%	0.19%
FindBugs 1.3.6	7688	72.78%	1.42%	iText 2.1.4	4643	85.18%	1.54%
Lucene 2.4.0	2965	74.16%	1.50%	Mockito 1.6	1408	68.32%	1.35%
ProGuard 4.3	4148	45.34%	2.65%	Stripes 1.5	1600	89.31%	2.09%

- The percentiles used to classify attribute fraction rank (Sect. 3.4) can be skewed.

Whether or not something classifies as a naming bug is subjective. What is *not* subjective, is the fact that all reported issues will be rare, and therefore worthy of reconsideration. To discern false positives from genuine naming bugs, we must rely on our on best judgement. To get an idea of the severity of the problem, we manually investigated 50 reported naming bugs chosen at random. We found that 30% of the reported naming bugs in the sample were false positives, suggesting that the approach holds promise (even though, due to the limited size of the sample, the true false positive rate might be significantly higher or lower). The false positives were primarily *getters* that were slightly complex, but not inappropriately so in our eyes, and methods containing logging code.

5.4   Threats to Validity

There are three major threats to the validity of our results:

- Does the pragmatic view of how meaning is constructed apply to Java programming?
- Is the corpus representative of real-world Java programming?
- Is the attribute model a suitable approximation of the actual semantics of a method?

Our basic assumption is that canonical usage of a method name is also meaningful and appropriate usage; this relates to the pragmatic view that meaning stems from actual use. We establish the meaning of phrases using a crude democratic process of voting. This approach is not without problems. First, it is possible for individual idiosyncratic applications to skew the election. In particular, code generation can lead to problems, since it enables the proliferation of near-identical clones. While we can spot gross examples of this (see Sect. 4), code generation on a smaller scale is hard to detect, and can affect the results for individual phrases. This in turn can corrupt our notion of canonical usage, leading to corrupt rules and incorrect reports of naming bugs. Second, there might be individual applications that use a language that is both richer, more consistent and precise than the one used by the majority. However, the relative uniformity in the distribution of naming bugs seems to indicate that neither of these problems are too severe. Despite these problems, therefore, we believe that the pragmatic view of meaning applies well to Java programming. It is certainly more reasonable to use the aggregated ideas of many as an approximation of meaning than to make an arbitrary choice of a single application's idea.

When aggregating ideas, however, we must assume that the ideas we aggregate are representative. The business journalist Surowiccki argues that diversity of opinion, independence, decentralisation and an aggregation mechanism are the prime prerequisites to make good group decisions [25]. The corpus we use was carefully constructed to contain a wide variety of applications and libraries of various sizes and from many domains. We therefore believe it to fulfil Surowiecki's prerequisites and be reasonably representative of real-world Java programming.

Finally, we consider the suitability of the model for method semantics, which is a coarse approximation based on our knowledge of Java programming. Using attributes to characterise methods has several benefits, in particular that it reduces the practically endless number of possible implementations to a finite set of semantic profiles. Furthermore, the validation of a useful model must come in the form of useful results. As we have seen, the model has helped us identify real naming bugs with what appears to be a relatively low rate of false positives. We therefore believe that the model is adequate for the task at hand.

6   Related Work

Micro patterns, introduced by Gil and Maman [10], are a central source of inspiration for our work. Micro patterns are machine-traceable patterns on the level of Java classes. A pattern is machine-traceable if it can be expressed as a simple formal condition on some aspect of a software module. The presented micro patterns are hand-crafted by the authors to capture their knowledge of Java programming.

In our work, we use hand-crafted machine-traceable attributes to model the semantics of methods rather than classes. The attributes are similar to *fingerprints*, a notion used by the Sourcerer code search engine [1]. According to the Sourcerer website[4], the engine supports three kinds of fingerprint-based search, utilising control flow, Java type and micro pattern information respectively. Ma et al. [16] provide a different take on the task of searching for a suitable software artefact. They share our assumption that programmers usually choose appropriate names for their implementations, and therefore use identifier information to index the Java API for efficient queries.

Overall, there seems to be a growing interest in harnessing the knowledge embedded in identifiers. Pollock et al. [20] introduce the term *Natural Language Program Analysis* (NLPA) to signify program analysis that exploits natural language clues. The analysis has been used to develop tools for program navigation and aspect mining [23, 22]. The tools exploit the relationship between natural language expressions in source code (identifiers and comments) and information about the structure of the code.

Singer and Kirkham [24] investigate which type names are used for instances of micro patterns in a large corpus of Java applications. More precisely, the *suffixes* of the actual type names are used (the last *fragment* of the name in our terminology). The empirical results indicate that type name suffixes are indeed correlated to the presence of micro patterns in the code.

Caprile and Tonella [4] analyse the structure of function identifiers in C programs. The identifiers are decomposed into fragments that are then classified into seven lexical categories. The structure of the function identifiers are further described by a hand-crafted grammar.

Lawrie et al. [13] study the quality of identifiers in a large corpus of applications written in several languages. An identifier is assumed to be of high quality if it can be composed of words from a dictionary and well-known abbreviations. This is a better quality indicator than mere uniformity of lexical syntax, but does not address the issue of *appropriateness*. Deißenböck and Pizka [6] develop a formal model for identifier quality, based on *consistency* and *conciseness*. Unfortunately, this model requires an expert to perform manual mapping between identifiers and domain concepts.

Reiss [21] proposes an automatic approach for finding unusual code. The assumption is that unusual code is potentially problematic code. The approach works by mining common syntactic code patterns from a corpus of applications. Unusual code is code that is not covered by such patterns. Hence we see that there are similarities to our work, both in the assumption and the approach. A main difference is that we define unusual code in the context of a given method phrase.

---

[4] http://sourcerer.ics.uci.edu/

7   Conclusion

Natural language expressions get their meaning from how and when they are used in practice. Deviation from normal use of words and phrases leads to misunderstanding and confusion. In the context of software this is particularly bad, since precise understanding of the code is paramount for successful development and maintenance. We have therefore coined the term *naming bug* to describe unusual aspects of implementations for a given method name. We have presented a practical approach to *debugging method names*, by offering assistance both in finding and fixing naming bugs. To find naming bugs, we use name-specific implementation rules mined from a large corpus of Java applications. Naming bugs can be fixed either by changing the implementation or by using a different method name; for the latter task, we have also shown an approach to provide automatic assistance. To demonstrate that method name debugging is useful, we have applied the rules to uncover naming bugs both in the corpus itself and in other applications.

In this and previous work, we have exploited the fact that there is a shared vocabulary of terms and phrases, *Java Programmer English* [12], that programmers use in method names. In the future, we would like to investigate the adequacy of that vocabulary. In particular, there might be terms or phrases that are superfluous, while others are missing, at least from the common vocabulary of Java programmers. We know that there exists verbs (for instance *create* and *new*) that seem to be used almost interchangeably in method names. Our results reveal hints of this, by finding a shorter semantic distance between phrases that use such verbs. By analysing the corresponding method implementations, we could find out whether there are subtle differences in meaning that warrant the existence of both verbs in Java Programmer English. If not, it would be beneficial for Java programmers to choose one and eliminate or redefine the other. There are also verbs (and phrases) that are imprecise, in that they are used to represent many different kinds of implementations. For instance, the ubiquitous *getter* is much less homogenous than one might expect [11], indicating that it has a wide variety of implementations. It would be interesting to see if the verbs are simply used as easy resorts when labelling more or less random chunks of code, or if there are legitimate, identifiable sub-uses that would warrant the invention of new verbs. Or it might be that a minority of the Java community already has invented the proper verbs, and that they should be more widely adopted to establish a richer, more expressive language for all Java programmers to use.

Acknowledgements. We thank Jørn Inge Vestgården, Wolfgang Leister and Truls Fretland for useful comments and discussions, and the anonymous reviewers for their thoughtful remarks.

References

[1] Bajracharya, S.K., Ngo, T.C., Linstead, E., Dou, Y., Rigor, P., Baldi, P., Lopes, C.V.: Sourcerer: a search engine for open source code supporting structure-based search. In: Tarr, P.L., Cook, W.R. (eds.) OOPSLA Companion, pp. 681–682. ACM Press, New York (2006)

[2] Beck, K.: Implementation Patterns. Addison-Wesley Professional, Reading (2007)

[3] Bloch, J.: Effective Java. Prentice-Hall, Englewood Cliffs (2008)

[4] Caprile, B., Tonella, P.: Nomen est omen: Analyzing the language of function identifiers. In: Proceedings of the Sixth Working Conference on Reverse Engineering (WCRE 1999), Atlanta, Georgia, USA, 6-8 October 1999, pp. 112–122. IEEE Computer Society Press, Los Alamitos (1999)

[5] Collar, E., Valerdi, R.: Role of software readability on software development cost. In: Proceedings of the 21st Forum on COCOMO and Software Cost Modeling, Herndon, VA (October 2006)

[6] Deißenböck, F., Pizka, M.: Concise and consistent naming. In: Proceedings of the 13th IEEE International Workshop on Program Comprehension (IWPC 2005), pp. 97–106. IEEE Computer Society Press, Los Alamitos (2005)

[7] Eierman, M.A., Dishaw, M.T.: The process of software maintenance: a comparison of object-oriented and third-generation development languages. Journal of Software Maintenance and Evolution: Research and Practice 19(1), 33–47 (2007)

[8] Fellbaum, C.: WordNet: An Electronic Lexical Database. MIT Press, Cambridge (1998)

[9] Frege, G.: On sense and reference. In: Geach, P., Black, M. (eds.) Translations from the Philosophical Writings of Gottlob Frege, pp. 56–78. Blackwell, Malden (1952)

[10] Gil, J., Maman, I.: Micro patterns in Java code. In: Proceedings of the 20th Annual ACM SIGPLAN Conference on Object-Oriented Programming, Systems, Languages, and Applications (OOPSLA 2005), San Diego, CA, USA, October 16-20, 2005, pp. 97–116. ACM Press, New York (2005)

[11] Høst, E.W., Østvold, B.M.: The programmer's lexicon, volume I: The verbs. In: Proceedings of the Seventh IEEE International Working Conference on Source Code Analysis and Manipulation (SCAM 2007), Washington, DC, USA, pp. 193–202. IEEE Computer Society, Los Alamitos (2007)

[12] Høst, E.W., Østvold, B.M.: The Java programmer's phrase book. In: Proceedings of the 1st International Conference on Software Language Engineering (SLE 2008), Springer, Heidelberg (2008)

[13] Lawrie, D., Feild, H., Binkley, D.: Quantifying identifier quality: An analysis of trends. Journal of Empirical Software Engineering 12(4), 359–388 (2007)

[14] Lawrie, D., Morrell, C., Feild, H., Binkley, D.: What's in a name? A study of identifiers. In: Proceedings of the 14th International Conference on Program Comprehension (ICPC 2006), Athens, Greece, 14-16 June 2006, pp. 3–12. IEEE Computer Society Press, Los Alamitos (2006)

[15] Liblit, B., Begel, A., Sweeser, E.: Cognitive perspectives on the role of naming in computer programs. In: Proceedings of the 18th Annual Psychology of Programming Workshop, Sussex, United Kingdom, September 2006, Psychology of Programming Interest Group (2006)

[16] Ma, H., Amor, R., Tempero, E.D.: Indexing the Java API using source code. In: Australian Software Engineering Conference, pp. 451–460. IEEE Computer Society Press, Los Alamitos (2008)

[17] Manning, C.D., Schuetze, H.: Foundations of Statistical Natural Language Processing. MIT Press, Cambridge (1999)

[18] Martin, R.C.: Clean Code. Prentice-Hall, Englewood Cliffs (2008)

[19] McConnell, S.: Code Complete: A Practical Handbook of Software Construction, 2nd edn. Microsoft Press (2004)

[20] Pollock, L.L., Vijay-Shanker, K., Shepherd, D., Hill, E., Fry, Z.P., Maloor, K.: Introducing natural language program analysis. In: Proceedings of the 7th ACM Workshop on Program Analysis for Software Tools and Engineering (PASTE 2007), San Diego, California, USA, 2007, June 13-14, 2007, pp. 15-16. ACM, New York (2007)

[21] Reiss, S.P.: Finding unusual code. In: Proceedings of the 23rd IEEE International Conference on Software Maintenance (ICSM 2007), pp. 34-43. IEEE Computer Society Press, Los Alamitos (2007)

[22] Shepherd, D., Fry, Z.P., Hill, E., Pollock, L., Vijay-Shanker, K.: Using natural language program analysis to locate and understand action-oriented concerns. In: Proceedings of the 6th international conference on Aspect-oriented software development (AOSD 2007), pp. 212-224. ACM Press, New York (2007)

[23] Shepherd, D., Pollock, L.L., Vijay-Shanker, K.: Towards supporting on-demand virtual remodularization using program graphs. In: Proceedings of the 5th International Conference on Aspect-Oriented Software Development (AOSD 2006), pp. 3-14. ACM Press, New York (2006)

[24] Singer, J., Kirkham, C.: Exploiting the correspondence between micro patterns and class names. In: Proceedings of the Eight IEEE International Working Conference on Source Code Analysis and Manipulation (SCAM 2008), pp. 67-76. IEEE Computer Society Press, Los Alamitos (2008)

[25] Surowiecki, J.: The Wisdom of Crowds. Anchor (2005)

[26] Witten, I.H., Frank, E.: Data Mining: Practical Machine Learning Tools and Techniques, 2nd edn. Morgan Kaufmann, San Francisco (2005)

[27] Wittgenstein, L.: Philosophical Investigations. Prentice-Hall, Englewood Cliffs (1973)

MAPO: Mining and Recommending API Usage Patterns

Hao Zhong[1,2], Tao Xie[3,*], Lu Zhang[1,2], Jian Pei[4], and Hong Mei[1,2,*]

[1] Key Laboratory of High Confidence Software Technologies, Ministry of Education, China
[2] School of Electronics Engineering and Computer Science, Peking University, China
{zhonghao04,zhanglu,meih}@sei.pku.edu.cn
[3] Department of Computer Science, North Carolina State University, USA
xie@csc.ncsu.edu
[4] School of Computer Science, Simon Fraser University, Canada
jpei@cs.sfu.ca

Abstract. To improve software productivity, when constructing new software systems, programmers often reuse existing libraries or frameworks by invoking methods provided in their APIs. Those API methods, however, are often complex and not well documented. To get familiar with how those API methods are used, programmers often exploit a source code search tool to search for code snippets that use the API methods of interest. However, the returned code snippets are often large in number, and the huge number of snippets places a barrier for programmers to locate useful ones. In order to help programmers overcome this barrier, we have developed an API usage mining framework and its supporting tool called MAPO (Mining API usage Pattern from Open source repositories) for mining API usage patterns automatically. A mined pattern describes that in a certain usage scenario, some API methods are frequently called together and their usages follow some sequential rules. MAPO further recommends the mined API usage patterns and their associated code snippets upon programmers' requests. Our experimental results show that with these patterns MAPO helps programmers locate useful code snippets more effectively than two state-of-the-art code search tools. To investigate whether MAPO can assist programmers in programming tasks, we further conducted an empirical study. The results show that using MAPO, programmers produce code with fewer bugs when facing relatively complex API usages, comparing with using the two state-of-the-art code search tools.

1 Introduction

The modern software industry increasingly relies on third-party libraries and frameworks provided by companies or open source organizations. Programmers often need to cope with Application Programming Interfaces (APIs) of these libraries or frameworks to accomplish their daily work. Unfortunately, most of the API libraries are complex and difficult to use [30]. Typically, an API library or framework written in object-oriented languages often provides a large number of classes and methods. For example, the Eclipse 3.1 platform SDK provides more than 11,000 classes not to say

---

* Corresponding authors.

S. Drossopoulou (Ed.): ECOOP 2009, LNCS 5653, pp. 318–343, 2009.

its large external plug-in projects. Furthermore, API libraries or frameworks provided by different companies and organizations follow different styles. As a result, even experienced programmers may encounter problems when they are to use unfamiliar API libraries or frameworks.

Due to these issues, programmers often struggle with choosing proper methods provided by APIs (called API methods) and how to organize the API methods when invoking them together to implement a certain feature. In fact, if the API classes and methods have meaningful names, it might not be too difficult for the programmers to find useful API methods for a given task. However, it is often difficult for the programmers to pick out all the essential API methods and to organize these API methods properly for the task. Some API libraries or frameworks such as the .NET framework are well documented and have sample snippets, but for many API libraries or frameworks, no code snippet is provided or the provided code snippets exhibit only one usage. As an API method may have many usages, the provided usage may not be relevant to the task at hand. Therefore, the associated documentation of an API library or framework is insufficient for programmers.

Fortunately, as source files in open source projects contain various API usages, programmers can access code snippets of plenty of usages using code search engines such as Google code search [12] or code snippet recommenders such as Strathcona [15]. However, given an API method, as there often exist many code snippets using the method in various open source projects, it is challenging for existing code search tools to rank the code snippets by putting the ones with relevant usage at the top of the returned list. As a result, programmers may need to browse through a large number of code snippets to locate snippets with relevant usage.

At the same time, data mining [13] provides various techniques to mine a large volume of data into useful patterns. These techniques are potentially useful to help programmers in locating useful code snippets. In this paper, we propose an API usage mining framework and its supporting tool called MAPO to mine API usage patterns from a large number of code snippets. With the mined patterns, MAPO further guides programmers to locate useful code snippets.

This paper makes the following main contributions:

- **Extraction strategy.** A code analyzer and a set of strategies to extract API usage information from code snippets that include usages of API methods.
- **Mining technique.** A technique to mine API usage patterns from the collected API usage information, with the application of clustering on the collected API method call sequences.
- **Recommendation mechanism.** A user interface to recommend the API usage patterns and their associated code snippets to programmers.
- **Experimental study.** An experimental study on evaluating MAPO, where we applied MAPO on 20 open source projects (141K lines of code in total, which use Eclipse Graphical Editing Framework (GEF) [17]) and acquired 93 patterns, which include 157 API method call sequences and cover the usages of 856 API methods. We also compared MAPO with two state-of-the-art code search tools: Strathcona [15] and Google code search [12]. The experimental results show that the

```
public class DEditorActionContributor ... {
    public void contributeToMenu(IMenuManager menu) {
        super.contributeToMenu(menu);
        IMenuManager editMenu = menu.findMenuUsingPath(IWorkbenchActionConstants.M_EDIT);
        if(editMenu != null ){
            editMenu.add(new Separator());
            editMenu.appendToGroup("additions", fToggleInsertModeAction);
        }
    }
    ...
}
```

```
public class RubyEditorActionContributor ... {
    public void contributeToMenu(IMenuManager menuManager) {
        ...
        IMenuManager gotoMenu = menu.findMenuUsingPath("navigate/goTo");
        if(gotoMenu != null ){
            gotoMenu.add(new Separator("additions2"));
            gotoMenu.appendToGroup("additions2", fGotoMatchingBracket);
        }
    }
    ...
}
```

Fig. 1. Code snippets of "`appendToGroup`" returned by Google code search

patterns mined by MAPO are useful to help programmers locate useful code snippets more effectively than Strathcona and Google code search.

– **Empirical study.** An empirical study on evaluating MAPO, where we investigated whether MAPO can assist programmers to complete programming tasks. The results show that comparing with Strathcona and Google code search, MAPO helps programmers produce code with fewer bugs when API usages are relatively complex and these usages exist in code repositories.

The rest of the paper is organized as follows. Section 2 presents an example to illustrate our approach. Section 3 discusses related work. Section 4 presents our approach. Sections 5 and 6 describe our experimental study and empirical study, respectively. Section 7 discusses issues in API usage mining. Section 8 concludes.

2   Example

To compare the effectiveness of locating useful code snippets, we use an example to illustrate the situation when using Google code search [12] to locate some code snippets. Suppose that we plan to add an action item to the menu of the Eclipse IDE platform. After browsing Eclipse's platform API documentation[1], we find a potentially relevant interface IContributionManager based on its description: "*A contribution manager organizes contributions to such UI components as menus, toolbars and status lines*". By browsing methods defined in this interface, we find one method appendToGroup potentially relevant based on its description: "*Adds a contribution item for the given*

---

[1] http://tinyurl.com/5ltogx

```
public class ContextMenuProviderImpl ... {
    public void buildContextMenu(IMenuManager manager) {
        GEFActionConstants.addStandardActionGroups(manager);
        IAction action;
        action = actionRegistry.getAction(CreateAttributeAction.ID);
        if(action.isEnabled() )
            manager.appendToGroup(GEFActionConstants.GROUP_REST, action);
        ...
    }
    ...
}
```

```
public class LatticeContextMenuProvider ... {
    public void buildContextMenu (IMenuManager manager) {
        GEFActionConstants.addStandardActionGroups(manager);
        IAction action;
        action = actionRegistry.getAction(ShowMethodSignatureAction.TEXT);
        if(action.isEnabled() )
            manager.appendToGroup(GEFActionConstants.GROUP_VIEW, action);
        ...
    }
    ...
}
```

Fig. 2. Code snippets of "appendToGroup" returned by Google code search (Cont.)

action at the end of the group with the given name". We then use *"appendToGroup lang:java"* to query Google code search and it returns 151 code snippets[2].

After browsing these code snippets, we find two relevant code snippets as shown in Figure 1. Both snippets are put near the bottom of the returned list. In particular, the first snippet in Figure 1 is put as the 84th of the snippet list, and the second snippet in Figure 1 is put as the 104th of the snippet list. We further investigate the returned 151 snippets, and we find that there are many different usages of the API method appendToGroup. For example, the snippets in Figure 2 exhibit another usage of appendToGroup. The two snippets are put as the 11th and the 27th of the returned list. The snippets with different usages interlace with each other, and none of the four snippets are ranked as top 10 snippets by Google code search. As a result, in this particular example, we need to check 84 snippets to locate the first relevant code snippet. We next illustrate how MAPO addresses the preceding situation.

Pattern mining. To mine patterns, MAPO first clusters code snippets according to their similarities of each other (Section 4.2). The aim of the clustering is to cluster code snippets exhibiting different usages (such as the snippets in Figures 1 and 2) into different clusters. In Figure 1, the two snippets come from two methods with the same name (*i.e.*, contributeToMenu), and the two methods belong to two classes with similar names

---

[2] We used *"appendToGroup lang:java"* to query Google code search in January 2008. Note that given the same key words, Google code search may return different numbers of code snippets over time possibly due to the growth of Google code search's crawled repositories. The situation of using it for the described purpose becomes even worse with the growth of Google code search's crawled repositories. From more crawled repositories, Google code search returns more code snippets with more API usages for a given query. Code snippets of interest may be pushed to an even lower position by code snippets exhibiting other usages.

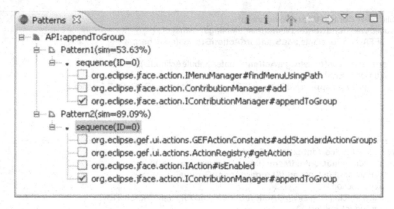

Fig. 3. Pattern index of "appendToGroup"

(*i.e.*, DEditorActionContributor and RubyEditorActionContributor). Similarly, we make the same observation in Figure 2. Although the four code snippets are from four different projects, they all follow the convention of using similar names for similar usages. In MAPO, the similarity metric used in clustering is mainly based on this convention. Here, if MAPO does not use these names for clustering and uses only method call sequences, it cannot mine patterns that are sensitive to programming contexts such as class names and method names.

For each cluster, MAPO adopts a frequent subsequence miner [7] to mine usage patterns from the code snippets in the cluster (Sections 4.2). For example, from each of the two clusters, MAPO acquires one usage pattern as shown in Figure 3. A mined pattern may have one or more frequent sequences of API method calls, and one frequent sequence describes one common usage exhibited by the snippets. For example, the frequent sequence under "*Pattern1*" in Figure 3 shows that in this usage, appendToGroup is often used with findMenuUsingPath and add, and when the three API methods are used together, they follow the sequential rule of findMenuUsingPath→ add →append- ToGroup (*i.e.*, the usage exhibited in the snippets of Figure 1).

Pattern recommendation. MAPO uses mined patterns as an index for their associated code snippets (Section 4.3). As mined patterns are usually much fewer than code snippets, programmers are able to locate their code snippets more effectively with the pattern index. For example, MAPO associates "*Pattern1*" in Figure 3 to the code snippets in Figure 1, and "*Pattern2*" in Figure 3 to the code snippets in Figure 2. When a programmer clicks a pattern, MAPO returns all the code snippets associated with the pattern to the programmer. In this example, as the second pattern exhibits the API usage of interest, a programmer needs to check only 2 snippets for the first relevant snippet. In addition, from a mined pattern, a programmer is able to find which methods are used together with appendToGroup and how to call these methods correctly. Code search engines such Google code search do not provide such a benefit directly to programmers. This example illustrates how MAPO is more effective than Google code search in helping write API client code.

3 Related Work

To our knowledge, our MAPO is the first approach that mines API usage patterns and uses mined patterns as an index for recommending associated code snippets to aid programming. Our approach is related to existing work on recommending code snippets since MAPO recommends code snippets organized according to API usage patterns mined from them. MAPO is also related to existing work on mining API properties since API usage patterns mined by MAPO have similar forms as API properties mined by existing work. We next discuss the major differences between MAPO and these existing related approaches.

Recommending code snippets. Strathcona developed by Holmes and Murphy [15] locates a set of relevant code snippets from a code snippet repository by matching the structure of the code under development with the code snippets in the repository. As MAPO returns code snippets given an API method name, it is more convenient to locate useful code snippets if a programmer wants to know the usages of a particular API method. In addition, like other code search engines, Strathcona returns a list of relevant code snippets, whereas MAPO extracts common patterns among the list of relevant code snippets returned by a code search engine or Strathcona. Our evaluation (Section 5) shows that the mined patterns help programmers locate useful code snippets more effectively than approaches that recommend raw code snippets (such as Strathcona and Google code search).

Prospector developed by Mandelin *et al.* [22] synthesizes solution jungloids from a jungloid query. A jungloid query is a pair (T_{in}, T_{out}) where T_{in} and T_{out} are source and target object types, respectively. The retrieval is accomplished by traversing a set of paths (API method call sequences) from T_{in} to T_{out}. XSnippet developed by Tansalarak and Claypool [32] extends Prospector and adds additional queries, ranking heuristics, and mining algorithms to query a code snippet repository for code snippets relevant to the programming task at hand. Instead of finding code snippets from a repository (with a limited set of snippets), PARSEWeb developed by Thummalapenta and Xie [33] uses Google code search for collecting relevant code snippets and mines the returned code snippets to find solution jungloids. These tools require programmers to translate a programming task into the form of a jungloid query (source and target object types), whereas MAPO returns ranked relevant patterns and code snippets given a query such as an API method name, complementing these existing tools.

Saul *et al.* [29] proposed an approach to find API methods that are closely related to a query API method of interest, by discovering API methods that share a caller or a callee with the query API method. Their approach recommends only a set of API methods without temporal information among them whereas MAPO recommends both API usage patterns with temporal information and their associated code snippets.

Mining API properties. Mining API properties has long been a research focus. Previous related approaches fall into categories as follows.

The first category is to mine association rules among software artifacts. Some approaches [19, 20, 24, 37] mine association rules among method calls. Some approaches [25] mine association rules among class inheritances. Some approaches [8] mine association rules among class collaborations. These previous approaches mine properties without temporal information, whereas MAPO mines more complicated API usage patterns involving multiple methods and temporal information.

The second category is to mine frequent call sequences from API client code or traces. To mine these frequent method calls, some approaches [27, 34] use existing sequence mining techniques [3], and other approaches [1, 10, 35, 39] adopt various customized techniques. MAPO also mines frequent call sequences, but there are two major differences between MAPO and the preceding approaches. One is that most of these preceding approaches mine patterns related to one or two API method calls, whereas MAPO mines patterns related to multiple API method calls. The other is that these approaches do not take programming contexts into consideration, whereas MAPO combines the frequent subsequence mining technique with the clustering technique, and thus MAPO alleviates the interlacement among different usages that are sensitive to programming contexts.

The third category is to mine automata from API client code or traces. To mine automata, some approaches [4, 5, 21] use the Angluin's algorithm [6], and other approaches [14, 36, 31, 9, 28, 11] adopt various customized techniques. These approaches are not as robust to noise (either an anomalous or buggy API method call) in traces as MAPO, because their underlying finite automaton learner is not as robust to noise as the frequent subsequence miner used by MAPO.

MAPO is extended from its previous version [38], and the main differences are as follows. First, we choose an offline mechanism to improve user experiences as it takes less time to query a mined pattern than to mine a pattern on demand. Second, we combine clustering with sequence mining to mine API usage patterns that are sensitive to programming contexts. Consequently, MAPO is now able to mine patterns that are useful under particular programming contexts. Finally, we further conduct various experiments to evaluate the effectiveness of our new approach.

4 Approach

MAPO (as shown in Figure 4) consists of a source code analyzer, an API usage miner, and an API usage recommender. The source code analyzer (Section 4.1) extracts the

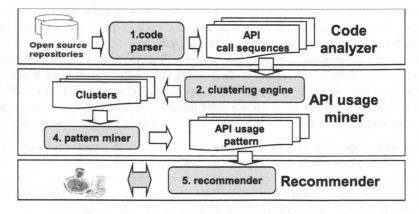

Fig. 4. Overview of MAPO

API usage information from code snippets (referred to as client code in the rest of this paper) that call API methods, and organizes the information according to the methods from which the information is collected. The API usage miner (Section 4.2) groups the API usage information into clusters and mines API usage patterns from each cluster separately. The mined API usage patterns are stored and fed to the recommender. The recommender (Section 4.3) is an Eclipse plug-in that recommends proper API usage patterns and their associated code snippets to programmers upon their requests.

4.1 Source Code Analyzer

Client code from open source projects provides valuable scenarios on how to use API methods. To extract API usage information from client code, we have developed a source code analyzer based on Eclipse's JDT compiler [2]. In MAPO, we consider the following program locations as API method calls:

- A super constructor call when the super class is provided by a third-party library or framework such as the Eclipse Graphical Editing Framework (GEF) [17].
- A class cast expression when the associated class is provided by a third-party library or framework.
- A method call when the declared class of the method is provided by a third-party library or framework.
- A class instance creation when the associated class is provided by a third-party library or framework.

As a practical matter, there are also some in-house API libraries or frameworks whose source files are available. Here, our definition emphasizes on third-party libraries or frameworks, and if an API library or framework is in-house, we can ignore its source code to treat it the same as third-party libraries or frameworks. We next present the details of extracting API method call sequences from method m.

Collecting third-party API method calls. We consider only method calls of third-party API methods (*i.e.*, API methods from third-party libraries or frameworks) in m. As a single statement may call more than one API method, MAPO performs a post-order traversal to collect API method call sequences. For example, the corresponding call sequence of statement `getGraphicalViewer().setRootEditPart( new ScalableRootEditPart())` is as follows:

```
@new org.eclipse.gef.editparts.ScalableRootEditPart
@org.eclipse.gef.ui.parts.GraphicalEditor#getGraphicalViewer
@org.eclipse.gef.EditPartViewer#setRootEditPart
```

In the sequence, the representation of each method call starts with @. A method's name is separated from its declaring class with #. When an API method call is a constructor call, the representation consists of new followed by the class name (*e.g.*, the first call in the preceding sequence).

Dealing with conditional statements. As there may be conditional statements in m, MAPO considers all the possible API method call sequences induced by these statements. Consider the following method body containing three if-statements.

```
public void fun(boolean cond1, boolean cond2, boolean cond3){
  i1;
  i2;
  if(cond1)
     if(cond2) i3
  else i4;
  if(cond3) i5;
     else i6;
}
```

Let $\{i_1, \ldots, i_6\}$ be the API method calls in method *fun*. There are six possible API method call sequences in *fun*: $\langle i_1, i_2, i_5 \rangle$, $\langle i_1, i_2, i_6 \rangle$, $\langle i_1, i_2, i_3, i_5 \rangle$, $\langle i_1, i_2, i_3, i_6 \rangle$, $\langle i_1, i_2, i_4, i_6 \rangle$, and $\langle i_1, i_2, i_4, i_5 \rangle$. Here we do not consider the dependency among *cond1*, *cond2*, and *cond3* for simplicity (thus infeasible paths/sequences may be produced like those produced by many other static analysis techniques). Similarly, we acquire possible API method call sequences for methods containing *switch*-statements. For loop statements such as *for*-statements, *while*-statements, and *do-while*-statements, as we do not know how many times they are to be executed at runtime, we treat them as conditional statements for simplicity (later we shall use conditional statements to refer to statements involving branching points for simplicity). That is to say, we view a loop statement as containing two branches: one for executing the loop once, and the other for not executing the loop at all. Once again, this simplification may also cause imprecision. However, we believe that it should not make a big difference for MAPO to mine patterns, since no matter whether we include the API method calls in the loop statement once or more than once in the sequence, the mined pattern tells the programmer only that these API methods are often used together. The programmer still needs to explore the associated code snippets to understand whether these API methods can be called many times.

Selecting a subset of sequences. After we acquire all the possible API method call sequences of m, we select a subset of sequences (that covers all API method calls) as the representative API method call sequences for each m. The reason for selecting a subset of sequences is to address the following two issues. The first issue is *method overweight*. As different methods may contain different numbers of (nested) conditional statements, we generate different numbers of possible API method call sequences for these methods. If we choose all the possible API method call sequences for each method, the methods with more sequences may have undesirable bigger impact on the mining process. The other issue is *common-path overweight*. In the preceding piece of source code, $\langle i_1, i_2 \rangle$ appears in all the six sequences, because $\langle i_1, i_2 \rangle$ is on the common path of execution, not because $\langle i_1, i_2 \rangle$ is a frequent usage pattern. However, if we pass all the six sequences to the miner, $\langle i_1, i_2 \rangle$ will be given a biased weight and may be recognized as a frequent pattern. To reduce this bias, we use a greedy strategy to select sequences. The strategy first selects the longest sequence. From the remaining sequences, the strategy iteratively selects the sequence that covers (*i.e.*, involves) the most un-covered API method calls until all the API methods are covered. We feed selected sequences to our pattern miner where the selection order does not have impact on the mined patterns.

Inlining non-third-party methods. As programmers may scatter their implementation of a feature into different (non-third-party) methods especially when using API frameworks, a single method may not contain all the involved third-party API methods of an API usage scenario. To address this issue, we employ a method inlining strategy. Our method inlining strategy is a recursive process. When constructing the API method call sequences of m, we need to inline the API method call sequences of each non-third-party method m' called by m. This strategy is also applied to construct the API method call sequences of m'. When m and m' are within the same class, MAPO traverses the parser tree of the class for m''s API method call sequences. When m and m' are not within the same class, MAPO resolves the declaring class of m' and then finds the declaring class's source file for m''s method body. After that, MAPO constructs m''s API method call sequences from its found method body. The iterations go on in the call graph till no non-third-party methods need to be inlined. Note that we deal with recursions among methods and repeating methods by avoiding inlining any method that has been inlined before. As MAPO analyzes client code statically, it ignores polymorphic method calls because these calls are determined at runtime. Here, we choose not to extract all possible sequences from a polymorphic call to avoid a similar overweight problem as common-path overweight.

4.2 API Usage Miner

Although the extracted API method call sequences contain valuable usage scenarios of API methods, it is difficult to mine patterns directly from these sequences because these sequences may include quite different API usage scenarios. If we mine all the sequences together, these different API usage scenarios may interfere with each other and thus impact the mining process negatively. As shown in Figure 4, to reduce the interference between different API usage scenarios, we first cluster the extracted API method call sequences and then mine patterns separately from each cluster.

Clustering API method call sequences. Clustering techniques [18] are to group a given collection of unlabelled items into meaningful clusters. Clustering is data-driven and the category labels are obtained solely from the similarities among data. Therefore, before we use existing techniques to cluster API method call sequences, we need to first define their quantified similarities. We next present the details of our similarity metric. **Names:** In both code snippets in Figure 1, appendToGroup is used with findMenuUsingPath and add, and the API method call order is findMenuUsingPath→ add→ appendToGroup. To effectively mine this pattern in MAPO, we need to cluster API method call sequences from these two code snippets and other similar snippets into one cluster. When we examine the names used in the two code snippets, we make the following observation. The first snippet illustrates the code for a method named contributeToMenu in a class named DEditorActionContributor, while the second snippet illustrates the code for a method named contributeToMenu in a class named RubyEditorActionContributor. The method names are the same, and the class names are very similar. Similarly, in both snippets in Figure 2, appendToGroup is used with getAction, isEnabled, and addStandardActionGroups. The method and class names used in the first snippet are buildContextMenu and ContextMenuProviderImpl, while the method and class names used in the second snippet are buildContextMenu and LatticeContextMenuProvider. Once again, the method names are the same, and the class names are very similar. We further study some more snippets, and we confirm the preceding observation: when two snippets have similar method names and similar class names, the two snippets often exhibit the same usage. The convenance comes partly from copy-paste programming and partly from class inheritances. In particular, although the classes named DEditorActionContributor and RubyEditorActionContributor are from two different projects, they both extend the class named org.eclipse.ui.editors.text.TextEditorActionContributor. The programmers of the two code snippets may refer to the extended class for naming their extending classes, so the two classes have similar names. The preceding observation forms our design rationale of choosing the similarities between method names and the similarities between class names as two sources for the definition of the similarities between API method call sequences.

When calculating the similarity between a pair of names, we split the names into words according to the capital letters in the names. MAPO chooses the Levenstein measure provided by Simmetrics[3] to calculate the similarity between two words. Then we calculate the similarity between two names as the average of the similarities of their pairwise split words.

Called API methods: Besides method names and class names, we choose called API methods as the third source for the definition of the similarities between API method call sequences. This design decision aims to deal with the following situation. When different programmers implement a similar feature, they may use a different set of API methods. For example, to parse XML files, programmers may use Jdom[4], Dom4j[5], or other API libraries to accomplish their task.

For two sequences (s_1 and s_2), we define their similarity metric as follows.

$$sim(s_1, s_2) = \frac{\# \; of \; API \; calls \; in \; I_1 \cap I_2}{\# \; of \; API \; calls \; in \; I_1 \cup I_2} \tag{1}$$

Here, I_1 and I_2 are the corresponding sets of API methods appearing in the two sequences. The number of API method calls appearing in both sets of called API methods is represented as "$\# \; of \; API \; calls \; in \; I_1 \cap I_2$". The number of API method calls appearing in either set of called API methods is represented as "$\# \; of \; API \; calls \; in \; I_1 \cup I_2$".

Based on the preceding definitions of similarities, given two API method call sequences, we calculate one similarity value based on the method names, one similarity value based on the class names, and one similarity value based on the called API methods. Using the three similarity values, we calculate the similarity of the two API method call sequences as the average of the three similarity values. Based on the similarity of any two API method call sequences, MAPO uses a classical hierarchical clustering technique [13] provided by the toolbox of Matlab[6].

Mining API patterns. Agrawal and Srikant [3] propose to mine sequential patterns in transaction databases and time-series databases. In these databases, transactions are ordered by transaction time and each transaction is a set of items. Here, the mining problem is to find all sequential patterns with a minimum user-defined support, which is the number of API method call sequences that contain the patterns. As shown in Figure 4, the API method call sequences in each cluster are fed into a frequent subsequence

---

[3] http://www.dcs.shef.ac.uk/~sam/simmetrics.html
[4] http://www.jdom.org
[5] http://www.dom4j.org
[6] http://www.mathworks.com/matlabcentral/fileexchange/7486

miner for mining frequent sequences. From each cluster, MAPO combines the mined frequent call sequences to produce a pattern.

In particular, to produce frequent API method call sequences, MAPO first encodes the call sequences of a cluster into the form of a transaction database and then feeds the database to an existing frequent subsequence miner [7]. In each cluster (C), the support of an API method call sequence (s) is defined as follows:

$$support(s) = \frac{\#\ of\ API\ call\ sequences\ with\ s}{\#\ of\ API\ call\ sequences\ in\ C} \qquad (2)$$

This definition is adapted from the classical definition of frequent sequences that is used by existing frequent subsequence miners. A frequent subsequence miner automatically mines the frequent sequences whose support values are greater than a threshold. After mining the frequent sequences, MAPO decodes each mined sequence into a frequent API method call sequence.

4.3 API Usage Recommender

This section presents the mechanism of MAPO to recommend associated snippets using the mined patterns as an index. Figure 5 shows MAPO's API usage recommender, which is a plug-in that integrates with the Eclipse IDE.

Instead of requiring programmers to check the snippets one by one, the recommender provides programmers with the capability to use the mined patterns as an index to locate snippets. For example, if a programmer wants to know the usages of appendToGroup, the programmer needs to type in "*appendToGroup*" into the method body under development. After that, the programmer selects "*appendToGroup*" and clicks "*Query API*

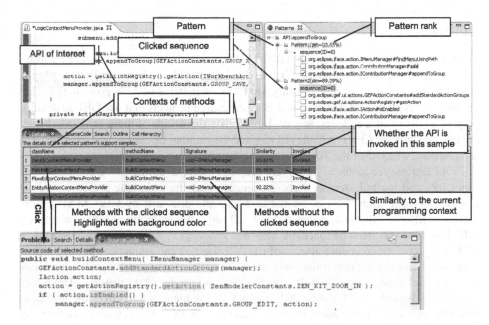

Fig. 5. MAPO recommender with annotations

patterns" of the context menu for the usages of "*appendToGroup*". Figure 5 shows an annotated screen snapshot of the preceding query. The returned relevant patterns with the pattern ranks are shown in the pattern view on the right side of Figure 5. The rank of a pattern is the average similarity of the supporting snippets to the current programming task. Here, we use the method names and the class names to calculate the similarity. For example, supposing that the programmer is implementing a method named m in class c, m and c will be compared with the method name and the class name of each supporting snippet to calculate a similarity value. The similarity definition is the same as the one in Section 4.2. From each pattern, MAPO lists its frequent method call sequences. One pattern may have more than one sequence, and MAPO recommends only sequences containing the API method of interest to the programmer.

The programmer can use the returned patterns as an index to locate snippets. In particular, the programmer can exploit a pattern's associated snippets by clicking on the pattern. The brief summaries of the associated snippets are listed in the "*details view*" on the bottom of Figure 5, and the snippets with the call sequence of interest are highlighted. Here, every entry in the "*details view*" denotes a snippet. The programmer can further exploit the source code of each snippet by clicking an entry with highlighted patterns. The source code is also highlighted with relevant API methods.

5   Experimental Study

We conducted an experimental study on MAPO, Strathcona [15], and Google code search [12]. The experimental study aims to investigate whether MAPO can help programmers locate code snippets of interest faster than the other two tools.

5.1   Setup

The Graphical Editing Framework (GEF) [17] is one of the sub-projects under Eclipse's tool project. Programmers can use GEF to develop graphical editors for Eclipse plug-in applications. In our experimental study, we focus on patterns of APIs provided by GEF. To mine the patterns of GEF, we used 20 open source projects that use GEF to develop graphical editors as a code repository. Table 1 lists the details of these projects, including project sources, Lines of Code (LOC), and the number of classes and methods. The total number of LOC of the 20 projects is about 141K.

From the source code of these 20 projects, MAPO extracted API method call sequences and built clusters of these sequences using the technique presented in Section 4.2. As our study focuses on patterns of APIs provided by GEF, MAPO automatically filtered out clusters that did not call any GEF APIs by checking whether a called method was from the package org.eclipse.gef. After filtering, MAPO used SPAM [7] to mine frequent patterns of the API method call sequences in each cluster separately, and the support value was set to 0.7. We choose the support value based on our initial experience. From the clusters, MAPO produced 93 patterns. The mined 93 patterns include 157 frequent API method call sequences and cover the usages of 856 API methods. In particular, in the 93 patterns, 26.9% patterns have more than one frequent API method call sequence. In the 157 frequent API method call sequences,

Table 1. Projects used to mine patterns

Project	Project source	LOC	#classes	#methods
Work flow	TU Berlin	10125	101	1017
Net Editor	TU Berlin	2867	35	359
Sequence Editor	TU Berlin	3921	46	486
Visual OCL	TU Berlin	11967	134	1077
PetriEditor	TU Berlin	3248	44	375
jLibrary (Client)	SourceForge	46213	503	3455
Green UML	SourceForge	10652	146	1151
Quantum	SourceForge	2380	33	225
GanttRCP	SourceForge	3760	72	510
OpenWFE (IDE)	SourceForge	9952	178	954
Jupe	SourceForge	8100	109	665
Schema Viewer	SourceForge	3358	48	338
Janus	SourceForge	1952	19	132
ZEN-kit	University of California	3991	151	314
SimpleGEF	Bonevich	851	20	120
cvsgrapher	Bonevich	1706	29	179
GEF tutorial	EclipseTeam	837	19	122
GEF example	EclipseTeam	1299	22	155
Hello GEF	EclipseTeam	1042	18	144
OAW sample	Eclipse GMT	12777	203	1196
Total		140998	1930	12974

61.8% frequent sequences describe usages of more than two API methods, and 70.7% frequent sequences describe usages of more than one class.

Strathcona is able to locate a set of relevant code snippets from a code repository. The returned snippets have a similar structure with the code under development. Strathcona can be installed through the instructions from its website[7]. From its repository information[8], we find that Strathcona covers all relevant APIs of GEF.

Google code search uses a much larger repository than MAPO. To make the study comparable, we restrict its search scope to the same projects as MAPO using Google code search's keyword, *package*[9]. As all our 20 projects are from the open source community, these projects can be crawled by Google code search. That is to say, in our experimental study, both MAPO and Google Code search use exactly the same code repository. For Google code search, we also tried to use class and method names presented in Section 4.2 to build the queries for the examples of Table 2. From these queries, no snippet is returned because Google code search uses these names as keywords to retrieve the exactly matched snippets and such snippets can hardly be found. As a result, in our experimental study, Google code search does not use these names to refine its results whereas MAPO does. This comparison may be somewhat unfair to Google code search, but using Google code search without these names reflects how it is actually used by its users in practice.

---
[7] http://tinyurl.com/6h2ybq
[8] http://tinyurl.com/5w56ye
[9] http://www.google.com/intl/en/help/faq_codesearch.html

For a given query, MAPO returns its relevant patterns and snippets within only a few seconds because it does offline mining (*i.e.*, mining patterns before a programmer makes a request on specific API methods). As these patterns are already mined, MAPO achieves good user experiences for programmers. As far as their runtime performances are concerned, all the three tools are comparable.

5.2   Quantitative Comparison

To compare the three tools quantitatively, we exploit a GEF book titled as *Eclipse Development using the Graphical Editing Framework and the Eclipse Modeling Framework*. This book is an IBM redbook[10] and is recommended by the GEF project as the first book on GEF[11]. In this book, the examples relevant to GEF are densely listed in its Chapter 4 titled as *GEF examples* and these examples cover many aspects of the usages of GEF. Based on all the 13 examples in the chapter, we prepared 13 programming tasks. In each task, we use the first API method call and the programming context in the example to query the three tools[12]. After that, we check the returned snippets for the matched one. Here, a matched snippet of an example should use the same set of API methods and the same API method call sequence as exhibited in the example.

Table 2. Comparison of Strathcona, Google code search, and MAPO

Example	First matched snippet			Second matched snippet			Total num. of items		
	Strat.	*Google*	*MAPO*	*Strat.*	*Google*	*MAPO*	*Strat.*	*Google*	*MAPO*
example 1	**5**	1	1	**n/a**	2	2	10	8	(2)
example 2	1	1	1	2	**n/a**	2	10	7	(1)
example 3	1	3	1	**5**	4	2	10	12	(4)(2)
example 4	n/a	4	n/a	n/a	10	n/a	10	11	n/a
example 5	1	7	2	3	**13**	3	10	33	(2)
example 6	n/a	9	n/a	n/a	11	n/a	10	33	n/a
example 7	2	4	2	**n/a**	**10**	3	10	39	(2)
example 8	n/a	n/a	n/a	n/a	n/a	n/a	10	18	(1)
example 9	**n/a**	3	1	**n/a**	4	2	10	28	(2)
example 10	1	1	1	2	2	2	10	16	(1)
example 11	**2**	**10**	1	**n/a**	**15**	2	10	39	(2)
example 12	**n/a**	1	1	**n/a**	2	2	10	27	(1)
example 13	2	2	2	3	**5**	3	10	70	(2)(1)

Effectiveness of locating the 1st matched snippet. Table 2 shows the results of the three tools to locate the 1st matched snippet. Column "Total num. of items" lists the returned items from each query. For its sub-columns, sub-columns "*Strat.*" and "*Google*" list the number of snippets returned by Strathcona and Google code search, respectively;

---

[10] http://www.redbooks.ibm.com/abstracts/sg246302.html

[11] http://www.eclipse.org/gef/reference/articles.html

[12] For the sixth example, we use the third API method call because its first and second API method calls overlap with the third example. In addition, as discussed before, we do not use the programming contexts to build queries for Google code search.

sub-column *"MAPO"* lists the returned patterns where a bracket pair denotes a pattern, and the number enclosed by a bracket pair denotes the number of frequent sequences (associated with the pattern) that contain the API method of interest.

Strathcona always returns 10 snippets, and its developers described that the limit of 10 was chosen informally [16]. Google code search returns much fewer snippets than expected due to two factors. One is that we restrict the search scope of Google code search for a fair comparison as explained in Section 5.1[13]. The other is that Google code search may have some techniques to filter out some snippets that match the given keywords, because when we restrict the search scope to *Jlibrary* and *Quantum*, it returns 3 snippets, but when we expand the search scope to all our 20 projects, the preceding 3 snippets are not returned. Google code search may use this filtering technique to control the number of returned snippets. Unlike Google code search, MAPO relies on mined patterns to achieve a similar goal. Generally, as MAPO mines patterns from raw snippets, MAPO returns fewer items to be checked than Strathcona and Google code search.

Column "First matched snippet" lists the numbers of snippets that need to be checked to find the first matched snippets among the snippets returned by Strathcona, Google code search, and MAPO. For Strathcona and Google code search, we check the snippets by their orders returned by these two tools. For MAPO, we check its returned snippets by the ranking order of the patterns. As MAPO highlights the snippets with a frequent call sequence automatically, only one highlighted snippet needs to be checked for each call sequence because all the highlighted snippets follow a similar usage.

From the results of MAPO and Strathcona, we find that in four examples, MAPO requires programmers to check fewer snippets for the first match than Strathcona, and in one example, MAPO requires to check more snippets for the first match than Strathcona. The results of Strathcona sometimes suffer from noisy snippets (*i.e.*, snippets that are not relevant but are matched based on search criteria used by the used code search tool). In particular, in Examples 9 and 12, many returned snippets from Strathcona have no method bodies, and these snippets can hardly show any correct API usage. We further check the snippets returned by MAPO, and we find that some snippets also contain noises but these noises do not affect the results of MAPO much. As it is rare that many snippets follow a similar noisy pattern, these noises are rarely mined as a pattern. As a result, the snippets with noises are rarely highlighted when we use patterns as an index for snippets.

From the results of MAPO and Google code search, we find that in five examples, MAPO requires programmers to check fewer snippets for the first match than Google code search, and in two examples, MAPO fails to find a match while Google code search succeeds. Strathcona also fails to find a match for these two examples. We investigate these two examples. We find that the usages of relevant API methods are quite complex, and a method call sequence cannot describe these API usages sufficiently. In Section 7, we further discuss this issue. In Example 8, all the three tools fail to find a match. The usage in this example may be rare and does not occur in any snippet in the 20 projects being mined.

In summary, generally, as MAPO uses patterns as an index for snippets, it requires less effort to locate the first match than the other two tools. In addition, as patterns are mined from raw snippets, these patterns are more robust to noises than raw snippets.

---

[13] Note that we do not restrict the search scope of Google code search for the example in Section 2.

The comparison also helps us understand cases where MAPO needs improvements in our future work to handle complex API usages.

Effectiveness of locating the 2nd matched snippet. For a critical programmer, it may be essential to recommend snippets with a similar usage of the first matched snippet's so that the programmer can have high confidence that the selected snippet embeds a common usage pattern. Table 2 shows the results of these tools to locate the second matched snippets. Column "Second matched snippet" lists the number of snippets to be checked to find the second match among the snippets returned by Strathcona, Google code search, and MAPO, respectively.

For Strathcona and Google code search, we still need to check the returned snippets one by one. For MAPO, as we can highlight the snippets with a particular pattern, after we find the first match, we need to check only the next highlighted snippet associated with the same pattern for the second match. From the results of MAPO and Strathcona, we find that in eight examples Strathcona fails to find the second match, while only in three examples MAPO fails to find the second match. In addition, for the five examples where both MAPO and Strathcona are able to find the second match, MAPO requires to check fewer or the same number of snippets for the second match than Strathcona. As Strathcona returns a limited set of snippets, Strathcona seems difficult to provide rematched snippets for critical programmers. From the results of MAPO and Google code search, we find that in seven examples, MAPO requires to check fewer snippets for the second match than Google code search.

As MAPO groups code snippets of a similar API usage into one cluster, programmers can easily find the the 2nd matched code snippet if they already find a matched code snippet. We do not further compare the effectiveness of these tools to locate the third code snippet and so on, although we anticipate to get similar results from the comparison.

In summary, MAPO requires less effort of a critical programmer to search for rematched snippets than the other tools. The rematched snippets provided by MAPO increase a programmer's confidence that a usage is correct and common because it is relatively rare that snippets from different projects all follow a similar noisy or buggy pattern to use API methods.

In fact, a code snippet recommending tool often faces the following dilemma. To help programmers find the first matched snippet as soon as possible, a code search engine may need to put the snippets with different usages on the top of its returned snippet list, but the rematched snippets may thus be put near the bottom of the snippet list. To help programmers find the rematched snippets as soon as possible, a code search engine may need to put the rematched snippets near the top of the returned snippet list, but the snippets with different usages may thus be put near the bottom of the returned snippet list. MAPO solves this dilemma, as MAPO clusters snippets and uses the mined patterns as an index for these snippets. From our experiences, in some extreme cases, MAPO returns about 20 patterns given a single query. However, it is still much fewer than the code snippets returned by a code search engine.

5.3 Significance of MAPO's Design Decisions

We next show the impacts of MAPO's design decisions on MAPO's effectiveness in locating the first and the second matches. For each task, we turn off MAPO's individual

Table 3. Impacts of MAPO's design decisions

Example	First matched snippet				Second matched snippet				Total num. of items			
	All	×S	×I	×C	All	×S	×I	×C	All	×S	×I	×C
example 1	1	1	**n/a**	1	2	2	**n/a**	2	(2)	(2)	**n/a**	(2)
example 2	1	1	1	1	2	2	2	2	(1)	(1)	(1)	(1)
example 3	1	1	1	**n/a**	2	2	2	**n/a**	(4)(2)	(4)(2)	(3)(1)	**(2)**
example 4	n/a	n/a	n/a	n/a	n/a	n/a	n/a	n/a	n/a	n/a	n/a	n/a
example 5	2	2	2	**n/a**	3	3	3	**n/a**	(2)	(2)	(2)	**n/a**
example 6	n/a	n/a	n/a	n/a	n/a	n/a	n/a	n/a	n/a	n/a	n/a	n/a
example 7	2	2	2	**n/a**	3	3	3	**n/a**	(2)	(2)	(2)	**n/a**
example 8	n/a	n/a	n/a	n/a	n/a	n/a	n/a	n/a	(1)	(1)	(1)	(1)
example 9	1	1	1	1	2	2	2	2	(2)	(2)	(2)	(2)
example 10	1	1	1	1	2	2	2	2	(1)	(1)	(1)	(1)
example 11	1	1	1	**n/a**	2	2	2	**n/a**	(2)	(2)	(2)	**n/a**
example 12	1	1	1	1	2	2	2	2	(1)	(1)	(1)	(1)
example 13	2	**n/a**	**n/a**	**n/a**	3	**n/a**	**n/a**	**n/a**	(2)(1)	**(1)**	**(1)(1)**	**(1)**

In this table, we highlight those affected values with the bold font.

internal techniques and compare the results with "*All*" where all techniques are turned on, and Table 3 shows the results. Column "First matched snippet" lists the number of snippets that require to be checked for the first match. Column "Second matched snippet" lists the number of snippets that require to be checked for the second match. Column "Total num. of items" lists the number of the total frequent sequences. For their sub-columns, sub-columns "×S", "×I", and "×C" show the results when we turn off the corresponding technique, respectively. Based on these results, we find the impacts of MAPO's design decisions on its effectiveness as follows.

Selection. We find that the result of Example 13 is affected by the selection technique. In this example, the related API methods are called within a branching statement. Let us use $|With(s)|$ to denote "*# of API method call sequences with s*" in Equation 2, and we use $|C|$ to denote "*# of API method call sequences in cluster C*". If we turn off the selection technique and extract all possible call sequences, $|C|$ increases while $|With(s)|$ does not change much. Consequently, s's support value decreases and s may not be mined as a frequent call sequence. From the observation, we find that the selection technique helps MAPO mine frequent API method call sequences when the API method of interest is often used within branches in conditional statements.

Inlining. We find that the results of Examples 1 and 13 are affected by the inlining technique. We further investigate the two examples' usages, and we find that API methods of the mined sequence from "*All*" are actually scattered in different methods of client code. Consequently, when we turn off inlining, these API method call sequences cannot be extracted and thus cannot be mined as frequent API method call sequences. From the observation, we find that the inlining technique helps MAPO mine API method calls from different methods of client code into frequent API method call sequences.

Clustering. We find that the results of Examples 3, 5, 7, 11, and 13 are affected by the clustering technique. For the ease of discussing this technique, let s_1 and s_2 be two mined frequent call sequences from clusters C_1 and C_2, respectively, and from Equation 2, their support values are $\frac{|With(s_1)|}{|C_1|}$ and $\frac{|With(s_2)|}{|C_2|}$. When we turn off clustering, C_1, C_2, and other clusters are merged into one. As a result, the support of s_1 changes to $\frac{|With(s_1)|}{|C_1|+|C_2|+|N|-|C_1\cap C_2|}$ where N is the set of sequences that also call API methods in s_1 from other clusters. For simplicity, we next focus only on cases for s_1. If s_1 and s_2 belong to the same pattern, C_1 and C_2 are the same cluster. After we turn off clustering, s_1's support value changes to $\frac{|With(s_1)|}{|C_1|+|N|}$. If $|N|$ is small, s_1's support value does not decrease much, and can still be mined as a frequent sequence. We find that Examples 1, 2, 9, 10, and 12 fall into this situation and their results are not affected. If $|N|$ is large, s_1's support value may decrease too much to be mined as a frequent sequence. We find that Examples 5, 7, and 11 fall into this situation and their results are affected. If s_1 and s_2 belong to two different patterns, C_1 and C_2 are two different clusters. After we turn off clustering, s_1's support value changes to $\frac{|With(s_1)|}{|C_1|+|C_2|+|N|}$. We see that the support value may decrease more than in previous examples. We find that Examples 3 and 13 fall into this situation and their results are affected. Based on these observations, we find that the clustering technique helps MAPO alleviate the interlacement among different usages that are sensitive to programming tasks.

As for the results of Examples 2, 10, and 12, their results are not affected by any the MAPO's internal techniques. We investigate these examples, and we find that their API usages are quite simple and straightforward. For example, after we investigate the related snippets of Example 10, we find the following facts regarding the call sequence of addRetargetAction. It is seldom used in different programming usages. Its relevant API methods are seldom scattered in different methods. It is even seldom used within branches of conditional statements. Consequently, its results are not affected by these techniques in MAPO.

In summary, MAPO's techniques help handle complex usages of API methods. In particular, the selection technique helps MAPO mine API frequent sequences when the API method of interest is often used within branches in conditional statements. The inlining technique helps MAPO mine API method calls from different methods of client code into frequent API method call sequences. The clustering technique helps MAPO alleviate the interlacement among different usages that are sensitive to programming contexts.

5.4 Threats to Validity

The threats to external validity primarily include the degree to which the projects being mined, the programming tasks being constructed, and existing code search tools being compared are representative of true practice. Although GEF is one of the popular sets of Eclipse APIs, only one set of APIs is used, and the recommendations are all on the use of GEF. Although we tried to be as objective as possible by exploiting all code snippets from a book to construct programming tasks, these code snippets are limited in number, and code snippets from books may omit rare usages that are also useful to programmers. Although Strathcona and Google code search are the publicly available tools related to MAPO in code searching with API method queries, some other code search engines or tools may perform better than these two tools. These threats could be reduced by more experiments on wider types of subjects and tools in future work. The threats to internal validity are instrumentation effects that may bias our results. To reduce these threats, we manually inspected all snippets returned by MAPO and Strathcona as well as most snippets returned by Google code search.

6 Empirical Study

Our empirical study aims to investigate whether MAPO can assist programmers to complete programming tasks. In general, the development time and the number of introduced bugs (reflecting the quality of completed code) are two major metrics for the evaluation of tools aiming at assisting programming activities. However, these two metrics can impact each other. Intuitively, given a tool, the more time a programmer spends for a given programming task, the more likely the programmer produces code with fewer bugs. Therefore, in our empirical study, we give the programmers a fixed time (one hour) and use the number of introduced bugs as the metric for the tools' usefulness of assisting programming. As all the tools aim at facilitating programming tasks concerning APIs, we focus on API-related bugs such as missing essential API methods and improper orders of these API methods.

To conduct the study, we prepared six programming tasks listed in Table 4. The detailed descriptions of these tasks can be found in another GEF book titled as *SWT/JFace in Action* [23], which is also recommended by the GEF project[14]. As GEF is a framework to create graphical editors, it is difficult to use it to implement an independent task. To prepare each task, we first implemented the task in a code base and then took out the code that is related to the task from the code base to form an incomplete code base. The code base had 2383 LOC. Here, to simulate the real usage of these tools, we did not choose an existing GEF project because the source code of an existing GEF project

Table 4. Tasks used in the empirical study

Task	Description	Essential API calls
1	Factor an incoming request	3
2	Start monitoring property changes	4
3	Update the name and the bounds of a figure	5
4	Add a context menu to an editor	5
5	Add a tool bar to an editor	5
6	Save the content of a editor	8

Table 5. Background of the subjects

	Group 1			Group 2		
	subject 1	subject 2	subject 3	subject 4	subject 5	subject 6
Java (Years)	4	3	2	3	1	3
GEF (Years)	2	0	0	0	0	1

---

[14] http://www.eclipse.org/gef/reference/articles.html

Table 6. Results of the empirical study

	Control Group				MAPO Group			
	subject 1	subject 2	subject 3	total	subject 4	subject 5	subject 6	total
Task 1	0	0	0	0	0	1	0	1
Task 2	0	1	1	2	0	1	1	2
Task 3	2	0	5	7	2	4	0	6
	MAPO Group				Control Group			
	subject 1	subject 2	subject 3	total	subject 4	subject 5	subject 6	total
Task 4	0	0	0	0	5	4	0	9
Task 5	0	0	0	0	0	4	0	4
Task 6	0	2	3	5	4	3	3	10

might be found in existing repositories. We chose these tasks because they cover many aspects of GEF's usages and they vary in their difficulties to implement. Column 3 of Table 4 lists the number of API methods that are essential to implement the tasks. These tasks are relatively small in size. Even for the 6th task that contains the most essential APIs, a programmer needs to write only less than one hundred lines of code.

We invited six graduate students (subjects) majoring in computer science from Peking University to complete the six tasks. None of the invited subjects was familiar with MAPO. All of them were shown a short demonstration on using the three tools just before the study. Table 5 shows the background of these subjects. Most of the subjects have some programming experience of Java but little experience of GEF. We divided these subjects into two groups with the goal of making each group to have comparably similar mixture of background.

To reduce the possible imbalance between the two groups, we introduced a crossover comparison that is used in existing empirical studies [26]. In particular, our study has two stages, and in each stage, the two groups exchange their roles as the MAPO group and the control group. In particular, in the first stage, Group 1 was asked to complete Tasks 1, 2, and 3 using Google code search and Strathcona, whereas Group 2 was asked to complete Tasks 1, 2, and 3 using MAPO. In the second stage, Group 1 was asked to complete Tasks 4, 5, and 6 using MAPO, whereas Group 2 was asked to complete Tasks 4, 5, and 6 using Google code search and Strathcona. The tasks and the copies of the incomplete code were assigned to the subjects just before the study began. These subjects worked on the tasks separately and were free to test and execute the programs when completing these tasks. In each stage, the subjects were allowed to use one hour to finish the incomplete code according to the assigned tasks.

After the subjects of the two groups finished the preceding tasks using the assigned tools, we checked the code written by these subjects. We did not classify their submitted tasks as complete or incomplete for comparison of these tools, as the classification may not be sufficiently objective. Instead, we prepared a test suite for each task, and if a completed program fails to pass a test case of a task, we count the failure as one found bug of the task. The test suites are carefully prepared for two goals. One is that the test suites should be designed to contain no redundant tests (*i.e.*, no two test cases cover the same behavior or expose the same bug), so that one bug will be less likely to be exposed (and thus counted) repeatedly by multiple test cases. The other is that a test suite of a task should try to cover comprehensive behaviors of the task. We carefully checked the failed test cases to ensure that they reveal difference defects, and Table 6 shows the results. Column "*subject x*" lists the numbers of failed test cases in completed projects of the *x*th subject. Column "*total*" lists the numbers of total failed test cases. From "*total*" of Table 6, in the first task, the MAPO group produced code with more bugs than the control group. In the second task, the MAPO group produced code with the same number of bugs with the control group. In all the remaining four tasks, the MAPO group produced code with fewer bugs than the control group.

Our observation confirms that MAPO is able to assist programmers to produce code with fewer bugs when implementing their programming tasks. After inspection of the introduced bugs, we find the impacts of these tools as follows. In Tasks 1 and 2, there is a little difference in performance between the MAPO group and the control group. We find that in the two tasks, the essential API methods are from the same package of an API framework, and their usages are relatively straightforward. The number of bugs is small, and the bugs are introduced because the subjects are unfamiliar to the incomplete code. As the subjects of the two groups have comparable background, almost the same number of bugs are introduced. In Task 3, there is also a little difference in performance between the MAPO group and the control group. We find that the API usage of this task is relatively complex and cannot be found in existing snippets or patterns. As a result, all the three tools cannot give the subjects much help, and the subjects of the two groups both introduce many bugs. In Tasks 4, 5, and 6, there is a significant difference in performance between the MAPO group and the control group. We find that in these tasks, the API usages are relatively complex. For example, in Task 4, before the API method `appendToGroup` is called to add an action to the menu, another API method `isEnable` should be called to check whether the action is enabled. As shown in Figure 3, MAPO mines this usage into a pattern. As a result, all the subjects of the MAPO group called this API method call, whereas only one subject of the control group did so. In Task 6, the API method `getEditorInput` is essential to be called to get the content of the editor, and another API method `markSaveLocation` is also essential to be called to mark the saved status of the editor after its content is saved. Two subjects of the MAPO group used both API method calls to complete their code because MAPO mines these API method calls into a pattern and highlights them in the recommended snippets, whereas no subjects of the control group used both API method calls in their code. It is tricky because the former API method `getEditorInput` is declared by the class `org.eclipse.ui.part.EditorPart`, whereas the latter API method `markSaveLocation` is declared by another class `org.eclipse.gef.commands.CommandStack`. As MAPO mines this API usage into a pattern, it helps the subjects of the MAPO group understand this usage better than the subjects of the control group.

In summary, in the three tasks of our empirical study, as API usages are straightforward or cannot be found in existing snippets, the three tools do not show many differences in effectiveness. In the other three tasks, as API usages are relatively complicated, MAPO successfully helps programmers produce code with fewer bugs than the other two tools. MAPO helps programmers understand complicated usages of APIs and thus assist programmers to complete programming tasks.

Threats to validity. As our empirical study shares the settings with the experimental study in Section 5, our empirical study shares the threats with the study in Section 5 as well. Besides these threats, our empirical study has four other threats to internal validity. First, our empirical study involves human subjects, and the particular programming capabilities of the human subjects may bias results. To reduce this threat, we invited as many human subjects as possible and used a crossover design. Second, the results observed in the empirical study may not be applicable to programming tasks other than those considered in the study, being a threat to the external validity. We can conduct empirical studies involving more subjects and more programming tasks to further reduce these threats. Third, due to the limit of human resources, we assign the six subjects into two groups, one of which is a control group. In the control group, we allow the subjects to use both Google code search and Strathcona, which may have negative impacts on the two tools. To reduce the threat, we plan to involve more subjects and to assign these subjects into three groups with one tool for each group. Fourth, the learning curve of the these subjects may affect the results. To reduce the threat, we balance the two groups with similar background. To further reduce the threat, we plan to give detailed training to the subjects.

7   Discussion and Future Work

Tuning the MAPO approach. Our MAPO approach chooses some data mining techniques and their parameters based on our initial experiences. We still need further investigations to confirm whether these selected techniques and parameters are the best choice. For mining techniques, we plan to try other clustering techniques such as K-means and DBSCAN, or to try some classifiers such as K-nn in the clustering stage[15]; we plan to try other miners such as Acharya *et al.* [1]'s partial order miner in the mining stage; and we plan to take other features such as class structure into consideration for clustering. For parameters, we plan to evaluate the significances of the selected weights and thresholds.

Quality of mined patterns. In the experiment, we do not show the quality of mined patterns directly. As most libraries do not provide usage patterns, there is no off-the-shelf golden standard for real patterns. We plan to conduct more experiments to show the quality of mined patterns when such a golden standard is available in future work.

Other object-oriented languages. Although the current implementation of MAPO analyzes only Java code, our MAPO approach may be generally applicable for other object-oriented languages since our approach relies on some common object-oriented features. We plan to adapt MAPO to other object-oriented languages in future work.

Mining uncommon API usages. As most existing mining approaches extract API usages from only API client code, these approaches may fail to mine API usage patterns that are not common among client code (but can be potentially inferred from API implementation code). In future work, we plan to develop techniques to mine API patterns based on both API client code and implementation code.

---

[15] Please refer to *Data Mining: Concepts and Techniques* [13] for the details of these techniques.

8   Conclusion

To help a programmer understand API usages and write API client code more effectively, we have developed a tool called MAPO. It mines API usage patterns from open source repositories automatically and recommends the mined patterns and their associated snippets on a programmer's requests. In particular, MAPO implements a mechanism that combines frequent subsequence mining with clustering to mine API usage patterns from code snippets. In addition, MAPO provides a recommender that integrates with the existing Eclipse IDE. Through MAPO's recommender, a programmer can retrieve patterns to help navigate their associated snippets to find the code snippet of interest effectively. We have conducted an experimental study on MAPO as well as Strathcona and Google code search, two state-of-the-art code searching tools. The results show that MAPO helps a programmer to locate useful code snippets more effectively than these two existing tools. To explore whether MAPO can assist programmers in programming tasks, we further conducted an empirical study. The results show that comparing with Strathcona and Google code search, MAPO helps programmers produce code with fewer bugs when API usages are relatively complex and these usages can be found in existing code snippets.

Acknowledgments

We thank the anonymous reviewers for their insightful comments. This material is based upon Tao Xie's work supported in part by the U. S. Army Research Laboratory and the U. S. Army Research Office under contract/grant number W911NF-08-1-0443. The authors from Peking University are sponsored by the National Basic Research Program of China (973) No. 2009CB320703, the High-Tech Research and Development Program of China (863) No. 2007AA010301 and No. 2006AA01Z156, the Science Fund for Creative Research Groups of China No. 60821003, and the National Science Foundation of China No. 90718016. Jian Pei's research was supported in part by an NSERC Discovery Grant and an NSERC Discovery Accelerator Supplement Grant.

References

[1] Acharya, M., Xie, T., Pei, J., Xu, J.: Mining API patterns as partial orders from source code: From usage scenarios to specifications. In: Proc. 7th ESEC/FSE, pp. 25–34 (2007)

[2] Aeschlimann, M., Baumer, D., Lanneluc, J.: Java tool smithing extending the Eclipse Java Development Tools. In: Proc. 2nd EclipseCon (2005)

[3] Agrawal, R., Srikant, R.: Mining sequential patterns. In: Proc. 7th ICDE, pp. 3–14 (1995)

[4] Alur, R., Černý, P., Madhusudan, P., Nam, W.: Synthesis of interface specifications for Java classes. In: Proc. 32nd POPL, pp. 98–109 (2005)

[5] Ammons, G., Bodik, R., Larus, J.R.: Mining specifications. In: Proc. 29th POPL, pp. 4–16 (2002)

[6] Angluin, D.: Learning regular sets from queries and counterexamples. Information and Computation 75(2), 87–106 (1987)

[7] Ayres, J., Flannick, J., Gehrke, J., Yiu, T.: Sequential pattern mining using a bitmap representation. In: Proc. 8th KDD, pp. 429–435 (2002)

[8] Bruch, M., Schäfer, T., Mezini, M.: FrUiT: IDE support for framework understanding. In: Proc. 4th ETX, pp. 55–59 (2006)

[9] Chang, R., Podgurski, A., Yang, J.: Finding what's not there: a new approach to revealing neglected conditions in software. In: Proc. ISSTA, pp. 163–173 (2007)

[10] Engler, D., Chen, D.Y., Hallem, S., Chou, A., Chelf, B.: Bugs as deviant behavior: a general approach to inferring errors in systems code. In: Proc. 8th SOSP, pp. 57–72 (2001)

[11] Gabel, M., Su, Z.: Javert: fully automatic mining of general temporal properties from dynamic traces. In: Proc. 16th FSE, pp. 339–349 (2008)

[12] Google Code Search Engine (2008), http://www.google.com/codesearch

[13] Han, J., Kamber, M.: Data mining: concepts and techniques. Morgan Kaufmann Publishers Inc., San Francisco (2000)

[14] Henzinger, T., Jhala, R., Majumdar, R.: Permissive interfaces. In: Proc. 5th ESEC/FSE, pp. 31–40 (2005)

[15] Holmes, R., Murphy, G.C.: Using structural context to recommend source code examples. In: Proc. 27th ICSE, pp. 117–125 (2005)

[16] Holmes, R., Walker, R.J., Murphy, G.C.: Approximate structural context matching: An approach to recommend relevant examples. IEEE Transactions on Software Engineering 32(12), 952–970 (2006)

[17] Hudson, R., Shah, P.: GEF in depth. In: Proc. 2nd EclipseCon (2005)

[18] Jain, A.K., Murty, M.N., Flynn, P.J.: Data clustering: a review. ACM Computing Surveys 31(3), 264–323 (1999)

[19] Li, Z., Zhou, Y.: PR-Miner: Automatically extracting implicit programming rules and detecting violations in large software code. In: Proc. 5th ESEC/FSE, pp. 306–315 (2005)

[20] Livshits, V.B., Zimmermann, T.: Dynamine: Finding common error patterns by mining software revision histories. In: Proc. 5th ESEC/FSE, pp. 296–305 (2005)

[21] Lo, D., Khoo, S.: SMArTIC: towards building an accurate, robust and scalable specification miner. In: Proc. 6th ESEC/FSE, pp. 265–275 (2006)

[22] Mandelin, D., Xu, L., Bodik, R., Kimelman, D.: Jungloid mining: helping to navigate the API jungle. In: Proc. PLDI, pp. 48–61 (2005)

[23] Matthew Scarpino, S.N., Holder, S., Mihalkovic, L.: SWT/JFace in Action. Manning (2005)

[24] McCarey, F., Cinnéide, M.Ó., Kushmerick, N.: Recommending library methods: An evaluation of the vector space model (VSM) and latent semantic indexing (LSI). In: Proc. 9th ICSR, pp. 217–230 (2006)

[25] Michail, A.: Data mining library reuse patterns using generalized association rules. In: Proc. 22nd ICSE, pp. 167–176 (2000)

[26] Ng, T., Cheung, S., Chan, W., Yu, Y.: Work experience versus refactoring to design patterns: a controlled experiment. In: Proc. 6th ESEC/FSE, pp. 12–22 (2006)

[27] Ramanathan, M.K., Grama, A., Jagannathan, S.: Path-sensitive inference of function precedence protocols. In: Proc. 29th ICSE, pp. 240–250 (2007)

[28] Reiss, S., Renieris, M.: Encoding Program Executions. In: Proc. 23rd ICSE, pp. 221–230 (2001)

[29] Saul, Z.M., Filkov, V., Devanbu, P., Bird, C.: Recommending random walks. In: Proc. 7th ESEC/FSE, pp. 15–24 (2007)

[30] Scaffidi, C.: Why are APIs difficult to learn and use? Crossroads 12(4), 4–4 (2005)

[31] Shoham, S., Yahav, E., Fink, S., Pistoia, M.: Static specification mining using automata-based abstractions. In: Proc. ISSTA, pp. 174–184 (2007)

[32] Tansalarak, N., Claypool, K.T.: XSnippet: Mining for sample code. In: Proc. 21st OOPSLA, pp. 413–430 (2006)

[33] Thummalapenta, S., Xie, T.: PARSEWeb: A programmer assistant for reusing open source code on the web. In: Proc. 22nd ASE, pp. 204–213 (2007)

[34] Wasylkowski, A., Zeller, A., Lindig, C.: Detecting object usage anomalies. In: Proc. 7th ESEC/FSE, pp. 35–44 (2007)
[35] Weimer, W., Necula, G.: Mining temporal specifications for error detection. In: Halbwachs, N., Zuck, L.D. (eds.) TACAS 2005. LNCS, vol. 3440, pp. 461–476. Springer, Heidelberg (2005)
[36] Whaley, J., Martin, M., Lam, M.: Automatic extraction of object-oriented component interfaces. In: Proc. ISSTA, pp. 218–228 (2002)
[37] Williams, C.C., Hollingsworth, J.K.: Recovering system specific rules from software repositories. In: Proc. 2nd MSR, pp. 1–5 (2005)
[38] Xie, T., Pei, J.: MAPO: Mining API usages from open source repositories. In: Proc. 3rd MSR, pp. 54–57 (2006)
[39] Yang, J., Evans, D., Bhardwaj, D., Bhat, T., Das, M.: Perracotta: mining temporal API rules from imperfect traces. In: Proc. 28th ICSE, pp. 282–291 (2006)

Supporting Framework Use via Automatically Extracted Concept-Implementation Templates

Abbas Heydarnoori, Krzysztof Czarnecki, and Thiago Tonelli Bartolomei

Generative Software Development Lab
University of Waterloo, Canada
{aheydarn,kczarnec,ttonelli}@gsd.uwaterloo.ca
http://gsd.uwaterloo.ca

Abstract. Application frameworks provide reusable concepts that are instantiated in application code through potentially complex implementation steps such as subclassing, implementing callbacks, and making calls. Existing applications contain valuable examples of such steps, except that locating them in the application code is often challenging. We propose the notion of *concept implementation templates*, which summarize the necessary implementation steps, and an approach to automatic extraction of such templates from traces of sample applications. We demonstrate the feasibility of the template extraction with high precision and recall through an empirical study with twelve realistic concepts from four widely-used frameworks. Finally, we report on a user experiment with twelve subjects in which the choice of templates vs. documentation had much less impact on development time than the concept complexity.

1   Introduction

Object-oriented frameworks allow the reuse of both designs and code and are one of the most effective reuse technologies available today. Frameworks provide *domain-specific concepts*, which are generic units of functionality. Framework-based applications are constructed by writing *completion code*, also known as *application code*, that instantiates these concepts. For example, a graphical user interface (GUI) framework such as *JFace* offers implementation for a set of GUI concepts, which include a text box, tree viewer, and context menu. The instantiation of such concepts requires various *implementation steps* in the completion code, such as subclassing framework-provided classes, implementing interfaces, and calling appropriate framework services.

Many existing frameworks are difficult to use because of their large and complex *Application Programming Interfaces* (APIs) and often incomplete user documentation. To cope with this problem, application developers frequently apply the *Monkey See/Monkey Do* rule [1]: "Use existing framework applications as a guide to develop new applications". Understanding how an existing application implements a concept requires the ability to quickly locate those parts of the application code that implement the concept. Unfortunately, locating the concept implementation can be challenging since the implementation is often scattered in the application code and tangled with the implementation of other concepts.

S. Drossopoulou (Ed.): ECOOP 2009, LNCS 5653, pp. 344–368, 2009.
© Springer-Verlag Berlin Heidelberg 2009

Several tools have been proposed to address this challenge. *Framework usage comprehension* tools such as Strathcona [2] and FrUiT [3] apply static analysis to the source code of sample applications and allow retrieving code snippets or usage rules for a particular API element. These tools can be very helpful to understand concept implementations, but require the developer to know at least the names of some of the API elements involved. They are less helpful if the developer has only a high-level idea of the concept that needs to be implemented or if the concept spans multiple classes or both. *Concept location* tools such as SNIAFL [4] or SITIR [5] can be used to locate the code implementing a concept of interest identified by higher-level characteristics such as usage scenarios or domain terms. These tools do not focus on framework API usage, however: the code identified will still include many application-specific elements that are irrelevant from the viewpoint of framework usage.

To address the above issues, we propose the notion of *concept implementation templates* and *FUDA (Framework Understanding through Dynamic Analysis)*, an approach to automatic extraction of such templates from traces of sample applications. A concept implementation template is a tutorial-like code example summarizing the *implementation steps* necessary to instantiate a given concept. Such a template can be used as a starting point to further investigate the concrete concept implementations in the sample applications.

The FUDA template extraction approach works by invoking the concept of interest in at least two different contexts in one or more sample applications, and recording all runtime interactions between the application code and the framework API. For instance, given the context menu in an Eclipse view as the desired concept, each trace could be collected by invoking a context menu in a different Eclipse view. The collected traces are then intersected. The calls in the intersection provide the basis for generating a template that specifies which packages to import, framework classes to subclass, interfaces to implement, and operations to call in order to implement the concept.

We have implemented the extraction approach as a tool for Java and used this tool in a study to evaluate the quality of the extraction. The study shows that the approach can produce templates with relatively few false positives and false negatives for realistic concepts by using only two sample applications.

Furthermore, we conducted a user experiment with twelve subjects comparing templates to framework documentation. For the studied sample, no statistically significant difference between using templates and documentation in terms of implementation time and number of introduced bugs could be detected. The analysis of additional data and feedback suggested that templates should be used together with the sample applications from which they were extracted rather than just by looking at the templates alone.

The contributions of the paper include (1) the notion of automatically extracted concept implementation templates, (2) an approach to automatic extraction of such templates from sample applications, (3) a prototype implementation of the extraction approach, (4) a study evaluating the precision and recall of the extraction approach, and (5) an experiment evaluating the usefulness of templates in comparison to framework documentation in assisting application developers.

In the remainder, we introduce our running example (Section 2) and present the notion of templates (Section 3). We then describe the extraction approach (Section 4) and present its evaluation (Section 5). Finally, we discuss several aspects of FUDA (Section 6), compare it with related work (Section 7), and conclude (Section 8).

2   Running Example

As an example, consider the code implementing a context menu using JFace (Figure 1). The menu is located in `SampleView`, which is a visual component that displays trees using a `TreeViewer` (l. 36). The code was generated using one of Eclipse's wizards. The lines implementing the context menu are marked by •. The lines marked by ○ implement a Welcome window and were manually added as an example of code that is completely unrelated to the context menu. The constituent parts of the view are created in `createPartControl()` (l. 190). In particular, this method calls `makeActions()` (l. 198) and `hookContextMenu()` (l. 199), which together create the context menu. In general, a context menu consists of one or more actions (l. 220, 225) and potentially one or more separators (l. 215, 217). It is constructed by a menu manager (l. 202, 208) and invoked by a menu listener (l. 204). The latter implements the `menuAboutToShow()` (l. 205) callback method which is called by the framework, i.e., JFace, when the user clicks to open the context menu.

The context menu example illustrates some of the challenges in locating concepts in code. The implementation of the menu is tangled with the implementation of the view and it involves a complex interaction of several objects, namely view, menu manager, menu listener, menu, actions, and separators. To complicate the matter, a concept implementation may also be scattered across several classes as in the case of Eclipse's drag&drop. Consequently, even though locating a concept in the GUI of a sample application may be easy, locating its implementation in the application code is often challenging and time consuming.

3   Concept Implementation Templates

A template for our context menu example is shown in Figure 2. The template was generated from two traces collected by invoking the context menu in two sample applications: `SampleView` (Figure 1) and `Console`, which is part of Eclipse. The generated template has the form of a tutorial-like example in Java-based pseudocode.

Templates specify the following implementation steps: packages to import (l. 1–8 in Figure 2), framework classes to subclass (l. 15), interfaces to implement (l. 9), methods to implement (l. 10), objects to create (e.g., l. 11), and methods to call (e.g., l. 12). Note that the specified steps involve only the elements of the framework API. For example, the method calls `makeActions()` and `hookContextMenu()` in Figure 1 are specific to that particular implementation and are not reflected in the template. The involved elements may be entirely framework-defined, e.g., the implementation of `Separator`, which is instantiated in line 11, resides in framework code. Alternatively, the elements may also reside in the application code, provided that they are *framework-stipulated*. In particular, such elements are (1) application classes that are subtypes of API-defined types; (2) application methods that implement API-defined operations or override API-defined methods; and (3) constructors of framework-stipulated classes. For example,

```
      ...
 35  public class SampleView extends ViewPart {
 36     private TreeViewer viewer;
 37     private DrillDownAdapter drillDownAdapter;
•38     private Action action1;
•39     private Action action2;
○40     private WelcomeWindow welcomeWindow;
      ...
 98     class ViewContentProvider
 99        implements IStructuredContentProvider, ITreeContentProvider {
      ...
162     }
163     class ViewLabelProvider extends LabelProvider {
      ...
189     }
190     public void createPartControl(Composite parent) {
○191       welcomeWindow = new WelcomeWindow();
○192       welcomeWindow.open();
193       viewer = new TreeViewer(...);
194       drillDownAdapter = new DrillDownAdapter(viewer);
195       viewer.setContentProvider(new ViewContentProvider());
196       viewer.setLabelProvider(new ViewLabelProvider());
197       viewer.setInput(getViewSite());
•198      makeActions();
•199      hookContextMenu();
200     }
•201    private void hookContextMenu() {
•202       MenuManager menuMgr = new MenuManager("#PopupMenu");
•203       menuMgr.setRemoveAllWhenShown(true);
•204       menuMgr.addMenuListener(new IMenuListener() {
•205          public void menuAboutToShow(IMenuManager manager) {
•206             SampleView.this.fillContextMenu(manager);
•207          }});
•208       Menu menu = menuMgr.createContextMenu(viewer.getControl());
•209       viewer.getControl().setMenu(menu);
•210       getSite().registerContextMenu(menuMgr, viewer);
•211    }
•212    private void fillContextMenu(IMenuManager manager) {
•213       manager.add(action1);
•214       manager.add(action2);
•215       manager.add(new Separator());
•216       drillDownAdapter.addNavigationActions(manager);
•217       manager.add(new Separator(IWorkbenchActionConstants.MB_ADDITIONS));
•218    }
•219    private void makeActions() {
•220       action1 = new Action() {
221          public void run() { showMessage("Action 1 executed"); }
•222       };
•223       action1.setText("Action 1");
•224       action1.setToolTipText("Action 1 tooltip");
•225       action2 = new Action() {
226          public void run() { showMessage("Action 2 executed"); }
•227       };
•228       action2.setText("Action 2");
•229       action2.setToolTipText("Action 2 tooltip");
•230    }
      ...
267  }
```

Fig. 1. Implementation of a sample Eclipse view with a context menu (•)

```
 1  import org.eclipse.jface.action.Separator;
 2  import org.eclipse.jface.viewers.Viewer;
 3  import org.eclipse.jface.action.Action;
 4  import org.eclipse.jface.action.MenuManager;
 5  import org.eclipse.swt.widgets.Menu;
 6  import org.eclipse.jface.resource.ImageDescriptor;
 7  import org.eclipse.jface.action.IMenuListener;
 8  import org.eclipse.swt.widgets.Control;

 9  public class AppMenuListener implements IMenuListener {          (l. 204)→
10    public void menuAboutToShow(menuManager) {                     (l. 205)→
11      Separator separator = new Separator(String)||(); //REPEAT    (l. 215, l. 217)→
12      menuManager.add(separator)||(appAction); //REPEAT       (l. 213-l. 215, l. 217)→
13    }
14  }

15  public class AppAction extends Action {                          (l. 220, l. 225)→
16  }

17  public class SomeClass {
18    public void someMethod() {
19      Viewer viewer = ...;
20      Control control = viewer.getControl(); //MAY REPEAT          (l. 208, l. 209)→
21      AppAction appAction = new AppAction(); //MAY REPEAT          (l. 220, l. 225)→
22      appAction.setText(String); //MAY REPEAT                      (l. 223, l. 228)→
23      appAction.setToolTipText(String); //MAY REPEAT               (l. 224, l. 229)→
24      MenuManager menuManager = new MenuManager(String)||(String,String)||();  (l. 202)→
25      menuManager.setRemoveAllWhenShown(boolean);                  (l. 203)→
26      AppMenuListener appMenuListener = new AppMenuListener();     (l. 204)→
27      menuManager.addMenuListener(appMenuListener);                (l. 204)→
28      Menu menu = menuManager.createContextMenu(control);          (l. 208)→
29    }
30  }
```

Fig. 2. A sample implementation template extracted for the concept context menu

AppAction is both defined (l. 15) and instantiated (l. 21) in the application code; however, JFace's design stipulates the creation of subclasses of the API-defined class Action in the application code. In addition to the basic implementation steps, the template also reflects (i) call nesting, e.g., add() is called directly or indirectly by menuAboutToShow() (l. 12); (ii) call order, e.g., the menu listener is added to the menu manager (l. 27) before creating the menu (l. 28); and (iii) parameter passing patterns, e.g., the control object passed to the menu creation method (l. 28) is obtained by a prior call to getControl() (l. 20). The comments REPEAT and MAY REPEAT indicate that the commented step appeared more than once in every or some of the traces used to generate the template, respectively.

Templates are rendered in ordinary Java with two main exceptions. First, the code uses the notation '||' to show that a method with a given name was called with different argument types. For example, add(separator)||(appAction) (l. 12 in Figure 2) is due to multiple calls to add() with different arguments (l. 213 and 215 in Figure 1). Second, what appears to be a local variable declaration in Java, such as appAction (l. 21), actually has global meaning in the template. For that reason, appAction can be used as a method argument in another method scope (l. 12).

A template extracted by FUDA is an approximation of the necessary implementation steps, and it can be incomplete or unsound or both. In particular, implementation

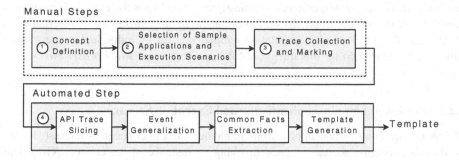

Fig. 3. FUDA overview

steps can be missing (*false negatives*) or unrelated steps (*false positives*) can be present in some cases. Given two traces, FUDA will filter out any steps that are not common to both traces. If a necessary implementation step, say component registration, can be achieved in more than one way, e.g., by calling different methods, such a step may get filtered out. Furthermore, FUDA relies on the assumption that input traces show the execution of the concept of interest in different contexts. For example, `SampleView`, which uses `TreeViewer`, and `Console` provide entirely different contexts for the context menu. In contrast, a template generated from `SampleView` and a view containing a `TableViewer`, which is graphically different from the `TreeViewer` of the `SampleView`, would also contain calls to `setContentProvider` and `setLabelProvider`. Although the calls to these two methods are not related to the context menu, they are contained both in code instantiating `TreeViewer` and in code instantiating `TableViewer`. Finally, some implementation details are still missing in a template. For example, although the calls in lines 21–23 are marked as candidates to be repeated, the template does not reflect that they should be repeated as a block, rather than individually. Nevertheless, the user can still extract the missing details from the actual sample code. The traceability links between the implementation steps in the template and the corresponding steps in the application code, as shown in Figure 2, can support this task.

4   The FUDA Template Extraction Approach

From a user perspective, FUDA's process consists of the four steps depicted in Figure 3. The first three steps are performed manually by the user; the last one is a composition of several automated sub-steps. We describe each step in detail next.

4.1   Concept Definition

A framework-provided concept may be implemented by one or more objects. FUDA can produce implementation templates covering the entire life cycle of a concept, which involves concept creation (creating and setting up its implementation objects), concept invocations (calling the objects) and concept destruction (tearing down and disposing the objects). The following *concept-defining question* asks for the entire life cycle of a concept: "*How does one implement a context menu in an Eclipse view?*" Alternatively, FUDA can also produce implementation templates covering individual concept invocations, as exemplified by this question: "*What events occur when a user clicks on a figure?*"

4.2   Selection of Sample Application(s) and Execution Scenarios

FUDA requires one or two applications implementing the concept of interest. It also needs two execution scenarios, each invoking an instance of the concept. Graphical concepts can be directly invoked, but FUDA is also applicable to non-graphical frameworks, as long as the concept of interest can be explicitly invoked from the sample applications' graphical or programmatic user interface.

The applications and the scenarios should be selected to achieve one or more of the following goals: (1) The scenarios are concept-focused: ideally the majority of the executed instructions are part of the concept. (2) The concept is invoked separately from others as part of the scenario and the invocation can be explicitly marked. (3) Each concept instance is invoked in a different context. A single application may already support the third goal, e.g., an application implementing a context menu in two different views would suffice. Because FUDA works by intersecting traces of the different executions, the more the contexts differ, the lower the possibility of false positives. For the same reason, it is important to select scenarios that contain a similar variant of the concept, which minimizes false negatives. For example, if a variant of the context menu concept with a separator is desired, scenarios that contain separators should be selected.

4.3   Trace Collection and Marking

This step involves running each sample application under a *tracer* and invoking the concept of interest. The user specifies the package(s) in which the framework resides, e.g., `org.eclipse.jface.*` for the context menu, and the package(s) in which the application resides. The tracer logs all calls that occur at the boundary between the application and the framework, which results in a *framework API interaction trace*, called *API trace* for short. If possible, pinpointing the moments before and after the concept invocation will improve the template extraction results, which is in fact essential for concepts whose defining question deals with the response to an event. For the context menu example, pinpointing amounts to instructing the tracer to *mark* subsequent events right before opening the menu and instructing it to stop marking right after the menu is open. If the moments before and after concept invocation cannot be pinpointed, the whole trace is marked. Concepts invoked through a programmatic interface can use the tracer tool to indicate the begin and end of the concept execution.

The API trace consists of *API interaction events*, which are runtime events corresponding to method or constructor calls executed at the boundary between the framework and application code. This boundary consists of (1) all calls to application methods and constructors that are framework-stipulated and (2) calls to API-defined methods and constructors from within the application. Each event has one of two directions: (1) an event is *outgoing* iff the call is made from within the application code;

e_1 ↑null:WelcomeWindow.<init>():1
e_2 ↑1:WelcomeWindow.open():2
e_3 ↓1:jface.window.Window.createContents(3):3
e_4 ↑1:WelcomeWindow.getShell():3
e_5 ↑null:jface.viewers.TreeViewer.<init>(4,5):6
e_6 ↑null:SampleView$ViewContentProvider.<init>(7):8
e_7 ↑6:jface.viewers.TreeViewer.setContentProvider(8):V
e_8 ↑null:SampleView$ViewLabelProvider.<init>(7):9
e_9 ↑6:jface.viewers.TreeViewer.setLabelProvider(9):V
e_{10} ↑6:jface.viewers.TreeViewer.setInput(10):V
e_{11} ↓8:jface.viewers.IContentProvider.inputChanged(6,10):V
e_{12} ↓8:jface.viewers.IStructuredContentProvider.getElements(10):11
e_{13} ↑8:SampleView$ViewContentProvider.getChildren(12):11
e_{14} ↓9:jface.viewers.ILabelProvider.getText(13):14
e_{15} ↓9:jface.viewers.ILabelProvider.getImage(13):15
e_{16} ↓8:jface.viewers.ITreeContentProvider.hasChildren(13):16
•e_{17} ↑null:SampleView$2.<init>(7):17
•e_{18} ↑17:jface.action.Action.setText(18):V
•e_{19} ↑17:jface.action.Action.setToolTipText(19)·V
•e_{20} ↑null:SampleView$3.<init>(7):21
•e_{21} ↑21:jface.action.Action.setText(22):V
•e_{22} ↑21:jface.action.Action.setToolTipText(23):V
•e_{23} ↑null:jface.action.MenuManager.<init>(24):25
•e_{24} ↑25:jface.action.MenuManager.setRemoveAllWhenShown(26):V
•e_{25} ↑null:SampleView$1.<init>(7):27
•e_{26} ↑25:jface.action.MenuManager.addMenuListener(27):V
•e_{27} ↑6:jface.viewers.TreeViewer.getControl():28
•e_{28} ↑25:jface.action.MenuManager.createContextMenu(28):29
•e_{29} ↑6:jface.viewers.TreeViewer.getControl():28
•e_{30} ↑6:jface.viewers.TreeViewer.getControl():28
•e_{31} **↓27:jface.action.IMenuListener.menuAboutToShow(25):V**
•e_{32} **↑25:jface.action.IMenuManager.add(17):V**
•e_{33} **↑25:jface.action.IMenuManager.add(21):V**
•e_{34} **↑null:jface.action.Separator.<init>():30**
•e_{35} **↑25:jface.action.IMenuManager.add(30):V**
e_{36} ↓8:jface.viewers.ITreeContentProvider.hasChildren(13):31
e_{37} ↓8:jface.viewers.ITreeContentProvider.hasChildren(13):32
•e_{38} **↑null:jface.action.Separator.<init>(33):34**
•e_{39} **↑25:jface.action.IMenuManager.add(34):V**
e_{40} ↓8:jface.viewers.IContentProvider.inputChanged(6,10):V
e_{41} ↓8:jface.viewers.IContentProvider.dispose():V
e_{42} ↑1:WelcomeWindow.close():35

Fig. 4. Framework API interaction trace

and (2) an event is *incoming* iff the call is made from within the framework code, i.e., a callback.

The complete API trace produced by running SampleView from Figure 1 and invoking its context menu is shown in Figure 4. Events are denoted as $D \ O{:}n(P){:}R$, where D represents the direction of the event, with "↓" for incoming and "↑" for outgoing events; O is the target object's ID or "null" for constructor and static method calls; n represents the fully qualified name of the target method or constructor; P is a list of IDs of objects passed as parameters; and R is the ID of the returned object or "V" if the return type is void. For brevity, the package prefix org.eclipse was removed from n for all JFace events. The events in bold face are those that were marked by informing the tracer about the moments just before and after the context menu was invoked.

Most of the events in Figure 4 can easily be traced back to their corresponding code lines in Figure 1. The events e_1–e_{30} are generated when the createPartControl()

is called, e.g., e_1 is due to line 191. The actual call to `createPartControl()` is not traced because it resides in `eclipse.ui`, which is not part of JFace. The calls in l. 209 and l. 210 are not traced for the same reason. Indentation denotes *event nesting*. For example, events e_3 and e_4 were generated in the control flow of the call to `welcomeWindow.open()` (l. 192). Anonymous classes are denoted by numbers separated from their host classes by \$, e.g., e_{17} constructs `action1` (l. 220).

The marked events (in bold face) were generated by the callback to `menuAboutTo-Show()`, which is called by JFace when a menu is being opened. That method calls `fillContextMenu()`, which generates the nested events e_{32}–e_{39}. The incoming events e_{36}–e_{37} are generated by the method called in l. 216, which is not part of JFace and thus not traced. The last three events, e_{40}–e_{42}, are generated during cleanup (code not shown).

4.4 Automated Trace Processing

The automated trace processing stage receives two or more of the collected traces and generates a concept implementation template. It consists of the following steps.

API Trace Slicing. The marked trace region (bold face) in Figure 4 contains the calls that occurred when the context menu was being opened. Selective marking improves the results by delimiting the interaction between application and framework that is relevant for the concept of interest. If the goal is to understand the complete life cycle of the concept, however, it is necessary also to consider calls related to the initialization and clean-up of the involved objects, which are not reflected in this marked region. For example, e_{17}–e_{22} create and initialize the context menu's actions.

We use *API trace slicing* to identify these additional calls based on the marked region. API trace slicing identifies all the unmarked calls in the input trace that involve any of the objects that are also involved in a marked call. The precise definition is based on the *object-connectedness* of two events. The two events $e_i = D_i \ O_i{:}n_i(P_i){:}R_i$ and $e_j = D_j \ O_j{:}n_j(P_j){:}R_j$ are object-connected iff they share any target, parameter, or returned objects, i.e., $(\{O_i, R_i\} \cup P_i) \cap (\{O_j, R_j\} \cup P_j) \setminus \{\text{null}, \text{V}\} \neq \emptyset$. Also, let *object-relatedness* be the transitive closure of object-connectedness. Then, a trace slice is defined as the portion of the input trace consisting of all the marked events and the unmarked events that are object-related to the marked events. In Figure 4, the unmarked events that are object-related to the marked ones are typeset in italic font. For example, e_5 is object-connected to e_7 through the object with ID 6, and e_7 is object-connected to e_{36} through object 8. Consequently, e_5 is object-related to the marked event e_{36} and thus part of the slice. Note that slicing eliminates the steps implementing the Welcome window (e_2–e_4, e_{42}), which are unrelated to the context menu. As can be seen in Figure 4, API trace slicing is an approximation of the actual dependencies between API calls. The approximation worked perfectly for the real framework APIs in our evaluation (Section 5), however: there was not a single false negative due to slicing. Slicing is optional since some concepts focus on the invocation only, in which case no slicing is needed and only the marked events are further processed. Also, if marking is not used, FUDA will process the entire trace.

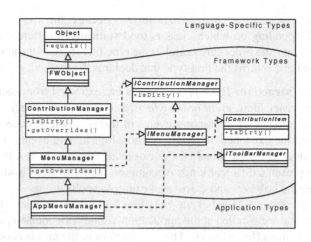

Fig. 5. Boundaries of application, framework, and language-specific types

Event Generalization. The generalization procedure allows the next processing stage to compare traces in terms of framework API types. This procedure is a static analysis that replaces the application-specific names of events with appropriate framework names. For example, the fully qualified name of e_6 in Figure 4 (SampleView$-ViewContentProvider.<init>) is application-specific and generalization replaces it by [jface.viewers.IStructuredContentProvider, jface.-viewers.ITreeContentProvider].<init>. The two names in brackets refer to the framework interfaces that ViewContentProvider implements (l. 99). Event generalization treats calls to instance methods, constructors, and static methods differently. We will explain it using Figure 5, which shows some menu-related classes.

Instance Methods. When generalizing an instance method call, the procedure aims at maximum generality and searches for the topmost types that declare the method. For example, the method equals in Java is declared by Object and although the method may be implemented in many subclasses, it conceptually belongs to Object. A method may have multiple topmost types. For example, generalization of a call to AppMenuManager.isDirty() identifies both IContributionManager and IContributionItem as topmost types since both interfaces declare the method.

Constructors. An application class may specialize many framework and application-specific types. For constructor calls, the procedure aims at minimum generality and selects all framework-defined supertypes of the target application class that are located at the bottom framework borderline of the type hierarchy. For example, for a call to the constructor of AppMenuManager, the procedure identifies MenuManager and IToolBarManager as the generalized framework types. The rationale for minimum generalization for constructors is that selecting the topmost types, even if only topmost *framework* types, would lose too much information. For example, assuming that all framework classes are derived from FWObject, the latter approach would yield FWObject for every constructor call to a subclass of a framework class.

Static Methods. Although a static method cannot be polymorphically called, it can be hidden by an equally named static method in a subclass. For example, in Figure 5, both

`MenuManager` and `ContributionManager` declare the `getOverrides()` static method. Depending on which class is used statically, a different method is really being used. Thus, the procedure searches the type hierarchy of the application class being instantiated and returns the first type that declares the method.

Common Facts Extraction. Three types of facts are extracted from each generalized trace: *event occurrence facts*, *event nesting facts*, and *event dependency facts*. The first represents the occurrence of interaction events in the generalized trace, while the remaining represent the existence of certain relationships among events. Then, *common facts* are computed as intersections of the extracted fact sets across the generalized traces. Figure 6 presents different kinds of common facts extracted from two generalized traces for `SampleView` and `Console` example applications.

Event occurrence facts, called *event facts* for short, are the names of the methods and constructors that were called at the application-framework boundary and the corresponding call directions (Figure 6(a)). They abstract away the numbers of occurrences, object IDs, and parameter and return types of the corresponding calls. The rationale is that two methods with the same name but different parameter or return types or numbers of parameters are likely to be conceptually equivalent within an API. An event fact D $t.n$, where t is a type name, is extracted from a generalized trace iff the trace contains one or more events D $O_i:[\ldots,t,\ldots].n:R_i$, where O_i is any object ID or "null" and R_i is any object ID or "V". We say that the events *match* such an event fact. For example, a_2 is extracted from the generalized trace due to its events corresponding to e_{18} or e_{21} in Figure 4. The events in Figure 4 that match the common event facts in Figure 6(a) are marked by •. The remaining events are effectively filtered out as they were unique to this trace.

Event nesting facts record the calling context for outgoing calls (Figure 6(b)). A nesting fact $a_i \rightarrow a_j$, where a_i and a_j are event facts, is produced whenever the generalized trace contains two events e_k and e_l such that (i) e_k and e_l match a_i and a_j, respectively; (ii) e_l is outgoing; and (iii) e_l is directly nested in e_k in the trace.

Event dependency facts represent call sequence and object passing patterns. There are nine dependency fact types: target-target (TT), target-parameter (TP), target-return (TR), parameter-target (PT), parameter-parameter (PP), parameter-return (PR), return-target (RT), return-parameter (RP), and return-return (RR). A target-target dependency fact $TT(a_i, a_j)$, where a_i and a_j are event facts, is produced whenever the generalized trace contains two events e_k and e_l such that (i) e_k and e_l match a_i and a_j, respectively; (ii) e_k precedes e_l in the trace; and (iii) both e_k and e_l have the same object as target. The analogous definitions for the remaining dependency fact types are obtained by modifying the third condition. For example, if the return object ID of e_k is used as a parameter in e_l, the resulting fact type is $RP(a_i, a_j)$. Dependency facts indicate sharing of objects and object passing; e.g., PR and TR may represent the registration of an object with a framework and subsequent retrieval. After the common facts are computed, the event facts that originated from the same generic events (because of multiple type names due to generalization) are collapsed and the affected common nesting and dependency facts are updated accordingly.

Template Generation. This section sketches the main steps of the template generation algorithm. Interested readers can refer to [6] for further details. The inputs to the

a_1 ↑jface.action.Action.<init>
a_2 ↑jface.action.IAction.setText
a_3 ↑jface.action.IAction.setToolTipText
a_4 ↑jface.action.MenuManager.<init>
a_5 ↑jface.action.IMenuManager.setRemoveAllWhenShown
a_6 ↑jface.action.IMenuListener.<init>
a_7 ↑jface.action.IMenuManager.addMenuListener
a_8 ↑jface.viewers.Viewer.getControl
a_9 ↑jface.action.MenuManager.createContextMenu
a_{10} ↓jface.action.IMenuListener.menuAboutToShow
a_{11} ↑jface.action.Separator.<init>
a_{12} ↑jface.action.IContributionManager.add

(a) Common event occurrence facts

$a_{10} \rightarrow a_{11}$
$a_{10} \rightarrow a_{12}$

(b) Common nesting facts

$RT(a_1, a_2)$	$RT(a_1, a_3)$	$RP(a_1, a_{12})$	$TT(a_2, a_3)$
$TP(a_2, a_{12})$	$TP(a_3, a_{12})$	$RT(a_4, a_5)$	$RT(a_4, a_7)$
$RP(a_4, a_{10})$	$RT(a_4, a_{12})$	$RT(a_4, a_9)$	$TT(a_5, a_7)$
$TT(a_5, a_9)$	$TP(a_5, a_{10})$	$TT(a_5, a_{12})$	$RP(a_6, a_7)$
$RT(a_6, a_{10})$	$TT(a_7, a_9)$	$PT(a_7, a_{10})$	$TP(a_7, a_{10})$
$TT(a_7, a_{12})$	$RP(a_8, a_9)$	$TP(a_9, a_{10})$	$TT(a_9, a_{12})$
$PT(a_{10}, a_{12})$	$RP(a_{11}, a_{12})$		

(c) Common dependency facts

Fig. 6. Common facts

algorithm are the three sets of common facts and the generalized traces. The common facts determine the overall structure of the template, and the traces are used to extract additional details as needed. The algorithm executes the following steps.

Create Classes. A class is created for each group of incoming event facts that are related by TT dependencies. The corresponding constructor calls are assigned using RT dependencies. For example, the class in l. 9 (Figure 2) is created for the fact a_{10}, which does not participate in any TT dependencies and thus forms its own group. The corresponding constructor call is a_6, due to $RT(a_6, a_{10})$. The remaining unassigned constructor calls for abstract classes or interfaces, which occur when instantiating anonymous classes, are grouped through RR dependencies and a class is created for each such group. For example, the class in l. 15 is created for a_1, a call to the constructor of the abstract class `Action`.

Create Methods and Constructors. For each incoming event fact assigned to a class in the previous step, a method is created in that class. For example, the method in l. 10 is created for a_{10}. A constructor is created in a class if nesting facts whose source is any of the constructor calls assigned to that class are present.

Create Statements. Outgoing calls are placed in methods based on the common nesting facts. For example, the nesting fact $a_{10} \rightarrow a_{12}$ places the call in l. 12. The generalized traces are then consulted to see whether the calls are repeated in a given calling context. For instance, the call to a_{12} is marked as REPEAT since a_{12} was called multiple times in every trace within the control flow of `menuAboutToShow()`. The additional class `SomeClass` (l. 17) is created to host calls corresponding to outgoing event facts for which no calling contexts are specified by the nesting facts. Within each method, calls are sorted in an order determined by the dependency facts. For example, the call order in the context menu template was obtained as a topological sort on the graph with event facts as nodes and the dependency facts as directed edges. Since multiple calls to a given method are collapsed in a single event fact, dependency facts may form cycles, in which case only a subset of the calls can be sorted. The calls that cannot be sorted according to the dependencies are listed in an arbitrary order and the user is warned.

Identify Supertypes. Superclass and interfaces for each class (except `SomeClass`) are determined by constructing a type hierarchy of target types of incoming method and constructor calls assigned to that class. The leaves of this type hierarchy identify the superclass and the interfaces for that class.

Generate Class and Variable Names. Each class is named by prepending `App` to its superclass name or one of its interface names if no superclass is present. Constructor calls and method calls whose return types are not void are made initializers of variable declarations. Variables are then given names that are the same as their types, but in lower case, e.g., `appAction` in l. 21 and `menu` in l. 28.

Broadcast Variables. The dependency facts, except RR, are used to identify object passing between calls. For example, `appAction` is passed as a parameter to `add` in l. 12 because of $RP(a_1,a_{12})$. New variables are introduced as needed. The notation ' | | ' is used to illustrate different argument types passed to a method or constructor call, e.g., in l. 12. Parameter objects of framework-stipulated types that were not returned by any other calls are provided by dummy declarations as in l. 19.

Identify Imports. Package imports are identified based on the fully qualified type names of the event facts.

5   Evaluation

The approach was evaluated through an experiment to assess the template extraction process (Section 5.1) and an additional experiment to analyze the usage of templates in the implementation of framework-provided concepts (Section 5.2).

5.1   Evaluation of Template Extraction

Experimental Design. This evaluation was designed to verify that *FUDA can extract templates with high precision and recall from only two traces and two sample applications*. We aim at keeping the number of traces per concept as small as possible since the collection of traces represents manual effort. In particular, the installation and execution of sample applications can be cumbersome. Also, in an earlier experiment [7] we showed that additional applications cause templates to concentrate on the minimal common implementation steps, without much improvement in terms of false positives or negatives. The evaluation consists of the following steps.

Selection of Frameworks and Concepts. The evaluation includes four widely used frameworks (Table 1). The JFace and Eclipse concepts, except Focus, were selected as representative for FUDA based on the authors' prior familiarity with these frameworks.

Table 1. Experimental data (* indicates concepts from developer forums)

Framework	Concept	Defining Question	In scope	Slicing	Frequent	Simple	Composite	Name	Source	No Slicing G	I	M	P	R	With Slicing G	I	M	P	R
JFace	Context Menu	How to implement a context menu in a view?	X	X	X	X	X	Tree View / Console	Eclipse Wizard / Eclipse UI	15	0 (4)	1 (1)	100 (73)	94 (92)	15	0 (4)	1 (1)	**100** (73)	**94** (92)
JFace	Toolbar Button	How to add a button to a view's toolbar?	X	X	X	X	X	Pkg Explorer / Crosscutting Comparison	Eclipse JDT / AJDT	18	5 (14)	3 (3)	72 (22)	81 (57)	13	1 (9)	3 (3)	**92** (31)	**80** (57)
JFace	Content Assist	How to develop a content assistant in a text editor?	X	X	–	–	X	Java editor / JSP editor	Eclipse JDT / Eclipse WTP	46	27 (30)	1 (1)	41 (35)	95 (94)	32	13 (16)	1 (1)	**59** (50)	**95** (94)
Eclipse	Table Viewer	How to develop a table viewer?	X	–	X	–	X	Editor List / Table View	eclipse-plugins / Eclipse Wizard	39	0 (23)	0 (0)	100 (41)	100 (100)	–	–	–	–	–
Eclipse	Tree Viewer	How to develop a tree viewer?	X	–	X	–	X	LDAP Brwsr / Tree View	eclipse-plugins / Eclipse wizard	45	0 (29)	1 (1)	100 (36)	98 (94)	–	–	–	–	–
Eclipse	Navigate	How to create the tree navigation buttons in a view's toolbar?	X	X	–	X	X	KTreeMap / SVN Repository	SourceForge / Subclipse	40	10 (20)	0 (0)	75 (50)	100 (100)	38	8 (18)	0 (0)	**79** (53)	**100** (100)
Eclipse	Focus*	What events happen by clicking on a view's titlebar?	X	–	X	X	–	LDAP Brwsr / Editor List	eclipse-plugins / eclipse-plugins	4	0 (0)	0 (0)	100 (100)	100 (100)	–	–	–	–	–
GEF	Select*	What events happen by clicking on a figure?	X	–	X	X	–	Flow / Shapes	GEF Examples / GEF Examples	7	0 (3)	0 (0)	100 (57)	100 (100)	–	–	–	–	–
GEF	Figure*	How to draw a figure in a GEF editor?	X	X	X	–	X	Flow / Shapes	GEF Examples / GEF Examples	83	25 (75)	0 (0)	70 (10)	100 (100)	68	10 (60)	0 (0)	**85** (12)	**100** (100)
GEF	Connection*	How to draw a connection between two figures?	X	X	X	–	X	Flow / Shapes	GEF Examples / GEF Examples	91	26 (82)	0 (0)	71 (10)	100 (100)	76	10 (66)	0 (0)	**87** (13)	**100** (100)
GEF	Title-Bar Color*	How to change the color of a GEF editor's title-bar?	–	–	–	X	–	–	–	–	–	–	–	–	–	–	–	–	–
Java 2D	Moving Shapes*	How to draw shapes and let the user drag them?	X	X	X	X	X	GTEditor / GeoSoft	Google Code / Google Search	25	7 (16)	4 (4)	72 (36)	82 (69)	18	3 (9)	4 (4)	**83** (50)	**79** (69)
Java 2D	Circle Drawing*	How to draw a red circle on a black background	X	X	X	X	X	JHotDraw / Scribble	SourceForge / Google Search	12	4 (9)	0 (0)	67 (25)	100 (100)	10	2 (7)	0 (0)	**80** (30)	**100** (100)
Java 2D	Rounded Image*	How to make the corners of an image rounded?	–	–	X	X	–	–	–	–	–	–	–	–	–	–	–	–	–

G: Template size; I: Num of false positives; M: Num of false negatives; P: Precision; R: Recall.

The remaining concepts (i.e., their defining questions) were sampled from developer forums of the respective frameworks and FUDA steps were performed for them without much prior knowledge of the corresponding frameworks.

The concepts were selected to cover a variety of characteristics, namely being *in scope* of FUDA's intended usage or not, requiring *slicing* or not, being *frequent* among existing applications or *rare*, being *simple* or *complex* in terms of implementation complexity measured as template size, or being *composite* in the sense of consisting of several variable subsets of implementation steps or *atomic*, if only a fixed set of steps is involved.

Tree Viewer and Table Viewer are the concepts in Table 1 where slicing was not used since the scenario involving view opening and closing spanned the entire view life cycle. Thanks to trace slicing, FUDA also works well for concepts having life cycles spanning beyond the marked trace region, which are those shown with "X" in the Slicing column. We also included two concepts, Focus and Select, for which only the marked region is used since the defining question asked for the response to an event. Obviously, FUDA works best for frequent concepts, in which case finding sample applications is likely easy. It may be applicable to rare concepts, too, if the user has already identified one or two applications with appropriate execution scenarios. For example, users may apply FUDA to find out the implementation of a rare concept that caught their eye in an existing application. Also, concepts that may appear rare at first might not be rare after all. For example, the choice of red and black in Circle Drawing may be rare, but setting background and figure colors is not. Most of the considered concepts are composite as they include variable parts. For example, a context menu may or may not include a separator. Concepts with only few implementation steps tend to be atomic and more complex ones are usually composite. Finally, Rounded Image and Title-Bar Color are out of scope because it is very unlikely to find applications and scenarios satisfying the three goals from Section 4.2 for them.

Selection of Applications and Execution Scenarios. The sample applications come from different sources (Table 1), such as framework-packaged examples for Eclipse's Graphical Editing Framework (GEF), applications listed in online repositories, e.g., `eclipse-plugins.org`, or part of a larger familiar environment, e.g., Java Development Tools (JDT). Application selection involved (i) reliance on prior familiarity with a given application (mostly for JFace and Eclipse), (ii) browsing and running the standard examples (e.g., GEF), (iii) searching or browsing in application repositories (e.g., GTEditor for Moving Shapes was identified on Google Code by the search keyword "shape" and seeing a screenshot of a drawing editor), or (iv) tips by others (e.g., WTP was suggested by a colleague). Selecting the applications for each concept took anywhere from no time for Eclipse JDT or wizards thanks to prior familiarity to up to an hour of searching and browsing for `eclipse-plugins.org` or `SourceForge.net`. The selection process had a significant learning effect: familiarity with framework-packaged examples or applications inspected for a given concept significantly reduced the selection time for the next concept. Some execution scenarios were already specified by the defining questions, e.g., *"How does one draw a figure in a GEF editor?"* In other cases, an action invoking the concept of interest had to be identified, e.g., the opening action for Context Menu.

Trace Collection. The tracer used to collect the traces was implemented using AspectJ. The user had to specify the packages in which the framework of interest and the sample application reside. All concepts in Table 1 involved trace marking, except Tree Viewer and Table Viewer for which full traces were used. Note that only the calls at the application-framework boundary are traced, which are drastically fewer than all the calls involved in the implementation of a concept. As a result, API tracing is quite efficient. For example, tracing all of GEF (`org.eclipse.gef.*`) was almost unnoticeable when using GEF applications on a laptop with a single-core Pentium M 1.6MHz processor, 1GB of RAM, and Windows XP. The applications ran two to three times slower when all of Eclipse was traced (`org.eclipse.*`), however. Collecting a single trace took anywhere from several seconds to a few minutes.

Template Generation. The template extraction algorithms described in this paper were implemented as an Eclipse plug-in. This tool was then used to generate the templates.

Development of Reference Templates. The precision and recall of the generated templates were calculated against reference templates. For each concept in scope a *mandatory* and an *optional* reference template were created. Mandatory reference templates represent the set of mandatory implementation steps, i.e., the ones that are essential to the instantiation of a concept: if the step is removed, the concept does not work as expected. For example, without calling the method `createContextMenu()` (l. 28 in Figure 2) a context menu cannot be realized. For concepts that relate to the response to an event, such as Focus and Select, the mandatory steps are the ones that always occur as a result to the event. Optional reference templates additionally include steps that are not essential but that are relevant to the concept and were present in the sample applications. For instance, Context Menu's optional reference template includes calls to create and register separators.

Reference templates were carefully created to minimize threats to the validity of the results. For all concepts, reference templates were created using documentation found online (usually third-party articles or solutions posted in forums or both) and manually inspecting sample applications. In order to guarantee their correctness, reference templates were used in the creation of sample implementations. The determination of mandatory steps was mostly obvious; dubious cases were verified by removing the step from the sample implementation and testing. Reference templates were then compared against the generated ones to identify optional features present in the sample applications. Each non-mandatory step found in the generated template was examined and classified as optional, if it was relevant to the concept, or *irrelevant*, otherwise. If not clear, we were conservative and the step was considered irrelevant.

Calculation of Precision and Recall. The calculation of precision and recall is based on counting the basic implementation steps contained in a template: subclass declarations, interface implementation declarations, method implementations (except `some-Method()`), method calls, and constructor calls. These steps are the main elements of a template. Call sequence and parameter passing patterns are considered supplementary information that makes templates more readable. The calculation of precision and recall is based on determining three numbers: G is the number of all implementation steps in the generated template; (ii) M is the number of steps present in the reference template but missing in the generated template (i.e., false negatives); and (iii) I is the number of steps incorrectly present in the generated template, but absent in the reference template (i.e., false positives). Precision is calculated as $P = (G - I)/G$, and *recall* is calculated as $R = (G - I)/(G - I + M)$.

Experimental Results. The precision and recall results are given in Table 1. For the concepts with slicing, we also include the numbers obtained by using full traces without slicing, for comparison. The final numbers are marked in bold, with precision ranging between 59% and 100% and recall ranging between 79% and 100% when optional reference templates are used. When mandatory reference templates are used (in parentheses), precision ranges between 12% and 100%, and recall ranges between 57% and 100%. Note that users are likely interested in templates similar to optional reference templates; the mandatory reference templates are used to establish a lower bound on the precision and recall. In the following, we concentrate on the results for optional reference templates.

In general, false positives were more frequent than false negatives. False positives were due to similarities among the sample applications that extend beyond the concept of interest. For example, the single false positive for Toolbar Button was due to calls to the method `IShellProvider.getShell()`, which are frequently used in Eclipse views. Slicing improved precision by eliminating between 20% and 80% of false positives, except for Context Menu, for which the sample applications were different enough to achieve 100% precision without slicing. Slicing was particularly useful for Figure and Connection since all GEF editors use common parts such as palette and action bar. While steps related to action bar were eliminated by slicing, some palette-related steps remained since palette was involved in all figure drawing scenarios.

The false negatives for JFace concepts represent the case when the user does not correctly identify the framework packages. For instance, for the concept Context Menu, the instruction `setMenu()` (l. 209 in Figure 4) is missing because it is in the Eclipse framework, not in JFace. The only false negative for the concept Tree Viewer was the method `getChildren()`: since the collected traces included only the outgoing calls to this method and not any incoming calls, the generated template did not contain this method as one that needs to be implemented. Two of the false negatives for Moving Shapes were caused by a limitation of AspectJ, which cannot introduce code into `java.awt.*` packages or any other package belonging to the Java runtime library. The other two false negatives for this concept were due to different instructions that our sample applications used to change the location of a shape. Similarly, although we did not have any false negatives for Circle Drawing, the analysis revealed that one false negative was likely. The reason is that there are multiple ways of implementing circle drawing, e.g., using `drawOval()` or `draw(new Ellipse)`, and the difference between these calls is not visible to the application user.

Threats to Validity. We see three main threats to validity. First, the selection of frameworks and concepts for the evaluation might not be representative of those used in real-world development. This threat is addressed by selecting frameworks that are widely used, by including concepts from developer forums, and selecting concepts with different properties. Second, the selection of applications and execution traces might not be representative. We minimize this threat by following the same identification strategies that would be applied in practice and use a mix of them in the evaluation. Third, the reference templates could be incorrect, which would impact the calculation of precision and recall values. We minimized this threat by (i) using three sources of knowledge for all concepts: manual inspection of sample applications, consulting existing documentation, and testing the implementation steps in sample implementations; (ii) having two of the authors independently check in several iterations the correctness of all the reference templates and the values calculated for precisions and recalls; and (iii) reporting not only the values for the comparison with the optional reference templates, but also to the mandatory reference templates.

5.2 Evaluation of Template Usage

Experimental Design. The previous experiment showed that implementation templates can be extracted from sample applications with high precision and recall. This experiment was designed to go further and evaluate the following research questions: (i) Are implementation templates as effective as framework documentation in aiding the development of framework-provided concepts? The rationale behind this question is that if templates are as effective as framework documentation, then they can serve as a substitute when no documentation is available. (ii) What is the influence of template quality and its usage strategies on the quality of resulting implementations? For instance, if templates are simply pasted into target applications, its false positives could pollute implementations with undesired code, and its false negatives could yield incomplete implementations.

Hypothesis and Measures. The experiment was designed to provide quantitative and qualitative evidence regarding the first research question, and qualitative data concerning the second question. Developers were recruited and asked to implement framework-provided concepts using one of the documentation aids, i.e., framework documentation or template. To answer the first research question, the effectiveness of each documentation aid was measured in terms of development time and functional correctness of resulting implementations. We defined three levels of functional correctness: *success*, if the resulting implementation behaved as specified; *buggy*, if the implementation did not perform as specified; and *incomplete*, if the developer did not finish the implementation. Since we had no expectations as to which documentation aid is superior we formulated the following two-sided null hypothesis:

H_0 : *The development time to implement a framework-provided concept supported by implementation templates equals the development time when supported by framework documentation.*

After the completion of the implementation, developers answered a questionnaire and went through a debriefing interview. To answer the second research question, this data was used to determine how developers employed the information contained in documentation and templates (usage strategies). We then analyzed how templates' quality and usage strategies affect the functional correctness of resulting implementations.

Procedure and Data Collection. We selected two simple concepts (Context Menu and Navigate) and two complex concepts (Content Assist and Table Viewer) that were used in the previous experiment (Table 1). We recruited twelve subjects: nine graduate students (S_1-S_6, S_8-S_{10}), two professionals (S_7, S_{12}), and one 4th-year undergraduate student (S_{11}). Before the experiment, subjects answered a background questionnaire to determine their experience. All subjects had between 4 and 10 years of Java programming experience and all subjects except subject S_8 had at least one year of industrial programming experience. The subjects were blocked into two groups depending on their experience levels with the JFace and Eclipse frameworks: subjects in the *experienced* group (S_1-S_6) had implemented both frequent concepts before (Context Menu and Table Viewer), but not the rare ones (Navigate and Content Assist); subjects in the *moderate* group (S_7-S_{12}) had not previously implemented any of the four concepts. All subjects were given a briefing about implementation templates. In this briefing, we focused on the information available in templates, but let subjects freely decide how to use it in their implementations.

The experiment used three independent variables with two factor levels each: *documentation aid* (framework documentation (D) and implementation template (T)), *concept complexity* (simple and complex) and *subject experience* (moderate and experienced). The templates used in the experiment were those automatically extracted in the first study (Table 1). The documentation for a given concept was identified in Eclipse Help, Eclipse Corner Articles[1], or third-party Eclipse articles (web search). The documentation length varied between 5 pages (for Navigate) and 28 pages (for Content Assist). Each document had a dedicated section for the concept of interest and included code examples. Each subject was assigned one simple and one complex concept, and used a template for implementing one concept and documentation for the other concept (in a balanced sequence). The experienced subjects were assigned the rare concepts and the moderate subjects were assigned the frequent concepts; however, the assignment was random and balanced over the simple and complex concepts within each subject group. For each concept, a concept instance specification and a target application were created. Each specification consisted of a screenshot showing the desired concept to be implemented and a short paragraph describing it. Each target application was of minimal size, ranging between 10 (for Content Assist) and 186 LOC (for Navigate), to help developers focus on implementing the assigned concept instead of navigating and investigating the target applications.

The subjects were asked to implement the specified concept instance within the corresponding target application. During the implementation, the only documentation aids the subjects could use were the respective documentation aid (D or T), the two sample applications for a given concept (Table 1), and the framework-provided JavaDoc documentation. In particular, they could not use Eclipse Help or search the web. Note that JavaDoc documentation does not explain how to implement concepts, but only how to use a given framework-provided programming element, such as an interface or a method. The sizes of the sample applications varied between 1 KLOC (EditorList for Table Viewer) and 66 KLOC (Subclipse for Navigate). The subjects were instructed to implement each assigned concept without interruptions and measure the time needed.

After the implementation, subjects filled a result questionnaire, asking whether the provided documentation aid was useful; how many of the sample applications were used; and how the templates could be improved. Finally, we tested and inspected the subjects' code to determine whether each concept was correctly implemented.

---

[1] http://www.eclipse.org/articles/

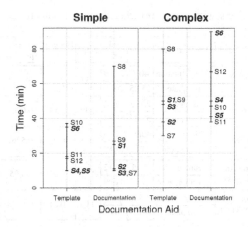

Fig. 7. Experimental results

Data Analysis. The qualitative aspects of the experiment were analyzed via inspection of resulting implementations, and careful examination of questionnaires and interviews. The quantitative assessment of development time was performed through univariate statistical analyses, which were applied to each independent variable. Unpaired, two-sample, two-sided *t-tests* [8] were performed. To reduce potential threats due to violation of t-test assumptions, we also applied the non-parametric Wilcoxon rank sum test [8]. For both hypothesis tests, we set the significance level to $\alpha = 0.05$ and presented the p-value. Furthermore, we measured the effect size as the percentage difference between means (*%diff*) and by calculating Hedge's *g* [9], which is defined as the difference between means divided by the pooled standard deviation.

Experimental Results. Due to space constraints, this section summarizes the most important results. A complete description of the data can be found elsewhere [6][10].

Discussion of Quantitative Results. Figure 7 shows the time measured for each implementation as a function of the documentation aid and concept complexity. Bold labels identify experienced subjects; solid lines indicate the variance. The descriptive statistics and the results of the statistical analyses are presented in Table 2. The three initial rows present data for the independent variables and the two last rows present additional data for documentation aid when isolating the complexity levels.

The first row presents the most important quantitative experimental results. The p-values for documentation aid are not significant ($p \gg 0.05$). On average, subjects using templates took 13% less time to implement the concept than subjects using documentation. The second row presents a different picture. The choice between a simple or complex concept has an extremely significant ($p = 0.0006 \ll 0.05$) impact on development time. Complex concepts take consistently longer than simple concepts to implement (avg. 124.6%), regardless of documentation aid and experience. This outcome inspired the analysis presented in the last two rows, where we isolate the complexity levels. The results show that, within a complexity level, subjects using templates were 11% or 17% faster on average, but these two results are statistically not significant, as in the first analysis. All these trends can also be clearly verified by inspecting the diagram in

Table 2. Descriptive statistics and univariate analysis results for development time

Independent Variable	Factor Level	Mean	Std. Dev.	%diff	Hedge's g	t-test (p-value)	Wilcoxon (p-value)
Documentation Aid (All Concepts)	Documentation	40.5	25.79	-13.0	-0.22	0.5855	0.6851
	Template	35.25	20.33				
Concept Complexity	Simple	23.33	17.71	124.6	1.58	0.0006	0.0006
	Complex	52.42	17.84				
Subject Experience	Moderate	40.92	22.49	-14.9	-0.25	0.5267	0.5431
	Experienced	34.83	23.82				
Documentation Aid (Simple Concepts)	Documentation	25.5	23.12	-17.0	-0.22	0.695	1.0000
	Template	21.17	11.99				
Documentation Aid (Complex Concepts)	Documentation	55.5	19.71	-11.1	-0.31	0.5748	0.7466
	Template	49.33	17				

Figure 7, where complexity deeply impacts time, while documentation aid does not. Note that the diagram also allows the identification of individual trends (e.g., subject S_8 takes usually longer to perform the tasks).

The fact that H_0 could not be rejected with high significance in our experiment implies that no evidence could be provided regarding the difference (or equality) in effectiveness between templates and documentation when providing aid for developers to implement framework-provided concepts. The experiment shows that the impact of concept complexity is far greater than the choice of documentation aid, however, which indicates that if there is indeed difference, its impact on the development time is likely to be small.

Discussion of Qualitative Results. We first investigated the impact of templates' false positives and false negatives on the implementation. Table 1 shows the number of false positives and negatives for each template. In general, false negatives prevent the full instantiation of the concept, as in the case of Context Menu and Table Viewer. False positives either cause runtime errors (as in Content Assist) or pollute the concept instantiation with unnecessary code (as in Navigate). Further, the questionnaires and interviews allowed the determination of template usage strategies. Subjects used the templates essentially in two ways, either by pasting them directly into a target application or as an entry point to inspect sample applications. When using templates as an entry point, subjects either copied sample application code into the target application or wrote their own code based on what they learned. Some subjects who pasted templates directly into target applications also investigated sample applications before executing the code. Other subjects tried to execute the code and only investigated sample applications after a runtime error occurred or an unintended behavior appeared. Only subject S_4 pasted template code without verifying against sample applications.

The resulting implementations were executed and manually inspected. Most implementations followed the specified functional requirements and were classified as *success*. Only two were *buggy*. The task specification was not correctly followed by subject S_6 in the Content Assist (complex/documentation) implementation. Subject S_4 implemented Navigate (simple/template) with an additional button. This error arose because S_4 pasted the template code without verifying sample applications, and Navigate contained false positives that included unwanted code. This observation suggests that templates should always be used together with sample applications since they help understanding what is missing and detecting unneeded code.

Threats to Validity. The main threat to internal validity concerns the distribution of subjects over the tasks. This threat was minimized by blocking subjects according to experience and randomizing the remaining distribution. The main threat to construct validity is related to the measurement of effectiveness and the definition of documentation. We used implementation time to measure effectiveness and it is clear that different notions could be used, such as code quality, that could affect the results. The definition of documentation sought to maximize its familiarity and conciseness by selecting standard documents dedicated to the concept at hand. The principal threats to external validity refer to the generalization from students to professionals and from a laboratory to a real setting and to the small sample size. We minimized these threats by selecting a sample that resembles our target population (i.e., experienced subjects) and using realistic concepts and a state-of-the-art development environment (Eclipse JDT). Our sample of twelve subjects is sufficient to produce preliminary results and qualitative insights, but a larger sample is required to provide conclusive results.

6   Discussion

Strengths and Weaknesses. The results of template extraction evaluation presented in Section 5.1 indicate that FUDA can retrieve concept implementation templates with relatively high precision and recall from only two traces and two sample applications. Furthermore, the processing of the traces is fully automatic and the instrumentation does not impose significant overhead on the application execution since only the API interaction rather than full traces are recorded. Given a set of applications and scenarios, the amount of time needed to retrieve templates is mainly determined by the time it takes to execute the scenarios on the applications. Furthermore, dynamic analysis detects the API elements that are actually being invoked. This is important since frameworks typically use polymorphism and reflection, which can render static analysis less precise.

Nevertheless, the approach has some potential drawbacks as well. Most importantly, it relies on the ability to find appropriate sample applications. The quality of the results may depend on the selection of the applications and concept invocation scenarios. In particular, the scenarios might require careful design to isolate the API instructions of interest in the context of composite concepts. Second, all dynamic approaches are dependent on the input data and generalizing from this data might not be safe. In particular, FUDA may fail to retrieve optional API instructions. Both issues are discussed further shortly. Finally, dynamic approaches require the setup of the runtime environment, which might not be easy in some situations. Therefore, being able to retrieve useful concept implementation templates from only few application executions is particularly important.

Scenario Design Considerations. The nature of the concept and the ways in which it is implemented by the applications can influence the results. Ideally, the concept is atomic, its invocation is easily delimitable (for marking), and the sample applications have only this concept in common. In this case, FUDA will yield best results. In general, concepts are composites of other concepts, the invocation of a concept might not be easily demarcated, and the sample applications may have several concepts in common. For a composite concept, developers should select applications that vary those of its components that should be eliminated. If the concept of interest is part of a composite concept, developers should be able to demarcate the boundaries of the concept execution. If these scenario design goals are only partially satisfied, the resulting false positives and false negatives may still be identified by following the traceability links in the template and studying the actual sample application code.

7   Related Work

Framework documentation and completion approaches support framework users passively or actively or both. For instance, *framework-specific modeling languages* (FSMLs) [11] document framework-provided concepts as hierarchies of mandatory and optional features and actively support users in instantiating the concepts through round-trip engineering. Further, *reuse contracts* [12] and *collaboration contracts* [13] help ensure that frameworks are used correctly. Nonetheless, the main difficulty of these approaches is that framework documentation requires manual effort and, consequently, documentation of the framework may become outdated. FUDA attempts to fill this gap by allowing users to generate implementation templates when the framework documentation is missing.

   Framework usage comprehension is supported by several approaches such as XSnippet [14], Strathcona [2], Prospector [15], PARSEWeb [16], and FrUiT [3]. Both XSnippet and Strathcona are context-sensitive code assistant tools that allow developers to query a repository of code snippets that are relevant to the programming task at hand. Given two API types τ_{in} and τ_{out} as a query, both Prospector and PARSEWeb mine for call sequences transforming an object of type τ_{in} to another object of type τ_{out}. FrUiT mines for frequent API usage patterns as association rules, e.g., *subclass A $\Rightarrow$ call m*. It then uses such rules to suggest implementation steps for a class under development. All these approaches are mainly code assistants in the context of a programming task at hand, such as how to call a specific framework method or how to instantiate a particular framework class. In contrast to FUDA, they do not provide a complete code snippet or implementation template for instantiating an entire, large concept, which may span multiple framework methods or even classes. Moreover, whereas all these approaches use static analysis, FUDA applies primarily dynamic analysis. The advantage of static analysis is that it can cope with a large body of applications and potentially incomplete code. The advantage of dynamic analysis is that it can handle highly polymorphic and reflective code, which is often part of modern frameworks. Additionally, contrary to FUDA, static analysis does not support concept identification by invoking concepts directly from the user interface.

   Specification mining is concerned with automatically discovering the protocols or rules that a program must follow when interacting with an API. Existing techniques can be classified into static [17][18] and dynamic [19][20][21] ones. Examples of static approaches include inferring ordering patterns among method calls [17] or detecting function precedence protocols [18]. Examples of dynamic approaches contain mining temporal API rules from dynamic traces [19], mining iterative patterns from traces [20], or inferring declarative specifications of the API behavior for target concepts such as the raising of an exception [21]. In contrast to specification mining approaches, FUDA does not recover API interaction protocols. The latter are important for library API usage, but less so for frameworks. Frameworks typically follow *inversion of control* by enforcing protocols in framework rather than application code. Although FUDA extracts total orders of calls, it does so to improve readability of templates by sorting calls within method bodies. Additionally, dynamic specification mining techniques often require several runtime traces in order to recover different legal execution sequences. On the other hand, FUDA aims to keep the number of traces as small as possible to make the approach attractive in practice.

Concept location concentrates on understanding how a certain concept or functionality is implemented in the source code of an application. Existing approaches can be mainly categorized into static (e.g., [4]), dynamic (e.g., [22]), and hybrid ones (e.g., [5][23]). One can refer to [5] for a good literature overview. We focus only on the most related dynamic and hybrid techniques. Most of these techniques use two or more traces to filter out irrelevant events, e.g., [22][23]. SITIR [5] gets away with only one trace by filtering it using the textual similarity to a keyword query. Unlike FUDA, all these techniques focus on retrieving concepts in general application code rather than framework-provided concepts. Therefore, the result may contain many application-specific instructions that are irrelevant from the viewpoint of framework usage. FUDA avoids this problem by focusing on API interaction traces and removing the application-specific content from those traces through the event generalization. Furthermore, we are unaware of other techniques using the combination of API trace marking with API trace slicing. In particular, SITIR [5] uses the runtime trace marking to reduce the size of the traces, but it misses the relevant events to the implementation of the desired concept that are not marked at runtime. FUDA is able to identify such relevant events by applying the API trace slicing.

8   Conclusion

This paper presented FUDA, an approach for extracting implementation templates from traces obtained by invoking concepts of interest in sample applications. FUDA was tested on twelve concepts of four widely-used frameworks. The concept sample included both simple and complex ones. Six concepts corresponded to questions found at developer forums. The experimental evaluation shows that, for the considered concepts, FUDA can extract templates with high precision (59-100%) and recall (79-100%) from only two traces and two sample applications per concept. Finally, we reported on a user experiment with twelve subjects in which the choice of templates vs. documentation had much less impact on development time than the concept complexity. The experiment also suggested that the templates should be used together with the sample applications from which they were extracted.

Acknowledgements. The authors would like to acknowledge Eric Eide, James Noble, and the anonymous reviewers for their valuable suggestions for improving the paper. We also thank Shoja Chenouri who helped in the statistical analyses.

References

1. Gamma, E., Beck, K.: Contributing to Eclipse: Principles, Patterns, and Plugins. Addison-Wesley, Reading (2003)
2. Holmes, R., Murphy, G.C.: Using structural context to recommend source code examples. In: ICSE (2005)
3. Bruch, M., Schafer, T., Mezini, M.: FrUiT: IDE support for framework understanding. In: ETX (2006)
4. Zhao, W., Zhang, L., Liu, Y., Sun, J., Yang, F.: SNIAFL: Towards a static noninteractive approach to feature location. TOSEM 15(2) (2006)
5. Liu, D., Marcus, A., Poshyvanyk, D., Rajlich, V.: Feature location via information retrieval based filtering of a single scenario execution trace. In: ASE (2007)
6. Heydarnoori, A.: Supporting Framework Use via Automatically Extracted Concept-Implementation Templates. PhD thesis, University of Waterloo, Canada (February 2009)
7. Heydarnoori, A., Bartolomei, T.T., Czarnecki, K.: Comprehending object-oriented software frameworks API through dynamic analysis. Technical Report CS-2007-18, School of Computer Science, University of Waterloo (2007)
8. Montgomery, D.C.: Design and analysis of experiments, 6th edn. Wiley, Chichester (2004)
9. Hedges, L.V.: Distribution theory for Glass's estimator of effect size and related estimators. Journal of Educational Statistics 6(2) (1981)
10. Generative Software Development Lab: FUDA supporting material (2008), http://gsd.uwaterloo.ca/~aheydarn/fuda/
11. Antkiewicz, M., Bartolomei, T.T., Czarnecki, K.: Automatic extraction of framework-specific models from framework-based application code. In: ASE (2007)
12. Steyaert, P., Lucas, C., Mens, K., D'Hondt, T.: Reuse contracts: managing the evolution of reusable assets. In: OOPSLA (1996)
13. Hondt, K.D.: A Novel Approach to Architectural Recovery in Evolving Object-Oriented Systems. PhD thesis, Vrije Universiteit Brussel, Belgium (1998)
14. Sahavechaphan, N., Claypool, K.: XSnippet: Mining for sample code. In: OOPSLA (2006)
15. Mandelin, D., Xu, L., Bodík, R., Kimelman, D.: Jungloid mining: Helping to navigate the API jungle. In: PLDI (2005)
16. Thummalapenta, S., Xie, T.: PARSEWeb: A programmer assistant for reusing open source code on the web. In: ASE (2007)
17. Wasylkowski, A., Zeller, A., Lindig, C.: Detecting object usage anomalies. In: FSE (2007)
18. Ramanathan, M.K., Grama, A., Jagannathan, S.: Path-sensitive inference of function precedence protocols. In: ICSE (2007)
19. Yang, J., Evans, D., Bhardwaj, D., Bhat, T., Das, M.: Perracotta: Mining temporal API rules from imperfect traces. In: ICSE (2006)
20. Lo, D., Khoo, S.C., Liu, C.: Efficient mining of iterative patterns for software specification discovery. In: KDD (2007)
21. Sankaranarayanan, S., Ivanči, F., Gupta, A.: Mining library specifications using inductive logic programming. In: ICSE (2008)
22. Wilde, N., Scully, M.C.: Software reconnaissance: Mapping program features to code. JSM 7(1) (1995)
23. Eisenbarth, T., Koschke, R., Simon, D.: Locating features in source code. TSE 29(3) (2003)

Stepping Stones over the Refactoring Rubicon
Lightweight Language Extensions to Easily Realise Refactorings

Max Schäfer, Mathieu Verbaere, Torbjörn Ekman, and Oege de Moor

Programming Tools Group, University of Oxford, UK
{max.schaefer,mathieu.verbaere,torbjorn,oege}@comlab.ox.ac.uk

Abstract. Refactoring tools allow the programmer to pretend they are working with a richer language where the behaviour of a program is automatically preserved during restructuring. In this paper we show that this metaphor of an extended language yields a very general and useful implementation technique for refactorings: a refactoring is implemented by embedding the source program into an extended language on which the refactoring operations are easier to perform, and then translating the refactored program back into the original language. Using the well-known *Extract Method* refactoring as an example, we show that this approach allows a very fine-grained decomposition of the overall refactoring into a series of micro-refactorings that can be understood, implemented, and tested independently. We thus can easily write implementations of complex refactorings that rival and even outperform industrial strength refactoring tools in terms of correctness, but are much shorter and easier to understand.

1 Introduction

According to its classic definition, refactoring is the process of improving the design of existing code by behaviour-preserving program transformations, themselves called refactorings. Applying refactorings by hand is error-prone since even very simple operations such as renaming a program entity can affect large parts of the refactored program and may interact with existing program structure in subtle ways, leading to uncompilable code or, even worse, to code that still compiles but behaves differently.

For many years now, popular Integrated Development Environments such as JetBrains' IntelliJ IDEA [10], Eclipse [2], or Sun's NetBeans [17] have provided support for automated refactorings in which the user specifies the refactoring operation to perform, and the refactoring engine performs the requested transformation while checking that program behaviour is actually preserved.

Traditionally [19], this is done by checking preconditions that are thought sufficient to preserve some invariants, which in turn ensure behaviour preservation. However, as we have pointed out before [21], this approach has severe weaknesses. Deriving the correct preconditions relies on a global understanding of the object language in which programs to be refactored are written, and has to account for all corner cases that might possibly lead to an incorrect refactoring. In a complex modern language like Java this is an arduous task even for very simple refactorings, and we found in an informal survey that none of the most popular IDEs solves it satisfactorily [3]. Even if sufficient preconditions are found, further evolution of the language is likely to introduce new

S. Drossopoulou (Ed.): ECOOP 2009, LNCS 5653, pp. 369–393, 2009.
© Springer-Verlag Berlin Heidelberg 2009

constructs and concepts that impact refactoring in subtle ways, and make it necessary to revise the preconditions.

We believe that it is more beneficial to think about refactorings directly in terms of invariant preservation rather than preconditions. The ultimate invariant to be preserved is still, of course, the semantics of the input program, but this criterion is too deep and too far removed from the program as a syntactic entity to be useful. We should rather search for more syntactic invariants whose preservation we can see as ensuring the correctness of the refactoring. In previous work, we have shown how this approach can be used to tackle the *Rename* refactoring: From the abstract criterion of binding preservation, i.e. the requirement that in the renamed program every name still refer to the same declaration as before, we obtain a concrete implementation that correctly refactors many programs on which industrial strength tools fail.

In this paper, we follow this line of work and show how it can be extended to cover more complex refactorings, among them the *Extract Method* refactoring, that was dubbed "Refactoring's Rubicon" by Fowler [7], who proclaimed it to be the yardstick of "serious" refactoring tools.

Our key idea is to treat refactorings not as transformations on programs in the object language that the programmer writes them in, but instead as transformations on programs translated into a richer language that offers some additional language features to ease their implementation. The implementation of the refactoring itself then becomes much simpler, but some effort has to be invested into the translation back from the enriched language to the base language.

As an example, first consider renaming. If we extend our basic language with *bound* names, i.e. names that do not follow the normal lookup rules, but directly bind to their target declaration (preventing accidental shadowing or capture), renaming becomes trivial to implement: First, all names in the input program are replaced by their bound equivalents (their bindings are "locked"). Now the renaming can be performed without having to worry about altering the binding structure, since all references in the program are fixed. Finally, we need to go back to the language without bound names, replacing them with possibly qualified names in the base language that have the same binding behaviour (their bindings are "unlocked"). If unlocking cannot be performed, the transformation is unsafe and has to be aborted and rolled back.

Of course, the unlocking step is highly non-trivial to perform and hard to implement, but a general translation from "Java with Bound Names" to plain Java is very useful in the context of other refactorings as well. Consider, for example, the *Push Down Method* refactoring, in which a method m is moved from a class A to its subclass B. Its crucial correctness property is again binding preservation, since we want to ensure that all calls to m still resolve to the right method after pushing, and that all references to fields, variables, types, and methods inside m itself still refer to the same targets as before. Again, this is easily achieved in Java with Bound Names: we simply lock all calls to m and all names within m itself, then move the definition of m from A to B, and unlock, using the same translation from Java with Bound Names to plain Java originally developed for *Rename*.

In this paper we show how this idea of refactorings as transformations on a richer language can be extended to more complex refactorings, most prominently *Extract*

Method, Inline Method, Extract Local Variable, and *Inline Local Variable.* Although binding preservation is still important, these refactorings are more challenging in that they move code relative to other code. As a criterion to preserve behaviour, we suggest control flow and data flow preservation: All statements in the affected methods should maintain their control flow predecessors and successors throughout the refactoring, and all variables should have the same reaching definitions.

Our aim is not to prove that this is a sufficient criterion for behaviour preservation. If we wanted to do that, we would have to restrict our attention to a suitably well-behaved subset of the language, since in full Java even the introduction of a number of extra push instructions that would be needed to realise the call to an extracted method in byte code, could possibly lead to an out-of-memory error, which would alter the behaviour of the program.

We rather take flow preservation as a common-sense criterion that is to guide our implementation; since it can be effectively checked, it also provides a safety net for our refactoring engine. By judicious introduction of additional language extensions we can further decompose the overall transformation into micro-refactorings that each perform a small, well-defined task. These language extensions are lightweight in that they cannot occur in source programs and no code is generated for them, but they are introduced and eliminated again during the process of refactoring.

This decomposition brings with it the usual benefits of modularity, as it eases implementation and testing . We were thus able to implement all four of the above-mentioned refactorings in less than 3000 lines of code, most of which is reused heavily between the individual refactorings, as part of our JastAdd-based refactoring engine, and pass all applicable tests in the internal test suites of both Eclipse and IntelliJ IDEA.

The main novel contributions of this paper are:

- A presentation of refactorings solely based on **invariant preservation**, which provides a more flexible implementation guideline than traditional precondition-based approaches.
- The use of **lightweight language extensions** as a device to simplify and modularise refactoring implementations.
- An **analysis of Extract Method** in terms of this general approach, showing how the overall refactoring can be decomposed into micro-refactorings that are easy to implement, understand, and test.
- A high-quality **implementation of Extract Method** and **related refactorings** based on this analysis, that is very compact, yet supports the whole Java 5 language and is on par with well-known Java IDEs in terms of correctness.

We structure this paper as follows: Section 2 introduces refactoring challenges, illustrated with the example of *Extract Method.* Section 3 shows how these challenges can be met using a decomposition of the whole refactoring into a series of well-defined micro-refactorings, and Section 4 provides a more in-depth discussion of how this can be done for method extraction. Section 5 puts these concepts into context and discusses how similar strategies can be used on related refactorings. Section 6 evaluates our implementation in terms of code size and correctness, comparing it against some other well-known Java refactoring engines. Section 7 discusses some related work directions for future work before we conclude in Section 8.

2 Challenges

We begin by introducing refactoring challenges through our running example, the *Extract Method* refactoring for the Java language. It is used to simplify complicated methods by extracting a contiguous range of statements into a new method, and replace the original statements by a call to that method. As a simple example, consider the method m in Figure 1 on the left, and assume we want to extract the body of the **for** loop into a new method processItem.

```
class A {
  void m() {
    int total = 0;
    for(Item i : getItems()) {
      System.out.println("item "
        + i.getDescription());
      total += i.getValue();
    }
    System.out.println("total: "
      + total);
  }

  (...)
}
```

⟹

```
class A {
  void m() {
    int total = 0;
    for(Item i : getItems()) {
      total = processItem(i, total);
    }
    System.out.println("total: "
      + total);
  }

  int processItem(Item i, int total) {
    System.out.println("item "
      + i.getDescription());
    total += i.getValue();
    return total;
  }

  (...)
}
```

Fig. 1. An example program before and after *Extract Method*

This is relatively easy; all we need to do is provide i and total as parameters to the new method, and return the value of total to update the original variable after the method returns. Thus the resulting program should look like the one shown in the same figure on the right.

But even this simple example shows that *Extract Method* is much more than just cut-and-paste. In general, we can identify three different kinds of problems to be handled, that can all be cast as preservation problems: we need to preserve name bindings, control flow, and data flow.

2.1 Name Binding Preservation

Since the refactoring introduces new names and declarations into the program, care has to be taken not to accidentally change existing name bindings. Take, for example, the program in Figure 2 on the left; the method m in class A constructs an instance of the locally declared class X and returns it.

In NetBeans, extracting the declaration of X to a method n yields the program on the right, where the instance constructed is no longer of the local class X, but of the global class of the same name. This particular program does not change its behaviour, but slightly extended examples either make NetBeans produce an output program that does not compile (which is annoying to the user, if comparatively harmless), or that still does compile but behaves differently.

```
class X { }                                    class X { }
class A {                                      class A {
  Object m() {                                   Object m() {
    class X { }          " ⟹ "                      return new X();
    return new X();                              }
  }                                              void n() {
}                                                  class X { }
                                                 }
                                               }
```

Fig. 2. How not to preserve name binding during method extraction

Other IDEs employ simple heuristics to guard against this kind of situation, but no systematic binding preservation seems to be attempted, and similar bugs can be discovered in all cases [3].

2.2 Control Flow Preservation

While Java mostly uses structured control flow, it also provides the unstructured branching statements **break** and **continue**. The former exits from an enclosing loop (which can be further specified by a label), while the latter only exits from the current iteration and starts the next one. These "**goto**s in disguise" cannot be moved into the newly created method blindly: If their target loop is not also moved, the resulting program will not compile.

Even more subtle is the **return** statement: If types match, an extracted method with an embedded return will still compile, but of course the statement now returns from the *extracted* method, not the original method as it did before. As an example, consider the program in Figure 3 on the left, and assume we want to extract the **if** statement into a method n. A naive implementation might produce the program on the right, which has different behaviour from the original program: while originally calling m(23) would return immediately, it now prints 23.

A precondition-based approach might categorically forbid extraction of any code that contains these branching statements, but that would reject many potentially useful refactorings: As a simple example, consider the program in Figure 4 on the left, and assume we want to extract the whole body of m into a new method n. This can easily be done if, instead of replacing the extracted code by the method invocation n(i), we instead replace it by **return** n(i).

Thus a more advanced precondition might be to allow extraction if all control paths end in a **return** statement. But this is again too stringent a requirement, as the example

```
                                       class A {
                                         void m(int i) {
class A {                                  n(i);
  void m(int i) {                          System.out.println(i);
    if(i == 23)        " ⟹ "             }
      return;                             void n(int i) {
    System.out.println(i);                 if(i == 23)
  }                                           return;
}                                          }
                                       }
```

Fig. 3. How not to preserve control flow during method extraction

```
class A {                          class B {
  int m(int i) {                     void x(int j) {
    if(i == 23)                        if(j == 42)
      return 42;                         return;
    return i + 1;                      System.out.println(j);
  }                                  }
}                                  }
```

(a)   (b)

Fig. 4. Preserving control flow during method extraction

program in the same figure on the right shows. Our preconditions would not allow us to extract the whole body of x into a new method y, although this would actually be unproblematic, since the code to be extracted is right at the end of the enclosing method anyway.

These examples show that precondition based refactoring engines are doomed to play an ultimately pointless game of tag in which preconditions have to be progressively relaxed as desirable refactorings are discovered. It is all too easy to introduce unsoundness this way, especially if new language versions introduce constructs that influence control flow (such as the **assert** statement in Java 1.4).

We instead propose preservation of control flow as the goal to aim for during method extraction: every statement in the extracted method should have the same control flow predecessors and successors as before the extraction. This immediately rules out **break** and **continue** statements whose target is not in the new method: their control flow successors will no longer be defined at all. For the two examples above, it can however be seen that their control flow successors do not change during the proposed refactorings, although flow sometimes has to be "rerouted" by inserting extra statements like the **return** of the first example.

Since refactorings work on a source-level representation of the program, not its generated byte code, some care has to be taken in determining control flow information, which we will discuss in more detail in Section 3.

2.3 Data Flow Preservation

One of the most intricate aspects of the *Extract Method* refactoring is to determine the parameters of the extracted method. Intuitively, it is clear that we need to pass the new method the values of any local variables it might need, and that the new method in turn should return the values of any local variables it has changed, if they are needed for further computation.

In previous work [23] we have given criteria for selecting parameters and return values in terms of familiar data flow concepts such as liveness and def/use sites. As it turns out, these criteria can be given a more basic justification in terms of data flow preservation.

Analogous to control flow successors and predecessors, we define data flow successors and predecessors: The data flow predecessors of a variable use are its reaching

```
class A {                                    class A {
  void m(boolean b) {                          void m(boolean b) {
    int i = 22;                                  int i = 22;
    int n = 40;                                  int n = 40;
    try {                                        try {
      // from                                      i = f(b, i, n);
      ++i;                                         System.out.println(i+n);
      if(b) {                                    } catch(Exception e) {
        n += 2;                                  }
        throw new Exception();               }
      }                      ⟹            int f(boolean b, int i, int n)
      // to                                       throws Exception {
      System.out.println(i+n);                 ++i;
    } catch(Exception e) {                     if(b) {
    }                                            n += 2;
  }                                              throw new Exception();
}                                              }
                                               return i;
                                             }
                                           }
```

Fig. 5. A refactoring rejected by Eclipse

definitions, i.e. all definitions of this variable that might influence the value of the variable at this point in the program. Similarly, the data flow successors of a variable definition are all uses that might be reached without an intervening definition.

We can now specify that a variable should become a parameter to the extracted method if it has a use within the code to be extracted whose data flow predecessor lies before the extracted selection, and it should be returned if it has a definition whose data flow successor comes after the selection. This is a natural criterion, since those data flow edges would be "broken" by method extraction, and hence have to be rerouted through parameters in order to be preserved.

Again, we leave it to Section 3 to make this basic idea more precise and show how it can be implemented at the abstract syntax tree level. That this is not a trivial problem can be illustrated by a simple example: Assume that in the program in Figure 5 on the left we want to extract the code between the comments. We note that all of b, n, and i have to become parameters to the new method, and i should be returned so that its new value is available for the println statement, as shown in the program on the right.

The value of n, however, does *not* need to be returned: if n is changed by the extracted code, an exception is immediately thrown and control transfers to the **catch** clause; in other words, the assignment to n has no data flow successor, and hence its value does not need to be returned. Eclipse, for example, does not detect this, and determines that both values need to be returned. This is not easily accomplished in Java, and hence the refactoring is rejected.

3   Our Approach

As outlined in the last section, the main challenge in implementing the *Extract Method* refactoring and its brethren is the intertwining of name binding, control flow, and data flow, which are all delicate by themselves, and even more so in conjunction.

By using our existing naming framework, we can easily achieve binding preservation where necessary, so we can concentrate on preserving control and data flow. It is a

natural idea to simplify this task by splitting the refactoring into two parts that deal
with control flow and data flow separately. Unfortunately, this is difficult to achieve in
plain Java: At some point during the refactoring, the statements to be extracted have
to be moved into a new method, and at that point both their control and data flow will
change at the same time.

We hence introduce *anonymous methods* into the language as a lightweight extension
that helps breaking up the transformation. Just as an anonymous class is a class that
is defined and instantiated at the same time and may access local variables from the
surrounding method, an anonymous method is a method that is defined and invoked
at the same time, and (besides its own parameters and local variables) can also access
variables from the surrounding method.

In control flow terms it behaves like an ordinary method, in particular **break** and
continue statements can not escape the anonymous method. In data flow terms, however, it behaves like a block in that it can access variables from the enclosing scope in a
lexically scoped fashion.

Thus an anonymous method provides a convenient half-way point for the *Extract
Method* refactoring: If we can package up the statements to be extracted into an anonymous method, it means that we have successfully preserved the control flow. We can
then tackle the task of preserving data flow by successively introducing parameters and
return values as needed. Once the anonymous method does not reference any local variables from the surrounding method anymore, it can safely be promoted to a normal
method without disturbing either control or data flow.

While we leave a detailed exposition of the different steps involved in extracting a
method to the next section, we will briefly describe the general procedure by using our
initial example. Here is the original program, with the statements to be extracted framed
by comments:

```
class A {
  void m() {
    int total = 0;
    for(Item i : getItems()) {
      // from
      System.out.println("item " + i.getDescription());
      total += i.getValue();
      // to
    }
    System.out.println("total: " + total);
  }

  (...)
}
```

As a first step, it will be convenient to turn the sequence of statements to extract
into a block so that we can analyse it and operate on it as a single abstract syntax tree.
This first step, a micro-refactoring we will refer to as *Extract Block*, is fairly easy to
implement, since blocks do not affect control and data flow, and yields the following
program:

```
class A {
  void m() {
    int total = 0;
    for(Item i : getItems()) {
      {
        System.out.println("item " + i.getDescription());
```

```
        total += i.getValue();
    }
  }
  System.out.println("total:␣" + total);
}

(...)
}
```

Now we turn the extracted block into an anonymous method without parameters, carefully preserving control flow in the process. This micro-refactoring, called *Introduce Anonymous Method*, yields this:

```
class A {
  void m() {
    int total = 0;
    for(Item i : getItems()) {
      (() : void ⇒ {
        System.out.println("item␣" + i.getDescription());
        total += i.getValue();
      })();
    }
    System.out.println("total:␣" + total);
  }

  (...)
}
```

We write the anonymous method as (() : **void** ⇒ ...) (), indicating that it has no formal parameters, is of return type **void**, and is applied to an empty list of arguments. Note that this syntax is for presentation purposes only, and anonymous methods cannot appear in user programs.

Our next task is to reroute dataflow edges that go across the boundaries of the anonymous method, i.e. to do a lambda lifting [11]. To ease this step, we allow our anonymous methods to have *reference* parameters like in C#. Thus we get the following:

```
class A {
  void m() {
    int total = 0;
    for(Item i : getItems()) {
      ((int i, ref int total) : void ⇒ {
        System.out.println("item␣" + i.getDescription());
        total += i.getValue();
      })(i, total);
    }
    System.out.println("total:␣" + total);
  }

  (...)
}
```

The anonymous method now has two parameters i and total, both of type **int**, to which the arguments i and total from the surrounding method are assigned. In the former case, the parameter i and the argument i are entirely different entities, whereas in the latter case the reference parameter total is aliased to the variable total to make sure that any changes to the parameter are reflected in the variable.

Before we can lift the anonymous method to a named method, we need to eliminate reference parameters, which are not supported in normal Java. The easiest way is to require that there be at most one such parameter, and turn it into a return value, yielding the following result:

```
class A {
  void m() {
    int total = 0;
    for(Item i : getItems()) {
      total = ((int i, int total) : int ⇒ {
        System.out.println("item " + i.getDescription());
        total += i.getValue();
        return total;
      })(i, total);
    }
    System.out.println("total: " + total);
  }

  (...)
}
```

Now the anonymous method's body does not reference any local variables from the surrounding method, thus its control and data flow both behave as with a named method, and we can, in a final step, lift it out to complete the extraction.

```
class A {
  void m() {
    int total = 0;
    for(Item i : getItems()) {
      total = n(i, total);
    }
    System.out.println("total: " + total);
  }
  int n(int i, int total) {
    System.out.println("item " + i.getDescription());
    total += i.getValue();
    return total;
  }

  (...)
}
```

We would like to particularly emphasise that we do not propose to add anonymous methods as a general mechanism to the Java language standard. It is rather a lightweight extension that we use to simplify the implementation of refactorings. There is no parsing syntax for anonymous methods, hence they can never occur in user programs, and no code can be generated for them. All we need to specify is their behaviour in terms of name binding, control flow, and data flow.

Although we have described only the *Extract Method* refactoring here and will continue to concentrate on it as our running example, other refactorings that deals with code movement, in particular *Inline Method*, *Extract Local Variable*, and *Inline Local Variable*, face exactly the same kind of problems, and can indeed be treated in the same way.

4   *Extract Method* in Small Pieces

Using the concepts introduced in the previous section, we will now take a more detailed look at the implementation of *Extract Method*. Our refactoring engine is implemented as an extension to the JastAddJ Java compiler [4], hence it can work on the abstract syntax tree produced by the compiler frontend, and use all of the static analysis machinery provided by the compiler. In particular, this includes name lookup to easily navigate from a name to its declaration.

We also make use of a new implementation of the intra-procedural control flow analysis library presented in [18]. This library provides for every AST node two attributes `pred` and `succ`, that compute the nodes preceding resp. succeeding this node in terms of control flow. In particular, this allows us to compute, for any statement, its preceding and succeeding statements. For a given node n, if the node s is contained within the set `n.succ()`, we say that there is a *"succ edge"* from n to s, and similar for `pred`.

We can now implement a "locking" and "unlocking" mechanism somewhat similar to the bound names framework [21]: Before performing a transformation, we compute the control flow predecessors and successors of the statements that the transformation acts upon. Then after the transformation we recompute this information and verify that it has not changed, aborting the refactoring if any change has occurred[1].

A certain category of syntax tree nodes can be categorised as *flow-through* nodes, which purely contribute to the program's control flow without influencing any other aspect of the semantics. Examples are nodes corresponding to **break** and **continue** statements, but also nodes corresponding to **return**[2]. When checking for control flow preservation, we disregard such nodes, thus creating the opportunity to "fix" control flow by inserting additional flow-through nodes.

Note that the *post hoc* flow preservation check makes the refactoring robust in the face of future language extensions: if additional control flow constructs appear which are not handled by the refactoring, the transformation will be aborted instead of producing incorrect results.

On top of the control flow analysis we have implemented a lightweight dataflow analysis for local variables and parameters which provides two attributes `dataPred` and `dataSucc` for every variable node in the syntax tree. The former computes all assignment statements for the same variable that can be reached by walking along `pred` edges without encountering any intervening assignments to this variable; the latter does the reverse and computes a set of variable nodes that may use the value assigned to a variable in an assignment. Thus, `dataPred` gives us all reaching definitions of a variable use, whereas `dataSucc` computes the set of reached uses of a variable definition.

This flow analysis framework, together with the naming toolkit, provides the basis on which we build our implementation of method extraction. The extraction process is split up into five smaller refactorings:

1. *Extract Block* pulls the statements to be extracted together into a block.
2. *Introduce Anonymous Method* turns that block into an anonymous method without parameters.
3. *Close Over Variables* eliminates any references to local variables from within the anonymous method by introducing parameters.
4. *Eliminate Reference Parameters* gets rid of parameters that need to be passed by reference, since this is not supported by Java.

---

[1] It is enough to perform intra-procedural flow analysis, since the naming framework guarantees that method calls are resolved to the same method before and after the refactoring, which means that inter-procedural control flow will not change.

[2] However, for a statement **return** e;, the node corresponding to e (and its children) are *not* flow-through, since they correspond to actual computation taking place.

5. *Lift Anonymous Method* turns the anonymous method into a named method within the same type as the method we are extracting from.

The whole *Extract Method* refactoring is simply a sequential composition of these five sub-refactorings, which we now are going to discuss in greater detail. The control flow and data flow analyses are run before and after each refactoring step to ensure that the invariants are preserved.

4.1   Extract Block

The *Extract Block* refactoring takes as its input a block b (represented by its node in the abstract syntax tree) composed of statements b_1 to b_n and two indices i and j such that $1 \leq i \leq j \leq n$. The goal of the refactoring is to put statements b_i to b_j into a new block b' and insert it into b to replace the original statements.

This refactoring can itself be composed from even simpler operations: In a first step, we insert an empty block after statement b_j, then we successively move the statements b_j to b_i into this new block. For every statement to be moved, we want to ensure that its flow and bindings do not change, so we lock flow and binding information, move it into the block, and then unlock it; this operation can be encapsulated into a micro-refactoring *Push Statement into Block*.

As an example, consider the program in Figure 6 (a), and assume we want to wrap the first three statements of m into a block. We create an empty block and push the third

```
class A {
   int x = 23;
   int m() {
      x = 42;
      int x = 55;
      ++x;
      return x;
   }
}
```

(a)

```
class A {
   int x = 23;
   int m() {
      x = 42;
      int x = 55;
      {
         ++x;
      }
      return x;
   }
}
```

(b)

```
class A {
   int x = 23;
   int m() {
      x = 42;
      int x;
      x = 55;
      {
         ++x;
      }
      return x;
   }
}
```

(c)

```
class A {
   int x = 23;
   int m() {
      int x;
      this.x = 42;
      {
         x = 55;
         ++x;
      }
      return x;
   }
}
```

(d)

```
class A {
   int x = 23;
   int m() {
      int x;
      {
         this.x = 42;
         x = 55;
         ++x;
      }
      return x;
   }
}
```

(e)

Fig. 6. *Extract Block* in action

statement into it, which does not violate binding or flow preservation and yields the intermediate program in (b).

The next statement cannot be pushed into the block directly: it declares the variable x which is referenced after the block; if we were to push the whole statement into the block, x would become invisible, and the resulting program would fail to compile. Hence we first employ a micro-refactoring *Split Variable Declaration*, that turns a variable declaration with initialisation into a "pure" declaration without initialiser followed by an assignment, yielding program (c).

Now the statement x = 55; can be pushed into the block without any problems. We also need to move the declaration up to the beginning of the selection to clear the way for pushing the remaining statements. This, of course, creates a problem, since the local variable x would now shadow the field x in the assignment x = 42. Fortunately, our naming framework takes care of this automatically, and after unlocking we get (d).

Moving the last statement into the block does not present any particular difficulties, and we obtain our final program in (e).

Of the three minor refactorings discussed here, *Extract Block* might be considered a useful refactoring in its own right to clarify code structure. *Push Statement Into Block* and *Split Declaration*, on the other hand, are pure building blocks that are not very useful to the programmer; they can, however, be reused in the context of other refactorings.

4.2   Introduce Anonymous Method

Next we want to convert the block created in the previous step into an anonymous method without parameters. JastAddJ, of course, has no built-in support for anonymous methods, since they are not part of the Java language. Its very extensible implementation, however, makes it extremely easy to add language extensions.

Support for anonymous methods can be added by providing an additional production for an abstract syntax tree node in the object language:

```
AnonymousMethod : Expr ::= Parameter:ParameterDeclaration*
       ReturnType:Access Exception:Access* Block Arg:Expr*;
```

In words, this production says that anonymous methods are a kind of expression, i.e. they can occur anywhere the Java language grammar allows an expression to occur. They contain a list of parameters, represented by the same node type as parameters for plain Java methods and constructors; a return type which is an Access, i.e. a possibly qualified name; a list of thrown exceptions, likewise given as accesses; a body given as a Block; and finally a list of arguments, which may be arbitrary expressions.

We do not specify any parsing rules for anonymous methods, since we do not want to make them available for programmers, but for presentation purposes we use the concrete syntax $(\overline{p} : r \textbf{ throws } \overline{x} \Rightarrow b)(\overline{e})$ to represent an anonymous method with body b that takes parameters $\overline{p}$, is invoked with arguments $\overline{e}$, throws exceptions $\overline{x}$ and has return type r.

To defer the handling of multiple return values, we introduce another language extension in the form of *output* and *reference* parameters, marked with the modifiers **out** and **ref**, respectively. The argument given for such parameters must be a variable of the enclosing scope, and any changes the anonymous method makes to the parameter are reflected in that argument, thus these arguments are (conceptually) passed by reference.

Parameters marked **ref** may be read before they are assigned, which is not possible for **out** parameters. These two kinds of parameters behave like their counterparts in C#, but they only occur as ephemeral language constructs during refactoring, not as genuine language features. A parameter that is marked neither **out** nor **ref** is called a *value parameter*.

Conceptually, control flow for an anonymous method works like for a normal method call: parameters are bound to arguments, the body is executed, and may return a value by executing a **return** statement. Exception handling likewise works as for methods, exceptions thrown but not caught within the anonymous method propagate to the enclosing scope and onwards until a corresponding **catch** clause is found. Like a normal method, an anonymous method may declare and use local variables in addition to its parameters, and it may also access any variable or field visible in the surrounding method, subject to lexical scoping.

To turn a block into an anonymous method without parameters, we do not need to adjust any data flow or name bindings: all these work the same way for blocks as they do for anonymous methods. We do, however, need to make sure that control flow is preserved. Hence, we lock down control flow in the block, computing and caching the predecessor and successor statements of every statement in the block, then wrap it into an anonymous method, and unlock control flow, recomputing all predecessor and successor statements to make sure they have not changed.

More precisely, given a block b in a context with return type T^3, we perform the following steps:

1. Lock all control flow in b.
2. Compute all uncaught checked exceptions thrown in b, and use the naming framework to compute locked accesses $e_1, \ldots, e_n$ for them.
3. Construct an anonymous method C of the form

   $$(() : R \textbf{ throws } e_1, \ldots, e_n \Rightarrow b)()$$

   where R is T if b cannot complete normally[4], or **void** otherwise.
4. If b can complete normally, replace it by C;, otherwise by **return** C;.
5. Unlock control flow, aborting the refactoring if the flow has changed.

In the second example program of Figure 4, for example, the block can complete normally, so we perform the following transformation:

```
class A {                              class A {
  void m(int i) {                        void m(int i) {
  {                                        (() : void => {
    if(i == 23)                              if(i == 23)
      return;          =>                       return;
    System.out.println(i);                   System.out.println(i);
  }                                        })();
}                                        }
}                                      }
```

---

[3] That is, T is either the return type of the enclosing method, or it is **void** if b is not inside a method.

[4] That is, if every control flow path through b ends in a control transfer statement like **return**; for the precise definition see the Java Language Specification[8].

In the program on the left, the only control flow successor of both the **return** statement and the `println` statement is the "exit node" of the enclosing method, which is a pseudo-statement indicating that control flow has reached the end of the method (see [18] for more details on this point). The same is true in the refactored program on the right, and since all the other predecessor and successor statements are likewise preserved, the refactoring can continue.

In the first example program of Figure 4, the block *cannot* complete normally (both control paths end in a **return** statement), hence we transform as follows:

```
class A {                                      class A {
  void m(int i) {                                int m(int i) {
  {                                                return (() : int => {
    if(i == 23)                                      if(i == 23)
      return 42;                  ⟹                    return 42;
    return i + 1;                                    return i + 1;
  }                                                }) ();
}                                                }
}                                              }
```

Again, we can verify that control flow successors have not changed: the newly inserted **return** is a flow-through node, and hence does not disrupt control flow.

4.3 Close over Variables

We now want to perform lambda lifting on the anonymous method produced by the previous step, to make explicit any dependencies on local variables from the surrounding scope. In data flow terms, we need to handle two situations:

- The anonymous method might read a local variable x from the surrounding scope, whose value was set before executing the method; thus it has an incoming dataflow edge that crosses the boundaries of the anonymous method.
- The anonymous method might write a local variable y from the surrounding scope whose value is read after the method has finished executing; thus it has an outgoing data flow edge that crosses the method's boundaries.

In the first case, x needs to be made a value parameter of the method, in the second case y should become an output parameter. Of course, both situations may apply to the same variable, which should then be classified as a reference parameter.

We can implement these conditions in terms of the dataflow framework: For a given occurrence of a variable x in the anonymous method,

- x should be made a value parameter if any of its data flow predecessors come before the entry of the anonymous method,
- x should be made an output parameter if any of its data flow successors come after the exit of the anonymous method,

and it should be made a reference parameter if both situations apply.

After all variables have been treated in this manner, we are guaranteed that all data flow edges have been safely rerouted. There might, however, still be references to local variables from the enclosing scope in the body; this happens if the use of a local variable

```
class A {                              class A {
  int k;                                 int k;
  void m(boolean b) {                    void m(boolean b) {
    int n = 23, m;                         int n = 23, m;
    (() : void ⇒ {                         ((boolean b, ref int n) : void ⇒ {
      if(b)                                  int m;
        n += 19;            ⇒                 if(b)
      m = k = 56;                              n += 19;
    })();                                    m = k = 56;
    System.out.println(n);                 })(b, n);
  }                                        System.out.println(n);
}                                        }
                                       }
```

Fig. 7. Closing over local variables

inside the anonymous method is independent of its use in the enclosing method, and we can then safely make it a local variable of the anonymous method instead.

As an example, consider the program in Figure 7 on the left. The *Close Over Variables* refactoring considers the three references to b, n, and m inside the anonymous method (but not the reference to k, since it is a field).

– b has an incoming dataflow edge; the parameter declaration counts as a definition, there are no intervening definitions of b, and the definition is outside the anonymous method. It has no outgoing dataflow edge, since it is never used afterwards.
– n has both an incoming and an outgoing dataflow edge; its data flow predecessor is its declaration, which is outside the anonymous method; its data flow successor is the println statement, which is likewise outside the anonymous method.
– m has neither incoming nor outgoing dataflow edges, since it has no data flow predecessors or successors.

Thus, b should be made a value parameter, n a reference parameter, and m a local variable, yielding the program on the right.

Note that control flow cannot be influenced by the transformations done in this step, so no control flow locking and unlocking is needed. Also, we forgo binding preservation in this step: uses of local variables from the surrounding scope will now bind to the corresponding parameters instead. In all the preceding (and most of the following) steps, however, we do indeed want to preserve binding. Our decomposition of the refactoring helps to clarify this situation and makes it possible to precisely pinpoint at which stages binding preservation is required, and where we have deliberately chosen to relax it.

4.4 Eliminate Reference Parameters

Our refactoring process has now reached its apogee from the Java language specification: not only are we working with an anonymous method, a construct unknown to the JLS, but it even might feature output and reference parameters, which are likewise not supported by the language. It is now our task to safely remove these extra features to bring our program back into the fold of standard compliant Java programs.

In this step, we eliminate **out** and **ref** parameters. The basic idea is that a **ref** parameter can be simulated by a value parameter whose value is returned to the surrounding method, and there assigned to the corresponding variable; an **out** parameter is a local variable whose value is passed back in the same fashion.

More precisely, we perform the following steps:

1. If there is no output or reference parameter, the refactoring is a no-op. If there is more than one such parameter, abort (since Java methods can only return a single value).
2. If the anonymous method already has a non-**void** return type, abort likewise, for the same reason.
3. Let x be the only non-value parameter. If it is a reference parameter, change it into a value parameter. Otherwise make it into a local variable of the anonymous method and remove the corresponding argument.
4. Change the return type of the anonymous method to the type of x.
5. Insert a statement to return x and wrap the whole anonymous method into an assignment to the corresponding variable in the surrounding method.

All these steps are quite straightforward to implement; for example, the program from Figure 7 becomes

```
class A {
  int k;
  void m(boolean b) {
    int n = 23, m;
    n = ((boolean b, int n) : int ⇒ {
      int m;
      if(b)
        n += 19;
      m = k = 56;
      return n;
    })(b, n);
    System.out.println(n);
  }
}
```

As explained, this refactoring step rejects any anonymous method that needs to return the value of two or more variables, which results in a behaviour similar to Eclipse. An alternative would be to package up the necessary return values into a wrapper object, return that object, and unwrap it again in the calling method.

4.5 Lift Anonymous Method

To finally turn our refactored program back into a normal Java program, we need to eliminate the anonymous method. We know that it has only value parameters and its body does not reference any local variables from the enclosing scope; hence it is semantically equivalent to a call to a named method with the same body and parameters and the same arguments.

Assuming that we want to extract the anonymous method to a method named f, we simply convert $(\overline{p} : r \textbf{ throws } \overline{x} \Rightarrow \overline{b})(\overline{e})$ into the method call $f(\overline{e})$, and insert the definition

r $f(\bar{p})$ **throws** $\bar{x}$ {
$\quad \bar{b}$

}

into the surrounding class declaration. Our naming framework is put to use to ensure that the call to f really binds to the newly inserted method f (and that there are no overriding methods), and that all type bindings are preserved; this will, for example, detect (and reject) a refactoring that tries to extract a statement that throws a locally declared exception type.

The example program from above, of course, poses no such problems, and we can successfully complete the refactoring:

```
class A {
  int k;
  void m(boolean b) {
    int n = 23, m;
    n = f(b, n);
    System.out.println(n);
  }
  int f(boolean b, int n) {
    int m;
    if(b)
      n += 19;
    m = k = 56;
    return n;
  }
}
```

4.6   Putting It All Together

The micro-refactorings introduced above are all implemented as methods on AST node types, which are just Java classes. For example, the *Extract Block* refactoring is a method in class `Block` with the signature

```
Block extractBlock(int i, int j) throws RefactoringException
```

When invoked as b.extractBlock(i, j), the method extracts statements i to j of block b into a new block, and returns it as a result. If, at any point, the refactoring cannot proceed (for example due to an invariant violation), an exception is thrown.

The other refactorings are implemented in a similar way, so that the complete *Extract Method* refactoring can be realised as a one-liner (although we introduce some line breaks for æsthetic reasons):

```
MethodDecl extractMethod(int i, int j, String n, String v)
    throws RefactoringException {
  return extractBlock(i, j).extractAnonymous().
      closeVariables().eliminateOut().lift(n, v);
}
```

This method again belongs to class `Block`, and is invoked on the block from which we want to extract statements i to j. The parameter n determines the name of the new method, and v its visibility. Since all the micro-refactorings return the result they produce, an invocation chain can be used to implement their sequential composition.

Space constraints prevent us from showing more code, but the entire refactoring framework is available at http://jastadd.org/refactoring-tools.

5 Discussion

The previous two sections have discussed in some detail an implementation of *Extract Method* as a sequential composition of five component refactorings that make essential use of several lightweight language extensions to achieve better separation of concerns, and to get a clearer picture of how the refactoring preserves certain syntactic invariants to achieve behaviour preservation.

The same approach works equally well for other refactorings. Let us take a short look at *Inline Method*. It is the inverse of *Extract Method* in that it takes an invocation of a method and inlines the method body, substituting it for the invocation expression. It can likewise be decomposed into five micro-refactorings, that are precisely inverse to their counterparts from *Extract Method*:

1. *Anonymise Method* turns a method call that can be statically resolved into an anonymous method with the same body, parameter list and exception list as the named method being invoked, applied to the same arguments.
2. *Introduce Reference Parameter* removes return statements and replaces them with assignments to an output parameter.
3. *Open Variables* substitutes actual arguments for formal parameters, using the locking framework to ensure that name binding and data flow remain unaffected.
4. *Inline Anonymous Method* replaces an invocation of an anonymous method without parameters by its body, preserving control flow.
5. *Inline Block* inlines all statements within a block into the surrounding block.

As another example of a similar pair of inverse refactorings we have *Extract Local Variable*, which extracts an expression into a local variable, and *Inline Local Variable*, which eliminates all uses of a local variable by substituting its value. Both were very easy to implement in our framework.

In all these cases, the use of anonymous methods allows us to separate the concerns of data flow preservation and control flow preservation, and as before both the name binding framework and the control and data flow library see heavy use. Several smaller language extensions are also used: For example, when inlining method parameters during *Open Variables* it is useful to introduce temporary local variables whose names should not conflict with any other variables in scope. We introduce such non-shadowing variables as an additional language construct which can be turned into a normal declaration by choosing a fresh name.

These language extensions only exist at the level of abstract syntax. It is hard to imagine a good syntactic representation, e.g., for a bound name that explicitly specifies its binding target, and it would certainly not be conducive to a source program's clarity to explicitly contain such constructs. But that is not their goal: Bound names and bound control flow exist only to raise the level of abstraction for implementing refactorings and to address in one place issues that occur in several different refactorings.

The situation is a bit different for anonymous methods and their support for reference and output parameters: again, these only exist in the abstract syntax tree and cannot be used in source programs. Programming languages like C# or Smalltalk, on the other hand, come with built-in support for this kind of language feature, which could potentially simplify the implementation of refactorings like *Extract Method*. However, it may be the case that the complexity of handling closures in the analysis outweighs the benefit of using them for decomposition.

It is perhaps interesting to observe that our use of an intermediate language for refactoring goes against the usual trend: For static analysis, for example, one would normally choose an intermediate language that is *simpler* than the source language, abstracting away from its idiosyncrasies and simplifying it down to a core language. We work instead on a *richer* language that introduces new features which we find useful for structuring the refactoring process.

However, this does not complicate the implementations of the refactorings proper. While there are numerous statements in Java that affect control flow, from the refactoring point of view it is sufficient to abstract them as nodes in a control flow graph. Similarly, all expressions in Java that contain an assignment as a side effect can be abstracted as reaching definitions.

The challenge of refactoring a rich language with various extensions thus boils down to implementing name binding, control flow analysis, and data flow analysis for the full language. These analyses can all be implemented in a modular and extensible way, taking advantage of the compiler infrastructure [21,18].

While the analyses provide these abstractions and use them to enforce invariants, the micro-refactorings build on top of these abstractions and therefore only need to deal with a much smaller language. For example, *Extract Method* needs to be aware of concepts such as methods, parameters, return values, and exceptions; the remaining language features can be abstracted as their effect on control and data flow.

This abstract view is sufficient for the refactoring developer. The invariant checking provides a safety net that guards against corner cases and surprising interactions between language features. For example, if the developer did not implement the *Close Over Variables* micro-refactoring, method extraction would still be possible for a limited number of cases, and reject cases were lambda lifting is needed.

The developer could then further improve the transformation to cover more cases without the danger of inadvertently allowing unsound refactorings. This stands in sharp contrast to a precondition-based approach where unanticipated situations easily lead to incorrect transformations.

6   Evaluation

For evaluating our approach, we first present some statistics on the amount of code needed to implement the discussed refactorings.

The naming framework is the biggest component, requiring about 1700 lines of code[5]; this excludes code that is specific to the *Rename* refactorings. The implementation of the control flow analysis contributes around 550 lines of code, whereas the data flow analysis for local variables is implemented in 200 lines of code. Note that the former two components were written well before we started implementing the refactorings discussed in this paper, only the data flow analysis was implemented specifically for this project.

---

[5] This and all following code size measurements were generated using David A. Wheeler's 'SLOCCount'.

The implementation of anonymous methods requires about 150 lines of code, for the definition of corresponding AST node types, pretty printing, name analysis, and control and data flow analysis.

The size of the individual refactorings we have implemented is summarised in Figure 8: for each refactoring we show its decomposition in micro-refactorings, and the size of each micro-refactoring.

Extract Method takes around 500 lines of code, quite evenly distributed between the individual micro-refactorings: *Extract Block* needs about 140 lines (including the code for *Push Statement Into Block* and *Split Declaration*), *Introduce Anonymous Method* and *Close Over Variables* around 100 lines each, whereas *Eliminate Reference Parameters* and *Lift Anonymous Method* each are implemented in less than 90 lines.

Similar numbers obtain for *Inline Method*, shown in the same figure on the right, which is overall a bit smaller than *Extract Method*; *Extract Local Variable* and *Inline Local Variable* are significantly smaller, at about 80 lines of code each.

These numbers compare very favourably both to Eclipse's implementation of *Extract Method*, which comprises more than 1500 lines of code, and other implementations like the one presented by Juillerat [12] that seems to offer less functionality for only a subset of Java at around 1000 lines of code.

To test the correctness of our refactorings, we put together a suite of about 90 tests for *Extract Method* and its constituent micro-refactorings, and several dozen for the other refactorings, in particular including all the test cases for bugs in the refactoring engines of popular IDEs [3].

We also ran our engine on the test suite for Eclipse 3.4, which is publicly available, and some tests from the test suite for IntelliJ IDEA 8.0, which JetBrains kindly provided for us to use.

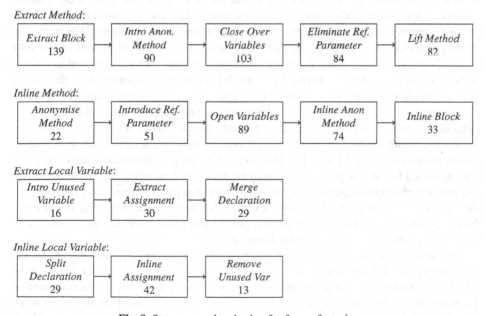

Fig. 8. Structure and code size for four refactorings

The former includes 395 test cases for *Extract Method*, of which 23 test functionality that we do not support yet: Two test cases concern the extraction of a method into a surrounding class other than the immediate host class. Another 21 cases test duplicate elimination, where a number of occurrences of the same expression are jointly extracted into a method. This feature is largely orthogonal to the extraction process proper and relies on clone detection [1], which we have not implemented in our framework yet. All of the remaining 372 test cases are handled correctly by our implementation, among them three on which Eclipse's own refactoring engine fails with a null pointer exception, and one on which it produces a wrong result.

The test cases that JetBrains provided to us comprise 74 tests for *Extract Method*, of which 19 again concern duplicate elimination. We pass all the remaining 55 tests.

Where our engine did not produce identical code to Eclipse or IntelliJ, we manually checked to make sure that our output is equally valid. Such discrepancies are mostly due to a different ordering of the parameters of the extracted method or similar syntactic variations.

In summary, we can say with confidence that our implementation is at least as good as these two industrial-strength implementations, and in some cases manages to detect and properly handle situations they fail to address.

7   Related and Future Work

Refactoring literature usually presents statement-level refactoring like *Extract Method* as primitive transformations useful in the composition of larger-scale refactorings [19,13]. We are, however, by no means the first to advocate the decomposition of that kind of refactoring into yet smaller components. In [20], Perera paints a compelling picture of how the use of micro-refactorings changes the way refactorings are used by the programmer, with method extraction in Java as one of his examples. His proposed building blocks, *e.g. Push Statement into Method* for moving statements one by one into a freshly created method, are still quite complex, however, as they still need to yield a valid Java program at each intermediate step. It is hence not obvious that his decomposition actually makes it easier to implement a behaviour preserving refactoring engine. By comparison, our use of lightweight language extensions makes the individual micro-refactorings much simpler and easier to think about and implement.

Such decomposition of statement-level refactorings is also addressed by Ettinger in his inspirational PhD thesis [5], in which he develops a theoretical framework for slicing-based behaviour-preserving transformations. Noteworthily, he chose to embed the concept of liveness directly into programs, by explicitly stating variables that cannot be local to a statement. Rather than tackling a full mainstream language like we do, however, Ettinger focuses on proving the correctness of transformations for programs written in a simple *ad hoc* imperative language.

The concept of control and data flow preservation features prominently in the influential paper of Komondoor and Horwitz [14] on procedure extraction. Under their idealising assumptions, they can indeed prove that flow preservation entails semantics preservation, which, as we have discussed, is not the case for Java. However, their work mostly focuses on moving statements together to arrange them into a contiguous block suitable for extraction; the actual process of extracting into a procedure they dismiss as "straightforward".

Our use of language extensions like bound names bears a certain resemblance to work by Mens and others on implementing transformations on graph representations of programs [16]. The graph they propose, however, only encodes part of the program, namely its high-level structure, as none of the refactorings they discuss actually require control and data flow information. Furthermore, their work does not address the problem of translating back the graph representation into a source-level program, which is essential for the purposes of a refactoring engine.

The composition of smaller refactorings into larger ones has been the focus of work by Kniesel and Koch [13]. For the refactorings we have considered in this paper, a very simple form of sequential composition is sufficient, which they call AND-sequence. Their work is also concerned with composing the pre- and post-conditions of constituent refactorings, which does not directly apply to our invariant-based presentation.

An invariant-based approach to structural refactoring has been suggested some time ago by Griswold [9]. He provides a small catalogue of simple "program restructurings" that preserve data and control dependencies as captured in a Program Dependence Graph [15]. While these restructurings are quite similar in scope and intent to our micro-refactorings, they are presented for a very small and well-behaved object language (a first-order subset of Scheme), where they are much easier to implement and reason about than with Java.

For future work, we would like both to explore the implementation of new refactorings and to extend our current implementations. There is still a number of structural refactorings that our engine does not support, for example *Encapsulate Field* or *Move Method*, but it seems that most of these should be easy to implement using our by now well-developed toolbox of name binding and flow analyses.

A more interesting challenge would be to implement the *Extract Slice* refactoring [6], which does away with the restriction of *Extract Method* that only consecutive statements can be extracted. Slice extraction needs to freely rearrange statements, so it does not preserve control flow in general; an invariant-based presentation would hence need to consider more subtle preservation criteria.

A more straightforward extension to our current implementation would be to implement duplicate elimination as provided by Eclipse and IntelliJ. As mentioned, this extension would not seem to necessitate any extensions to the extraction mechanism proper, but only requires the implementation of a clone detection algorithm [1].

Finally, it would be interesting to see if the decomposition we have achieved for our four example refactorings could help with their verification. Since each micro-refactoring performs a very small but independent and well-defined transformation on the program it is tempting to try and verify their correctness separately, and then compose their proofs into a correctness proof of the whole refactoring. Such a proof could also make use of our previous work on formalising Java name binding [22].

8 Conclusions

We have presented a general approach to implementing software refactorings by viewing them as invariant-preserving transformations on programs in an enriched language.

Such an enriched language offers extensions to the base language that make the implementation of refactorings easier, for example by providing implicit invariant checking, or language constructs that can be used to better decompose the transformation performed by a refactoring. We have implemented a framework that offers several such extensions to the Java 5 language, and have used it to implement non-trivial refactorings such as *Extract Method*. The implementations are concise and well-structured; they support the complete Java 5 language; and our tests show that in terms of correctness they rival or even surpass widely known refactoring engines. We are confident that our approach is flexible enough to allow easy implementation of any structural refactoring that modifies name binding, control flow, and data flow.

We agree with Fowler's assessment that the *Extract Method* refactoring is a paradigmatic example of a refactoring that is simple, yet requires non-trivial analysis. But we have shown that there is no need to cross this Rubicon in one huge leap; we can instead pass it on stepping stones, one micro-refactoring at a time, with the principle of invariant preservation as our guide rope.

Acknowledgements

We would like to thank Emma Nilsson-Nyman and Ting Ting Mao, who implemented the control flow package that our refactoring implementation depends so vitally on, and Dmitry Jemerov of JetBrains, who graciously gave us access to IntelliJ's test suite. Damien Sereni provided important feedback on the ideas presented in this paper from the early stages. We thank him as well as Ran Ettinger, James Noble and the anonymous reviewers, who gave insightful comments on a draft version, which helped us improve the final paper in many ways. Finally, we would like to praise our poetic pal Pavel, without whom this paper would have a very dull title.

References

1. Baxter, I.D., Yahin, A., Moura, L., Sant'Anna, M., Bier, L.: Clone Detection Using Abstract Syntax Trees. In: ICSM, Washington, DC, USA, p. 368. IEEE Computer Society Press, Los Alamitos (1998)
2. Eclipse (2008), http://www.eclipse.org
3. Ekman, T., Ettinger, R., Schäfer, M., Verbaere, M.: Refactoring bugs (2008), http://progtools.comlab.ox.ac.uk/refactoring/bugreports
4. Ekman, T., Hedin, G.: The JastAdd Extensible Java Compiler. In: OOPSLA (2007)
5. Ettinger, R.: Refactoring via Program Slicing and Sliding. D.Phil. thesis, Computing Laboratory, Oxford, UK (2007)
6. Ettinger, R., Verbaere, M.: Untangling: a slice extraction refactoring. In: Aspect-Oriented Software Development (AOSD), pp. 93–101 (2004)
7. Fowler, M.: Crossing Refactoring's Rubicon (2001), http://martinfowler.com/articles/refactoringRubicon.html
8. Gosling, J., Joy, B., Steele, G., Bracha, G.: The Java Language Specification (2005)
9. Griswold, W.G.: Program Restructuring as an Aid to Software Maintenance. Ph.D. thesis, University of Washington (1991)
10. IntelliJ IDEA (2008), http://www.jetbrains.com

11. Johnsson, T.: Lambda Lifting: Transforming Programs to Recursive Equations. In: Jouan-naud, J.-P. (ed.) FPCA 1985. LNCS, vol. 201, pp. 190–230. Springer, Heidelberg (1985)
12. Juillerat, N., Hirsbrunner, B.: Improving Method Extraction: A Novel Approach to Data Flow Analysis Using Boolean Flags and Expressions. In: WRT (2007)
13. Kniesel, G., Koch, H.: Static Composition of Refactorings. The Science of Computer Programming 52(1-3), 9–51 (2004)
14. Komondoor, R., Horwitz, S.: Semantics-preserving Procedure Extraction. In: POPL, pp. 155–169. ACM Press, New York (2000)
15. Kuck, D.J., Kuhn, R.H., Leasure, B., Padua, D.A., Wolfe, M.: Dependence Graphs and Compiler Optimizations. In: POPL, January 1981, pp. 207–218 (1981)
16. Mens, T., DeMeyer, S., Janssens, D.: Formalising behaviour preserving program transformations. In: Corradini, A., Ehrig, H., Kreowski, H.-J., Rozenberg, G. (eds.) ICGT 2002. LNCS, vol. 2505, pp. 286–301. Springer, Heidelberg (2002)
17. NetBeans (2008), http://www.netbeans.com
18. Nilsson-Nyman, E., Ekman, T., Hedin, G., Magnusson, E.: Declarative Intraprocedural Flow Analysis of Java Source Code. In: Proceedings of 8th Workshop on Language Descriptions, Tools and Applications (LDTA 2008) (2008)
19. Opdyke, W.F.: Refactoring Object-Oriented Frameworks. PhD thesis, University of Illinois at Urbana-Champaign (1992)
20. Perera, R.: Refactoring: to the Rubicon.. and beyond! In: OOPSLA 2004: Companion to the 19th annual ACM SIGPLAN conference on Object-oriented programming systems, languages, and applications, pp. 2–3. ACM Press, New York (2004)
21. Schäfer, M., Ekman, T., de Moor, O.: Sound and Extensible Renaming for Java. In: Kiczales, G. (ed.) OOPSLA. ACM Press, New York (2008)
22. Schäfer, M., Ekman, T., de Moor, O.: Formalising and Verifying Reference Attribute Grammars in Coq. In: Castagna, G. (ed.) ESOP 2009. LNCS, vol. 5502, pp. 143–159. Springer, Heidelberg (2009)
23. Verbaere, M., Ettinger, R., de Moor, O.: JunGL: a Scripting Language for Refactoring. In: ICSE (2006)

Program Metamorphosis

Christoph Reichenbach*, Devin Coughlin, and Amer Diwan

University of Colorado, Boulder, CO 80309, USA
{reichenb,devin.coughlin,diwan}@colorado.edu

Abstract. Modern development environments support refactoring by providing atomically behaviour-preserving transformations. While useful, these transformations are limited in three ways: (i) atomicity forces transformations to be complex and opaque, (ii) the behaviour preservation requirement disallows deliberate behaviour evolution, and (iii) atomicity limits code reuse opportunities for refactoring implementers.

We present 'program metamorphosis', a novel approach for program evolution and refactoring that addresses the above limitations by breaking refactorings into smaller steps that need not preserve behaviour individually. Instead, we ensure that sequences of transformations preserve behaviour together, and simultaneously permit selective behavioural change.

To evaluate program metamorphosis, we have implemented a prototype plugin for Eclipse. Our analysis and experiments show that (1) our plugin provides correctness guarantees on par with those of Eclipse's own refactorings, (2) both our plugin and our approach address the aforementioned limitations, and (3) our approach fully subsumes traditional refactoring.

Keywords: Refactoring, Program Evolution.

1   Motivation

Modern programming methodologies, such as Extreme Programming [2], use *refactoring* to prepare software for impending change or to eliminate "bad smells" in source code. Fowler *et al.* [4] defines refactoring as:

> A change made to the internal structure of software ... without changing its observable behaviour

To automate this process, integrated development environments such as Eclipse [14] and refactoring engines such as HaRe [8] provide machine support for refactoring. These systems implement refactoring as atomic transformations guarded by preconditions. The underlying assumption is that if the precondition holds, the transformation will preserve behaviour. If the precondition does not hold, the IDE disallows the transformation. This approach prevents some forms of unintended behavioural change but presents several problems to refactoring users and developers:

---

* Supported by NSF Career Grant CCR-0133457 and NSF Grant ST-CRTS 0540997.

S. Drossopoulou (Ed.): ECOOP 2009, LNCS 5653, pp. 394–418, 2009.

```
class A {                    class A { }
  private int x;
  void f()                   class B {
  { x = C.g(); }               private int x;
}                              void f()
                               { x = C.g(); }
class B { }                  }
```

Fig. 1. The chicken-or-egg problem: fields and methods must be moved simultaneously

1. **The chicken-or-egg problem.** Atomic transformations with preconditions may prohibit safe refactorings. Consider the program in Figure 1: if we wish to move field "x" and method "f" from class "A" to class "B", we would like to employ the 'Move Method' and 'Move Field' refactorings [4]. If we move "f" first, "B.f()" will not be able to see "x", so 'Move Method' will disallow the move. However, if we move "x" first, the process fails for the converse reason. This chicken-or-egg problem is exacerbated if additional fields or mutually recursive methods are affected, and while refactoring users can sometimes find workarounds, they may find it easier to abandon the promised behaviour preservation of refactorings in favour of faster manual editing. Some refactoring implementations address this problem by attempting to predict which additional methods and fields must be moved simultaneously to atomically perform the refactoring, but these fixup heuristics are complex, error-prone, and may run contrary to the user's wishes.

2. **The selective behaviour evolution problem.** The user may want to exploit the automation provided by refactorings without necessarily preserving all behaviour. For example, in theory a refactoring must never allow the user to rename a public method since some independent source code (perhaps in a plugin) might reference this method by name. In practice, a user might accept this change and yet still want to prevent other forms of behavioural change, such as a renamed method overriding a method it didn't override before. This is a dilemma for refactoring engine designers: they must anticipate the degree to which users value safety over versatility.

3. **The predictive analysis problem.** Since traditional behaviour preservation checks are implemented as preconditions, they must predict the effect of the transformation in order to determine if it will cause problems. To do this exhaustively is quite difficult. For example, in the case of 'Rename', a precondition must consider all the possible ways in which a name could be captured and check to see if that will happen. As Schäfer et al. [13] point out, a less error-prone approach is to first perform the transformation and then check after the fact to see if any names have been captured.

This paper shows how a small twist to the "classical" refactoring implementation strategy allows us to solve the above problems. We achieve this by:

1. Capturing the approximate program behaviour in a program model,
2. Applying a series of possibly non–behaviour-preserving program metamorphosis steps (PM steps for short),
3. Using *postconditions* to compare the original program model to the current program model to see if behaviour has changed.

This twist yields a new view on refactoring: instead of treating refactoring as the application of atomic refactorings that must preserve behaviour by themselves, we can think of refactoring as a *process* of gradual application of PM steps. As part of this process, users may check for behaviour preservation at any time. Thus, users may decide to first transform their program as they desire (e.g., moving fields and methods) and then either recover behavioural equivalence, if necessary, or expressly and selectively accept some or all behavioural change.

Program metamorphosis provides three main benefits over the traditional approach to refactorings:

1. It allows safe transformations through intermediate stages whose behaviour differs from the intended behaviour,
2. It allows safe transformations through intermediate stages that may not even compile,
3. It allows the user to selectively evolve behaviour.

In this paper, we provide the following contributions: we describe the process of program metamorphosis (Section 2) and demonstrate the benefits it offers over traditional refactoring (Section 3). We then sketch a theory that allows us to view program metamorphosis as a decomposition of refactorings and show that our approach is at least as safe as traditional refactoring, if we base it on refactorings that we can decompose in a certain way (Section 4). Next, we describe a prototype Eclipse plugin that demonstrates that program metamorphosis is practical to implement (Section 5). Finally, we describe several refactorings we implemented using our prototype; where possible, we compare the quality of their behaviour preservation promises against those provided by Eclipse's refactorings by applying both to Java projects with comprehensive unit test suites (Section 6). Section 7 reviews related work and Section 8 concludes.

2   The Process of Program Metamorphosis

Before we look at concrete examples of program metamorphosis, it is helpful to consider the structure of the underlying process. A program metamorphosis system consists of three main components:

1. a mechanism for generating *program models* that describe the approximate behaviour of a program,
2. a *consistency checker* that compares two program models and extracts the inconsistencies (if any) between them,
3. a suite of small *PM steps*, each of which transforms the program in a possibly non–behaviour-preserving way.

Program metamorphosis uses the consistency checker and program model generator to help the user compose PM steps into a sequence of transformations that, taken as a whole, preserves behaviour.

2.1   Combining Multiple PM Steps

Unlike traditional refactorings, which use preconditions to check the legality of the transformation, program metamorphosis uses postconditions. Specifically, program metamorphosis constructs a model of the program's behaviour before the transformation, transforms the program, and then constructs another model after the transformation, possibly re-using parts of the earlier model. If the two models do not match, then the program's behaviour may have been changed. This approach, illustrated in Figure 2, allows program metamorphosis to safely combine multiple transformations as follows:

1. We first calculate a model for the program and save it as the "desired program model." We call this the "desired" model since we ultimately want the transformed program to end up with the same model.
2. When the user applies a PM step, we compare the desired program model with the calculated current program model, reporting any inconsistencies to the user. If there are inconsistencies then the user may:
   (a) Revert the previous step,
   (b) Apply another PM step, or
   (c) Accept any or all of the reported inconsistencies as behavioural change by updating the desired model to incorporate the change in behaviour.

The key benefit of program metamorphosis is that after the user has applied any particular PM step, the program's current behaviour may not match its original behaviour, but *the user can continue applying steps until it does.* In this way, PM allows the composition of simple, possibly non-behaviour preserving steps into a sequence that does, in its entirety, preserve behaviour.

Figure 3 visualises the advantages of our approach. In this figure, every vertex represents a program; either well-formed (black) or ill-formed (white), while edges represent PM steps. Programs with 'equivalent' behaviour are grouped into equivalent classes. To refactor program p_a to program p_b, we can choose

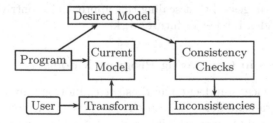

Fig. 2. Consistency checking process for program metamorphosis

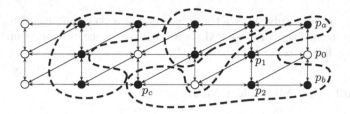

Fig. 3. Program metamorphosis. Black vertices represent well-formed programs; white vertices represent ill-formed programs. Solid edges represent the application of PM steps. Dashed lines group programs with equivalent behaviour.

two PM steps: from p_a to p_0, then to p_b, since we may 'pass through' ill-formed programs. With refactoring, we must always remain well-formed and in the same equivalence class, so we have to take a longer route through p_1 and p_2 instead (Section 3.1 gives a concrete example of this scenario). Worse, we can never hope to reach p_c from p_a with refactoring, while there are many ways to get there with program metamorphosis (Section 5.3 gives a concrete example of this scenario).

2.2   Recovery Plans

In addition to relying on the user to apply additional steps when the current model does not match the desired model, a program metamorphosis system can automatically attempt to recover consistency in several ways:

1. *Disallow/retract PM steps* that fail to preserve behaviour.
2. *Heuristically apply supporting PM steps.* For example, Schäfer *et al.* [13] describe a particular technique that can be used to automatically fix name capture after 'Rename'. In some cases, heuristic changes may have undesired side-effects; if so, the user must undo them later. In a similar vein, existing refactoring tools, such as Eclipse, predict conflicts that will happen and heuristically pre-apply other refactorings in order to avoid them.
3. *Search for recovery plans.* Recovery plans are short sequences of PM steps that will satisfy the postconditions. The user can then pick which plan (if any) she wants to enact. This approach falls within the realm of *AI Planning*; to be practical, it requires heuristics to guide the planning process.
   One of our earlier prototypes incorporated such facilities, though our initial experiments suggested that scaling this approach is nontrivial. We expect to explore this idea further in future work.

2.3   Challenges in Comparing Program Models

Program equivalence is undecidable; thus, we cannot be fully precise when comparing two program models. We can choose to err either on the side of being *pessimistic*, i.e., making conservative worst-case assumptions, or on the side of being *optimistic*. Both approaches have their merits: being pessimistic means that we will always be safe, while being optimistic means that we can be more flexible. In Java we must be optimistic, at least in some respects; otherwise dynamic class loading and reflection render most interesting refactorings impossible.

Traditional refactorings have only two options: they can be pessimistic and safe, or optimistic and flexible. Program metamorphosis adds a third option: it can be pessimistic and safe, but also allow users to accept inconsistencies as behavioural change and thereby also be flexible.

We show in Section 4 that at least in theory program metamorphosis is as safe as refactorings; we show in Section 6 that our first prototype is also as safe as refactorings.

3   Examples of Program Metamorphosis

In the following, we present three examples to illustrate our approach in practice. First, we illustrate transformations that temporarily change behaviour (Section 3.1). Next, we consider transformations that temporarily render the program ill-formed (Section 3.2). Finally, we examine the use of selective behaviour evolution (Section 3.3).

3.1   Transformations through Non-equivalent Programs

Consider the program below and assume that the user wants to swap the names of the totalValue instance variable and the total method parameter. In the following, we have labelled important declarations and variable references with $[\cdot]^n$.

```
class Receipt {
  [int totalValue]¹;
  void setTotal([int total]²) {
    [totalValue]³ = [total]⁴;
  }
}
```

A rename refactoring using atomic preconditions would disallow starting the transformation by renaming either totalValue to total or total to totalValue because in both cases the parameter (2) would capture the left-hand side of the assignment (3), possibly changing the behaviour of the program. This transformation *could* be accomplished via refactorings, albeit awkwardly, by first renaming one of the variables to a temporary name, renaming the other to the first name, and then renaming the temporary name to the second name, but this work-around requires three steps rather than two and forces the user to plan ahead when refactoring.

PM can perform the transformation safely in two steps using postconditions. It starts by creating the following program model, which captures the binding of variable uses to declaration (here $n \rightarrow m$ indicates that the variable used at n refers to the declaration at m).

| Desired Name Model | $3 \rightarrow 1, 4 \rightarrow 2$ |

The user can then apply a rename step to change the total field declaration (1) to be called totalValue. PM now computes the model for the transformed program and compares it to the desired model, reporting any inconsistencies to the user. In this case, the rename has caused the reference on the left-hand side of the assignment (3) to be captured: it previously referred to the the field (declaration 1) but now refers to the parameter (declaration 2).

```
class Receipt {
  [int totalValue]¹;
  void setTotal([int totalValue]²) {
    [totalValue]³ = [totalValue]⁴;
  }
}
```

Desired Name Model	$3 \rightarrow 1, 4 \rightarrow 2$
Current Name Model	$3 \rightarrow 2, 4 \rightarrow 2$
Inconsistencies	3 captured by 2

The program's behaviour has now been changed: calling setTotal() will no longer update the totalValue field. To ensure behaviour preservation, the user can either revert the rename transformation, or apply another rename step to rename the left-hand side totalValue (3) to total.

PM steps have access to the desired program model, which helps them in transforming programs. In the case of rename, we use the mappings in the *desired model*, rather than the current model, to decide which occurrences of totalValue need to be changed. Thus renaming (3) to total updates both (3) and the field declaration (1), since (3) is mapped to (1) in the desired model, while leaving (2) unaffected:

```
class Receipt {
  [int total]¹;
  void setTotal([int totalValue]²) {
    [total]³ = [totalValue]⁴;
  }
}
```

Desired Name Model	$3 \rightarrow 1, 4 \rightarrow 2$
Current Name Model	$3 \rightarrow 1, 4 \rightarrow 2$
Inconsistencies	None

The current model now matches the desired model. We have achieved the desired transformation safely and naturally in only two steps, which would be impossible with a traditional Rename refactoring since atomic preconditions prohibit transforming through an intermediate stage that does not preserve behaviour.

3.2   Transformations through Ill-Formed Programs

Sometimes it makes sense to temporarily transform into a program that will not even compile. Consider the case below where the user wants to move both the setTotal() method and the total field from the Receipt class to the Bill class.

Preconditions, as in traditional refactorings, would disallow first moving the method, since there is no total field in Bill, but would also prohibit first moving the total field, since that would leave behind an unresolved reference to that field in Receipt.

```
class Receipt {
  [int total]¹;
  void setTotal([int totalValue]²) {
    [total]³ = [totalValue]⁴;
  }
}

public class Bill { }
```

Desired Name Model	$3 \rightarrow 1, 4 \rightarrow 2$

By using postconditions and a program model, program metamorphosis avoids this chicken-or-egg problem: the user can move either the field or the method first, and then move the other. Suppose she moves setTotal() first: this step will will result in an unknown name inconsistency and the compiler will complain that it can't resolve the reference to total (3).

```
class Receipt {
  [int total]¹;
}

class Bill {
  void setTotal([int totalValue]²) {
    [total]³ = [totalValue]⁴;
  }
}
```

Desired Name Model	$3 \rightarrow 1, 4 \rightarrow 2$
Current Name Model	$3 \rightarrow ?, 4 \rightarrow 2$

Inconsistencies	Unknown name 'total' at 3

The user can now apply a second move step to move the total field to Bill. After this step, the current model matches the desired model and the program is again well-formed.

```
class Receipt { }

class Bill {
  [int total]¹;
  void setTotal([int totalValue]²) {
    [total]³ = [totalValue]⁴;
  }
}
```

Desired Name Model	$3 \rightarrow 1, 4 \rightarrow 2$
Current Name Model	$3 \rightarrow 1, 4 \rightarrow 2$
Inconsistencies	None

3.3 Selective Behaviour Evolution

Refactorings are not, by definition, permitted to change program behaviour, but sometimes this is desirable. Consider the case where the user wants to rename a public class: technically this should not be allowed since there may be independent code (such as a plugin) that relies on the existence of that class. If we care about preserving our public APIs, we can extend the program model to account for class visibility. Suppose, in the example below, that the user wants to change the Bill class to be called Invoice instead.

```
public class Bill {
  [private int total]¹;
  private void setTotal([int totalValue]²) {
    [total]³ = [totalValue]⁴;
  }
}
```

Desired Visibility Model	public $\rightarrow$ {Bill}, protected $\rightarrow$ {}

After renaming Bill to Invoice, the current and desired models no longer match:

Desired Visibility Model	public → {Bill}, protected → {}
Current Visibility Model	public → {Invoice}, protected → {}
Inconsistencies	Extra public class Invoice Missing public class Bill

Program metamorphosis now reports two inconsistencies between the current and desired program models. First, there is a new public class, Invoice, whose presence could prevent a plugin that already defines its own Invoice class from loading. This may be an acceptable behaviour change (after all, library implementers frequently add classes in order to provide new features). Second, Bill is no longer a public class; this change is more troubling since it would break existing plugins that rely explicitly on the Bill functionality.

Rather than revert the transformation, with program metamorphosis the user can *selectively* accept behavioural change by modifying the desired program model to indicate that there should be a public class called Invoice. All future program models will be compared against this new model.

Desired Visibility Model	public → {Bill, Invoice}, protected → {}
Current Visibility Model	public → {Invoice}, protected → {}
Inconsistencies	Missing public class Bill

Even after modifying the desired model, the 'Missing public class Bill' inconsistency remains; the user could choose to clear this up by, say, introducing a new version of Bill that delegates to an instance of Invoice.

Compare this user experience to that offered by traditional refactoring implementations: those typically require the user to make an all-or-nothing choice to apply an unsafe transformation after warning her that it may change behaviour. She must then determine how the program text was transformed, discern how these alterations would change program behaviour, and decide if that new behaviour is acceptable. In contrast, program metamorphosis determines how the program *behaviour* has been changed and allows the user to approve or reject those behavioural changes individually.

3.4   Reusing Equivalence Checks

One benefit of using program models rather than the predictive analyses required by preconditions is that they are often agnostic as to how the program is transformed. The name model is constructed in the same way regardless of whether a name could be captured via a rename, a field move, or a pull-up method. Similarly, it doesn't matter to the visibility model whether a class's visibility was changed because it was deleted or because it was renamed. This is advantageous because as we add new PM steps, they can reuse the same program models and get existing behaviour preservation checks "for free." While refactorings can also sometimes exploit commonalities [7], it is much less obvious how source code for predictive analyses can be re-used.

3.5 Summary

By using postconditions and program models to check for behavioural equivalence, program metamorphosis allows users to safely compose sequences of transformational steps that may not preserve behaviour individually. This approach is more natural than that used by traditional refactorings because it does not force users to plan ahead; instead, program metamorphosis notifies them whenever they have arrived at a non-equivalent or even ill-formed program and allows them to continue transforming until the problem has been corrected. Further, this approach enables an elegant mechanism of informing users about possible behavioural changes and allows them to selectively choose which, if any, of those changes are acceptable.

4 Program Metamorphosis and Refactoring

As we have seen, our PM steps are quite different from traditional refactorings, even though they achieve similar goals. In this section, we investigate the relation between these two classes of transformations on a high level. We first take refactorings apart and show how their components relate to the components of a program metamorphosis system (Section 4.1), and then formally derive the notion of a program metamorphosis system from the resulting building blocks (Section 4.2). We establish some basic properties about this formalism (Section 4.3) and finally 'close the circle' by showing how we can build refactorings from PM steps (Section 4.4).

4.1 How Refactorings Work

Abstractly, a refactoring is a pair $\langle P, t \rangle$. P is a safety precondition that determines whether or not the refactoring is applicable to a given program. t transforms the program.

Since refactorings should preserve behaviour, P should ensure that the program has the same behaviour before and after applying t:

$$P(p) \implies [\![t(p)]\!] = [\![p]\!]$$

where $[\![-]\!]$ maps a program to its behaviour. Refactoring implementers then typically implement P such that

$$P(p) \implies V(p) \wedge V(t(p)) \wedge (p \equiv t(p))$$

i.e., the precondition $P(p)$ holds only if the input program p is well-formed ($V(p)$) and the the resulting program will both be well-formed and (in some sense) equivalent to the input program ($p \equiv t(p)$); ideally, but not necessarily, by exhibiting precisely the same behaviour (cf. Section 2.3).

If we examine existing refactoring implementations in more detail, we observe that they implement both the validity predicates and the notion of equivalence via an intermediate step, namely the construction of a model. This model is typically a set or slice of some relevant properties of the current program; refactoring developers choose those properties so that they can check for well-formedness and predict the outcome of the transformation. For example, Griswold [5] uses a Program-Dependence Graph to determine relevant relationships that might be affected by the refactoring, while Eclipse uses a comprehensive name and type model provided by its JDT library[1]. Let us assume that we compute such a program model m with a program analysis properties, i.e., $m = \text{properties}(p)$. Then the above implication becomes

$$P(p) \implies V(m) \land V(t'(m)) \land (m \equiv t'(m))$$

(modulo overloading of our predicate V and equivalence relation $\equiv$). Here, t' is a simulation of the effect of transformation t on the program model:

$$\text{properties} \circ t = t' \circ \text{properties}$$

i.e., we should arrive at the same model if we first compute the program model and then apply t' as if we first transform the program and then compute a program model from the result.

In practice, refactoring implementors usually don't need to make the modified model $t'(m)$ explicit, since they can use domain knowledge to (a) re-compute only the relevant slice of the program model that might have been affected by the transformation and (b) manually deforest [16] their code to directly check for possible changes at the same time as computing the effect the transformation would have on the model.

4.2   Towards Program Metamorphosis

Such optimisations lead to tightly integrated t', V and ($\equiv$). But if we make all three explicit, we obtain the building blocks for program metamorphosis.

To see this, recall our example from Section 3.2 of moving a method together with the field the method depends on. Let t_m be the move for the method and t_f the move for the field. Then we have that

$$V(t'_m(p)) \text{ does } NOT \text{ hold}$$

i.e, our program is ill-formed after the first transformation step (because the method can no longer see the field from its new location). However,

$$V(t'_f \circ t'_m(p)) \text{ and, moreover, } m \equiv t'_f \circ t'_m(m)$$

i.e., the composition of both transformation steps preserves behaviour. Here, we exploit that program well-formedness (V) is independent of any preceding transformations.

---

[1] http://www.eclipse.org/jdt/overview.php

4.3   Soundness and Derivation

In this section, we find that we can always construct a program metamorphosis system from an existing set of refactorings if we can decompose the refactorings appropriately, and that the resulting metamorphosis system gives the same consistency promises as the original set of refactorings. We make this more concrete in the following:

First, assume that properties : $L \to \mathcal{M}$ computes a program model $m \in \mathcal{M}$ from a program $p \in L$.

Definition 1. *A program metamorphosis system is a tuple* $\langle \mathcal{M}, \text{properties}, \equiv, V \rangle$ *such that* $V(\text{properties}(p))$ *iff the program p is well-formed.*

To simplify our exposition, we overload $V(p) \iff V(\text{properties}(p))$ and $p \equiv p' \iff \text{properties}(p) \equiv \text{properties}(p')$.

As we have discussed previously, our analyses and equivalence relations can be 'pessimistic' or 'optimistic'. For pessimistic metamorphosis systems we can utilise the above intuition to show a useful property regarding the strength of our consistency promises:

Definition 2. *A program metamorphosis system is* sound *wrt a language semantics* $[\![-]\!]$ *iff, for all programs $p, p' \in L$ such that p' can be reached from p with program metamorphosis steps,*

$$V(p) \wedge V(p') \wedge (p \equiv p') \implies [\![p]\!] = [\![p']\!]$$

Conveniently, we can construct metamorphosis systems from refactoring preconditions such that the metamorphosis systems are sound whenever the preconditions are sound. Recall our earlier decomposition of preconditions:

$$P(p) \iff V(p) \wedge V(t(p)) \wedge (p \equiv t(p))$$

If we set $(-) = (\equiv_{[\![-]\!]})$, where $p \equiv_{[\![-]\!]} p' \iff [\![p]\!] = [\![p']\!]$, we have the "perfect" predicate for *any* refactoring. This relation is undecidable, so we must choose another. If we choose not to be conservative (i.e., if we do not guarantee behaviour preservation), we may pick any relation. If we are conservative, we must pick a $(\equiv) \subset (\equiv_{[\![-]\!]})$, i.e., a conservative approximation that distinguishes some programs that would be semantically equivalent. We can then immediately see the following:

Theorem 1. *Given the decomposition of refactoring preconditions $P_1, \ldots, P_n$, we can construct a metamorphosis system that is sound if $P_1, \ldots, P_n$ are conservative, and allows at least as many transformations as $P_1, \ldots, P_n$ allow.*

Proof. Let $(\equiv_1), \cdots, (\equiv_n)$ be the equivalence relations used in $P_1, \ldots, P_n$. Then we set

$$(\equiv) = (\equiv_1) \cup \cdots \cup (\equiv_n)$$

All $(\equiv_i)$ are conservative approximations of $(\equiv_{[\![-]\!]})$, so $(\equiv)$ inherits this property. Furthermore, for any programs p_1, p_2 we have that $p_1 \equiv_i p_2$ $(1 \le i \le n)$ implies $p_1 \equiv p_2$.

In the above, we did not specify how the program models and **properties** functions of the various preconditions should be combined. In theory, we can always resort to a straightforward cartesian product on the program model (as suggested by our construction of the combined ($\equiv$)), but in practice this is wasteful: most program models can be factored into common components (for example, practically all refactorings need a name model, and most need a type model). The net result of this observation is that the complexity and size of our model apparatus never increases (and often decreases) relatively to the number of transformations every time we merge two metamorphosis systems.

4.4   Back to Refactoring

Having separated refactorings into individual program transformations, equivalence predicates and program validity checks, we can now reconstruct refactorings as compositions of transformations with a post-hoc equivalence check, by slightly adjusting our combination scheme from Section 2.1:

1. Record the initial program.
2. Apply all PM steps that make up the refactoring following appropriate heuristics.
3. Determine whether the resulting program is both valid and equivalent to the initial one; otherwise roll back.

In Sections 5.2 and 6.1 we give concrete examples that illustrate this idea.

5   Program Metamorphosis in Practice

To experiment with stateful program metamorphosis, we implemented a number of prototype systems [11]. Below, we detail the most mature of our systems, a stateful program metamorphosis system for Java that functions as a plugin for the Eclipse IDE (version 3.2.2). We employ the same infrastructure that Eclipse's built-in refactorings use in order to make a comparison between the two approaches meaningful.

5.1   Program Metamorphosis in Java

We first describe our prototype's program model, our consistency promises, and the PM steps it supports, followed by a discussion of our user interface and a demonstration of the flexibility of our system compared to traditional refactorings.

Program model. Our program model includes the results of name, Use-Def, and Def-Use analyses. For name analysis, we use Eclipse's built-in bindings mechanism to determine the declaration for each use of a name and store a mapping between names and declarations. For Def-Use and Use-Def chains, we calculate intra-procedural reaching definitions and similarly store a mapping between uses and definitions. We recompute the model when the program changes; our model equivalence test reports an inconsistency whenever the newly computed mappings do not match the original ones.

Consistency promises. Our prototype tracks whether variables, classes, type variables and methods refer to the same entities as before metamorphosis. Since it is impossible in general to determine the precise dynamic type of an expression, our system uses static types to resolve dispatch; thus, we are sometimes inaccurate when determining whether two methods refer to the same piece of functionality before and during metamorphosis. Our system may therefore conservatively issue inconsistencies where there are none; the user can review such inconsistencies and override them as (potential) behavioural change.

We further track re-ordering among read and write operations in local variables, which can arise when we move code fragments via PM-Cut and PM-Paste (see below).

PM steps. We have focussed on implementing small, composable transformations that, when combined, can match and exceed the expressive power of common refactorings. To that end, our current prototype supports the following PM steps:

- *PM-Rename*: change the name of a type or variable and its uses. This step is similar to the 'Rename' refactoring except that it uses the current program model to link names to declarations. Unlike the 'Rename' refactoring, PM-Rename allows name changes that result in name captures or other inconsistencies. Since this step does not alter the *desired* program model, we lose no information when a renaming causes names to conflict.
- *PM-Split*: take a single assignment and convert it into a declaration and initialiser (such as "x = y + 500;" $\longrightarrow$ "int x = y + 500;"). Unlike the 'Split Temporary' refactoring, this step does not introduce a new variable name for the declaration.
- *PM-Delegate*: replace a method call on implicit *this* with the same method call on another object or vice versa (e.g. "bar()" $\leftrightarrow$ "foo.bar()").
- *PM-Cut*: remove a statement, field, or method, along with its associated program model fragment, and place it in a clipboard. There is no analogue to PM-Cut in refactoring.
- *PM-Paste*: retrieve the statement, field, or method from the current clipboard and paste it and the program model fragment into a class or method body. There is no analogue to PM-Paste in refactoring.

Our PM steps act on both the AST and the program model. For example, PM-Split replaces an assignment AST node with a variable declaration node, but also updates the name mappings in the model so that each name that uses the definition now maps to the new declaration.

We have by no means implemented the complete set of useful PM steps. However, as Kiezun et al. point out [6], the fraction of 'Rename' and 'Move' refactorings among all refactorings used in practice is very high, "perhaps as high as 90% of all refactorings". We chose to provide PM-Rename and PM-Cut/PM-Paste to support these refactorings. PM-Cut and PM-Paste also permit great flexibility in program evolution and demonstrate that program metamorphosis has utility beyond mere refactoring. PM-Delegate followed from PM-Cut/PM-Paste; it is very useful for clearing up inconsistencies when moving code between different classes and methods. We implemented PM-Split to provide support for the 'Split Temporary' refactoring and to illustrate that our notion of program models scales to program properties other than name analysis mappings.

User interface. Our prototype attempts to mirror the user interface workflow of Eclipse's refactorings as much as possible. The user selects a portion of program text in the main editor and then chooses a PM step from an Eclipse menu. This brings up a modal "wizard" box that requests additional information (e.g., the new name in a PM-Rename step), if necessary. The user can then review a list of textual changes that the PM step will perform and can choose to apply or abort the step.

If the user chooses to apply the step, we ask Eclipse to perform these textual changes. We then recompute the model and compare it to the desired model, listing any differences as "Problem Markers" in the Eclipse pane for syntax errors and warnings. The user may choose to accept any of these differences as a change in program behaviour using Eclipse's "Quick Fix" interface and/or apply additional PM steps to resolve them.

In order to maintain our consistency guarantees, we must prevent the user from free-form editing the program text. While it may sometimes be possible to map arbitrary edits into appropriate program model updates (borrowing ideas from [15]), we cannot expect such approaches to work in general. Consider a program with name capture: if the user writes a new statement referencing the captured name, it is unclear which declaration she means.

5.2   Flexibility

Using the five PM steps supported by our system (cf. Section 5.1) we found that we can implement some refactorings completely, while offering partial support for others. Our prototype supports seven standard refactorings [4]: 'Rename', 'Pull Up Method', 'Pull Up Field', 'Push Down method', 'Push Down Field' (all described in Section 6), as well as 'Move Field' and 'Split Temporary'. Note that the 'Push Down' refactorings are currently limited to pushing down to a single class due to an implementation limitation (Section 6). We currently have no facility for adding or removing classes; but if the user manually adds empty classes and uninitialised fields before beginning program metamorphosis and manually deletes other classes afterward, we can support two additional refactorings, 'Tease Apart Inheritance' (Section 5.3) and 'Extract Class'. For many other refactorings, such as 'Move Method', 'Inline Method', or 'Replace Inheritance With Delegation', our system can provide significant support.

That we do not support all standard refactorings is a limitation of our prototype and not of program metamorphosis in general. With additional PM steps (e.g. steps to introduce new classes, methods, and declarations) and a more sophisticated program model (e.g. global value numbering) we could fully support more refactorings.

Our prototype puts a similar amount of effort into preserving program behaviour as existing refactoring tools do (Section 6). Like traditional refactorings, we ensure that the final program is well-formed (largely relying on Eclipse's existing facilities to do so), preserve unique references to methods, fields, and variables, and make no attempt to maintain library APIs. Unlike Eclipse's automated refactorings, we preserve the order of reads and writes to local variables.

5.3   Teasing Apart Inheritance

Fowler [4] lists a "big refactoring" called 'Tease Apart Inheritance', for cleaning up class hierarchies that do not clearly separate responsibilities. This refactoring is hard to fully support with traditional refactoring approaches but useful for showcasing some of the strengths of our approach. For example, consider a class "NetworkServer" with subclasses "TCPChatServer" and "UDPDataServer": here we have hardwired application protocols (Chat/Data) to transport protocols (TCP/UDP).

Figure 4 illustrates this idea and the desired program evolution on an abstract level: the upper part of the figure shows the class hierarchy of "N" and its children "A×X" and "B×Y" before changing the program. Assume that the method "f" in both "A×X" and "B×Y" has the following form:

```
void f() { ... g(); ... }
```

Since our classes "A×X" and "B×Y" combine functionality that should be handled orthogonally, we wish to tease them apart, by moving the different implementations of method "g" into a separate inheritance hierarchy. Figure 4 again illustrates this idea: We extract "g" into separate classes "X" and "Y"

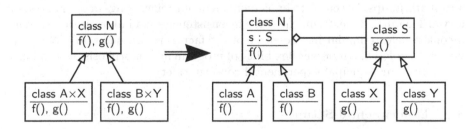

Fig. 4. Teasing Apart Inheritance: we extract functionality "X" and "Y" into a new class hierarchy underneath "S". The refactored class "N" then aggregates an instance of "S".

beneath a new, common (abstract) superclass "S" and insert a field "s" of type "S" into class "N".

With program metamorphosis, we can do this straightforwardly: we PM-Cut and PM-Paste all relevant methods as shown in Figure 4, and then apply 'PM-Delegate' to the calls to "g()" in "f()":

```
void f() { ...  s.g();  ... }
```

Our system still gives us inconsistencies for "s.g()", since we use the static type of "s" to determine which "g" we are calling. We can address these inconsistencies easily by accepting them as a potential behavioural change.

Our current prototype provides all relevant functionality for this process, except for introducing the field "s". Also, introducing and/or deleting classes during metamorphosis currently invalidates our consistency promises, so we must add new classes before and obsolete old classes afterwards.

We are not aware of any way to implement the above directly using only traditional refactorings, and no refactoring engine we have experimented with supports 'Tease Apart Inheritance' directly.

6   Prototype Correctness

As we have suggested in Sections 4 and 5.3, refactorings can always be embedded into a program metamorphosis system, and often split into smaller, more flexible parts (Section 5.2). Program metamorphosis is thus (in theory) intrinsically at least as flexible as traditional refactoring; as we have seen in Section 5.2, it is (in practice) more flexible. However, this flexibility might be a trade-off with safety: despite our argument in Section 4.3 that it is *possible* to be as safe as refactoring, it might not be *practical* to implement a program metamorphosis system that indeed achieves a comparable level of safety.

To investigate this concern, we opted to compare the safety of our PM steps with refactorings provided by an established refactoring system. Since PM steps are more fine-grained than refactorings, we constructed three standard refactorings out of the metamorphosis steps provided by our prototype. There are many ways to construct such refactorings in practice, if we include all possible automatic fixups. We chose to implement all of our refactorings in a very straightforward manner: transform, check for inconsistencies, and abort if there are any inconsistencies (simulating the effect of a refactoring precondition). While this does not exploit the inherent flexibility of program metamorphosis, it is sufficient to address our principal experimental concern, safety.

6.1   Experimental Setup

For our experiments, we paired our manually constructed refactorings with refactoring built into Eclipse 3.2.2 (since our system was developed for the Eclipse 3.2 infrastructure). Our refactorings were as follows:

- **Rename**. Our 'Rename' refactoring simply performs a PM-Rename step, but does not attempt to avoid or resolve any name capture. We configured Eclipse's Rename to rename all other relevant identifiers, including identifiers of overriding and overridden methods in super- and subclasses, which our renaming does not do implicitly. Eclipse also provides a feature that will rename occurrences of a class name in a string or external text file. This option is meant to address uses of reflection, wherein Java may instantiate a class, invoke a method, or read from or write to a variable designated by a string value. Since this mechanism is unsafe in practice, we left it disabled.
- **Pull Up Field**. Our 'Pull Up Field' refactoring moves a field to a superclass (PM-Cut followed by PM-Paste), then iterates over all subclasses of the target class to identify fields of the same name. For each such field it tests if the initialiser is identical to the initialiser of the initially selected field, and, if so, deletes the field in the subclass (per PM-Cut).

  For Eclipse's 'Pull Up Field', we instructed Eclipse to also pull up dependent methods and fields, if necessary (in practice, this should only be needed if those entities are used in the field's initialiser.)
- **Pull Up Method**. Our Pull Up Method refactoring implementation is analogous to Pull Up Field, except that we also determine all methods and fields transitively referenced in the method and pull those up afterwards.

  We configured Eclipse's Pull Up Method to also move all dependent entities.

We then instructed our system to randomly locate opportunities for applying such refactorings in a given program. Our mechanisms for choosing such opportunities were as follows:

- **Rename**: For every 'Rename', we identified a possibly renameable entity (a 'SimpleName', in Eclipse JDT nomenclature) anywhere in the program. We skipped package names because of limitations of our testing infrastructure, but included class names and names of entities external to the program (such as the 'toString()' in java.lang.Object).

  We then decided a new name as follows: with a probability of 0.5 we chose a fresh name, otherwise we chose a random name from the same compilation unit. These names were chosen the same way that renameable entities were chosen; in particular, names that occur frequently in a class had a higher probability of being chosen. If the new name was identical to the original name, we instead chose a fresh name.
- **Pull Up**: For pulling up, we identified pairs of types (interfaces, abstract classes, concrete classes) in a nontrivial supertype relationship (i.e., the classes were not identical) together with a method or field that could be moved from one type to the other, as required by the specific refactoring.

To test the correctness of a refactoring, we tested for whether the refactoring aborted, succeeded, or failed. We say that a refactoring *aborted* if the refactoring indicated that it was not applicable / would change behaviour. In traditional refactoring terms, this is usually expressed as the precondition failing. We say that a refactoring *succeeded* if the refactoring applied, and the program was both statically well-formed and dynamically behaved the same as before, as far as we could tell (see below). We say that a refactoring *failed* if the refactoring applied (i.e., the precondition did not fail) but the resulting program was statically ill-formed or did not preserve its dynamic behaviour.

To determine whether dynamic behaviour had changed, we ran the unit test suite shipped with the programs in question. If any unit test failed, we assumed that dynamic behaviour had changed in an unintended way and that the refactoring had therefore failed.

We also automatically asserted that all non–aborted transformations had indeed modified the program and manually sampled the results to ensure that the transformations were reasonably close to our expectations.

Our specific approaches for determining refactoring results were as follows:

- **Eclipse refactoring**: For Eclipse's refactoring, we attempted to apply the refactoring (using the refactoring scripting interface) atomically. If the attempt failed (usually because a precondition failed), we marked the refactoring as *aborted*. Otherwise we ran Eclipse's own static checks on the program and any unit tests. If either the static checks or the unit tests failed, the refactoring *failed*, otherwise it *succeeded*.
- **Program metamorphosis**: For our own refactorings, we applied all relevant transformations (usually several) in sequence, disregarding any inconsistencies until the end. After we had finished transforming, we ran our own inconsistency checks as well as Eclipse's static checks. If either indicated an error or inconsistency, we *aborted*. Otherwise we ran the unit tests to determine whether the refactoring had *failed* or *succeeded*.

Note that we interpreted the results of Eclipse's own correctness checks differently for program metamorphosis and traditional Refactoring. This reflects the program metamorphosis philosophy and highlights an advantage of our approach: by definition, a traditional refactoring must preserve behaviour if its preconditions trigger – in particular, it must produce a well-formed program. Program metamorphosis, on the other hand, need only be able to determine whether the program is well-formed or not *after the fact*. As we observed with Eclipse, this allows us to exploit traditional IDE correctness checks to augment our own checks for program model equivalence (Section 5.1).

6.2 Results

We ran our experiments against the following programs:

- Functional Analyzer [10], a flexible tool for fast analysis of trace information and similar numerical data, developed by one of the authors (7714 loc[2]).
- Apache Commons: Discovery 0.4, a library for detecting and managing plugins, developed by the free Apache Commons project (2543 loc).

---

[2] Lines of non-comment non-whitespace source code, computed with `sloccount`.

- Apache Commons: Validator 1.3.1, a general-purpose validation library for structured data, particularly XML (8874 loc).
- Apache Commons: Chain 0.4, a chain-of-responsibility implementation, again part of the Apache Commons project (8010 loc).
- Apache Commons: Digester 1.8, a configurable XML configuration file interpreter (12342 loc).

We chose the above programs by availability and presence of substantial unit test suites.

For each experiment, we configured our system to perform 200 random transformations for each refactoring. Table 5 summarises our results.

As we can see from our results, our (fairly straightforwardly) PM-scripted refactorings are competitive with Eclipse's. In the majority of the cases we tested, both systems behaved equivalently. Where they didn't, the differences were mostly due to Eclipse being more flexible by providing additional fixups or Eclipse being less conservative (particularly when pulling up) and thus being simultaneously more flexible and more error-prone. For 'Pull Up', our primitive dependency analysis was sometimes fooled, most commonly by this references, resulting in additional aborts. In all instances that that we observed, a human programmer, driven by our inconsistencies, would have been able to identify and rectify the situation straightforwardly. In other instances, less-than-ideal interfacing between our module and the Eclipse parser prevented our prototype from matching up code from before and after a transformation (particularly in Rename). With respect to the focus of our tests, we observed that PM-scripted refactorings were safer than Eclipse's traditional refactorings: averaging over all of our tests, the cases in which the PM-scripted refactorings failed and Eclipse's refactorings succeeded or aborted made up 0.1%, while the cases in which Eclipse's refactorings failed and the PM-scripted refactorings aborted or succeeded made up 24.4% of all tests.

- **Pull Up Field.** Pulling up, Eclipse attempts to merge fields from all subclasses, whether or not those fields have the same initialisers. This frequently introduces bugs, not all of which are caught by unit tests. If the common fields' types mismatch, Eclipse aborts, while our simple pull-up heuristic skips the fields if their initialisers differ, accounting for a few cases in which our PM-scripted refactoring is more flexible. In other cases, Eclipse implicitly changed field visibility (from private to protected) if needed, which was not part of our PM scripting.
- **Pull Up Method.** For 'Pull Up Method', both refactoring implementations failed consistently when pulling up unit test methods into superclasses for which not all subclasses satisfied the test, in the Commons Validator. When pulling up methods, Eclipse again suffered from its implicit merging of fields when pulling up dependent entities, while our PM-scripted refactoring's refusal to implicitly change visibility accounted for much of its lack of flexibility. Eclipse's 'Pull Up Method' further changes requests to pull up a method into an interface into a request to add a method

Refactoring	Identical				More Flexible		More Failures	
	abort	success	failure	total	PM	Eclipse	PM	Eclipse
Pull Up Field								
Functional Analyzer	9.0%	4.0%	0.0%	13.0%	2.0%	7.0%	0.0%	80.0%
Commons Discovery	13.5%	9.0%	0.0%	22.5%	0.0%	37.0%	0.0%	40.5%
Commons Validator	31.5%	4.5%	0.0%	36.0%	18.5%	32.5%	0.0%	31.5%
Commons Chain	16.5%	0.0%	0.0%	16.5%	1.5%	40.0%	0.0%	43.5%
Commons Digester	3.0%	19.0%	0.0%	22.0%	0.0%	43.0%	0.0%	35.0%
average	14.7%	7.3%	0.0%	22.0%	4.4%	31.9%	0.0%	46.1%
Pull Up Method								
Functional Analyzer	55.0%	3.0%	0.0%	58.0%	0.0%	20.5%	0.0%	21.5%
Commons Discovery	51.5%	0.0%	0.0%	51.5%	0.0%	20.0%	0.0%	28.5%
Commons Validator	46.0%	29.0%	7.5%	82.5%	0.0%	9.0%	0.0%	8.5%
Commons Chain	51.5%	0.5%	0.0%	52.0%	1.5%	5.0%	0.0%	42.5%
Commons Chain	46.0%	4.5%	2.5%	53.0%	0.0%	19.5%	0.0%	27.5%
average	50.0%	7.4%	2.0%	59.4%	0.3%	14.8%	0.0%	25.7%
Rename								
Functional Analyzer	17.0%	60.5%	0.5%	78.0%	0.0%	21.5%	0.0%	0.5%
Commons Discovery	29.0%	59.5%	2.0%	90.5%	0.0%	9.0%	0.0%	0.5%
Commons Validator	30.5%	60.5%	1.5%	92.5%	0.5%	5.5%	0.5%	1.5%
Commons Chain	43.0%	50.0%	1.0%	94.0%	0.5%	2.0%	0.5%	3.0%
Commons Chain	29.0%	59.0%	1.0%	89.0%	0.5%	9.5%	0.5%	1.0%
average	29.7%	57.9%	1.2%	88.8%	0.3%	9.5%	0.3%	1.3%

Fig. 5. Benchmarking results for Eclipse's refactoring suite (Eclipse) and refactoring scripted from program metamorphosis steps (PM). **Identical** identifies cases in which both tools behaved equivalently. **More Flexible** identifies cases in which one tool permitted a transformation while the other tool aborted that transformation. **More Failures** identifies cases in which one tool caused behavioural change. Note that **Identical(total)**, **More Flexible** and **More Failures** sometimes add up to more than 100% in cases where both tools performed the transformation but one tool produced an incorrect result (we counted this as the correct tool being both safer and more flexible). Considering cases where Eclipse failed, this accounts for all of the cases in which PM was more flexible in 'Pull Up Field', as well as for 1% of the 'Pull Up Method' cases in the Commons Chain. Considering cases where PM-scripted refactoring failed, this accounted for two cases in 'Rename' (cf. our discussion).

declaration of the same interface to the interface, again adding to its flexibility (an actual 'Pull Up Method' into an interface is only possible for abstract methods).

– **Rename.** For renaming, our system primarily suffered from two limitations: first, our prototype will not refactor constructors in some cases, and secondly, we do not enforce the override status of overriding methods in subclasses.

Refactoring constructors requires renaming the class and all related constructors. A limitation of the Eclipse parser that we have not yet addressed sometimes prohibits this in classes with multiple constructors; this issue accounts for 3% of the aborted rename attempts (total) in the Functional Analyzer, 10.5% in Commons Discovery, 13% in the Commons Validator, 16.5% in the Commons Chain package, and 12% in the Commons Digester. Note that these failures also account for some of its increased safety in the presence of reflection. Since reflection allows classes to be looked up by names read from external files, it is notoriously hard to support in any kind of refactoring process. (All of our test cases utilise reflection to some extent.)

Another current limitation is that our inconsistency checks do not enforce the overriding status of methods when renaming methods of a subclass. In the presence of an @Override annotation, this usually leads to static errors, but in two cases it allowed the PM-scripted refactoring to introduce a dynamic failure. We expect to extend our program model to add either explicit 'method-X-overrides-method-Y' information or global value numbering to increase the strength of our correctness promises overall.

We also experimented with 'Push Down Method' and 'Push Down Field'. Due to an unresolved issue in our prototype, our 'Push Down' operations are currently overly conservative when pushing to multiple subclasses: copying (rather than cutting and pasting) generates 'fresh' methods and fields, resulting in spurious inconsistency warnings that cannot be accepted as behavioural change. Conversely, Eclipse's 'Push Down' refactoring cannot be constrained to push down to one particular subclass: instead, it always pushes down to all immediate subclasses, though users can interactively choose to suppress parts of the textual diff after the refactoring has terminated. We could thus not directly compare the two sets of functionality, though we have no reason to assume that a corrected PM-scripted 'Push Down' would ultimately exhibit correctness or performance characteristics different from the PM-scripted 'Pull Up'.

While our results overall indicate that our scripted refactorings are less flexible than Eclipse's refactorings, we note the following:

– Our prototype is, on average, safer than Eclipse's refactorings.
– Our prototype permits us to quickly script refactorings that are as flexible as Eclipse's refactorings in most of the cases we examined, without including any automated fixups or complex analyses as part of the scripting.

6.3 Practicality

One goal of our Java prototype is to examine whether program metamorphosis is practical to implement and useful for evolving real-world programs. Here, we evaluate our prototype in terms of code size and resource consumption.

The main component of the memory cost for program metamorphosis is the need to keep an AST of the entire program in memory at all times. Our prototype requires two copies of the full AST in memory during equivalence checking. Using the the Eclipse JDT's built-in memory queries, we have determined that a single instance of the Functional Analyzer AST requires approximately 4MB of memory, which we consider to be acceptable on modern machines.

Our prototype (excluding unit tests) consists of 3829 lines of Java across 53 files and relies significantly on Eclipse's infrastructure to perform program analysis and to interact with the user. This shows that a useful set of PM steps can be implemented in a relatively small amount of code and that PM can be compatible with existing program analysis frameworks and program evolution tools. For this reason, we have favoured ease of implementation and tight integration with Eclipse over speed. For example, we used the JDT's built-in name analysis even though it requires re-parsing to get updated analysis. We could reduce our runtime overhead by comparing only altered parts of the program and recomputing program models lazily. This would decrease execution times and memory usage at the cost of added complexity.

To ensure that our prototype is practical for interactive use, we measured execution times for the correctness tests from Section 6. We summarise these results in Figure 6. All experiments were run on a 2.4GHz Intel Core 2 Quad with 4GB of RAM, running Java 1.6.0_03-b05 on Ubuntu 7.1 with Linux 2.6.24.

Refactoring	Program	Eclipse			PM		
		min	avg	max	min	avg	max
Pull Up Field	Functional Analyzer	0.11s	0.32s	1.15s	2.05s	2.29s	2.81s
	Commons Discovery	0.13s	0.24s	0.52s	0.86s	0.97s	1.37s
	Commons Validator	0.18s	0.45s	0.96s	2.70s	3.07s	4.55s
	Commons Chains	0.36s	0.47s	0.83s	2.39s	2.49s	2.64s
	Commons Digester	0.15s	0.31s	1.51s	3.09s	3.44s	7.87s
	total	0.11s	0.36s	1.51s	0.86s	2.45s	7.87s
Pull Up Method	Functional Analyzer	0.12s	0.32s	0.83s	1.90s	2.55s	3.35s
	Commons Discovery	0.14s	0.32s	2.95s	n/a	n/a	n/a
	Commons Validator	0.22s	0.47s	1.93s	2.73s	3.79s	11.65s
	Commons Chains	0.39s	0.64s	1.74s	2.18s	2.38s	2.59s
	Commons Digester	0.19s	0.55s	1.62s	3.09s	4.83s	10.43s
	total	0.12s	0.46s	2.95s	1.90s	3.39s	11.65s
Rename	Functional Analyzer	0.09s	0.34s	2.71s	1.10s	1.36s	2.92s
	Commons Discovery	0.02s	0.15s	0.85s	0.43s	0.53s	1.53s
	Commons Validator	0.06s	0.20s	0.69s	1.46s	1.71s	1.98s
	Commons Chains	0.06s	0.26s	0.98s	1.14s	1.35s	2.12s
	Commons Digester	0.12s	0.28s	1.66s	1.72s	1.95s	2.58s
	total	0.02s	0.25s	2.71s	0.43s	1.38s	2.92s

Fig. 6. Minimum, average, and maximum refactoring execution times, for both Eclipse's built-in refactorings and program metamorphosis

For program metamorphosis, the execution time is the sum of the execution times of all intermediate steps. The **total** line gives the overall minimum, maximum, and average of the averages (as summarised per program).

Our unoptimised prototype executes most transformation steps well within the time limits of what we can expect from an interactive tool. While some transformations may take more than two seconds to complete overall, note that both of our pull-up refactorings are multi-step transformations in program metamorphosis, as we explained in Section 6; except for two Renames (one in the Functional Analyzer and one in the Commons Digester), no individual transformation execution time was more than 2.5s per PM step (including re-parsing and AST re-matching for the entire program after each step).

7   Related Work

There is a large body of related work on refactoring (cf. [9] for a survey), including many implementations, such as HaRe [8] and Eclipse [14]. The observation that more information than immediately visible to the eye is needed to perform correct transformations was already employed by Griswold [5], who used Program Dependence Graphs [3] for this purpose. These systems consider refactorings to be individual macroscopic transformations. Some other program transformation approaches [1, 17] look specifically for atomic transformations, but remain entirely semantics-preserving.

Composing transformations to achieve a certain goal is the central theme of AI Planning (cf. [12] for a high-level overview). The composition of refactorings in particular has also been considered [7], but only for traditional approaches to refactoring, without allowing intermediate invalidation of correctness properties.

8   Conclusion

We have presented a novel approach to program evolution in which users interactively combine small program transformations, *PM steps*, while a consistency checking mechanism tracks behavioural change that they introduce. As part of this process, users can choose to explicitly alter behaviour rather than to preserve it. Since our approach differs from refactoring (a) by allowing users to transform more liberally and (b) by permitting explicit behavioural change, we give it a different name, *program metamorphosis*. We have further described an Eclipse plugin that implements program metamorphosis for Java. Our experimental results suggest that program metamorphosis is a practical and viable approach for supplanting traditional machine support for refactoring.

Acknowledgements

The authors are indebted to Daniel von Dincklage, William Griswold, Jeremy Siek, Philipp Wetzler, and the anonymous ECOOP, POPL and ICFP referees for their valuable feedback on this work.

References

[1] Arsac, J.J.: Syntactic source to source transforms and program manipulation. Commun. ACM 22(1), 43–54 (1979)

[2] Beck, K.: eXtreme Programming eXplained, Embrace Change. Addison-Wesley, Reading (2000)

[3] Ferrante, J., Ottenstein, K.J., Warren, J.D.: The program dependence graph and its use in optimization. ACM Trans. Program. Lang. Syst. 9(3), 319–349 (1987)

[4] Fowler, M., Beck, K., Brant, J., Opdyke, W., Roberts, D.: Refactoring: Improving the Design of Existing Code. Addison-Wesley, Reading (1999)

[5] Griswold, W.G., Notkin, D.: Program Restructuring as an Aid to Software Maintenance. Technical report, Univ. of Wash (1990)

[6] Kiezun, A., Fuhrer, R.M., Keller, M.: Advanced Refactoring in Eclipse: Past, Present and Future. In: First Workshop on Refactoring Tools, Berlin (2007), https://netfiles.uiuc.edu/dig/RefactoringWorkshop/Presentations/AdvancedRefactoringInEclipse.pdf

[7] Kniesel, G., Koch, H.: Static composition of refactorings. Sci. Comput. Program. 52(1-3), 9–51 (2004)

[8] Li, H., Reinke, C., Thompson, S.: Tool Support for Refactoring Functional Programs. In: Jeuring, J. (ed.) ACM Sigplan Haskell Workshop, pp. 27–38 (2003)

[9] Mens, T., Tourwe, T.: A survey of software refactoring. IEEE Trans. Softw. Eng. 30(2), 126–139 (2004)

[10] Mytkowicz, T., Sweeney, P.F., Hauswirth, M., Diwan, A.: Time interpolation: So many metrics, so few registers. In: MICRO 2007: Proceedings of the 40th Annual IEEE/ACM International Symposium on Microarchitecture, Washington, DC, USA, pp. 286–300. IEEE Computer Society Press, Los Alamitos (2007)

[11] Reichenbach, C., Diwan, A.: Program Metamorphosis. Technical Report CU-CS-1036-07, University of Colorado at Boulder (2007)

[12] Russell, S., Norvig, P.: Artificial Intelligence: A Modern Approach, 2nd edn. Prentice-Hall, Englewood Cliffs (2003)

[13] Schäfer, M., Ekman, T., de Moor, O.: Sound and Extensible Renaming for Java. In: Kiczales, G. (ed.) 23rd Annual ACM SIGPLAN Conference on Object-Oriented Programming, Systems, Languages, and Applications (OOPSLA 2008). ACM Press, New York (2008)

[14] Shavor, S., D'Anjou, J., Fairbrother, S., Kehn, D., Kellerman, J., McCarthy, P.: The Java Developers Guide to Eclipse. Addison-Wesley, Reading (2003)

[15] Taneja, K., Dig, D., Xie, T.: Automated detection of API refactorings in libraries. In: ASE 2007: Proceedings of the twenty-second IEEE/ACM international conference on Automated software engineering, pp. 377–380. ACM Press, New York (2007)

[16] Wadler, P.: Deforestation: Transforming programs to eliminate trees. Theoretical Computer Science 73, 344–358 (1990)

[17] Ward, M.P., Zedan, H.: MetaWSL and Meta-Transformations in the FermaT Transformation System. In: COMPSAC (1), pp. 233–238 (2005)

From Public to Private to Absent: Refactoring JAVA Programs under Constrained Accessibility

Friedrich Steimann and Andreas Thies

Lehrgebiet Programmiersysteme
Fakultät für Mathematik und Informatik
Fernuniversität in Hagen
D-58084 Hagen
steimann@acm.org, Andreas.Thies@fernuni-hagen.de

Abstract. Contemporary refactoring tools for JAVA aiding in the restructuring of programs have problems with respecting access modifiers such as public and private: while some tools provide hints that referenced elements may become inaccessible due to the intended restructuring, none we have tested prevent changes that alter the meaning of a program, and none take steps that counteract such alterations. To address these problems, we formalize accessibility in JAVA as a set of constraint rules, and show how the constraints obtained from applying these rules to a program and an intended refactoring allow us to check the preconditions of the refactoring, as well as to compute the changes of access modifiers necessary to preserve the behaviour of the refactored program. We have implemented our framework as a proof of concept in ECLIPSE, and demonstrated how it improves applicability and success of an important refactoring in a number of sample programs. That our approach is not limited to JAVA is shown by comparison with the constraint rules for C# and EIFFEL.

"Moving state and behavior between classes is the very essence of refactoring." [4]

1 Introduction

In object-oriented programming languages like C++, JAVA, and C#, information hiding [17] is supported by access modifiers such as public and private. Their disciplined use contributes to modularization and, thus, the design of a program.

Refactorings change a program's design without altering its (externally visible) behaviour [4]. Insofar as the change affects the division of the program into modules, access modifiers must be updated during the refactoring process to reflect the new modularization. However, while insufficient accessibility is routinely reported by the compiler, excessive accessibility is usually not and therefore often forgotten [1]. Worse still, in JAVA the change of access modifiers can have an effect on static and dynamic binding, changing the meaning of a program [1, 14, 19].

Refactoring tools are metaprograms aiding the programmer in the often tedious and error-prone refactoring process. Contemporary IDEs such as ECLIPSE [3], NETBEANS [15], and INTELLIJ IDEA [9] come with various refactoring tools, usually including

S. Drossopoulou (Ed.): ECOOP 2009, LNCS 5653, pp. 419–443, 2009.
© Springer-Verlag Berlin Heidelberg 2009

support for renaming program elements, moving elements, and modifying the type hierarchy. However, as we will see, when it comes to maintaining accessibility most refactoring tools are flawed, not only in rare corner cases. As we will also see, the problem is not caused by negligence of the programmers who implemented the tools, but the tremendous complexity of the programming languages used today, and the myriad of different constructions they allow.

In this paper, we present a constraint-based approach to modelling the access control[1] rules of JAVA that makes it easy for a refactoring tool to respect them. In particular, we show how a *change of accessibility* of a declared entity, as well as how a *change of location* of a declared entity and its contained references, propagate through a program, and how these changes are constrained by references to the declared entities and by other declarations. This enables us to enhance important refactorings such as MOVE TYPE/MEMBER and PULL UP/PUSH DOWN MEMBER by adding necessary preconditions that are currently unconsidered, and also by adding mechanics enabling applications that currently lead to failure. Our approach is analogous to that taken by the type-related refactorings described in [22], but remains completely orthogonal in the problems it addresses. Also, our definition of foresight rules anticipating the changes performed by an intended refactoring appears to be novel.

The remainder of this paper is organized as follows. In Section 2, we motivate our work by presenting a number of basic problems current refactoring tools have, and by arguing why existing related work does not address them sufficiently. In Section 3, we develop our formal framework of accessibility constraints and present the constraint rules that model JAVA's access control. In Section 4 we show how these constraints and their generation integrate into the refactorings we aim to improve. Section 5 presents the implementation of our framework in ECLIPSE's JAVA DEVELOPMENT TOOLS (JDT) and shows how we have tested and evaluated it. Section 6 discusses our work, its limitations, and its potential for performing systematic programming language comparisons.

2   Motivation

2.1   Problems

Moving a class without adapting accessibility can break the code. For instance, moving class B in the JAVA program

```
package a;
class A {
  B b;
}

package a;
class B {}
```

to another package with the corresponding refactoring tools of ECLIPSE, NETBEANS and IDEA will produce a compilation error, since for the class B to be accessible from other packages, it needs to be declared public, which the tools ignore (only IDEA

---

[1] not to be confused with access rights [11]

issues a warning that B will become inaccessible for A). Note that this is not a problem of JAVA's language design, but a necessary consequence of modularization: access across packages should be restricted to elements declared public. Moving B therefore either breaks the designed modularization and should be prevented, or it constitutes a design change that should be reflected in a change of the corresponding access modifiers.

While the above problem is detected by the compiler and easily responded to, the situation becomes more complex when members of B are accessed. For instance, moving class B in

```
package a;
public class A {
  void n() { (new B()).m("abc"); }
}

package a;
public class B {
  public void m(Object o) {…}
  void m(String s) {…}
}
```

to another package will not produce a compilation error, but instead change the meaning of the program: rather than the method n in A calling m(String) in B as before the change, m(Object) gets invoked instead. The corresponding refactoring tool of ECLIPSE performs the change without warning; NETBEANS displays that B.m(String) is referenced and IDEA warns that it becomes inaccessible from A, but neither indicates that the refactoring will change the meaning of the program.

The change of meaning can be detected by observing that the static binding of the method call has changed. However, this alone is not sufficient, as the following example shows:

```
package a;
public class A {
  void m(String s) {…}
  void n() { ((A) new B()).m("abc"); }
}

package a;
public class B extends A {
  void m(String s) {…}
}
```

Again, moving B to another package changes the meaning of the program, yet this time not because the binding changes, but because m(String) in A changes its status from being overridden in B to not being overridden, so that calling m(String) on a receiver of static type A is no longer dispatched to the implementation in B. In ECLIPSE and NETBEANS, this change of meaning goes unnoticed, IDEA notes that class A contains a reference to class B, but this is not indicative of the problem.

While all the above sample problems can be easily fixed by adapting the accessibility of members to preserve program meaning, in real programs there may be ripple effects that are difficult to oversee, and also unobvious conditions that prevent such changes. For instance, if

```
package a;
public class C extends B {
  void m(String s) {…}
  public void m(Object o) {…}
}
```

is added to the previous example, the accessibility of m(String) in B cannot be increased to public without also increasing its accessibility in C. However, increasing accessibility of m(String) in C may be contraindicated, as it can change meaning of another call:

```
package b;
class D {
    void n() { (new C()).m("abc"); }
}
```

Although all three IDEs offer a refactoring for changing accessibility of methods (as part of changing their signature), none of them notes the change of binding this entails.

It should be clear from these examples that for larger programs, the situation quickly becomes unmanageable for a human programmer. Reliable tool support is therefore needed.

2.2 Related Work

That moving classes, fields, and methods of an object-oriented program can be a nontrivial problem was already recognized by Opdyke in his doctoral thesis [16]. However, despite a presentation of formal preconditions, these seem to be only loosely related to a concrete language (C++), and do not seem to be thoroughly checked for completeness. For instance, the preconditions for pulling up a member variable (field) state that "the variable is defined identically in all subclasses where it is defined" and that "the variable isn't already defined locally in (as a private member of) the superclass" [p. 73]. However, if one of the subclasses has another superclass with a variable of the same name (that was previously hidden), an ambiguity arises for accesses of the variable from the subclass (cf. Section 3.1, Inh-2). Also, Opdyke's treatment of access modifiers and how they are to be handled in refactorings is only cursory.

Contemporary refactoring tools such as those integrated in the ECLIPSE JDT [3], in NETBEANS [15], and in IDEA [9] all include some basic precondition checking (in IDEA including the issuing of warnings when a declared entity is moved out of reach), and some (notably IDEA) also present a list of references potentially directly affected by a refactoring, but none of them correctly predicts the change of semantics provoked by the examples of the previous subsection and the subsections that follow, and none offers a change of access modifiers that would prevent such changes or avoid compilation errors. The understanding of the consequences of such refactorings is therefore the duty of the programmer.

The problem of maintaining accessibility is related to, yet sufficiently different from, making sure that all bindings are preserved under the RENAME refactoring [18]. It is similar in that each reference must refer to the same declared entity before and after a refactoring (or otherwise the meaning of the program changes). It is different in that maintaining static binding alone is not enough (as the above example with the lost dynamic binding suggests), and that it is not achieved by changing references to a declared entity (by renaming them as well, or by adding necessary qualification [18]), but by changing the (accessibility of) the declared entity itself. Also, as the last of the above examples suggested, changes of accessibility may be constrained by the accessibility of other declared entities, so that the refactoring may have ripple effects. Inversion of the lookup of a declared entity as resorted to in [18] does not point to these indirect constraints and is therefore insufficient to solve our problem.

That reverse lookup is indeed insufficient became clear to us during the development of our ACCESS MODIFIER MODIFIER (AMM), a smell detection and refactoring tool that marks all methods with excessive accessibility and offers its reduction to the lowest level tolerated by the program [1]. The AMM maintains reverse lookup tables for every method, pointing from that method to its references. However, to deal with the binding problems sketched above, we had to implement additional lookups and checks reflecting the relevant rules of the language specification. Since the checks and lookups were hard-coded for a specific problem, namely the independent change of accessibility of a single method, retrofitting them to a different purpose (such as precondition checking for general MOVE refactorings), or even to a different target language, amounts to rewriting them. Because the problem itself seems rather general, we thought that a more generic, problem-independent formulation of the conditions under which accessibility could be changed would be desirable.

Such a formulation has been delivered as part of a formal model of JAVA written for the theorem prover ISABELLE/HOL [19]. Using this formalization, some interesting runtime properties of JAVA programs concerning access integrity could be shown. However, both model and theorem prover are rather heavy-weight and have to our knowledge not yet been utilized in refactoring tools.

A much lighter declarative approach to controlling access has been pursued in KACHEK/J, a tool that infers object encapsulation properties for JAVA programs [7]. KACHEK/J uses constraints to express a set of rules that allow the inference of confinement, i.e., that no aliases to instances of a confined type exist outside its defining package. The constraints basically make sure that confined types are neither declared public nor cast to non-confined supertypes, that they cannot be the types of public or protected members, and that methods inherited by them cannot leak aliases to the this pointer. While these constraints add confinement as a new property to the language (rather than model existing ones, as we intend), to improve this property in existing programs the first author of [7] has developed the JAVA ACCESS MODIFIER INFERENCE TOOL (JAMIT) [7, 8], which also builds on constraints. However, the constraints of JAMIT model only those aspects of JAVA access modifiers that are relevant to the virtual machine (JAMIT operates on byte code), and do not deal with possible changes of bindings that result from moving program elements.

3   Accessibility Constraints

Following the approach of JAMIT [8], we model the access control rules of JAVA using constraints, making our above identified refactoring problems solvable by constraint programming. Constraint programming usually consist of two parts:
1. the generation of the constraints describing the problem, and
2. constraint satisfaction, i.e., the computation of a solution for the generated constraints.

Each generated constraint constrains one or more variables by setting up relations between them or assigning constant values to them. Through shared variables, the generated constraints form a network, referred to as *constraint set* hereafter; the solution of a constraint set consists of assignments to the variables that satisfy all constraints. Generally, a constraint set can have arbitrarily many (including no) solutions; in case more than one solution exists, one is usually interested in one that satisfies certain additional conditions (not expressed as constraints). Although the solution of a constraint set is generally problem-independent, the additional conditions can lead to algorithms finding the best solution efficiently.

The constraints describing a particular refactoring problem are usually generated from the program to be refactored by applying a set of *constraint generating rules*, or *constraint rules* for short [22]. The variables in the generated constraints represent those parts of the program that can be changed to solve the problem. Constraint generation also assigns the variables of the constraints initial values; these values reflect the program as it is at the outset of the problem (when the constraints were generated), that is, before the refactoring is performed.

A constraint set generated from a (syntactically and semantically) correct program always has a solution, and in particular all constraints are satisfied by the initial variable assignments, or otherwise the constraint rules are inconsistent. Vice versa, any assignment to variables that solves the constraint set must represent a correct program, or otherwise the constraint rules are incomplete. Therefore, given a complete set of constraint rules, if another than the initial solution has been found, adapting the original program to the changed variable values (so that constraint generation would have extracted these values as initial had it been applied to the adapted program) will lead to a (syntactically and semantically) correct program. We refer to adapting the program so as to reflect the variable values of a new solution as *writing back the solution*.

3.1 Generating Accessibility Constraints

Basics For our purposes, an object-oriented program consists of a set, D, of declared entities [6, §6.1] d, d_1, etc., and a set, R, of references r, r_1, etc. referring to declared entities. The set of declared entities D is partitioned into a set of classes, C, a set of interfaces, I, a set of methods (including constructors), M, and a set of fields, F.[2] D also contains a subset of declared entities (including all constructors) declared as static, S. We express the binding of a reference r to a declared entity d by a function

$$\beta: R \rightarrow D \qquad \text{(binding)}$$

where $\beta(r) = d$ means that reference r binds to declared entity d. One common invariant of refactorings is that bindings are not changed.

A program is further divided into a set, L, of locations l, l_1, etc. Each $d \in D$ is declared, and each $r \in R$ resides, in a location $l \in L$.[3] In languages allowing nesting of declarations, the location is conveniently expressed by a path expression involving all

---

[2] The set of variables (temporaries and formal parameters) is not contained in D, since their access cannot be modified.

[3] The location of a declaration element is sometimes referred to as its declaration space [13], and is not to be confused with its scope.

containing declarations. To facilitate reading, we tag declared entities and references in the code we are referring to using comments, as in

```
package a; class /*d1*/A { /*r1*/B b; }
```

We refer to the location of so tagged entities and references by the function

$$\lambda: D \cup R \to L \qquad \text{(location)}$$

For instance, the location of d_1 (class A) in the above program, $\lambda(d_1)$, is a (the containing package) and that of r_1, $\lambda(r_1)$, is a.A (the containing class).

In JAVA the accessibility of a declared entity is determined by an access modifier preceding its declaration. We write $\langle d \rangle$ for the declared access modifier of d. The set of available access modifiers, A, is $\{public, protected, package, private\}$.[4] Its elements are totally ordered: $public > protected > package > private$, where $>$ means granting greater access. As usual, we write $\geq$ to denote greater than or equal.

Whether a reference can access a declared entity is determined by the access rules of the language. In order to maintain a certain language independence (and also because they are quite intricate in the case of JAVA), we model the access rules as a function

$$\alpha: L \times L \to A \qquad \text{(required access modifier)}$$

where the first argument is the location of the reference, the second is the location of the referenced declared entity, and where $\alpha(\lambda(r), \lambda(d))$ computes the smallest access modifier for d granting r access to d. α may be considered an inverse of the so-called *accessibility domain* [13], mapping a declared entity and its declared accessibility to all locations in the program text in which access to the member is permitted. We model α as a function of a pair of locations rather than of $R \times D$ since the access modifier required for accessibility does not depend on individual references or declared entities, but where they are located.[5] Also, as we will see, not the references or declared entities, but their locations are the variables of our constraints.

For a declared entity d that is a member of a type, the location of a reference r to d may be insufficient to determine d's accessibility — the (static) type through which d is accessed is also significant. We model this through a function

$$\rho: R \to L \qquad \text{(receiver)}$$

computing the location corresponding to the body of the receiver type. For instance, in the program

```
class A {
  B b = new B();
  int i;
  void m() { /*r1*/i = 1; /*r2*/b.i = 2; }
class B extends A {}
```

$\rho(r_1)$ evaluates to A and $\rho(r_2)$ evaluates to B.

We are now equipped to state our first constraint rule.

---

[4] Not every declaration element can use every access modifier — the domain of legal access modifiers depends on the kind of element that is declared, and where it is declared. As will be seen below, we model this as a constraint rule.

[5] The one exception, access to protected members, is modelled as a constraint rule (Acc-2).

Accessing   Accessing a declared entity d via a reference r requires that the declared accessibility of d, $\langle d \rangle$ (its access modifier) is equal to or greater than the accessibility required by the language's access rules. To express this, we introduce the following constraint rule:

$$\beta(r) = d \quad \Rightarrow \quad \langle d \rangle \geq \alpha(\lambda(r), \lambda(d)) \tag{Acc-1}$$

Applied to the JAVA program

```
package a; class A { /*r1*/B b; }
package a; class /*d1*/B {}
```

we obtain the constraint $\langle d_1 \rangle \geq \alpha(\lambda(r_1), \lambda(d_1))$. The variables of the constraint are:
- $\langle d_1 \rangle$, the declared access modifier of d_1,
- $\lambda(r_1)$, the location of r_1, and
- $\lambda(d_1)$, the location of d_1.[6]

As noted above, for the initial assignments of the variables derived from a syntactically and semantically correct program, constraints are always solved; note how this is indeed the case for the above example, in which $\langle d_1 \rangle = \alpha(\lambda(r_1), \lambda(d_1)) = package$.

Now a refactoring may change the values of one or more variables, possibly violating the constraint. For instance, when class A is moved to another package, $\lambda(r_1)$ changes its value so that α evaluates to *public* and the constraint is no longer satisfied. To satisfy it, either the declared access modifier $\langle d_1 \rangle$ has to be changed to *public*, or class B has to be moved to the same location.[7] While the constraint itself is neutral to the chosen solution, the constraint satisfaction algorithm can be adapted to compute the one that is required (or makes most sense) for the given refactoring.

In the special case of protected access, it must be made sure that a "protected member or constructor of an object may be accessed from outside the package in which it is declared only by code that is responsible for the implementation of that object" [6, §6.2.2]. This is achieved by the additional constraint rule

$$\beta(r) = d \wedge \alpha(\lambda(r), \lambda(d)) = protected \wedge d \notin S \wedge \rho(r) \notin subclasses(\lambda(r)) \cup \{\lambda(r)\} \quad \Rightarrow$$
$$\langle d \rangle = public \tag{Acc-2}$$

in which subclasses($\lambda(r)$) represents the union of the locations corresponding to the bodies of (true) subclasses of the class whose body corresponds to $\lambda(r)$. Note that Acc-2 does not replace Acc-1 in case of accessing protected members — it only adds a stronger constraint.

Inheritance   JAVA's access rules require accessibility of an inherited member as if it were accessed as a member of the base class [6, 14, 19]. Therefore, Acc-1 covers access of inherited members as well. For instance, in

---

[6] Note that in JAVA, the default constructor of a class may be implicitly accessed by its subclasses' constructors. In these cases, corresponding constraints must be created without presence of explicit references.

[7] Note that if class B is moved first, the constraint generated from Acc-1 only requires that r_1 is also moved. Other rules of the language may require that r_1 must remain within the body of its owning class, so that class A must be moved with it. However, this constraint is unrelated to access control and therefore out of scope. We will return to this issue in Section 3.2.

```
package a; class A {}
package b; class B extends a.A { protected /*d1*/void m() {...} }
package b; class C { void n() { (new B()).m(); } }
```

pulling up d_1 is correctly prevented by Acc-1 (but nevertheless performed without warnings by ECLIPSE, NETBEANS, and IDEA). However, Acc-1 is insufficient to maintain inheritance under refactoring, as the following example shows (note how i can be accessed from B even though i is protected and B is in a different package):

```
package a;
public class A {
  protected /*d1*/int i;
  void n() { /*r1*/(new b.B()).i = 1; }
}

package b;
public class B extends a.A {}
```

Here, reducing the declared accessibility of d_1 produces an error, even though $\alpha(\lambda(r_1), \lambda(d_1)) = private$. The reason for this is that after the reduction, B, the type through which i is accessed, no longer inherits i. The reduction of accessibility and the concomitant loss of inheritance are prevented by the constraint rule

$$\beta(r) = d \wedge \rho(r) \neq \lambda(d) \quad \Rightarrow \quad \langle d \rangle \geq \alpha(\rho(r), \lambda(d)) \qquad \textbf{(Inh-1)}$$

which, in the above example, requires at least *protected* for $\langle d \rangle$. As above, Inh-1 does not replace Acc-1 in case of accessing inherited members — it adds to it, effectively requiring that $\langle d \rangle$ is greater than the maximum of $\alpha(\lambda(r), \lambda(d))$ and $\alpha(\rho(r), \lambda(d))$.

However, there is another problem with inheritance, namely that access of a static field can become ambiguous if it is inherited both from a superclass and from an interface [6, §8.3.3.3]. For instance, in

```
class A { private /*d1*/static int i = 1; }
interface I { /*d2*/static int i = 2; }
class B extends A implements I {void m() { int j = /*r1*/i; } }
```

in which $\beta(r_1) = d_2$, the accessibility of d_1 must not be increased. While the compiler detects and denies such ambiguous access, a refactoring changing the accessibility of the field in the superclass so that it is inherited by the subclass (where it was not prior to the refactoring must foresee this problem and refuse its application. This is achieved by the constraint rule

$$\{d, d'\} \subseteq F \cap S \wedge \iota(d) = \iota(d') \wedge \beta(r) = d \wedge \lambda(d') \in \text{superclasses}(\rho(r)) \quad \Rightarrow$$
$$\langle d' \rangle < \alpha(\lambda(r), \lambda(d')) \qquad \textbf{(Inh-2)}$$

in which $\iota(d)$ refers to the unqualified identifier (simple name) of d and superclasses(.) has the obvious meaning (analogous to subclasses(.) in Acc-2). Note that for qualified references r to d, $\rho(r)$ corresponds to an interface, so that Inh-2 is not applicable (because superclasses($\rho(r)$) is undefined). Also note that $\langle d' \rangle$ depends on $\lambda(r)$, not $\rho(r)$, since access, not inheritance, may become ambiguous.

There is a variant of the above example in which d_1 does not exist in class A prior to the refactoring, for instance because it is yet to be pulled up from a subclass. To prevent such a refactoring (which would affect the binding of r_1), Inh-2 must be applied to a declared entity d' (d_1 in the above example) that is not yet there (or, rather, that has as yet another location), so that r cannot yet bind to it. We call such constraint rules, which anticipate a refactoring, *foresight rules*. They can only be applied when the intended refactoring is known.

Subtyping   A rather straightforward constraint rule expresses that in JAVA, the accessibility of an overriding or hiding method must not decrease ([6, §8.4.8.3]). This is expressed by the constraint rule

$$\{d, d'\} \subseteq M \wedge (\text{overrides}(d', d) \vee \text{hides}(d', d)) \;\;\Rightarrow\;\; \langle d' \rangle \geq \langle d \rangle \quad \textbf{(Sub-1)}$$

in which overrides(.,.) and hides(.,.) have the obvious meanings. Note that the subtyping rule does not apply to fields in JAVA; however, as we will see below, hiding (including that of fields) gives rise to another constraint rule. Also note that, as for Inh-2 above, there is a foresight application of this rule, namely when the method d is pulled up from a sibling class.

A rather subtle implication of subtyping in JAVA is that a method inherited by a class that implements an interface requiring that method must remain publicly accessible. This is expressed by the constraint rule

$$\{d, d'\} \subseteq M \wedge \text{subsignature}(d', d) \wedge \{c, c'\} \subseteq C \wedge i \in I \wedge \lambda(d) = i \wedge \lambda(d') = c'$$
$$\wedge\ \text{implements}(c, i) \wedge \text{inherits}(c, d', c') \;\;\Rightarrow\;\; \langle d' \rangle = \text{public} \quad \textbf{(Sub-2)}$$

in which subsignature(.,.) is defined as in [6, §8.4.2] and implements(.,.) as well as inherits(.,.,.) have their obvious meanings.

Dynamic binding   Since constraints work in both directions, the above subtyping constraint rule Sub-1 equally states that the access modifier of an overridden method must always be less than or equal to that of the overriding method. Thus, if the access modifier for an overriding method should be decreased for any reason, the access modifier of the overridden method may also have to decrease.

There are however bounds to this decrease, set by JAVA's rules for dynamic binding. For example, given the JAVA code

```
class A {
    /*d1*/void m() {...}
    void n() {/*r1*/m();}
}
class B extends A {
    /*d2*/void m() {...}
}
```

changing accessibility of d_1 to *private* is syntactically correct, but changes the meaning of the program, since the call of m() in n() is no longer dispatched to the implementation of m() in B, if n() is invoked on an instance of B. Therefore, we add a constraint rule

$$\text{overrides}(d', d) \;\;\Rightarrow\;\; \langle d \rangle \geq \alpha(\lambda(d'), \lambda(d)) \quad \textbf{(Dyn-1)}$$

This models the requirement that for a method to be overridden, it must be accessible from the overriding subclass [6, §8.4.8.1]. Note that whether the loss of dynamic binding actually leads to a change of meaning of the program depends on the dynamic types of the receiver objects, and thus on conditions that cannot generally be decided statically. Therefore, Dyn-1 is a conservative rule that prohibits illegal refactorings, but may also prevent legal ones.

Accidentally losing overriding and dynamic binding has a converse problem, namely accidentally introducing it: if in the program

```
class A {
    private /*d1*/void m() {...}
    void n() {/*r1*/m();}
}
class B extends A {
    /*d2*/void m() {...}
}
```

accessibility of d_1 is increased to *package*, the meaning of the program changes for invocations of n() on instances of B. This is prevented by the constraint rule

$$\lambda(d) \in \text{superclasses}(\lambda(d')) \land \text{subsignature}(d', d) \land \neg\text{overrides}(d', d) \quad \Rightarrow$$
$$\langle d \rangle < \alpha(\lambda(d'), \lambda(d)) \qquad \textbf{(Dyn-2)}$$

Note that Dyn-1 and Dyn-2 are not only useful for preventing a change of access modifiers that changes the status of dynamic binding — they are also capable of correcting access modifiers when moving subclasses to other packages, so as to maintain (absence of) overriding. For instance, Dyn-1 requires increasing the access modifier of d_1 in

```
public class A {
    /*d1*/void m() {...}
    void n() {
        A a = new B();
        /*r1*/a.m();
    }
}
public class B extends A {
    /*d2*/void m() {...}
}
```

to *protected* when class B is moved to another package, which otherwise would prevent execution of d_2 (example adapted from [14]). Note that the concomitant required increase of the accessibility of d_2 is mandated by Sub-1, requiring that $\langle d_2 \rangle \geq \langle d_1 \rangle$.

Further note that because Dyn-1 and Dyn-2 have mutually exclusive antecedents, they can never introduce a direct (i.e., not involving other declared entities or references) contradiction. This is different, however, for Sub-1 and Dyn-2: since their antecedents can both be fulfilled for the same pair (d, d'), one might be concerned about unforeseen interactions. However, due to the declarative nature of constraints, this is not necessary: if all rules are correct, the result of their combined application is also correct (even if the resulting constraints are unsolvable; see below for an example of this). Constraints are inherently modular.

Overloading   In addition to overriding, JAVA allows overloading, which poses its own problems. For example, in the JAVA program

```
class A {
    /*d1*/void m(Object o) {...}
}
class B extends A {
    /*d2*/void m(String s) {...}
}
class C {
    void n() { /*r1*/(new A()).m("abc"); }
}
```

430   F. Steimann and A. Thies

where all classes reside in the same package, $\beta(r_1) = d_1$. However, when d_2 is pulled up from B to A, the binding of r_1 changes to d_2, changing the meaning of the program.

The problem here is similar to that of inheriting two static fields (Inh-2) in that neither reference r nor declared entity d of an existing binding $\beta(r) = d$ changes location or accessibility — instead, a new declared entity d' becomes accessible, affecting the binding of r. Therefore, as with Inh-2 we have to create a constraint limiting the accessibility of the new declared entity d' (or a declared entity in a new location) so that it remains inaccessible for references that would otherwise be re-bound to d'. This is done by the constraint rule

$$\{d, d'\} \subseteq M \wedge \text{overloads}(d', d) \wedge \beta(r) = d \wedge \lambda(d') \in \text{superclasses}(\rho(r)) \cup \{\rho(r)\} \quad \Rightarrow$$
$$\langle d' \rangle < \alpha(\lambda(r), \lambda(d')) \qquad \textbf{(Ovr)}$$

in which overloads(d', d) is defined as in [6, §8.4.9]. As for Inh-2, a constraint generated from Ovr constrains accessibility of a declared entity in a constraint set in which variable values have been updated to reflect the refactoring (in the above example, $\lambda(d_2)$ has changed to a new location). The constraint may be invalid before the refactoring in the sense that it does not adequately reflect the program as is (in the above example, there is no reason to restrict, on the basis of r_1, accessibility of d_2 where it *is* located). Because its application must foresee the refactoring to be performed, Ovr is a foresight rule that, like Inh-2 and Hid, can only be applied to a program when the planned refactoring is known.[8]

The overloading constraint rule Ovr has an interesting consequence: it can require access modifiers to be less than *private*, which basically means that the so modified entity must not be there. While this may seem paradoxical, it makes perfect sense in certain situations: for instance, if $\lambda(r_1)$ in the above example were class A, Ovr would produce $\langle d_2 \rangle < private$, meaning that m(String) must not be declared in A (which is the only correct solution to the problem). In order for all constraints generated by our rules to be satisfiable, we introduce a new value to our set of access modifiers, A, which is smaller than *private*. We call this access modifier *absent*.[9] Note that a constraint requiring an existing declared entity to be absent can only be generated by foresight rules (because otherwise the program from which it were created, having an entity it must not have, would be incorrect), and that no constraint variable can have the initial value *absent*.

Hiding The overloading rule Ovr has another interesting application: if we extended the antecedent to cover overriding methods, Ovr could prevent the pulling up of d_2 in

```
class A {
  /*d1*/void m() {...}
}
class B extends A {
  void n() { /*r1*/m(); }
}
```

---

[8] Note that the converse problem, namely that binding of r to d' is redirected to d because d' became inaccessible, is prevented by Acc-1.

[9] Satisfiability with abnormal values like *absent* is different from lack of satisfiability, since it provides a diagnosis of the problem and points to a possible solution. Cf. Section 6.1 for a discussion.

```
class C extends B {
    /*d2*/void m() {…}
}
```

which would lead to a change of binding of r_1. The pulling up would be prevented by Ovr because its application would produce the constraint $\langle d_2 \rangle < \alpha(\lambda(r_1), \lambda(d_2))$, which is at conflict with the constraints generated by Sub-1, $\langle d_1 \rangle \leq \langle d_2 \rangle$, and Acc-1, $\langle d_1 \rangle \geq \alpha(\lambda(r_1), \lambda(d_1))$ (= $\alpha(\lambda(r_1), \lambda(d_2))$), so that the refactoring would lead to an unsolvable constraint set (meaning that pulling up d_2 is not allowed).

Rather than extending Ovr as suggested above, we introduce a separate constraint rule that also covers static methods and fields, whose introduction in a type can likewise lead to a change of binding (called *hiding* in [6] or *hiding through inheritance* in [13]). However, other than with overloading, with hiding there will never be solutions consisting of reducing accessibility of the hiding declared entity to a level above *absent*. Therefore, the new constraint rule reads

$$\iota(d) = \iota(d') \wedge \beta(r) = d \wedge \lambda(d') \in (\text{superclasses}(\rho(r)) \cup \{\rho(r)\}) \setminus \text{superclasses}(\lambda(d))$$
$$\Rightarrow \quad \langle d' \rangle = absent \qquad \qquad \textbf{(Hid)}$$

where $\iota(d) = \iota(d')$ means that d and d' have the same name or are override-equivalent [6, §8.4.2]. Again, that a declared entity that hides must be absent may seem paradoxical, but just as with inheritance (Inh-2) and overloading (Ovr), Hid is not applied to a program as is, but rather to the changes introduced by the refactoring were it performed (a kind of internal preview). It is thus a foresight rule, here one preventing that a certain declared entity is introduced, or moved, to a certain location.

Note that so-called *shadowing* and *obscuring* [6] (called *hiding by nesting* in [13]) cannot be prevented by adjusting access modifiers and are therefore out of scope for this paper.

Miscellaneous   A number of constraints follow directly from the JAVA language specification (JLS) [6] and are easily formalized:
- The accessibility of an array type equals the accessibility of its element type [6, §6.6.1].
- The accessibility of all fields declared in the same field declaration must be equal [6, §8.3].
- All main methods must be publicly accessible [6, §12.1.4].
- Only that top level type of a compilation unit whose name equals the name of the compilation unit may be declared public [6, §7.6].[10]
- A singly imported type and imported static members must be accessible by the importing compilation unit [6, §7.5].

Not so easily formalized (and omitted here for spatial reasons) is the rule that for multiple on-demand imports [6, §7.5], if a simple name in the importing compilation unit refers to a declared entity imported by one of the imports, the same entity must not be accessible through any of the other on-demand imports [6, §6.5].

For open programs (libraries, frameworks, etc.) it is necessary to keep other entry points than the main methods accessible. We therefore interpret certain annotations as constraints keeping the accessibility of the annotated entity constant; the @API annotation introduced in [1], as well as the @Test annotation of JUNIT, are examples of this.

---

[10] Note that in our formalization, compilation units have not been included as locations.

Last but not least (and as announced in Footnote 4), the set of admissible access modifiers for a declared entity depends on its kind and where it is declared, which is modelled by a corresponding constraint rule. Note that the allowable modifiers of d may change should the location of d change, for instance when d is a method pulled up to an interface.

3.2 Solving Accessibility Constraints

Solutions to finite constraint sets over variables with finite domains are trivially found by generating all possible variable assignments and by testing for each assignment whether it solves the constraint set. Clearly, the computational complexity of such a procedure is exponential in the number of variables, and therefore rarely acceptable. However, while general constraint satisfaction problems are known to be NP-complete, in practice, highly efficient algorithms that can solve finite domain constraint satisfaction problems such as ours with thousands of variables in acceptable time are available off the shelf (see, e.g., [5]), so that we will not go into details here. With one notable exception.

Since our constraint rules only model one aspect of JAVA, namely its access control, the constraints generated from these rules cannot be expected to prevent changes to programs violating syntactic or semantic rules unrelated to accessibility (examples of this are given in Footnote 7 and in Section 6.3). In particular, generated constraint sets may have solutions involving the changed location of elements that translate to incorrect programs, even if no access constraint is violated. Therefore, we restrict constraint solving to computing new values for the variables representing the declared access modifiers of entites, $\langle . \rangle$, and keep the variables representing locations of declared entities and references, $\lambda(.)$, constant (unless of course the change of location is the purpose of a refactoring). Since the sets of possible locations for references and declared entities are usually large, this reduces the complexity of our constraint satisfaction problems considerably.

4   Refactoring with Accessibility Constraints

Traditionally, the specification of a refactoring consists of a set of preconditions and an algorithmic part that describes its "mechanics" [4].[11] The preconditions are checked before the refactoring is performed; their purpose is to exclude applications of the refactoring to constellations in which the refactoring cannot work.

For constraint-based approaches to refactoring, precondition checking and mechanics rely on the same characterization of the problem: precondition checking amounts to finding out whether a generated constraint set with the intended changes applied is solvable, and performing the mechanics amounts to writing a solution of the constraint set (i.e., the found variable values) back to the program. If checking solvability

---

[11] Being an algorithm, the complete specification of a refactoring would also involve a set of postconditions. However, postconditions of refactorings are rarely found in the literature.

and finding a solution are considered one, refactoring with constraints consists of four steps:

1. the generation of constraints and initial variable values from the program to be refactored (resulting in a solved constraint set);
2. a change of variable values and the addition of foresight constraints reflecting the planned refactoring (possibly resulting in an unsolved constraint set);
3. the solution of the constraint set under the side conditions of the refactoring (including which constraint variables are fixed and which can be changed as part of the solution); and
4. the writing back of the found solution, if any.

The refactoring may involve user interaction, namely answering questions as to whether certain changes should be allowed (such as the change of access modifiers due to ripple effects). Since the constraints required for each particular refactoring, which variables of these constraints are actually changeable, and the possible user interaction depend on the concrete refactoring, we clarify these issues separately for each refactoring.

4.1   The CHANGE ACCESSIBILITY Refactoring

The most primitive refactoring relating to accessibility is changing the access modifier of a declared entity. It is a refactoring because, as noted in the introduction, the change represents a change of design and because it requires a careful prior analysis (it can change the meaning of the program, which a refactoring must not do).

The constraints to be generated for this refactoring are those involving the entity d whose declared accessibility $\langle d \rangle$ is to be changed, and recursively all those that are directly or indirectly (through shared constraint variables) related to it. If the user chooses that no other declared entities d' may be touched in the course of the refactoring, the set of constraints needing to be generated is reduced to the ones in which d is directly involved; the declared access modifiers $\langle d' \rangle$ of the d' participating in these constraints are then marked as constant.

The computation of the solution is initiated by assigning the constraint variable $\langle d \rangle$ representing the declared accessibility of the entity d to be refactored the value corresponding to the target accessibility. If the new value leaves the constraint set solved, the changed value can be written back and the refactoring is performed. If it is unsolved, a new solution must be computed. To express that the solution should involve as few and as small changes as possible (a side condition of the refactoring), the number of changes must be counted and the constraint solver instructed to find a solution that minimizes this count. If no solution exists, the refactoring must be refused; otherwise, the solution is written back and the refactoring performed.

Regarding the foresight rules preventing a change of binding (Inh-2 and Ovr; Hid is irrelevant here, because it can only prevent changes of location), only those constraints need be generated that constrain declared entities d whose accessibility may change during the course of the refactoring. For Inh-2, this amounts to checking all superclasses of $\rho(r)$ for all r with $\beta(r) = d$, for the presence of a static field with the same name as d. If present, a corresponding constraint is added. For Ovr, the check is analogous, but limited to overloaded methods. For instance, if in the program

```
package a;
public abstract class A {
  protected /*d1*/abstract void m(String s);
}

package a;
public class B extends A {
  public /*d2*/void m(Object o) {...}
  protected /*d3*/void m(String s) {...}
}

package b;
public class C {
  void n() { /*r1*/(new a.B()).m("abc"); }
}
```

accessibility of d_1 is to be increased to *public*, application of Ovr adds the constraint $\langle d_3 \rangle < \alpha(\lambda(r_1), \lambda(d_3))$ (because Sub-1 inserted $\langle d_3 \rangle \geq \langle d_1 \rangle$, implying a change of $\langle d_3 \rangle$). Since $\alpha(\lambda(r_1), \lambda(d_3)) = public$, the refactoring is prevented.

A special case of changing accessibility is the HIDE METHOD refactoring, which suggests making "each method as private as you can" [4]. In previous work of ours, we have implemented a refactoring that attempts to hide all methods of a program in one step [1]. However, due to the imperative character of the implementation (cf. Section 2.2), it did not consider ripple effects (i.e., one reduction that required another reduction as a prior step), so that it had to be repeated after each application to see whether any new reductions had become possible. By contrast, the constraint approach we are presenting here addresses this chaining through constraint propagation, so that accessibility of all declared entities can be reduced to their smallest possible levels in a single refactoring step.

4.2 The MOVE TYPE/MEMBER and PULL UP/PUSH DOWN MEMBER Refactorings

As far as accessibility is concerned, there is no difference between moving and pulling up or pushing down members (a distinction that is made in [4] and also in many refactoring tools): the constraint rules to be applied are precisely the same. The difference lies in which other elements must be moved as well, but this is independent of access modification and hence outside the scope of our work (cf. Sections 3.2 and 6.3). Therefore, we do not distinguish between these refactorings here.

Moving one or more declared entities d means that the constraint variables representing their locations, $\lambda(d)$, are assigned new values. If the declared entities contain references r, their locations $\lambda(r)$ change as well. All constraints directly or indirectly involving the changed $\lambda(d)$ or $\lambda(r)$ must be generated. If the user selects that no access modifiers may be changed as part of the refactoring, the set of constraints to be generated is restricted to the ones directly involving the moved locations and the values of all variables $\langle d \rangle$ are considered constant. All this is more or less analogous to the CHANGE ACCESSIBILITY refactoring (cf. above).

The situation is significantly different, however, for the foresight rules: here, Inh-2, Sub-1, Ovr, and Hid must be applied to the *moved* program elements, referring to their updated locations. This implies that search for overloaded or override-equivalent methods and for fields of the same name must be commenced in the target, rather than the original, location. For instance, if the intended refactoring for the program

```
package a;
public class A {
  public /*d1*/void m(Object o) {...}
  void n() { /*r1*/(new b.B()).m("abc"); }
}

package b;
public class B extends A {}

package a;
public class C extends B {
  public /*d2*/void m(String s) {...}
  void n() { /*r2*/(new C()).m("abc"); }

}
```

is to pull up d_2 to class B, application of Ovr to r_1, d_1, and d_2 in its new location, class B, produces the constraint $\langle d_2 \rangle < \alpha(\lambda(r_1), \lambda(d_2))$ (= *public*; note that this constraint is not justified for the program before the refactoring). Since application of Acc-1 produced $\langle d_2 \rangle \geq \alpha(\lambda(r_2), \lambda(d_2))$ (= *protected*), the pulling up of d_2 is possible, but only if $\langle d_2 \rangle$ is reduced to *protected*. Since we restricted the moving of program elements to the ones the user required to be moved (cf. Section 3.2), for all others the foresight rules must be applied as if the refactoring were CHANGE ACCESSIBILITY (because this is all that can happen). In the above example, there are no other foresight rules to be applied.

4.3 Renaming Declared Entities and Changing Method Signatures

A number of standard refactorings have the potential to change bindings. Perhaps the most prominent is the RENAME refactoring, which has to deal with issues such as hiding, shadowing, and obscuring [6, 18]. In certain cases, a change of accessibility can prevent such changes of binding, but these cases are rather rare. Also, the choice of names should not have an impact on accessibility and thus modularity, so that we do not pursue this further here.

Somewhat related is the problem of changed bindings due to a change of method signatures, either due to user request or as a side effect of refactorings such as GENERALIZE DECLARED TYPE or USE SUPERTYPE WHERE POSSIBLE [21]. In languages with single dispatch, the change of binding is limited to overloaded methods, and therefore can be dealt with using our constraint rules (in particular Ovr). However, as will be discussed in Section 6.2, other means of preventing or solving such problems may be more adequate.

4.4 Enabling other Refactorings

Although not themselves concerned with changing access modifiers, some refactorings have preconditions requiring a certain level of accessibility of involved declared entities. For instance, the REPLACE INHERITANCE WITH DELEGATION [10] refactoring requires that the inheriting class or its subclasses do not need access to protected members inherited before the refactoring (because these are no longer accessible after inheritance has been replaced by delegation). A corresponding case study showed that

Table 1. Space and time requirements of the approach as currently implemented (see text).

| | SPACE | | | TIME | | | |
| | No. of | | | Avg. Time$^\$$ in msec to | | | Avg. No. of |
Project	$\lambda(.)$	$\langle.\rangle$	Constraints	Build	Check*	Solve*	Steps to Solve*
JUNIT 3.8.1	2553	1332	4949	10593	30	599	5293360
JESTER 1.37b	1475	761	2293	1127	9	81	6837
JHOTDRAW 6.01b	9594	4995	26816	21246	199	6452	25582800
APACHE.IO 1.4	4315	2181	12877	17843	129	2486	57052

$^\$$ on a contemporary Wintel machine with 2GHz clock speed and 1GB of main memory for the JVM
* averaged over the refactorings performed to obtain the data of Table 2

in more than 15% of all inheriting classes, this precondition was violated [10]. Increasing accessibility of the (formerly) inherited member to *public* would satisfy the precondition; however, this presupposes that such a change does not change the meaning of the program. This can easily be checked by our constraints.

5   Implementation

As a proof of concept, we have implemented our constraint-based model of accessibility in JAVA as a plug-in to ECLIPSE's JDT, and tested and evaluated it by using it as the basis of several systematic refactorings of a set of sample programs.

5.1   Constraint Generation

Section 4 described in abstract terms how the constraints required for a specific refactoring are determined. Basically, an implementation would have to start with an initial set of variables whose change of value models the intended refactoring, generate all constraints from the program that constrain these variables, add their other (changeable) variables to the variable set, and so forth until no more constraints can be added. For instance, if the declared accessibility $\langle d \rangle$ of an entity d is to be changed, the program must be scanned for matches of the preconditions of all constraint rules containing d. For Acc-1 with precondition $\beta(r) = d$ this means that all references r binding to d must be found, for Inh-1 that additionally the static type of the receiver must be looked up, and so forth. As it turns out, the required searches and lookups can be quite expensive, especially if the AST does not maintain inverted indices pointing from declared entities to their references (cf. the discussion in Section 2.2). Since the space and time requirements for building and keeping such indices can be substantial (see [1] for some measurements), and since the JDT's search functions also rely on scanning the AST (so that successive searches for references to different declared entities are rather expensive), we decided to generate all constraints in a single sweep of the AST, regardless of whether they are actually needed by the concrete refactoring problem. As can be seen from Table 1, this poses some non-negligible spatial and temporal limits on our implementation.

5.2 Auxiliary Functions

Except for α, the auxiliary functions and predicates occurring in the antecedents of our constraint rules (namely β, λ, ρ, ι, subclasses, superclasses, implements, inherits, hides, overrides, overloads, and subsignature) are implemented using corresponding API methods of the JDT. The function α computing the required accessibility level for a reference to a declared entity is unpleasant to specify (as was its extraction from the JLS [6]); because it is of no theoretical interest, we do not present it here.

5.3 Constraint Solution

For constraint set solution, we adopted Naoyuki Tamura's class library for constraint programming in JAVA, called CREAM [20]. CREAM offers various implementations of efficient solvers for finite domain (especially integer) constraint satisfaction problems, of which our accessibility constraint sets (with the finite and totally ordered A as their domain) are a special case. As can be seen from Table 1, CREAM is capable of computing a new solution for a constraint set invalidated by the change of variable values and the addition of foresight constraints modelling an intended refactoring in acceptable time. However, better performance can be expected from creating fewer constraints (cf. Section 5.1), and from devising problem-specific constraint solvers.

5.4 Testing

In the absence of a formal proof of the completeness and correctness of our constraint rule set, we tested it thoroughly, exploiting the invariants mentioned at the end of the introduction to Section 3. In particular:

1. We generated all constraints and initial variable values from existing programs and checked whether the resulting constraint sets were solved given the initial assignments. This gave us an idea of the correctness of our constraint rules.
2. We computed all solutions for constraint sets generated from programs covered by test suites and wrote back the solutions to the code, checking whether the programs still compiled and their test suites still passed. This gave us an idea of the completeness of our constraint rule set. Note that, because behaviour-preserving change of location is not only constrained by accessibility (cf. Sections 3.2 and 6.3), we only computed new values for the variables $\langle . \rangle$ representing the declared access modifiers.[12]
3. We automatically performed refactorings enhanced with accessibility constraints for precondition checking and for computing the necessary mechanics on several programs covered by accompanying test suites, and checked whether the refactorings left the meaning of the programs (as specified in the test cases) unchanged.

---

[12] Due to the exponentially growing number of possible solutions, we had to limit testing to small programs (mostly variants of the programs used as examples in this paper, but also subsets of JUNIT and other small programs). We complemented these tests by tests on much larger programs, in which we changed only one access modifier at a time.

All three approaches contributed to identifying and shaping our constraint rules, whose original extraction from the JLS [6] turned out to be difficult and error-prone.

For the automated application of refactorings to sample programs, we used our REFACTORING TOOL TESTER (RTT) program. RTT is an ECLIPSE plugin that automatically applies a given ECLIPSE refactoring tool to all those elements of a test program for which it is intended, and checks whether the program still compiles after the refactoring and whether its unit tests still pass (approximating behaviour preservation). In its purpose, RTT competes with ASTGEN [2], but its design is different in that it uses existing, rather than specially generated, programs. Using the RTT on a large set of test programs increases the likelihood of covering rare cases (the designers of the generators for ASTGEN may not even have conceived of). However, since this approach primarily tests the refactorings and only indirectly the constraints used to compute preconditions and necessary changes, and because these refactorings have bugs unrelated to accessibility, the results of this automated testing require a careful interpretation. We defer this to the next subsection.

5.5 Evaluation

Although our examples of Section 2.1 should have provided sufficient evidence for the usefulness of a formal capture of accessibility and its integration into refactoring tools, we have also conducted some experiments using real programs, giving us an impression of how often a user of these tools will actually benefit. For this, we have adapted our above described RTT to apply two ECLIPSE refactoring tools, MOVE CLASS and PULL UP METHOD, in three variants to a set of sample programs: variant 1 (*pure*) applies the refactorings as they are currently deployed with [3] (including their built-in precondition checking); variant 2 (*prec*) enhances them with our constraint-based precondition checking allowing no changes of access modifiers, and variant 3 (*mech*) enhances them with precondition checking and constraint-solution based mechanics adjusting access modifiers so as to make the refactoring possible. Thus, we get for each potential application (*appl*) of a refactoring six outcomes, namely for each variant one pair stating whether it passed the preconditions (p) and whether it was successful (s). The counts of these outcomes for the sample programs are summarized in Table 2.

Due to the nature of the problem, we can expect the number of precondition passes, p, to decrease from *pure* to *prec*, and the number of successes, s, to stay the same (if it decreased, our preconditions would likely be too strong). Thus, the relative number of successful applications should increase. When moving from *prec* to *mech*, p should increase, as should s. However, because the refactorings can fail for other reasons (see below), the relative number of successful applications can change in either direction.

For MOVE CLASS, the results from Table 2 confirm our expectations: the passing of preconditions drops by 15% on average when moving from *pure* to *prec*[13], and increases by 17% when moving from *prec* to *mech*. This means that if the refactoring is allowed to change access modifiers, preconditions predict that it can be applied in 99% of all cases, compared to 85% if no changes are allowed. The success rate, which

---

[13] The inhibiting constraint rules were Acc-1 (52×), Dyn-1 (7×), and Inh-1 (4×).

Table 2. Number of passed (*p*) and successful (*s*) refactorings as applied to several test projects (see text).

Project	appl	MOVE CLASS						appl	PULL UP METHOD					
		pure		prec		mech			pure		prec		mech	
		p	s	p	s	p	s		p	s	p	s	p	s
JUNIT 3.8.1	38	38	23	23	23	36	36	148	20	20	14	14	20	20
JESTER 1.37b	31	31	26	26	26	31	31	5	3	3	3	3	3	3
JHOTDRAW 6.01b	235	235	213	208	208	235	235	1167	199	187	147	139	168	160
APACHE.IO 1.4	73	73	64	64	64	73	73	102	14	14	14	14	14	14
total	377	377	326	321	321	375	375	1422	236	224	178	170	205	197

is only 86% for *pure*, increases to 100% for *prec* and *mech*. The decrease of successful applications from *pure* to *prec* by 2% in the case of JHOTDRAW turned out to be due to measurement error: the five surplus applications of *pure* changed the meaning of the program (an were thus in fact unsuccessful), but this was neither caught by the compiler (in the form of compile-time errors) nor by the test cases. The two illegal applications of *pure* that could not be legalized by *mech* (both from JUNIT) were due to unsatisfiable constraints introduced by application of Acc-1 and Dyn-2.

The picture is rather different for PULL UP METHOD: while applicability also decreases from *pure* to *prec* (by 24% on average[14]), the loss of applicability is not reverted by *mech*: of the 58 applications inhibited by *prec*, only 27 could be legalized by adapting access modifiers. The remainder was prevented by unsatisfiable constraints of the above kind, and also by the 16 constraints introduced by Hid (cf. Footnote 14), which are generally unsatisfiable for referenced entities (cf. Section 3.1). The high success rate of *pure* (95%) is explained by the fact that the original refactoring tool changes the access modifier of the pulled up method if this is deemed necessary (which avoids many compile-time errors), and that introduced binding errors are not caught by tests (recall that Dyn-1 and Dyn-2 may be too strict so that their violation may not even present an error). The eight unsuccessful applications for *prec* and *mech* are caused by errors introduced by the pure refactoring tool that are unrelated to accessibility (and thus can neither be prevented by *prec* nor fixed by *mech*), such as disregarding the changed type of this (cf. Section 6.3) and the incompatibility of exceptions thrown by the pulled up method and an override-equivalent method in a sibling class.

6   Discussion

6.1   The Value of *absent*

The existence of *absent* as an access modifier allows the elegant formulation of certain preconditions of refactorings as *solvable* constraints (cf. Footnote 9). For in-

---

[14] with Ovr (365×), Acc-1 (125×), Sub-1 (18×) and Hid (16×) inhibiting the application

stance, if a foresight constraint requires that a certain entity's declared accessibility must be less than *private*, and if no other constraint requires that it must be at least *private* (because the entity is never referenced), the constraint solver will assign it the value *absent*, suggesting that the element should be (and can be!) deleted. Without *absent*, the constraint set would be unsolvable and the possible solution, the removal of a declared entity, would remain unconsidered.

Beyond this, *absent* also has its own value. Analogous to JAMIT [8], our constraint rules are capable of detecting dead code, simply by searching for solutions of a program's constraint set that assigns *absent* to the access modifiers of declared entities. However, with the access rules as is, dead code can remain undetected due to circular referencing.

Declared entities that are sustained by circular references not fed by a reference into the circle can be reduced to *absent* by modifying the accessibility rule Acc-1 such that it allows *absent* for a $\langle d \rangle$ even though there is an r such that $\beta(r) = d$, if r resides in the location of a declared entity that is itself modified with *absent* (expressed by absent(r)):

$$\beta(r) = d \;\Rightarrow\; \langle d \rangle \geq \alpha(\lambda(r), \lambda(d)) \vee \langle d \rangle = absent \text{ if absent}(r) \qquad \textbf{(Acc-1')}$$

However, since all constraints are generated by a rather simple static analysis of the program, our dead code removal will always be inferior to that achieved by more sophisticated tools, so that we do not pursue this further here.

6.2   Too Strong Preconditions

One might argue that the requirement expressed by some of our constraint rules, that declared entities must be made inaccessible or even eliminated to allow certain refactorings, is unnecessarily strong. Indeed, the reference to an overloaded method can be forced to bind to a certain implementation by inserting upcasts to the formal parameter types of that particular implementation, and the reference to a hidden entity can be maintained by inserting qualified names (as described in [18] for the RENAME refactoring; cf. Section 2.2). However, this would require a change of the reference rather than a change of accessibility, and is therefore a different story (one in which references themselves are modelled as variables).

6.3   Boundaries of Accessibility Constraints

Controlling access modifiers does not solve all refactoring problems related to accessing members. For instance, in the left program of

```
class A {}                        class A { B b; }

class B extends A {               class B extends A {
    /*d1*/void m() {/*r1*/n();}       /*d1*/void m() {/*r1*/b.n();}
    /*d2*/void n() {}                 /*d2*/void n() {}
}                                 }
```

with classes A and B residing in the same package, pulling up m() does not violate the access rules of JAVA (B.n() is accessible from A), but nevertheless results in a semantic error — the problem here is that the implicit receiver of calling n(), this, is of type B before the refactoring and of type A after. Were n() called on a variable of type B as on the right, the program would still work after the refactoring. While a constraint-based solution to this problem is likely possible, it is independent of access modification and therefore out of scope for this paper.

6.4   Formal Comparison of Languages

Our capture of access control as a set of constraint rules allows the compact comparisons of programming languages. Table 3 provides such a comparison of JAVA, C#, and EIFFEL. The inclusion of EIFFEL may seem surprising, since EIFFEL does not have access modifiers, but uses selective export of features (to the listed classes and their subclasses, to all, or to no classes) instead [12]. However, it nevertheless fits nicely into our framework: in EIFFEL, the domain of the accessibility variables $\langle . \rangle$, A, is $\wp(C)$, the powerset of the set of classes (see Table 3).

Table 3 also reveals that C#, although rather similar to JAVA, avoids certain of its problems. For instance, violation of Dyn-1 resulting in a change of behaviour in JAVA leads to a semantic error reported by the compiler, and violation of Dyn-2 is impossible. Similarly, violation of Hid issues a warning suggesting that the new modifier be used. A constraint rule of C# not found in JAVA requires that the accessibility of a member is at most the accessibility of its declared type. This prevents the breaching of non-accessibility made possible by chained method calls in JAVA, through which an instance of an inaccessible type can be accessed.

7   Conclusion

Refactoring the design of a program typically involves the moving of classes and/or their members. This requires regard of the access control rules specified by the programming language. In JAVA, disregard of these rules cannot only lead to access violations (reported as errors by the compiler), it can also lead to a change of meaning of a program, which a refactoring must always avoid. By capturing the access control of JAVA in the form of constraint rules, we have provided a framework for checking the preconditions of refactorings affecting the accessibility of program elements, and for safely adapting declared accessibility as part of the mechanics of a refactoring that would otherwise be impossible. Our framework involves so-called foresight applications of rules that model the changes intended by a refactoring, and an additional access modifier *absent* suggesting the deletion of program elements that are in the way of a refactoring without being used by the program. By conducting systematic experiments, we have shown how our approach can improve applicability and correctness of at least one important refactoring tool; where it falls short, it may be possible that additional constraint rules (unrelated to access modification) can fix the problems.

Table 3. Comparing JAVA, C#, and EIFFEL by contrasting their accessibility constraint rules

	JAVA	C#	EIFFEL
A	set of access modifiers of which $\langle.\rangle$ is an element *public > protected > package > private*	*public > protected internal >* *{protected, internal} > private*	$\wp(C)$
Acc-1	accessing $\beta(r) = d \;\Rightarrow\; \langle d\rangle \geq \alpha(\lambda(r), \lambda(d))$	same as JAVA	$\beta(r) = d \;\Rightarrow\; \lambda(r) \in \langle d\rangle$
Acc-2	$\beta(r) = d \wedge \alpha(\lambda(r), \lambda(d)) = protected \wedge d \notin S \wedge \rho(r)$ $\notin subclasses(\lambda(r)) \cup \{\lambda(r)\} \;\Rightarrow\; \langle d\rangle = public$	analogous to JAVA, taking *protected internal* into account	not applicable
Inh-1	accessing inherited members $\beta(r) = d \wedge \rho(r) \neq \lambda(d) \;\Rightarrow\; \langle d\rangle \geq \alpha(\rho(r), \lambda(d))$	no additional constraint	no additional constraint
Inh-2	accessing multiply inherited static fields $\{d, d'\} \subseteq F \cap S \wedge \iota(d) = \iota(d') \wedge \beta(r) = d \wedge \lambda(d') \in$ $superclasses(\rho(r)) \;\Rightarrow\; \langle d'\rangle < \alpha(\lambda(r), \lambda(d'))$	not applicable (no implementation can be inherited from an interface)	not applicable (features inherited from more than one superclass must be renamed)
Sub-1	subtyping $\{d, d'\} \subseteq M \wedge (overrides(d', d) \vee hides(d', d))$ $\Rightarrow \langle d'\rangle \geq \langle d\rangle$	$\{d, d'\} \in M \wedge (overrides(d', d) \vee hides(d', d))$ $\Rightarrow \langle d'\rangle \;\boxed{=}\; \langle d\rangle$ (access modifiers of methods cannot be changed in subclasses)	$overrides(d', d) \;\Rightarrow$ $\langle d'\rangle \supseteq \langle d\rangle \vee$ check for CAT-calls
Dyn-1	losing dynamic binding $overrides(d', d) \;\Rightarrow\; \langle d\rangle \geq \alpha(\lambda(d'), \lambda(d))$	same; upon violation, compiler reports an error, since lack of accessibility conflicts with virtual modifier necessary for overriding	not applicable, since all features are inherited and dynamic binding is independent of accessibility
Dyn-2	introducing dynamic binding $\lambda(d) \in superclasses(\lambda(d')) \wedge subsignature(d', d)$ $\wedge \neg overrides(d', d) \;\Rightarrow\; \langle d\rangle < \alpha(\lambda(d'), \lambda(d))$	not applicable, since overriding would require adding a virtual modifier	see above
Ovr	overloading $\{d, d'\} \subseteq M \wedge overloads(d', d) \wedge \beta(r) = d \wedge \lambda(d')$ $\in superclasses(\rho(r)) \cup \{\rho(r)\} \Rightarrow \langle d'\rangle < \alpha(\lambda(r), \lambda(d'))$	same as JAVA	no overloading in EIFFEL
Hid	hiding $\iota(d) = \iota(d') \wedge \beta(r) = d \wedge \lambda(d') \in (superclasses(\rho(r))$ $\cup \{\rho(r)\})$ superclasses$(\lambda(d)) \;\Rightarrow\; \langle d'\rangle = absent$	same as JAVA, but violation issues a warning suggesting use of the new modifier (not for PULL UP)	same as C#, but hiding feature must be introduced using redefine $\langle d\rangle \leq \langle type(d)\rangle$ where $type(d)$ is the entity representing the declared type of d

Acknowledgements

We are indebted to Naoyuki Tamura for making available his CREAM library, and for pointing us to its neighbourhood search facility.

References

1. Bouillon, P., Großkinsky, E., Steimann, F.: Controlling accessibility in agile projects with the Access Modifier Modifier. In: Proc. of TOOLS, vol. 46, pp. 41–59 (2008)
2. Daniel, B., Dig, D., Garcia, K., Marinov, D.: Automated testing of refactoring engines. In: Proc. of ESEC/SIGSOFT FSE, pp. 185–194 (2007)
3. Eclipse Java Development Tools Version 3.4.1, http://www.eclipse.org
4. Fowler, M.: Refactoring: Improving the Design of Existing Code. Addison-Wesley, Reading (1999)
5. Frühwirth, T., Abdennadher, S.: Essentials of Constraint Programming. Springer, Berlin (2003)
6. Gosling, J., Joy, B., Steele, G., Bracha, G.: The Java Language Specification, http://java.sun.com/docs/books/jls/
7. Grothoff, C., Palsberg, J., Vitek, J.: Encapsulating objects with confined types. ACM Trans. Program. Lang. Syst. 29(6), 32 (2007)
8. Grothoff, C.: Introducing: the Java Access Modifier Inference Tool, http://grothoff.org/christian/xtc/jamit/
9. IntelliJ IDEA Version 8, http://www.jetbrains.com/idea/
10. Kegel, H., Steimann, F.: Systematically refactoring inheritance to delegation in Java. In: Proc. of ICSE, pp. 431–440 (2008)
11. Koved, L., Pistoia, M., Kershenbaum, A.: Access rights analysis for Java. In: Proc. of OOPSLA, pp. 359–372 (2002)
12. Meyer, B.: Object-Oriented Software Construction, 2nd edn. Prentice Hall International, Englewood Cliffs (1997)
13. Microsoft C# Language Specification v1.2, http://download.microsoft.com
14. Müller, P., Poetzsch-Heffter, A.: Kapselung und Methodenbindung: Javas Designprobleme und ihre Korrektur. In: Java-Informations-Tage, pp. 1–10 (1998)
15. NetBeans Integrated Development Environment Version 6.5, http://www.netbeans.org
16. Opdyke, W.: Refactoring Object-Oriented Frameworks. Ph.D. thesis, University of Illinois at Urbana-Champaign (1992)
17. Parnas, D.L.: On the criteria to be used in decomposing systems into modules. Commun. ACM 15(12), 1053–1058 (1972)
18. Schäfer, M., Ekman, T., de Moor, O.: Sound and extensible renaming for Java. In: Proc. of OOPSLA, pp. 277–294 (2008)
19. Schirmer, N.: Analysing the Java package/access concepts in Isabelle/HOL. Concurrency — Practice and Experience 16(7), 689–706 (2004)
20. Tamura, N.: Cream: Class Library for Constraint Programming in Java, http://bach.istc.kobe-u.ac.jp/cream/
21. Tip, F., Kiezun, A., Bäumer, D.: Refactoring for generalization using type constraints. In: Proc. of OOPSLA, pp. 13–26 (2003)
22. Tip, F.: Refactoring using type constraints. In: Riis Nielson, H., Filé, G. (eds.) SAS 2007. LNCS, vol. 4634, pp. 1–17. Springer, Heidelberg (2007)

Java on 1000 Cores:
Tales of Hardware/Software Co-design

Cliff Click

Azul Systems

Azul Systems designs and builds systems for running business logic applications written in Java. Unlike scientific computing, business logic code tends to be very large and complex (> 1MLOC is *common*), display very irregular data access patterns, and make heavy use of threads and locks. The common unit of parallelism is the transaction or thread-level task. Business logic programs tend to have high allocation rates which scale up with the amount of work accomplished, and they are sensitive to Garbage Collection max-pause-times. Typical JVM implementations for heaps greater than 4 Gigabytes have unacceptable pause times and this forces many applications to run clustered.

Our systems support heaps up to 600 Gigabytes and allocation rates up to 35 Gig/s with pause times in the dozen-millisecond range. We have large core counts (up to 864) for running parallel tasks; our memory is Uniform Memory Access (as opposed to the more common NUMA), cache-coherent, and has supercomputer-level bandwidth. The cores are our own design; simple 3-address RISCs with read- and write-barriers to support GC, hardware transactional memory, zero-cost high-rez profiling, and some more modest Java-specific tweaks.

This talk is about the business environment which drove the design of the hardware (e.g. why put in HTM support? why our own CPU design and not e.g. MIPS or X86?), some early company history with designing our own chips (1st silicon back from the fab had problems like the bits in the odd-numbered registers bleeding into the even-numbered registers), and finally some wisdom and observations from a tightly integrated hardware/software co-design effort.

S. Drossopoulou (Ed.): ECOOP 2009, LNCS 5653, p. 444, 2009.

Loci: Simple Thread-Locality for Java

Tobias Wrigstad, Filip Pizlo, Fadi Meawad, Lei Zhao, and Jan Vitek

Computer Science Dept.
Purdue University

Abstract. This paper presents a simple type system for thread-local data in Java. Classes and types are annotated to express thread-locality and unintended leaks are detected at compile-time. The system, called Loci, is minimal, modular and compatible with legacy code. The only change to the language is the addition of two new metadata annotations. We implemented Loci as an Eclipse plug-in and used it to evaluate our design on a number of benchmarks. We found that Loci is compatible with how Java programs are written and that the annotation overhead is light thanks to a judicious choice of defaults.

1 Introduction

Statically determining whether part of a computation takes place solely inside a single thread is desirable for several reasons. Not only does it simplify reasoning, but it enables optimizations that are only possible in sequential code, for example, to improve the performance of automatic memory management algorithms [17,32] or remove unnecessary synchronization [2,1]. Java has supported *thread-local fields* with the `ThreadLocal` class since version 1.2 of the language. Using this API, each thread can have its own copy of a field and use that in a race-free manner. Another example of use is the detection of deadlock and shutdowns in a CORBA implementation [25].

When used with simple or immutable data types, the `ThreadLocal` API offers sufficient protection. However, when used with mutable complex data types the safety offered by the `ThreadLocal` API can be likened to that of name-based encapsulation: the *field* is guaranteed to be thread-local, but not its *contents*. For example, a reference obtained from a thread-local field can subsequently be shared across threads, which may violate thread-locality assumptions elsewhere in the program. This also means that compilers can not rely on thread-locality in their optimizations.

In this paper, we propose a simple, statically checkable set of annotations that lets programmers express thread-locality. Our system, Loci, was designed with Java in mind, but should apply to Java-like languages with only a modicum of changes. We extend Java with two annotations: `@Thread`, to denote potentially thread-local objects and `@Shared` to denote shared objects. Classes that do not leak `this` to shared fields can be marked `@Thread` to denote that they are safe to use for thread-local computation. Annotations on fields, parameters, local variables and method returns are then used to express thread-locality of objects

S. Drossopoulou (Ed.): ECOOP 2009, LNCS 5653, pp. 445–469, 2009.

in the program. Loci statically verifies that a program's thread-local behavior corresponds to the programmer's intentions and thus enforces proper use of Java's ThreadLocal API. Experiments with Loci on ≥45 000 lines of Java code validate our design and suggest improvements.

The design of Loci was driven by a quest for simplicity and practical applicability. To minimize syntactic overhead, and increase reusability of code and libraries, Loci uses a default annotation system on types controlled by class-level annotations. In many cases, a single class-level annotation is necessary to make a class suitable for use in thread-local computation. Furthermore, the defaults have been chosen so that all existing Java programs are valid Loci programs. Loci is an ownership types system that uses *threads* as owners, instead of objects, similar in spirit to [30,14]. This paper makes the following contributions:

1. It proposes Loci, a simple annotation system for Java-like languages that can statically express and enforce proper use of thread-local data and integrates reasonably well with legacy code, specifically, all existing Java programs have a valid Loci semantics.
2. An implementation of Loci in an Eclipse plug-in which integrates error reporting with the Eclipse IDE and performs bytecode-level rewriting of thread-local field accesses and thread-local methods.
3. Reports on experimental results from annotating classes in existing Java programs. We have refactored some benchmark programs by hand and, in parallel, we have implemented an inference algorithm as well as a dynamic tracking algorithm.

The main motivation for our work is to statically enforce thread-locality in Java. Loci allows programmers to declare their intentions with respect to thread-locality and checks statically that those intentions are never violated. The knowledge that some of the data manipulated by a system is guaranteed to be race-free is a big help for programmers as they need not worry about concurrency control for those parts of the system.

There are other potential benefits to thread-locality that we intend to explore. For starters, we believe that thread-locality information can be used to improve performance. Trivially, thread-local objects are free from data races and no locks need to be acquired for such objects. Thread-locality also has positive effects on garbage collection. For example, collecting thread-local data can be done in parallel without synchronization. In a reference counted collector, reference counts on thread-local objects can be modified directly without a compare-and-swap. Previous work [17] shows overall speedups of 50% when using thread-local heaps in Java. As a last example, thread-locality could be used to cache field reads for local manipulation in methods, before written back.

Another interesting future application of thread-locality lies in real-time computing. Run-time facilities used to execute Java programs typically have a very fast path that speculatively assumes properties that would be implicit with thread locality. For example, thin locks [3] and biased locks [29] assume a lack of contention. While this results in good performance for systems in which only the overall throughput is important, it is of no use to systems in which the worst-case performance is the more interesting property. Thread-locality can aid the worst-case analysis of real-time programs, by assuring the developer that the slow-path will never be taken. Typical Java programs use locking in the form of the synchronized statement freely under the assumption that it is cheap. Unfortunately, locking is only cheap when it is uncontended. Proving this with a static analysis is hard, but can be made easy for a large subset of the program by using Loci. While real-time garbage collection is gaining acceptance, its performance is still lagging. Using thread-local heaps, or similar variants thereof [27,30], increases both mutator utilization and scalability. Existing systems accomplish this with a combination of run-time checks, analyzes performed at run-time on object graphs, and extremely strict confined types systems. Loci could be used to achieve a similar effect with more expressive power and less work on the part of the programmer.

2   Informal Introduction to Loci

We now informally describe the Loci system, its logical run-time view of the heap and the annotation system.

2.1   Example

As first example, Fig. 1 shows Loci preventing a supposedly thread-local variable from a thread's run method to be leaked. The class Leaky is a thread with a field unsafe of type String[]. The run() method stores a reference to an object that was intended to be thread-local into that field, thus making it possible for another thread to read the field and perform concurrent updates on the array.

In many cases, the only variable that needs to be explicitly annotated in Loci is the root variable on the bottom stack-frame in the thread's run-method. The Loci class Safe is a thread where the field unsafe has been marked @Shared. This means that it is a field that can be read by multiple threads. In the method run, the local variable is marked @Thread to denote that it is intended to be thread-local. Loci will flag the assignment of line 6 as a compile-time error because it breaks the thread-locality guarantee on local.

In cases where the thread needs to explicitly store thread-local variables on the heap, a @Thread field can be used. Class NotSoLeaky is a correct implementation of Leaky that uses the ThreadLocal API explicitly to store the contents of the local variable in a thread-local field. The same effect can be achieved in Loci by annotating a field as @Thread. This is done in class Safe where the field safe is thread-local. In this case, Loci will silently transform the code written by the programmer (at compile-time) into equivalent code which uses ThreadLocal.

To sum up, Loci guarantees that the contents of any field or variable annotated @Thread is and will remain thread-local. For variables this is done entirely at compile-time (by restricting assignments) and for fields the guarantee is obtained by translation into using the ThreadLocal API.

```
1   class Leaky extends Thread {        class Safe extends Thread {
2     String[] unsafe;                    @Shared String[] unsafe;
3                                          @Thread String[] safe;
4     public void run() {                  public void run() {
5       String[] local = ...;                @Thread String[] local = ...;
6       unsafe = local; // leak             unsafe = local; // wont compile
7                                            safe = local; // OK
8   } }                                  } }
9   ...                                  ...
10  Leaky t;                             Safe t;
11  ... = t.unsafe;                      ... = t.unsafe;
12                                       ... = t.safe; // no leak
```

```
1   class NotSoLeaky extends Thread {
2     ThreadLocal<String[]> safe = new ThreadLocal<String[]>();
3
4     public void run() { String[] local = ...; safe.set(local); }
5   }
6   ...
7   NotSoLeaky t = ...;
8   ... = t.safe.get();
```

Fig. 1. Enforcing thread-locality with Loci. Line 6 marked Leak in the leftmost example is prevented statically. On Line 12, the assignment from safe does not cause a leak, as different threads get different values when reading a thread-local field. Class NotSoLeaky is safe as it uses the the ThreadLocal API, Loci provides more convenient syntax for the same. Whenever ever a field is annotated @Thread, the Loci compiler will turn it into a ThreadLocal.

2.2   Logical View of the Heap

In Loci, the heap of a program with n threads is *logically* partitioned into n number of isolated heaps, called "heaplets", plus a shared heap. There is a one-to-one mapping between threads and heaplets. From now on, *heap* refers to the shared heap accessible by all threads, and *heaplets* refers to thread-local heaps. The Loci annotation system enforces the following simple properties on Java programs, shown in Fig. 2:

1. References from one heaplet into another are not allowed ($\longrightarrow$);
2. References from heaplets to the shared heap are unrestricted ($--\rightarrow$);
3. References from the shared-heap into a heaplet must be stored in a thread-local field ($\bullet--\rightarrow$).

The third property above ensures that even though a reference into a heaplet ρ_i may exist on the shared heap, it is only accessible to the thread i to which ρ_i belongs. If another thread j reads the same field, it will either get a reference into its own heap ρ_j that it had written there before, or a thread-local copy of the

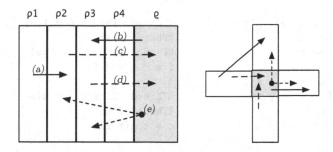

Fig. 2. Thread-Local Heaplets and a Shared Heap. The teal area (ϱ) is the shared heap, white areas ($\rho_1..\rho_4$) represent the thread-local heaplets. Solid arrows are invalid and correspond to property 1 in Sec. 2.2, dashed arrows are valid pointers into the shared heap (property 2), respectively from the shared heap into heaplets (property 3, when "anchored" in a bullet). The right-most figure is a Venn diagram-esque depiction of the same program to illustrate the semantics of the shared heap.

default value of the field (which may be `null`). Effectively, there is a copy of each thread-local field for each active thread in the system and writes and reads of the same thread-local field by different threads access different copies. Together, these simple properties make heaplets effectively thread-local, and objects in the heaplets are thus safe from race conditions and data races.

2.3   Annotations

Loci uses two annotations, `@Thread` and `@Shared`, their semantics is summarized in Table 1. We distinguish between class-level annotation and annotations on types in declarations. Class-level annotations control how instances of a class can be used. Instances of classes annotated `@Shared` always live in the shared heap. Instances of classes annotated `@Thread` may live on the shared heap, or

Table 1. Loci annotations

Annotation	Level	
@Shared	Class	Instances are always allocated in the shared heap.
@Thread	Class	Instances can be allocated either in the shared heap or in heaplets.
—	Class	Equivalent to @Shared.
@Shared	Field	May point into the heap or into a heaplet.
@Thread	Field	Must refer to a heaplet-allocated value. Access to the object is through the `ThreadLocal` API.
—	Field	Treated as @Shared if the enclosing class is @Shared, and as a @Thread local variable otherwise. (@Context in the formalism.)
@Shared	Local	May point into the heap or into a heaplet.
@Thread	Local	Must refer to a heaplet-allocated value.
—	Local	Treated as @Shared if the enclosing class is @Shared, and @Thread otherwise. (Called @Context in the formalism.)

```
1  @Thread class Foo { Foo f; }      @Shared class S { S f; }
2  @Shared Foo x;                    @Shared S x;
3  @Thread Foo y;                    @Thread S y; // Illegal
4  Foo z;                            S z = x = x.f;
5  @Shared Foo xx = x.f;
6  @Thread Foo yy = y.f;             @Thread class C { C m(S) { ... } }
7  Foo zz = z.f;                     @Thread C c;
8  yy.f = z; // Illegal              c = c.m(x.f);
```

Fig. 3. Loci by example. *Left:* f in Foo will live on same heap(let) as the enclosing obj. Thus, 5–7) are valid. Depending on the current context, z can be both shared and unshared. Thus, 8) is illegal. However, when we know the nature of the context, we can figure out the precise type (y in 6). *Right:* Line 3) demonstrates that @Shared classes cannot be pointed to by @Thread variables. Line 4) shows that an unannotated field in a @Shared class will also be shared. Line 6) trivially shows viewpoint adaptation.

on a thread-local heap. The class-level annotations control the implicit defaults used on types in the class. In a @Shared class, all types are implicitly shared. Unless explicitly declared @Thread, fields in a @Shared class point to objects in the shared heap. Fig. 3 contains some example uses of the annotations. In @Thread-annotated classes, the default annotation is empty (@Context in the formalism), which is a non-annotation only used implicitly. Empty is equivalent to owner in ownership types systems and means "the same as the enclosing instance." If f is an unannotated field in an instance o of a @Thread class, f will point to an object in the same heaplet as o, or into the shared heap iff o is in the shared heap. In practice, the implicit default value is right most of the time. Oftentimes, a single class-level annotation is all that is necessary. When accessing an unannotated field of a @Thread variable, the field's annotation will automatically default to @Thread. We refer to this as *viewpoint adaptation* and it is a simplified version of σ-substitution found in several ownership types formalisms [12,13,34,26].

Rather than splitting classes into thread-local and not, a @Thread class can be used to instantiate both thread-local and shared objects. This makes code more flexible and reusable in both shared and unshared context which is important for library classes. The main restriction for @Thread classes is that they may not assign from this in a way that could invalidate isolation. This is simple to check statically—disallow values whose annotation is unknown to be stored in explicitly annotated fields or variables. Since globals are always @Shared, a @Thread class may not leak this into them and so the only way to invalidate thread-locality is by storing this in a constructor argument. To that end, if a constructor takes 0 arguments or all @Thread arguments, the new object will be thread-local. Otherwise it will be shared.

Fields, variables, parameters and return types annotated @Thread or @Shared point to thread-local respectively shared objects. If the annotation is empty, it is effectively the same as the current this. To maintain compatibility with existing Java code, the default class-level annotation is @Shared. Thus, the class Thread

```
@Thread class RayTracerRunner extends RayTracer {
  @Shared Barrier br = null; # Barrier is shared between threads
  ...
}
...
// was thobjects[i] = new RayTracerRunner(i, wdt, hgt, brl);
thobjects[i] = new Thread() {
  public void run() {
    @Thread RayTracerRunner _ = new RayTracerRunner(i, wdt, hgt, brl);
    _.run(); // Start thread-local computation
  }
};
...
```

Fig. 4. Code from Raytracer in JavaGrande refactored with Loci annotations

is shared (which is the only sensible option), and as subclassing must preserve annotations in Loci (modulo for `Object`, see below), the derived thread classes in Fig. 1 must also be `@Shared`.

The root class `Object` is annotated `@Thread`. We treat it specially in that we allow it to be extended as `@Shared`. This is type safe, and as subtyping preserves annotations, cannot be used to confuse the type system.

Finally, Fig. 4 shows an example from Raytracer in the JavaGrande benchmarks where RayTracer classes all the classes that are used by RayTracer are annotated `@Thread`, modulo the shared barrier. The computation is thus entirely thread-local. The arrays of threads contain threads that simply start the thread-local computation.

2.4 Migrating Objects

Some concurrent programming idioms are characterized by phased access to objects. For example, in a producer-consumer pattern, an object is first accessed exclusively by the producer thread before being handed out to the consumer thread which then has sole access to the object. This goes beyond the kind of thread-locality expressible directly in Loci or most simple ownership type systems. Approaches based on linearity are feasible but they would overly complicate the type system. In Loci, when thread-local objects must migrate between threads it is necessary to perform a deep copy via the heap. Fig. 5 shows a method that copies an instance of `Foo` from Fig. 3 from a heaplet to the shared heap. Copying an object *directly* across heaplets is not yet supported, but we plan to investigate simple ways of doing this in the future.

For now, two threads in a producer-consumer relationship wishing to transfer unshared objects across via for example a shared queue, must copy the objects twice and place them on the shared heap. As noted in Sec. 2.3, most newly created instances of `@Thread` classes can safely be stored anywhere.

Two minor technicalities prevent us from doing direct inter-heaplet migration. Firstly, we cannot name a field belonging to another thread. Second, the

```
1  @Shared Foo copyToShared(Cache cache) {
2    if (cache.hasKey(this)) return cache.get(this);
3    @Shared Foo copy = new Foo();
4    cache.put(this, copy);
5    if (f != null) {
6      copy.f = f.copyToShared(cache);
7    }
8    return copy;
9  }
```

Fig. 5. A simple deep copy method for `Foo` that makes a shared copy of a possibly thread-local object. Cache is a `@Thread` map from keys to `@Shared` objects. Removing `@Shared` would make the method return a thread-local copy, as `Foo` is a `@Thread` class.

annotations can only express references into the current thread's heaplet or the shared heap. Extending the system to allow both is relatively straightforward. Writing to another thread's field can be as simple as extending `ThreadLocal` with a `put(Thread t, Object val)` method. A `@StackLocal` annotation could also be employed to type the `put()` method, and at the same time obviate the need for two deep copy methods, but would further complicate the system, especially when preserving aliasing through a cache like in Fig. 5.

2.5 Run-Time Overhead

Loci does not add run-time overhead over the equivalent Java programs. It does not need to store to what heap(let) an object belongs at run-time. `@Thread`-annotated local variables, parameters and method returns all live on the stack and are thus effectively thread-local without the need for any additional magic. Most notably, implicitly thread-local fields (e.g., `f` in Fig. 3) in `@Thread`-annotated classes do not incur any additional overhead. The key realization is that access to the enclosing object acts as a guard (similar observations have been done elsewhere, e.g., [13,34,16,18]):

> *If the enclosing object is only reachable by its "owning thread", the same holds for all objects pointed to by its non-@Shared fields.*

The overhead of `@Thread`-annotated *fields* is due to their implementation using Java's `ThreadLocal` API. Micro benchmarks suggest that access to a thread-local field is about 8 times slower than a regular field access. In our experience, fields only need to be annotated `@Thread` in the places where the Java program would have used the `ThreadLocal` API explicitly.

3 A Formal Account of Loci

We formalize our system in a subset of Java. For brevity, we omit commonly omitted features, such as overriding, interfaces, exceptions, final variables, primitive data types, arrays and generics. Generics is not yet supported by Loci as Java does not yet support annotations on type parameters. Should JSR 308, "Type Annotations" be accepted, adding support for annotating type parameters would be straightforward and would improve our story for collection classes.

3.1 Syntax and Static Semantics

Loci's syntax is shown in Fig. 6. For simplicity, we use an explicit annotation @Context, instead of implicit annotations. Without loss of generality, we use a "named form," where the results of field and variable accesses, method calls and instantiations must be immediately stored in a variable or field. For simplicity, all rules have an implicit program P in which classes are looked up. We use the right-associative viewpoint-adaptation operator $\oplus$ to expand the default @Context annotation thus:

$$\alpha_1 \oplus \alpha_2 \ c = \begin{cases} \alpha_1 \ c \text{ if } \alpha_2 = \text{@Context} \\ \alpha_2 \ c \text{ otherwise} \end{cases} \qquad \alpha_1 \oplus \alpha_2 \oplus \alpha_3 \ c = \alpha_1 \oplus (\alpha_2 \oplus \alpha_3 \ c)$$

For brevity, we assume that fields$(c) = \overline{\tau}\,\overline{f}$ where $\overline{f}$ are all fields in c and super classes of c. We use the shorthand fields$(c.f) = \tau$ to say that field f in class c has the type τ. For methods, we assume the existence of mtype$(c.m) = \overline{\tau} \to \tau$ and mbody$(c.m) = (\overline{x}, s;\text{return } x)$ where $\tau \ m(\overline{\tau}\,\overline{x})\{ \ s;\text{return } x \ \}$ is declared in the most direct superclass to c that declares m. We sometimes write (SUB-*) to denote all rules starting with "SUB" and (*-VAR) for all rules ending with "VAR."

We say that a program P is well-formed if all class definitions are well formed. By construction, all class hierarchies are rooted in Object. For simplicity, Object is an empty class with no superclasses that is annotated @Thread. A user-defined class is well-formed if it abides by (T-CLASS).

$$
\begin{array}{llr}
P & ::= \overline{cd} & program \\
cd & ::= \alpha \ \textbf{class} \ c \ \textbf{extends} \ d \ \{ \ \overline{fd} \ \overline{md} \ \} & class\ declaration \\
fd & ::= \tau f & field \\
md & ::= \tau \ m(\overline{\tau}\,\overline{x}) \ \{ \ s;\textbf{return} \ y \ \} & method \\
s & ::= s;s \ | \ \textbf{skip} | \ x = y.f \ | \ x = y \ | \ y.f = z \ | \ \tau \ x \ | & statement \\
& \quad x = \textbf{new} \ \tau() \ | \ x = y.m(\overline{z}) \ | \ x = \textbf{start} \ c() & \\
\tau & ::= \alpha \ c & type \\
\alpha & ::= \texttt{@Thread} \ | \ \texttt{@Shared} \ | \ \texttt{@Context} & annotations \\
\\
E & ::= [] \ | \ E[x : \tau] & local\ type\ environment \\
\end{array}
$$

Fig. 6. Loci's syntax. c, d are class names, f, m are field and method names, and x, y, z are names of variables or parameters respectively, where $x \neq$ this. For simplicity, we assume that names of classes, fields, methods and variables are unique. The special variable ret and return only appears in the dynamic syntax and semantics.

$$(\text{T-CLASS})$$
$$\text{fields}(d) = fd_2 \quad \text{methods}(d) = md_2 \quad \text{annote}(d) = \alpha_2$$
$$\forall m \in \text{names}(\overline{md_1}) \cap \text{names}(\overline{md_2}).\ \text{mtype}(c.m) = \text{mtype}(d.m)$$
$$\text{names}(\overline{fd_1}) \cap \text{names}(\overline{fd_2}) = \emptyset$$

$$\frac{\alpha_1 \neq \text{@Context} \quad (\alpha_1 = \alpha_2 \vee d = \text{Object}) \quad \alpha_1 \vdash \overline{fd_1} \quad \alpha_1\ c \vdash \overline{md_1}}{\vdash \alpha_1\ \text{class } c \text{ extends } d \ \{ \ \overline{fd_1}\ \overline{md_1}\ \}}$$

Notably, subclassing and overriding must preserve annotations, overriding is not supported, and @Context is not a valid class-level annotation.

$$(\text{T-FIELD}) \qquad\qquad\qquad (\text{T-METHOD})$$

$$\frac{\vdash \alpha_1 \oplus \alpha_2\ c}{\alpha_1 \vdash \alpha_2\ c\ f} \qquad \frac{(\alpha_1 = \text{@Thread} \wedge \alpha_2 = \text{@Context}) \vee \alpha_2 = \text{@Shared}}{\alpha_1\ c \vdash \tau\ m(\overline{\tau}\ \overline{x})\{\ s;\text{return } y\ \}}$$
$$\text{this} : \alpha_2\ c, \overline{x} : \overline{\tau} \vdash s;\ E \qquad E(y) \leq \alpha_2 \oplus \tau$$

(T-FIELD) uses the viewpoint-adaptation operator $\oplus$ on annotations and types. α_2 is the annotation on the field and α_1 is the annotation of the declaring class used if α_2 is @Context. The class of the field must be valid with respect to the resulting annotation. This is similar to σ-substitution found in ownership types type systems and is used frequently in the formalism.

In (T-METHOD), the type of this depends on the enclosing class. In a @Thread class, this is @Context and otherwise @Shared. This is because @Thread classes can be used to create both shared and thread-local instances.

Statements. The statements should be straightforward to follow for anyone familiar with Java. Remember, $x \neq$ this.

$$(\text{T-SEQUENCE}) \qquad\qquad (\text{T-SKIP}) \qquad\qquad (\text{T-ASSIGN})$$

$$\frac{E \vdash s_1; E_1 \quad E_1 \vdash s_2; E_2}{E \vdash s_1; s_2; E_2} \qquad \frac{}{E \vdash \text{skip}; E} \qquad \frac{E(y) \leq E(x)}{E \vdash x = y; E}$$

$$(\text{T-SELECT}) \qquad\qquad (\text{T-UPDATE}) \qquad\qquad (\text{T-DECL})$$

$$\frac{\begin{array}{c} E(y) = \alpha\ c \\ \text{fields}(c.f) = \tau' \\ \alpha \oplus \tau' \leq E(x) \end{array}}{E \vdash x = y.f; E} \qquad \frac{\begin{array}{c} E(y) = \alpha\ c \\ \text{fields}(c.f) = \tau \\ E(z) \leq \alpha \oplus \tau \end{array}}{E \vdash y.f = z; E} \qquad \frac{\begin{array}{c} x \notin dom(E) \\ E(\text{this}) = \alpha\ c \\ E' = E[x : \alpha \oplus \tau] \end{array}}{E \vdash \tau\ x; E'}$$

(T-SELECT) and (T-UPDATE) applies $\oplus$ to the annotation on the target and the field to possibly expand @Contexts. Note that (T-DECL) replaces @Context with the annotation of the current this (which may be @Context).

$$(\text{T-CALL}) \qquad\qquad\qquad (\text{T-FORK})$$
$$(\text{T-NEW}) \qquad E(y) = \alpha\ c \quad \text{mtype}(c.m) = \overline{\tau} \to \tau' \quad \text{mtype}(c.\text{run}) = \epsilon \to \tau$$

$$\frac{\vdash \tau \quad \tau \leq E(x)}{E \vdash x = \text{new } \tau(); E} \qquad \frac{E(\overline{z}) \leq \alpha \oplus \overline{\tau} \quad \alpha \oplus \tau' \leq E(x)}{E \vdash x = y.m(\overline{z}); E} \qquad \frac{E(x) = \text{@Shared } c}{E \vdash x = \text{start } c(); E}$$

Similar to how Java deals with threads, the start operation only works on classes that have a 0-arity run method (denoted by ϵ parameter types).

Subtyping, Types. The subtyping relation $\leq$ is the transitive relation closed under the rules below. annote(c) returns the annotation on the class c or @Thread if $c = $ Object.

$$
\frac{\alpha \text{ class } c \text{ extends } d \ \cdots}{c \leq d} \quad \text{(SUB-DIRECT)}
$$

$$
\frac{c \leq c' \quad c' \leq d}{c \leq d} \quad \text{(SUB-TRANS)}
$$

$$
\frac{}{c \leq c} \quad \text{(SUB-SELF)}
$$

$$
\frac{\vdash \alpha \, c \quad \vdash \alpha \, d \quad c \leq d}{\alpha \, c \leq \alpha \, d} \quad \text{(SUB-ANNOTE)}
$$

$$
\frac{\text{annote}(c) = \text{@Shared} \Rightarrow \alpha = \text{@Shared}}{\vdash \alpha \, c} \quad \text{(TYPE)}
$$

By (SUB-ANNOTE), subtyping must preserve annotations. Most importantly, though, Object may be subclassed as both @Shared and @Thread.

3.2 Dynamic Semantics

We formulate Loci's dynamic semantics as a small-step operational semantics. See Fig. 7 for syntax. A Loci configuration $H; \overline{T}$ consists of a single heap H of locations mapped to objects tagged to denote to what heap(let) they belong to and a collection of threads. Each thread T has its own stack, plus a thread id denoted ρ. An object belonging to the thread ρ will be tagged ρ in its second compartment. We use ϱ in the syntactic category ρ to denote the shared heap. Thread-scheduling is modeled as a non-deterministic choice in (D-SCHEDULE). A configuration with a thread scheduled to run is denoted $H; T; \overline{T}$. For convenience, we write $H(\iota.f)$ as a shorthand for $H(\iota)(f)$ and $H(\iota.f) := v$ for $H[\iota \mapsto o[f \mapsto v]]$. We denote the look-up of a non-existent field $H(\iota.f) = \bot$ (where $\bot \neq v$), which can happen due to lazy creation of thread-local fields. The initial configuration has the form $[]; (\langle [], s; \texttt{return } x \rangle, \rho)$, i.e., there is only one thread on start-up, and the initial stack frame and heap are empty. The relation $(\rightarrow)$ is the reduction step on configurations.

The rule (D-SCHEDULE) non-deterministically picks one thread for execution. The rules (D-FINISH) and (D-DEAD) remove threads that are fully reduced from the system. NPE is a thread that's dead from a null-pointer error.

$$
\frac{H; \overline{T} \, T' \, T \rightarrow H'; \overline{T''}}{H; \overline{T} \, T \, T' \rightarrow H'; \overline{T''}} \quad \text{(D-SCHEDULE)}
$$

$$
\frac{}{H; \overline{T} \, (\langle F, \texttt{return } x \rangle, \rho) \rightarrow H; \overline{T}} \quad \text{(D-FINISHED)}
$$

$$
\frac{}{H; \overline{T} \, (\text{NPE}, \rho) \rightarrow H; \overline{T}} \quad \text{(D-DEAD)}
$$

$H ::= [] \mid H[\iota \mapsto o]$	*heap*	$F ::= [] \mid F[y \mapsto v]$	*stack frame*
$T ::= (S, \rho) \mid (\text{NPE}, \rho)$	*thread*	$o ::= c(\rho, F)$	*object*
$S ::= \epsilon \mid S \langle F, s \rangle$	*stack*	$v ::= \iota \mid \texttt{null}$	*value*

Fig. 7. Syntax for heaps, threads, stacks, frame, objects and values. For brevity, we unify stack frame and object fields. To distinguish, we use f for fields and y for variables.

Local variable declaration and assignment offer no surprises.

$$\frac{F(y) = v \qquad T = (S \langle F[x = v], s \rangle, \rho)}{H; \overline{T} (S \langle F, x = y; s \rangle, \rho) \to H; \overline{T} T} \text{(D-ASSIGN)}$$

$$\frac{T = (S \langle F[x \mapsto \text{null}], s \rangle, \rho)}{H; \overline{T} (S \langle F, \tau \ x; s \rangle, \rho) \to H; \overline{T} T} \text{(D-DECL)}$$

$$\text{(D-SKIP)}$$
$$\overline{H; \overline{T} (S \langle F, \text{skip}; s \rangle, \rho) \to H; \overline{T} (S \langle F, s \rangle, \rho)}$$

We model thread-local variables as zero or more variables indexed by the thread id ρ—a thread ρ accessing a @Thread field f returns the contents of the field f_ρ.

$$\text{sel}(\iota, c.f, H, \rho) = \begin{cases} \text{null} & \text{if fields}(c.f) = \text{@Thread } d \wedge H(\iota.f_\rho) = \bot \\ v & \text{if fields}(c.f) = \text{@Thread } d \wedge H(\iota.f_\rho) = v \\ v' & \text{if } H(\iota.f) = v' \end{cases}$$

The predicate $\text{sel}()$ returns the value of the request field, or, if the field is thread-local, the value of the field indexed by the current thread.

$$\frac{F(y) = \iota \quad H(\iota) = c(\cdots) \quad \text{sel}(\iota, c.f, H, \rho) = v \quad T' = (S \langle F[x = v], s \rangle, \rho)}{H; \overline{T} (S \langle F, x = y.f; s \rangle, \rho) \to H; \overline{T} T'} \text{(D-SELECT)}$$

Missing thread-local fields are given the value null. An alternative would be to create a copy for every thread in the system, but the above solution felt somewhat closer to the semantics of the ThreadLocal API, which calls initialValue() on the first read of a field by a particular thread. Like reading, writing a @Thread field updates the copy of the field indexed by the current thread's id.

$$\text{upd}(\iota, c.f, H, \rho, v) = \begin{cases} H(\iota.f_\rho) := v & \text{if fields}(c.f) = \text{@Thread } c \\ H(\iota.f) := v & \text{otherwise} \end{cases}$$

$$\frac{F(y) = \iota \quad H(\iota) = c(\cdots) \quad H' = \text{upd}(\iota, c.f, H, \rho, F(z))}{H; \overline{T} (S \langle F, y.f = z; s \rangle, \rho) \to H'; \overline{T} (S \langle F, s \rangle, \rho)} \text{(D-UPDATE)}$$

We have omitted constructors (see Sec. 4.1 for a discussion on how to deal with them). Thus, a new instance is always thread-local and can subsequently be placed either on the shared heap or in the current heaplet. This is decided by the annotation of the target variable for the instantiation.

$$\text{reg}(\alpha, \rho, \rho_1) = \begin{cases} \rho & \text{if } \alpha = \text{@Thread} \\ \rho_1 & \text{if } \alpha = \text{@Context} \\ \varrho & \text{if } \alpha = \text{@Shared} \end{cases}$$

The predicate reg() "registers" a newly created instance with a certain thread.

$$\text{(D-NEW)}$$
$$\frac{H(F(\texttt{this})) = d(\rho_1, F_1) \quad \iota \text{ is fresh} \quad \text{names}(\text{fields}(c)) = \overline{f} \quad H' = H[\iota \mapsto c(\text{reg}(\alpha, \rho, \rho_1), \overline{f} \mapsto \overline{\texttt{null}})]}{H; \overline{T} \, (S \, \langle F, x = \texttt{new } \alpha \; c(); s \rangle, \rho) \rightarrow H'; \overline{T} \, (S \, \langle F[x \mapsto \iota], s \rangle, \rho)}$$

If the target variable is @Context-annotated, the class is stored in the same heap or heaplet as the current this. We use the special variable ret to capture return values. The only assignment to ret is through a return which assigns the ret of the underlying stack frame.

$$\text{(D-RETURN)}$$
$$\frac{F(y) = v \qquad T = (S \, \langle F'[\texttt{ret} \mapsto v], s' \rangle, \rho)}{H; \overline{T} \, (S \, \langle F', s' \rangle \langle F, \texttt{return } y \rangle, \rho) \rightarrow H; \overline{T} \, T}$$

$$\text{(D-CALL)}$$
$$\frac{F(y) = \iota \quad F(\overline{z}) = \overline{v} \quad H(\iota) = c(\cdots) \quad \text{mbody}(c.m) = (\overline{x'}, s'; \texttt{return } y') \quad F' = \texttt{this} \mapsto \iota, \overline{x'} \mapsto \overline{v} \quad S' = S \, \langle F, x = \texttt{ret}; s \rangle}{H; \overline{T} \, (S \, \langle F, x = y.m(\overline{z}); s \rangle, \rho) \rightarrow H; \overline{T} \, (S' \, \langle F', s'; \texttt{return } y' \rangle, \rho)}$$

An invocation $x = y.m()$ is rewritten into $x = \texttt{ret}$ and the method's body is executed on a new stack frame eventually assigning ret as the result of a return.

$$\text{(D-FORK)}$$
$$\frac{\iota, \rho' \text{ are fresh} \quad \text{names}(\text{fields}(c)) = \overline{f} \quad H' = H[\iota \mapsto c(\varrho, \overline{f} \mapsto \overline{\texttt{null}})] \quad \text{mbody}(c.\texttt{run}) = (\epsilon, s'; \texttt{return } y') \quad T = (\langle [\texttt{this} \mapsto \iota], s'; \texttt{return } y' \rangle, \rho')}{H; \overline{T} \, (S \, \langle F, x = \texttt{start } c(); s \rangle, \rho) \rightarrow H'; \overline{T} \, T \, (S \, \langle F[x \mapsto \iota], s \rangle, \rho)}$$

The (D-FORK) operations adds a thread to the system and is a simplified union of Java's new and start. The new thread object is created on the shared area, forcing its thread-local data to be stored either on the stack of the run method, or in a thread-local field. Adding thread-local threads to the system would be as simple as introducing a start operation that returns null.

For brevity, null-pointer exceptions kill the entire thread rather than propagate an error through the execution. The semantics is effectively the same.

$$\text{(D-SELECT-NPE)}$$
$$\frac{}{H; \overline{T} \, (S \, \langle F[y \mapsto \texttt{null}], x = y.f; s \rangle, \rho) \rightarrow H; \overline{T} \, (\text{NPE}, \rho)}$$

$$\text{(D-UPDATE-NPE)}$$
$$\frac{}{H; \overline{T} \, (S \, \langle F[y \mapsto \texttt{null}], y.f = z; s \rangle, \rho) \rightarrow H; \overline{T} \, (\text{NPE}, \rho)}$$

$$\text{(D-CALL-NPE)}$$
$$\frac{}{H; \overline{T} \, (S \, \langle F[y \mapsto \texttt{null}], x = y.m(\overline{z}); s \rangle, \rho) \rightarrow H; \overline{T} \, (\text{NPE}, \rho)}$$

3.3 Meta-theory

Well-Formedness Rules. We now present the rules for well-formed configurations, heaps and stacks. Γ is the store-type and has the syntax $\Gamma ::= \epsilon \mid \Gamma[\iota : \tau]$.

$$\mathrm{tid}(H, \iota) = \begin{cases} \rho & \text{if } H(\iota) = c(\rho, F) \\ \bot & \text{otherwise} \end{cases} \qquad \mathrm{tid}(T) = \begin{cases} \rho & \text{if } T = (S, \rho) \\ \rho & \text{if } T = (\mathrm{NPE}, \rho) \end{cases}$$

In the following rules, we make use of the auxiliary function $\mathrm{tid}(T)$ that extracts a thread's id, and $\mathrm{tid}(H, \iota)$, that looks up the thread id of an object on the heap. (WF-CONFIG) states that a configuration is well-formed if there is a well-formed store typing Γ which type the heap H and if all threads have distinct ids and are well-formed.

$$\frac{\vdash \Gamma \qquad \Gamma; H \vdash H \qquad \mathrm{tid}(\overline{T}) \text{ distinct} \qquad \forall (S, \rho) \in \overline{T} \,.\, \Gamma; H \vdash_\rho S}{\Gamma \vdash H; \overline{T}} \text{ (WF-CONFIG)}$$

$$\frac{}{\vdash []} \text{ (WF-}\Gamma\text{-0)} \qquad \frac{\vdash \Gamma \quad \vdash \alpha\, c \quad \alpha \neq \texttt{@Context}}{\vdash \Gamma[\iota : \alpha\, c]} \text{ (WF-}\Gamma\text{-1)} \qquad \frac{}{\Gamma; H \vdash_\rho []} \text{ (WF-THREAD-0)} \qquad \frac{\Gamma; H \vdash_\rho S \quad \Gamma; H; E \vdash_\rho F \quad E \vdash s; E'}{\Gamma; H \vdash_\rho S \langle F, s\rangle} \text{ (WF-THREAD-1)}$$

An object is well-formed if all its fields point to locations on the heap. Thread-local objects must have the same id as the current thread or, otherwise, the id of the shared heap. Note that @Context does not appear on types in Γ.

$$\frac{}{\Gamma; H' \vdash_\rho []} \text{ (WF-HEAP-}\epsilon\text{)} \qquad \frac{\Gamma; H' \vdash_\rho H \quad \Gamma(\iota) = \texttt{@Shared}\, c \quad \mathrm{fields}(c) = E \quad \Gamma; H'; E \vdash_\varrho F}{\Gamma; H' \vdash_\rho H[\iota \mapsto c(\varrho, F)]} \text{ (WF-HEAP-SHARED)} \qquad \frac{\Gamma; H' \vdash_\rho H \quad \Gamma(\iota) = \texttt{@Thread}\, c \quad \mathrm{fields}(c) = E \quad \Gamma; H'; E \vdash_\rho F}{\Gamma; H' \vdash_\rho H[\iota \mapsto c(\rho, F)]} \text{ (WF-HEAP-THREAD)}$$

Due to the treatment of thread-local fields, rules for well-formed fields are a bit more complex that usual for a Java-like language. (WF-FIELD-ϵ) captures that thread-local fields may not yet have been initialized.

$$\frac{}{\Gamma; H; E \vdash_\rho []} \text{ (WF-FIELD-}\epsilon\text{)} \qquad \frac{\Gamma; H; E \vdash_\rho F \quad E(f) = \tau}{\Gamma; H; E \vdash_\rho F[f \mapsto \texttt{null}]} \text{ (WF-FIELD-NULL)} \qquad \frac{\Gamma; H; E \vdash_\rho F \quad E(f) = \tau}{\Gamma; H; E \vdash_\rho F[f_{\rho'} \mapsto \texttt{null}]} \text{ (WF-FIELD-THREAD-NULL)}$$

$$\frac{\Gamma; H; E \vdash_\rho F \quad E(f) = \tau \quad \mathrm{tid}(H, \iota) = \rho' \quad \Gamma(\iota) \leq \tau}{\Gamma; H; E \vdash_\rho F[f_{\rho'} \mapsto \iota]} \text{ (WF-FIELD-THREAD)}$$

$$\frac{\Gamma; H; E \vdash_\varrho F \quad E(f) = \texttt{@Shared}\, c \quad \Gamma(\iota) \leq \texttt{@Shared}\, c \quad \mathrm{tid}(H, \iota) = \varrho}{\Gamma; H; E \vdash_\rho F[f \mapsto \iota]} \text{ (WF-FIELD-SHARED)} \qquad \frac{\Gamma; H; E \vdash_\rho F \quad E(f) = \texttt{@Context}\, c \quad \Gamma(\iota) \leq \alpha\, c \quad \mathrm{tid}(H, \iota) = \rho}{\Gamma; H; E \vdash_\rho F[f \mapsto \iota]} \text{ (WF-FIELD-CONTEXT)}$$

Notably, @Shared fields point to objects on the shared heap, @Context fields point to objects on the same heap(let) as the current this, and @Thread fields have ≥ 0 copies subscripted with the same thread id as the object they point to.

For stack frames, a pointer in a @Shared field points to an object on the shared heap and a pointer in a non-shared field points to an object on the same heap(let) as the current this.

$$(\text{WF-FRAME-1})$$
$$\Gamma; H \vdash_\rho E, F$$
$$\text{tid}(H, \iota) = \rho' \quad \Gamma(\iota) \leq \alpha\, c$$

(WF-FRAME-0) $\qquad \alpha = \text{@Shared} \Rightarrow \rho' = \varrho \qquad (\text{WF-FRAME-2})$

$$\dfrac{}{\Gamma; H \vdash_\rho [],[]} \qquad \dfrac{\alpha \neq \text{@Shared} \Rightarrow \rho' = \rho}{\Gamma; H \vdash_\rho E[y:\alpha\, c], F[y \mapsto \iota]} \qquad \dfrac{\Gamma; H \vdash_\rho E, F}{\Gamma; H \vdash_\rho E[y:\tau], F[y \mapsto \text{null}]}$$

Invariants Informally, Loci enforces the following property:

> A thread ρ can only access objects in heaplet ρ or on the shared heap ϱ.

We formulate this in two theorems, the first of which says that pointers in variables on a stack frame in a thread ρ either point to objects in ρ or in ϱ, and the second that evaluating a field access in thread ρ results in a pointer to either an object in ρ or in ϱ (or is a null-pointer).

Theorem 1. *Local variables point into shared heap or current heaplet. If $\Gamma; E \vdash H; \overline{T}(S\langle F, s\rangle, \rho)$, then $\forall \iota \in rng(F)$. $\text{tid}(H, \iota) \in \{\varrho, \rho\}$.*

Proof. Follows by straightforward induction on s. (WF-FRAME-1) and (WF-FRAME-2) are key. □

Theorem 2. *Field accesses yield pointers to shared heap or current heaplet. Let s be a field access $x = y.f$. If $\Gamma; E \vdash H; \overline{T}(S\langle F, s\rangle, \rho)$, $H; \overline{T}(S\langle F, s\rangle, \rho) \rightarrow H'; \overline{T'}(S'\langle F', s'\rangle, \rho)$, and $F'(x) = \iota$, then $\text{tid}(H', \iota) \in \{\varrho, \rho\}$.*

Proof. The proof is by derivation on $\Gamma; E \vdash H; \overline{T}(S\langle F, x = y.f\rangle, \rho)$ relying on the fact that ρ is threaded through a computation and that @Context-annotated fields point to the heaplet of its enclosing object. By the rules for well-formed configurations, heaps and fields, $H(F(y).f) = \iota$ and $\text{fields}(c.f) = \alpha\, c'$ implies $\text{tid}(H, \iota) = \rho'$ s.t. (a) $\alpha = \text{@Shared}$ implies $\rho' = \varrho$, (b) $\alpha = \text{@Context}$ implies $\rho' = \rho''$ s.t. $\text{tid}(H(F(y))) = \rho''$, and (c) $\alpha = \text{@Thread}$ implies $f = f_\rho \wedge \rho' = \rho$. Cases (a) and (c) immediately satisfy the theorem and case (b) follows immediately from Theorem 1 that gives $\rho'' \in \{\rho, \varrho\}$. □

Type Soundness. We prove type soundness in the standard fashion of progress plus preservation [33]. In this context, preservation means that reduction does not invalidate the store typing.

Theorem 3. *Preservation. If $\Gamma \vdash H; \overline{T}$, and $H; \overline{T} \rightarrow H'; \overline{T'}$, then there exists a Γ' s.t. $\Gamma' \vdash H'; \overline{T'}$.*

Proof. The proof is straightforward by structural induction. There are no surprising cases. □

Theorem 4. *Progress. If* $\Gamma \vdash H;\overline{T}$, *then there exists a reduction such that* $H;\overline{T} \to H';\overline{T'}$.

Proof. The proof is straightforward by structural induction on the shape of T where most cases are immediate. The slightly more intricate cases, (T-SELECT), (T-UPDATE) and (T-CALL) are all guarded by (*-NPE) versions of the rule that deal with null-dereferencing. By (WF-HEAP-*) and (WF-FIELD-*), a well-formed object $c(\rho, F)$ has all non-@Thread fields in F. By (SELECT-FIRST-THREAD), accessing an "undefined" thread-local field does not get stuck. Last, the only ways in which (D-NEW) or (D-FORK) could get stuck is if we cannot produce fresh ι's or ρ's, which is not modeled by our system. □

4   Loci for Eclipse

We have implemented Loci as an Eclipse plug-in. The plug-in supports most of Java, modulo generics, checking of native code, and reflection. The tool implements static checking of @Shared, @Thread, and the implicit @Context annotation. Currently, the tool gives a warning rather than an error when it detects a violation. Fig. 8 shows how @Thread fields are desugared into uses of the ThreadLocal API before compilation. The tool ignores primitive types and immutables, like strings and boxed primitives. To minimize the annotation burden, in a @Thread class, @Context is the implicit default annotation for a type of @Thread class, and @Shared for a type of @Shared class. In a @Shared class, the implicit annotation

```
1   @Thread class Foo {
2     @Thread Foo foo = null;
3
4
5
6
7
8     Object x;
9     void bar() {
10        @Thread Foo f = foo;
11        foo = f;
12    }
13  }
```

```
1   @Thread class Foo {
2     @Thread ThreadLocal<Foo> foo =
3       new ThreadLocal<Foo>() {
4         Foo initialValue() {
5           return null;
6         }
7       };
8     Object x;
9     void bar() {
10        @Thread Foo f = foo.get();
11        foo.set(f);
12    }
13  }
```

Fig. 8. Sugared view and corresponding desugared view of a @Thread class. "Ensugar" and "desugar" buttons in the tool allows the user to switch back and forth between these views. Notably, @Thread-annotated local variables (f above) do not need to be implemented using the ThreadLocal API.

is @Shared. Notably, there is no keyword for @Context, it is only used implicitly. While it would have been more reasonable to default unannotated classes to @Thread, this would have had the drawback of requiring invasive changes to legacy code. To give existing Java programs a valid Loci interpretation, unannotated classes are implicitly @Shared, with the exception of Object.

4.1   Extending Loci to Full Java

In this section, we address some of the interplay with Java not visible from the formalization, due to simplifications or Java conventions.

Anonymous classes. Loci fully supports anonymous classes. Anonymous classes automatically inherit the annotation of the superclass or interface. In the case of an interface without a class-level annotation, Loci currently requires the resulting instance to be stored immediately in a local variable and infers the annotation from the variable's type. Ambiguous instantiations of this kind could be solved by annotating the instantiated type.

Arrays. Loci supports three kinds of arrays (of any dimension):

1. Thread-local arrays of pointers to shared objects or primitives
2. Thread-local arrays of pointers to thread-local objects
3. Shared arrays of pointers to shared objects or primitives

If Foo and Bar are a @Shared respectively a @Thread class, then @Thread Foo[] is an array of the first kind, @Thread Bar[] the second, and @Shared Foo[] and @Shared Bar[] are of the third kind. The reason why @Shared Bar[] is a shared array of shared objects rather than an shared array of thread-local objects is because this case can be easily modeled by @Thread Bar[]. This frees @Shared Bar[] up to allow using Bar as a shared class in @Shared arrays. When using array initializers, Loci will inspect the annotations on the values used to initialize the array to infer whether the compartments of the array should be @Thread or @Shared, similar to constructor arguments in instantiation.

Interfaces. Unless explicitly annotated, we treat Java interfaces as implicitly annotated @Context, even on the class level (this is supported in the tool but omitted from the formalism since it does not deal with interfaces). When implemented, we apply the $\oplus$ operator using the annotation of the implementing class to get the annotation to which the implementing class must correspond. This allows us to reuse interfaces across different classes with different thread-local behavior.

Constructors and Instantiation. As @Shared classes are semantically equivalent to Java classes, their constructors require no special treatment. For @Thread classes, the story is different. Modulo constructor arguments, it is easy to see that a @Thread class instance constitutes a "free" value. The type of this is @Context SomeClass and as the types of static fields and methods must use either @Shared or @Thread, the class is effectively prevented from leaking itself. If a class "uses" @Context to annotate types of parameters to its constructor, we can derive the annotation of the new instance by looking at how these parameters are instantiated. If a new is only valid if the instance was shared (i.e., it binds a @Shared argument to a @Context parameter), the new object lives in the shared heap and the result type of the instantiation is @Shared. If @Context parameters are bound only to @Context, the resulting type is @Context. If both bindings are required, the instantiation is invalid as the object's type would have to be both @Shared and @Thread.

Inner and Nested classes. @Shared classes can have nested @Thread classes and vice versa. The inverse poses a problem, though, as the nested class instance has access to the enclosing instance, which could be thread-local. For this reason, Loci only allows instantiating @Shared inner classes inside non-thread-local instance. For example, given

```
@Thread class Foo { @Shared class Bar { } }
@Thread Foo f1;
@Shared Foo f2;
Foo f3;
```

we are allowed to do f2.new Bar() but not f1.new Bar() as the resulting shared instance would break thread-locality of the object in f1. Naturally, f3.new Bar() is only allowed if we can determine that f3 is shared.

Nested classes can be annotated @Thread and @Shared just like regular classes. They can access static variables of the enclosing classes.

Static Fields, Blocks and Methods. In static context, the implicit annotation is @Shared rather than @Context. Static fields and variables can still be @Thread, but never @Context. The downside of this design is that static methods used to implement pure functions can never manipulate @Context data (see Sec. 5).

Generics and Collections. As stated above, Loci does not yet support Java generics. The reason is that Java does not (yet) support annotations on type parameters. Once Java does, extending Loci to work with generics is straight-forward and will mostly follow the style of [28]. On the downside, support for generics will require the introduction of additional annotations to our system to serve as "annotation parameters." The reason is to enable expressing that the annotations on two different types should be bound to the same annotation.

Java's Thread API. As we saw in Fig. 1, Thread is a shared class. The same holds for Runnable. This is natural, since instances of both will (potentially) be shared between at least two threads. Rather than using thread-local fields in a Thread object, a programmer should insert an extra level of indirection pointed to by a @Thread local variable in the run() method. (This pattern emerged in our evaluation.) As a result of these default annotations, Loci works naturally with Java ThreadPools. Java's InheritableThreadLocal also works well with the annotations as inherited values are fresh thread-local copies for the new thread. Extending Loci to support InheritableThreadLocal is straightforward.

5 Evaluation of Type System Design

To evaluate the type system design and our defaults, we have annotated parts of the JavaGrande benchmark and Lucene Search from the DaCapo Benchmark suite [5]. We have also implemented an inferencer for our system. The results are shown in Tab. 2. In short, they show us that the design of the Loci type system is largely compatible with how Java code is written.

Tab. 2 shows our results from annotating large chunks of Java code. We used code coverage tools to make sure we annotated parts of the code that was actually being executed. We also annotated parts of Xalan, a $\geq 100\,000$ LOC XSLT processor, but this work is unfinished at the time of writing. As is visible from the table, the number of annotations is small—80 annotations in total for 44 245 LOC, which is less than 1 annotation per 500 LOC. The annotation of Lucene Search was driven by the desire to only annotate the parts of the code that execute as part of thread-local computation and leave the rest of the code unannotated. We were able to annotate 19 classes as @Thread that perform thread-local computation inside instances of **IndexReader**. Due to lack of an annotated Java API, some classes could not be annotated without getting warnings from the Loci tool, notably the index reader itself. Most notably, both classes stored in thread-local fields in the original source (**TermsVectorReader** and **SegmentTermEnum**) could be annotated @Thread. The two thread-local fields in Lucene Search in Tab. 2

Table 2. Results from experiments with annotating Java programs with Loci. The upper right table shows results from applying a conservative analysis to infer annotations to GNU classpath. The bottom shows results of dynamic analysis for DaCapo benchmarks [5]. We measure both the average rate at which objects are thread-local, and the average number of bytes that belong to thread-local objects. In the entire DaCapo suite, 69% of all objects are thread-local.

	LOC	Classes	@Thread	@Shared	Default		Inferred	Classes
Raytracer	1496	16	16	0	0		@Thread	5996
Lucene Search	42749	285	19	0	266		@Shared	1289
Total	44245	301	35	0	266		Total	7285

	@Thread Annotations				@Shared Annotations			
	Fields	Params	Returns	Vars	Fields	Params	Returns	Vars
Raytracer	0	0	0	1	1	1	1	1
Lucene Search	2	0	4	5	0	20	0	9
Total	2	0	4	6	1	21	1	10

Average Thread-locality Rate										
	ANTLR	BLOAT	Eclipse	Apache FOP	HSQLDB	Jython	Lucene Index	Search	PMD	Xalan
Objects	79%	82%	63%	78%	88%	77%	78%	74%	83%	66%
Bytes	71%	77%	64%	76%	85%	73%	71%	51%	81%	69%

were uses of `ThreadLocal` that were there from the start and none were added. The two key reasons why a class could not be annotated `@Thread` is because it stores itself in a hash map or extends vector. Both these problems can be solved by annotating the standard library. Raytracer is a much smaller application (only 1496 LOC). Here, all classes could be annotated `@Thread`. There were no uses of `ThreadLocal` to begin with, and none were added.

Though we have not annotated the entire DaCapo suite, we wanted to see what fraction of objects are effectively thread-local. To measure this, we instrumented revision 15.182 of Jikes RVM [21] to report the fraction of live objects that have been used from multiple threads. Detecting object accesses was done using a read barrier. These measurements also include objects used by the VM, which itself is heavily multi-threaded, hence even for single-threaded benchmarks like ANTLR, BLOAT, and others, the rate is not 100%. As Tab. 2 shows, all benchmarks have at least half of their heaps occupied by thread-local objects—including heavily multi-threaded ones like Lucene Search. Perhaps unsurprisingly, our results show that small objects tend to be more likely to be thread-local, as evidenced by the rate of object thread-locality being higher than the rate of heap usage by thread-local objects.

Class-Level Annotation Inference. To further test our assumption that most classes can be annotated `@Thread`, we implemented a conservative backwards-flow analysis to detect leakage of `this`. Classes that could leak `this`, or extended `@Shared` classes, were marked `@Shared`. The remaining classes were marked `@Thread`. Applying the analysis on the GNU Classpath version of the Java standard API, 82% of all classes could be annotated `@Thread`, notably all collection classes. For simplicity, we assumed that native code did *not* leak `this`. Assuming native code always leaks, the number is 77% and e.g., all collection classes are shared because of sparse uses of native code in some collection implementations. We have also used our Jikes RVM instrumentation to check that all objects annotated thread-local were indeed accessed by a single thread, and we found that this was the case. Thus, it seems that our implementation is correct.

We now briefly report on the most important realizations from annotating the programs.

Static Methods. Our experiments with Loci shows that our simple defaults-to-`@Shared` approach for static methods caused problems in many cases where static methods were used as global functions. For example, the `Vec` class in Raytracer, frequently uses methods like this:

```
public static Vec sub(Vec a, Vec b) {
  return new Vec(a.x - b.x, a.y - b.y, a.z - b.z);
}
```

Since the `a` and `b` in the code about would be `@Shared` by default from being in a static context, any thread-local vectors are precluded from using this purely functional method. The simple solution for this problem was to simply make these methods instance methods, which was a simple refactoring, but an annoying one. Similar refactorings were done for Lucene Search as well. In the spirit of simplicity, a possible solution to this problem is to allow explicit uses of @Context (they must be explicit to preserve all-shared semantics of unannotated Java programs) on parameters to static methods. The existing type system would prevent leakage as is. A more general but less lightweight solution is a parametric approach using "annotation parameters." This also has use for the problem with equals methods.

Exceptions. The Xalan benchmark uses exceptions to propagate broken XML nodes to a problem reporter. As Exception defaults to shared in our system, this caused a problem for making the XML parsing a thread-local computation as thread-locality would be lost for a broken node wrapped in a shared exception. This practice, and the fact that exceptions cannot propagate into another thread short of being stored on the heap, caused us to rethink this default. We are currently investigating the possibility of annotating Throwable and its subclasses as @Thread and the default annotation on exceptions will be @Context.

Equals Methods. In a @Thread class C, the type of this is @Context C. This automatically prevents the leaking of this into @Shared variables, but there are also downsides. Consider the typing of Java's equals method. If the parameter to equals has type @Context, then a @Thread class cannot pass this to the equals of a shared object, nor vice versa. This turned out to be a rare problem and occurred only twice in Lucene and was solved by ignoring the warnings after having manually inspected the code. Furthermore, we can only compare objects living in the same heap(let), which is unfortunate.

A flexible solution to this problem is supporting annotation-polymorphic methods[1]. This also solves problems with static methods discussed above. An alternative solution is to use a different equals method for the three possible combinations. As Java does not allow dispatching on annotations, these methods must be differently named, but since which method to use can be statically determined, calls to equals can be automatically rewritten under the hood by the tool to use the right version, and the different equals methods automatically inferred from the @Shared case. Notably, unless we allow @Context to be used explicitly in @Shared classes, receiver and argument on equals calls on @Shared receivers with @Context arguments would have to be switched.

5.1 Removing Unnecessary Synchronization

For flexibility for library classes, @Thread classes can be used to create both shared and thread-local objects. This requires extra work to elide locks in Loci. To this end, we introduce a "shadow method," a duplicate of a method where synchronization on @Context objects is removed. Calls on thread-local receivers will call shadow methods, prefixed Shadow_ if they exist. In shadow methods, this is thread-local and thus all @Context variables are too. Loci creates these methods

---

[1] Since Loci only has one annotation per type, this would not break polymorphism as is the case for full-blown ownership types systems, see [35].

```
1   @Thread class Foo {                 1   @Thread class Foo {
2     @Thread Foo foo = null;           2     @Thread ThreadLocal<Foo> foo = ...
3     @Thread Foo synchronized m1() {   3     @Thread Foo synchronized m1() {
4       this.m2();                      4       this.m2();
5       if (foo != null) m1();          5       if (foo.get() != null) m1();
6       return foo;                     6       return foo.get();
7     }                                 7     }
8                                       8     @Thread Foo Shadow_m1() {
9                                       9       this.Shadow_m2();
10                                      10      if (foo.get() != null)
11                                      11        Shadow_m1();
12                                      12      return foo.get();
13                                      13    }
14    synchronized void m2() {          14    synchronized void m2() {
15      this.m1();                      15      this.m1();
16    }                                 16    }
17                                      17    void Shadow_m2() {
18                                      18      this.Shadow_m1();
19                                      19    }
20  }                                   20  }
```

Fig. 9. "Ensugared" and "desugared" view of a class with synchronized methods. Desugaring of line 2 is omitted since it is shown in Fig. 8.

automatically and transparently. Fig. 9 shows the "ensugared" (standard view) and the "desugared" view of a piece of code. We have implemented this scheme in Loci and tested it on our annotated programs. Without sufficiently annotated Java standard libraries, we will not see any measurable performance benefits due to default-to-@Shared. For example, the IndexReader class in Lucene Search, which would be key to avoid a fair amount of synchronized methods calls, cannot be annotated @Thread due to uses of library use in its methods and methods of its subclasses.

6   Related Work

Domani et al. [17] propose thread-local heaps where each thread is given it own chunk of memory in which to allocate objects. The goal is to remove locking from the GC for thread local objects. They use a dynamic analysis to track thread-locality and do not enforce it. Several researchers have employed compile-time escape analysis to identify local and global objects [6,7,10,32,11]. These proposals target compiler optimizations (e.g., the removal of unnecessary synchronization) and memory management, and do not support static checking of programmer intentions with respect to thread-locality. Currently, JVMs performs similar analyzes under the hood (see e.g., [8,20]), but cannot enforce correct usage of ThreadLocal or does not give any feedback to the programmer to help verify her programs. Recently, Flanagan et al. [18] extended ATOMICJAVA [19] with support for thread-local data for full-on Java. They target method atomicity and their system is powerful and distinguishes between five different kinds of atomicities. Their system is more powerful than ours and allows any object to act as a guard, whereas we only allow `this` to act as a guard for fields. As a result, their system is more complicated and comes at the price of additional complexity and annotation overhead.

Loci is simple ownership type system [24,15]. Several approaches using ownership types for concurrency control have been proposed [4,9,30,16,14]. None of these systems use a thread-as-owners approach, nor focuses on thread-local data. Guava [4] presents as an informal collection of rules which would require a significantly more complex type system than the one we present here. STREAM-FLEX [30] use a minimal notion of ownership, with little need for annotations, to simplify memory management in a real-time setting. Cunningham et al. [16] employ Universe Types to "carve up a heap" for safe locking. Their system is similar to ours in that it is based on a simple ownership system [23], but focuses on eliminating data races rather than checking thread-locality. Joëlle [14] proposes a minimal ownership types system in the active objects setting that guarantees that only the thread of an active object will access its representation. The system is built on a different set of principles—sharing is impossible, and all inter-thread communication must be asynchronous or the thread-locality assumption is void. Kilim [31] gives thread-locality through a linear type system for actor-style programming in Java. Kilim replaces copying by transfer of ownership. Sadly, Kilim's requirement that unique messages be tree-structured (due to linearity) forces regular object structures used as internal representations of communicating actors to be cloned into trees, at least on the sender's side, before being transferred.

7   Conclusion

We have presented Loci, a simple type system for thread-local data in Java and Java-like languages. We have shown its formal semantics, and stated and proven its crucial properties. Furthermore, we have described our realization of Loci as an Eclipse tool and described how the Loci annotations apply to full-on Java. Experiences with using Loci on known benchmarks showed that the system is compatible with current Java practices, but that further extensions are needed. We will continue to develop Loci while continuing the balance act between simplicity of the annotations, usefulness and legacy integration.

In future work we intend to explore synergies of thread locality information with other optimizations. If a dynamic analysis can make up for its overhead, we envisioning allowing "casts" on the annotations. This will allow a simpler system but also open up for run-time errors. We will also extend Loci to support generics and experiment with the practical usefulness of adding a `@Free` annotation.

Acknowledgments. We thank the ECOOP reviewers for their suggestions which helped improve the presentation of this paper. The impetus for this work came from discussion with Doug Lea. The paper benefited from comments and discussion with Johan Östlund. The authors were partially supported by grants NSF CPA 0811631, NSF CPA 0811691 and NSF 0720652.

References

1. Java theory and practice: Synchronization optimizations in mustang, http://www-128.ibm.com/developerworks/java/library/j-jtp10185/
2. Aldrich, J., Chambers, C., Sirer, E.G., Eggers, S.J.: Static analyses for eliminating unnecessary synchronization from Java programs. In: SAS, pp. 19–38 (1999)
3. Bacon, D.F., Konuru, R., Murthy, C., Serrano, M.: Thin locks: Featherweight synchronization for Java. In: PLDI, pp. 258–268 (1998)
4. Bacon, D.F., Strom, R.E., Tarafdar, A.: Guava: a dialect of Java without data races. In: OOPSLA, pp. 382–400 (2000)
5. Blackburn, S.M., et al.: The DaCapo benchmarks: Java benchmarking development and analysis. In: OOPSLA, pp. 169–190 (2006)
6. Blanchet, B.: Escape analysis for object-oriented languages: application to Java. In: OOPSLA, pp. 20–34 (1999)
7. Bogda, J., Hölzle, U.: Removing unnecessary synchronization in Java. In: OOPSLA, pp. 35–46 (1999)
8. Borman, S.: Sensible sanitation – understanding the IBM Java garbage. IBM DeveloperWorks (August 2002)
9. Boyapati, C., Lee, R., Rinard, M.: Ownership Types for Safe Programming: Preventing Data Races and Deadlocks. In: OOPSLA, pp. 211–230 (2002)
10. Choi, J.-D., Gupta, M., Serrano, M., Sreedhar, V.C., Midkiff, S.: Escape analysis for Java. In: OOPSLA, pp. 1–19 (1999)
11. Choi, J.-D., Gupta, M., Serrano, M.J., Sreedhar, V.C., Midkiff, S.P.: Stack allocation and synchronization optimizations for Java using escape analysis. ACM Trans. Program. Lang. Syst. 25(6), 876–910 (2003)
12. Clarke, D.: Object Ownership and Containment. PhD thesis, University of New South Wales, Australia (2001)
13. Clarke, D., Wrigstad, T.: External uniqueness is unique enough. In: Cardelli, L. (ed.) ECOOP 2003. LNCS, vol. 2743, pp. 176–200. Springer, Heidelberg (2003)
14. Clarke, D., Wrigstad, T., Östlund, J., Johnsen, E.B.: Minimal Ownership for Active Objects. Technical Report SEN-R0803, CWI (2008)
15. Clarke, D.G., Potter, J., Noble, J.: Ownership types for flexible alias protection. In: OOPSLA, pp. 48–64 (1998)
16. Cunningham, D., Drossopoulou, S., Eisenbach, S.: Universe Types for Race Safety. In: VAMP 2007, September 2007, pp. 20–51 (2007)
17. Domani, T., Goldshtein, G., Kolodner, E.K., Lewis, E., Petrank, E., Sheinwald, D.: Thread-local heaps for Java. In: ISMM, pp. 76–87 (2002)
18. Flanagan, C., Freund, S.N., Lifshin, M., Qadeer, S.: Types for atomicity: Static checking and inference for Java. ACM TOPLAS 30(4), 1–53 (2008)
19. Flanagan, C., Qadeer, S.: A type and effect system for atomicity. In: PLDI, pp. 338–349 (2003)
20. Goetz, B.: Java theory and practice: Urban performance legends, revisited. IBM DeveloperWorks (September 2005)
21. Jikes RVM homepage, http://jikesrvm.org/
22. Joisha, P.G.: Compiler optimizations for nondeferred reference: counting garbage collection. In: ISMM, pp. 150–161 (2006)

23. Müller, P.: Modular Specification and Verification of Object-Oriented Programs. Springer, Heidelberg (2002)
24. Noble, J., Vitek, J., Potter, J.: Flexible alias protection. In: Jul, E. (ed.) ECOOP 1998. LNCS, vol. 1445, pp. 158–185. Springer, Heidelberg (1998)
25. OpenJDK, http://openjdk.java.net/
26. Östlund, J., Wrigstad, T., Clarke, D., Åkerblom, B.: Ownership, uniqueness and immutability. In: TOOLS (2007)
27. Pizlo, F., Hosking, A.L., Vitek, J.: Hierarchical real-time garbage collection. In: LCTES, pp. 123–133 (2007)
28. Potanin, A.: Generic Ownership—A Practical Approach to Ownership and Confinement in OO Programming Languages. PhD thesis, Victoria University of Wellington (2007)
29. Russell, K., Detlefs, D.: Eliminating synchronization-related atomic operations with biased locking and bulk rebiasing. In: OOPSLA, pp. 263–272 (2006)
30. Spring, J.H., Privat, J., Guerraoui, R., Vitek, J.: StreamFlex: High-throughput Stream Programming in Java. In: OOPSLA, pp. 211–228 (2007)
31. Srinivasan, S., Mycroft, A.: Kilim: Isolation-typed actors for java. In: Vitek, J. (ed.) ECOOP 2008. LNCS, vol. 5142, pp. 104–128. Springer, Heidelberg (2008)
32. Steensgaard, B.: Thread-specific heaps for multi-threaded programs. In: ISMM, pp. 18–24 (2000)
33. Wright, A.K., Felleisen, M.: A syntactic approach to type soundness. Inf. Comput. 115(1), 38–94 (1994)
34. Wrigstad, T.: Ownership-Based Alias Management. PhD thesis, Royal Institute of Technology, Kista, Stockholm (2006)
35. Wrigstad, T., Clarke, D.: Existential owners for ownership types. Journal of Object Technology 4(6), 141–159 (2007)

Failboxes: Provably Safe Exception Handling*

Bart Jacobs** and Frank Piessens

Department of Computer Science, Katholieke Universiteit Leuven, Belgium
{bart.jacobs,frank.piessens}@cs.kuleuven.be

Abstract. The primary goal of exception mechanisms is to help ensure that when an operation fails, code that depends on the operation's successful completion is not executed (a property we call *dependency safety*). However, the exception mechanisms of current mainstream programming languages make it hard to achieve dependency safety, in particular when objects manipulated inside a try block outlive the try block.

Many programming languages, mechanisms and paradigms have been proposed that address this issue. However, they all depart significantly from current practice. In this paper, we propose a language mechanism called failboxes. When applied correctly, failboxes have no significant impact on the structure, the semantics, or the performance of the program, other than to eliminate the executions that violate dependency safety.

Specifically, programmers may create failboxes dynamically and execute blocks of code in them. Once any such block fails, all subsequent attempts to execute code in the failbox will fail. To achieve dependency safety, programmers simply need to ensure that if an operation B depends on an operation A, then A and B are executed in the same failbox. Furthermore, failboxes help fix the unsafe interaction between locks and exceptions and they enable safe cancellation and robust resource cleanup. Finally, the Fail Fast mechanism prevents liveness issues when a thread is waiting on a failed thread.

We give a formal syntax and semantics of the new constructs, and prove dependency safety. Furthermore, to show that the new constructs are easy to reason about, we propose proof rules in separation logic. The theory has been machine-checked.

1 Introduction

If a program is seen as a state machine, a programmer's job may be seen as writing code to deal with each of the states that the program may reach. However, programmer time is limited and some states are less likely to occur during production than others. Therefore, in many projects it is useful to designate the most unlikely states as *failure states* and to deal with all failure states in a uniform way, while writing specific code only for non-failure (or *normal*) states.

An extreme form of this approach is to simply ignore failure states and not care what the program does when it reaches a failure state (i.e., when it *fails*). This

---

* We used the term *subsystems* in preliminary work.
** Bart Jacobs is a Postdoctoral Fellow of the Research Foundation - Flanders (FWO).

S. Drossopoulou (Ed.): ECOOP 2009, LNCS 5653, pp. 470–494, 2009.
© Springer-Verlag Berlin Heidelberg 2009

is often what happens when subroutines indicate failure conditions as special return values, and programmers have no time to write code at call sites to check for them.

A major problem with this approach is that it is *unsafe*: a failure may lead to the violation of any and all of the program's intended safety properties. Specifically, the approach violates *dependency safety*, the property which says that when an operation fails, code that depends on the operation's successful completion is not executed.

To fix this, modern programming languages offer constructs that make it easy for programmers to indicate that a state is a failure state, and deal with failure states by terminating the program by default. The underlying assumption is that termination is always safe. For example, in Java, a failure state is indicated by throwing an unchecked exception. We will focus on the Java language in this paper; the related work section discusses other languages.

Whereas by default, when a program throws an exception it terminates immediately, the programmer can override this default through the use of try-catch statements and try-finally statements. Furthermore, in a multithreaded program, when a thread's main method completes abruptly (i.e., an exception was thrown and not caught during its execution), only that thread, not the entire program, is terminated. Also, when a synchronized block's body completes abruptly, the lock is released before the exception is propagated further.

These deviations from strict termination behavior are useful and are used for two reasons. Firstly, not all exceptions indicate failure. Sometimes, programmers throw and catch exceptions to implement the program's functional behavior. Typically, in Java, checked exceptions are used for this. Secondly, programmers sometimes wish to increase the program's robustness by not considering the program to be a single unit of failure but rather by identifying multiple smaller units of failure. Common examples are extensible programs, where poorly written or malicious plugins (such as applets or servlets) should not affect the base system; and command-processing applications (such as request-response-based servers, GUI applications, or command-line shells) where a failure during the processing of a command should simply cause an error response to be returned, while continuing to process other commands normally.

However, by continuing to execute after a failure, the risk of safety violations reappears. In particular, safety violations are likely if the code that fails leaves a data structure in an inconsistent state and this data structure is then accessed during execution of a finally block or after the exception is caught, or by another thread. In other words, there is a safety risk if a try block manipulates an object that outlives the try block. More generally, if we define *dependency safety* as the property that if an operation fails, no code that depends on the operation's successful completion is executed, then dependency safety may be violated if pieces of code outside a try block depend on particular pieces of code inside the try block either not executing at all or executing to completion successfully. This is the problem we address in this paper.

To remedy this, we propose a language mechanism called *failboxes*. Programmers may create failboxes dynamically and execute blocks of code in them. Once any such block fails, all subsequent attempts to execute code in the failbox will fail. To achieve dependency safety, programmers simply need to ensure that if an operation B depends on an operation A, then A and B are executed in the same failbox. Furthermore, failboxes help fix the unsafe interaction between locks and exceptions and they enable safe cancellation and robust resource cleanup. Finally, the Fail Fast mechanism prevents liveness issues in the presence of failure in cooperating concurrent computations.

Failboxes are very lightweight: a failbox can be implemented as an object with a boolean field indicating if the failbox has failed, and a parent pointer. Executing a code block in a failbox essentially means that before and after executing the block, the thread-local variable that designates the current failbox is updated, and before a failbox is made current, it is checked that it has not failed.

We give a formal syntax and semantics of the new constructs, and prove dependency safety. Furthermore, to show that the new constructs are easy to reason about, we propose separation logic proof rules and prove their soundness.

The rest of the paper is structured as follows. In Section 2, we illustrate the problem with an example and discuss existing approaches. In Section 3, we introduce failboxes. We show additional aspects and benefits of the approach for multithreaded programs in Section 4. Section 5 briefly discusses how the approach enables safe cancellation and robust compensation. To show that it is easy to reason about the new constructs, we propose separation logic proof rules for the envisaged usage patterns in Section 6. We end the paper with sections on implementation issues (Section 7), related work (Section 8), and a conclusion (Section 9).

The theory of this paper has been machine-checked using the Coq proof assistant [12].

2   Problem Statement

Consider the example program in Figure 1. It shows a program that continuously receives commands and processes them. The code for processing commands is not shown, except that it involves calls of *compute* and calls of *addEntry* on a *Database* object *db* that is shared across all command executions. If the processing of a command fails, e.g. because it requires too much memory, the exception is caught, an error message is shown to the user, and the next command is received.

This program is unsafe. Specifically, some executions of this program violate the intended safety property that at the start of each loop iteration, object *db* is *consistent*, i.e., satisfies the property that *count* is not greater than the length of *entries*. In particular, consider an execution where method *addEntry* is called in a state where *entries* is full. This means *count* equals *entries.length*. As a result, after incrementing *count*, *addEntry* will attempt to allocate a new, larger array. Now assume there is not enough memory for this new array and an *OutOfMemoryError* occurs at location A. At this point, *count* is greater than the

```
class Database {
  int count;
  int[] entries := new int[10];
  /* invariant: count ≤ entries.length */
  void addEntry(int entry) {
    count++;
    if (count = entries.length + 1) {
      int[] es := new int[count * 2];   // *** A ***
      System.arraycopy(entries, 0, es, 0, entries.length);
      entries := es;
    }
    entries[count − 1] := entry;   // *** B ***
  } ... }
class Program {
  public static void main(String[] args) {
    Database db := new Database();
    while (true)
      /* invariant: db is consistent */
    {
      String cmd := readCommand();
      try {
        ··· compute(cmd); ···
        ··· db.addEntry(···); ···
      } catch (Throwable e) { showErrorMessage(e); }
}} ... }
```

Fig. 1. An unsafe program

length of *entries* and the *Database* object is inconsistent. Next, the exception is caught in method *main* and the loop is continued, violating the safety property.

Note: In this case, the safety violation results in an *ArrayIndexOutOfBounds-Exception* at location *B* in each subsequent call of *addEntry*; however, in general, safety violations might remain undetected and lead to data corruption, incorrect results, or sending incorrect commands to hardware devices.

The following approaches exist to deal with this complication:

- **Never catch unchecked exceptions.** Never catching unchecked exceptions makes it easier to preserve safety properties, since the many implicit control flow paths created by catching unchecked exceptions are avoided. However, catching unchecked exceptions can be useful, as in the example. Note also that **try-finally** blocks are equivalent to **try-catch** blocks that catch unchecked exceptions; specifically, assuming S_1 does not jump out of the **try** block, a statement

$$\textbf{try } \{ \ S_1 \ \} \textbf{ finally } \{ \ S_2 \ \}$$

  is equivalent to

$$\textbf{try } \{ \ S_1 \ \} \textbf{ catch } (\textit{Throwable } t) \ \{ \ S_2 \textbf{ throw } t; \ \} \ S_2$$

and is subject to the same complication: S_2 might depend on the successful completion of certain sub-computations within S_1. Never catching unchecked exceptions would imply never using **try-finally** blocks, or modifying their semantics so that they ignore unchecked exceptions. The semantics of synchronized blocks would need to be updated similarly.

- **Always maintain consistency.** It is often possible to ensure that objects used across try-catch blocks, like the *Database* object in the example, are in a consistent state at all times. Often it is sufficient to reorder assignments; e.g., in the example, moving the count increment after the assignment to *entries* preserves consistency. Another approach is to use a functional programming-like approach, where a new object state is built up separately and then installed into the object using a single assignment. In the example, method *addEntry* would return a new *Database* object rather than updating the existing one. Yet another approach is to use transaction-like technologies, such as software transactional memory [19, 5]. However, these approaches either require the programmer to perform non-trivial additional reasoning and/or programming work, or impose a potentially significant performance overhead.

- **Never fail during critical sections.** It might be possible in some cases to guarantee absence of failure at points where failure would violate safety. This requires careful programming to avoid operations that might encounter resource or implementation limitations, such as heap or stack memory allocations or operations on bounded integers, or to move these operations out of the critical section. Furthermore, this might require virtual machine support if the virtual machine may perform resource allocations implicitly. For example, the .NET Framework's JIT compiler may allocate memory at any time to store a newly compiled piece of code. Therefore, starting with version 2, the .NET Framework offers constructs to "prepare" a piece of code that must execute without failure [21]. However, this approach imposes a significant burden on the programmer.

- **Ensure dependent code is not executed.** In this approach, steps are taken to ensure that if a computation fails with an unchecked exception, then no computations that depend on the failed computation's successful completion ever get to run. There are at least two ways to achieve this:

  - **Use separate threads.** In this approach, threads are adopted as the units of failure. Within a thread, unchecked exceptions are never caught; that is, an exception in the thread causes the entire thread to die. All data structures are local to threads. Instead of running a block of code in a try-catch block, it is run in a separate thread. During this time, the original thread waits for the termination of the child thread; additionally, the original thread may accept messages on a message queue. If the child thread needs to perform an operation whose failure should cause the parent thread to fail (such as an *addEntry* call on the *Database* object), the child thread may perform a remote procedure call into the parent thread via the parent thread's message queue. This is more or less the approach used in operating systems, in the Erlang language [1], and in the SCOOP multithreading approach for Eiffel [17].

- **Guard dependent code manually.** The programmer can manually arrange to ensure that dependent code is not executed. For example, the programmer could associate a boolean flag with each object used across try-catch blocks that tracks whether the object is in a consistent state, and check this flag before accessing the object [13]. If the flag is false, an exception is thrown.

In this paper we present a new approach in the fourth category, which, like the use of separate threads and manually guarding dependent code, supports catching exceptions and does not require that consistency be maintained always or that failures be avoided, but which has less programming and run-time overhead than the use of separate threads and which has less programming overhead than manually guarding dependent code.

3   Failboxes

In our approach, the language is extended with a notion of *failboxes*. Constructs are added for creating a new failbox and for running a piece of code in a designated failbox. As soon as one such piece of code fails (i.e., completes abruptly with an unchecked exception), any subsequent attempt to run code in the failbox fails. To ensure dependency safety, the programmer simply needs to ensure that if a computation B depends on a computation A, then A and B run in the same failbox.

To facilitate composition of program modules, failboxes are ordered hierarchically. When creating a new failbox, a parent may be specified. If an exception occurs in a failbox, both it and its transitive children are marked as failed.

3.1   Syntax and Semantics

The syntax of the new constructs is as follows:

$$s ::= \ldots$$
$$\mid x := \textbf{currentfb}; \ \mid x := \textbf{newfb}; \ \mid x' := \textbf{newfb}(x);$$
$$\mid \textbf{enter } (x) \ \{ \ \bar{s} \ \} \ \textbf{catch } \{ \ \bar{s}' \ \}$$

where s ranges over statements, $\bar{s}$ ranges over sequences (i.e., sequential compositions) of statements, and x and x' range over local variable names.

Note: For simplicity, we ignore checked exceptions and exception objects in the formal developments.

A program state is a tuple of the form

$$(L, \Sigma, \Phi, T)$$

where L, the *lock map*, is a partial function that contains a pair (o, t) if thread t holds the lock of object o; Σ is a partial function that maps each allocated failbox to its parent failbox (and a root failbox to itself); Φ is the set of *failed failboxes*; and T is a partial function that maps each thread to its current state. (We omit the heap since our constructs do not interact with it.)

A thread state is a tuple of the form

$$(f, V, \overline{s}, \overline{b}, \overline{F})$$

where f is the thread's *current failbox*, V is a total function that maps each variable name to a value, $\overline{s}$, the *continuation*, is the sequence of statements to be executed by the thread, $\overline{b}$ is the sequence of *enclosing blocks*, and $\overline{F}$ is the sequence of enclosing activation records.

The syntax of an enclosing block is as follows:

$$b ::= \textbf{enter} \ (f) \ \textbf{catch} \ \{ \ \overline{s} \ \} \ \overline{s}' \mid \textbf{synchronized} \ (o); \ \overline{s}$$

where an enclosing enter block records the failbox f that was current prior to the enter statement (*not* the failbox that was entered), the catch block body $\overline{s}$, and the statements $\overline{s}'$ that are to be executed after completion of the enter statement; and an enclosing synchronized block records the object o whose lock was acquired, and the statements $\overline{s}$ that are to be executed after completion of the synchronized statement.

In the initial program state of a program with main method body $\overline{s}$, the lock map is empty, there is a single failbox f, whose parent is itself, no failbox is marked as failed, and there is one thread t whose current failbox is f; all of the thread's local variables are bound to **null**, and it has no enclosing blocks and no enclosing activation records:

$$\frac{\text{main } \overline{s}}{\text{initial } (\emptyset, \{(f, f)\}, \emptyset, \{(t, (f, (\lambda x.\textbf{null}), \overline{s}, \epsilon, \epsilon))\})}$$

The statement $x := \textbf{currentfb};$ assigns the current failbox to variable x:

CURRENTFB
$$\frac{(t, (f, V, x := \textbf{currentfb}; \ \overline{s}, \overline{b}, \overline{F})) \in T}{(L, \Sigma, \Phi, T) \to (L, \Sigma, \Phi, T(t := (f, V(x := f), \overline{s}, \overline{b}, \overline{F})))}$$

The statement $x := \textbf{newfb};$ creates a new root failbox and assigns it to x:

NEWFB-ROOT
$$\frac{(t, (f, V, x := \textbf{newfb}; \ \overline{s}, \overline{b}, \overline{F})) \in T \qquad f' \notin \text{dom}(\Sigma) \qquad \Sigma' = \Sigma(f' := f')}{(L, \Sigma, \Phi, T) \to (L, \Sigma', \Phi, T(t := (f, V(x := f'), \overline{s}, \overline{b}, \overline{F})))}$$

If x is bound to a failbox f' and f' is not marked as failed, the statement $x' := \textbf{newfb}(x);$ creates a new child failbox of f' and assigns it to x':

NEWFB-CHILD
$$\frac{(t, (f, V, x' := \textbf{newfb}(x); \ \overline{s}, \overline{b}, \overline{F})) \in T \\ V(x) = f' \qquad f' \notin \Phi \qquad f'' \notin \text{dom}(\Sigma) \qquad \Sigma' = \Sigma(f'' := f')}{(L, \Sigma, \Phi, T) \to (L, \Sigma', \Phi, T(t := (f, V(x' := f''), \overline{s}, \overline{b}, \overline{F})))}$$

If x is bound to a failbox f', and f' is not marked as failed, then statement
enter (x) { $\bar{s}'$ } **catch** { $\bar{s}''$ } records the current failbox, the catch block body
$\bar{s}'$, and the current continuation in a new enclosing block, makes f' the current
failbox, and starts executing the enter block body $\bar{s}'$:

ENTER
$$\frac{(t, (f, V, \textbf{enter } (x) \{ \bar{s}' \} \textbf{ catch } \{ \bar{s}'' \} \bar{s}, \bar{b}, \overline{F})) \in T \quad V(x) = f' \quad f' \notin \Phi \quad \bar{b}' = (\textbf{enter } (f) \textbf{ catch } \{ \bar{s}'' \} \bar{s}) \cdot \bar{b}}{(L, \Sigma, \Phi, T) \to (L, \Sigma, \Phi, T(t := (f', V, \bar{s}', \bar{b}', \overline{F})))}$$

On normal completion of an enter block body, the former current failbox is
restored and the catch block is skipped, provided that the former current failbox
is not marked as failed:

ENTER-COMPLETE-NORMAL
$$\frac{(t, (f, V, \epsilon, (\textbf{enter } (f') \textbf{ catch } \{ \bar{s}' \} \bar{s}'') \cdot \bar{b}, \overline{F})) \in T \quad f' \notin \Phi}{(L, \Sigma, \Phi, T) \to (L, \Sigma, \Phi, T(t := (f', V, \bar{s}'', \bar{b}, \overline{F})))}$$

where ϵ denotes the empty sequence.

We model the occurrence of an exception as the replacement of the current
continuation with a throw statement. An exception can occur at any time; this
reflects the fact that in Java a *virtual machine error* can be thrown at any time
[10, §11.3.2].

FAIL
$$\frac{(t, (f, V, \bar{s}, \bar{b}, \overline{F})) \in T \quad \bar{s} \neq \textbf{throw};}{(L, \Sigma, \Phi, T) \to (L, \Sigma, \Phi, T(t := (f, V, \textbf{throw};, \bar{b}, \overline{F})))}$$

If variable x is not bound to a failbox, or it is bound to a failbox but the failbox
is marked as failed, then both $x' := \textbf{newfb}(x);$ and **enter** (x) { $\bar{s}$ } **catch** { $\bar{s}'$ }
throw an exception (of type *FailboxException*); this is covered by rule FAIL.

On abrupt completion of an enter block body with an exception, the current
failbox and its descendants are marked as failed, the former current failbox is
restored, and the catch block is executed, provided the former current failbox is
not marked as failed:

ENTER-COMPLETE-ABRUPT
$$\frac{(t, (f, V, \textbf{throw};, (\textbf{enter } (f') \textbf{ catch } \{ \bar{s}' \} \bar{s}'') \cdot \bar{b}, \overline{F})) \in T \quad \Phi' = \Phi \cup (\Sigma^{-1})^*(f) \quad f' \notin \Phi'}{(L, \Sigma, \Phi, T) \to (L, \Sigma, \Phi', T(t := (f', V, \bar{s}' \ \bar{s}'', \bar{b}, \overline{F})))}$$

where $(\Sigma^{-1})^*(f)$ denotes the set of f's descendants, including f itself.

On normal completion of an enter block body, if the former current failbox is marked as failed, it is restored but the catch block is skipped and a
FailboxException exception is thrown:

ENTER-COMPLETE-NORMAL-FAIL
$$\frac{(t, (f, V, \epsilon, (\textbf{enter } (f') \textbf{ catch } \{ \bar{s}' \} \bar{s}'') \cdot \bar{b}, \overline{F})) \in T \quad f' \in \Phi}{(L, \Sigma, \Phi, T) \to (L, \Sigma, \Phi, T(t := (f', V, \textbf{throw};, \bar{b}, \overline{F})))}$$

On abrupt completion of an enter block body with an exception, if after marking the current failbox as failed, the former current failbox is marked as failed, the former current failbox is restored but the catch block is skipped and a *FailboxException* exception is thrown:

ENTER-COMPLETE-ABRUPT-FAIL

$$\frac{(t, (f, V, \mathbf{throw}; , (\mathbf{enter}\ (f')\ \mathbf{catch}\ \{\ \overline{s}'\ \}\ \overline{s}'') \cdot \overline{b}, \overline{F})) \in T \qquad \varPhi' = \varPhi \cup (\Sigma^{-1})^*(f) \qquad f' \in \varPhi'}{(L, \Sigma, \varPhi, T) \rightarrow (L, \Sigma, \varPhi', T(t := (f', V, \mathbf{throw}; , \overline{b}, \overline{F})))}$$

3.2 Syntactic Sugar

We remove try-catch statements and try-finally statements from the language as separate statements. Instead, we define them as syntactic sugar over the new constructs. Specifically, the statement

$$\mathbf{try}\ \{\ \overline{s}\ \}\ \mathbf{catch}\ \{\ \overline{s}'\ \}$$

is defined as

$$x := \mathbf{currentfb};\ x' := \mathbf{newfb}(x);\ \mathbf{enter}\ (x')\ \{\ \overline{s}\ \}\ \mathbf{catch}\ \{\ \overline{s}'\ \}$$

where x and x' are fresh. That is, a try-catch statement executes the try block in a new child failbox of the current failbox.

The statement

$$\mathbf{try}\ \{\ \overline{s}\ \}\ \mathbf{finally}\ \{\ \overline{s}'\ \}$$

is defined as

$$\mathbf{try}\ \{\ \overline{s}\ \}\ \mathbf{catch}\ \{\ \overline{s}'\ \mathbf{throw};\ \}\ \overline{s}'$$

This means that a try-finally statement executes its try block in a new child failbox of the current failbox.

Furthermore, we define the following shorthands:

$$\mathbf{enter}\ (x)\ \{\ \overline{s}\ \}\ \equiv\ \mathbf{enter}\ (x)\ \{\ \overline{s}\ \}\ \mathbf{catch}\ \{\ \mathbf{throw};\ \}$$
$$\mathbf{reenter}\ (x)\ \{\ \overline{s}\ \}\ \equiv\ \mathbf{enter}\ (x)\ \{\ \overline{s}\ \}\ \mathbf{catch}\ \{\}$$

In words, an enter statement propagates exceptions, and a reenter statement does not. Note: in real implementations, a reenter statement would not cause exception information to be lost, since the exception object would be associated with the failbox at the time the failbox is marked as failed, and an API would be provided to retrieve the stored exception object of a failed failbox.

3.3 Terminology

We use the following terminology: We say that an event in a thread t occurs *in a failbox f* or a statement is executed (or executes) in f if the event occurs or the statement execution starts at a time when f is the current failbox of t. We say that *a failure occurs* in *t* when an unchecked exception is thrown (i.e., the continuation of *t* is a throw statement). We say that a statement execution *fails* if it completes abruptly because of an unchecked exception. We say that a failbox *f* *fails* when a failure occurs in *f*. We say that an execution step *enters* a failbox *f* if *f* is the current failbox after the step and was not the current failbox before the step. Similarly, we say that an execution step *leaves* a failbox *f* if is not the current failbox after the step and was the current failbox before the step.

3.4   Example

The approach is illustrated and motivated by the example in Figure 2. (Note: In the examples we use a more conventional syntax.) It shows how the unsafe program of Figure 1 can be made safe using failboxes. A failbox *f* is created and then both the main loop and calls of *addEntry* are executed in *f*. This ensures that if a call of *addEntry* fails, the main loop terminates.

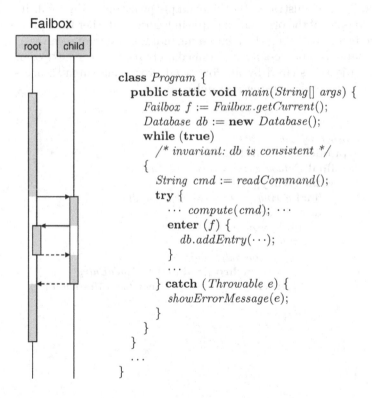

```
                                class Program {
                                  public static void main(String[] args) {
                                    Failbox f := Failbox.getCurrent();
                                    Database db := new Database();
                                    while (true)
                                      /* invariant: db is consistent */
                                    {
                                      String cmd := readCommand();
                                      try {
                                        ··· compute(cmd); ···
                                        enter (f) {
                                          db.addEntry(···);
                                        }
                                        ···
                                      } catch (Throwable e) {
                                        showErrorMessage(e);
                                      }
                                    }
                                  }
                                  ···
                                }
```

Fig. 2. The example of Figure 1, fixed using failboxes. When an *addEntry* call fails, failbox *f* is marked as failed. When control subsequently exits the try block, this is considered an attempt to enter *f*; therefore, a *FailboxException* is thrown. As a result, the catch block is skipped, the loop is exited, and the program terminates safely. The sequence diagram shows the failbox transitions.

The example motivates why on entry to a try block, the failbox in which the try-catch statement executes is no longer considered the current failbox. This ensures that failures in method *compute* are properly caught by the try-catch statement, and do not cause the program to terminate.

4   Multithreading

4.1   Synchronized Statements: Safety Issues

One common way that the strict termination approach of dealing with failures is overridden, is through the use of **synchronized** blocks. A **synchronized** (*o*) *S* block in Java acquires the lock of object *o*, executes statement *S*, and then releases the lock of *o*, even if *S* failed. This helps prevent deadlocks, but it creates a safety risk. In particular, if a failure occurs while *o* is inconsistent, the commonly intended safety property that shared objects whose lock is not held are consistent, is violated.

The problem is illustrated by the example program in Figure 3. It is a multi-threaded version of the original example in Figure 1. Rather than processing each command before receiving the next command, the program receives a command, spawns a thread to process it, and immediately receives the next command. The *Database* object is shared by all command processing threads; accesses to the object are synchronized using a **synchronized** block.

```
class Program {
  public static void main(String[] args) {
    final Database db := new Database();
    while (true) {
      final String cmd := readCommand();
      new Thread() {
        public void run() {
          try {
            ··· compute(cmd); ···
            ··· synchronized (db) { db.addEntry(···); } ···
          } catch (Throwable e) { showErrorMessage(e); }
        }
      }.start();
    }
  }
  ···
}
```

Fig. 3. An unsafe program. A failure in *compute* is handled correctly, but if a failure occurs in method *addEntry* while the *Database* object is inconsistent, the object's lock is released, causing threads that subsequently acquire the lock to see the object in an unexpected state, violating safety.

This program is unsafe. In particular, in some executions, the intended safety property that whenever a shared object's lock is not held by any thread, the object is consistent, is violated. This property is relied on to guarantee that method *addEntry* is called only on objects that are consistent. Specifically, suppose a failure occurs in method *addEntry* while the *Database* object is inconsistent. This causes the lock to be released. Subsequent command processing threads that acquire the lock will then see the *Database* object in an inconsistent state.

4.2   Failboxes Approach for Safe Synchronized Statements

Failboxes can be used to write safe lock-based multithreaded programs, by associating each shared object with a failbox and running the code that accesses a shared object within the associated failbox. This way, when a failure occurs, the failbox is marked as failed, so that when another thread subsequently attempts to enter the failbox in order to access the object, an exception is thrown and the thread is prevented from seeing inconsistent state. The modified safety property is that whenever no thread holds a shared object's lock, either the object is consistent or its associated failbox is marked as failed.

The approach is illustrated in Figure 4. It is the example of Figure 3, made safe using failboxes. Specifically, the example uses an enter statement to execute the *addEntry* calls in the main thread's root failbox. When an *addEntry* call fails, this failbox is marked as failed before the lock is released. When another thread

```
class Program {
  public static void main(String[] args) {
    final Failbox f := Failbox.getCurrent();
    final Database db := new Database();
    while (true) {
      final String cmd := readCommand();
      new Thread() {
        public void run() {
          try {
            ··· compute(cmd); ···
            ··· synchronized (db) { enter (f) { db.addEntry(···); } } ···
          } catch (Throwable e) { showErrorMessage(e); }
        }
      }.startInCurrentFailbox();
    }
    ···
  }
}
```

Fig. 4. The example of Figure 3, made safe using failboxes. If a call of *addEntry* fails, failbox *f* is marked as failed and subsequent attempts by other threads to enter the failbox will fail. Furthermore, by the Fail Fast feature, a *stop f* signal is sent to all threads running in the failed failbox *f* or a descendant of *f*. In the example, this means the program terminates.

subsequently acquires the lock and attempts to enter the failbox, an exception is thrown, so that the thread is prevented from unsafely calling *addEntry*.

4.3 Multithreaded Failboxes

In a multithreaded program, it is possible for computations in multiple threads to be executing in the same failbox f concurrently. If this happens, we say f is multithreaded. The question then arises as to what happens when one of these computations fails. There are two distinct concerns involved in this matter: preserving the program's intended safety properties, and ensuring useful progress.

4.4 Multithreaded Failboxes: Safety

In a well-written program, a failure in one thread should not have safety implications for operations executing concurrently in other threads. Specifically, in a *data-race-free* program, where the program synchronizes accesses to shared memory using the language's synchronization constructs, an operation can see the data that was being manipulated by a computation that failed only if the operation is not concurrent with the failure, i.e., the operation was synchronized with the failed computation. (Formally, the failure *happens-before* the operation.) Therefore, to ensure safety, it is sufficient that synchronization constructs perform the necessary failboxes bookkeeping to ensure that if a failure happens in a failbox, no operation that is ordered after this failure through synchronization runs in this failbox. To achieve this, we specify the semantics of synchronized statements with respect to failboxes as follows: after acquiring the lock, the statement checks that the current failbox has not failed; otherwise, it throws a *FailboxException*. Furthermore, before releasing the lock, if the body completed abruptly with an exception, the current failbox is marked as failed. The step rules are shown in Figure 5.

4.5 Properties

We are now ready to state and sketch the proof of the main properties of the failboxes approach.

We first define some terms. An *execution* is a finite or countably infinite sequence of program states. An *execution point* is a nonnegative integer that serves as an index into an execution. A *thread execution point* (k, t) is a pair of an execution point k and a thread identifier t.

Definition 1 (Happens-Before). *The happens-before relation* $\overset{\text{hb}_E}{\to}$ *on thread execution points of an execution* $E = C_0, C_1, \ldots$ *is the smallest transitive relation that satisfies the following properties:*

- *Any thread execution point of a thread* t *happens-before any subsequent thread execution point of* t

$$k_1 < k_2 \Rightarrow (k_1, t) \overset{\text{hb}_E}{\to} (k_2, t)$$

SYNCHRONIZED

$$\frac{(t, (f, V, \mathbf{synchronized}\ (x)\ \{\ \overline{s}'\ \}\ \overline{s}, \overline{b}, \overline{F})) \in T}{\quad V(x) = o \quad o \notin \mathrm{dom}(L) \quad f \notin \Phi \quad \overline{b}' = (\mathbf{synchronized}\ (o);\ \overline{s}) \cdot \overline{b}}{(L, \Sigma, \Phi, T) \overset{t:\mathrm{acq}(o)}{\to} (L(o := t), \Sigma, \Phi, T(t := (f, V, \overline{s}', \overline{b}', \overline{F})))}$$

SYNCHRONIZED-REENTRANT

$$\frac{(t, (f, V, \mathbf{synchronized}\ (x)\ \{\ \overline{s}'\ \}\ \overline{s}, \overline{b}, \overline{F})) \in T \quad V(x) = o \quad (o, t) \in L}{(L, \Sigma, \Phi, T) \to (L, \Sigma, \Phi, T(t := (f, V, \overline{s}'\ \overline{s}, \overline{b}, \overline{F})))}$$

SYNCHRONIZED-COMPLETE-NORMAL

$$\frac{(t, (f, V, \epsilon, (\mathbf{synchronized}\ (o);\ \overline{s}) \cdot \overline{b}, \overline{F})) \in T}{(L, \Sigma, \Phi, T) \overset{t:\mathrm{rel}(o)}{\to} (L \setminus \{(o, t)\}, \Sigma, \Phi, T(t := (f, V, \overline{s}, \overline{b}, \overline{F})))}$$

SYNCHRONIZED-COMPLETE-ABRUPT

$$\frac{(t, (f, V, \mathbf{throw}; , (\mathbf{synchronized}\ (o);\ \overline{s}) \cdot \overline{b}, \overline{F})) \in T}{\Phi' = \Phi \cup (\Sigma^{-1})^*(f) \quad T' = T(t := (f, V, \mathbf{throw}; , \overline{b}, \overline{F}))}{(L, \Sigma, \Phi, T) \overset{t:\mathrm{rel}(o)}{\to} (L \setminus \{(o, t)\}, \Sigma, \Phi', T')}$$

Fig. 5. Step rules for synchronized statements

- *If execution step k_1 is a release of some lock o by some thread t_1, and subsequent execution step k_2 is an acquire of o by some thread t_2, then (k_1, t_1) happens-before $(k_2 + 1, t_2)$*

$$C_{k_1} \overset{t_1:\mathrm{rel}(o)}{\to} C_{k_1+1} \Rightarrow C_{k_2} \overset{t_2:\mathrm{acq}(o)}{\to} C_{k_2+1} \Rightarrow k_1 < k_2 \Rightarrow (k_1, t_1) \overset{\mathrm{hb}_E}{\to} (k_2 + 1, t_2)$$

- *If at execution step k thread t starts a new thread t' (see Figure 6), then (k, t) happens-before $(k + 1, t')$*

$$C_k \overset{t:\mathrm{fork}(t')}{\to} C_{k+1} \Rightarrow (k, t) \overset{\mathrm{hb}_E}{\to} (k + 1, t')$$

The Main Lemma states that once an exception occurs in a failbox, no code executes in that failbox "afterwards".

Lemma 1 (Main Lemma). *Consider an execution E of a program π of the extended language, and consider two thread execution points (k_1, t_1) and (k_2, t_2) in E, such that (k_1, t_1) happens-before (k_2, t_2). If t_1 is executing in some failbox f_1 in state k_1, and t_2 is executing in some descendant f_2 of f_1 in state k_2, then if t_1 is failing in state k_1, then t_2 is failing in state k_2.*

$$\mathrm{exec}(\pi, E) \Rightarrow (k_1, t_1) \overset{\mathrm{hb}_E}{\to} (k_2, t_2) \Rightarrow$$
$$C_{k_1} = (L_1, \Sigma_1, \Phi_1, T_1) \Rightarrow T_1(t_1) = (f_1, V_1, \mathbf{throw}; , \overline{b}_1, \overline{F}_1) \Rightarrow$$
$$C_{k_2} = (L_2, \Sigma_2, \Phi_2, T_2) \Rightarrow T_2(t_2) = (f_2, V_2, \overline{s}_2, \overline{b}_2, \overline{F}_2) \Rightarrow$$
$$f_2 \in (\Sigma_2^{-1})^*(f_1) \Rightarrow \overline{s}_2 = \mathbf{throw};$$

Proof. It suffices to prove for every prefix of some path from (k_1, t_1) to (k_2, t_2) in the happens-before graph, that at the thread execution point (k_3, t_3) at the end of the prefix, one or more of the following hold:

- the thread is failing and the current failbox is f_1
- failbox f_1 and its descendants have been marked as failed and one or more of the following hold:
  - the current failbox is not f_1 or a descendant of f_1, or
  - the thread is failing.

This can be proved easily by induction on the length of the prefix and case analysis on the last edge.

Now consider an execution E of a program π and a *dependency relation* D on the thread execution points of E. We say E *uses failboxes correctly* with respect to D, if whenever thread execution point p_2 depends on thread execution point p_1, the current failbox at p_2 is a descendant of the current failbox at p_1. We say E is *dependency-safe* with respect to D if whenever p_2 depends on p_1, and p_1 happens-before p_2, and p_1 is failing, then p_2 is failing. We then have the Soundness Theorem: if E uses failboxes correctly with respect to D, then E is dependency-safe with respect to D. This follows directly from the Main Lemma.

A machine-checked proof of these properties is available online [12].

4.6 Multithreaded Failboxes: Ensuring Useful Progress

Even if a computation is safe, it might not be contributing to the useful work of the application. Specifically, if multiple computations are running in the same failbox, then this is taken to mean that they depend on each other for useful progress. As a result, if one of them fails, there is no point for the others to continue, so they should be stopped to free up CPU cycles, memory, and other resources these computations may be using. Therefore, in our approach, at the time a failbox f is marked as failed, a *stop f* signal is sent to all threads currently running in f or a descendant of f. When the signal arrives, this results in a *FailboxException* being thrown in the target thread, provided it is still running in f or a descendant. To allow efficient implementations, we do not impose timing constraints on the delivery of the signal, except that it must arrive eventually. We call this mechanism the Fail Fast mechanism (after the Fail Fast principle [20]).

The usefulness of the Fail Fast mechanism is illustrated by the example in Figure 4. Once failbox f has failed, all subsequent attempts to access the database fail. Assuming most commands access the database, this means the program's functionality is severely degraded. Therefore, it seems appropriate to escalate the failure and terminate the program. This typically signals a system administrator or service management daemon to restart the program in a clean state, hopefully restoring full service. In the example, this behavior is achieved by running not just the *addEntry* calls, but the main loop as well, in failbox f. When an *addEntry* call fails, an asynchronous exception is thrown in the main thread, which causes the loop to terminate.

FORK

$$t' \notin \mathrm{dom}(T) \qquad \frac{(t, (f, V, \mathbf{fork} \ \{ \ \overline{s}' \ \} \ \overline{s}, \overline{b}, \overline{F})) \in T}{T' = T(t := (f, V, \overline{s}, \overline{b}, \overline{F}), t' := (f, V, \overline{s}', \epsilon, \epsilon))}$$

$$(L, \Sigma, \Phi, T) \overset{t:\mathrm{fork}(t')}{\rightarrow} (L, \Sigma, \Phi', T')$$

THREAD-COMPLETE-ABRUPT

$$\frac{(t, (f, V, \mathbf{throw};, \epsilon, \epsilon)) \in T \qquad f \notin \Phi \qquad \Phi' = \Phi \cup (\Sigma^{-1})^*(f)}{(L, \Sigma, \Phi, T) \rightarrow (L, \Sigma, \Phi', T)}$$

$\mathbf{fork}* \ \{ \ \overline{s} \ \} \equiv \mathbf{fork} \ \{ \ x := \mathbf{newfb}; \ \mathbf{reenter} \ (x) \ \{ \ \overline{s} \ \} \ \}$ where x is fresh

Fig. 6. Step rules for thread creation

In fact, since the existing command processing threads are unlikely to be able to run to completion successfully, it makes sense to terminate these as well. This is achieved in the example by running the command processing threads in failbox f as well, by using method *startInCurrentFailbox* (added by our language extension) instead of *start* to start these threads. (To ensure backward compatibility, method *start* starts the new thread in a newly created root failbox, so that failure of the new thread does not cause a stop signal to be sent to the original thread.)

In the example, the failbox hierarchy is as follows. Failbox f, a root failbox, has one child for each try block execution. This ensures, as before, that exceptions in method *compute* do not cause the program to terminate.

The step rules for thread creation are shown in Figure 6. In the formal language, statement **fork** corresponds with method *startInCurrentFailbox*, and **fork*** corresponds with method *start*.

4.7   Wait Dependency Safety

A sub-concern of the concern of ensuring useful progress is the concern of ensuring progress. Specifically, one of the correctness properties that are difficult to achieve in the presence of unchecked exceptions is *wait dependency safety*, the property that if, in a given program execution, a wait operation W depends on a computation A, then, assuming that W terminates if A does not fail, W terminates. Analogously to the dependency relation used in the definition of dependency safety, the wait dependency relation used here is an application-specific relation; the intention is that if a wait operation W depends on a computation A, this means that, abstractly speaking, W waits for a signal to be sent by A. In Java, a typical example of this is when W is an *Object.wait* call on some object o and A at some point performs an *Object.notifyAll* call on o.

Failboxes can be used to achieve wait dependency safety. We say that a program *uses failboxes correctly* for the purpose of wait dependency safety if whenever in a given program execution, a wait operation W depends on a computation A, then A runs in a failbox f and W runs in a descendant of f. We then have the property that if a program uses failboxes correctly for the purpose of wait dependency safety, then the program is wait-dependency-safe. Indeed, if

A fails, a stop signal is sent to the thread that is running W. As a result, when the signal arrives, either W has already terminated, or W is terminated by the *FailboxException* thrown by the Fail Fast mechanism. We call this property the soundness of the Fail Fast mechanism.

A machine-checked proof of this property is available online [12].

5   Cancellation and Compensation

We propose the use of failboxes in programs to make them safe for failures. However, it turns out that if failboxes are applied correctly in a program, then this also enables safe *cancellation* of computations, with no extra effort, and without the need for polling, through the Fail Fast mechanism. In order to enable cancellation of a computation, the program runs it in a dedicated failbox; to cancel the computation, it calls the *Failbox* object's *cancel* method, which simulates the occurrence of a failure in the failbox and triggers the Fail Fast mechanism. This achieves the convenience of the deprecated *Thread.stop* approach, without the safety risk.

Consider for example the program of Figure 4. The main loop repeatedly receives a command and starts a command thread to process it. The processing is done inside a try-catch statement, and therefore in a per-command child failbox of the root failbox. This program could be extended to enable cancellation of commands as follows. In order to cancel a command, the program calls the command failbox's *cancel* method. If the command thread is executing in the command failbox, it is stopped; however, if it is executing inside the database, it is allowed to continue to execute until it leaves the root failbox and re-enters the command failbox, at which point an exception is thrown. Contrast this with calling *stop* on the command thread, which would stop the thread even if it was running in the database, causing the entire program to fail.

The failboxes mechanism also enables *safe compensation*. By compensation, we refer to the scenario where a client computation invokes a service offered by a provider computation, which changes the provider's state. This imposes the obligation on the client to invoke a compensating service to restore the provider's state, after the client is done using the service. The conventional approach to compensation is through try-finally statements. However, an unchecked exception can cause the compensation action to be skipped, if the exception occurs after the action that is to be compensated, but before the try block is entered, or if it occurs after the finally block is entered, but before the compensation action completes.

This may be addressed using the failboxes mechanism by performing the following transformation:

```
init();                          enter (provider) {
try {                              init();
    // Use the service             reenter (client) {
} finally {            ⇒              // Use the service
    compensate();                  }
}                                  compensate();
                                 }
```

Before invoking the service, the thread running the client computation enters the provider's failbox. After the service is invoked, it re-enters the client failbox using a nested reenter statement where the client uses the service. When the client is done using the service, it leaves the nested enter statement, causing the thread to re-enter the provider failbox, perform the compensating action, and finally leave the outer enter statement, re-entering the client failbox. This approach guarantees that either the compensation occurs or the provider failbox is marked as failed. If an exception occurs while the client uses the service, the client failbox is marked as failed, but the exception is not propagated by the reenter statement. This ensures that compensation is not skipped. When the thread leaves the outer enter statement, it enters the client failbox, which was marked as failed, and therefore the exception is propagated from that point, as in the case of the try-finally statement.

6   Proof Rules

To show that it is easy to reason about programs that use failboxes, in this section we propose separation logic proof rules for the main envisaged usage patterns.

Recall the semantics of separation logic assertions: **emp** describes the empty heap, and the separate conjunction $P * Q$ describes a heap that can be split into one that satisfies P and one that satisfies Q:

$$s, h \vDash \textbf{emp} \Leftrightarrow h = \emptyset \quad s, h \vDash P * Q \Leftrightarrow \exists h_1, h_2 \bullet h = h_1 \uplus h_2 \wedge s, h_1 \vDash P \wedge s, h_2 \vdash Q$$

We extend the syntax of correctness judgments (but not the syntax of assertions) to be failboxes-aware. Specifically,

$$\Sigma; f \vdash \{\Gamma\} \; \overline{s} \; \{Q\}$$

denotes the correctness of statement list $\overline{s}$ under commitment list Σ, current failbox f, precondition P, and postcondition Q. The syntax of commitment lists is as follows:

$$\Sigma ::= \epsilon \mid \Sigma, f : P$$

We say that assertion P is committed to failbox f. Informally, this means that to access the resources of P, f must first be entered. Failboxes are denoted using logical variables.

The above correctness judgment implies the following validity statement:

$$[\![\Sigma]\!] * P \Rightarrow \mathsf{valid}(\overline{s}, [\![\Sigma]\!] * Q, [\![\Sigma]\!] * \textbf{true})$$

(under the assumption that $\overline{s}$ does not assign to any variables that Σ depends on) where Σ is here interpreted as a separation logic assertion as follows:

$$[\![\epsilon]\!] \equiv \textbf{emp} \qquad [\![\Sigma, f : P]\!] \equiv [\![\Sigma]\!] * (f \in \Phi \vee P)$$

i.e., for each commitment $f : P$, either P holds (and is owned by the current thread) or f has failed. $\mathsf{valid}(\bar{s}, Q, R)$ is true under a given heap, failed set, and variable environment, if after executing $\bar{s}$ in this state, upon normal completion Q holds and upon abrupt completion R holds.

A throw statement always satisfies partial correctness.

C-THROW
$$\Sigma; f \vdash \{P\} \textbf{ throw}; \{Q\}$$

For verifying a try-catch statement, the heap is split into two parts: part P_{f} is accessed by the try block only inside **enter** (f) statements, and part P is accessed freely. The second premise of the rule ensures soundness for normal completion of the try block. The third is for the case where the try block fails.

C-TRYCATCH
$$\frac{\forall f' \bullet \Sigma, f : P_{\mathsf{f}}; f' \vdash \{P\}\, \bar{s}\, \{Q\} \qquad P_{\mathsf{f}} * Q \Rightarrow Q' \qquad \Sigma; f \vdash \{P_{\mathsf{f}}\}\, \bar{s}'\, \{Q'\}}{\Sigma; f \vdash \{P_{\mathsf{f}} * P\} \textbf{ try } \{\, \bar{s}\, \} \textbf{ catch } \{\, \bar{s}'\, \} \{Q'\}}$$

(under the assumption that P_{f} does not depend on any variables that $\bar{s}$ assigns to).

An enter block can access the piece of heap associated with the failbox being entered.

C-ENTER
$$\frac{\Sigma; f \vdash \{P * P_{\mathsf{f}}\}\, \bar{s}\, \{Q * P_{\mathsf{f}}\}}{\Sigma, f : P_{\mathsf{f}}; f' \vdash \{P \wedge x = f\} \textbf{ enter } (x)\, \bar{s}\, \{Q\}}$$

The compensation pattern can be verified as follows.

C-COMPENSATION
$$\frac{\begin{array}{c}\Sigma; f \vdash \{P * P_{\mathsf{f}}\}\, \bar{s}_1\, \{Q_1 * P_{\mathsf{f}}' \wedge y = f'\} \\ \Sigma, f : P_{\mathsf{f}}'; f' \vdash \{Q_1\}\, \bar{s}_2\, \{Q\} \qquad \Sigma; f \vdash \{P_{\mathsf{f}}'\}\, \bar{s}_3\, \{P_{\mathsf{f}}\}\end{array}}{\begin{array}{c}\Sigma, f : P_{\mathsf{f}}; f' \vdash \\ \{P \wedge x = f\} \textbf{ enter } (x)\, \{\, \bar{s}_1 \textbf{ reenter } (y)\, \{\, \bar{s}_2\, \}\, \bar{s}_3\, \}\, \{Q\}\end{array}}$$

(under the assumption that P_{f}' does not care about any variables that $\bar{s}_2$ assigns to). The compensation pattern allows the commitment $f : P_{\mathsf{f}}$ to be replaced temporarily with the commitment $f : P_{\mathsf{f}}'$.

A machine-checked soundness proof of these proof rules is available online [12].

We developed a prototype verifier based on these ideas [12].

7 Implementation Issues

We created a prototype implementation of the approach on the .NET Framework as a C# 3.0 library. C# 3.0's lambda expression syntax can be used to write reasonably concise enter statements.

A major complication for achieving a fully correct implementation of the approach in the form of a library, is the fact that the .NET Framework Common Language Runtime may throw an exception at any program point, due to an internal resource limit being reached or an internal error being discovered within the execution engine [21]. (The same holds for the Java Virtual Machine. See the Java Virtual Machine Specification, Second Edition [14], Section 2.16.2.) Specifically, if an enter block completes abruptly with an exception, no internal exception must intervene between catching the exception and marking the failbox as failed; otherwise, the enter statement completes without marking the failbox as failed, breaking dependency safety.

Version 2.0 of the .NET Framework introduced constructs specifically for writing code that must execute reliably in the presence of internal exceptions [21]. We used these constructs in our prototype implementation to ensure that on abrupt completion of the body of an enter statement, the failbox and its descendants are marked as failed and stop signals are sent to other threads executing in the failbox or its descendants. Specifically, we used the following API:

$$ExecuteCodeWithGuaranteedCleanup(t, c, u)$$

where t and c are delegates (similar to function pointers in C) and u is arbitrary user data that is passed to t and c. The API first executes t. When t completes, either normally or abruptly, the cleanup delegate c is executed. The API guarantees that no internal exceptions occur during the execution of c, provided that c satisfies certain constraints, such as: no heap memory allocation, and no unbounded call stack memory allocation. Unfortunately, these constraints have not been spelled out very precisely anywhere; we had to make some assumptions as to what can reasonably be executed without the risk of internal exceptions.

We have performed a few microbenchmark performance tests. These indicate the following approximate timings for the following statements:

Statement	Timing	Timing*
try {} catch {}	$13\mu s$	$1.9\mu s$
try { enter (f) {} } catch {}	$23\mu s$	$3.4\mu s$

To measure the impact of the *ExecuteCodeWithGuaranteedCleanup* construct, we replaced it with a dummy that uses a simple try-finally statement. The resulting timings are shown in the third column. It turns out that the overhead of this construct dominates the run time.

Even though the current performance is probably acceptable for most real-world applications, we believe it can still be improved significantly, in particular if the constructs are implemented directly in the virtual machine rather than as a library. Performing such an implementation is future work.

We have also prepared a prototype implementation of failboxes as a library on the Java virtual machine. However, due to the absence of constructs to prevent internal or asynchronous exceptions on this platform, the implementation is not safe in the presence of such exceptions.

The prototype implementations are available on line [12].

8   Related Work

To the best of our knowledge, failboxes are the first approach for programmers to achieve dependency safety of their Java-like programs that combines low programming overhead, low performance overhead, and low reasoning overhead, and is compositional (i.e. failboxes can be nested arbitrarily).

Languages as operating systems. Many extensions of Java have been proposed that support running multiple programs or *tasks* in the same virtual machine. These can typically be used to enforce dependency safety. However, in contrast to failboxes, all of these have goals beyond dependency safety, typically including protection against malicious code, and accounting of memory and other resources. As a result, they impose greater programming and performance overhead on communication between tasks than the overhead of switching between failboxes.

Perhaps the most closely related such system is Luna [11]. To support memory accounting and immediate guaranteed memory reclamation when a task is killed, the heap is logically partitioned among the tasks; the only way for one task to access an object belonging to another task is through a *remote pointer*, which is distinguished from local pointers through its type. When a task is killed, remote pointers pointing into it are *revoked*, so that if the task was holding a lock, other tasks do not see inconsistent state. Failboxes offer no memory accounting or guaranteed memory reclamation, but in turn impose a lower programming and performance overhead. Specifically, passing data across tasks requires either copying or the use of remote pointers, both of which incur a programming and performance overhead; failboxes, in contrast, allow data to be passed around freely.

DrScheme [8, 7] is a Scheme environment designed for programs that serve as platforms for other programs. In DrScheme, it is possible for two child programs to share a mutable data structure and yet be killed independently. The solution is to host the data structure in a separate thread, and to access it only via message passing with this thread. DrScheme's contribution is that it enables two untrusted child programs to set up such a shared data structure without circumventing resource policies and without the need for the shared structure to be trusted by the kernel. However, from a dependency safety point of view, the situation is as in Java: DrScheme requires either the use of message passing between separate threads or manually guarding dependent code.

Erlang [1] is a language focused on reliability. Inconsistent data structures within a process are ruled out because the language has no destructive update. Processes communicate through asynchronous message passing. Fail-fast is achieved by linking processes: when a process dies, an exit signal is sent to linked processes, causing those to die as well by default.

Non-compositional approaches. Marlow et al. [16] propose an extension of concurrent Haskell with constructs that make it possible to write safe programs where one thread throws an asynchronous exception in another thread. The block e construct disables asynchronous exceptions during execution of e; e can use unblock e' to re-enable them during execution of a sub-expression e'. Unlike failboxes, the block construct is not compositional; for example, in the program of Figure 4, the *addEntry* call could be protected against cancellation of jobs using block; however, imagine the command processing program is part of a larger system. Then one may want to cancel the program as a whole, including any *addEntry* calls. This is possible with failboxes (by cancelling failbox f, which cancels its descendants as well), but not with the block construct. Also, the construct does not help in dealing with failures; for example, a failure during the *addEntry* call would not prevent further accesses to the database. However, the block construct, or something similar, is useful and even necessary to be able to robustly implement failboxes as a library in a given language.

Starting with version 2, the .NET Framework includes reliability features that make it possible to write cleanup routines that are guaranteed to execute even in the presence of failure or cancellation [21]. However, like the block construct, the approach is not compositional: these cleanup routines cannot be cancelled; furthermore, they must be carefully coded to rule out failures within the cleanup routines themselves since those are not dealt with safely. The mechanism is intended only for manipulation of execution environment resources; it is not for general application use.

Three further reliability-related features in .NET Framework version 2 are the following. Firstly, cancellation is disabled during finally blocks. This enables safe cleanup in the presence of cancellation (but not failure). Secondly, an unhandled exception in one thread kills all other threads, without executing catch or finally blocks. However, in the thread that throws the unhandled exception, finally blocks are executed normally and locks are released, leaving a time window between the release of the lock and the time the exception reaches the toplevel (possibly after executing other finally blocks) where other threads can see inconsistent state. Thirdly, a method *Environment.FailFast* was added, which terminates the program immediately.

Rudys et al. [18] propose weaving code into an untrusted plugin (such as an applet) that polls a cancellation request flag to enable forcibly cancelling the plugin. The flag is also checked whenever the host system calls into the plugin. In our approach, a thread running in one failbox may protect itself from cancellation of its failbox by entering an ancestor failbox to which it has a reference; however, separate techniques (e.g., perhaps by associating permissions with failboxes) could be used to prevent this in case the thread is running untrusted code.

The SCOOP multithreading approach for Eiffel [17] has a notion of *subsystems*. A subsystem in SCOOP is a thread and a set of objects handled by that thread. Brooke and Paige [3] suggest marking an object as "dead" when the processing of an asynchronous incoming call fails, causing subsequent calls to fail immediately. SCOOP subsystems cannot be nested.

Other related work. Garcia et al. [9] provide a survey of exception mechanisms. However, the authors do not discuss the dependency safety issue. In fact, most modern imperative and/or object-oriented languages have inherited the exception mechanism of CLU [15] and therefore suffer from the problems addressed by our approach.

Class-handlers, as proposed by Dony [4] and others, are exception handlers associated with classes rather than blocks of statements; they apply to all methods of the class. They would facilitate manually guarding dependent code. For example, a class-handler on the *Database* class could set a *failed* field to *true* when an unchecked exception is caught and then re-throw the exception. The field would still need to be checked manually on entry to each method.

Weimer and Necula [22] propose *compensation stacks* to make it easier to write effective cleanup code. However, they do not address the safety issues identified in Section 5.

Fetzer et al. [5] assume the viewpoint that "exception handling is only effective if the premature termination of a method due to an exception does not leave an object in an inconsistent state". The paper proposes techniques to detect and "mask" *non-atomic exception handling*, i.e. violations against *failure atomicity*. The paper assumes that after catching an exception, the entire application should be in a consistent state, whereas we allow *failed failboxes* to remain in an inconsistent state, while preventing control from entering a failed failbox. The authors find a large number of Java methods that are not failure atomic. This would strengthen the case for failboxes, because it indicates that exceptions do indeed commonly leave objects in an inconsistent state.

An alternative way to deal with failures is to roll the state of the objects involved back to a consistent state, through the use of transactions (e.g. Shavit and Touitou [19], Welc et al. [23], Fetzer et al. [5]). However, this has a greater performance overhead; also, it presents problems when the computation that failed performed I/O. Our failboxes approach is more conservative from a semantic and performance point of view.

This work was inspired by our research in program verification for Java-like languages that is sound in the presence of failures. To the best of our knowledge, no existing program verifiers for Java-like languages (including ESC/Java [6] and Spec# [2]) have this property. In Jacobs et al. [13], we propose a verification approach for Java programs where the programmer manually guards dependent code using flag variables that track an object's consistency. The present work addresses the programming overhead of that approach.

9   Conclusion

We propose a language extension, called *failboxes*, that facilitates writing sequential or multithreaded programs that provably preserve intended safety properties and that do not leak resources, even in the presence of failure, and that perform safe cancellation of computations. To the best of our knowledge, it is the first such extension of a Java-like language that combines low programming, performance, and reasoning overhead, and that is compositional.

Future work includes gaining experience with our prototype implementation, mainly to assess the applicability and the usability of the approach. We anticipate the possible need to facilitate the placement of enter blocks, perhaps through annotations on methods, classes, or packages, or through some inference scheme.

Other work includes applying the failboxes idea to the problem of exception handling in asynchronous and callback patterns.

Acknowledgements

The authors would like to thank Jan Smans, Marko van Dooren, Scott Owens, and the Cambridge programming languages group for their helpful comments. This research is partially funded by the Interuniversity Attraction Poles Programme Belgian State, Belgian Science Policy.

References

[1] Armstrong, J.: Making reliable distributed systems in the presence of software errors. PhD thesis, Royal Institute of Technology, Stockholm, Sweden (2003)

[2] Barnett, M., Chang, B.-Y.E., DeLine, R., Jacobs, B., Leino, K.R.M.: Boogie: A modular reusable verifier for object-oriented programs. In: de Boer, F.S., Bonsangue, M.M., Graf, S., de Roever, W.-P. (eds.) FMCO 2005. LNCS, vol. 4111, pp. 364–387. Springer, Heidelberg (2006)

[3] Brooke, P.J., Paige, R.F.: Exceptions in Concurrent Eiffel. Journal of Object Technology 6(10), 111–126 (2007)

[4] Dony, C.: Exception handling and object-oriented programming: a synthesis. In: Proc. OOPSLA (1990)

[5] Fetzer, C., Högstedt, K., Felber, P.: Automatic detection and masking of non-atomic exception handling. In: Proc. Intl. Conf. Dependable Systems and Networks (DSN) (2003)

[6] Flanagan, C., Leino, K.R.M., Lillibridge, M., Nelson, G., Saxe, J.B., Stata, R.: Extended static checking for Java. In: Proc. PLDI, pp. 234–245 (2002)

[7] Flatt, M., Findler, R.B.: Kill-safe synchronization abstractions. In: Proc. PLDI (2004)

[8] Flatt, M., Findler, R.B., Krishnamurthi, S., Felleisen, M.: Programming languages as operating systems (or Revenge of the son of the Lisp machine). In: Proc. Intl. Conf. on Functional Programming (ICFP) (1999)

[9] Garcia, A.F., Rubira, C.M.F., Romanovsky, A.B., Xu, J.: A comparative study of exception handling mechanisms for building dependable object-oriented software. Journal of Systems and Software 59(2), 197–222 (2001)

[10] Gosling, J., Joy, B., Steele, G., Bracha, G.: The Java Language Specification, 3rd edn. Prentice Hall PTR, Englewood Cliffs (2005)

[11] Hawblitzel, C., von Eicken, T.: Luna: a flexible Java protection system. In: Proc. OSDI (2002)

[12] Jacobs, B., Piessens, F.: Failboxes: Prototype implementations, prototype verifier, machine-checked metatheory (July 2008), http://www.cs.kuleuven.be/~bartj/failboxes

[13] Jacobs, B., Müller, P., Piessens, F.: Sound reasoning about unchecked exceptions. In: Proc. ICFEM (2007)

[14] Lindholm, T., Yellin, F.: The Java Virtual Machine Specification, 2nd edn. Addison-Wesley, Reading (1999), http://java.sun.com/docs/books/jvms/

[15] Liskov, B., Snyder, A.: Exception handling in CLU. IEEE Trans. Software Eng. 5(6), 546–558 (1979)

[16] Marlow, S., Jones, S.P., Moran, A., Reppy, J.: Asynchronous exceptions in Haskell. In: Proc. PLDI (2001)
[17] Meyer, B.: Eiffel: The Language. Prentice-Hall, Englewood Cliffs (1992)
[18] Rudys, A., Clements, J., Wallach, D.S.: Termination in language-based systems. In: Network and Distributed System Security Symposium (NDSS) (February 2001)
[19] Shavit, N., Touitou, D.: Software transactional memory. In: Proc. PODC, pp. 204–213 (1995)
[20] Shore, J.: Fail fast. IEEE Software (September 2004)
[21] Toub, S.: Keep your code running with the reliability features of the .NET Framework. MSDN Magazine (October 2005)
[22] Weimer, W., Necula, G.C.: Finding and preventing run-time error handling mistakes. In: Proc. OOPSLA, pp. 419–431 (October 2004)
[23] Welc, A., Jagannathan, S., Hosking, A.L.: Transactional monitors for concurrent objects. In: Odersky, M. (ed.) ECOOP 2004. LNCS, vol. 3086, pp. 518–541. Springer, Heidelberg (2004)

Are We Ready for a Safer Construction Environment?

Joseph (Yossi) Gil[1,2] and Tali Shragai[2]

[1] Google, Inc.
[2] The Technion

"Unfortunately, the mainstream languages C# *and* Java *give access to the object being constructed (through this) while construction is ongoing."*
Fähndrich and Leino [12]

Abstract. The semantics of many OO languages dictates that the constructor of a derived class is a refining extension of one of the base classs constructors. As this base constructor runs, it may invoke dynamically bound methods which are overridden in the derived class. These invocations receive an "half baked object", i.e., an object whose derived class portion is uninitialized. Such a situation may lead to confusing semantics and to hidden coupling between the base and the derived. Dynamic binding within constructors also makes it difficult to enhance the programming language with advanced mechanisms for expressing design intent, such as *non-null annotation* (denoting reference values which can never be null), *read-only annotation* for fields and variables (expressing the intention that these cannot be modified after they are completely created) and *class invariants* (part of the famous design by contract methodology). A read-only field for example becomes immutable only after the creation of the enclosing object is complete.

We investigate the current programming practice in JAVA of calling dynamically bound methods. In a data set comprising a dozen software collections with over sixty thousand classes, we found that although the potential for such a situation is non-negligible (prevalence > 8%), i.e., there are many constructors that make calls to methods which *may* be overridden in derived classes, actual such dynamic binding is scarce, found in less than 1.5% of all constructors, inheriting from less than 0.5% of all constructors. Further, we find that over 80% of these incidents fall into eight "patterns", which can be relatively easily transformed into equivalent code which refrains from premature method invocation.

A similar predicament occurs when a constructor exposes the self identity to external code, which then invokes methods overridden in the derived class. Our estimate on the prevalence of this exposition is less accurate due to the complexity of interprocedural dataflow analysis. Although the estimate is high, there are indications that it arises from a relatively small number of base constructors.

1 Introduction

Women who have given birth can testify that the process is not infinitesimally short. Objects are no different than babies in this respect: it takes time to mature a raw memory block into a live object, and during that time computation may occur.

Consider a class D which inherits from a class B. Then, in most OO languages the construction of a D-object is what we call a *refinement* of the construction of a B object, in that the body of any constructor of D is executed only after an explicit or implicit

S. Drossopoulou (Ed.): ECOOP 2009, LNCS 5653, pp. 495–519, 2009.

invocation of one of the constructors of B. [1] What is the status of the D object in the course of this invocation? On one hand, this object cannot be thought of as a mature, ordinary object of class D, since D's constructor was not invoked yet. On the other hand, thinking of the object as an instance of class B, may lead to surprising results, e.g., in the case that B is an abstract class. Concretely, suppose that B's constructor invokes a dynamically bound member function implemented in both B and D. The dominating *thesis*, taken by languages such as JAVA [1] and C$^\#$ [15], is that of *dynamic binding* within constructors, i.e., D's implementation is executed. The *anti-thesis* of *static binding*, taken in languages such as C++ [26], dictates that B's implementation is executed.

This research sets its objective in understanding how such "half-baked" objects are used in actual programs. Our research method is primarily *empirical*: Following the tradition of works such as [5, 6, 2, 10] we apply static analysis techniques combined with manual inspection to a large software data set. The interest in the study is raised by the inherent limitations of both the dynamic- and the static- binding approaches. We briefly describe here a *synthesis* of the approaches which addresses these limitations. But before this or any other new, competing proposal, can be considered, it must be evaluated against the common programming practice which this research tries to discover.

1.1 The Static vs. the Dynamic Binding Semantics within Constructors

Object creation can be divided into three conceptual stages: *(i)* memory allocation, *(ii)* preliminary field initialization, and *(iii)* establishing invariants. Allocation is often automatic, especially in languages with memory management. Preliminary initialization also depends on the language model (vacuous in C++, as opposed to default zero initialization in Java), and is not very interesting. What we are interested in here is the final stage, that of establishing invariants, which often involves some computation. This final stage is realized by the user-defined constructor. This section serves as a brief reminder of the distinction, in the context of constructors, between static- and dynamic-binding semantics and its consequences.

Somewhat paradoxically, the static binding approach of C++ may compromise static type safety, as demonstrated in Fig. 1. In the figure, we see an abstract class `Shape` containing an abstract ("pure virtual" in the C++ jargon) function `draw` (Line 2) which is then realized (Line 7) in the inheriting concrete class `Circle`. Instantiating `Circle` here results in a runtime error: `Circle`'s constructor implicitly invokes the default constructor of `Shape`, which in turn, as a consequence of the static binding semantics of C++, invokes the pure virtual function `Shape::draw`. [2] Clever compilers (GCC [25] is a case in point) may detect and warn the programmer against this particular case in which the call to a pure virtual function from within the constructor is so obvious. The general case, which may involve a chain of aliases and virtual function calls is intractable [13].

---

[1] It could be the case that this constructor of B invokes yet another constructor of B, which may invoke yet another constructor B, or of a parent of B, in which case we say that the constructor of D refines all of these constructors.

[2] More precisely, the C++ semantics attributes this error to the attempt to dynamically invoke a pure virtual function, rather than to the fact that this function has no body; for various reasons, C++ allows defining pure-virtual functions with body, but the runtime error would have occurred *even* if `Shape::draw` had body!

The C++ design choice of static binding semantics within constructors is probably due to the language defines no default initial value of data members. In languages with such a default value, the dynamic binding approach makes sense: an object is in some defined state even prior to actual invocation of the construction. The JAVA equivalent of Fig. 1 behaves as follows when an instance of `Circle` is created: first the constructor of `Shape` is invoked, which then invokes the `Circle`'s version of `draw`; then the constructor of `Circle` is completed.

The difficulty with this approach is that with modern software architectures, the predefined state, i.e., `null` in all reference fields, 0 in numerical fields, etc., is too degenerate to be useful. In our little example, it is not clear that a circle can be drawn before the constructor of this class has set crucial data such as location and radius. More generally, this predefined state contradicts non-null promises, `final` guarantees, etc.

Dynamic binding in constructors means that methods may be called prematurely. When this happens, methods are restricted since they cannot rely on any of the fields of the derived class for being properly initialized, and in general should be ready to deal with an object whose invariant was not fully established. The working of the constructor is complicated by its coupling with dynamically bound methods. The fact that the constructor is a method called precisely once for each object, whereas other methods may be invoked any number of times may add to the complexity.

```
1 class Shape { public: Shape() { draw(); }
2                public: virtual void draw() = 0;
3 };

5 class Circle: public Shape {
6     public: Circle() { cout << "Circle::Circle()\n"; }
7     public: void draw() { cout << "Circle::draw()\n";
    }
8 };
```

Fig. 1. Pure virtual function call in C++

Fig. 2 demonstrates the confusing situation of a prematurely called method in actual industrial code. In the figure we see (parts of) class `Compiler`, drawn from package `org.eclipse.jdt.internal.compiler` of the Eclipse JDT. Note that the last statement of the constructor of this class, calls function `initializeParser`, which as its name indicates, is in charge of initializing instance variable `parser`.

Consider now the implementation of the derived class `CodeSnippetCompiler`, as depicted in Fig. 3. We see in the figure (lines 3–6) that this class overrides function `initilializeParser`, specializing the `parser` field with a parser suitable for parsing code

```
1 public class Compiler {
2     public Parser parser;
3     public void initializeParser() {
4         this.parser = ...;
5     }
6     public Compiler ( ...constructor's arguments omitted for brevity ... ) {
7         // create a problem handler given a handling policy
8         this.options = new CompilerOptions(settings);
9         //...
10        initializeParser(); // call to a non−final function
11    }
12 }
```

Fig. 2. A base class invoking a polymorphic function

```
 1 public class CodeSnippetCompiler extends Compiler {
 2   public void initializeParser() {
 3     this.parser = new CodeSnippetParser(
 4        this.problemReporter, this.evaluationContext,
 5        this.options.parseLiteralExpressionsAsConstants,
 6        this.codeSnippetStart, this.codeSnippetEnd);
 7   }
 8   EvaluationContext evaluationContext;
 9   int codeSnippetStart, codeSnippetEnd;

11   public CodeSnippetCompiler( ...initial arguments omitted for brevity ...
12        EvaluationContext evaluationContext,
13        int codeSnippetStart, int codeSnippetEnd
14   ) {
15        super(environment, policy, settings, requestor, problemFactory);
16        this.parser = new CodeSnippetParser(
17             this.problemReporter, evaluationContext,
18             this.options.parseLiteralExpressionsAsConstants,
19             codeSnippetStart, codeSnippetEnd);
20        this.parseThreshold = 1;
21   }
22 }
```

Fig. 3. A derived class overriding a function called from the base constructor

snippets. Three data members are passed to the constructor of of CodeSnippetParser in the overridden version initilializeParser. These are: evaluationContext, codeSnippetStart and codeSnippetEnd (defined in lines 8–9).

The constructor of this class starts by calling the base constructor in Line 15. This refined base constructor calls the overridden version of initializeParser(), but this function cannot complete its mission correctly, since the three data members it relies on belong to the derived class and could not have been initialized yet.

In fact, we see that the constructor of CodeSnippetCompiler repeats (lines 16–19) the body of function initializeParser (that is lines 3–6), immediately after the call to the refined constructor. The fact that the constructor of CodeSnippetCompiler forgets to initialize the three said data members, even though it receives the values for these from its arguments is probably an indication that the code was corrected after it was discovered that the language does not support the design behind Compiler.

The "bad smell" code in figures 2 and other bugs (e.g., a call to an abstract function to retrieve a member value—omitted from this excerpt) we found in our study show that the dynamic binding is confusing. The fact that JAVA forbids making a call to a member function when refining a base constructor or in delegating to another constructor of the same class[3] is also an indication that a call to an overridden function was not intended to be allowed.

But, beyond the confusing semantics, and arguably more importantly, the dynamic binding approach makes it difficult to introduce notions such as non-null [12, 6, 20], immutability (e.g.,JAVARI [3, 28] and JAC [18]) and class invariant [22, 19] guarantees into the language. Such guarantees are typically achieved by the constructor. But,

---

[3] that is, the code **class D extends** B { D() {**super**(f()); }} is illegal if f is a function member of either B or D

the possibility of methods being executed before the constructor even begun, makes it impossible to rely on these guarantees. This is the reason that much of this work introduces non-standard types and annotations to deal with half-baked objects, e.g., Fähndrich and Leino introduce [Raw] methods types [12] and Zibin and colleagues @AssignsFields annotations [30].

1.2 Hardhat Constructors and Destructors

Problems of this sort may occur not only when the constructor calls, directly or indirectly, methods overridden in the derived class. It could also be the case that the constructor reveals **this** to code external to the class, either by passing it as a parameter to an external function, or by storing it in an externally accessible field, making it possible to invoke overridden methods before construction is complete. Detecting cases of this sort could be difficult, especially in a multithreaded execution environment.

A similar problem occurs in C++ which imposes a refining semantics on destructors: a class destructor implicitly invokes the destructor of the parent class after its body completed execution. Runtime errors due to a call to a pure virtual function may thus occur in the course of a destructor's execution. The situation is exacerbated by the fact that destructors are typically called implicitly, e.g., as part of stack unrolling due to exception handling.

A natural and appealing resolution of the dilemma in choosing between the static and dynamic approaches is in a *synthesis* which *forbids* the processes of object creation and destruction from making any computation in which there is a difference between the two binding semantics. (An interesting alternative is offered by EIFFEL [16] in which the creation of a derived class does not involve a creation of a subobject of the base class.) We propose a language model enforcing constructors and destructors in which no polymorphic calls could be made, what we call *hardhat* execution. Thus, in this model, the premature call to draw in Fig. 1 is simply signalled by the compiler. The advantages should be clear:

1. *Type Safety.* The hardhat semantics avoids the type safety problem of the static binding approach.
2. *Reduced Coupling with Base Classes.* A method defined in a class D can be certain that it receives a D object (more precisely, an object for which a constructor of D has at least begun its operation, or that the destructor of D has not finished its execution.). This reduces and simplifies the dynamic binding's typical coupling between the class and its base, and makes the analysis of multithreaded programs a bit easier.
3. *Crisp Boundary Between Initialization and Use.* Hardhat constructors are consistent with the OO thinking by which objects are created and only then used. The predicaments of a prematurely called method are avoided: a method should not be aware of the fact that it may be called from a constructor of a base class, and the analysis of multithreaded programs become
4. *Simplified Language Extensions.* With hardhat constructors the introduction of non-nullity, immutability and invariant statement is simplified. (The problem in introducing these is not completely solved, since one still has to address the problem of a method being called from a constructor of the class itself).

This paper is concerned mostly with the *cost* to be paid in introducing hardhat constructors into languages such as JAVA. Towards this end, we try to estimate the prevalence of constructors which deviate from the hardhat model in existing code, and to characterize the use of dynamic binding within constructors.

Our search for transgressing constructors in actual code relies on the following definition of hardhat execution:

> A *constructor is* hardhat *if it is both* monomorphic *(that is, it does not make any chain of of* this *method calls which raises the binding question) and* modest *(that is, it does not expose the* this *reference by storing it in a variable or passing it as an explicit parameter).*

The auxiliary notions of monomorphism and modesty are explained in greater detail below, but the intuition should be clear: The examples set in Fig. 1 and in Fig. 2 and Fig. 3 demonstrate cases of polymorphic behavior during construction. To see why we would like constructors to be "modest", consider for example the standard JAVA class Thread, depicted in part in Fig. 4.

```
1 public class Thread {
2    public Thread() {
3       init(null, null, "Thread-" + nextThreadNum(), 0);
4    }
5    private void init(ThreadGroup g, Runnable t, String n, long s) {
6       //...
7       setPriority(priority);
8       //...
9    }
10   public final void setPriority(int newPriority) {
11      checkAccess();
12      //...
13   }
14   public final void checkAccess() {
15      SecurityManager security = System.getSecurityManager();
16      if (security != null)
17         security.checkAccess(this);
18      //...
19   }
20   //...
21 }
```

Fig. 4. A constructor revealing a self reference

The no-arguments constructor invokes function init, which invokes setPriority which then invokes function checkAccess. This calls' chain poses no polymorphic construction risk, since all functions in the chain are either final or private. But, further inspection may be more difficult, since the runtime type of variable security is unknown: function checkAccess() delegates (Line 17) part of its mission to an external class through the security.checkAccess(this) call. The implementation of checkAccess in class SecurityManager may choose to invoke methods on the passed parameter. If the invoked methods are overridden in descendants of Thread, then they these may be surprised to find that their receiver is an incomplete object.

To make constructors hardhat, we need to make a concrete language definition forbidding both polymorphic calls and identity exposition from within construction. There is a variety of ways in which such concretization can be made: A naïve, and probably too restrictive, approach is to disallow any function calls from within constructors. A more permissive alternative is to allow constructors to invoke only `final` methods which are also *anonymous*, where anonymous methods are defined by Bokowski and Vitek's constraints [4]:

$\mathcal{A}1$ *"The reference* `this` *can only be used for accessing fields and calling anonymous methods of the current instance."*

$\mathcal{A}2$ *"Anonymity declarations must be preserved when overriding methods."*

$\mathcal{A}3$ *"The constructor called from an anonymous constructor must be anonymous as well."*

$\mathcal{A}4$ *"Native methods must not be declared anonymous."*

An amalgam of the two extremes is in e.g., introducing of a new method tag `init` (which could be realized as an annotation for example) which is to be used for a complete separation of the construction process from the invocation of methods on a constructed object. The requirements are then that *(i)* `init` methods are called only by constructors and other `init` methods; *(ii)* constructors and `init` cannot call non-`init` methods; *(iii)* `init` methods cannot be overridden; and *(iv)* `init` are anonymous in the Bokowski-Vitek sense. Or, one may also consider replacing requirement *(iii)* by the demand that `init` methods "semi-static methods" (sometimes called *raw* in the literature), i.e., methods which are bound dynamically yet are not allowed to access neither `this` nor any non-`static` fields or methods. (Obviously, in languages with destructors, there should also be methods tagged as `destruct`, with similar requirements. But, for simplicity, we shall henceforth concentrate in constructors.)

There is also an alternative perspective in which constraints are placed only on constructors which are invoked by constructors of a derived class; this requires a mechanism for denoting a constructor as "final", meaning that it cannot be refined in derived classes. The language design space is further enriched by the many other variants for providing the means that the self reference is not aliased: Bokowski and Vitek alone enumerate and compare six different methods of alias control, and the body of literature on aliasing and ownership (see e.g., a dedicated journal issue [23] or a survey in [29]) is still increasing at a staggering rate.

1.3 This Research

The evolution of programming language constructs tends to follow a three stage life cycle: (a) intuitive understanding, (b) language legalese and (c) formalization. This research begins from the premise that such concrete language definitions and placement of restrictions on software designers require better understanding of how "half-baked" objects are actually used in practice; our primary focus is on this study. Issues of the actual language definition, and careful weighing of the relative merits of alternatives sketched above and their formalization are left to future work.

This choice of ours is guided by our belief that greater care should be exercised before introducing language constructs preventing self-aliasing in *all* constructors for example, than in adding e.g., confined types which do not pertain to all code.

Accordingly, two hypotheses were initially set out for examination: *(i)* constructors which are not hardhat in actual code are rarities, and *(ii)* most of these can be easily made safe. Verification of the first conjecture should make the notion of hardhat constructors a candidate worthy of inclusion in new languages. Verification of the second should help encourage changes in the semantics of current programming languages. Alternatively, the understanding of actual use of non-hardhat constructors in code should help to evaluate the price of placing the hardhat requirement in a new language on the customers..

Experiments were run in a software corpus comprising circa 75,000 JAVA user defined types featuring some 85,000 class constructors assembled from a dozen different collections drawn from a variety of application domains. Two principal kinds of measures are reported: First, our estimates on the *number of cases* of use of polymorphism and immodesty should help in appreciation of the penalty designers have to pay if safe constructors become in effect. A second kind of measure, should be indicative of the *amount of work* required to correct and eliminate such unsafe behavior from the code.

It is difficult in general to define the relative size of a code fragment in which a certain phenomena occurs. Cabral and Marques [5] relied on line counts for measuring the relative code size dedicated to exception handling. Unfortunately, such a number may be dependent on formatting style—the relative increase in line count due to a decision to locate curly brackets on a separate line is not the same in small and large counts. A better measure could be the number of tokens, but this number is still influenced by style. More stable is the number of classes, functions and constructors; fortunately, unlike the problem that Cabral and Marques [5] faced, this measure is suitable for our case. This is the reason that our estimates of "unsafe" behavior are both class- and constructor- based. We believe that both may be useful, and may be used together in appreciating the tendency of unsafe constructors to accumulate in the same class.

Our investigation here concentrates on the occurrence of polymorphic behavior in constructors. Nevertheless, we report quantitative data of immodest behavior in constructors and classes. As it turns out, our conservative estimates of the prevalence of these are high, which made the task of manual analysis of these more difficult.

Outline. The remainder of this article is organized as follows: Sec. 2 describes the software corpus used in our study. Sec. 3 presents our results on the prevalence of polymorphic behavior in constructors, while Sec. 4 describes the results of our manual analysis of a large portion of these cases. Our finding on immodest constructors is presented in Sec. 5. Sec. 6 concludes.

2   The Software Corpus

The software corpus used in our empirical study was assembled from the union of collections used in the empirical study of Chalin and James [6] and that of Gil and Maman [14]. We decided however to eliminate the *SoenEA* project from the ensemble of Chalin and James in the interest of reproducibility—an official web page describing the project could not be found. The impacts of this omission should be negligible since this collection is relatively small (52 classes).

Overall, the corpus comprises twelve collections of JAVA code, all of which are freely available on the web at least in binary form: *JRE 1.6.0_01* [4] (used in almost all empirical studies of JAVA, e.g., [14, 8, 21, 2]); although naturally, each such experiment uses a different version of the library); *JBoss 3.2.6* [5] (circa 1,000 packages of sources were not available); *Eclipse 3.0.1* [6] (note that Eclipse was used in the empirical study of Chalin and James [6], although, in contrast with their work which examined just the JDT core, circa 1130 classes, we used the entire Eclipse implementation); *Poseidon 2.5.1 community edition* [7] (sources of were not available, binaries were apparently obfuscated by an automatic tool); *Tomcat 5.0.28* [8]; *Scala 1.3.0.4* Just like Poseidon, sources of the SCALA [24] distribution were largely unavailable, but this is because the compiler itself is written in SCALA; *JML 5.5* (a set of software tools used for the implementation of the JAVA Modeling Language [19]); *ANT 1.6.2*[9]; *MJC 1.3* (MultiJAVA is a JAVA language extension [7] which adds open classes and symmetric multiple dispatch to the language; MJC is multiJAVA the compiler); *JEdit 4.2*; *ESC 2.0b2* (the Extended Static Checker programming tool that tries to check some of JML assertions through static analysis); and *Koa* [10] (the Koa Tallying subsystem is a Dutch Internet voting application).

Tab. 2 summarizes the size properties of the software collections comprising our corpus. Overall, we have more than 75,000 user defined types organized in some 3,500 packages. We also see that the total number of constructors is greater than 85,000 and that there are a total of more than 66,000 classes.

Examining the table we see that the software collections vary in size: the largest collection is JBoss with close to 16,000 classes, while the smallest has less than forty (the median size is 3,000 classes). We can also see that the majority of the code in our corpus is drawn from three large collec-

Table 1. Size statistics of the twelve collections in the corpus

Collection	Packages	Types	Classes	Interfaces	Constructors	Avg. No. of Constructors
JBOSS	997	18,697	15,786	2,911	22,089	1.40
JRE	740	16,816	14,603	2,034	20,388	1.39
ECLIPSE	587	16,049	14,232	1,817	15,840	1.11
POSEIDON	593	10,045	8,686	1,359	11,078	1.28
TOMCAT	280	4,335	3,756	579	5,198	1.38
SCALA	96	3,379	2,754	625	3,144	1.14
JML	67	2,316	2,127	189	2,938	1.38
ANT	120	1,968	1,611	357	2,015	1.25
MJC	41	1,140	1,025	115	1,436	1.40
JEDIT	23	805	776	29	895	1.15
ESC	35	643	632	11	713	1.13
KOA	2	37	36	1	38	1.06
Total	3,581	76,230	66,024	10,027	85,772	1.30
Median	108	2,847	2,440	468	3,041	1.26

tions: JRE, JBoss and Eclipse, which are of relatively the same size. The other collections are smaller.

The constructor count was produced by a binary analysis of the bytecode representation of the software. (In general, all automatic analysis reported in this work was done on this representation. We turned to the source for manual inspection as necessary and as described below.) In this representation, with the exception of interfaces, all classes

---

[4] http://download.java.net/jdk6

[5] http://www.jboss.org

[6] http://www.eclipse.org

[7] http://www.gentleware.com

[8] http://jakarta.apache.org

[9] http://ant.apache.org

[10] http://sort.ucd.ie

have at least one constructor, since a default, no-arguments constructor is generated by the compiler for every class that has no programmer defined constructors.

Note that the number of constructors is close to the number of classes, but the numbers are not the same: a class has on average 1.3 constructors. This does not necessarily mean that the relative number of constructors in which half-baked objects are used is the same as the relative number of classes in which such objects are used.

As reported previously [14], there are inevitably duplications in the corpus: certain classes occur more than once in the different collections. These repetitions are often due to different versions of the same software base. There were even a few cases in which the same class occurred more than once in the same collections. Nevertheless, repetitions were not too frequent (less than 10%) and since we are trying to determine the prevalence of a rather rare phenomena, the error in not eliminating these is small.

Tab. 2 shows how many base classes and how many "base constructors" were found in the collections in the software corpus. That is to say, counts of the actual number of classes that have subclasses in each of the collections, and the number of constructors in those classes.

Table 2. Base classes and constructors in the corpus

Collection	Internal		External		Total	
	Classes	Ctor's	Classes	Ctor's	Classes	Ctor's
JBOSS	1,809	2,857	180	469	1,989	3,326
JRE	2,212	3,583	0	0	2,212	3,583
ECLIPSE	1,537	1,952	61	143	1,598	2,095
POSEIDON	1,140	1,714	308	689	1,448	2,403
TOMCAT	543	819	71	185	614	1,004
SCALA	350	428	81	251	431	679
JML	391	578	70	211	461	789
ANT	230	328	39	102	269	430
MJC	149	233	63	195	212	428
JEDIT	41	66	71	223	112	289
ESC	106	126	31	91	137	217
KOA	2	2	13	39	15	41
Total	8,510	12,686	988	2,598	9,498	15,284
Median	370.5	503	66.5	190	446	734

The three column groups in the table demonstrate an interesting experimental difficulty, raised in its full gravity by this study. As might be expected, other than the JRE, software collections are not self contained: inevitably, there are classes in each such collection which inherit from classes found in other libraries (most often the JRE). The interaction between constructors of base classes found in one library with constructors of derived classes found in another library may makes reasoning a bit more difficult.

As suggested by the table, our analysis considers also "external base classes". In most collections, the majority of base classes are internal. In JEDIT and in KOA however, most base classes are external: JEDIT is a typical GUI application, with many of its classes inheriting from the GUI classes of the JRE. KOA also relies on GUI and XML processing services of the JRE, inheriting from the appropriate classes. We see that in JEDIT the number of external bases is disproportionally large; in KOA, the number of external base constructors is much greater than internal base constructors. This however does not happen in other collections, and the relative number of external constructors and external bases is typically small, with median and median value of the relative number of external bases, both constructors and classes, is in the 1%–3% range.

It is a fundamental property of JAVA that every non-final class (with at least one non-private constructor) may be subclassed. It is also fundamental that every such constructor may be refined. But, how many classes are subclassed in practice? How many constructors are actually refined? Theoretically, the minimal number of classes with no descendants and unrefined constructors is one. In practice, it can be inferred from Tab. 2

hat about 15% of internal constructors are constructors of base classes. The fraction of base constructors increases to about one in five if "external constructors" are included. Also, even if a collection is augmented with all bases, only about one in seven classes serves as a base for other classes.

The observation that even in large software collections most classes do not have descendants, and the majority of constructors are not refined guided our analysis and we have separate measurements of constructors with potentially for non-hardhat behavior and constructors in which this potential is realized.

Comparing the total number of external base classes (988) with the total number of constructors found in these classes (2,598), we find that the average number of constructors in these classes is 2.63, i.e., much greater that the 1.30 average over all classes (as can be computed in Tab. 2). If only internal base classes and base constructors are considered, the average is still high: 1.49. If all bases, internal and external, are considered together, then the average is 1.61. We conjecture that this phenomenon is explained by two properties of JAVA software (a) most classes are not intended to serve as bases (as argued above), and (b) classes with more constructors are more likely to serve as bases.

Applying the standard χ^2-test to compare the distribution of the number of constructors in classes with no children, and classes with children, supports claim (b). The test reveals a significant difference between the two distributions and that the fraction of classes with two constructors or more is significantly (99.99% confidence level) higher in classes which serve as bases.

3 Polymorphic Constructors

Having described the data set, we turn now to the description of the research method and results. This section is devoted to the study of the prevalence of *polymorphic constructors*. We say that a constructor is polymorphic if it may execute differently due to overriding, that is if there is a chain of method calls with this as the receiver, starting at the constructor which leads to a call to an overridden method.

In the following section we explain how such polymorphic behavior may be eliminated. We exclude from our attention here and in the next section cases in which the call to an overridden method occurs as a result of assigning this to a variable or passing it as a parameter, and then using this variable or parameter as a receiver. This kind of non-hardhat behavior is the subject of Sec. 5.

3.1 Definitions

As explained above, the polymorphic behavior during the construction process occurs while a derived constructor refines a base constructor. To capture the subtleties of this interaction we distinguish between three kinds of "polymorphic" constructors:

Polymorphic Pitfall Constructors. Recall that only one in seven classes have descendants, and that the majority of constructors are not refined at all. There are therefore many constructors that bear the potential for polymorphic behavior, but the polymorphic behavior may, or may not be manifested, depending on whether the enclosing class has any derived classes, and whether any of these derived classes overrides any of the potentially polymorphic methods invoked by the constructor.

We say that a constructor of a certain class is a *polymorphic pitfall* if it calls, directly or indirectly, a method of its class and of an ancestor class which *might* be overridden in a derived class, i.e., a method which is non-`final`, non-`static` and non-`private`. Determining whether a constructor is a polymorphic pitfall, does not require whole-world analysis; only the class itself and its ancestors must be inspected. In the example of Fig. 1, the constructor `Shape::Shape()` is a polymorphic pitfall.

Polymorphic Falls Constructors. The definition of polymorphic constructors puts the "blame" on the polymorphic behavior on the refined constructor, which by definition must be a polymorphic pitfall. Still, even though the fault occurs at the refined constructor; the problem is manifested only when the refining constructor is invoked. We therefore say that a constructor of a derived class is a *polymorphic fall* if it refines a polymorphic pitfall constructor, in such a way that the refined constructor makes a method call chain in which a message, which is bound to different methods in the base and in the derived classes, is sent to `this`. Again, determining whether a constructor is a *polymorphic fall* can be decided by inspecting its enclosing class and all its bases.

The constructor `Shape::Shape()` in Fig. 1 is not a polymorphic fall since it refines no other constructors. In contrast, the no-arguments constructor of the derived class, `Circle::Circle()` is a polymorphic fall since it refines the polymorphic constructor `Shape::Shape()` which calls method `draw` whose implementations in the base `Shape` and the derived `Circle` are different. The constructor of class `CodeSnippetCompiler` is likewise a polymorphic fall.

The case of `abstract` classes is somewhat special in that even if a constructor of such a class may demonstrate polymorphic behavior, we classify it as a pitfall, since this polymorphic behavior can only be realized if this constructor is refined.

With the above two definitions, we can give an alternative characterization of polymoprhic constructors: A *polymorphic constructor* is a polymorphic pitfall constructor for which we found one or more refining *polymorphic fall constructors*. Thus, the decision of whether a polymorphic fall constructor is indeed polymoprhic is relative to the code base.

3.2 Method

Our analysis was carried out first on the binary representation of the code, using the *Java Tools Language* (JTL) [9]—a declarative language for code analysis. JTL itself is implemented on top of the *Byte Code Engineering Library* (BCEL)[11], formerly known as *JavaClass*—a toolkit for static analysis and dynamic creation or transformation of JAVA class files. The analysis was then completed by manual inspection of the source.

The JTL code in Fig. 5 demonstrates how the search for polymorphic fall constructors was conducted. The unary predicate `polymorphic_fall_constructor_class` matches all classes which have a polymorphic fall constructor. A constructor of a base class which makes a call to a non-final non-static function, will thus be included in our report each time a derived class overrides this function.

---

[11] http://jakarta.apache.org/bcel/index.html

```
polymorphic_fall_constructor_class := !abstract class {
    exists constructor refines* C and infringes C;
};

refines* C := refines C | refines C' and C' refines* C;

refines C := invokespecial C, C constructor and
             declared_in T, C declared_in T', T extends T';

infringes C :=
             declared_in T, C internal_call* M, M overridden_in T;

internal_call* M := internal_call M
                  | internal_call* M', M' internal_call M;

internal_call M := declared_in T, invoke M, M declared_in T;

overridden_in T := T declares M, M overrides #;
```

Fig. 5. A JTL query for finding classes with polymorphic fall constructors

It is important to note that the search is conservative: predicate `refines` is supposed to match cases in which a constructor relies on a constructor of a base class to create its `this` parameter. The predicate, however, also captures cases in which a constructor of a base class is invoked for other purposes. Similarly, in tracing the chain of internal calls by predicates `internal_call*` and `internal_call`, no attempt is made to ensure that these are invoked on the implicit `this` parameter.

The analysis represented by Fig. 5 may therefore flag false positives, but it will not allow any polymorphic fall constructors to go undetected. In our manual inspection of 226 cases of polymorphic falls in constructors found in the JRE only 24 false positives were found, i.e., the accuracy of the analysis in this collection is about 90%. In 259 such cases inspected manually in the Eclipse collection, only one such false positive was found. We therefore estimate the accuracy of the algorithm as being at least 85%.

The JTL equivalent for finding polymorphic pitfalls is much simpler and is not provided here. Polymorphic classes were found by analyzing the report of constructor falls.

3.3 Findings

Tab. 3 shows the prevalence of polymorphic behavior in constructors in each of the collections in the software corpus.

The third column of the table tells us that in total, a polymorphic fall occurred in only 1,200 constructors, which constitute slightly less than 1.4% of the total of 85,772 constructors in the corpus. The variety among the different collections is not too large: in some collections no polymorphic construction behavior was found at all, and the maximum ratio of such constructors is 2.91%, achieved at JEDIT. The relatively high rate at this collection is explained by its heavy reliance and inheritance from GUI classes with polymorphic behavior.

In the second column of the table we see the number of constructors which caused these falls. In total, there were 390 such bad constructors, which make 0.45% of all constructors. The second column in the table also shows the fraction of polymorphic constructors from base constructors only. With 1.64% median value, even this fraction is small.

Table 3. Absolute and relative prevalence of polymorphic behavior in constructors (conservative analysis)

Collection	Polymorphic Constructors	Polymorphic Fall Constructors	Polymorphic Pitfall Constructors
JBOSS	70 (2.10%)	140 (0.63%)	1,570 (7.11%)
JRE	120 (3.35%)	396 (1.94%)	1,314 (6.44%)
ECLIPSE	86 (4.11%)	302 (1.91%)	1,671 (10.55%)
POSEIDON	55 (2.29%)	209 (1.89%)	1,281 (11.56%)
TOMCAT	12 (1.20%)	32 (0.62%)	335 (6.44%)
SCALA	9 (1.33%)	37 (1.18%)	259 (8.24%)
JML	25 (3.17%)	35 (1.19%)	260 (8.85%)
ANT	5 (1.16%)	10 (0.50%)	148 (7.34%)
MJC	7 (1.64%)	13 (0.91%)	141 (9.82%)
JEDIT	1 (0.35%)	26 (2.91%)	107 (11.96%)
ESC	0 (0.00%)	0 (0.00%)	27 (3.79%)
KOA	0 (0.00%)	0 (0.00%)	3 (7.89%)
Total	390 (2.55%)	1,200 (1.40%)	7,116 (8.30%)
Median	9 (1.48%)	32 (1.04%)	259 (8.07%)

Comparing the second and the third column we see that on average, every polymorphic pitfall is responsible to about three polymorphic falls..

The fourth column of the table gives the numbers of constructors (internals and externals combined) which are polymorphic pitfalls, that is may cause a polymorphic fall by descendants. We see that the numbers in this column are much higher, with median prevalence exceeding 8%.

Every polymorphic constructor is necessarily a polymorphic pitfall, so it is no wonder that the numbers in the fourth column are greater than those reported in the second. But, a striking conclusion can be drawn from comparing the relative values: the density of polymorphic constructors within base constructors is invariably smaller than the density of polymorphic pitfalls among all constructors. For example, in Eclipse, only about 4% of base constructors created a polymorphic fall, whereas more than 10% of all constructors in this collection have a polymorphic pitfall.

The fact that actual polymorphic behavior is smaller than what might be expected by the potential for it can be attributed to two, non-mutually exclusive, reasons:

1. *Few Descendants Conjecture.* Classes with polymorphic pitfall constructors are less likely to be extended
2. *Unrealized Potential Conjecture.* Potentially polymorphic constructors do not realize this potential in full during inheritance, because the potentially polymorphic methods invoked from a constructor of the base are not always overridden.

An experiment or measurement to verify the second conjecture is not simple. Our research continued to test the first explanation against the null hypothesis by which the occurrence of potentially polymorphic behavior within constructors does not change the probability of a class serving as a base.

Consider now Tab. 4 which is similar to Tab. 3 except that it revolves around classes instead of constructors. That is, in Tab. 4 we report on the number of classes whose constructors can be categorized according to the three varieties of polymorphic behavior.

Table 4. Prevalence of classes with polymorphic behavior in their constructors (conservative analysis)

Collection	Classes with Polymorphic Constructors		Classes with Polymorphic Fall Constructors		Classes with Polymorphic Pitfall Constructors	
JBOSS	44	(2.21%)	122	(0.77%)	1,192	(7.55%)
JRE	89	(4.02%)	262	(1.79%)	968	(6.63%)
ECLIPSE	67	(4.19%)	265	(1.86%)	1,498	(10.53%)
POSEIDON	43	(2.97%)	155	(1.78%)	1,119	(12.88%)
TOMCAT	9	(1.47%)	27	(0.72%)	256	(6.82%)
SCALA	9	(2.09%)	24	(0.87%)	236	(8.57%)
JML	18	(3.90%)	32	(1.50%)	199	(9.36%)
ANT	5	(1.86%)	10	(0.62%)	105	(6.52%)
MJC	7	(3.30%)	13	(1.27%)	124	(12.10%)
JEDIT	1	(0.89%)	18	(2.32%)	103	(13.27%)
ESC	0	(0.00%)	0	(0.00%)	24	(3.80%)
KOA	0	(0.00%)	0	(0.00%)	3	(8.33%)
Total	292	(3.07%)	928	(1.41%)	5,827	(8.83%)
Median	9	(2.15%)	24	(1.07%)	199	(8.45%)

Note again that the number of classes with polymorphic constructors is presented in the table as a fraction of the total number of base classes. The 292 such classes are however only 0.44% of the total of 66,024 classes of our corpus and only 0.38% of the 76,230 types in the corpus.

Also take note that each base class with a polymorphic constructor is, on average, "responsible" for three classes in which an actual polymorphic call occurs.

A comparison of the totals line in tables 3 and 4 shows that the relative prevalence of constructors and classes is quite similar. The prevalence of polymorphic, polymorphic falls and polymorphic pitfalls constructors is (respectively) 2.55%, 1.40%, and 8.30% whereas the corresponding numbers for classes in which this behavior is found are 3.07%, 1.41% and 8.83%. The similarity also occurs in the median line, and (to a lesser extent) in each of the prevalence values.

The similarity is a bit suspicious, since, as observed above (Sec. 2), classes which serve as bases tend to have more constructors. We should therefore have expected that base classes would be more prone to have at least one polymorphic constructor.

To better understand the situation, we applied a statistical test to check whether classes with polymorphic behavior in one of their constructors have the same number of descendants as other classes.

1. Classes with polymorphic pitfalls constructors tend to have **more** descendants than classes without such constructors.
2. Classes with polymorphic constructors have a **greater** number of descendants than other base classes.

Both results were found to be statistically significant (with confidence level of at least 99%) by a variant of the of the Mann-Whitney test for comparing ordinal non-normally distributed unpaired data sets. These findings indicate that the second conjecture is more likely to be true: polymorphic pitfalls are not realized as often as they can be during inheritance.

3.4 Summary

Our experimental findings in this corpus show that polymorphic constructors are rather rare—the prevalence of this phenomena is between 1% and 2%, depending on how the measurements are made. More precisely, we found that:

- About 98.6% of all constructors in the corpus do not have a polymorphic fall; also, about 98.6% of all classes do not have a polymorphic fall.
  The complement of this ratio is indicative of the total amount of work required to eliminate such falls.
- These polymorphic falls are caused by the 390 polymorphic constructors; 99.55% of all constructors are monomorphic; the ratio of classes with such behavior is similar.
  The complement of this ratio is indicative of the number of distinct cases to be considered if such falls are to be eliminated. On average each such case involves three descendant classes and four refining constructors.
- About 8% of all constructors are a polymorphic pitfall, that is, pose a risk to have descendants with polymorphic falls. Still, even though classes with polymorphic pitfall constructors tend to have more descendants, the fall is not realized in all of these descendants.

Recall that these conclusions are drawn based on a conservative code analyzer, whose errors are only false reports on polymorphic behavior. The true results are probably (slightly) better, in the sense that polymorphic behavior is scarcer than the above numbers indicate.

4 Patterns of Polymorphic Behavior in Constructors

In order to better understand the nature of polymorphic calls in the code base, we conducted a detailed manual inspection of 485 cases of polymorphic failures. A *case of polymorphic failure* is defined as a triple of (i) a constructor of a base class, (ii) a refining constructor of a derived class, and (iii) a method called by the base constructor with different implementation in the base and the derived class. 226 of these cases were drawn from the JRE; the remaining 259 cases were taken from Eclipse.

4.1 Polymorphic Solutions Patterns

Our manual inspection of the said cases revealed that the polymorphic behavior during construction appears in a relatively small number of patterns. We have identified those patterns and created a group of solutions targeted at each pattern: CONSTANT INITIALIZER, SEMI-CONSTANT INITIALIZER, INITIALIZER OBJECT, FUNCTION OBJECT, MULTIFUNCTION OBJECT, FACTORY and INLINE DATA.

Fig. 6 depicts the relationship between these patterns. An arrow from one such pattern to another indicates that the former generalizes the latter.

The most general pattern is MULTIFUNCTION OBJECT, while the most specific one is CONSTANT INITIALIZER. Patterns FUNCTION OBJECT and INITIALIZER OBJECT both generalize NON-CONSTANT INITIALIZER, while MULTIFUNCTION OBJECT generalizes and unifies the behavior both. FACTORY and INLINE DATA are isolates in the sense that they do not generalize, nor are being generalized by, any of the other patterns.

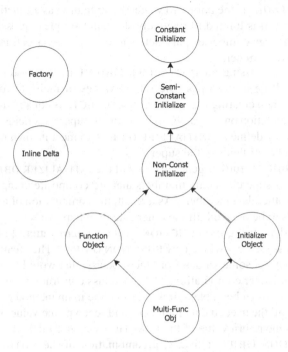

Fig. 6. Design patterns for devirtualization constructors

1. CONSTANT INITIALIZER: the most common type of virtual methods called inside a constructor are methods that return a constant value, or a static field, that is known in the subclass only, and needed by the superclass. Examples for this type of behavior may be found in some of the large inheritance star shaped topologies such as those rooted by JRE's `com.sun.jmx.snmp.Enumerated` and `com.sun.org.apache.xml.internal.security.utils.ElementProxy` and Eclipse's `org.eclipse.jdt.core.dom.ASTNode`.
   These virtual calls may be avoided by adding a parameter to the super constructor and passing the constant value or static data member in the call to `super(...)`.

2. SEMI-CONSTANT INITIALIZER: similarly to the previous case, a no-argument method invoked from a superclass constructor may return different newly created objects, depending on the subclass implementation. The overriding methods in each subtype contain a single `new` statement to create and return a new object of a type specific for each subclass. Furthermore, the constructor invocation uses no receiver fields.
   An alternative for this is implemented as done for the CONSTANT INITIALIZER, by making the `new SomeField(...)` expression a parameter of the `super()` call.

3. NON-CONSTANT INITIALIZER: a more general case requires the subclass to perform computation on its constructor arguments or static data members. As in the previous case, this is performed inside the overridden method, resulting in a value used for the superclass constructor.
   Such polymorphism can be resolved as in the previous pattern: the computation itself can be written as an argument in the call to `super(...)`, thus passing the computed value from the subclass to the superclass as a constructor parameter.

4. INITIALIZER OBJECT: the ability to write a computation as a function argument to the super(...) call is limited to relatively short and simple expressions. Additionally, passing a large number of parameters to the super(...) call may be inconvenient for the programmer.

   An alternative is passing an INITIALIZER OBJECT as the super(...) parameter. This object will be used to pass the setting values of multiple superclass fields. Additionally, when creating the INITIALIZER OBJECT, its constructor may perform any type of calculation on the values to be set in the superclass fields. In this manner, any subclass may define an INITIALIZER OBJECT to meet its own needs, and use it to set any number of fields in the superclass.

5. FUNCTION OBJECT: further generalization of the INITIALIZER OBJECT is targeted at the setting of superclass data members that are composite components, and are dependent on other data members. As a result, the computation of a dependent data member needs to be delayed till the other data members are set.

   This may be done using the FUNCTION OBJECT micro pattern [14]: the subclass would call for super(...) with a new FUNCTION OBJECT. The creation of the Function Object may set some values from the subclass, that would be used for the superclass data member computation. The superclass constructor will start by setting independent data members. Next, it will invoke the main method of the FUNCTION OBJECT, pass all the needed data members, and received the value of the composite component as the return value of the FUNCTION OBJECT method.

6. MULTIFUNCTION OBJECT: finally, a combination of the INITIALIZER OBJECT and the FUNCTION OBJECT can be implemented using a MULTIFUNCTION OBJECT. The MUTLIFUNCTION-FUNCTION OBJECT is different than the FUNCTION OBJECT because it externalizes more than just a single component initialization method, and thus may be used for the setting of all the superclass's data members, as done by the INITIALIZER OBJECT for the simpler data members (which are independent of other date members).

7. FACTORY: this solution is required when the construction process of the object may conceptually be divided into two phases. The Factory is an auxiliary wrapper class, which is responsible of creating and initializing objects of the superclass or the subclasses types, without the need for their constructors to be public. Having the construction wrapped by the Factory allows for the removal of polymorphic initialization methods from the base constructor, as the Factory itself will handle the second phase of the initialization.

8. INLINE DELTA: a derived class may refine a method invoked from its base class for the purpose of adding on to the superclass functionality with initialization of the derived class's own data members. This implies that the fields of the subclass are set during superclass construction, rather than during the construction of the derived class itself. This case follows a pattern of an overriding method starting by invoking the superclass's version, and then adding a delta of subclass-specific initialization. The solution for this type of polymorphic call is simply to inline the section regarding the subclass into the subclass constructor, and thus avoid overriding the base class version of it.

Table 5. Applying the devirtualization design patterns on JRE and Eclipse

Collection	JRE		Eclipse		Total	
Constant-initializer	82	(40.59%)	110	(42.64%)	192	(41.74%)
Function-object	44	(21.78%)	28	(10.85%)	72	(15.65%)
Inline-delta	19	(9.41%)	59	(22.87%)	78	(16.96%)
Native	14	(6.93%)	0	(0.00%)	14	(3.04%)
Unresolved	14	(6.93%)	23	(8.91%)	37	(8.04%)
Non-constant-initializer	9	(4.46%)	5	(1.94%)	14	(3.04%)
Code-rewrite	9	(4.46%)	1	(0.39%)	10	(2.17%)
Semi-constant-initializer	5	(2.48%)	13	(5.04%)	18	(3.91%)
Redundant	5	(2.48%)	8	(3.10%)	13	(2.83%)
Multi-function-object	1	(0.50%)	1	(0.39%)	2	(0.43%)
Initializer-object	0	(0.00%)	5	(1.94%)	5	(1.09%)
Factory	0	(0.00%)	5	(1.94%)	5	(1.09%)

Tab. 5 depicts the prevalence of the various patterns found in our manual inspection.

The most common pattern is also the simplest— CONSTANT INITIALIZER, appearing in over 40% of the cases in both JRE and Eclipse. The next most common pattern is the FUNCTION OBJECT, which allows for a delayed execution of computation inside the base constructor through an object that was passed by the derived class. This pattern was found in 21.78% of the JRE cases, but only 10.85% of the Eclipse cases. The rest of the patterns are less prevalent, and used to resolve a smaller number of specific cases.

Tab. 5 also includes some cases where the techniques described above were not applied:

1. A "code rewrite" solution applies for cases where the super constructor invokes a public method that is part of the class interface. In such cases, the derived class overrides the original implementation, but in fact, when invoked through the constructor of the base class, only the original implementation is executed. For example, take class JDialog from the JRE's javax.swing package. Its method setLayout() is invoked (indirectly) through the constructor of class Window (from java.awt package). The implementation of the overridden version of setLayout() is depicted in Fig. 7. This implementation queries a boolean data member in Line 9. This boolean is initialized to **false**, and is set only through the constructor of JDialog. As a result, when JDialog::setLayout() is invoked through the super constructor, the value of

```
1 class JDialog {
2 protected boolean rootPaneCheckingEnabled = false;

4 protected boolean isRootPaneCheckingEnabled() {
5     return rootPaneCheckingEnabled;
6 }

8 public void setLayout(LayoutManager manager) {
9     if(isRootPaneCheckingEnabled())
10        getContentPane().setLayout(manager);
11    else
12        super.setLayout(manager);
13    }
14 }
```

Fig. 7. Overriding setLayout() in JDialog

the boolean data member will always be `false`, and so only the super version of `setLayout()` is executed (Line 12).

The suggested code rewrite solution is done on the base class `Window`. An alternative to the invocation of `setLayout()` from the constructor of `Window` would be to use a private method which contains the complete implementation of the original `setLayout()`. Then, this private method may be invoked from both the public `setLayout()` and from the constructor of `Window`.

2. A "native" case describes a case where the base class invokes an abstract method whose implementation in a derived class is declared `native`. Since in these cases we have no access to the native code, we could not analyze it. This case was encountered only in JRE and appeared in nine concrete subclasses of WComponentPeer in sun.awt package (where the method create() is `native`), and in the superclass of WCustomCursor from the same package (by invoking createNativeCursor()).

3. The "unresolved" cases are those where the overriding methods contains a complex series of actions that are also very different than the original base implementation. We marked 6.9% of the falls identified for JRE as "unresolved", and less than 9% in Eclipse.

5   Immodest Constructors

Coding and maintenance is complicated when a constructor refines a polymorphic constructor, since in such a class methods may be executed before any of its own constructors started executing. Our search for polymorphic behavior during construction in Sec. 3 was restricted to chains of direct message sends to the created object. But, such half-baked objects can also be encountered through aliasing—an exposed reference can be used to invoke dynamically bound methods on a half-baked object.

This section describes the results of our search for constructors which expose the `this`-identity, what we call *immodest* constructors.

5.1   Definitions

Sec. 3.1 defined three varieties of polymorphic behavior during construction. The three kinds of exposition defined are similar in nature.

Immodesty Pitfall Constructors. We say that a constructor is an *immodesty pitfall* if it exposes the `this` identity, by assigning it into a variable, which may be accessed by external code or serve as a target of an internal method, or by passing it as a parameter to external code.

Immodest Fall Constructors. We say that a constructor is an *immodest fall* if it refines a an immodesty pitfall constructor, and overrides a method defined by the class of the pitfall constructor.

Immodest Constructors. A constructor is *immodest* if (i) it is an immodesty pitfall constructor *and* (ii) it is a refined by an immodest fall constructor.

Consider for example the JAVA class `Frame` depicted in Fig. 8 (drawn from the `java.awt` package). Then, both constructors of this class are immodesty pitfalls: The first since

```
1  public class Frame {
2      public void init(String title, GraphicsConfiguration gc) {
3          this.title = title;
4          SunToolkit.checkAndSetPolicy(this, false);
5      }
6      public Frame(String title) throws HeadlessException {
7          init(title, null);
8      }
9      public Frame() throws HeadlessException {
10         this("");
11     }
12 }
```

Fig. 8. Constructors revealing a self reference in JAVA

it invokes method `init` which exposes the `this` pointer to an external class. The second constructor is such pitfall since it delegates its construction task to the first constructor. Observe however that both constructors are monomorphic.

To understand why immodesty is undesirable, consider again Fig. 8 and a subclass of `Frame`. If this subclass does not override function `init`, then all of its constructors are immodest falls since they necessarily refine one of `Frame`'s constructors which exposes the `this` identity. If however, the said subclass overrides `init`, then all of its constructors are by definition polymorphic falls (which would also make `Frame`'s constructors polymorphic).

Note that the above reasoning also shows that there are constructors which are *both* polymorphic and immodest. Since the overlap was small, we chose to categorize all such cases as being polymorphic.

5.2 Method

What is known in the JTL jargon as *pedestrian patterns* were used to identify cases in which constructors invoke, directly or indirectly, polymorphic member functions. A more sophisticated analysis involving dataflow analysis (using scratches as they are called in JTL), was used to identify cases in which constructors allow external code, i.e., code which is not part of the ancestors chain of a class, to access a half-baked object.

Our conservative search for incidents of immodesty used inexact yet conservative interprocedural analysis starting at the base constructor and exact intraprocedural dataflow analysis. The analysis was complemented by a laborious manual inspection of the violating code.

5.3 Findings

Tab. 6 shows the prevalence of immodest behavior in constructors in each of the collections in the software corpus.

Examining the second column of the table we see that there is a great variance in the prevalence of immodest constructors, ranging from 0% to 9%; even the median (2.42%) is very different from the average prevalence (5.94%). Comparing this average with the average prevalence of polymorphic constructors (2.55% see Tab. 3) we see that there are more than twice as many immodest constructors than there are polymorphic constructors.

Table 6. Prevalence of immodest behavior in constructors (conservative analysis)

Collection	Immodest Constructors		Immodest Fall Constructors		Immodest Pitfall Constructors	
JBOSS	129	(3.88%)	718	(3.25%)	957	(4.33%)
JRE	283	(7.90%)	1,111	(5.45%)	1,178	(5.78%)
ECLIPSE	186	(8.88%)	906	(5.72%)	1,704	(10.76%)
POSEIDON	215	(8.95%)	1,384	(12.49%)	1,351	(12.20%)
TOMCAT	10	(1.00%)	109	(2.10%)	81	(1.56%)
SCALA	53	(7.81%)	298	(9.48%)	402	(12.79%)
JML	15	(1.90%)	90	(3.06%)	183	(6.23%)
ANT	1	(0.23%)	18	(0.89%)	30	(1.49%)
MJC	6	(1.40%)	56	(3.90%)	130	(9.05%)
JEDIT	7	(2.42%)	131	(14.64%)	189	(21.12%)
ESC	3	(1.38%)	13	(1.82%)	21	(2.95%)
KOA	0	(0.00%)	4	(10.53%)	4	(10.53%)
Total	908	(5.94%)	4,838	(5.64%)	6,230	(7.26%)
Median	10	(2.16%)	109	(4.67%)	183	(7.64%)

These two phenomena occur also in the third column of the table: the prevalence of immodest fall constructors is large (from less than 2% to almost 15%), and their total number is greater than the number of polymorphic fall constructors by a factor greater than 4.

Interestingly, the prevalence of immodest constructors with immodest behavior when compared to the entire constructors population is still small and is equal to about 1.06%. The prevalence of immodest pitfalls constructors is not quite as small: 5.64%.

Perhaps surprisingly, in examining the fourth column we find the number of *immodest pitfall constructors* is smaller (!) than the number of *polymorphic pitfall constructors*. But, the variety in this column is even greater than in the other columns (from less than 1.5% to more than 21%).

Tab. 7 shows the prevalence of classes with constructors with immodest behavior.

Table 7. Prevalence of classes with constructors with immodest behavior (conservative analysis)

Collection	Classes with Immodest Constructors		Classes with Immodest Fall Constructors		Classes with Immodest Pitfall Constructors	
JBOSS	61	(3.07%)	582	(3.69%)	650	(4.12%)
JRE	100	(4.52%)	894	(6.12%)	649	(4.44%)
ECLIPSE	117	(7.32%)	821	(5.77%)	1,374	(9.65%)
POSEIDON	115	(7.94%)	1,146	(13.19%)	1,018	(11.72%)
TOMCAT	7	(1.14%)	88	(2.34%)	61	(1.62%)
SCALA	43	(9.98%)	274	(9.95%)	312	(11.33%)
JML	9	(1.95%)	82	(3.86%)	98	(4.61%)
ANT	1	(0.37%)	15	(0.93%)	23	(1.43%)
MJC	4	(1.89%)	51	(4.98%)	74	(7.22%)
JEDIT	3	(2.68%)	123	(15.85%)	152	(19.59%)
ESC	1	(0.73%)	12	(1.90%)	15	(2.37%)
KOA	0	(0.00%)	4	(11.11%)	4	(11.11%)
Total	461	(4.85%)	4,092	(6.20%)	4,430	(6.71%)
Median	8	(2.68%)	105	(5.77%)	125	(7.22%)

The data in this table can be summarized as follows: The same phenomena we found for immodest constructors in Tab. 6, including great variety in the prevalence of immodest and immodest falls types of behavior, and a higher incidence rate in these than in their polymorphic counterpart.

The comparison of the finding regarding constructors and the findings regarding classes indicate that an immodest constructor is "responsible" on average to almost six actual immodesty falls, and that every class with immodest constructor has on average almost 9 classes with immodesty pitfall constructors. This indicates that in immodest constructors tend to be grouped together in a smaller number of classes.

6 Conclusions and Further Research

Our main conclusion is that polymorphic construction is scarce, occurring in about 1.4% of all classes and 1.4% constructors. The base constructors and base classes responsible for this behavior are even scarcer; their prevalence is less than 0.5%. This prevalence is in interesting contrast with the fact that the potential for such a polymorphic behavior occurs with at least 8% prevalence, *and* the fact that classes with potentially polymorphic behavior tend to have (with statistical significance greater than 99%) more descendants.

It might be useful to repeat our study in a framework set of mind, That is, examine polymorphic pitfall constructors manually, concentrating on those for which no corresponding falls were found, in attempt to determine whether the pitfalls were intentional, serving a "hot-spot" purpose.

Unfortunately, the results of the analysis of exposure were not as striking. We found that there is a *potential* of leaking the this reference to external code in about 6% of the constructors. It is not clear however whether this potential leakage is significant, since it could be the case that the external code does not actually make use of this reference. For example, this could be assigned to one of the class's fields, as is often done in initializing a circular linked list, but even though this field has default visibility, no other class in the package uses it as a receiver, or even reads this field. Also, even if the external code sends a message to the leaked this, this sending could be done only after the class was fully constructed. Clearly, more work is required in this direction.

Based on an initial manual exploratory findings of immodest behavior we conjecture that in the majority of immodesty cases, the external code does not send any messages to the revealed reference, and if such messages are sent, they are rarely overridden in any of the derived classes. If this conjecture is contradicted, and the incidents are found to be of sufficient importance then perhaps the time is ripe for introducing two initialization phases: one in which the object is constructed internally, and another in which the object initial interconnection network is established. This second phase could be useful e.g., for a model-view-controller architecture, in which the construction of each view component includes storing its address in the update list of the model component. We suspect however that such cases are rare, and could be addressed by construction patterns tailored for this purpose.

We discussed alternatives for enforcing modest behavior on constructors (so to speak), a prime alternative being a model similar to Bokowski and Vitek's confined types. The

518   J. Gil and T. Shragai

data we collected shows that the phenomena is sufficiently prevalent that designers of new languages should consider appropriate way of addressing it.

In light of our finding regarding polymoprhic constructors, language designers should consider introducing `init` (and `destruct`) methods is in setting a clear cut boundary between between the construction (and destruction) process and the normal object's life time. The variety of ways of doing that are discussed briefly in the opening section of this article. An inspection of the patterns of polymorphic behavior in constructors and their coverage rate suggest that such semantics may be even feasible in existing language with extensive code base (probably as compiler option or extension).

We also believe that the time may is ripe for introducing what we have called *semi-Static Methods*, i.e., functions which are *dynamically* bound, but are allowed to invoke only static and semi-static methods of the class. Semi-static methods are prohibited from accessing instance methods and variables. A familiar example is JAVA's `getClass()` method. Such a feature is useful in constructors, as demonstrated by the construction patterns that can be more readily implemented using this feature.

References

1. Arnold, K., Gosling, J.: The Java Programming Language. The Java Series. Addison-Wesley, Reading (1996)
2. Baxter, G., Frean, M., Noble, J., Rickerby, M., Smith, H., Visser, M., Melton, H., Tempero, E.: Understanding the shape of Java software. In: Tarr and Cook [27]
3. Birka, A., Ernst, M.D.: A practical type system and language for reference immutability. In: Vlissides, J.M., Schmidt, D.C. (eds.) Proc. of the 19th Ann. Conf. on OO Prog. Sys., Lang., & Appl (OOPSLA 2004), Vancouver, BC, Canada, October 2004. ACM SIGPLAN Notices, vol. 39 (10) (2004)
4. Bokowski, B., Vitek, J.: Confined types. In: Proc. of the 14th Ann. Conf. on OO Prog. Sys., Lang., & Appl (OOPSLA 1999), Denver, Colorado, November 1-5, 1999. ACM SIGPLAN Notices, vol. 34 (10), pp. 82–96. ACM Press, New York (1999)
5. Cabral, B., Marques, P.: Exception handling: A field study in Java and.NET. In: Ernst [11], pp. 151–175
6. Chalin, P., James, P.R.: Non-null references by default in Java: Alleviating the nullity annotation burden. In: Ernst [11], pp. 227–247
7. Clifton, C., Millstein, T., Leavens, G.T., Chambers, C.: MultiJava: Design rationale, compiler implementation, and applications. ACM Trans. Prog. Lang. Syst. 28(3) (May 2006)
8. Cohen, T., Gil, J.: Self-calibration of metrics of Java methods. In: Proc. of the 37th Int. Conf. on Technology of OO Lang. and Sys (TOOLS 2000 Pacific), Sydney, Australia, November 20-23, 2000, pp. 94–106. Prentice-Hall, Englewood Cliffs (2000)
9. Cohen, T., Gil, J.Y., Maman, I.: JTL—the Java tools language. In: Tarr and Cook [27]
10. Eckel, N., Gil, J.: Empirical study of object-layout strategies and optimization techniques. In: Bertino, E. (ed.) ECOOP 2000. LNCS, vol. 1850, pp. 394–421. Springer, Heidelberg (2000)
11. Ernst, E. (ed.): ECOOP 2007. LNCS, vol. 4609. Springer, Heidelberg (2007)

12. Fähndrich, M., Leino, K.R.M.: Declaring and checking non-null types in an object-oriented language. In: Crocker, R., Steele Jr., G.L. (eds.) Proc. of the 18th Ann. Conf. on OO Prog. Sys., Lang., & Appl (OOPSLA 2003), October 2003. ACM SIGPLAN Notices, vol. 38 (11) (2003)
13. Gil, J., Itai, A.: The complexity of type analysis of object oriented programs. In: Jul, E. (ed.) ECOOP 1998. LNCS, vol. 1445, pp. 601–634. Springer, Heidelberg (1998)
14. Gil, J., Maman, I.: Micro patterns in Java code. In: Johnson and Gabriel [17], pp. 97–116
15. Hejlsberg, A., Wiltamuth, S., Golde, P.: The C# Programming Language, 2nd edn. Addison-Wesley, Reading (2003)
16. ISE. ISE EIFFEL The Language Reference. ISE, Santa Barbara, CA (1997)
17. Johnson, R., Gabriel, R.P.: Proc. of the 20th Ann. Conf. on OO Prog. Sys., Lang., & Appl (OOPSLA 2005), San Diego, California. ACM SIGPLAN Notices (2005)
18. Kniesel, G., Theisen, D.: JAC access right based encapsulation for Java. Softw. Pract. Exper. 31(6), 555–576 (2001)
19. Leavens, G.T., Baker, A.L., Ruby, C.: Preliminary design of JML: A behavioral interface specification language for Java. ACM SIGSOFT Software Engineering Notes 31(3), 1–38 (2006)
20. Male, C., Pearce, D.J.: Non–null type inference with type aliasing for java. Technical report, Computer Science, Victoria University of Wellington, NZ (August 2007)
21. Melton, H., Tempero, E.: Static members and cycles in Java software. In: International Symposium on Empirical Software Engineering and Measurement, pp. 136–145 (2007)
22. Meyer, B.: Object-Oriented Software Construction, 2nd edn. Prentice-Hall, Englewood Cliffs (1997)
23. Noble, J., Lea, D.: Editorial: Aliasing in object-oriented systems. Soft. Practice & Experience 31(6), 505 (2001)
24. Odersky, M., Altherr, P., Cremet, V., Emir, B., Maneth, S., Micheloud, S., Mihaylov, N., Schinz, M., Stenman, E., Zenger, M.: An overview of the Scala programming language. Technical Report IC/2004/64, EPFL Lausanne, Switzerland (2004)
25. Stallman, R.M.: Using the GNU Compiler Collection (GCC): GCC Version 4.1.0. Free Software Foundation (2005)
26. Stroustrup, B.: The C++ Programming Language, 3rd edn. Addison-Wesley, Reading (1997)
27. Tarr, P.L., Cook, W.R. (eds.): Proc. of the 21st Ann. Conf. on OO Prog. Sys., Lang., & Appl. (OOPSLA 2006), Portland, Oregon, October 22-26. ACM SIGPLAN Notices (2006)
28. Tschantz, M.S., Ernst, M.D.: Javari: Adding reference immutability to Java. In: Johnson and Gabriel [17]
29. Wrigstad, T.: Ownership-Based Alias Managemant.[12] PhD thesis, KTH, Computer and Systems Sciences (May 2006)
30. Zibin, Y., Potanin, A., Ali, M., Artzi, S., Kieżun, A., Ernst, M.D.: Object and reference immutability using Java generics. In: ESEC/FSE 2007: Proceedings of the 11th European Software Engineering Conference and the 15th ACM SIGSOFT Symposium on the Foundations of Software Engineering, Dubrovnik, Croatia, September 5–7 (2007)

---

[12] http://www.diva-portal.org/kth/theses/abstract.xsql?dbid=3956

Type-Based Object Immutability with Flexible Initialization

Christian Haack[1,2,*] and Erik Poll[1,*]

[1] Radboud University, Nijmegen
[2] Aicas GmbH, Karlsruhe

Abstract. We present a type system for checking object immutability, read-only references, and class immutability in an open or closed world. To allow object initialization outside object constructors (which is often needed in practice), immutable objects are initialized in lexically scoped regions. The system is simple and direct; its only type qualifiers specify immutability properties. No auxiliary annotations, e.g., ownership types, are needed, yet good support for deep immutability is provided. To express object confinement, as required for class immutability in an open world, we use qualifier polymorphism. The system has two versions: one with explicit specification commands that delimit the object initialization phase, and one where such commands are implicit and inferred. In the latter version, all annotations are compatible with Java's extended annotation syntax, as proposed in JSR 308.

1 Introduction

1.1 Motivation

Immutable data structures greatly simplify programming, program maintenance, and reasoning about programs. Immutable structures can be freely shared, even between concurrent threads and with untrusted code, without the need to worry about modifications, even temporary ones, that could result in inconsistent states or broken invariants. In a nutshell, immutable data structures are simple. It is therefore not surprising that favoring immutability is a recommended coding practice for Java [3].

Unfortunately, statically checking object immutability in Java-like languages is not easy, unless one settles for supporting only a restricted programming style that can be enforced through `final` fields. Clearly, objects are immutable if all their fields are `final` and of primitive type. Additionally, one can allow `final` fields of immutable types, this way supporting immutable recursive data structures. Thus, Java's `final` fields support a style of programming immutable objects that mimics datatypes in functional languages and is advocated, for instance, by Felleisen and Friedman [15].

Many immutable objects, however, do not follow this style. A prominent example are Java's immutable strings. An immutable string is a wrapper around a character array. While `final` fields can prevent that a string's internal character array is replaced by another character array, `final` fields cannot prevent that the array elements themselves are mutated. Moreover, Java's type system provides no means for preventing representation exposure of the character array, which would allow indirect mutation of a string

---

* Supported by IST-FET-2005-015905 Mobius project.

S. Drossopoulou (Ed.): ECOOP 2009, LNCS 5653, pp. 520–545, 2009.

through aliases to its (supposedly) internal character array. Preventing this, not just for arrays but for any internal mutable data structures, requires a richer type system with support for object confinement.

It is also quite common to have immutable data structures that are not instances of immutable classes. Examples include immutable arrays, immutable collections that are implemented in terms of Java's mutable collection classes (but are never mutated after initialization), and immutable cyclic data structures, e.g., doubly linked lists, graphs or trees with parent references. Concrete examples are given on pages 527, 529 and Figure 3.

This article presents the design of a pluggable type system for Java to specify and statically check various immutability properties. A pluggable type checker operates on Java's abstract syntax trees and is optionally invoked after the standard type checker, to ensure additional properties. A pluggable checker for object immutability guarantees that immutable objects never mutate.

Syntactically, our immutability type system can be handled with Java's extended annotation syntax as proposed by JSR 308 [19], to be included in Java 7, which allows annotations on all occurrences of types. While in this paper we slightly deviate from legal annotation syntax (for explanatory reasons), all proposed annotations are in syntactic positions allowed by JSR 308.

1.2 Kinds of Immutability

The following classification of immutability properties has been used in various places in the literature [34,22]:

- *Object immutability:* An object is immutable if its state cannot be modified.
- *Class immutability:* A class is immutable if all its instances in all programs are immutable objects.
- *Read-only references:* A reference is read-only if the state of the object it refers to cannot be modified through this reference.

Examples of *immutable classes* are Java's String class and the wrapper classes for primitive types, e.g., Integer and Boolean. All instances of immutable classes are immutable objects.

Conversely, *immutable objects* need not be instances of immutable classes. For example, immutable arrays are not instances of an immutable class, and neither are immutable collections that are implemented in terms of Java's mutable collection libraries. Immutable objects that are not instances of immutable classes typically have public, non-final fields or public mutator methods, but the pluggable type system disallows assignments to these fields and calls to these methods.

An example for a *read-only reference* is the reference created by Java's static method Collection unmodifiableCollection(Collection c), which generates a wrapper around collection c. This wrapper refers to c through a read-only reference.

For class immutability, we further distinguish between an open and a closed world [25]:

- Class immutability *in a closed world* assumes that all program components follow the rules of the pluggable type system.

- Class immutability *in an open world* assumes that immutable classes and the classes they depend on follow the rules of the pluggable type system, but clients of immutable classes are unchecked (i.e., they only follow Java's standard typing rules).

Unchecked class clients may for instance be untrusted applets. Note that the closed world assumption only makes sense if *all* code is checked with the additional type rules. Java's classes String, Integer and Boolean are immutable in an open world. For class immutability in an open world it is essential that instances of immutable classes encapsulate their representation objects. Open-world-immutable classes necessarily have to initialize their instances inside constructors or factory methods, and they should not provide accessible mutator methods or fields. Note also that, in an open world, object immutability without class immutability can only be achieved for objects that are never exposed to unchecked clients, because unchecked clients cannot be prevented from calling mutator methods or assigning to accessible fields if these exist. Similarly, in an open world, read-only references can only be achieved for references that are never exposed to unchecked clients.

1.3   Specifying Immutability with Type Qualifiers

Following our earlier work [18], we support the distinction between mutable and immutable objects through *access qualifiers* on types:

Access qualifiers:
$p, q ::=$ RdWr   read-write access (default)
          Rd   read-only access
          $\cdots$

Types:
$T ::= q\,C$ C-object with q-access
$C \in$ ClassId   class identifiers

Objects of type Rd C are called Rd-objects, and have immutable fields. Our type system is designed to guarantee the following soundness property (see Theorem 2):

Well-typed programs never write to fields of Rd-objects.

For instance, the method bad() attempts an illegal write to a Rd-object and is forbidden by our type system. On the other hand, good() legally writes to a RdWr-object:

```
class C { int f; }
static void bad(Rd C x) {
    x.f = 42; // TYPE ERROR
}
```
```
static void good(RdWr C x) {
    x.f = 42; // OK
}
```

An additional type qualifier, Any, represents the least upper bound of Rd and RdWr:

$p, q ::= \cdots$

          Any   "either Rd or RdWr"

Subqualifying:

Rd $<:$ Any   RdWr $<:$ Any

Subtyping:

$$\frac{p <: q \qquad C <: D}{p\,C <: q\,D}$$

A reference of a type Any C may refer to a Rd-object or a RdWr-object, so writes through Any-references are forbidden. Beware of the difference between Rd and Any. A reference of type Any C is a *read-only reference*, meaning you cannot write to the object through this particular reference. A reference of type Rd C is a reference to a read-only object, i.e. to an object that *nobody* has write-access to.[1]

The following example shows how Any-references can be useful. The method m() creates a RdWr-array and then applies the method foo() to the array. From the type of foo() we can tell that foo() does not mutate the array: [2]

```
interface Util {              static void m(Util util) {
    void foo(int Any [] a);       int[] a = new int RdWr [] {42,43,44};
}                                 util.foo(a);
                                  assert a[0] == 42;
                              }
```

In this example, we assume a closed world. In an open world, where there may be unchecked classes that do not play by the additional rules our type system imposes, there is still the possibility that foo() writes a to some heap location of type Any, so that unchecked class could modify a[0] concurrently. Preventing foo() from writing its parameter to the heap can be achieved by a more general method type that uses qualifier polymorphism, as will be discussed in Section 2.3.

1.4 Flexible Object Initialization with Stack-Local Regions

A common problem of type systems for object immutability [4,18,34,22] and for non-nullness (more generally, object invariants) [13,14,28] is object initialization. Whereas in traditional type systems, values have the same types throughout program execution, this is not quite true for these systems. Type systems for non-nullness face the difficulty that all fields are initially null; type systems for object immutability face the difficulty that even immutable objects mutate while being initialized. In these systems, each object starts out in an uninitialized state and only obtains its true type at the end of its initialization phase. Thus, objects go through a *typestate transition* from "uninitialized" to "initialized".

Object initialization is often the most complicated aspect of otherwise simple type systems, see for instance Fähndrich and Leino's non-nullness type system [13]. Some of the above type systems require that initialization takes place inside object constructors [13,18,34]. Unfortunately, this does not really simplify matters because object constructors in Java-like languages can contain arbitrary code (which may, for instance, leak self-references or call dynamically dispatched methods). Moreover, initialization inside constructors is often too restrictive in practice. For instance, cyclic data structures often get initialized outside constructors, and array objects do not even have constructors.

One contribution of this paper is a simple but flexible object initialization technique for immutability, using stack-local memory regions. Object initialization with stack-local regions supports a programming style that is natural for programmers in mainstream OO languages. In particular, programmers do not have to mimic destructive reads, as required by type systems where object initialization is based on unique references [4,22]. Statically checking object initialization with stack-local regions is simple, as it does not require tracking aliasing on the heap, which is needed in more general

---

[1] IGJ [34] uses the same three qualifiers, calling them @Mutable, @Immutable, and @ReadOnly instead of Rd, RdWr and Any.

[2] Following JSR 308 syntax, the qualifier of an array type C[] is written before the [].

typestate-like systems based on static capabilities [10,29,6,11,5,7,2]. In order to facilitate modular static checking, these systems use additional program annotations in the form of constraints, effects, or pre/postconditions. Our system, on the other hand, only uses standard type annotations, largely hiding the typestate change from "uninitialized" to "initialized" from programmers. To this end, we have designed an inference algorithm that automatically infers the end of object initialization phases (see Section 3.4).

1.5   Object Confinement with Qualifier-Polymorphic Methods

A type system for class immutability in an open world must enforce several confinement properties [3]. Specifically, it must guarantee that instances of immutable classes encapsulate their representation objects and that their object constructors do not leak self-references. In our earlier paper [18], we enforced these properties using two type-based confinement techniques (in addition to the access qualifiers Rd and RdWr), namely a dedicated ownership type system for enforcing encapsulation of representation objects, and so-called anonymous methods [32] for confining self-references during object construction. Unfortunately, the resulting type system was more complex than one would desire. One of the insights of this article is that, when combined with flexible object initialization, the various confinement properties for class immutability can be expressed in terms of methods that are polymorphic in access qualifiers.

To get an idea how polymorphism helps with confinement, consider the following qualifier-polymorphic method signature:

$$\text{<q> void foo(char q [] arg)}$$

where <q> denotes universal quantification of the qualifier variable q, making the method polymorphic in q. For a qualifier hierarchy without greatest element, this signature tells us that foo() does not write its parameter to a heap location, because the type of such a location would need a single qualifier annotation that is greater than all other qualifiers.[3] This observation can be exploited to confine representation objects of immutable objects and to confine self-references to constructors of immutable objects.

To support *deep immutability* we treat the access qualifier as an implicit class parameter. It is interesting that this single class parameter in combination with qualifier-polymorphic methods and flexible object initialization suffices for satisfactorily encoding class immutability. In particular, we do not need separate ownership annotations, because the required confinement properties can be expressed in terms of these primitives, in a similar way as in ownership type systems. Flexible initialization is a crucial ingredient, as it allows us, for instance, to treat the internal character array of a string as an *immutable* object (rather than as a *mutable* object that is owned by an immutable one). This would not be possible if object initialization was tied to object constructors, because then all arrays would necessarily be mutable[4]. As a result of treating the character array inside a string as immutable, our type system can, for instance, easily support

---

[3] Any is actually not the greatest element of our qualifier hierarchy, but the greatest qualifier for *initialized* objects. We still name this qualifier Any (rather than Initialized). Fortunately, qualifiers for uninitialized objects are inferred and never need to be written by programmers.

[4] Supporting immutable arrays initialized by array initializers is not enough for the constructor String(char[] c) of Java's String class, because the length of c is not known statically.

different strings sharing the same, immutable, character array for their representation, which is often problematic with ownership types.

1.6 Summary of Contributions

Based on the ideas sketched in this introduction, we have designed a pluggable immutability type system for Java-like languages. The primitives of the type language are the type qualifiers Rd, RdWr and Any for specifying object access rights. The features of the system are:

- *expressiveness:* the system supports object immutability, read-only references, and class immutability in a closed and open world;
- *simplicity and directness:* the system only needs the type qualifiers Rd, RdWr and Any plus qualifier polymorphism; its formal typing rules are simple; annotations are only required on field types and in method signatures; no annotations are required inside method bodies;
- *flexible initialization:* object initialization is not tied to object constructors; while the type system is necessarily flow-sensitive in order to support object initialization, it works for concurrency, too, because it enforces that threads only share initialized objects and because types of initialized objects are persistent.

On the technical side, our contributions are:

- *type system formalization and proof of soundness for object immutability:* we formalize a subset of the type system for a small model language; this subset focuses on what we believe is the most critical part of the system, namely, the initialization phase; we prove that the system is sound for object immutability: *well-typed programs never write to* Rd-*objects*;
- *a local annotation inference algorithm:* we present a local annotation inference algorithm that automatically infers the end of object initialization phases; we have formalized this algorithm for our model language and proven it sound.

Outline. The rest of the paper has two parts. Section 2 informally discusses the type system design. Section 3 contains the technical contributions: it formalizes the type system for a small model language, presents the annotation inference algorithm, and states soundness theorems, whose detailed proofs are contained in the companion report [17]. Section 4 compares to related work and Section 5 concludes.

2   Informal Presentation

We carry on with the informal presentation, as started in Section 1.3.

2.1   Access Qualifier as Class Parameter

For aggregate object structures, it is desirable to associate a single access qualifier with the entire aggregate, especially if the internal structure of the aggregate is hidden from object clients. In order to support *access control for aggregates through single access qualifiers*, we treat the access qualifier as an implicit class parameter. We have already proposed this in [18] and so has IGJ [34]. Technically, we introduce a *special access variable* myaccess that refers to the access qualifier of this. The scope of this variable is the entire class body. In particular, the myaccess variable can be used in field types and signatures of methods and constructors. In the Square class below, myaccess annotates the type Point of its fields. Method m() takes an Any-square, so can neither write to the Point-fields of the square, nor to the int-fields of its points.

```
class Point { int x; int y; }
class Square { myaccess Point upperleft; myaccess Point lowerright; }
static void m(Any Square s) {
    s.upperleft = s.lowerright; // TYPE ERROR
    s.upperleft.x = 42; // TYPE ERROR
}
```

It is also possible to assign a single access right to a cyclic structure. For instance:

```
class Person { myaccess Person partner; }
class Couple { myaccess Person husband; myaccess Person wife; }
```

Old-fashioned couples stick with each other forever: they have type Rd Couple. Modern couples can divorce and the partners can re-marry: they have type RdWr Couple.

The access qualifier is a *covariant class parameter*. Generally, covariant class parameters are unsound, because upcasting a class parameter allows ill-typed writes to fields whose types depend on this class parameter. Here, treating the access qualifier covariantly is sound, because access qualifiers that permit write-access are minimal elements of the qualifier hierarchy. Thus, *upcasting access qualifiers makes object references read-only*.

2.2 Flexible Initialization

For sound object initialization, we adapt a technique from region-based memory management [30], allowing initialization of immutable objects inside *stack-local memory regions* (closely related to *lexically scoped regions*). A stack-local region is a part of the heap that cannot be reached from the rest of the heap. All references into a stack-local region are on the stack. Each stack-local region is *owned* by a method (or a constructor), namely, the lowest method on the call stack that holds references into this region. All objects inside a stack-local region have the same special type qualifier. The method that owns the region (and only this method) is permitted to change this type qualifier to some other qualifier, uniformly for all objects in the same region. When this typestate change is performed, the owning method is on the top of the call stack, so all references into the stack-local region come from local variables of this owning method. This means that all references into the stack-local region at the time of the typestate change are statically known: the static type system can easily modify the type qualifiers of these references.

Technically, to support flexible initialization, we add Fresh-qualifiers. These have a name as an argument, which we call an *initialization token*.

$$p, q ::= \cdots$$

Fresh(n)	fresh object under initialization
$n \in$ Name	token for initializing a set of related objects

An initialization token can be viewed as an identifier for a stack-local region that contains Fresh(n)-objects. The token n is secret to the method that owns the associated region and grants permission to commit $Fresh(n)$ to q, for any q. To syntactically capture this semantics, we introduce two *specification commands*:

newtoken n	create a new initialization token
commit Fresh(n) as q	globally convert Fresh(n) to q

These are specification commands, i.e., they operate on auxiliary state ("ghost state") and have no runtime effect on concrete state or control flow. Our inference algorithm can infer all specification commands, so they need not be written by the programmer. In fact, all annotations inside method bodies can be inferred, so that programmers only have to write qualifiers in field declarations and method signatures. In the examples below, all inferred annotations are shaded gray.

The following method, for instance, creates an immutable array; it uses the flexible initialization technique, to initialize the array r outside a constructor.

```
static char Rd [] copy (char Any [] a) {
    newtoken n;
    char[] r = new char Fresh(n) [a.length];
    for (int i=0; i++; i < a.length) r[i] = a[i];
    commit Fresh(n) as Rd;
    return r;
}
```

To initialize immutable cyclic data structures, we use the same initialization token for all members of the structure. Using the flexible initialization technique, we can set cross-references (here husband and wife) *after* the constructors have been called:[5]

```
newtoken n;
Person alice = new <Fresh(n)>Person();
Person bob = new <Fresh(n)>Person();
alice.partner = bob; bob.partner = alice;
Couple couple = new <Fresh(n)>Couple();
couple.husband = bob; couple.wife = alice;
commit Fresh(n) as Rd;
```

Note that field types and method signatures cannot contain $Fresh(n)$-annotations, because n is out-of-scope in field types and method signatures:

```
class C {
    Fresh(n) D x; // TYPE ERROR: n out of scope
    static Rd C commit(Fresh(n) C x) { // TYPE ERROR: n out of scope
        commit Fresh(n) as Rd; return x; }
}
```

Because we do not allow methods that are parametrized by initialization tokens, each initialization token is confined to a single method. As a result, only the method that "owns" a $Fresh(n)$-region can commit it, which is crucial for the soundness of commit.

Figure 1 sketches a runtime configuration before a commit-statement. In this configuration, the heap has three regions: a region of initialized objects, and two Fresh regions with associated initialization tokens n1 and n2. The picture shows possible

---

[5] Person() is a qualifier-polymorphic constructor, hence the angle brackets. See Section 2.4.

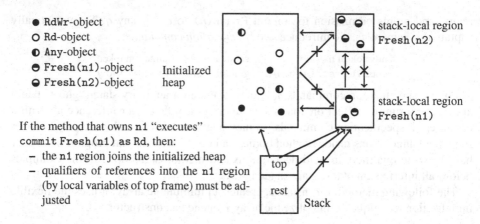

- RdWr-object
- Rd-object
- Any-object
- Fresh(n1)-object
- Fresh(n2)-object

Initialized heap

stack-local region Fresh(n2)

stack-local region Fresh(n1)

top

rest

Stack

If the method that owns n1 "executes" commit Fresh(n1) as Rd, then:

- the n1 region joins the initialized heap
- qualifiers of references into the n1 region (by local variables of top frame) must be adjusted

Fig. 1. Committing the fresh region owned by the top stack frame

inter-region references. Importantly, the type system ensures that there are *no incoming references from the heap into* Fresh *regions*. Furthermore, when the top of the stack owns region n1, there are no references from the rest of the stack into this region. When the commit-statement is executed, region n1 is merged with the initialized region. The type system then has to adjust the qualifiers of all references into region n1. Fortunately, this can be done statically, because all references into this region come from local variables in its owning method.

2.3 Qualifier Polymorphism for Methods

Consider the following method:

```
static void copy(Point src, Point dst) {
    dst.x = src.x; dst.y = src.y;
}
```

This method could accept both RdWr-points and Fresh-points as dst-parameters. To facilitate this, we introduce *bounded qualifier polymorphism for methods*. The Hasse diagram in Figure 2.3 depicts the qualifier hierarchy, including qualifier bounds. The syntax for qualifier-polymorphic methods is as in Java Generics:

$$<\bar{\alpha} \text{ extends } \bar{B}> T \ m(\bar{T} \ \bar{x}) \ q\{\dots\} \quad \textit{(method declaration)}$$

We usually omit the qualifier bound Qual, writing <a extends Qual> as <a>. The qualifier q is associated with the receiver parameter, that is, $e.m()$ can only be called if e's access qualifier is a subqualifier of q. Receiver qualifiers are not present in static methods. For subclassing, method types are treated contravariantly in the qualifiers on input types (including the receiver qualifier) and covariantly in the qualifier on the output type. These variances are as in IGJ [34]. We can now type copy() as follows:

```
static <a, b extends Writeable> void copy(a Point src, b Point dst) {
    dst.x = src.x; dst.y = src.y;
}
```

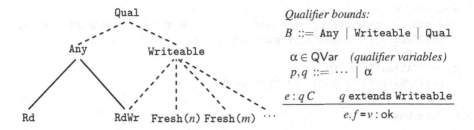

Fig. 2. The qualifier hierarchy. `Qual` and `Writable` are qualifier *bounds*, not qualifiers, so they cannot be used as type qualifiers, only in `extends`-clauses.

Note that `Writeable` can only be used as a qualifier bound, but not as a qualifier. Allowing `Writeable` as qualifier would lead to unsoundness for two reasons: Firstly, `Writeable` would be a *non-minimal qualifier that allows writes*, which would make covariance of the `myaccess` class parameter unsound. Secondly, `Writeable` could be used as an annotation on field types. This would open the door for violating stack locality of `Fresh`-regions, which would make the typestate transition at `commits` unsound.

Signatures of qualifier-polymorphic methods tell us which method parameters are potentially mutated by the method. In addition, they also provide information about which method parameters are potentially written to the heap. For instance:

- `static <a> void foo(int a [] x);`
  - does not write to object x through reference x
  - does not write object x to the heap
- `static void faa(int Any [] x);`
  - does not write to object x through reference x
  - may write object x to the heap (into Any-fields)
- `static <a extends Writeable> void fee(int a [] x);`
  - may write to object x through reference x
  - does not write object x to the heap

The method $foo(x)$ cannot write x to the heap, because the qualifier hierarchy does not have a greatest element, which would be needed as the type of a location that x can be written to. Similarly, $fee(x)$ cannot write x to the heap, because there is no qualifier that bounds all writeable qualifiers.

In the following example, we use the qualifier for the receiver parameter to distinguish between inspector and mutator methods. Inspectors can be called on any receivers, whereas mutators can only be called on writeable receivers:

```
class Hashtable<K,V> {
    <a> V get(K key) a { ... }  // inspector
    <a extends Writeable> V put(K key, V value) a { ... }  // mutator
}
```

To create an immutable hash table we can use flexible initialization outside the constructor:

```
newtoken n;
Hashtable<String,String> t = new <Fresh(n)>Hashtable<String,String>();
t.put("Alice", "Female"); t.put("Bob", "Male");
commit Fresh(n) as Rd;
t.get("Alice"); // OK
t.put("Charly", "Male"); // TYPE ERROR
```

2.4 Constructors

Constructor declarations have one of the following two forms:

<table>
<tr><td>$<\bar{\alpha}\ \text{extends}\ \bar{B}>\ q\ C(\bar{T}\ \bar{x})\ p\ \{\ body\ \}$</td><td>(caller-commit constructor)</td></tr>
<tr><td>$<\bar{\alpha}\ \text{extends}\ \bar{B}>\ q\ C(\bar{T}\ \bar{x})\{\ \text{newtoken}\ n;\ body\ \}$</td><td>(constructor-commit constructor)</td></tr>
</table>

Caller-commit constructors are more common. In their signature, p represents the qualifier of this when the constructor body starts executing. The typechecker assumes this qualifier initially when checking the constructor body, and enforces that constructor callers, through super() or this(), establish this precondition. The postcondition q represents the qualifier of this when the constructor terminates.

A typical instance of caller-commit constructors looks like this:

$$<\alpha\ \text{extends}\ \text{Writeable}>\ \alpha\ C(\bar{T}\ \bar{x})\ \alpha\ \{\ \dots\ \}$$

In particular, the default no-arg constructors have this form. Note that, if in the above constructor signature α does not occur in any of the parameter types $\bar{T}$, then we know that the constructor does not leak references to this[6]. This is often desired for constructors. Constructors that deliberately leak this could have the following form (which prevents the creation of immutable class instances):

$$\text{RdWr}\ C(\bar{T}\ \bar{x})\ \text{RdWr}\ \{\ \dots\ \}$$

Constructor-commit constructors enforce that the object is committed inside the constructor. This is useful in an open world to prevent object clients from ever seeing an uninitialized object. In constructor-commit constructors, the precondition is omitted. Instead, the constructor begins by generating a fresh token n. The body then initially assumes that this has qualifier Fresh(n). The scope of n is the constructor body, and therefore n cannot be mentioned in the constructor postcondition. To establish the postcondition, the body is forced to commit Fresh(n) before it terminates. The type system disallows calling constructor-commit constructors through super() or this(). Therefore, constructor-commit constructors are particularly suited for final classes.

Figure 3 shows an example with a caller-commit constructor. An immutable tree with parent pointers is constructed from the bottom up. A single initialization token is used for all nodes and is committed only after the root node has been initialized. This example is interesting because Qi and Myers [28] identify it as a problematic initialization pattern for other type systems [14]. It causes no problems for our system.

---

[6] If α occurs in $\bar{T}$, the constructor could for instance leak this to a field $x.f$ of a constructor parameter $\alpha\ D\ x$, in case f's type in C is annotated with myaccess.

```
class Tree {
    myaccess Tree parent, left, right;
    <a extends Writeable> a Tree (a Tree left, a Tree right) a {
        this.left = left; this.right = right;
        if (left != null) left.parent = this;
        if (right != null) right.parent = this;
    }
}

newtoken n;
Tree left_leaf = new <Fresh(n)>Tree(null, null);
Tree right_leaf = new <Fresh(n)>Tree(null, null);
Tree root = new <Fresh(n)>Tree(left_leaf, right_leaf);
root.parent = root;
commit Fresh(n) as Rd;
```

Fig. 3. Bottom-up initialization of a tree with parent pointers

2.5 Class Immutability in an Open World

In his book "Effective Java" [3], Bloch presents rules that ensure class immutability. These rules require that fields of immutable classes are private and final, that public methods are inspectors, that methods and constructors do not leak representation objects, that public constructors do not leak this, and that the behaviour of instances of immutable classes does not depend on overridable methods. Some of these rules (e.g., that all fields are private and final) can very easily be checked automatically. The conditions that methods of immutable classes are inspectors, that instances of immutable classes do not leak representation, and that constructors of immutable classes do not leak this can be expressed and checked by our type system.

If we specify class immutability with a class annotation Immutable, we could for instance declare an immutable String class like this:

```
Immutable final class String {
    private final char myaccess [] value;
    ...
}
```

Semantically, the Immutable annotation is meant to specify that String is an immutable class in an open world, i.e., that all instances of String are Rd-objects that cannot be mutated by possibly unchecked clients. In order to tie the access modifier for the value array to the access modifier for the enclosing string, it is important that we annotate the value field with myaccess instead of Rd. In combination with the requirements on method and constructor signatures below, this prevents representation exposure of the character array.

The following rules guarantee class immutability:

- immutable classes must be final and direct subclasses of Object
- methods and constructors may only call static or final methods or methods of final classes (transitively)

```
static <a, b extends Writeable>
void arraycopy(a Object src, int srcPos, b Object dst, int dstPos, int l);

public <a> Rd String(char a value[]) {
    newtoken n;
    int size = value.length;
    char[] v = new char Fresh(n) [size];
    System.arraycopy(value, 0, v, 0, size);
    this.offset = 0; this.count = size; this.value = v;
    commit Fresh(n) as Rd;
}
```

Fig. 4. A constructor of Java's immutable `String` class

– all fields must be final
– public constructors must have the following form:

$<\bar{\alpha}$ extends $\bar{B}>$ Rd $C(\bar{T}\ \bar{x})\{$ newtoken $n;\ldots;$ commit Fresh(n) as Rd; $\}$
where myaccess does not occur in $\bar{T}$

– types of public methods must have the following form:

$<\alpha,\bar{\beta}$ extends $\bar{B}>$ $U\ m(\bar{T}\ \bar{x})\ \alpha\{\ldots\}$

We use the `String` example to explain the constructor rule: The rule ensures that public constructors do not assign previously existing character arrays to the string's value field. This would only be possible, if the class parameter myaccess occurred in one of the parameter types $\bar{T}$, which is forbidden. For instance, the constructor `String(char value[])` is forced to make a defensive copy of its input parameter, as shown in Figure 4. Furthermore, constructors can not assign `this` or `this.value` to heap locations outside the stack-local `Fresh(n)`-region. This would only be possible if one of the parameter types $\bar{T}$ mentioned myaccess, or if the commit-statement were executed somewhere in the middle of the constructor, in which case the constructor could write `this.value` or `this` to the heap as a Rd-object after the commit.

As for the method rule, we have already argued that the above method type enforces that m is an inspector. Furthermore, the type forbids that m assigns the value array to the heap, because the qualifier hierarchy does not have a greatest element. Note that method types of the form $U\ m(\bar{T}\ \bar{x})$ Any$\{\ldots\}$ do not prevent representation exposure, because they enable writing the value array to Any-fields, which is dangerous in an open-world. Similarly, if the value field were annotated with Rd instead of myaccess, the value array could be written to Rd-fields or Any-fields.

2.6 Threads

For type soundness in multi-threaded programs, we must ensure that thread-shared objects are initialized, i.e., they must have types Rd, RdWr or Any, but not Fresh. This suffices for soundness, because types of initialized objects never change. As all thread-shared objects are reachable from the sharing Thread-objects and as the initialized region is closed under reachability[7], it suffices to require that Thread-objects are initialized when threads get started. Furthermore, we must assume this fact as the precondition for verifying the body of Thread.run():

```
class Thread {
    void run() RdWr { }
    void start(); // Treated specially. Type system uses run()'s type.
}
```

Subclasses of Thread may override run() with receiver qualifier RdWr or Any (by contravariance)[8]. Calling start() on a receiver o, whose static type is a subtype MyThread of Thread, requires that o has run()'s receiver qualifier from MyThread. Note that treating Thread.start() specially is not a random special case, because conceptually Thread.start() is a *concurrency primitive for dynamic thread creation* (a.k.a. fork or spawn), which is always treated specially in verification systems for concurrency.

3   The Formal Model

We formalize our system for a model language that is deliberately simple. The main objective is to prove soundness of the flexible initialization technique in a very simple setting, to describe the local inference algorithm in the small as a high-level blueprint for an implementation, and to prove soundness of the inference algorithm. Our simple language is based on recursively defined records with nominal types, recursive function definitions, and a simple command language. We include conditionals and while-loops, because the type system and the associated inference algorithm are flow-sensitive, and so branching and repetition are interesting.

Mathematical Notation. Let $X \to Y$ be the set of functions from X to Y, and $X \rightharpoonup Y$ the set of partial functions, and $\mathsf{SetOf}(X)$ the set of all subsets of X. Functions $f \in X \rightharpoonup Y$ induce functions in $\hat{f} \in \mathsf{SetOf}(X) \to \mathsf{SetOf}(Y)$: $\hat{f}(X') = \{f(x) \mid x \subset X' \cap \mathrm{dom}(f)\}$. We usually omit the hat when the context resolves ambiguities. For $f \in X \rightharpoonup Y$ and Z some set, let $f|Z$ be the restriction of f to Z: $f|Z = \{(x,y) \in f \mid x \in Z\}$. For $f \in X \rightharpoonup Y$ and $g \in Y \to Z$, let $g \circ f = \{(x,g(f(x))) \mid x \in \mathrm{dom}(f)\}$. Note that $g \circ f \in X \rightharpoonup Z$. For $f, g \in X \rightharpoonup Y$, let $f[g] = g \cup (f \mid \{x \mid x \notin \mathrm{dom}(g)\})$. Let $x \mapsto y = \{(x,y)\}$. We write $f, x \mapsto y$ instead of $f[x \mapsto y]$ when we want to indicate that $x \notin \mathrm{dom}(f)$. If f is a type environment, we write $f[x:y]$ and $f,x:y$ instead of $f[x \mapsto y]$ and $f,x \mapsto y$. We write π_1 and π_2 for the first and second projection that map pairs to their components.

3.1   A Model Programming Language with Access Qualifiers

Our model is based on records. We refer to named record types as classes, and to records as objects. Record types are of the form $q\,C$, where q is an access qualifier and C a class identifier. The void-type has only one element, namely null. We define a mapping

---

[7] In this discussion, we ignore Java Generics. See [17] for a discussion of generics.

[8] It would also be sound to use Rd as the receiver qualifier for Thread.run(). However, this would be too restrictive, because it would globally enforce that threads never write to fields of their Thread-objects.

$$\Delta ::= \varepsilon \mid \Delta, \alpha \vartriangleleft B \mid \Delta, n : \text{Token} \quad \textit{(qualifier environments)}$$

$$\frac{}{\Delta, \alpha \vartriangleleft B, \Delta' \vdash \alpha \vartriangleleft B} \qquad \frac{}{\Delta, n : \text{Token}, \Delta' \vdash n : \text{Token}}$$

$$\frac{}{q <: \text{Any}} \qquad \frac{\Delta \vdash q \vartriangleleft B}{} \qquad \frac{}{\Delta \vdash n : \text{Token}}$$

$$\frac{}{\Delta \vdash q \vartriangleleft \text{Any}} \qquad \frac{}{\Delta \vdash q \vartriangleleft \text{Qual}} \qquad \frac{}{\Delta \vdash \text{RdWr} \vartriangleleft \text{Writeable}} \qquad \frac{}{\Delta \vdash \text{Fresh}(n) \vartriangleleft \text{Writeable}}$$

Fig. 5. Qualifier typing, $\Delta \vdash q \vartriangleleft B$ and $\Delta \vdash n : \text{Token}$

that erases qualifiers from types: $|q\, C| = C$ and $|\text{void}| = \text{void}$. *Subqualifying* is the least partial order such that $\text{Rd} <: \text{Any}$ and $\text{RdWr} <: \text{Any}$. *Subtyping* is the least partial order such that $p\, C <: q\, C$ for all $p <: q$. A *class table* is a set of class declarations for distinct class identifiers. Class declarations may be (mutually) recursive. A *method table* is a set of (mutually) recursive function declarations for distinct identifiers. The syntax of the model language is shown below. The identifiers x and n in the forms $(C\ x; e)$ and $(\texttt{newtoken}\, n; e)$ are binders with scope e, and we identify expressions up to renaming of bound identifiers[9]. The judgment in Figure 5 formalizes boundedness (writing $\vartriangleleft$ for `extends`) and ensures that arguments n of $\texttt{Fresh}(n)$ represent initialization tokens.

$$n, o \in \text{Name} \quad \textit{(names)} \qquad \alpha, \beta \in \text{QVar} \quad \textit{(qualifier variables, including myaccess)}$$
$$p, q \in \text{Qual} ::= \text{Rd} \mid \text{RdWr} \mid \text{Any} \mid \text{Fresh}(n) \mid \alpha \quad \textit{(access qualifiers)}$$
$$f, g \in \text{FieldId} \quad \textit{(field identifiers)} \qquad C, D \in \text{ClassId} \quad \textit{(class identifiers)}$$
$$class ::= \text{class}\, C\, \{\bar{T}\, \bar{f}\} \quad \textit{(class declarations)} \qquad T \in \text{Ty} ::= q\, C \mid \text{void} \quad \textit{(types)}$$
$$B \in \text{QualBound} ::= \text{Writeable} \mid \text{Any} \mid \text{Qual} \quad \textit{(qualifier bounds)}$$
$$m \in \text{MethodId} \quad \textit{(method identifiers)} \qquad x \in \text{Var} \quad \textit{(local variables)}$$
$$method ::= <\bar{\alpha} \vartriangleleft \bar{B}>\, T\, m(\bar{T}\, \bar{x})\, \{e\} \quad \textit{(method declarations)}$$

$$v \in \text{OpenVal} ::= \text{null} \mid n \mid x \qquad\qquad\qquad \textit{(open values)}$$
$$e \in \text{Exp} ::= v \mid C\, x; e \mid \texttt{newtoken}\, n; e \mid h; e \qquad \textit{(expressions)}$$
$$h \in \text{HdExp} ::= x{=}v \mid x{=}v.f \mid v.f{=}v \mid x{=}<\bar{q}>m(\bar{v}) \mid x{=}\text{new}\, q\, C \mid \quad \textit{(head expressions)}$$
$$\qquad\qquad\qquad \text{if}\, v\, e\, e \mid \text{while}\, v\, e \mid \text{commit}\, \text{Fresh}(n)\, \text{as}\, q$$

Derived form, $e; e'$: $v; e \stackrel{\Delta}{=} e \quad (h; e); e' \stackrel{\Delta}{=} h; (e; e') \quad (C\, x; e); e' \stackrel{\Delta}{=} C\, x; (e; e')$ if x not free in e'
$\qquad\qquad\qquad\quad (\texttt{newtoken}\, n; e); e' \stackrel{\Delta}{=} \texttt{newtoken}\, n; (e; e')$ if n not free in e'
Derived form, $e;$: $e; \stackrel{\Delta}{=} e; \text{null}$

Note that declarations of local variables associate a class C with the variable, but no access qualifier q. The reason for this design choice is that local variables may change their qualifier at commit-statements. We would find it misleading if our system fixed an access qualifier for a local variable at its declaration site, even though later the variable refers to objects with incompatible access qualifiers.

Our system also permits qualifier changes at assignments to local variables. This seems a natural design choice, given that we have flexible qualifiers for local variables anyway. When a local variable x is used, the type system assumes the access qualifier of the object that most recently got assigned to x. For instance, assuming a context where local variables r and w have types Rd Point and RdWr Point, respectively:

```
Point p; p=w;    // now p has type RdWr Point
p.x=42;          // this typechecks
p=r;             // now p has type Rd Point
p.x=42;          // type error: illegal write to Rd-object
```

---

[9] See also the remark on the operational semantics of `newtoken` at the end of Section 3.2.

3.2 Operational Semantics

Heaps are functions from names to objects. Each object is tagged with an access qualifier. These tags are auxiliary state in the sense that they have no effect on concrete program state or control flow, that is, they are erasable. The operational semantics also tracks the pool of tokens that have so far been generated. Token pools are erasable.

$$v \in \mathsf{Val} ::= \mathtt{null} \mid n \qquad obj \in \mathsf{Object} \triangleq \mathsf{Qual} \times (\mathsf{FieldId} \rightharpoonup \mathsf{Val}) ::= q\{\bar{f}{=}\bar{v}\}$$

$$h \in \mathsf{Heap} \triangleq \mathsf{Name} \rightharpoonup \mathsf{Object} \qquad t \in \mathsf{TokenPool} \triangleq \mathsf{SetOf}(\mathsf{Name})$$

Commit-environments are functions from names to access qualifiers. They are used to track `Fresh`-qualifiers that have been committed.

$$\delta \in \mathsf{CommitEnv} \triangleq \mathsf{Name} \rightharpoonup \mathsf{Qual}$$

Commit-environments δ induce functions $\hat{\delta}$ in $\mathsf{Qual} \rightarrow \mathsf{Qual}$, $\mathsf{Ty} \rightarrow \mathsf{Ty}$ and $\mathsf{Object} \rightarrow \mathsf{Object}$: $\hat{\delta}(\mathsf{Fresh}(n)) = q$ if $\delta(n) = q$, $\hat{\delta}(q) = q$ otherwise; $\hat{\delta}(q\,C) = \hat{\delta}(q)\,C$, $\hat{\delta}(\mathtt{void}) = \mathtt{void}$; $\hat{\delta}(q\{\bar{f}{=}\bar{v}\}) = \hat{\delta}(q)\{\bar{f}{=}\bar{v}\}$. If the context resolves ambiguities, we omit the hat.

A *stack frame* is a pair of a local store σ and an expression e:

$$\sigma \in \mathsf{Var} \rightharpoonup \mathsf{Val} \qquad fr \in \mathsf{Frame} \triangleq (\mathsf{Var} \rightharpoonup \mathsf{Val}) \times \mathsf{Exp} \qquad s \in \mathsf{Stack} ::= \mathtt{nil} \mid fr :: s$$

We extend the domain of functions σ to $\mathsf{OpenVal}$, by setting $\sigma(v) = v$ for $v \in \mathsf{Val}$. *Configurations* are triples of stacks, heaps and token pools.

$$cfg \in \mathsf{Configuration} \triangleq \mathsf{Stack} \times \mathsf{Heap} \times \mathsf{TokenPool}$$

The rules in Figure 6 define the small-step operational semantics on configurations. In the rules (Red Dcl) and (Red New Token), we implicitly use a bound-variable convention that allows us to rename bound variables and names appropriately.

(Red Dcl)
$$(\sigma, C\,x;e) :: s,h,t \rightarrow ((\sigma,x \mapsto \mathtt{null}),e) :: s,h,t$$

(Red New Token) $\quad n \notin t$
$$(\sigma, \mathtt{newtoken}\,n;e) :: s,h,t \rightarrow (\sigma,e) :: s,h,t \cup \{n\}$$

(Red Set Local)
$$(\sigma, x{=}v;e) :: s,h,t \rightarrow (\sigma[x \mapsto \sigma(v)],e) :: s,h,t$$

(Red Get) $\quad v \neq \mathtt{null} \quad \sigma(v) = n$
$$(\sigma, x{=}v.f;e) :: s,h,t \rightarrow (\sigma[x \mapsto \pi_2(h(n))(f)],e) :: s,h,t$$

(Red Set) $\quad v \neq \mathtt{null} \quad \sigma(v) = n$
$$(\sigma, v.f{=}w;e) :: s,h,t \rightarrow (\sigma,e) :: s,h[n \mapsto (\pi_1(h(n)), \pi_2(h(n))[f \mapsto \sigma(w)])],t$$

(Red Call) $\quad <\bar{\alpha} \triangleleft \bar{B}> U\,m(\bar{T}\,\bar{x})\{e'\}$
$$(\sigma, x{=}{<}\bar{q}{>}m(\bar{v});e) :: s,h,t \rightarrow (\bar{x} \mapsto \sigma(\bar{v}),e'[\bar{q}/\bar{\alpha}]) :: (\sigma,x{=}{<}\bar{q}{>}m(\bar{v});e) :: s,h,t$$

(Red Return)
$$(\sigma,w) :: (\sigma',x{=}{<}\bar{q}{>}m(\bar{v});e) :: s,h,t \rightarrow (\sigma'[x \mapsto \sigma(w)],e) :: s,h,t$$

(Red New) $\quad \mathtt{class}\,C\{\bar{T}\,\bar{f}\} \quad n \notin dom(h)$
$$(\sigma, x{=}\mathtt{new}\,q\,C;e) :: s,h,t \rightarrow (\sigma[x \mapsto n],e) :: s,(h,n \mapsto q\{\bar{f}{=}\mathtt{null}\}),t$$

(Red If True) $\quad \sigma(v) = \mathtt{null}$
$$(\sigma,(\mathtt{if}\,v\,e\,e');e'') :: s,h,t \rightarrow (\sigma,e;e'') :: s,h,t$$

(Red If False) $\quad \sigma(v) \neq \mathtt{null}$
$$(\sigma,(\mathtt{if}\,v\,e\,e');e'') :: s,h,t \rightarrow (\sigma,e';e'') :: s,h,t$$

(Red While True) $\quad \sigma(v) = \mathtt{null}$
$$(\sigma,(\mathtt{while}\,v\,e);e') :: s,h,t \rightarrow (\sigma,e;(\mathtt{while}\,v\,e);e') :: s,h,t$$

(Red While False) $\quad \sigma(v) \neq \mathtt{null}$
$$(\sigma,(\mathtt{while}\,v\,e);e') :: s,h,t \rightarrow (\sigma,e') :: s,h,t$$

(Red Commit) $\quad \delta = (n \mapsto q)$
$$(\sigma, \mathtt{commit}\,\mathtt{Fresh}(n)\,\mathtt{as}\,q;e) :: s,h,t \rightarrow (\sigma,e) :: s,(\delta \circ h),t$$

Fig. 6. Operational semantics

3.3   Type System

A *type environment* is a function from variables and names to types.

$$\iota \in \mathsf{Var} \cup \mathsf{Name} \qquad \Gamma \in \mathsf{TyEnv} \triangleq (\mathsf{Var} \cup \mathsf{Name}) \to \mathsf{Ty}$$

Let $\Gamma <: \Gamma'$ whenever $\mathrm{dom}(\Gamma) = \mathrm{dom}(\Gamma')$ and $\Gamma(\iota) <: \Gamma'(\iota)$ for all ι in $\mathrm{dom}(\Gamma)$. We extend the domain of type environments to include $\mathtt{null}$: $\Gamma(\mathtt{null}) = \mathtt{void}$.

We define: $\Delta \vdash q : \mathtt{ok}$ iff $\Delta \vdash q \triangleleft \mathtt{Qual}$; $C : \mathtt{ok}$ iff C is declared; $\Delta \vdash q\, C : \mathtt{ok}$ iff $\Delta \vdash q : \mathtt{ok}$ and $C : \mathtt{ok}$; $\Delta \vdash \mathtt{void} : \mathtt{ok}$ always; $\Delta \vdash \Gamma : \mathtt{ok}$ iff $\Delta \vdash \Gamma(\iota) : \mathtt{ok}$ for all ι in $\mathrm{dom}(\Gamma)$; $\Delta \vdash \delta : \mathtt{ok}$ iff $\Delta \vdash n : \mathtt{Token}$ and $\Delta \vdash \delta(n) : \mathtt{ok}$ for all x in $\mathrm{dom}(\delta)$.

Typing judgments for expressions have the following formats:

$$\Sigma \vdash \{\Gamma, \delta\} e : T\{\Gamma', \delta'\} \qquad \Sigma \vdash \{\Gamma, \delta\} h \{\Gamma', \delta'\}$$

(Γ, δ) represents the configuration before executing the expression, and (Γ', δ') the one afterwards. We refer to (Γ, δ) as the precondition of the expression, and to (Γ', δ') as its postcondition. Recall that we permit local variables to change the qualifier components of their types. This is why we need to include type environments in postconditions. We write $\Delta; \Gamma \vdash v : T$ to abbreviate $\Delta \vdash \{\Gamma, \emptyset\} v : T\{\Gamma, \emptyset\}$.

Now we can present the typing rules for expressions:

(Null)
$$\frac{\Delta \vdash \Gamma, \delta, T : \mathtt{ok}}{\Delta \vdash \{\Gamma, \delta\}\mathtt{null} : T\{\Gamma, \delta\}}$$

(Id)
$$\frac{\Delta \vdash \Gamma, \delta : \mathtt{ok}}{\Delta \vdash \{\Gamma, \delta\}\iota : \Gamma(\iota)\{\Gamma, \delta\}}$$

(Sub)
$$\frac{\Delta \vdash U, \Gamma'' : \mathtt{ok} \quad T <: U \quad \Delta \vdash \{\Gamma, \delta\} e : T\{\Gamma', \delta'\} \quad \Gamma' <: \Gamma''}{\Delta \vdash \{\Gamma, \delta\} e : U\{\Gamma'', \delta'\}}$$

(Dcl)
$$\frac{\Delta \vdash q\,C : \mathtt{ok} \quad \delta(q) = q \quad \Delta \vdash \{(\Gamma, x : q\,C), \delta\} e : T\{(\Gamma', x : U), \delta'\}}{\Delta \vdash \{\Gamma, \delta\} C\, x; e : T\{\Gamma', \delta'\}}$$

(Seq) $\quad \Delta \vdash \Gamma, \delta : \mathtt{ok}$
$$\frac{\Delta \vdash \{\Gamma, \delta\} h\{\Gamma', \delta'\} \quad \Delta \vdash \{\Gamma', \delta'\} e : T\{\Gamma'', \delta''\}}{\Delta \vdash \{\Gamma, \delta\} h; e : T\{\Gamma'', \delta''\}}$$

(New Token)
$$\frac{\Delta \vdash \Gamma, \delta, \Gamma', \delta' : \mathtt{ok} \quad \Delta, n : \mathtt{Token} \vdash \{\Gamma, (\delta, n \mapsto \mathtt{Fresh}(n))\} e : T\{\Gamma', (\delta', n \mapsto q)\}}{\Delta \vdash \{\Gamma, \delta\}\mathtt{newtoken}\, n; e : T\{\Gamma', \delta'\}}$$

In the rule (Dcl), we assume that the newly declared local variable initially has type $q\,C$, where q can be chosen appropriately. An automatic typechecker needs to delay the choice of an appropriate q until the new variable first gets assigned to. This delayed choice of q is subsumed by the inference algorithm in Section 3.4. The premise $\delta(q) = q$ ensures that q is not a previously committed $\mathtt{Fresh}$-qualifier.

In the typing rules for head expressions, note that we update the qualifiers of local variables after assignments, implementing flexible qualifiers of local variables, as discussed earlier. Crucially, the rule (Set) checks that the object is writeable:

(Set Local)
$$\frac{|\Gamma(v)| = |\Gamma(x)|}{\Delta \vdash \{\Gamma, \delta\} x = v\{\Gamma[x : \Gamma(v)], \delta\}}$$

(Get) $\mathtt{class}\ C\{..\,T\,f..\}$
$$\frac{\Gamma(v) = q\,C \quad U = T[q/\mathtt{myaccess}] \quad |U| = |\Gamma(x)|}{\Delta \vdash \{\Gamma, \delta\} x = v.f\{\Gamma[x : U], \delta\}}$$

(Set) $\mathtt{class}\ C\{..\,T\,f..\}$
$$\frac{\Gamma(v) = q\,C \quad \Delta \vdash q \triangleleft \mathtt{Writeable} \quad \Delta; \Gamma \vdash w : T[q/\mathtt{myaccess}]}{\Delta \vdash \{\Gamma, \delta\} v.f = w\{\Gamma, \delta\}}$$

(Call) $<\bar{\alpha} \triangleleft \bar{B}>\, U\, m(\bar{T}\ \bar{x})\{e\}$
$$\frac{\delta(\bar{q}) = \bar{q} \quad \Delta \vdash \bar{q} \triangleleft \bar{B} \quad \Delta; \Gamma \vdash \bar{v} : \bar{T}[\bar{q}/\bar{\alpha}] \quad V = U[\bar{q}/\bar{\alpha}] \quad |V| = |\Gamma(x)|}{\Delta \vdash \{\Gamma, \delta\} x = <\bar{q}> m(\bar{v})\{\Gamma[x : V], \delta\}}$$

(New)
$$\frac{\Delta \vdash q\,C : \mathtt{ok} \quad \delta(q) = q \quad C = |\Gamma(x)|}{\Delta \vdash \{\Gamma, \delta\} x = \mathtt{new}\, q\,C\{\Gamma[x : q\,C], \delta\}}$$

(If)
$$\frac{\Delta; \Gamma \vdash v : T \quad \Delta \vdash \{\Gamma, \delta\} e : \mathtt{void}\{\Gamma', \delta'\} \quad \Delta \vdash \{\Gamma, \delta\} e' : \mathtt{void}\{\Gamma', \delta'\}}{\Delta \vdash \{\Gamma, \delta\}\mathtt{if}\, v\, e\, e'\{\Gamma', \delta'\}}$$

(While)
$$\frac{\Delta; \Gamma \vdash v : T \quad \Delta \vdash \{\Gamma, \delta\} e : \mathtt{void}\{\Gamma, \delta\}}{\Delta \vdash \{\Gamma, \delta\}\mathtt{while}\, v\, e\{\Gamma, \delta\}}$$

Well-typed stack frames, $\Delta;\Delta';\Gamma;\Gamma' \vdash fr : T$ **and** $\Delta;\Delta';\Gamma;\Gamma' \vdash fr : T \to U$:

$$\frac{\Delta,\Delta';\Gamma,\Gamma' \vdash \sigma : \Gamma'' \quad \Delta,\Delta' \vdash \{\Gamma'',\delta\}e : T\{\Gamma''',\delta'\} \quad \text{dom}(\delta) \subseteq \text{dom}(\Delta') \quad \delta \circ \Gamma'' = \Gamma''}{\Delta;\Delta';\Gamma;\Gamma' \vdash (\sigma,e) : T}$$

$$\frac{fr = (\sigma, x = <\bar{q}>m(\bar{v});e) \quad \Delta;\Delta';\Gamma;\Gamma' \vdash fr : U \quad <\bar{\alpha}\lhd\bar{B}> T\ m(\bar{V}\ \bar{x})\{e'\}}{\Delta;\Delta';\Gamma;\Gamma' \vdash fr : T[\bar{q}/\bar{\alpha}] \to U} \qquad \frac{\Delta \vdash \Gamma : \text{ok} \quad (\forall x \in \text{dom}(\sigma))(\Delta;\Gamma \vdash \sigma(x) : \Gamma'(x))}{\Delta;\Gamma \vdash \sigma : \Gamma'}$$

Well-typed stacks, $\Delta;\Gamma \vdash s : \text{ok}$ **and** $\Delta;\Gamma \vdash s : T \to \text{ok}$:

$$\frac{\Delta \vdash \Gamma, T : \text{ok}}{\Delta;\Gamma \vdash \text{nil} : T \to \text{ok}} \qquad \frac{\Delta;\Delta';\Gamma;\Gamma' \vdash fr : T \quad \Delta;\Gamma \vdash s : T \to \text{ok}}{\Delta,\Delta';\Gamma,\Gamma' \vdash fr :: s : \text{ok}} \qquad \frac{\Delta;\Delta';\Gamma;\Gamma' \vdash fr : T \to U \quad \Delta;\Gamma \vdash s : U \to \text{ok}}{\Delta,\Delta';\Gamma,\Gamma' \vdash fr :: s : T \to \text{ok}}$$

Well-typed objects, $\Delta;\Gamma \vdash obj : T$:

$$\frac{\text{class}\ C\ \{\bar{T}\ \bar{f}\} \quad \Delta;\Gamma \vdash \bar{v} : \bar{T}[q/\text{myaccess}]}{\Delta;\Gamma \vdash q\{\bar{f}=\bar{v}\} : q\ C}$$

Well-typed heaps, $\Delta;\Gamma \vdash h : \text{ok}$:

$$\frac{\text{dom}(\Gamma) = \text{dom}(h) \quad (\forall n \in \text{dom}(h))(\Delta;\Gamma \vdash h(n) : \Gamma(n))}{\Delta;\Gamma \vdash h : \text{ok}}$$

Well-typed token pools, $\Delta \vdash t : \text{ok}$:

$$\frac{\text{dom}(\Delta) = \text{dom}(t) \quad (\forall n \in t)(\Delta \vdash n : \text{Token})}{\Delta \vdash t : \text{ok}}$$

Well-typed configurations, $cfg : \text{ok}$:

$$\frac{\Delta;\Gamma \vdash s : \text{ok} \quad \Delta;\Gamma \vdash h : \text{ok} \quad \Delta \vdash t : \text{ok}}{s,h,t : \text{ok}}$$

Fig. 7. Typing rules for configurations

(Commit)
$$\frac{\delta(n) = \text{Fresh}(n) \quad \Delta \vdash q : \text{ok} \quad \delta(q) = q \quad \delta' = n \mapsto q}{\Delta \vdash \{\Gamma,\delta\}\text{commit Fresh}(n)\ \text{as}\ q\{\delta' \circ \Gamma, \delta' \circ \delta\}}$$

In the (While) rule, note that the environments are an invariant for the loop body. Consequently, it is disallowed to commit inside a loop body a token that was generated outside the loop body (as this would modify the commit-environment). On the other hand, it is allowed to commit tokens that were generated inside the loop body, because the rule (New Token) removes such tokens from pre- and postcondtions.

For checking class and method declarations, we use the following rules:

(Class)
$$\frac{\text{myaccess}\lhd\text{Qual} \vdash \bar{T} : \text{ok}}{\text{class}\ C\ \{\bar{T}\ \bar{f}\} : \text{ok}}$$

(Method)
$$\frac{\bar{\alpha}\lhd\bar{B} \vdash U,\bar{T} : \text{ok} \quad \bar{\alpha}\lhd\bar{B} \vdash \{\bar{x}:\bar{T},\emptyset\}e : U\{\Gamma,\emptyset\}}{<\bar{\alpha}\lhd\bar{B}>\ U\ m(\bar{T}\ x)\{e\} : \text{ok}}$$

Soundness. We extend the type system to configurations, as shown in Figure 7. The judgment for stack frames has the format $\Delta;\Delta';\Gamma;\Gamma' \vdash fr : T$. The type T is the type of the return value. Whereas Δ and Γ account for tokens and objects that are known to stack frames below *fr*, the environments Δ' and Γ' account for tokens and objects that have been generated in *fr* or in stack frames that were previously above *fr* and have been popped off the stack. The premise $\text{dom}(\delta) \subseteq \text{dom}(\Delta')$ in the first typing rule for stack frames captures formally that the commit-environment for the top frame never contains initialization tokens that have been generated in the rest of the stack. This is important for the soundness of (Commit). Another judgment for stack frames has the form $\Delta;\Delta';\Gamma;\Gamma' \vdash fr : T \to U$. Intuitively, it holds when $\Delta;\Delta';\Gamma;\Gamma' \vdash fr : U$ and in addition *fr* currently waits for the termination of a method call that returns a value of type T.

We can now prove the following preservation theorem:

Theorem 1 (Preservation). *If cfg* : ok *and cfg* $\to$ *cfg', then cfg'* : ok.

The proof of the preservation theorem is mostly routine and contained in the companion report [17]. The following theorem says that the type system is sound for object immutability: *well-typed programs never write to fields of* Rd-*objects*. The theorem is a simple corollary of the preservation theorem and the fact that a configuration is ill-typed when the head expression of its top frame instructs to write to a field of a Rd-object.

Theorem 2 (Soundness for Object Immutability). *If cfg* : ok, *cfg* $\rightarrow^*$ $(\sigma, v.f = w; e)$ :: s, h, t *and* $\sigma(v) = n$, *then* $\pi_1(h(n)) \neq$ Rd.

3.4 Local Annotation Inference

Figure 8 presents the syntax for annotation-free expressions E, as obtained from the expression syntax by omitting the specification statements newtoken and commit, as well as the qualifier arguments at call sites and the qualifier annotations at object creation sites. The function $e \mapsto |e|$ erases specification commands and annotations from annotated expressions. This section presents an algorithm that infers the erased information, deciding the following question: Given Δ, Γ, E, T such that $\Delta \vdash \Gamma, T$: ok. Are there e, Γ' such that $|e| = E$ and $\Delta \vdash \{\Gamma, \emptyset\} e : T \{\Gamma', \emptyset\}$?

We have proven that our algorithm answers this question soundly: if the inference algorithm answers "yes", then the answer to this question is indeed "yes". We believe that the converse also holds (completeness), but cannot claim a rigorous proof. The algorithm constructs an annotated expression e whose erasure is E. An implementation does not have to really construct e, because knowing that e exists suffices. There are, of course, many annotated expressions that erase to the same annotation-free expression. So what is the strategy for inserting the specification commands without restricting generality? Conceptually, the algorithm parses the unannotated E from left to right, inserting specification commands newtoken and commit as needed.

Inserting Commits. For commits, we use a lazy strategy and only insert a commit if this is strictly necessary. For instance, we never insert commits in front of local variable assignment, because commits and local variable assignments can always be commuted without breaking well-typedness or changing the erasure. The spots where commits do get inserted are: (1) in front of field assignments when a value of type Fresh(n) is assigned to a field of type q where $q \neq$ Fresh(n), (2) in front of method calls when the method signature forces to commit types of arguments, (3) in front of the return value when the return type forces to commit the type of the return value, (4) at the end of conditional branches to match commits that have been performed in the other branch, (5) at the end of loop bodies (for tokens generated inside the loop) to establish the loop invariant, and (6) in front of loop entries (for tokens generated outside the loop) to establish the loop invariant. Consider the following example with a while-loop:

```
void r(Rd C x);      void w(RdWr C x);      <a ◁ Writeable> f (a C x);
C x; x = new C; while x ( f(x); w(x); );
```
Generated annotated expression:
```
newtoken m; newtoken n; C x; x = new Fresh(n) C;
commit Fresh(n) as RdWr; while x ( <RdWr>f(x); w(x); );
commit Fresh(m) as Any;
```

$E \in$ AfreeExp ::= $v \mid C \, x;E \mid H;E$ *(annotation-free expressions)*

$H \in$ AfreeHdExp ::= $x = v \mid x = v.f \mid v.f = v \mid x = m(\bar{v}) \mid$ *(annotation-free head expressions)*
                 $x = \text{new} \, C \mid \text{if} \, v \, E \, E \mid \text{while} \, v \, E$

$|\cdot| : \text{Exp} \to \text{AfreeExp}$

$|v| \overset{\triangle}{=} v$ $|C \, x;e| \overset{\triangle}{=} C \, x;|e|$ $|\text{newtoken} \, n;e| \overset{\triangle}{=} |e|$ $|\text{commit Fresh}(n) \, \text{as} \, q;e| \overset{\triangle}{=} |e|$

$|h;e| \overset{\triangle}{=} |h|;|e|$, if $h \neq \text{commit Fresh}(\_) \, \text{as} \, \_$

$|\cdot| : \text{HdExp} \to \text{AfreeHdExp}$

$|x = \langle \bar{q} \rangle m(\bar{v})| \overset{\triangle}{=} x = m(\bar{v})$ $|x = \text{new} \, q \, C| \overset{\triangle}{=} x = \text{new} \, C$ $|\text{if} \, v \, E \, E'| \overset{\triangle}{=} \text{if} \, v \, |E| \, |E'|$

$|\text{while} \, v \, E| \overset{\triangle}{=} \text{while} \, v \, |E|$ $|h| \overset{\triangle}{=} h$, otherwise

Fig. 8. Annotation-free expressions and erasure

In the above expression, the method call w(x) inside the loop body forces a commit in front of the loop.[10] In contrast, the following expression does not typecheck, because the loop body forces x to have both a Writeable type and type Rd, which is impossible.

```
C x; x = new C; while x ( f(x); r(x); ); // TYPE ERROR
```

One could deal with while-loops by a fixed point computation that requires two iterations over the loop body, one to discover a candidate loop invariant and another one to check if the candidate grants the access permissions required by the loop body. Our algorithm is syntax-directed, because this is simpler to implement on top of the JSR 308 checkers framework [23].

Generating Tokens. Concerning the generation of initialization tokens, there are two questions to answer. Firstly, when does the algorithm generate new initialization tokens, and secondly, where does the algorithm insert the newtoken statements that bind the tokens. Generation happens (1) at variable declaration sites, (2) at object creation sites, and (3) at call sites for instantiation of qualifier parameters that occur in the method return type but not in the method parameter types. At such sites, the algorithm generates a new token n and uses Fresh(n) as the type of the newly declared variable, the newly created object or the method return value. In the above example, m and n are the tokens that were generated at the variable declaration site for x and at the object creation site that follows it. Note that tokens generated at variable creation sites often do not occur in the program text. Using Fresh(n) as the qualifier for newly created objects (and similarly for variable declarations and method returns) is no restriction, because the following type- and erasure-preserving transformation replaces qualifiers q at object creation sites by Fresh(n):

$$x = \text{new} \, q \, C \to \text{newtoken} \, n; x = \text{new Fresh}(n) \, C; \text{commit Fresh}(n) \, \text{as} \, q$$

As for where to insert newtoken, observe that these can always be pulled out of conditional branches by the following type- and erasure-preserving transformation:

if v (newtoken $n;e$) $e' \to$ newtoken $n;$ if $v \, e$ ($e';$ commit Fresh(n) as $\delta(n);$)
where δ is the commit environment in the postcondition of e (as found in the type derivation)

---

[10] Technically, the inference algorithm delays the generation of the prefix newtoken m;newtoken n; and the postfix commit Fresh(m) as Any. These get inserted at the top level, see Theorem 3.

$$\boxed{f;g} \qquad f;g \overset{\Delta}{=} (g \circ f) \cup g \quad \text{if } \mathrm{dom}(f) \cap \mathrm{dom}(g) = \emptyset$$

$$\boxed{ts \in \mathsf{Scopes} ::= t \mid t :: ts} \qquad |t| \overset{\Delta}{=} t \quad |t :: ts| \overset{\Delta}{=} t \cup |ts| \qquad \mathrm{rest}(t) \overset{\Delta}{=} \emptyset \quad \mathrm{rest}(t :: ts) \overset{\Delta}{=} |ts|$$

$$\mathrm{newtokens}(t); e \overset{\Delta}{=} \mathtt{newtoken}\ n_1; \ldots; \mathtt{newtoken}\ n_k; e \qquad\qquad \text{if } t = \{n_1, \ldots, n_k\}$$
$$\mathrm{commit}(\delta) \overset{\Delta}{=} \mathtt{commit\ Fresh}(n_1)\ \mathtt{as}\ q_1; \ldots; \mathtt{commit\ Fresh}(n_k)\ \mathtt{as}\ q_k; \quad \text{if } \delta = \{n_1 \mapsto q_1, \ldots, n_k \mapsto q_k\}$$

Fig. 9. Helpers

We cannot pull `newtoken` out of loops, though, because the typing rules prevent loop bodies to commit tokens that were generated outside the loop. Consider the following variation of the earlier example:

```
C x; while x ( x = new C; f(x); r(x); );
```

In contrast to the erroneous expression further up, this expression is well-typed. The inference algorithm generates the following annotated expression for it:

```
newtoken m; C x; commit Fresh(m) as Rd; while x (
    newtoken n; x = new Fresh(n) C; <Fresh(n)>f(x);
    commit Fresh(n) as Rd; r(x); );
```

The `newtoken` command commutes with all other commands, and therefore the inference algorithm generates `newtoken` at the beginning of loop bodies only (leaving token generation at the beginning of method bodies implicit).

Subqualifying Constraints. To deal with subqualifying the inference algorithm generates subqualifying constraints. We extend qualifiers by existential variables:

$$?\alpha \in \mathsf{ExVar} \quad \text{(existential variables)} \qquad p, q \in \mathsf{Qual} ::= \cdots \mid ?\alpha \qquad \Delta \vdash ?\alpha \lhd \mathsf{Qual}$$

We partition the set of qualifiers into the sets PQual of *persistent qualifiers* and TQual of *transient qualifiers*:

$$\mathsf{TQual} \overset{\Delta}{=} \{\mathtt{Fresh}(n) \mid n \in \mathsf{Name}\} \qquad \mathsf{PQual} \overset{\Delta}{=} \mathsf{Qual} \setminus \mathsf{TQual}$$

A *substitution* is a function from existential variables to closed persistent qualifiers:

$$\rho \in \mathsf{Subst} \overset{\Delta}{=} \mathsf{ExVar} \rightharpoonup (\mathsf{PQual} \setminus \mathsf{ExVar})$$

Note that existential variables range over persistent qualifiers only. Substitutions ρ induce functions $\hat{\rho}$ in $\mathsf{PQual} \to \mathsf{PQual}$: $\hat{\rho}(?\alpha) = \rho(?\alpha)$ if $?\alpha \in \mathrm{dom}(\rho)$; $\hat{\rho}(q) = q$ otherwise. Let $\hat{\rho}(T)$ (resp. $\hat{\rho}(e)$) denote the type (resp. expression) obtained by substituting all qualifier occurrences q by $\hat{\rho}(q)$. We omit the hat when no ambiguities arise.

A *constraint set* contains pairs of the forms (q, B) and (p, q):

$$C \in \mathsf{Constraints} \overset{\Delta}{=} \mathsf{SetOf}(\mathsf{PQual} \times \mathsf{QualBound} \cup \mathsf{PQual} \times \mathsf{PQual})$$

A Δ-*solution* of a constraint set C is substitution ρ such that $\Delta \vdash \rho(q) \lhd B$ and $\rho(p) <: \rho(q)$ for all $(q, B), (p, q)$ in C.

Inference Algorithm. The inference judgment has the following format, where ts, Γ, δ_{pre} and T are inherited attributes, and the other attributes are synthesized.

$$ts; \Gamma \vdash E : T \Downarrow (\Gamma', \delta, ts', t, C)^{\text{for} (\delta_{pre} \vdash e)}$$

The synthesized annotated expression e is such that $|E| = e$. An implementation does not need to compute e or track δ_{pre}, as the other attributes do not depend on them.

- (Γ, δ_{pre}) represents the precondition for e.
- $(\Gamma', (\delta_{pre}; \delta))$ represents the postcondition for e.
- ts contains the tokens in scope before e. ts has a stack structure that reflects the nesting of enclosing while loops.
- ts' contains the tokens in scope after e.
- t contains all tokens n in $\text{rest}(ts')$ such that the type derivation for e has a leaf of the form $\Delta \vdash \text{Fresh}(n) \triangleleft \text{Writeable}$. These tokens must be tracked because they cannot be committed to Rd in front of enclosing while-loops. (See the example on page 539.)
- C are the subqualifying constraints required for well-typedness of e.

For the details of the inference algorithm we refer to our report [17], where the following soundness theorem is proven:

Theorem 3 (Soundness of Inference). *Suppose* $\text{ran}(\Delta) \subseteq \text{QualBound}$, $(\Delta \vdash \Gamma, T : \text{ok})$, Γ, T *do not contain existential variables,* $\emptyset; \Gamma \vdash E : T \Downarrow (\Gamma', \_, t, \_, C)^{\text{for}(\emptyset \vdash e)}$ *and* ρ Δ-*solves* C. *Then* $(\Delta \vdash \{\Gamma, \emptyset\} \text{newtokens}(t); \rho(e); \text{commit}(\delta) : T\{(\delta; \rho) \circ \Gamma', \emptyset\})$ *for* $\delta = \{(n, \text{Any}) \mid n \in t, \hat{\delta}(n) = \text{Fresh}(n)\}$.

4 Related Work

Immutability. Our type system supports class immutability, object immutability, and read-only references, allows flexible object initialization, and is simple and direct (building only on the access qualifiers Rd, RdWr and Any). To the best of our knowledge, no existing type system for a Java-like language meets all these goals at once: Our earlier system Jimuva [18] supports object immutability and open-world class immutability, but requires immutable objects to be initialized inside constructors and does not meet the goal of simplicity and directness, as it requires ownership types, effect annotations and anonymity annotations in addition to access qualifiers. IGJ [34] is simple, direct and supports both object immutability and read-only references, but requires immutable objects to be initialized inside constructors and its support for deep immutability is limited. For instance, IGJ has no way of enforcing that the character array inside an immutable string is part of the string and should thus be immutable. This would either require immutable arrays or a special treatment of owned mutable subobjects, neither of which IGJ supports[11]. SafeJava [4] and Joe₃ [22] are ownership type systems that support immutable objects with long initialization phases, where the transition from "uninitialized" to "initialized" is allowed through unique object references. In order to maintain

---

[11] IGJ supports immutable arrays initialized by array initializers. This is not enough to check the String-constructor String(char[] c), because the length of c is not known statically.

uniqueness they use destructive reads, which is a rather unnatural programming style in Java-like languages. These systems build on top of expressive ownership type systems, thus violating our design goals of simplicity and directness. Frozen objects [20] support immutable objects with long initialization phases, but builds on the Boogie verification methodology [1], so is not suitable for an independent pluggable type system. The Universe type system [21] features read-only references. In particular, Generic Universe Types [12] support covariant class parameters if the main modifier of the supertype is Any (which is essentially what we and IGJ [34] do).

Unkel and Lam [31] automatically infer stationary fields, i.e., fields that may turn immutable outside constructors and after previous assignments, and thus are not necessarily final. Their fully automatic analysis requires the whole program. It only detects fields that turn stationary before their objects have been written to the heap, and is in this respect more restrictive than our system, which can deal with stack-local *regions*, as needed for initializing cyclic structures. On the other hand, our system only works at the granularity of objects. Interestingly, non-final stationary fields are reportedly much more common than final fields.

Our system does not address *temporary immutability*, which would require heavier techniques in order to track aliasing on the heap. On an experimental level, statically checking temporary immutability has been addressed by Pechtchanski and Sarkar [24]. On a theoretical level, it is very nicely supported by fractional permissions [5].

Object confinement and ownership. For open-world class immutability, we use qualifier polymorphism to express several confinement properties. Firstly, we express a variant of so-called anonymous methods [32] in terms of qualifier polymorphism. Anonymous methods do not write this to the heap. Our variant of anonymity for constructors of immutable classes is slightly weaker and forbids that this is written to the heap outside the Fresh region in which the instance of the immutable class is constructed. Secondly, by combining the myaccess class parameter with conditions on method types, we can express that representation objects of immutable objects are encapsulated, thus avoiding the need to include both access qualifiers *and* ownership annotations in the system. To this end, we make use of qualifier-polymorphic methods, similar to owner-polymorphic methods in ownership type systems [4,9,18,27,33].

It is not clear if the myaccess parameter alone is enough to express tree-structured ownership hierarchies in general, as facilitated in parametric ownership type systems (e.g., [8], [4]) through instantiating the owner class parameter by rep or this, and in the Universe type system [21] through the rep-modifier. Potanin's system FGJ+c for package-level confinement [26] is based on a static set of owner constants (formally similar to Rd and RdWr but without the additional access semantics). It seems that very similar confinement properties as in FGJ+c could be expressed purely in terms of qualifier-polymorphic methods and without the owner constants. A subtle difference, however, is this: FGJ+c, as most ownership type systems, allows methods to return confined objects, ensuring safety by preventing "outside" class clients from calling such methods. Our system, on the other hand, prevents methods from returning confined objects in the first place. In an open world, where class clients may not follow the rules of the pluggable type system, the latter is the only safe choice.

Type systems for flexible object initialization. There are several articles on initialization techniques for non-nullness type systems [13,14,28]. Fähndrich and Xia's system of "delayed types" [14] is most closely related to our work, like us using lexically scoped regions for safe typestate changes, and using a class parameter representing a "delay time", similar to our myaccess parameter. Unlike us, Fähndrich and Xia do not address local annotation inference. Our system is considerably simpler than theirs, because the initialization problem for immutability seems inherently simpler than the initialization problem for object invariants. Intuitively, there are two reasons for this: Firstly, whereas for object immutability the end of the initialization phase is merely associated with the disposal of a write permission, for object invariants it is associated with an *obligation* to prove the invariant. Secondly, a major complication in [14] is the need to permit inserting uninitialized objects into initialized data structures. This is essential to satisfactorily support cyclic data structures, but requires the use of existential types. Fortunately, this complication does not arise for immutability, because no objects (whether uninitialized or not) ever get inserted into *immutable* data structures.

J\mask [28] is a type-and-effect system for reasoning about object initialization. It is based on a rich language for specifying partial object initialization, including primitives for expressing that fields may or must be uninitialized, as well as conditional assertions. It is designed to guarantee that well-typed programs never read uninitialized fields. It is not designed for immutability, and consequently offers no support for specifying deep immutability or object confinement, as needed for object and class immutability. J\mask (based on a rich specification language for partial object initialization) is quite different in nature to Fähndrich and Xia's delayed types (based on a variant of lexically scoped regions combined with dependent types). Qi and Myers rightly claim that J\mask supports some initialization patterns that delayed types do not, giving bottom-up initialization of trees with parent pointers as an example where delayed types cannot establish object invariants in the required order. This example causes no problems for our immutability system, see Figure 3. In fact, our annotations for this example avoid conditional assertions and are thus simpler than J\mask's (but this comparison is not quite fair, as J\mask and our system have different goals).

Lexically scoped regions. Stack-local regions are closely related to lexically scoped regions [30] for region-based memory management (see also [16]). Whereas, in region-based memory management, lexical scoping is used to statically determine when memory regions can safely be deallocated, here we use it to statically determine when the types of memory regions can safely be changed. Lexically scoped regions do not have a separate commit-statement, but associate the end of region lifetimes with the end of region name scopes. We opted for a separate commit-statement, because it simplifies the description of our inference algorithm, which works by a left-to-right pass over the abstract syntax tree, inserting commits when field or method types enforce this.

5 Conclusion

We presented a pluggable type system for immutable classes, immutable objects, and read-only references. The system supports flexible initialization outside constructors by means of stack-local regions. Our system shows, for the first time, that support for the various forms of immutability, including open-world class immutability, is possible without building on top of an expressive ownership type system (though the class parameter myaccess effectively provides some notion of confinement) and without using effect annotations or unique references. A lesson we have learned is that parametric qualifier polymorphism is a very expressive tool, both for flexibility and confinement.

Acknowledgments. We thank the anonymous ECOOP referees and James Noble for their careful reviews, and comments and critique that helped improve the paper.

References

1. Barnett, M., DeLine, R., Fähndrich, M., Leino, K.R.M., Schulte, W.: Verification of object-oriented programs with invariants. Journal of Object Technology 3(6), 27–56 (2004)
2. Bierhoff, K., Aldrich, J.: Modular typestate verification of aliased objects. In: OOPSLA, pp. 301–320 (2007)
3. Bloch, J.: Effective Java. Addison-Wesley, Reading (2001)
4. Boyapati, C.: SafeJava: A Unified Type System for Safe Programming. Ph.D thesis, MIT (2004)
5. Boyland, J.: Checking interference with fractional permissions. In: Cousot, R. (ed.) SAS 2003. LNCS, vol. 2694, pp. 55–72. Springer, Heidelberg (2003)
6. Boyland, J., Noble, J., Retert, W.: Capabilities for sharing: A generalisation of uniqueness and read-only. In: Knudsen, J.L. (ed.) ECOOP 2001. LNCS, vol. 2072, pp. 2–27. Springer, Heidelberg (2001)
7. Boyland, J., Retert, W.: Connecting effects and uniqueness with adoption. In: POPL, pp. 283–295 (2005)
8. Clarke, D., Potter, J., Noble, J.: Ownership types for flexible alias protection. In: OOPSLA, pp. 48–64 (1998)
9. Clarke, D., Wrigstad, T.: External uniqueness is unique enough. In: Cardelli, L. (ed.) ECOOP 2003. LNCS, vol. 2743, pp. 176–200. Springer, Heidelberg (2003)
10. Crary, K., Walker, D., Morrisett, G.: Typed memory management in a calculus of capabilities. In: POPL, pp. 262–275 (1999)
11. DeLine, R., Fähndrich, M.: Enforcing high-level protocols in low-level software. In: PLDI, pp. 59–69 (2001)
12. Dietl, W., Drossopoulou, S., Müller, P.: Generic universe types. In: Ernst, E. (ed.) ECOOP 2007. LNCS, vol. 4609, pp. 28–53. Springer, Heidelberg (2007)
13. Fähndrich, M., Leino, K.R.M.: Declaring and checking non-null types in an object-oriented language. In: OOPSLA, pp. 302–312. ACM Press, New York (2003)
14. Fähndrich, M., Xia, S.: Establishing object invariants with delayed types. In: OOPSLA, pp. 337–350. ACM, New York (2007)
15. Felleisen, M., Friedman, D.: A Little Java, A Few Patterns. MIT Press, Cambridge (1997)
16. Grossman, D., Morrisett, G., Jim, T., Hicks, M., Wang, Y., Cheney, J.: Region-based memory management in Cyclone. In: PLDI, pp. 282–293 (2002)
17. Haack, C., Poll, E.: Type-based object immutability with flexible initialization. Technical Report ICIS-R09001, Radboud University, Nijmegen (January 2009)
18. Haack, C., Poll, E., Schäfer, J., Schubert, A.: Immutable objects for a Java-like language. In: De Nicola, R. (ed.) ESOP 2007. LNCS, vol. 4421, pp. 347–362. Springer, Heidelberg (2007)
19. JSR 308 Expert Group. Annotations on Java types. Java specification request, Java Community Process (December 2007)

20. Leino, K.R.M., Müller, P., Wallenburg, A.: Flexible immutability with frozen objects. In: Shankar, N., Woodcock, J. (eds.) VSTTE 2008. LNCS, vol. 5295, pp. 192–208. Springer, Heidelberg (2008)
21. Müller, P., Poetzsch-Heffter, A.: Universes: A type system for alias and dependency control. Technical Report 279, Fernuniversität Hagen (2001)
22. Östlund, J., Wrigstad, T., Clarke, D., Åkerblom, B.: Ownership, uniqueness, and immutability. In: TOOLS Europe, pp. 178–197 (2008)
23. Papi, M., Ali, M., Correa, T., Perkins, J., Ernst, M.: Practical pluggable types for Java. In: International Symposium on Software Testing and Analysis, pp. 201–212 (2008)
24. Pechtchanski, I., Sarkar, V.: Immutability specification and applications. Concurrency and Computation: Practice and Experience 17, 639–662 (2005)
25. Porat, S., Biberstein, M., Koved, L., Mendelson, B.: Automatic detection of immutable fields in Java. In: CASCON 2002. IBM Press (2000)
26. Potanin, A., Noble, J., Clarke, D., Biddle, R.: Featherweight generic confinement. J. Funct. Program. 16(6), 793–811 (2006)
27. Potanin, A., Noble, J., Clarke, D., Biddle, R.: Generic ownership for generic Java. In: OOPSLA, pp. 311–324 (2006)
28. Qi, X., Myers, A.: Masked types for sound object initialization. In: POPL. ACM, New York (2009)
29. Smith, F., Walker, D., Morrisett, G.: Alias types. In: Smolka, G. (ed.) ESOP 2000. LNCS, vol. 1782, pp. 366–381. Springer, Heidelberg (2000)
30. Tofte, M., Talpin, J.-P.: Region-based memory management. Information and Computation 132(2), 109–176 (1997)
31. Unkel, C., Lam, M.: Automatic inference of stationary fields: a generalization of Java's final fields. In: POPL, pp. 183–195. ACM, New York (2008)
32. Vitek, J., Bokowski, B.: Confined types in Java. Softw. Pract. Exper. 31(6), 507–532 (2001)
33. Wrigstad, T.: Ownership-Based Alias Management. Ph.D thesis, KTH Stockholm (2006)
34. Zibin, Y., Potanin, A., Ali, M., Artzi, S., Kiezun, A., Ernst, M.: Object and reference immutability using Java generics. In: ESEC/FSE 2007, pp. 75–84. ACM, New York (2007)

Security Monitor Inlining for Multithreaded Java

Mads Dam[1], Bart Jacobs[2,*], Andreas Lundblad[1], and Frank Piessens[2]

[1] KTH, Sweden
{mfd,landreas}@kth.se
[2] K.U. Leuven, Belgium
{bartj,frank}@cs.kuleuven.be

Abstract. Program monitoring is a well-established and efficient approach to security policy enforcement. An implementation of program monitoring that is particularly appealing for application-level policy enforcement is monitor inlining: the application is rewritten to push monitoring and policy enforcement code into the application itself. The intention is that the inserted code enforces compliance with the policy (security), and otherwise interferes with the application as little as possible (conservativity and transparency).

For sequential Java-like languages, provably correct inlining algorithms have been proposed, but for the multithreaded setting, this is still an open problem. We show that no inliner for multithreaded Java can be both secure and transparent. It is however possible to identify a broad class of policies for which all three correctness criteria can be obtained. We propose an inliner that is correct for such policies, implement it for Java, and show that it is practical by reporting on some benchmarks.

1 Introduction

Program monitoring is a well-established and efficient approach to prevent potentially misbehaving software clients from causing harm, for instance by violating system integrity properties, or by accessing data to which the client is not entitled [1,2]. The conceptual model is simple: Potentially dangerous actions by a client program are intercepted and routed to a policy decision point in order to determine whether the actions should be allowed to proceed or not. In turn, these decisions are routed to a policy enforcement point, responsible for ensuring that only policy-compliant actions are executed. For the purpose of this paper, we will assume that policies are given as security automata in the style of Schneider [3].

Program monitoring can be implemented in different ways. The monitor can be external to the program being monitored: it could for instance be implemented as a proxy API, as part of a virtual machine, or as part of an operating system kernel.

---

* Bart Jacobs is a Postdoctoral Fellow of the Research Foundation - Flanders (FWO).

S. Drossopoulou (Ed.): ECOOP 2009, LNCS 5653, pp. 546–569, 2009.

An alternative implementation approach which is particularly appealing for application-level policy enforcement is monitor inlining [2]. Here, code rewriting is used to push policy relevant functionality into the client programs themselves.

For sequential programs, external monitoring and inlined monitoring enforce the same class of policies [4].[1] We show that, somewhat surprisingly, this is not true for multithreaded programs. The fact that the inlined monitor can only influence the scheduler indirectly – by means of the synchronization primitives offered by the programming language – has the consequence that certain policies cannot be enforced securely and transparently by an inlined reference monitor.

We give a simple example of a policy which an inliner is either unable to enforce securely, or else the inliner will need to affect scheduling by locking across the entire method call. This, however, can result in loss of transparency, performance degradation and, possibly, deadlocks. It is, however, possible to identify a large class of policies for which inlining remains a practical and efficient enforcement technique. We propose one such class, the *race-free policies*, and show that policies in this class can be enforced correctly by inlining in multithreaded Java. Moreover, we argue that the class of race-free policies is in fact the largest class of policies that is meaningful in a multi-threaded setting; the non-race-free policies by definition rely on execution constraints that go beyond those enforceable by inlining.

In particular, for many existing inlined monitoring systems whose formal treatment did not include multithreading but whose implementations could deal with multithreading [5,6,7], a non-race-free policy does most likely *not* express what the policy writer intended.

In summary, the paper makes the following contributions:

- We show that inlined monitoring in multithreaded Java is strictly less powerful than external monitoring.
- We characterize a class of policies that can be correctly enforced by inlining.
- We describe the design of an inlining algorithm and prove it correct for the identified class of policies.
- We report on our experience with a prototype implementation.

Finally, we believe that our study of the impact of multithreading on program rewriting in the context of monitor inlining is a first step towards a formal treatment of more general aspect implementation techniques in a multithreaded setting. Indeed, our policy language is a domain-specific aspect language, and our inliner is a simple aspect weaver.

1.1 Related Work

Schneider [3] proposed the use of automata as a tool to formalize security policies, and monitor inlining to enforce such policies was examined in [2,8]. The PoET/PSLang toolset by Erlingsson [8] implements monitor inlining for Java.

---

[1] If we consider broader classes of policies than those expressible by security automata, program rewriting can enforce strictly more policies.

That work represents security automata directly in terms of Java code snippets, making it difficult to formally prove correctness properties of the approach. Subsequent work on monitor inlining that addresses correctness properties includes [9] and [10], but these papers only consider sequential programs. Several papers [8,11,7,12] report on inliner implementations for multithreaded Java-like programs with locking regimes that appear essentially identical to the one used in our example algorithm. None of these works, however, analyze the implications of multithreading and locking on the enforceable class of policies. In previous work [13] we have examined the implication of locking across security relevant method calls, and to which extent transparency can be preserved in such a setting.

Edit automata [14,15] are examples of security automata that go beyond pure monitoring, as truncations of the event stream, to allow also event suppressions and insertions. As a consequence, edit automata can enforce a richer class of policies, the infinite renewal policies. A practical implementation of edit automata based on inlining is the Polymer system [6]. The main point of Polymer is to support composition of policies, and studying the impact of concurrency is left for future work.

There are many policy enforcement techniques, and the question of what classes of policies each policy enforcement technique can handle has received a considerable amount of attention. Schneider [3] kicked off this line of research, and his results were refined and extended by Viswanathan [16], Hamlen et al. [4] and others. Hamlen et al. distinguish three classes of enforcement mechanisms: static analysis, execution monitoring and program rewriting. They prove that when an execution monitor is afforded the same collection of intervention capabilities as an inliner, the inlining approach is strictly more powerful. This paper identifies an important domain where an external execution monitor has *more* intervention capabilities: in particular, an external execution monitor can freeze all threads in a program, whereas an inliner can only influence other threads by means of the synchronization primitives offered by the programming language.

Finally, inlining is closely related to aspect weaving. Aspects have been proposed by many authors as an implementation technique for security policy enforcement [14,17,18,19]. Other authors have generalized the events that an inlined monitor can see from method invocations and returns to program events specified by more general pointcut expressions [12].

1.2   Overview of the Paper

The rest of this paper is structured as follows. In Section 2, we briefly discuss the formal model of the Java Virtual Machine that we use in the rest of the paper. Next, in Section 3, we discuss what security policies we consider in this paper, and we introduce notation for them. Then we define the notion of inliner, and the correctness properties for inliners. Section 5 shows that these correctness criteria cannot be met for the policies and programs that we consider. The following section introduces the class of race-free policies, and Section 7 proposes an inlining algorithm and shows it is correct for all race-free policies. Then we report on experience with our implementation, and we offer a conclusion.

2   Program Model

We want to prove properties of inliners that operate on Java bytecode. The inlined code will monitor the interaction of the bytecode with a given API. We abstract from the API implementation: it will in many cases be a native implementation as policies typically talk about methods that perform IO.

Hence, our formal model is a standard model of the JVM extended with facilities to call an external API. Most of the results in this paper do not depend on the details of this formal model: the limitations we identify for monitor inlining in a multithreaded setting hold for a wide class of imperative programming languages and execution environments. In this section, we discuss those aspects of the formal model that are relevant for the paper. An appendix gives a more detailed exposition, as well as proofs for the correctness of the example inliner that necessarily depend on these details.

The formal model is a standard small-step operational semantics that defines a transition relation $\rightarrow_{\text{JVM}}$ on JVM configurations. An *execution* E of a program P is a (possibly infinite) sequence of JVM configurations $C_0 C_1 \ldots$ where C_0 is the initial configuration. The external API is modeled as a set of classes (disjoint from that of the client program) for which we have access only to the signature, but not the implementation, of its methods. It is essential that we perform API calls in two steps, to correctly model the fact that API calls are non-atomic in a multithreaded setting. When an API method is called in some thread a special API method stack frame is pushed onto the call stack, as detailed in the appendix. The thread can then proceed by returning or throwing an exception. When the call returns, an arbitrary return value of appropriate type is pushed onto the caller's evaluation stack; alternatively, when it throws an exception, an arbitrary, but correctly typed exceptional activation record is returned.

For the purpose of this paper, we assume sequential consistency of the JVM memory. This means we can reason about multithreaded executions as interleavings of single-thread executions, compatible with the happens-before order. The *happens-before order* [20] is a partial order on the transitions in an execution. It consists of the program order (ordering of two actions performed by the same thread) and the synchronizes-with order (order induced by synchronization constructs), and the transitive closure of the union of these.

The real Java memory model is weaker and this impacts our work in interesting ways, but studying this impact is left for future work.

The JVM execution steps that are of interest in this paper are the steps where an API method is entered or exited. Given an execution E the *observable trace* $\omega(E)$ of E is defined as follows:

$$
\begin{aligned}
\omega(C) &= \varepsilon \\
\omega(CC'E) &= \alpha\,\omega(C'E) \quad \text{if } C \xrightarrow{\alpha}_{\text{JVM}} C' \\
\omega(CC'E) &= \omega(C'E) \quad \text{if } C \xrightarrow{\tau}_{\text{JVM}} C'
\end{aligned}
$$

where a transition from C to C' performs an observable action α, denoted $C \xrightarrow{\alpha}_{\text{JVM}} C'$, if and only if it transitions from the client code to the API or vice versa. Specifically, we represent a call from client code bound at run time to an API method $c.m$ on an object o with arguments $\mathbf{v}$ by a thread tid as $C \xrightarrow{(tid,c.m,o,\mathbf{v})^{\uparrow}}_{\text{JVM}} C'$, and a normal return from this call with return value r as $C'' \xrightarrow{(tid,c.m,o,\mathbf{v},r)^{\downarrow}}_{\text{JVM}} C'''$. We represent an exceptional return from this call with exception object t as $C'' \xrightarrow{(tid,c.m,o,\mathbf{v},t)^{\Downarrow}}_{\text{JVM}} C'''$. All transitions other than the above are non-observable, denoted $C \xrightarrow{\tau}_{\text{JVM}} C'$.

We refer to actions $(tid,c.m,o,\mathbf{v})^{\uparrow}$, $(tid,c.m,o,\mathbf{v},r)^{\downarrow}$, and $(tid,c.m,o,\mathbf{v},t)^{\Downarrow}$ as before actions, after actions, and exceptional actions, respectively, and we collect them in sets $\Omega^{\uparrow}$, $\Omega^{\downarrow}$, and $\Omega^{\Downarrow}$. We refer to after and exceptional actions together as *end actions*, and we use *start action* as a synonym for before action.

The set of executions of a program P is $exec(P)$. We define the set $\mathcal{T}(P)$ of traces of P as $\mathcal{T}(P) = \{\omega(E) \mid E \in exec(P)\}$.

We will assume for simplicity that program and API do not share fields. This is not a restriction, as shared data can be modeled using fields defined in the API implementation and accessed with getters and setters. This effectively makes these field accesses observable.

In our program model all interactions between client code and API happen through method invocations, and in such a setting sets of traces as defined above are an adequate model for program behavior [21,22]: two programs with the same set of traces are observationally equivalent.

3   Security Policies

In this paper we consider only security policies that can be represented as security automata [3]. A *security automaton* is an automaton $\mathcal{A} = (Q, \delta, q_0)$ where Q is a countable (not necessarily finite) set of states, $q_0 \in Q$ is the initial state, and $\delta : Q \times \Omega \rightharpoonup Q$ is a (partial) transition function, where $\Omega = \Omega^{\uparrow} \cup \Omega^{\downarrow} \cup \Omega^{\Downarrow}$. All states $q \in Q$ are viewed as accepting. Note that our notion of policy assumes that policies only talk about API method invocations and returns. Many existing enforcement systems make the same assumption ([8,6]). This design decision limits our abilities to, for instance, perform any detailed data flow tracking. Policies in such a framework are typically sparse: Only a small number of API calls are actually security relevant, and calls to these methods are infrequent. But, the framework is sufficiently rich to allow a wide range of interesting policies to be expressed, and, in particular, it serves well as a generic setting in which to examine the effects of multithreading.

Our work uses the ConSpec language [23] for policy specification. ConSpec is similar to PSlang [8], but it has a formal semantics mapping ConSpec specifications to security automata.

An example of a ConSpec specification is given in Figure 1. The syntax is intended to be largely self-explanatory: The specification in Figure 1 states that the program has to ask the user for permission each time it intends to send a file over bluetooth. It does so by storing after a confirmation dialog what file the user has authorized to be sent, and to what URL it can be sent. Before an

```
SECURITY STATE    String requestorURL,
                  String requestedFile;

BEFORE BluetoothToolkit.sendFile(String destURL, String file)
    PERFORM
        requestorURL.equals(destURL) &&
        requestedFile.equals(file) -> { }

AFTER reply = JOptionPane.showConfirmDialog(String query)
    PERFORM
        reply != 0 && goodFileQuery(query) -> {
            requestedFile = queryFile(query);
            requestorURL = queryRequestor(query) }
        true -> { }
```

The macro `goodFileQuery(query)` returns true iff `query` is a well formulated file send query and `queryRequestor(query)` and `queryFile(query)` returns the requestor and file substrings of `query` respectively.

Fig. 1. A security specification example written in ConSpec

invocation of the sendFile method, it is checked that the actual parameters of the invocation correspond to the stored filename and URL. Hence, if the program would not pop up a confirmation dialog before sending, or if it would send a different file or send to a different URL than those confirmed in the dialog, the policy will block the send.

The example has two security relevant methods, `JOptionPane.showConfirm-Dialog` and `BluetoothToolkit.sendFile`. We refer to invocations and returns of such security relevant methods as *security relevant actions*. The specification expresses the constraints on security relevant actions in terms of guarded commands where the guards are boolean expressions and the updates are lists of assignments to security state variables. Both the guards and the assignments may mention the security state and the method call parameters. For an after action they may also mention the return value. In case the specification needs to talk about the current thread identifier, a ConSpec policy can call the `Thread.currentThread()` method. The only operation defined on thread identifiers is equality testing, so a policy can specify for instance that two invocations should happen in the same thread.

The *security state* declaration is a list of variable declarations. These variables represent the state space of the security automaton. For simplicity, we require that the initial values for the security state variables specified by the policy are the default initial values for their corresponding Java types. For example, the `requestedFile` variable in Figure 1 will initially be `null`.

An *event clause* defines how the security automaton reacts to a security relevant action. The event modifiers `BEFORE`, `AFTER` and `EXCEPTIONAL` specify if the event clause applies to a before action, after action or exceptional action. The method signature following the event modifier specifies the method that the event clause applies to. A sequence of guarded updates specifies the behaviour of the security automaton in response to actions matching the event clause. Guards are evaluated top to bottom, in order to obtain a deterministic semantics. For the first guard that evaluates to true, the corresponding update block is executed. If no clause guards hold, the call is violating, i.e. the security automaton does not accept the action. We restrict our attention to security automata that always accept return and exceptional actions. That is, we require that if the event modifier is AFTER or EXCEPTIONAL, the guards are exhaustive.

A security automaton can be derived from a ConSpec policy in the obvious manner. We refer to [9] for details.

Definition 1 (Policy Adherence). *The program P adheres to security policy S, if for all executions E of P, $\omega(E)$ is accepted by S.*

We identify a policy S with the language of traces of observable actions that it accepts, and hence we write policy adherence as $T(P) \subseteq S$.

4   Inlining Correctness Properties

A security policy specified as a security automaton can be enforced by an *execution monitor* [3]. An execution monitor is an enforcement mechanism that can monitor the observable steps that a target program takes, and that can terminate the program if a step does not comply with the policy. Such a monitor could for instance be implemented in the Java Virtual Machine.

An alternative implementation mechanism for execution monitoring is *inlined reference monitors* [5]. *Inlining* refers to the procedure of compiling a policy into a bytecode based reference monitor and embedding it into a target program. Formally, an inliner is a function $\mathcal{I}$ which for each policy S and program P produces an inlined program $\mathcal{I}(S, P)$. The intention is that the inserted code enforces compliance with the policy, and otherwise interferes with the execution of the target program as little as possible.

In this section we look at traditional correctness properties for inlined monitors. There are three correctness properties of fundamental interest (cf. [15],[4]): namely, the inliner should enforce policy adherence (security), it should not add new behavior (conservativity), and it should not remove policy-adherent behavior (transparency). More formally:

Definition 2 (Inliner Correctness Properties). *An inliner $\mathcal{I}$ is:*

- Secure *if, for every program P, every trace of the inlined program $\mathcal{I}(S, P)$ adheres to S, i.e. $T(\mathcal{I}(S, P)) \subseteq S$.*
- Conservative *if, for every program P, every trace of the inlined program $\mathcal{I}(S, P)$ is a trace of P, i.e. $T(\mathcal{I}(S, P)) \subseteq T(P)$.*
- Transparent, *if every adherent trace of the client program is also a trace of the inlined program, i.e. if $T(P) \cap S \subseteq T(\mathcal{I}(S, P))$.*

Inliners are only allowed to rewrite the program, and not the API. This is a realistic restriction. Even if an inliner rewrites all Java code, including the Java API implementation, native calls for instance for IO will remain. In our model, the Java API would then be considered part of the program, and the monitored

API would only consist of the natively implemented methods. In principle it would be possible to rewrite the native implementations as well, but the same issues would reoccur at the level of system calls, or, ultimately, of physical IO.

An upshot of the model is that an inliner can never prevent an API method from returning: inlined code can only be executed after the call has returned. This is why we impose the restriction on policies that after actions and exceptional actions should always be allowed (have exhaustive guards in ConSpec, i.e. at least one guard should evaluate to true). These actions can still specify updates to the security state. In particular, they might cause the automaton to enter a state from which no further actions are possible.

5   Limitations of Inlining in a Multithreaded Setting

In this section, we show that the traditional correctness criteria for inlined monitors are too strong in a multithreaded setting. While it is possible to securely and transparently enforce any policy specified as explained in Section 3 by an *external* monitor implemented as part of the Java Virtual Machine, it is impossible to do this with an inlined monitor.

A key factor that explains why there are policies that cannot be enforced by inlining is the fact that the inlined code can only control the scheduler indirectly through locking (whereas an external monitor can "freeze" the execution of the program while taking security decisions). Here is an example that illustrates this. Consider the policy in Figure 2. This policy says that $C.n()$ can only be called after a call to $C.m()$ has been initiated (but not necessarily returned). So the trace $T_1 = (tid, C.m, o, \mathbf{v})^\uparrow, (tid', C.n, o', \mathbf{v}')^\uparrow$ is allowed, but the trace $T_2 = (tid', C.n, o', \mathbf{v}')^\uparrow, (tid, C.m, o, \mathbf{v})^\uparrow$ is not allowed by the policy.

But it is impossible to write any program P that has the trace T_1 but that does not have the trace T_2 (unless API method $C.m$ collaborates, for instance by releasing a lock that is visible to the client on entry to $C.m$. But clearly this is not something one can assume about every API method).

Consider an example program P_{ex} that has trace T_1, for instance the program that starts two independent threads where one calls $C.m()$ and the other calls $C.n()$. Assume also that no lock is shared between the API and the client program. There is no way an inliner can rewrite this program to securely and transparently enforce this policy, because the inliner has no way of synchronizing with the end of the before action of the $C.m()$ call. The inliner *can* synchronize

```
SECURITY STATE
    boolean ok = false;

BEFORE C.m()
    PERFORM
        true -> { ok = true; }
BEFORE C.n()
    PERFORM
        ok -> {}
```

```
SECURITY STATE
    boolean ok = false;

AFTER C.m()
    PERFORM
        true -> { ok = true; }
BEFORE C.n()
    PERFORM
        ok -> {}
```

Fig. 2. Not enforceable by inlining   **Fig. 3.** Enforceable by inlining

with the return from $C.m()$, for instance by acquiring a lock across the call to $C.m()$ and forcing the thread that calls $C.n()$ to wait for that lock. But in that case, the inliner is actually enforcing the stronger policy shown in Figure 3.

The key observation is that such synchronization is impossible for the policy in Figure 2 (unless with help from the API, but the inliner cannot rewrite the API), and hence the ordering of the two before actions is up to the scheduler. Whatever the inliner does to the program, the inlined program will either have both traces (and thus the inliner was not secure) or it will have neither of the two traces (and thus the inliner was not transparent).

Lemma 1. *Any program that has an observable trace with two consecutive before actions, also has the same observable trace with these two before actions swapped.*

Proof. Two consecutive before actions are necessarily in different threads: within one thread, a before action is either the final action of that thread, or it is followed by an after or exceptional action.

For two consecutive before actions in different threads, there can be no happens-before relation between the two actions. This follows from the fact that the only way to introduce such a happens-before relation would be the synchronization on a lock: one thread would have to acquire the lock before doing the before action, and the other thread would have to release the lock after doing the before action. However, this would imply that this lock is shared between client program and API (as a thread is in client code immediately before a before action, and in the API immediately after a before action). Since we have ruled out such sharing, the result follows.   □

The assumption that there is no shared lock between client and API is a reasonable assumption for many API's, and in particular for the native API.

Theorem 1. *No inliner can be secure and transparent for the policy in Figure 2.*

Proof. Consider the output P'_{ex} of the inliner for the given policy and for the example program P_{ex} above. The program P_{ex} has the traces T_1 and T_2 discussed above. By lemma 1, P'_{ex} either has both T_1 and T_2 (and hence the inliner was not secure on P_{ex}), or it has neither of these traces (and hence the inliner was not transparent for P_{ex}.)   □

6 Race-Free Policies

6.1 Definitions and Properties

Generalizing from the example in Figure 2, the key issue is that no client program (not even after inlining) can arbitrarily constrain the set of observable traces. Given a certain trace of observable actions, in general there will be permutations of that trace that are also possible traces of the client program no matter what synchronization efforts the client does. These permutations that are always possible are captured by the notion of *client-order-preserving* permutations. (Recall that start actions are before actions, and that end actions are after or exceptional actions.)

Definition 3. *A permutation $\pi(T)$ of a trace T of observable actions is client-order-preserving if, for any i and j such that $i < j$ and T_i is an end action and T_j is a start action, $\pi(i) < \pi(j)$.*

The intuition behind the definition is the following: the client can control start actions, and can only observe end actions. If a start action comes later than an end action, the client *could* have synchronized to ensure this ordering. The client cannot perform such synchronization for concurrent before actions or concurrent after actions. The definition also implies that actions within a single thread can never be permuted: within a thread, start and end actions are strictly interleaved.

If a policy accepts a given trace, but rejects a client-order-preserving permutation of the trace, then that policy is not securely and transparently enforceable by inlining client code. This is captured by the following definition:

Definition 4. *A policy is race-free iff, for any trace T and any client-order-preserving permutation T' of T, if T is allowed, then T' is allowed.*

As an example, the policy in Figure 1 is race-free. As a broader class of examples consider the class of policies where the security state is a set of permissions, before actions require a permission to be present in this set and cause the permission to be removed, and after actions restore the permission. Such policies are race-free. This can be checked for instance by using Proposition 2 below.

We show further that the class of race-free policies is a lower bound on the class of policies enforceable by inlining by constructing an inliner that is secure, transparent and conservative for this class of policies.

The bound is tight if we want the inliner to work for all possible API implementations. This follows from the following theorem.

Theorem 2. *No inliner can be secure and transparent for a non-race-free policy for all possible API implementations.*

Proof. Let T be a trace accepted by the policy, and T' a client-order preserving transformation of T that is not accepted. Consider an API implementation that performs no synchronization. By an argument similar to the one in Lemma 1, any program that has the trace T necessarily also has the trace T': a client-order preserving permutation is always compatible with the happens-before ordering if the API does not perform any synchronization. Then, consider any program P that has trace T. In order to be transparent, the inliner has to produce an inlined P' that has T. But then P' also has T' and hence the inliner is not secure.   □

An interesting question is how to check if a policy is race-free.

Proposition 1. *It is a necessary and sufficient condition for race-freedom that all start actions are right-movers and all end actions are left-movers in the set of allowed observable traces. (I.e., if a trace T is allowed, then swapping a pair of consecutive actions x, y in different threads where x is a start action or y is an end action yields an allowed trace.)*

Proof. Such swappings generate the client-order preserving permutations.   □

In particular, if such swappings always have the same effect on the policy state, we know the policy is race-free:

Proposition 2. *The following is a sufficient condition for race-freedom. For any state s_1 of the security automaton corresponding to the policy, and for any pair of transitions with different thread identifiers starting in that state, $s_1 \xrightarrow{x}\xrightarrow{y} s_2$ where x is a start action or y is an end action, it holds that $s_1 \xrightarrow{y}\xrightarrow{x} s_2$.*

Proof. These conditions imply the conditions from Proposition 1.   □

Sufficient syntactical conditions for the conditions of proposition 2 are easily identified. For example, for the common case where the security state is a set of permissions, a sufficient condition is that start actions only consume permissions from the set, and after actions only add permissions.

6.2 Discussion

Are there interesting or practically relevant policies that are not race-free? A policy that is not race-free imposes constraints not only on the client program, but also on the API implementation and even on the scheduler. Hence, we argue that such policies never make sense. Even if an enforcement mechanism (such as an external execution monitor) could enforce the policy, the result of the enforcement is most likely not what the policy writer intended to express. Policies impose constraints on API method invocations because of the effects (such as writing a file, reading from the network, activating a device, ...) that these API implementations have. A policy such as the policy in Figure 2 intends to specify that initiation of one effect should come after the initiation of another effect. But without further information about the API implementations and the operation of the scheduler, there is no guarantee that enforcing this ordering on the API invocations will also enforce this ordering on the actual effects.

In other words, the race in the policy that makes it impossible for an inliner to enforce the policy, also makes it impossible to interpret method invocations soundly as initiations of effects.

Hence, a policy that is not race-free either indicates a bug in the policy (for instance, the policy writer intended to specify policy 3 instead of policy 2 – an easy mistake to make as in the single-threaded setting both policies are equivalent), or it is an indication of a misunderstanding of the policy writer (for instance the policy writer considers the start of the API method invocation as a synonym of the start of the effect the API method implements).

As a consequence, the practicality of inlining as an enforcement mechanism is not at stake, and detection of races in policies is useful as a technique to detect bugs in policies.

7 Example Inliner

In this section we propose an inlining scheme that is secure, conservative and transparent for race-free policies.

The state of the inlined reference monitor might possibly be updated by several threads concurrently. The updates to this state must therefore be protected by a global lock. A key design choice is whether to keep holding this lock during the API call, or to temporarily release the lock during the call and reacquire it after the call has returned.

The first choice (locking across calls) is easier to prove secure, as there is a strong guarantee that the updates to the security state happen in the correct order. We will see below that this is much trickier for an inliner that releases the lock during API calls. However, an inliner that locks across calls can introduce deadlocks in the inlined program and is thus not transparent. Consider for instance an API with a *barrier* method B that allows two threads to synchronize as follows: When one thread calls B, the thread blocks until the other thread calls B as well. Suppose this method is considered to be security-relevant, and the inliner, to protect its state, acquires a global lock while performing each security-relevant call. For a client program that consists of two threads, each calling B and then terminating, the inliner will introduce a deadlock, as one thread blocks in B while the other thread blocks on the global lock introduced by the inliner.

Even if it does not lead to deadlock, acquiring a global lock across a potentially blocking method call can cause serious performance penalties.

For this reason, our algorithm releases the lock before calling an API method. In fact, our algorithm ensures that the global lock is only held for very short periods of time. The design and security proof of an inliner locking across calls is given in [13].

It is worth emphasizing that the novelty in this section is not the inlining algorithm itself: the algorithm is similar to existing algorithms developed in the sequential setting [10,5,6,9] and the locking strategy is relatively straightforward. The novelty is the correctness proof. The same proof will be applicable to other inliners showing that, when one restricts oneself to race-free policies, these inliners are also correct.

7.1   The Inlining Algorithm

In order to enforce a policy through inlining, it is convenient to be able to statically decide whether a given policy clause applies to a given call instruction. Therefore, in this example inliner, we impose the restriction on policies that they should have simple call matching. We say a policy has simple call matching if for any security-relevant method $c.m$, an `invokevirtual` $d.m$ call is bound at run time to method $c.m$ if and only if $d = c$. Essentially, this means that we ignore the issues surrounding inheritance and dynamic binding. These are orthogonal to the results of this paper, and it has been described elsewhere how to deal with them [10].

The inliner we propose, $\mathcal{I}_{Ex}$, replaces each instruction $L :$ `invokevirtual` $c.m$ where $c.m$ is security-relevant by JVML code corresponding to the code in Figure 4. The replacement contains blocks of code to update the security state according to the before, after and exceptional clauses respectively. These three

Inlined label Instruction	Inlined label Instruction
L: ldc *SecState* monitorenter astore 0 ⋮ astore $n-1$ *beforeG₁*: [eval before G_1] ifeq *beforeG₂* [before update 1] goto beforeEnd ⋮ *beforeGᵢ*: [eval before G_i] ifeq *exit* [before update i] *beforeEnd*: aload $n-1$ ⋮ aload 0 ldc *SecState* monitorexit *invoke*: invokevirtual *c.m* *invokeDone*: ldc *SecState* monitorenter astore n *afterG₁*: [eval after G_1] ifeq *afterG₂*	[after update 1] goto *afterEnd* ⋮ *afterGⱼ*: [eval after G_j] ifeq *exit* [after update j] *afterEnd*: aload n ldc *SecState* monitorexit *afterReleased*: goto *done* *exceptionalG₁*: ldc *SecState* monitorenter [eval exceptional G_1] ifeq *exceptionalG₂* [exceptional update 1] goto *exceptionalEnd* ⋮ *exceptionalGₖ*: [eval exceptional G_k] ifeq *exit* [exceptional update k] *exceptionalEnd*: ldc *SecState* monitorexit *exceptionalReleased*: athrow *exit*: iconst -1 invokestatic *System.exit* *done*:

Added entries in exception handler array:

From	To	Target	Type
invoke	invokeDone	exceptionalG₁	any
L	exceptionalReleased	exit	any
exit	done	exit	any

Fig. 4. The inlining replacement of L: invokevirtual *c.m*

blocks are referred to as blocks of inlined code. The security state is maintained as static fields of an auxilliary class called *SecState*, created by the inliner. The inliner locks the security state by acquiring the lock associated with the *SecState* class, and stores arguments to the method call for use in event handler code. Each piece of event code evaluates guards by reference to the security state and the stored arguments, and updates the state according to the matching clause, or exits, if no matching clause is found.

The Java Virtual Machine Specification [24] states that some unchecked exceptions such as InternalError or UnknownError can occur at any instruction. In the theoretical development, we will ignore this possibility, i.e. we assume an error-free JVM. Our implementation defensively catches any such exception and exits the program. With such an implementation, security is guaranteed even on JVM's that do throw such exceptions, but clearly transparency is no longer guaranteed should the JVM not be error-free.

7.2 Correctness Properties

In this section we show that the inliner presented above is conservative, transparent, and secure for race-free policies. In view of theorem 2 this is the best we can do: The assumption of race freedom cannot be lifted without losing transparency. As mentioned, other design choices are possible: For instance we may choose to lock across the security relevant call [13]. Such a design choice sacrifices transparency in favour of security.

To first prove security, the key observation is the following: While the sequence of actions seen by the monitor might be different from the sequence of actual actions happening, the second is actually a client-order preserving permutation of the first. And hence, by the definition of race-free policy, if the first is accepted by the monitor, then the second is necessarily also accepted by the policy. So if the monitor allows the execution, it is actually compliant with the policy.

Theorem 3. *The example inliner $\mathcal{I}_{Ex}$ is secure for race-free policies.*

The full proof of the theorem is provided in the appendix of this paper. For conservativity, our proof is based on the observation that there is a strong correspondence between executions of an inlined program, and executions of the underlying program before inlining. From an execution of the inlined program, one can *erase* all the inlined instructions and the security state, and arrive at an execution of the underlying program. Moreover, such an execution and its erasure have the same observable trace of actions, hence conservativity follows.

Theorem 4. $\mathcal{I}_{Ex}$ *is conservative.*

Again, a full proof is provided in the appendix. Finally, for transparency:

Theorem 5. *The example inliner $\mathcal{I}_{Ex}$ is transparent.*

Proof. Consider a policy-adherent execution E of P. Insert policy checking steps into E to obtain a sequence of configurations E'. Then E' is an execution of the inlined program. This follows, by induction on the length of E, from the fact that E adheres to the policy.   □

8 Case Studies and Benchmarks

The inlining algorithm described above has been implemented in Java using the ASM framework [25]. We present some results and benchmarks of this inliner in four case studies. The inliner was designed and implemented as part of the S^3MS project, a project that investigates the applicability of inlined reference monitoring for Java applications on mobile phones. Hence, the case studies are all Java Micro Edition applications. The applications and the corresponding security policies are available at http://www.csc.kth.se/~landreas/inlining. The inlining was performed off-device on an Intel Core 2 CPU at 1.83 GHz with 2 Gb memory. All policies were successfully enforced by our inliner.

560   M. Dam et al.

ImageExchange (IE) ImageExchange is a combined server/client application that allows users to exchange images over a Bluetooth connection.

The policy in this case study restricts the program to only send the file that was last approved by the user. We adapt the bluetooth and gui API's slightly to allow this policy to be conveniently formulated.

Snake (SN) This is a classic game of snake in which the player may submit the current score to a server over a network connection.

The policy prevents data from being sent over the network after reading from phone memory.

MobileJam (MJ) The MobileJam application is a Bluetooth GPS based traffic jam reporter which utilizes the online Yahoo! Maps API.

The policy prevents the application from connecting to any URLs other than those starting with `http://local.yahooapis.com`

BatallaNaval (BN) BatallaNaval is a multiplayer battleship game that communicates through SMS messages.

In this case the policy restricts the number of sent SMS's to a constant.

The benchmarks for the case studies are summarized in table 1.When the security relevant methods perform IO the runtime overhead of the monitor is dwarfed by the IO overhead, and is too small to be measured. Since most policies talk about methods that perform IO, it is fair to say that in practice, there is close to no performance penalty.

To determine the runtime overhead impact of inlining more precisely, a program that invoked an empty dummy security relevant method in a loop was constructed. The execution time of this loop was then measured before and after inlining. The inlining caused the execution time to increase from 407 ms to 1358 ms when the loop was iterated 10^6 times. This indicates an overhead in this experiment of 951 nanoseconds per security relevant call. This includes the time needed to do call disambiguation in the presence of dynamic binding (something we left out of scope for the theoretical study, see Section 7). Given that security relevant calls in our framework typically occur at session rate, this suggest that the runtime overhead of inlining is in practice negligible.

To summarize, our experiments support the existing evidence [5,6] that inlining is a practical enforcement technique, even in a multithreaded setting.

Table 1. Benchmarks for the case studies

	IE	SN	MJ	BN
Security Relevant Invokes	2	2	4	2
Original Size of Binaries (kb)	35.2	23.2	196.2	210.7
Inlining Duration (s)	0.56	0.49	1.84	1.42
Size increase (%):	1.1	0.7	4.0	0.9

9   Conclusions and Future Work

Inlining is a powerful and practical technique to enforce security policies. Several implementations of inliners exist, even for multithreaded programs. Hence, the study of the correctness of inlining algorithms is important, and has received a substantial amount of attention the past few years. But, these efforts have focused on inlining in a sequential setting.

This paper shows that inlining in a multithreaded setting brings a number of additional challenges. Not all policies can be enforced by inlining in a manner which is both secure and transparent. Fortunately, these non-enforceable policies do not appear very important in practice: They are policies that constrain not just the program, but also the API or the scheduler. We have identified a class of so-called race-free policies that do allow effective enforcement by inlining, and we have exhibited a concrete inlining algorithm which satisfies the required correctness properties.

A number of extensions of this work merit attention. First, we do not yet address inheritance. This extension is relatively straightforward: In order to evaluate the correct event clause, runtime checks on the type of the callee object would be interleaved with the checks of the guards. This is spelled out for the sequential setting in [10] for C#. We do not expect any issues to carry this over to the multithreaded setting.

Another interesting direction is to consider proof-carrying code (PCC) for monitor inlining. The advantage of such a framework would be to allow inlining to be performed outside the application loader's trust boundary. We have already realized this for the case of sequential Java, and an extension to multithreaded Java is currently under way.

Acknowledgments. Thanks to Irem Aktug, Dilian Gurov and Dries Vanoverberghe for useful discussions on many topics related to monitor inlining. Thanks to Jan Smans and Fabio Massacci for providing useful feedback on a draft of this paper.

The work of Dam, Lundblad, and Piessens was partially supported by the S³MS project. Bart Jacobs is a Postdoctoral Fellow of the Research Foundation - Flanders (FWO). Jacobs and Piessens were partially funded by the Interuniversity Attraction Poles Programme Belgian State, Belgian Science Policy. Dam holds a research position with the Swedish Research Council (VR) and is affiliated with the VR Linnaeus Center ACCESS. Lundblad was partially supported by VR grant 2007-6436.

References

1. Evans, D., Twyman, A.: Flexible policy-directed code safety. In: IEEE Symposium on Security and Privacy, pp. 32–45 (1999)
2. Erlingsson, Ú., Schneider, F.B.: SASI enforcement of security policies: a retrospective. In: Proc. Workshop on New Security Paradigms (NSPW 1999), pp. 87–95. ACM Press, New York (2000)

3. Schneider, F.B.: Enforceable security policies. ACM Trans. Information and System Security 3(1), 30–50 (2000)
4. Hamlen, K.W., Morrisett, G., Schneider, F.B.: Computability classes for enforcement mechanisms. ACM Trans. Program. Lang. Syst. 28(1), 175–205 (2006)
5. Erlingsson, Ú.: The inlined reference monitor approach to security policy enforcement. Ph.D thesis, Dept. of Computer Science, Cornell University (2004)
6. Bauer, L., Ligatti, J., Walker, D.: Composing security policies with polymer. In: PLDI, pp. 305–314 (2005)
7. Hamlen, K.W., Morrisett, G., Schneider, F.B.: Certified in-lined reference monitoring on .NET. In: PLAS, pp. 7–16 (2006)
8. Erlingsson, Ú., Schneider, F.B.: IRM enforcement of Java stack inspection. In: IEEE Symposium on Security and Privacy, pp. 246–255 (2000)
9. Aktug, I., Dam, M., Gurov, D.: Provably correct runtime monitoring. In: Cuellar, J., Maibaum, T., Sere, K. (eds.) FM 2008. LNCS, vol. 5014, pp. 262–277. Springer, Heidelberg (2008)
10. Vanoverberghe, D., Piessens, F.: A caller-side inline reference monitor for an object-oriented intermediate language. In: Barthe, G., de Boer, F.S. (eds.) FMOODS 2008. LNCS, vol. 5051, pp. 240–258. Springer, Heidelberg (2008)
11. Chen, F., Rosu, G.: Java-MOP: A monitoring oriented programming environment for Java. In: Halbwachs, N., Zuck, L.D. (eds.) TACAS 2005, vol. 3440, pp. 546–550. Springer, Heidelberg (2005)
12. Hamlen, K.W., Jones, M.: Aspect-oriented in-lined reference monitors. In: PLAS, pp. 11–20 (2008)
13. Dam, M., Jacobs, B., Lundblad, A., Piessens, F.: Provably correct inline monitoring for multithreaded Java-like programs. Journal of Computer Security (2009)
14. Ligatti, J., Bauer, L., Walker, D.: Edit automata: enforcement mechanisms for run-time security policies. Int. J. Inf. Sec. 4(1-2), 2–16 (2005)
15. Ligatti, J.A.: Policy Enforcement via Program Monitoring. Ph.D thesis, Princeton University (2006)
16. Viswanathan, M.: Foundations for the run-time analysis of software systems. Ph.D thesis, University of Pennsylvania (2000)
17. Verhanneman, T., Piessens, F., De Win, B., Joosen, W.: Uniform application-level access control enforcement of orginzationwide policies. In: Twenty-First Annual Computer Security Applications Conference, pp. 389–398 (2005)
18. Dantas, D.S., Walker, D.: Harmless advice. In: POPL, pp. 383–396 (2006)
19. Shah, V., Hill, F.: An aspect-oriented security framework. In: Proceedings of the DARPA Information Survivability Conference, pp. 143–145 (2004)
20. Gosling, J., Joy, B., Steele, G., Bracha, G.: Java Language Specification, 3rd edn. Prentice Hall, Englewood Cliffs (2005)
21. Jeffrey, A., Rathke, J.: Java Jr: Fully abstract trace semantics for a core Java language. In: ESOP, pp. 423–438 (2005)
22. Jeffrey, A., Rathke, J.: A fully abstract may testing semantics for concurrent objects. Theor. Comput. Sci. 338(1-3), 17–63 (2005)
23. Aktug, I., Naliuka, K.: ConSpec – a formal language for policy specification. Electron. Notes Theor. Comput. Sci. 197(1), 45–58 (2008)
24. Lindholm, T., Yellin, F.: Java Virtual Machine Specification. Addison-Wesley Longman Publishing Co., Inc., Boston (1999)
25. ObjectWeb: Asm - home page (February 2008)
26. Freund, S.N., Mitchell, J.C.: A type system for object initialization in the Java bytecode language. ACM Trans. Program. Lang. Syst. 21(6), 1196–1250 (1999)
27. Leroy, X.: Java bytecode verification: Algorithms and formalizations. J. Autom. Reasoning 30(3-4), 235–269 (2003)

Appendix

This appendix contains the definitions for our formal model of the Java Virtual Machine, and proofs of the security and conservativity theorems for our example inliner.

9.1   Formal Model of the JVM

We assume that the reader is familiar with Java bytecode syntax, the Java Virtual Machine (JVM), and formalisations of the JVM such as [26]. Here, we only present components of the JVM, that are essential for the definitions in the rest of the text. A few simplifications have been made in the presentation. In particular, to ease notation a little we ignore issues concerning overloading.

Preliminary Conventions. We use c for class names, m for method names, and f for field names. For our purpose it suffices to think of class names as fully qualified.

To each method is associated a method definition as a pair of an instruction array and an exception handler array. Exception handlers (b, e, t, c) catch exceptions of type c (and its subtypes) raised by instructions in the range $[b, e)$ and transfer control to address t, if the handler is the topmost handler in the exception handler array that handles the instruction for the given type.

The set of values (of Java primitives and object references) is ranged over by v. Values of object type are (typed) locations o, or the value **null**. Locations are mapped to objects, or arrays, by a heap h. Objects are finite maps of non-static fields to values. Static fields are identified with field references of the form $c.f$. To handle those, heaps are extended to assignments of values to static field references.

Configurations and Transitions. A *configuration* $C = (h, \Lambda, \Theta)$ of the JVM consists of a *heap* h, a *lock map* Λ which maps an object o to a thread id *tid* iff *tid* holds the lock of o, and a *thread configuration map* Θ which maps a thread identifier *tid* to its thread configuration $\Theta(tid) = \theta$. A thread configuration θ is a stack R of activation records. For normal execution, the activation record at the top of an execution stack has the shape (M, pc, s, l), where:

- M is a reference to the currently executing method.
- The *program counter pc* is an index into the instruction array of M.
- The *operand stack* $s \in Val^*$ is the stack of values currently being operated on.
- l is an array of *local variables*. These include the parameters.

For exceptional configurations, the top frame of an execution stack has the form (o) where o is the location of an exceptional object, i.e. of class Throwable.

Activation records for API calls are special and are discussed below.

Definition of the transition relation. We only present the rules for the bytecode instructions mentioned in the paper. The rules for the other bytecode instructions are similar and straightforward.

Notation. Besides self-evident notation for function updates, array lookups etc. the transition rules use the following auxiliary operations and predicates:

- $v :: s$ pushes v on top of stack s
- $handler(M, h, o, pc)$ returns the proper target label given M, heap h, throwable o and pc pc in the standard way:
  $handler(M, h, o, pc) = handler2(H, h, o, pc)$ with H the exception handler array of M
  $handler2(\epsilon, h, o, pc) = \bot$
  $handler2((b, e, t, c) \cdot H, h, o, pc) =$
  $$\begin{cases} t & \text{if } b \leq pc < e \text{ and } h \vdash o : c \\ handler2(H, h, o, pc) & \text{otherwise} \end{cases}$$
- **v** is an argument vector
- Stack frames have one of three shapes (M, pc, s, l), (o) (where o is throwable in the current heap), and $(\Box)$ (used for API calls).

Local Variables and Stack Transitions

$$\frac{\Theta(tid) \to \theta}{(h, \Lambda, \Theta) \to (h, \Lambda, \Theta[tid \mapsto \theta])}$$

$$\frac{M[pc] = \texttt{aload } n}{(M, pc, s, l) :: R \to (M, pc + 1, l(n) :: s, l) :: R}$$

$$\frac{M[pc] = \texttt{astore } n}{(M, pc, v :: s, l) :: R \to (M, pc + 1, s, l[n \mapsto v]) :: R}$$

$$\frac{M[pc] = \texttt{athrow}}{(M, pc, o :: s, l) :: R \to (o) :: (M, pc + 1, o :: s, l) :: R}$$

$$\frac{M[pc] = \texttt{goto } L}{(M, pc, s, l) :: R \to (M, L, s, l) :: R}$$

$$\frac{M[pc] = \texttt{iconst\_}n}{(M, pc, s, l) :: R \to (M, pc + 1, n :: s, l) :: R}$$

$$\frac{M[pc] = \texttt{ldc } c}{(M, pc, s, l) :: R \to (M, pc + 1, c :: s, l) :: R}$$

$$\frac{M[pc] = \texttt{ifeq } L \qquad n = 0}{(M, pc, n :: s, l) :: R \to (M, L, s, l) :: R}$$

$$\frac{M[pc] = \texttt{ifeq } L \qquad n \neq 0}{(M, pc, n :: s, l) :: R \to (M, pc + 1, s, l) :: R}$$

Heap transitions

$$\frac{\Theta(tid) = (M, pc, v :: s, l) :: R \qquad M[pc] = \texttt{putstatic } c.f}{(h, \Lambda, \Theta) \rightarrow (h[c.f \mapsto v], \Lambda, \Theta[tid \mapsto (M, pc + 1, s, l) :: R])}$$

$$\frac{\Theta(tid) = (M, pc, s, l) :: R \qquad M[pc] = \texttt{getstatic } c.f}{(h, \Lambda, \Theta) \rightarrow (h, \Lambda, \Theta[tid \mapsto (M, pc + 1, h[c.f] :: s, l) :: R])}$$

Locking instructions

$$\frac{\begin{array}{c} \Theta(tid) = (M, pc, v :: s, l) :: R \\ M[pc] = \texttt{monitorenter} \qquad \Lambda(v) = \bot \end{array}}{(h, \Lambda, \Theta) \rightarrow (h, \Lambda[v \mapsto tid], \Theta[tid \mapsto (M, pc + 1, s, l) :: R])}$$

$$\frac{\begin{array}{c} \Theta(tid) = (M, pc, v :: s, l) :: R \\ M[pc] = \texttt{monitorexit} \qquad \Lambda(v) = tid \end{array}}{(h, \Lambda, \Theta) \rightarrow (h, \Lambda[v \mapsto \bot], \Theta[tid \mapsto (M, pc + 1, s, l) :: R])}$$

Exceptional Transitions

$$\frac{\begin{array}{c} \Theta(tid) = (o) :: (M, pc, s, l) :: R \\ pc' = handler(M, h, o, pc) \qquad pc' \neq \bot \end{array}}{(h, \Lambda, \Theta) \rightarrow (h, \Lambda, \Theta[tid \mapsto (M, pc', s, l) :: R])}$$

$$\frac{\begin{array}{c} \Theta(tid) = (o) :: (M, pc, s, l) :: R \\ handler(M, h, o, pc) = \bot \end{array}}{(h, \Lambda, \Theta) \rightarrow (h, \Lambda, \Theta[tid \mapsto (o) :: R])}$$

API calls API calls are treated specially, as discussed in Section 2. The rules below only deal with invocation of API methods. Other invocations (client code calling client code) are standard, and we don't spell out the rule here.

$$\frac{\begin{array}{c} \Theta(tid) = (M, pc, o :: \mathbf{v} :: s, l) :: R \\ M[pc] = \texttt{invokevirtual } c.m \qquad c \in API \end{array}}{(h, \Lambda, \Theta) \rightarrow (h, \Lambda, \Theta[tid \mapsto (\Box) :: (M, pc + 1, s, l) :: R])}$$

Exceptional return from an API method:

$$\frac{\Theta(tid) = (\Box) :: R}{(h, \Lambda, \Theta) \rightarrow (h, \Lambda, \Theta[tid \mapsto (o) :: R])}$$

Normal return from an API method:

$$\frac{\Theta(tid) = (\Box) :: (M, pc, s, l) :: R}{(h, \Lambda, \Theta) \rightarrow (h, \Lambda, \Theta[tid \mapsto (M, pc, v :: s, l) :: R])}$$

Programs and Executions. For the purpose of this paper we can view a *program* P as a set of class declarations determining types of fields and methods belonging to classes in P, and a method environment assigning method definitions to each method in P. An *execution* E of a program P is a (possibly infinite) sequence of JVM configurations $C_0 C_1 \ldots$ where C_0 is an initial configuration consisting of a single thread with a single, normal activation record with an empty stack, no local variables, M as a reference to the main method of P, $pc = 0$, and for each $i \geq 0$, $C_i \to_{\text{JVM}} C_{i+1}$. We restrict attention to configurations that are *type safe*, in the sense that heap contents match the types of corresponding locations, and that arguments and return/exceptional values for primitive operations as well as method invocations match their prescribed types. The Java bytecode verifier serves, among other things, to ensure that type safety is preserved under machine transitions (cf. [27]).

Thread creation. To support thread creation we assume that there is a distinguished API method that has, besides the standard effect of an API call discussed above, an additional side effect of creating an additional thread in the configuration. The newly created thread starts with a single normal activation record initialized to call the run() method of the object passed as a parameter to the API method.

9.2   Proof of the Security Theorem

Since our inliner does not synchronize across security-relevant API method calls, it is not guaranteed that updates to the inlined security state are completely synchronized with the actual security relevant actions. For instance, if two security relevant method invocations m_1 and m_2 happen concurrently, the following scenario is possible. First, the inlined code before the m_1 call is executed, then the inlined code before the m_2 call is executed, then m_2 is invoked, and then m_1 is invoked. In other words, the sequence of actions as considered by the monitor might not be equal to the sequence of actions as it actually happens. An immediate consequence of this is that some policies cannot be enforced securely by our inliner: for instance the policy in Figure 2 can not be securely enforced.

Fortunately, for the class of race-free policies, we can show that our inliner is secure. The key observation is the following: while the sequence of actions seen by the monitor might be different from the sequence of actual actions happening, the second is actually a client-order preserving permutation of the first. And hence, by the definition of race-free policy, if the first is accepted by the monitor, then the second is necessarily also accepted by the policy. So if the monitor allows the execution, it is actually compliant with the policy. We set out to prove this.

First some notation: We have to distinguish clearly between the actual security relevant API actions (the *observable actions* of the program invoking the API) and the execution of the corresponding *monitor actions* (the inlined code manipulating the inlined security state). We use the notation $\text{mon}(\alpha)$ for the monitor action corresponding to the observable action α. We define a monitor action to take place at the step in the execution that performs the inlined monitorexit instruction. We refer to these points in an execution as the *policy commit points*.

The policy commit points can be seen as the points where the monitor "sees" an observable action: at the policy commit point, the changes to the inlined security state for a given observable action are made visible by releasing the lock on the inlined security state.

An execution E now gives rise to two traces: the trace of the actual security relevant observable actions T_s, and the trace of the monitor actions T_m. In addition, the given execution E determines an ordering that allows us to merge these two traces into the full trace T_f.

For example, in the scenario discussed above, if we let α_1 be the observable action of calling m_1 and α_2 the observable action of calling m_2, then the trace $T_f = \text{mon}(\alpha_1), \text{mon}(\alpha_2), \alpha_2, \alpha_1$ is the full trace that illustrates that observable actions and monitor actions can occur in different orders.

Lemma 2. *The trace T_m of monitor actions in an inlined program always complies with the policy.*

Proof. All updates to the security state are done under a single lock, and hence can be serialized. Since the actions seen by the monitor correspond to the monitorexit steps on that single lock, they are synchronized with the updates to the security state. So this lemma is equivalent to saying that the inlined code correctly implements the security automaton in a sequential setting.   □

For a given execution, we first want to make sure that any start actions that have been monitored but not yet executed are added to the traces T_f and T_s. More precisely: if there are $\text{mon}(\alpha)$ actions with α a start action by a thread *tid* in T_f such that no action by *tid* succeeds this action in T_f, then for any such action add α to the end of T_f and to the end of T_s. Call the resulting traces T_f' and T_s'. It follows that T_f is a prefix of T_f' and T_s is a prefix of T_s'.

In a similar way, if there are end actions α by a thread *tid* in T_f such that no action by *tid* succeeds this action in T_f, then add $\text{mon}(\alpha)$ to the end of T_f and to the end of T_m. Call the resulting traces T_f'' and T_m'. It follows that T_f is a prefix of T_f'' and T_m is a prefix of T_m'. T_m' complies with the policy because of Lemma 2, and because after actions can only update the security state, they can not break compliance with the policy.

Lemma 3. *For each $\text{mon}(\alpha)$ action with α a start action by a thread tid in T_f'', there is exactly one immediately succeeding action by tid in T_f'', and this is the action α. Furthermore, for each $\text{mon}(\alpha)$ action with α an end action by tid in T_f'', there is exactly one immediately preceding action by tid in T_f'', and this is the action α.*

Proof. By induction on the length of the execution E.   □

As mentioned before, the trace T_m of monitor actions is not necessarily identical to the observable trace $T_s = \omega(E)$. But we show that T_s' is a client-order preserving permutation of T_m'.

Lemma 4. *Consider an execution E of an inlined program. The trace T_s' is a client-order preserving permutation of T_m'.*

Proof. Because of Lemma 3, we can define a function f from T_m' to T_s' that maps each monitor action $mon(\alpha)$ to the immediately succeeding action within the same thread (for α a start action), or to the immediately preceding action in the same thread (for α an end action).

f is injective, since for any start action by a thread tid in T_f'', only one action by tid precedes it immediately, and similarly for return actions. Because of the construction of T_m' and T_s', f is also surjective, hence it is a bijection. Hence, when we consider T_m' and T_s' as sequences of observable actions (and we don't care anymore about the distinction of whether this action is seen by the monitor and hence in T_m', or an actual observable action and hence in T_s'), f is a permutation.

We show that f is a client-order preserving permutation from T_m' to T_s'. Consider an after action i in T_m' and a before action j in T_m' such that $i < j$. We must now prove that $f(i) < f(j)$.

Let us call i_m and i_s the injections from T_m' and T_s' in T_f''. Then $i_m(i) < i_m(j)$. We also have that, since i is an after action, $i_s(f(i)) < i_m(i)$, and since j is a before action, $i_m(j) < i_s(f(j))$. Therefore, we have that $i_s(f(i)) < i_s(f(j))$. Since i_s is order-preserving, we have that $f(i) < f(j)$. This means T_s' is a client-order preserving permutation of T_m'. $\qquad\square$

Theorem 6. *The example inliner $\mathcal{I}_{Ex}$ is secure for race free policies.*

Proof. For any execution of the inlined program, by lemma 2, T_m complies with the policy. Since T_m' extends T_m only with after actions, T_m' also complies with the policy.

From Lemma 4 we know that T_s' is a client-order preserving permutation of T_m'. Hence, by the definition of race-free policy, T_s' also complies with the policy. Finally, since T_s is a prefix of T_s', it also complies with the policy. $\qquad\square$

9.3   Proof of Conservativity

Our proof of conservativity is based on the observation that there is a strong correspondence between executions of an inlined program, and executions of the underlying program before inlining. From an execution of the inlined program, one can *erase* all the inlined instructions and the security state, and arrive at an execution of the underlying program. Moreover, such an execution and its erasure have the same observable trace of actions, hence conservativity follows.

To make this precise, we first define the notion of the *erasure* of an execution of an inlined program.

Definition 5. *Given an execution E of $\mathcal{I}_{Ex}(\mathcal{S}, P)$. We define the erasure E' of E by recursion on the length of E. The erasure of an execution with a single configuration C is C, with the $\mathtt{SecState}$ removed from the heap. Consider an execution EC_nC_{n+1}'. Let $E'C'$ be the erasure of EC_n. Let tid be the thread that performes the step C_nC_{n+1}. Then we define the erasure of EC_nC_{n+1} as*

- $E'C'$ if the pc of tid in C_n points to an inlined instruction
- $E'C'$ followed by the configuration obtained by letting tid perform one step in the context of the original program and state C'.

It follows that E' is an execution of the uninlined program.

Definition 6. *Given an activation record $r = (M, pc, l, s)$ of $\mathcal{I}_{Ex}(\mathcal{S}, P)$ and an activation record $r' = (M', pc', l', s')$ of P, we say that r' corresponds to r iff*

- $M = M'$
- l' is l without the local variables introduced by the inliner
- if pc points to a non-inlined instruction then pc' points to the same instruction and s' is equal to s, otherwise pc' and s' equal the states of pc and s as they were right before entering the block of inlined code. For instance if pc equals beforeG_1 then pc' equals L and s' equals $l[0 \ldots n-1]s[n \ldots]$.

Definition 7. *Given a configuration $C = (h, \Lambda, \Theta)$ of an execution of the inlined program and a configuration $C' = (h', \Lambda', \Theta')$ of the original program P we say C' corresponds to C iff*

- h' is the heap obtained by removing the SecState from h
- Λ' is the lock map obtained by removing the SecState from Λ
- $Dom(\Theta') = Dom(\Theta)$ and for each $(tid, R) \in \Theta$ there is an R' such that $(tid, R') \in \Theta'$, $|R| = |R'|$ and for each $i \in [0, |R|)$, R'_i corresponds to R_i.

Lemma 5. *Given a partial execution EC of the inlined program $\mathcal{I}_{Ex}(\mathcal{S}, P)$, then for the erasure $E'C'$ of EC it holds that C' corresponds to C and $\omega(E'C') = \omega(EC)$.*

Proof. By induction on the length of EC. The base case is trivial. Consider an execution EC_nC_{n+1} of the inlined program. Let $E'C'$ be the erasure of EC_n. By the induction hypothesis, we may assume that C' corresponds to C_n and that $\omega(E'C') = \omega(EC_n)$. We have two cases

(1) if C_nC_{n+1} is an execution of an inlined instruction then the erasure of EC_nC_{n+1} equals $E'C'$. We prove that C' corresponds to C_{n+1} and that $\omega(EC_nC_{n+1}) = \omega(E'C')$ by case analysis on the label of the inlined instruction.
(2) otherwise, let $E'C'C''$ be the erasure of EC_nC_{n+1}. We prove that C'' corresponds to C_{n+1} and that $\omega(E'C'C'') = \omega(EC_nC_{n+1})$ by case analysis on the non-inlined instruction.

$\square$

Theorem 7. *$\mathcal{I}_{Ex}$ is conservative.*

Proof. For any execution of the inlined program, Lemma 5 gives us an execution of the uninlined program with the same trace. $\square$

EventJava: An Extension of Java for Event Correlation*

Patrick Eugster and K.R. Jayaram

Department of Computer Science, Purdue University, West Lafayette, IN 47906
{peugster,jayaram}@cs.purdue.edu

Abstract. Event correlation has become the cornerstone of many reactive applications, particularly in distributed systems. However, support for programming with complex events is still rather specific and rudimentary. This paper presents EventJava, an extension of Java with generic support for event-based distributed programming. EventJava seamlessly integrates events with methods, and broadcasting with unicasting of events; it supports reactions to combinations of events, and predicates guarding those reactions. EventJava is implemented as a framework to allow for customization of event semantics, matching, and dispatching. We present its implementation, based on a compiler transforming specific primitives to Java, along with a reference implementation of the framework. We discuss ordering properties of EventJava through a formalization of its core as an extension of Featherweight Java. In a performance evaluation, we show that EventJava compares favorably to a highly tuned database-backed event correlation engine as well as to a comparably lightweight concurrency mechanism.

1 Introduction

Events demark incidents in the execution of software, a change of state in some component. In a *distributed event-based system* (DEBS), software components communicate by transmitting and receiving event notifications, which reify the events and describe the observed changes in state. Some examples of events in different domains are (*i*) the reading from a temperature sensor, (*ii*) a stock quote, (*iii*) a link failure in a network monitoring system, (*iv*) change of relationship status in a social networking tool, or (*v*) drop in inventory below a defined threshold. Interacting objects in a DEBS can act in two roles, namely as (a) *sources* (notifying events), and/or (b) *sinks* (manifesting interest in being notified of events). Event notifications describe state changes by *attributes* attached to them. *Explicit* attributes represent application-specific data; e.g, a stock quote event has the name of the organization, the price of the stock and the opening price as explicit attributes. These are sometimes paired with *implicit* attributes conveying contextual information, such as wall clock time, logical time,

---

* Financially supported by National Science Foundation (NSF) through grants number 0644013 and number 0834529.

geographical/logical coordinates, or sources. Henceforth, we will use the term *events* to refer to both the incidents underlying such events as well as to their incarnations and notifications.

Sinks are not always interested in single events. Events can be *correlated* with other events, resulting in *complex events*. Examples are:[1]

– Average of temperature readings from 10 sensors inside a boiler.
– Average of temperature readings from a sensor within a 10 minute interval.
– The price of a stock decreases for 10 successive stock quotes immediately after a negative analyst report.
– Two insider trades of a large volume (≥ 10000) immediately after a stock price hits its 52 week high.
– Release of a new TV followed by 5 positive reviews in 1 month.

Event correlation is widely used in algorithmic trading and financial services, patient flow monitoring in hospitals, routing and crew scheduling in transportation, monitoring service level agreements in call centers, consumer behavior in on-line retailing and airline baggage handling, network monitoring and intrusion detection [1] just to name a few. In pervasive computing, events are often viewed as an adequate interaction abstraction due to their strongly asynchronous nature [2]. Examples of specialized event correlators in the database community are Cayuga [3], Aurora [4], and Borealis [5].

In DEBS, decoupling between the interacting objects (sources, sinks) is desired because it can lead to greater scalability. Because of this decoupling between components, interaction between them is asynchronous and often anonymous – sources and sinks do not need to know the identities of each other. Anonymous interaction is enabled by *groups* formed between sources and sinks. For example, the object that publishes stock quotes and objects which monitor stocks (at several stock brokers) are in a group – managed either using a group communication middleware (e.g. Spread [6]) or a specialized event dissemination middleware (e.g. Hermes [7], ActiveMQ [8]). The middleware is responsible for delivering events to sinks and providing fault tolerance.

In support of an increasing family of programs based on events and event-correlation in particular, we propose in this paper a novel extension of the mainstream Java programming language, called EventJava. This paper presents its design, semantics and implementation, starting by an illustration of its features through examples. The technical contributions of EventJava and this paper are:

1. An object-oriented programming model with generic support for event-based interaction. This model is implemented as an extension to Java, EventJava, incorporating features for event correlation, broadcast and unicast of events.
2. An implementation *framework* for event correlation promoting customizable propagation and matching of events. A reference implementation of this framework is presented, based on the Rete pattern matching algorithm [9]

---

[1] Source: www.thecepblog.com, www.complexevents.com, www.event-based.org

in the Jess expert system shell [10], and the JGroups [11] group communication system. Empirical evaluation shows that these custom off-the-shelf components can be used to achieve performance and scalability comparable to highly specialized correlation engines or lightweight concurrency mechanisms, illustrating the adequacy of the abstractions proposed in EventJava.

3. Formal semantics of event correlation in EventJava expressed as an extension to Featherweight Java (FJ) [12]. We present a *default* semantics of Event-Java, where events are correlated non-deterministically, and broadcast interaction between sources and sinks does not preserve the *ordering* of events of the middleware layer. We then present the precise semantics for a more deterministic event correlation in our *reference* implementation, showing that it preserves the ordering properties of the underlying middleware layer.

The remainder of this paper is organized as follows. Section 2 presents EventJava through examples. Section 3 details its syntax and semantics. Section 4 presents an implementation of EventJava based on a framework for semantics customization. Section 5 evaluates the performance of EventJava. Section 6 explains some of our design decisions and discusses various options in EventJava. Section 7 presents related work and Section 8 draws conclusions. A companion technical report [13] provides further details such as type checking rules.

2   EventJava by Example

This section gives an overview of EventJava, introducing its features stepwise through simplified examples.

2.1   Event Methods

An application event type is implicitly defined by declaring an *event method*, a special kind of asynchronous method. The formal arguments of event methods correspond to the explicit attributes of the event type.

Handling events. Consider the example below of a travel agency which notifies its customers of severe weather in cities that are part of their flight itineraries. Instances of the `Alerts` class react to simple `severeWeather` events by retrieving the email addresses of flight passengers (in- or outbound for the city) from a database and sending emails to them. Sinks can specify additional constraints on event attributes through *predicates*, which follow the **when** keyword.

```
class Alerts {
    ItineraryDatabase db;
    event severeWeather(String city, String description, String source)
        when (source == "weather.com") {
            Iterator<Itinerary> it = db.getItinerariesByCity(city).iterator();
            while(it.hasNext()) { Messenger.sendEmail(it.getAssociatedEmail());}
        }
}
```

In this example, the travel agency only trusts alerts from weather.com. The method body is called a *reaction* and is executed asynchronously in a separate thread (typically from a thread pool) upon occurrence of an event satisfying the predicate. Arguments are considered to be values, i.e., of primitive types or conforming to `Serializable`, to enable event notification across address spaces. Events (event method invocations) that match the predicate are consumed by the reaction.

Unicast. Invoking an event method on an object notifies the event to that object. To that end, the source object needs a reference to the sink – a stub if the sink is remote. For example, a `severeWeather` event can be notified to an instance a of `Alerts` as follows:

```
a.severeWeather("Chicago", "Snow Storm 15 inches", "weather.com");
```

Broadcast. The same `severeWeather` event can be notified to all instances of `Alerts` just like a static method call:

```
Alerts.severeWeather("Chicago", "Snow Storm 15 inches",
"weather.com");
```

When an event method $e()$ is invoked on a class C it is broadcast to all live instances of C and all instances of any subclass C' of C. By all instances of a class C, we mean all local instances and all remote instances of C within the group (see Section 4 for remote interaction and Section 6 for bootstrapping). When the invocation happens on an interface I, the event is broadcast to all instances of all classes C implementing I.

2.2 Complex Events and Correlation Patterns

Complex events are defined by *correlation patterns*, comma-separated lists of event method headers, e.g. $e_1(), e_2(), ..., e_q()$, preceded by the keyword **event**. As we will detail later, the correlation semantics can be sensitive to order.

Consider an algorithmic trading example comparing `earningsReport` and `analystDowngrade` events. If a stock has a negative earnings report (the actual earnings per share, `epsAct`, is less than the estimate `epsEst`), followed by an analyst downgrade to "Hold", then the algorithm recommends selling the stock.

```
class StockMonitor {
    Portfolio p;
    event earningsReport(String firm, float epsEst, float epsAct, String period),
        analystDowngrade(String firm1, String analyst, String from, String to)
    when (earningsReport < analystDowngrade && firm == firm1 &&
            epsAct < epsEst && to == "Hold") {
        p.RecommendSell(firm);
    }
}
```

The first condition `earningsReport<analystDowngrade` compares an event `earningsReport` with an `analystDowngrade` event. It is a shorthand notation for `earningsReport.time < analystDowngrade.time`. The `time` attribute is a default implicit event attribute representing timestamps for events (explained shortly). `firm` can be used in lieu of `firm1` in `analystDowngrade`, but then the event name followed by the attribute must be used in the predicate and reaction for disambiguation, as in `earningsReport.firm` and `analystDowngrade.firm`.

We refer to a predicate which compares attributes of two different events as a *Type-B* predicate (e.g. firm == firm1). Predicates which compare an attribute to a constant are referred to as *Type-A* predicates. As a comparison, our companion technical report [13] sketches a possible implementation of the same correlation pattern in standard Java.

Events that match the correlation pattern and satisfy the predicate are consumed by the reaction. Formal arguments of event methods can be similarly used in the reaction. An EventJava application developer is responsible for synchronizing accesses to shared data structures that occur *inside* the body of a reaction. One way to achieve synchronization is to add the **synchronized** keyword in front of the pattern; it applies to the reaction, ensuring mutual exclusion among its executions and those of other reactions and regular methods marked as synchronized.

2.3   Streams

EventJava also supports correlation over event *streams* through array-like indices on event methods in correlation patterns defining *windows*. Consider a simple pattern in fraud detection, which looks for 3 different insider trades of a stock with a combined volume ≥ 100000. This pattern specifies the number of insiderTrade events being correlated, and the attributes of each of the events are accessed in the predicate and reaction body using indices.

```
event insiderTrade[3](String firm, String name, String role, float price, long vol)
   when (insiderTrade[0].name != insiderTrade[1].name &&
   insiderTrade[1].name != insiderTrade[2].name &&
   insiderTrade[0].name != insiderTrade[2].name &&
   insiderTrade[0].firm == insiderTrade[1].firm == insiderTrade[2].firm &&
   insiderTrade[0].vol + insiderTrade[1].vol + insiderTrade[2].vol >= 100000){...}
```

A pattern of the form **event** $e[n]$ **when** (p) ... specifies that n events e are correlated such that:

- $\forall\, i, j \in \{0, ..., n-1\}$ $i < j$ implies $e[i]$.time $< e[j]$.time, for example with e=insiderTrade above.
- Although $e[i]$.time $< e[i+1]$.time, the n events need not be consecutive. For example, there can be another event e'=insiderTrade(...) which does not satisfy predicate p such that $e[0]$.time $< e'$.time $< e[1]$.time. If needed, windows of consecutive events can be achieved with additional predicates e.g. based on monotonically increasing counter values assigned as attributes to events of the same type.

Aggregated events can of course be correlated with non-aggregated ones. Consider the following algorithmic trading scenario which seeks a stock decreasing monotonically in value for 10 quotes after an analyst downgrade.

```
event analystDowngrade(String firm1, String analyst, String from,
String to),
      stockQuote[10](String name, float sPrice)
   when (analystDowngrade < stockPrice[0] &&
      for i in 0..8 stockQuote[i].sPrice > stockQuote[i+1].sPrice  &&
      for i in 0..9 stockQuote[i].name == analystDowngrade.name) {...}
```

A declaration $e()$ without window is in fact simply treated like $e[1]()$. Consider implementing the TV example from Section 1: *Release of a new TV followed by 5 positive reviews in 1 month.* We assume that on a scale of 0 to 5, a rating above 3.5 is considered positive:

```
event tvRelease(String model, float price, String date),
    tvReview[5](String model1, File review, float rating) when
        (for i in 0..3 tvReview[i].model1 == tvReview[i+1].model &&
        for i in 0..4 tvReview[i].rating >= 3.5 &&
        tvReview[4].time - tvReview[0].time = 30*24*60*60*1000 &&
        tvReview[0].model1 == tvRelease.model) {...}
```

2.4 Matching Semantics

Event correlation semantics have different parameters [14,15]. For instance, a pattern **event** $e_1()$, $e_2()$ can be matched by a sequence of events e_1^1, e_1^2, e_2^1 either as $\langle e_1^1, e_2^1 \rangle$ (FIFO) or $\langle e_1^2, e_2^1 \rangle$ (LIFO). In the latter case, one might even want to discard the superseded e_1^1. Different semantics can be of interest for different settings. In tightly coupled concurrency scenarios, the latter suggestion of discarding an event without consuming it seems wrong. In systems with dynamically joining and leaving participants and in the presence of predicates, it becomes infeasible in general to ensure that any event is consumed at least by one object, and obsolescence of events might be part of the application semantics.

To be able to accommodate various application types, matching in EventJava is implemented as part of a framework explained more in the following sections. Our *default* semantics presented in the next section are non-deterministic in that in the above example either outcome is possible. This reflects many concurrency settings where non-determinism is desired to achieve some form of fairness. The semantics of our *reference* implementation strike a balance between (a) static settings, i.e., where by design and deployment every event is assured to be consumed by at least one object (possibly by omitting predicates), and (b) dynamic distributed settings. They will be presented in Section 4.2.

2.5 Context

Events can have explicit and implicit attributes. In EventJava, implicit attributes form a *context*. The timestamps (`*.time`) used in Section 2.2 are but an example – though an important one. The ordering underlying our matching semantics rely on this notion.

Implicit event attributes are in fact fields defined globally by a `Context` class, of which an instance is passed along with every event. The code required to instantiate and pass this context is generated by our compiler. In the following simple class, an event is simply timestamped with the local physical clock. Please note that this is but a simple example, and that the notion of time is generally more complex and has to be closely aligned with the underlying communication infrastructure and the other parts of the framework (see Section 4).

```
public class Context implements Comparable<Context> , Serializable
{
    public long time;
    ... /* more fields */
    public Context() { this.time = System.currentTimeMillis(); }
    public Context(long time) { this.time = time; }
    public int compare(Context other) {
        if(timestamp == other.timestamp) return 0;
        ...
    }
    ...
}
```

The Context class is verified at compilation for well-formedness. Its **public** fields $f_1, f_2, ..., f_q$ (in the order of declaration) define the implicit event attributes. Constructors can have formal arguments corresponding to sub*sequences* of those fields. An event method declaration can optionally list the entire context, e.g. **event** $e()[f_1, ..., f_q]$, and an event method invocation in special cases may want to explicitly provide values for the context corresponding to a constructor, e.g. $e()[f_1, ..., f_j]$ ($j \in [1..q]$). Consider a Context class using geographic coordinates in addition to timestamps. The following example shows how a correlation pattern can use this context to collect rainfall readings from twenty different sensors located in a square region (see Figure 1: 55km North to 55km South and 55km East to 55km West) around the current location (which is denoted by C). The latitude and longitude are in the decimal degrees[2] format, in which $0.1° \doteq 11km$. Rainfall readings aggregated by the pattern should be within a 60 minute interval.

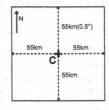

Fig. 1. Example with geographic coordinates

```
public class Context implements Comparable<Context> , Serializable
{
    public long time;
    public float latitude; //in decimal degree format
    public float longitude; //in decimal degree format
    ... //more fields and methods
}

class WeatherStats {
    float currLatitude;
    float currLongitude;
    event rainfall[20](float rainInMM, String place, int sensorID) when
        (for i in 0..19 Math.abs(rainfall[i].latitude - currLatitude) == 0.5 &&
         for i in 0..19 Math.abs(rainfall[i].longitude - currLongitude) == 0.5 &&
         for i in 0..18 rainfall[i].sensorID != rainfall[i+1].sensorID &&
         for i in 0..19 rainfall[i].time - currTime == 60 * 60 * 1000) {
            float sum = 0;
            for(int j = 0 ; j < 20 ; j++) sum += rainfall[j].rainInMM;
            float averageRainfall = sum/20;
            ...
    }
}
```

---

[2] http://en.wikipedia.org/wiki/Decimal_degrees

3 EventJava Syntax and Semantics

This section presents the syntax and semantics of EventJava in more detail, as an extension Featherweight Java (FJ) [12], dubbed Featherweight EventJava (FEJ). FEJ supports illustration, and reasoning about subtyping, inheritance, and matching semantics.

3.1 Featherweight EventJava (FEJ) Syntax

The major additions of EventJava to Java are reflected in Figure 2. As in FJ, **this** is a special variable x, and $\bar{o}$ represents a sequence $o_1 \ldots o_q$; separating symbols – if any – depend on the context. A given element of a sequence is referred to as o_j. Two-level nested sequences $\bar{\bar{o}}$ are also possible; in this case, an individual element can be referred to as o_j^k. The first bar above the o relates to the subscript index j, whereas the second one refers to the superscript index k; $\overline{o^k}$ thus unambiguously represents $o_1^k \ldots o_q^k$. We use $(o)_{1..q}$ instead of $\bar{o}$ to explicitly specify the size q of $\bar{o}$.

In FEJ, a program is a parallel execution of threads, where each thread is of the form $\mathtt{T}^i(\bar{t}_i)$; the parallel composition operator $\|$ is commutative and associative. In $\mathtt{T}^i(\bar{t}_i)$, i represents a unique identifier (not necessarily continuously assigned). Threads can be created explicitly (**new** $\mathtt{T}(\bar{t}_i)$) or by the system. Types (T) encompass classes (C), immutable classes (I), and value classes (D) which reflect primitive types. B, I, F, S for instance refer to booleans, integers, floats, and strings respectively. Instances of immutable and value classes are the only permissible terms for event attributes (N). Immutable classes are introduced to abstract serialization and avoid costly cloning. No assignments can occur to fields of such objects, and their fields have to be recursively immutable. (EventJava applies a simple static analysis to attempt to infer immutability and reverts to cloning if it fails.) Immutable classes cannot define patterns. FJ's call-by-value semantics are retained but as in other extensions (e.g. [16]), we introduce field assignments $(t.x := \ldots)$ and thus **new** $A(\ldots)$ terms evaluate to locations $l(A)$ in memory. The latter terms are not used explicitly in programs; when not germane to the discussion, the type A will be omitted for brevity.

Correlation patterns include a sequence of events E, a predicate, and a reaction. Events can either declare their context $(e_{[n]}(\overline{N\ x})_{[}\overline{N'\ x'}_{]})$, or omit it $(e_{[n]}(\overline{N\ x}))$. A predicate is a conjunction or disjunction $(b\text{-}op)$ of simpler predicates. Among those are comparisons of value objects $(v\text{-}op)$, and universal quantification (**for** i **in** $[n..n]$ p). An event e_j is always defined over a window of size $n_j \geq 1$, with n_j commonly 1. Predicates only allow u terms which represent a strict subgrammar of t, omitting for instance fields of **this**; even if type checking can ensure that a field f is of an immutable type, its value could otherwise change (by reassignment in another thread). In practice, the **final** modifier helps overcome this limitation.

3.2 Evaluation

Figure 3 presents auxiliary definitions for FEJ. We use contextual semantics to model dynamic semantics, introduced in Figures 4 and 5.

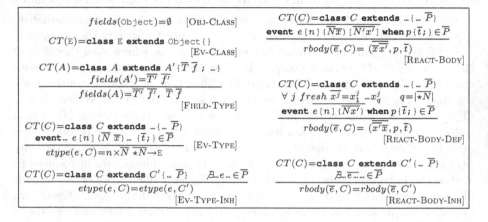

program	$Q ::= \emptyset \mid Q \parallel \mathtt{T}^i(\bar{t};)$	value	$v ::= l(A) \mid \mathbf{new}\ D\,(d)$
mutable	$L ::= \mathbf{class}\ C\ \mathbf{extends}\ C\{\bar{T}\ \bar{f};\ K\ \bar{M}\ \bar{P}\}$	type	$T ::= C \mid I \mid D$
immutable	$J ::= \mathbf{class}\ I\ \mathbf{extends}\ I\{\bar{N}\ \bar{f};\ K\ \bar{M}\}$	class	$A ::= C \mid I$
constructor	$K ::= A\,(\bar{T}\ \bar{f})\ \{\mathbf{super}\,(\bar{f});\ \mathbf{this}.\bar{f} := \bar{f};\}$	attribute	$N ::= I \mid D$
method	$M ::= T\ m\ (\bar{T}\ \bar{x})\ \{\bar{t};\ \mathbf{return}\ t;\}$	pattern	$P ::= \mathbf{event}\ \bar{E}\ \mathbf{when}\ p\{\bar{t};\}$
event	$E ::= e\,[n]\,(\bar{N}\ \bar{x})\,[\bar{N'}\ \bar{x'}] \mid e\,[n]\,(\bar{N}\ \bar{x})$		
filter	$u ::= u\,.\,f \mid (T)u \mid \mathbf{new}\ D\,(d) \mid x\,[n] \mid x\,[i]$		
predicate	$p ::= u\ \textit{v-op}\ u \mid p\ \textit{b-op}\ p \mid \,!\,p \mid \mathbf{for}\,i\,\mathbf{in}\,[n..n]\ p$		
term	$t ::= v \mid x \mid t\,.\,f \mid t\,.\,f := t \mid t\,.\,m\,(\bar{t}) \mid (T)\,t \mid t\,.\,e\,(\bar{t}) \mid t\,.\,e\,(\bar{t})\,[\bar{t}] \mid C\,.\,e\,(\bar{t})$		
	$\mid C\,.\,e\,(\bar{t})\,[\bar{t}] \mid \mathbf{new}\ A\,(\bar{t}) \mid \mathbf{new}\ \mathtt{T}\,(\bar{t};)$		

$$d \in \mathbb{D} \qquad (D, d, \mathbb{D}) \in \{(\mathtt{B}, b, \mathbb{B}), (\mathtt{I}, z, \mathbb{Z}), (\mathtt{F}, r, \mathbb{R}), (\mathtt{S}, s, \Sigma^*), ...\}$$
$$l \in \mathrm{dom}(\mathcal{L}) \qquad \textit{v-op} \in \{==, <=, <\}$$
$$n \in \mathbb{Z}^+ \qquad \textit{b-op} \in \{\&\&, \mid\mid\}$$

Fig. 2. Featherweight EventJava (FEJ) syntax

$fields(\mathtt{Object}) = \emptyset$ [OBJ-CLASS]

$CT(\mathtt{E}) = \mathbf{class}\ \mathtt{E}\ \mathbf{extends}\ \mathtt{Object}\{\}$
[EV-CLASS]

$$\frac{CT(A) = \mathbf{class}\ A\ \mathbf{extends}\ A'\{\bar{T}\ \bar{f}\ ;\ ...\} \qquad fields(A') = \bar{T'}\ \bar{f'}}{fields(A) = \bar{T'}\ \bar{f'},\ \bar{T}\ \bar{f}}$$
[FIELD-TYPE]

$$\frac{CT(C) = \mathbf{class}\ C\ \mathbf{extends}\ ...\{...\ \bar{P}\} \qquad \mathbf{event}...\ e\,[n]\,(\bar{N}\ \bar{x})\ ...\ \{\bar{t};\} \in \bar{P}}{etype(e, C) = n \times \bar{N}\ \star\bar{N} \to \mathtt{E}}$$
[EV-TYPE]

$$\frac{CT(C) = \mathbf{class}\ C\ \mathbf{extends}\ C'\{...\ \bar{P}\} \qquad \not\exists ...e... \in \bar{P}}{etype(e, C) = etype(e, C')}$$
[EV-TYPE-INH]

$$\frac{CT(C) = \mathbf{class}\ C\ \mathbf{extends}\ ...\{...\ \bar{P}\} \qquad \mathbf{event}\ e\,[n]\,(\bar{N}\bar{x})\,[\bar{N'}\bar{x'}]\ \mathbf{when}\ p\{\bar{t};\} \in \bar{P}}{rbody(\bar{e}, C) = (\bar{x}\bar{x'}, p, \bar{t})}$$
[REACT-BODY]

$$\frac{CT(C) = \mathbf{class}\ C\ \mathbf{extends}\ ...\{...\ \bar{P}\} \qquad \forall\, j\ fresh\ \bar{x^j} = x_1^j\ ...x_q^j \quad q = |\star\bar{N}| \qquad \mathbf{event}\ e\,[n]\,(\bar{N}\bar{x'})\ \mathbf{when}\ p\{\bar{t};\} \in \bar{P}}{rbody(\bar{e}, C) = (\bar{x'}\bar{x}, p, \bar{t})}$$
[REACT-BODY-DEF]

$$\frac{CT(C) = \mathbf{class}\ C\ \mathbf{extends}\ C'\{...\ \bar{P}\} \qquad \not\exists ...\overline{e...} \in \bar{P}}{rbody(\bar{e}, C) = rbody(\bar{e}, C')}$$
[REACT-BODY-INH]

Fig. 3. Auxiliary definitions for FEJ

Contextual semantics. Event methods are typed (*etype*) just like ordinary methods ([EV-TYPE], [EV-TYPE-INH]), since they don't have return values. E is used as a placeholder for **event** and has neither methods nor fields. Evaluation takes place on tuples; in the context of local evaluation $\longrightarrow$, such a tuple is a term together with an object store $\mathcal{L}$ and an event store $\mathcal{S}$ (see Figure 4). $\mathcal{S}(l)$ represents per-object queues of events of the form $(e, \overline{vv'}) \cdot (e, \overline{vv'}) \cdot ...$. Global evaluation $\Longrightarrow$ is similar to local evaluation, but relates programs instead of terms. $\longrightarrow^*$ is the transitive closure of $\longrightarrow$. $\mathcal{L}$ changes when vales are assigned to object fields ([FIELD-ASS-R]) and when new objects are created ([LOC-R]). In [FORALL-R], quantification over integers $n..n'$ is reduced to $n' - n + 1$ predicates. We sometimes use $(o)_{1..q}$ instead of $\bar{o}$ to make the size q of $\bar{o}$ explicit.

Contexts and broadcast. The context is represented by a set of terms $\overline{\nabla t}$ of types $\star\bar{N}$. In an event $e\,[n]\,(\bar{N}\ \bar{x})\,[\bar{N'}\ \bar{x'}]$, we assume, without loss of generality, that the first term of the context x_1' is used for ordering. In FEJ, values for the context variables are either specified explicitly $(t\,.\,e\,(\bar{t})\,[\bar{t}],\ C\,.\,e\,(\bar{t})\,[\bar{t}])$ or instantiated during reduction ([EV-DEF-R, EV-BCAST-DEF-R]). To simplify the calculus rules, we make two assumptions: (*i*) Either all events in a given pattern declaration specify the context or omit it. (*ii*) In all invocations of an event method, the context is either explicitly specified or instantiated during reduction. Rules [EV-DEF-R] and [EV-BCAST-DEF-R] mimic actions performed by the runtime/middleware in an implementation. In [EV-DEF-R] and [EV-BCAST-DEF-R], for a given object l, the ∇t_1^l terms assigned must evaluate to values that are totally ordered, in increasing order. In [EV-R], events are added to the queue corresponding to object l. Broadcast ([EV-BCAST-DEF-R, EV-BCAST-R]) is *semantically* equivalent to a sequence of unicasts ([EV-R]). Note that in both [EV-BCAST-DEF-R] and [EV-BCAST-R], broadcast is not *atomic*, because it takes q reduction steps, which can be interleaved with reduction steps of other threads running in parallel. So there is no *global* total order, i.e., events in different queues may be ordered differently.

Correlation. The core of the semantics is the reaction rule [REACT-R], which relies on the *match*() predicate, and uses a number of auxiliary definitions. $\pi_e \mathcal{S}(l)$ is a projection that simply extracts a subsequence of events of type e from an event queue $\mathcal{S}(l)$. Set complement $\mathcal{S}(l)\backslash(...)$ and inclusion $\in$ follow the usual intuition, but are specified to simplify understanding of the weaknesses of the present semantics and the refined semantics for our reference implementation presented in the next section. The *match*() predicate ([PATT-MATCH]) simply takes *any* set of events matching any pattern defined for a given object ($\in$), regroups the corresponding events ($\mathcal{N}$) and creates a corresponding variable substitution (Θ). In case the predicate for the pattern evaluates to *true*, [REACT-R] simply removes the events from the queue and creates a new thread (thread pool in practice) to execute the reaction. Note that [REACT-R] does not produce any side-effects in $\mathcal{L}$, due to the constraints on predicates. Given the non-deterministic nature of the event matching, paired by the simple reduction of an event broadcast to a multi-send in [EV-BCAST-R], two instances of a same class receiving identical sets of broadcast (only) events will not necessarily correlate the same events.

The matching semantics presented here are intentionally weak and serve mostly as illustration. The handling of broadcast for instance does not assume more than reliable point-to-point communication. Using expensive event dissemination protocols results in better ordering guarantees. The semantics of our reference implementation (Section 4.2) uses deterministic selection of matching events and total order broadcast to disseminate events, providing strong guarantees on the order of execution of reactions (Section 4.2). But, FEJ does not force the use of a specific dissemination protocol or protocol family, because the choice strongly depends on the application, and the underlying infrastucture and system model. Ordering guarantees, for instance, induce a sensible overhead most of the time. In specific cases, they may be achieved more easily or even spontaneously (e.g. if the basic communication mechanism is broadcast-based such as on a single Ethernet wire or in certain wireless settings) or simply not be needed. Ordering properties, just like correlation semantics in general, can not be automatically inferred from the application.

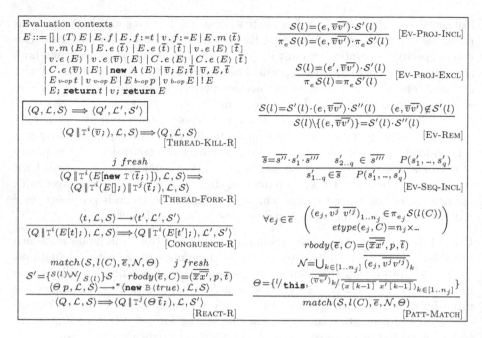

Fig. 4. Contextual semantics of FEJ

3.3 Constraints on Event Methods

Event methods are specific methods, and their declaration and implementation thus follows special restrictions.

R1 Event methods cannot throw exceptions and cannot return values. Their return type is **event**. This simplifies broadcast – the absence of exceptions and return values avoids dealing with multiple returns.

R2 Event method headers cannot be **synchronized**, as this would contradict their asynchronous nature. Reactions may be defined to be **synchronized** though by adding the keyword in front of the correlation pattern declaration.

R3 Similarly, **final** applies to correlation patterns. By prefixing a correlation pattern with that keyword, *all* event methods in the correlation pattern are transitively made final, and none of them can be overridden in a subclass correlation pattern.

R4 Predicates, like reactions, can not be defined in interfaces. An interface, or a class, can define an **abstract** event correlation pattern, which is strictly the same as defining the respective event methods individually.

R5 A reaction body can make a call to a reaction body of a pattern in its superclass through **super** only if the pattern *involves the same set of events*.

R6 An event method can only appear in a single correlation pattern within a class. Without this restriction, semantics become much more complicated, as elaborated in Section 6.

$$\boxed{\langle t, \mathcal{L}, \mathcal{S} \rangle \longrightarrow \langle t', \mathcal{L}', \mathcal{S}' \rangle}$$

$$\frac{\mathcal{L}(l) = [f_1 : v_1, ..., f_q : v_q]}{\langle l(A).f_j, \mathcal{L}, \mathcal{S} \rangle \longrightarrow \langle v_j, \mathcal{L}, \mathcal{S} \rangle} \quad \text{[Field-Acc-R]}$$

$$\frac{\mathcal{L}(l) = [f_1 : v_1, ..., f_q : v_q]}{\mathcal{L}' = \{[f_1 : v_1, ..., f_j : v', ..., f_q : v_q]/_l\} \mathcal{L}}{\langle l(C).f_j := v', \mathcal{L}, \mathcal{S} \rangle \longrightarrow \langle v', \mathcal{L}', \mathcal{S} \rangle} \quad \text{[Field-Ass-R]}$$

$$\frac{A \preceq T}{\langle (T) \, l(A), \mathcal{L}, \mathcal{S} \rangle \longrightarrow \langle l(A), \mathcal{L}, \mathcal{S} \rangle} \quad \text{[Obj-Cast-R]}$$

$$\frac{D \preceq T}{\langle (T) \, \mathbf{new} \, D\,(d), \mathcal{L}, \mathcal{S} \rangle \longrightarrow \langle \mathbf{new} \, D\,(d), \mathcal{L}, \mathcal{S} \rangle} \quad \text{[Val-Cast-R]}$$

$$\langle \overline{v}; \mathbf{return} \, v', \mathcal{L}, \mathcal{S} \rangle \longrightarrow \langle v', \mathcal{L}, \mathcal{S} \rangle \quad \text{[Ret-R]}$$

$$\frac{mbody(m, A) = (\overline{x}, \overline{t})}{\langle l(A).m\,(\overline{v}), \mathcal{L}, \mathcal{S} \rangle \longrightarrow \langle \{\overline{v}/_{\overline{x}}, \, l/\mathbf{this}\} \overline{t}, \mathcal{L}, \mathcal{S} \rangle} \quad \text{[Meth-R]}$$

$$\frac{\langle \mathbf{for} \, i \, \mathbf{in} \, [n..n'] \, p, \mathcal{L}, \mathcal{S} \rangle \longrightarrow}{\langle \{n/_i\} p \&\& ... \&\& \{n'/_i\} p, \mathcal{L}, \mathcal{S} \rangle} \quad \text{[Forall-R]}$$

$$\langle \, ! \, \mathbf{new} \, B\,(b), \mathcal{L}, \mathcal{S} \rangle \longrightarrow \langle \mathbf{new} \, B\,(\neg b), \mathcal{L}, \mathcal{S} \rangle \quad \text{[Bool-Neg-R]}$$

$$\frac{(b\text{-}op, \, a\text{-}op) \in \{(\&\&, \wedge), (||, \vee)\}}{\langle \mathbf{new} \, B\,(b) \, b\text{-}op \, \mathbf{new} \, B\,(b'), \mathcal{L}, \mathcal{S} \rangle \longrightarrow}{\langle \mathbf{new} \, B\,(b \, a\text{-}op \, b'), \mathcal{L}, \mathcal{S} \rangle} \quad \text{[Bool-Op-R]}$$

$$\frac{(v\text{-}op, \, a\text{-}op) \in \{(==, =), (<=, \leq), (<, \leq)\}}{\langle \mathbf{new} \, D\,(d) \, v\text{-}op \, \mathbf{new} \, D\,(d'), \mathcal{L}, \mathcal{S} \rangle \longrightarrow}{\langle \mathbf{new} \, B\,(d \, a\text{-}op \, d'), \mathcal{L}, \mathcal{S} \rangle} \quad \text{[Val-Op-R]}$$

$$\langle l.e\,(\overline{v}), \mathcal{L}, \mathcal{S} \rangle \longrightarrow \langle l.e\,(\overline{v}) \, [\overline{\nabla t^l}], \mathcal{L}, \mathcal{S} \rangle \quad \text{[Ev-Def-R]}$$

$$\frac{\mathcal{S}' = \{\mathcal{S}(l)\langle e, \overline{v} \; \overline{v'} \rangle/_l\} \mathcal{S}}{\langle l.e\,(\overline{v}) \, [\overline{v'}], \mathcal{L}, \mathcal{S} \rangle \longrightarrow \langle \mathbf{new} \, \mathbb{E}\,(), \mathcal{L}, \mathcal{S}' \rangle} \quad \text{[Ev-R]}$$

$$\frac{fields(A) = \overline{T} \, \overline{f} \quad l \notin dom(\mathcal{L})}{\mathcal{L}' = \{[f_1 : v_1, ..., f_q : v_q]/_l\} \mathcal{L}}{\langle \mathbf{new} \, A\,(\overline{v}), \mathcal{L}, \mathcal{S} \rangle \longrightarrow \langle l(A), \mathcal{L}', \mathcal{S} \rangle} \quad \text{[Loc-R]}$$

$$\frac{\overline{l} = \{l \mid l(C) \in \mathcal{L} \wedge C \preceq C'\}}{\langle C'.e\,(\overline{v}), \mathcal{L}, \mathcal{S} \rangle \longrightarrow}{\langle l_1.e\,(\overline{v}) \, [\overline{\nabla t^{l_1}}]; ...; l_q.e\,(\overline{v}) \, [\overline{\nabla t^{l_q}}], \mathcal{L}, \mathcal{S} \rangle} \quad \text{[Ev-Bcast-Def-R]}$$

$$\frac{\overline{l} = \{l \mid l(C) \in \mathcal{L} \wedge C \preceq C'\}}{\langle C'.e\,(\overline{v}) \, [\overline{v'}], \mathcal{L}, \mathcal{S} \rangle \longrightarrow}{\langle l_1.e\,(\overline{v}) \, [\overline{v'}]; ...; l_q.e\,(\overline{v}) \, [\overline{v'}], \mathcal{L}, \mathcal{S} \rangle} \quad \text{[Ev-Bcast-R]}$$

Fig. 5. Contextual semantics of FEJ (cont'd). $\preceq$ denotes subtyping, refer to the companion technical report [13] for the subtyping rules.

In FEJ, R1 is achieved by the introduction of the placeholder $\mathbb{E}$. R2 and R3 are abstracted, R4 and R6 are enforced by inheriting from FJ. R5 is abstracted in FEJ because FJ does not have **super**-calls.

3.4 Event Overloading, Event Overriding and Pattern Overriding

As in Java, an event method e_1 *overloads* e_2 if they have the same name but different type signatures (*etype* in Figure 3). In EventJava, they are treated as two different event methods and can appear in different correlation patterns in the same class (subject to restriction R6). Overriding an event method e (with window $[n]$) is possible (with $[n']$, $n' \geq n$) iff e is not in a **final** pattern in the (non-**final**) super-class. Consider a correlation pattern p_1 in class C containing event methods $e_1, ..., e_q$ with windows $n_1, ..., n_q$. Assume that class C' inherits from class C, and defines a pattern p_2 containing e_1. Then, we say that p_2 overrides p_1. But p_2 does not have to contain $e_2, ..., e_q$, which may be included in other patterns of C'. So, a pattern in C can be overridden by more than one pattern in C'. By restriction R6, since an event method can occur only in one correlation pattern per class, if C' does not define patterns containing $e_2, ..., e_q$, then they become abstract just like the subclass C' itself.

3.5 Global Progress

Consider an object $l(C)$ with a pattern **event** $\overline{e\,_{[n]}\,(\overline{N}\ \overline{x})\,_{[}\overline{N}\ \overline{x}]}$ **when** $p\{\overline{t}_;\}$ defined in C.

Definition 1 (Configurations). *We refer to* $\mathcal{C} = \langle Q, \mathcal{L}, \mathcal{S} \rangle$ *as a* configuration.

- $\mathcal{E}_j^k(Q, \mathcal{L}, \mathcal{S}) = \langle \mathrm{T}^i(E[d_j . e_j\,_{(\overline{v^j}\ \overline{v'^j})}]_k) \, \| \, Q, \mathcal{L}, \mathcal{S} \rangle$ *is an* event *configuration.*
- $\mathcal{R}_{l(C)}^{\overline{e}}(\Theta, Q, \mathcal{L}, \mathcal{S}) = \langle \mathrm{T}^{\langle l(C), \overline{e} \rangle}(\Theta \overline{t}_;...) \, \| \, Q, \mathcal{L}, \mathcal{S} \rangle$ *is a* reaction *configuration.*

Definition 2 (Run).
A run *is a succession of configurations* $\overline{\mathcal{C}} = \mathcal{C}_1 \Longrightarrow ... \Longrightarrow \mathcal{C}_q.$

Theorem 1 (Global progress). *Assume a run* $\overline{\mathcal{C}}$ *s.t.* $\forall j \in [1..q], k \in [1..n_j],$ (i) $d_j^k \in l(C) \cup \{C' \mid C \preceq C'\}$, (ii) $\exists \mathcal{L}_j^k(l)$, (iii) $\exists \mathcal{C} = \mathcal{E}_j^k(Q_j^k, \mathcal{L}_j^{\,k}, \mathcal{S}_j^k) \in \overline{\mathcal{C}}$, (iv) $\langle \{l/\,\textbf{this},\ \overline{(v^j v'^j)}_k/\,\overline{(\overline{x^j\,x'^j})}_{k\in[1..n_j]}\} p, ... \rangle \longrightarrow^* \langle \textbf{new}\ \texttt{B}(true), ... \rangle$. *Then* $\forall \overline{\mathcal{C}'} = \overline{\mathcal{C}} \Longrightarrow$ $\overline{\mathcal{C}''} \ni \mathcal{R}_l^{\overline{e}}(\Theta, Q, \mathcal{L}, \mathcal{S}) \in \overline{\mathcal{C}'}$

Proof by induction on derivation of $\Longrightarrow$. (The theorem reads "If a pattern of an object gets satisfied, the corresponding reaction will eventually be evaluated.")

4   Implementation

This section first presents the implementation framework underlying EventJava. Then, a reference implementation based on Jess [10] and JGroups [11] is presented along with its specific matching semantics, showing that these preserve total ordering properties of message dissemination in JGroups.

4.1 Implementation Framework

The EventJava compiler, implemented using Polyglot [17], translates EventJava programs to standard Java by (a) code transformations and (b) generation of application-specific helper classes (e.g. for broadcasting).

Framework components. The generated code represents the glue between EventJava programs and the framework components shown in Figure 6. An event notification/method invocation is forwarded to the communication *substrate*, JGroups in the case of our reference implementation, which takes care of remote communication including unicast and broadcast. In the broadcast case, the substrate delivers all the serialized event method invocations to the *resolver*, which determines the classes on which the methods were invoked and interacts with *broadcast objects* for those classes. Broadcast objects deliver the events to the sinks, where they are stored, typically but not necessarily, in event queues. The *matcher* — one instance per sink — checks the stored events for a match to any of the correlation patterns and spawns the reaction on its sink. Multi-threading can be used in various places, with synchronization depending on the desired semantics. While the substrate and

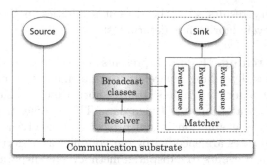

Fig. 6. The EventJava framework. Ovals represent the application. Shaded boxes represent fixed components; others are customizable.

matcher, like the context, are defined as an API, the resolver and broadcast classes are generated by our compiler to avoid costly dynamic invocations through reflection. The context of a given event is used and sometimes modified or augmented throughout the substrate and the matcher.

Code transformations. On the source side, each event method invocation is altered to create the context, serialize the explicit arguments, and invoke the substrate. All the instances of any class C which has at least one event method need to be tracked by its broadcast class. To that end, a static field instances is added to every such *sink class* to track all of its instances with weak references. Every **new** on a sink class is instrumented to add the created object to the class' instances set. Broadcast objects for sink classes recursively store references to broadcast objects for their sink subclasses.

Integration with Java RMI and garbage collection of sinks. Some constraints in EventJava come from its integration with the Java RMI framework [18]. This does not mean that remote communication in EventJava takes place over Java RMI. EventJava is merely integrated with the *interfaces*, for portability and interoperability with J2EE. The constraints introduced by this integration lead to a leaner and simpler model and do not reduce expressiveness to the extent of offsetting the benefits of the integration. The integration implies that events must be declared in interfaces subtyping java.rmi.Remote (omitted in the examples so far for brevity), which means that sinks are remote objects. Event methods become thereby **public**, and can not be **static**. These last two restrictions are ensured by FEJ, as bare FJ only supports such members. This integration with Java RMI also helps garbage collection of dead sinks, and ensures that events are not delivered to dead sinks. The **static** field instances added to the sink class uses weak references, which are periodically purged.

4.2 Deterministic Matching in the Jess Reference Implementation

While non-determinism might be desired in certain cases, a trading algorithm replicated for reliability by running several instances of the same class will yield contradictory results with the default semantics in Section 3.2, even if the application-level algorithm is deterministic.

Rete-based matching. Figure 7 presents an alternative deterministic dispatching semantics describing our reference implementation of the matcher on top of the Rete [9] algorithm in Jess [10]. In short, Rete treats events, with their explicit and implicit attributes as typed data. The matcher implementation ensures that predicate evaluation is synchronized for a given sink. Correlation patterns and predicates are encoded by our compiler as Jess rules. The matcher delivers the matched events to a dispatch method. The dispatch method, generated by our compiler, has code to receive matched events and use threads from a thread pool to execute the reaction bodies.

Semantics. In Figure 7, rules [Ev-Bcast-Def-R'], [Ev-Bcast-R'] and [Patt-Match'] replace [Ev-Bcast-Def-R], [Ev-Bcast-R] and [Patt-Match] respectively. Rules [React-R'$_1$] and [React-R'$_2$] replace [React-R]. In [Ev-Bcast-Def-R'] and [Ev-Bcast-R'], when an event is broadcast, the context terms are instantiated and the events are added to the corresponding per-object queues of S in a single atomic step, i.e., total order broadcast is used. This differs from the default semantics of FEJ where a multi-send is used. Again, in [Ev-Bcast-Def-R'], for a given object l, the ∇t_1^l terms assigned must evaluate to values that are totally ordered, in increasing order. This, in combination with the use of total order broadcast, ensures *global* total order, i.e., the events in all the queues of S are totally ordered.

In Rete-based matching, for pattern **event** $e_1()$,..., $e_q()$ **when** p, the *first* received instance of e_1 is chosen for which an instance of each remaining event type has been received such that the predicate p is matched. If there are several instances of e_2 for which instances of $e_3, .., e_q$ exist such that p holds, then the first one is chosen and so on. If an event e_j has an assigned window of size n_j then the algorithm of course looks for the first sequence of length n_j (relation $\in^1$ defined by [Ev-First-Seq-Incl]) such that there are instances of the remaining event types.

Once a match is determined for a given correlation pattern, any event which is of an event type within the correlation pattern and *older* than the respective matching one is discarded in addition to the matching one ($\binom{*}{}$). Otherwise, the total order determined by JGroups is not preserved. Furthermore, reactions for a same correlation pattern on a same object are executed sequentially in the order in which they are identified, by identifying threads by a $\langle object, pattern \rangle$ tuple ([React-R'$_{1,2}$]). Synchronization code has to consider this. *Total order* broadcast (as well as reaction serialization) can be disabled in our reference implementation if an application does not require the ordering guarantees. In the absence of ordering guarantees, an EventJava implementation could, for instance, choose to handle reactions like transactions with an optimistic concurrency model.

$$\overline{s}=\overline{s'''}\cdot s_1'\cdot\overline{s''''} \quad s_{2..q}'\in^1\overline{s''''} \quad P(s_1',...,s_q')$$

$$\nexists\, s_1''\in\overline{s'''}\;:\; \left(\begin{array}{c}\overline{s}=...s_1''\cdot\overline{s''''} \quad s_{2..q}''\in\overline{s''''} \\ P(s_1'',...,s_q'')\end{array}\right)$$

$$\frac{}{s_{1..q}'\in^1\overline{s}\;P(s_1',...,s_q')}$$
[Ev-First-Seq-Incl]

$$\frac{S(l)=S'(l)\cdot(e,\overline{vv'})\cdot S(l)'' \quad (e,\overline{vv'})\notin S'(l)}{S(l)\backslash^*\{(e,\overline{vv'})\}=S(l)''}$$
[Ev-Rem-All]

$$\overline{l}=\{l\mid l(C)\in\mathcal{L}\wedge C\preceq C'\}$$

$$\frac{S'=\{^{S(l_1\setminus e,\overline{v}\ \overline{\nabla t^{l_1}})}/_{l_1}\ ...\ ^{S(l_q\setminus e,\overline{v}\ \overline{\nabla t^{l_q}})}/_{l_q}\}S}{\langle C'.e\,(\overline{v}),\mathcal{L},\mathcal{S}\rangle\longrightarrow\langle\mathbf{new}\ \text{E}\,(),\mathcal{L},\mathcal{S}'\rangle}$$
[Ev-Bcast-Def-R']

$$\frac{\overline{l}=\{l\mid l(C)\in\mathcal{L}\wedge C\preceq C'\}\quad S'=\{^{S(l\setminus e,\overline{v}\ \overline{v'})}/_{\overline{l}}\}S}{\langle C'.e\,(\overline{v})\,[\overline{v'}],\mathcal{L},\mathcal{S}\rangle\longrightarrow\langle\mathbf{new}\ \text{E}\,(),\mathcal{L},\mathcal{S}'\rangle}$$
[Ev-Bcast-R']

$$match^1(\mathcal{S},l(C),\overline{e},\mathcal{N},\Theta) \quad Q=Q'\|\text{T}^{\langle l,\overline{e}\rangle}(\overline{t'};)$$
$$rbody(\overline{e},C)=(\overline{\overline{x}\,\overline{x'}},p,\overline{t}) \quad S'=\{^{S(l)\backslash^*}\mathcal{N}/_{S(l)}\}\mathcal{S}$$
$$\langle\Theta\,p,\mathcal{L},\mathcal{S}\rangle\longrightarrow^*\langle\mathbf{new}\ \text{B}\,(true),\mathcal{L},\mathcal{S}\rangle$$

$$\frac{}{\langle Q,\mathcal{L},\mathcal{S}\rangle\Longrightarrow\langle Q'\|\text{T}^{\langle l,\overline{e}\rangle}(\overline{t};\Theta\,\overline{t};),\mathcal{L},\mathcal{S}'\rangle}$$
[React-R'$_1$]

$$match^1(\mathcal{S},l(C),\overline{e},\mathcal{N},\Theta) \quad Q\neq Q'\|\text{T}^{\langle l,\overline{e}\rangle}(\overline{t'};)$$
$$rbody(\overline{e},C)=(\overline{\overline{x}\,\overline{x'}},p,\overline{t}) \quad S'=\{^{S(l)\backslash^*}\mathcal{N}/_{S(l)}\}\mathcal{S}$$
$$\langle\Theta\,p,\mathcal{L},\mathcal{S}\rangle\longrightarrow^*\langle\mathbf{new}\ \text{B}\,(true),\mathcal{L},\mathcal{S}\rangle$$

$$\frac{}{\langle Q,\mathcal{L},\mathcal{S}\rangle\Longrightarrow\langle Q\|\text{T}^{\langle l,\overline{e}\rangle}(\Theta\,\overline{t};),\mathcal{L},\mathcal{S}'\rangle}$$
[React-R'$_2$]

$$\left((e_j,\overline{v^j}\ \overline{v'^j})_{1..n_j}\in^1\pi_{e_j}S(l(C))\right)_{j=1..q}$$

$$\overline{e}=e_1..e_q \quad etype(e_j,C)=n_j\times...$$

$$rbody(\overline{e},C)=(\overline{\overline{x}\,\overline{x'}},p,\overline{t})$$

$$\mathcal{N}=\bigcup\nolimits_{k\in[1..n_j]}(e_j,\overline{v^j v'^j})_k$$

$$\Theta=\{^{l}/\mathbf{this},\overline{^{(\overline{vv'})k}/(\overline{x\,[k-1]}\ \overline{x'\,[k-1]})}_{k\in[1..n_j]}\}$$

$$\frac{}{match^1(\mathcal{S},l(C),\overline{e},\mathcal{N},\Theta)}$$
[Patt-Match']

Fig. 7. Deterministic matching semantics in the Jess reference implementation

Ordering properties. We can prove that ordering at the JGroups level is preserved by the matching semantics. Consider Definitions 1 and 2 for configurations and runs given in Section 3.5. Assume $l(C)$ and $l'(C)$, and a pattern **event** $e\,[n]\,(\overline{N}\ \overline{x})\,[\overline{N}\ \overline{x}]$ **when** $p\,\{\overline{t};\}$ defined in C.

Theorem 2 (Order preservation). *Assume a run $\overline{C}$ s.t. $\forall C=\mathcal{E}_j^k(Q,\mathcal{L},\mathcal{S})\in\overline{C}\ d_j^k\notin\{l(C),l'(C)\}$.*

Then $\forall\mathcal{C}_i,\mathcal{C}_{i'},\mathcal{C}_j,\mathcal{C}_{j'}\in\overline{C}\mid\mathcal{C}_i=\mathcal{R}_l^{\overline{e}}(\Theta,Q_i,\mathcal{L}_i,\mathcal{S}_i),\ \mathcal{C}_{i'}=\mathcal{R}_l^{\overline{e}}(\Theta',Q_{i'},\mathcal{L}_{i'},\mathcal{S}_{i'}),\ \mathcal{C}_j=\mathcal{R}_{l'}^{\overline{e}}(\Theta,Q_j,\mathcal{L}_j,\mathcal{S}_j),\ \mathcal{C}_{j'}=\mathcal{R}_{l'}^{\overline{e}}(\Theta',Q_{j'},\mathcal{L}_{j'},\mathcal{S}_{j'})\ i<i'\Leftrightarrow j<j'.$

Proof by induction on derivation of $\Longrightarrow$. (The theorem reads: "For two instances of a same class receiving only broadcast events, the objects will execute reactions to a given pattern in the same order.")

5   Evaluation

Given that there is a strong variance in workloads produced by distributed applications (same or different), over time depending on their deployment, we do not evaluate our system with specific applications, but rather use stress testing by varying the different parameters of the load. This section stress tests our reference implementation of EventJava (referred to as EventJava) by comparison with (a) the highly tuned Cayuga correlation engine [3] and (b) lightweight limited correlation for concurrency in Cω [22]. All tests use the more resource-demanding "\" semantics (see Section 6).

5.1 Cayuga

Cayuga [3] is a highly tuned, database-backed, correlation engine. The paper by
Demers et al. [3] shows that Cayuga outperforms other correlation engines like
Aurora [4] and Borealis [5]. All measurement scenarios and settings were taken
from [3] to not favor EventJava. Figure 8 compares the throughput of Event-
Java with Cayuga with respect to the number of different event methods/event
types involved per sink. This experiment was conducted on an iMac dual core
2.0Ghz with 2GB RAM. Sink classes were generated with 1000, ... ,150000 (non-
abstract) event methods and 4 event methods per correlation pattern, i.e. for the
sink class with 100,000 event methods, there were 25,000 correlation patterns.
The number of event methods and correlation patterns is relevant because it
directly affects the performance of the matcher – the time taken by any search
algorithm to match an event to a pattern. The throughput (number of events
processed per second) of EventJava remains well above 10,000 events/sec even
for the case involving 150,000 event methods and 37,500 correlation patterns,
even outperforming Cayuga. Note though that according to [3], Cayuga scales
relatively better than EventJava, performance with EventJava drops relatively
sharper beyond 150,000 event methods per sink. Cayuga's throughput drops beyond 10,000 event types, but Cayuga can scale even up to 400,000 event types
(their throughput is 2000 events/sec at 400,000 event methods). Also, Cayuga's
memory footprint is smaller than EventJava. We weren't able to reproduce these
results, and use the figures from [3] to plot the graph. Note that only one sink is
used because Cayuga has a single correlation engine and the goal is to compare
peak throughput of matching. We conclude that even when implemented with
custom off-the-shelf components such as Jess, the performance of EventJava is
comparable to a highly tuned correlation engine in substantial load scenarios.
This illustrates that the high-level programming abstractions of EventJava and
its resulting gains in safety, (e.g. when compared to queries expressed in SQL-like
grammars) do not entail any inherent penalty.

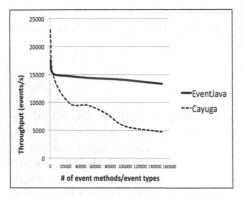

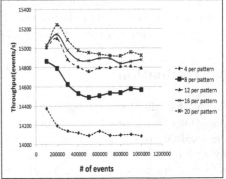

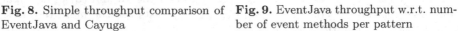

Fig. 8. Simple throughput comparison of EventJava and Cayuga

Fig. 9. EventJava throughput w.r.t. number of event methods per pattern

5.2   Complexity of Correlation Patterns

Figure 9 illustrates the scalability of EventJava with respect to the number of event methods in a correlation pattern. The experiment was conducted using a single sink with 100,000 different event methods. So, if there are 4 event methods per correlation patten, there are 25,000 correlation patterns. The throughput increases slightly with the number of events in the pattern, and in all cases the throughput is well above 14,000 events/sec. Figure 9 shows five such scenarios with 4, 8, 12, 16, and 20 event methods per pattern respectively. In Figure 9, we measure throughput by randomly generating events. The throughput remains fairly constant, irrespective of the number of events used in the measurement. For each scenario, we measure average throughput over streams of 100,000 events to 1 million events. The variation in throughput for any scenario is within 250 events per second, i.e., ∼2%. This shows that the throughput of EventJava does not decrease over time when it faces continuous streams of events. This experiment was conducted on an iMac 2.0 Ghz dual core with 2GB RAM.

5.3   Cω

Polyphonic C# [22], which is now part of Cω, implements the Join calculus [23] in C#. The key differences between (the Polyphonic-C# part of) Cω and Event-Java are (i) Cω does not support predicates (ii) Cω targets concurrent programming, supporting one synchronous method per pattern at most (iii) Cω does not explicitly support broadcast interaction (iv) Cω and EventJava differ in the algorithms used for the storage and matching of events, and (v) Cω has *stream types* which can be viewed as pointers to/iterators over a priori endless arrays, but they are not integrated with chords and correlation over streams is not supported. Correlation patterns without predicates are called *chords* in Cω terminology. Calls to asynchronous methods part of a pattern (a *chord* in Cω terminology) are queued, and a reaction can be dispatched when every method in the pattern has been called. In Figure 10, we measure the matching performance of Event-Java with Cω for predicate-less patterns which favors the concurrency scenarios aimed at by Cω. The measurements in this case were conducted on an HP PC with an Intel quad core 2.4Ghz processor and 3.5GB RAM. The throughput of EventJava is actually 18-19% higher than that of Cω, which shows the versatility of the reference implementation of EventJava. We conclude that EventJava can be an alternative to Cω for concurrent programming. Note that the introduction of predicates is in fact debated in [22], but not realized to retain the lightweight matching implementation.

5.4   EventJava Latency

For completeness, and to argue for the integration of a broadcast substrate in EventJava, we evaluate the end-to-end latency of EventJava in a distributed settting. Latency here is measured as the time interval between the production of the last event that instantiates a correlation pattern, and the dispatch of the

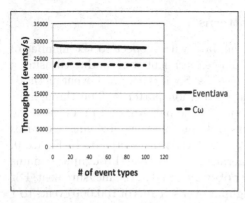

Fig. 10. Simple throughput comparison of EventJava and Cω

Fig. 11. End-to-end latency of EventJava application with respect to the number of sinks on different nodes

corresponding reaction at a possibly remote sink. For example if two events e_1, e_2 are used to match a pattern, and if the reaction at the remote sink is dispatched at time t, then the end-to-end latency is $t - max(e_1.\texttt{time}, e_2.\texttt{time})$. These measurements were conducted in a local area network, where clocks of hosts were closely synchronized. Figure 11 compares the average latency of EventJava with that of the same application implemented using Cω with .NET Remoting. The sink objects were distributed in groups of 100 on 1, 3, 5, 7, 9, 11 nodes and the source was on a different node. Each node was a Dell OptiPlex GX270 Workstation with a 3Ghz Pentium 4 processor and 512 MB RAM running Microsoft Windows XP. Figure 11 shows that average end-to-end latency remains closely constant in the EventJava application as the number of sinks increases, while average latency rapidly increases when performing a blunt multi-send with .NET Remoting.

6   Discussion

We discuss issues related to the design and implementation of EventJava, including three parameters for matching (M1, M2, M3) that can be set by the runtime.

Events in multiple patterns. As mentioned in Section 3.3, in a class, the same event method cannot be a part of more than one correlation pattern. Consider a class C, where an event method e occurs in more than one pattern p_1 and p_2. At runtime, the implementation has two alternatives when an event matches more than one pattern:

A1 *Non-deterministic choice:* Non-deterministically choose a pattern that consumes the event. This breaks the order preservation property of our reference implementation, which would defeat the purpose of many event dissemination protocols in the substrate. An application developer can easily separate p_1 and p_2 into two separate classes C_1 and C_2, and if non-determinism is desired, the developer can easily introduce it by randomization. But, reconstructing event order at the application level is much more complicated. If A1 can also create scenarios where a pattern is *starved*, i.e. does not consume any event for long periods of time.

A2 *Cloning:* Clone the event, thereby allowing all matching patterns to consume the event. This alternative can also break the order preservation property. Also, if events are cloned, the EventJava runtime has to maintain per-pattern data structures to store events, because the consumption of an event by one pattern is independent of other patterns. This degrades performance. A2 also complicates inheritance; if a class C defines two patterns p_1 and p_2, both containing event method e, and if class C' extends C and defines pattern p_3 containing e, does p_3 override p_1 or p_2? Both? Neither? We would need to add further syntax to EventJava to explicitly specify overridden events and patterns.

Because of these drawbacks, EventJava does not permit the same event method to occur in multiple patterns in a class.

Broadcast vs multicast. Through the presence of predicates in EventJava, broadcasting leads to *implicit* multicasting, as not all instances of a sink class C (and of its subclasses) will necessarily deliver a given event $C.e(\text{...})$. An intermediate case between unicast and implicit multicast consists in an *explicit* multicast where a select set of sinks are addressed – atomically as opposed to a multi-send as portrayed in rule [Ev-Bcast-R] of Figure 5. Several middleware systems propose such protocols natively, or they can be built on top. EventJava supports such interaction through specific proxies. As the invocation then occurs just like a regular unicast invocation (on the proxy) and many authors have elaborated on that in the past (e.g., [19,20]) we omit its presentation.

Bootstrapping and groups. Bootstrapping of EventJava components occurs like in any distributed application: a federated name is necessary for connecting parties. This name defines a group, which delimits an EventJava application and thereby also broadcasts. There are several ways of further reducing the scope of broadcasts. Two dynamic solutions are alluded to above. (1) By adding a *name* attribute to corresponding events, sinks can use predicates to specify *sub*groups of interest. (2) Creating explicit multicast groups by the use of proxies and libraries. Additionally, configuration files can be used to define boundaries for broadcasts on a per-event basis, e.g., through subnet masks.

Order. The ordering property stated above only holds for two instances of a same class, and with respect to individual patterns. By **matching following the patterns of a class in a deterministic order** (M1), which can be enabled in our implementation, the property can be widened to reactions to *all* patterns of two instances of a same class. Given the possibility of redistributing events across patterns and redefining predicates in subclasses, widening to subclasses is not possible straightforwardly. Similarly, *causal* order [21] is a useful property in asynchronous distributed systems devoid of synchronized clocks, e.g. for debugging. It can be inherently achieved with total order broadcast and *local* *order* [21], which our reference implementation provides, in settings considering *individual* events. As opposed to traditional message-wise delivery, correlation introduces the possibility of several and thus causally ordered events to be delivered *simultaneously* (in fact this is what many patterns are fishing for), but no two events $e_1 < e_2$ ($<$ representing a *happens-before* relation) can be handled by two subsequent reactions r_1 and r_2 in the inverse order, i.e., r_2 will not handle e_1 after r_1 handles e_2.

Event expiry. Predicates add to the possibility of events never being matched – or matchable. Events of a given type can accumulate if events of other types correlated with it are received at lower rates. Our reference implementation thus allows for the **setting of time-outs on events** (M2), by sources (context) and sinks. Furthermore, the deletion of all earlier events of a type when identifying the first one matching its pattern (" * " in rules [REACT-R'$_{1,2}$]) can be similarly disabled, leading to **retaining older non-matched events** (by using " \ " instead – M3). It is easy to show that this does not invalidate Theorem 2. However, the order of the *reaction executions*, though still total, can go against the total order determined on *events* by JGroups.

Language design issues. The `Context` class is not a superclass of all classes containing event methods because of ongoing extensions to EventJava where different event methods in a class can have different contexts. Another design choice would be to have an implicit join if the same parameter name is used in two event methods in a correlation pattern, rather than having it represent two variables that have to be disambiguated. Implicit joins are elegant, but programmers may accidentally use the same parameter name where a join is not intended.

7   Related Work

In this section, we present related work on programming language support for event-based programming with emphasis on correlation. An overview of the most closely related languages/frameworks is given in Table 1.

Concurrency. Like Cω [22], Join Java [26] faithfully implements the Join calculus [23] – providing a means to react to correlated asynchronous method invocations, without predicates, broadcast, and customizable matching. Functional languages like CML [28] and Erlang [34] provide powerful support for event-based programming, but do not explicitly support event correlation. In CML, events are essentially reified as function *evaluations* such as reads or writes on channels, which can be combined. Event correlation can be achieved by a *staged event matching*, in which a correlation pattern is matched in phases, where the occurrence of an event of a first type is a precondition for the remaining matching, which consumes that event. Staged event matching imposes an order on how events are matched to a correlation pattern. This gives the programmer much control over the exact matching semantics, but means implementing partial matching schemes repeatedly. In many cases, more advanced schemes expressed

Table 1. Overview of inherent event programming features of related programming languages/frameworks. Languages supporting broadcast also have unicast. Type-A and Type-B predicates are described in Section 2.2.

Language	Joins	Type-A predicates	Type-B predicates	Streams	Addressing
ECO [24]	-	✔	-	-	Broadcast
Java$_{PS}$ [25]	-	✔	-	-	Broadcast
Cω [22]	✔	-	-	-	Unicast
Join Java [26]	✔	-	-	-	Unicast
AWED [27]	✔	-	✔	-	Broadcast
CML [28]	✔ (staged)	✔	-	-	Broadcast
StreamFlex [29]	✔	-	-	✔	Unicast
StreamIt [30]	✔	-	-	✔	Unicast
Ptolemy [31]	✔ (staged)	-	-	-	Unicast
Scala Joins [32]	✔	✔	-	-	Unicast
Scala Actors [33]	✔ (staged)	✔	-	-	Unicast
Erlang [34]	✔ (staged)	✔	-	-	Unicast
EventJava	✔	✔	✔	✔	Broadcast

with staged matching can require "re-inserting" an event, which quickly complicates code. CML provides rich libraries with common operators to mitigate the issues above. Actor-based languages like Erlang [34] and Scala Actors [33] similarly support staged event matching. Scala Joins [32] provide Cω-like join patterns, but does not support Type-B predicates and broadcast interaction. Jeeg [35] is a concurrency extension of Java imposing ordering of method invocations based on patterns described in Linear Temporal Logic (LTL) in a way similar to the routines in many active object approaches, e.g., [36]. Like CML these approaches do however not allow for the atomic reaction to combinations of incoming calls/events. Responders [37] provide a means of writing responsive threads in a state-machine manner, yielding a safe and effective way of arranging event handling code. However, correlation is not supported, and reactions are synchronous to ensure determinism.

Publish/subscribe, streams and aspects. ECO (*events, constraints, objects*) [24] and Java$_{PS}$ [25] extend C++ and Java respectively for publish/subscribe-like distributed programming, i.e., reacting to singleton events.

StreamIt [30] is a dataflow language targeting fine-grained highly parallel stream applications and providing a highly optimizing native compiler (and a Java translator). While StreamIt programs can be parallelized automatically, the language is hardly suited for general purpose applications because of the lack of data types offered and the restricted programming model. Also, there is no support for event correlation or stream correlation. StreamFlex [29] is a Java API for stream processing inspired by StreamIt but providing high-predictability implemented on top of a real-time virtual machine. StreamIt provides `filters` and `channels`, leading to a similar programming model as CML. DirectFlow [38] is a domain specific language that simplifies programming information-flow components by hiding the control-flow interactions between them. Again, there is no explicit support for event correlation. AWED (*aspects with explicit distribution*) [27]) is an aspect language supporting the remote monitoring of distributed applications with distributed pointcuts and advice. EventJava can be viewed as AWED turned inside-out: applications are intentionally written to interact with specific events, which is achieved by the means of limited additional syntax. DJcutter [40] extends AspectJ's with remote joinpoints and pointcuts. However, at the runtime level, DJcutter proposes a centralized aspect-server, which constitutes a bottleneck in a large distributed systems; as many others of the others, DJcutter lacks consistency guarantees as a consequence of poor integration with distribution. Ptolemy [31] is an aspect-oriented language with quantified, typed events, but doesn't support correlation – joins can be performed in a staged manner as described earlier.

8   Conclusions and Outlook

We have presented EventJava, a generic language for event-based programming with event correlation. Our implementation framework allows for adaptation to various settings and systems. We are for instance in the process of implementing a lightweight version of EventJava for mobile computing. The notion of context allows us to easily accommodate *context-aware* applications.

We are currently pursuing two further axes of research, centered around matching semantics and the EventJava framework. First, we are devising annotations for flexibly configuring matching semantics on a per-pattern basis. Second, we are investigating the use of domain-specific aspects for context expression and propagation and other parts of our framework.

Acknowledgements

We would like to thank Ryan Maus at Allston Trading LLC for input on the algorithmic trading examples and Jacob Fancher for his contribution to the EventJava compiler. We would also like to thank William Cook, as well as the anonymous reviewers for their invaluable feedback, which helped improve the contents and presentation of this paper.

References

1. Trigeo: TriGeo Security Information Manager, Trigeo SIM (2007),
   http://www.trigeo.com/products/detailedf/
2. Gay, D., Levis, P., von Behren, R., Welsh, M., Brewer, E., Culler, D.: The *nesC* Language: A Holistic Approach to Networked Embedded Systems. In: PLDI, pp. 1–11 (2003)
3. Demers, A., Gehrke, J., Hong, M., Riedewald, M., White, W.: Towards Expressive Publish/Subscribe Systems. In: Ioannidis, Y., Scholl, M.H., Schmidt, J.W., Matthes, F., Hatzopoulos, M., Böhm, K., Kemper, A., Grust, T., Böhm, C. (eds.) EDBT 2006. LNCS, vol. 3896, pp. 627–644. Springer, Heidelberg (2006)

4. Abadi, D.J., Carney, D., Çetintemel, U., Cherniack, M., Convey, C., Lee, S., Stonebraker, M., Tatbul, N., Zdonik, S.: Aurora: A New Model and Architecture for Data Stream Management. VLDB Journal 12(2), 120–139 (2003)
5. Ahmad, Y., Berg, B., Çetintemel, U., Humphrey, M., Hwang, J.H., Jhingran, A., Maskey, A., Papaemmanouil, O., Rasin, A., Tatbul, N., Xing, W., Xing, Y., Zdonik, S.: Distributed Operation in the Borealis Stream Processing Engine. In: SIGMOD 2005, pp. 882–884 (2005)
6. Amir, Y., Danilov, C., Miskin-Amir, M., Schultz, J., Stanton, J.: The Spread Toolkit, http://www.spread.org
7. Pietzuch, P.R., Bacon, J.: Hermes: A Distributed Event-Based Middleware Architecture. In: ICDCSW 2002, pp. 611–618 (2002)
8. Apache: ActiveMQ (2008), http://activemq.apache.org/
9. Forgy, C.: Rete: A Fast Algorithm for the Many Patterns/Many Objects Match Problem. Artificial Intelligence 19(1), 17–37 (1982)
10. Friedman-Hill, E.: Jess (2008), http://www.jessrules.com/jess/
11. Ban, B.: JGroups - A Toolkit for Reliable Multicast Communication (2007), http://www.jgroups.org/javagroupsnew/docs/index.html
12. Igarashi, A., Pierce, B.C., Wadler, P.: Featherweight Java: A Minimal Core Calculus for Java and GJ. TOPLAS 23(3), 396–450 (2001)
13. Eugster, P., Jayaram, K.R.: EventJava: An Extension of Java for Event Correlation. Technical Report CSD TR #09-002, Department of Computer Science, Purdue University (2009), http://www.cs.purdue.edu/research/technical_reports/
14. Chakravarthy, S., Krishnaprasad, V., Anwar, E., Kim, S.K.: Composite Events for Active Databases: Semantics, Contexts and Detection. In: VLDB 1994, pp. 606–617 (1994)
15. Sánchez, C., Słanina, M., Sipma, H.B., Manna, Z.: Expressive completeness of an event-pattern reactive programming language. In: Wang, F. (ed.) FORTE 2005. LNCS, vol. 3731, pp. 529–532. Springer, Heidelberg (2005)
16. Welc, A., Hosking, A.L., Jagannathan, S.: Transparently reconciling transactions with locking for java synchronization. In: Thomas, D. (ed.) ECOOP 2006. LNCS, vol. 4067, pp. 148–173. Springer, Heidelberg (2006)
17. Nystrom, N., Clarkson, M.R., Myers, A.C.: Polyglot: An extensible compiler framework for java. In: Hedin, G. (ed.) CC 2003. LNCS, vol. 2622, pp. 138–152. Springer, Heidelberg (2003)
18. Sun: Java Remote Method Invocation, Java RMI (2004), http://java.sun.com/j2se/1.5.0/docs/guide/rmi/
19. Black, A., Immel, M.: Encapsulating plurality. In: Nierstrasz, O. (ed.) ECOOP 1993. LNCS, vol. 707, pp. 57–79. Springer, Heidelberg (1993)
20. Guerraoui, R., Garbinato, B., Mazouni, K.: GARF: A Tool for Programming Reliable Distributed Applications. Concurrency 5(4), 29–32 (1997)
21. Toinard, G.F.C.: A New Way to Design Causally and Totally Ordered Multicast Protocols. OSR 26(4), 77–83 (1992)
22. Benton, N., Cardelli, L., Fournet, C.: Modern Concurrency Abstractions for C#. TOPLAS 26(5), 769–804 (2004)
23. Fournet, C., Gonthier, C.: The Reflexive Chemical Abstract Machine and the Join Calculus. In: POPL 1996, 372–385 (1996)
24. Haahr, M., Meier, R., Nixon, P., Cahill, V., Jul, E.: Filtering and Scalability in the ECO Distributed Event Model. In: PDSE 2000, pp. 83–92 (2000)
25. Eugster, P.: Type-based Publish/Subscribe: Concepts and Experiences. TOPLAS 29(1) (2007)

26. Itzstein, S.V., Kearney, D.: The Expression of Common Concurrency Patterns in Join Java. In: PDPTA 2004, pp. 1021–1025 (2004)
27. Navarro, L., Südholt, M., Vanderperren, W., Fraine, B.D., Suvée, D.: Explicitly Distributed AOP using AWED. In: AOSD 2006, pp. 51–62 (2006)
28. Reppy, J.H., Xiao, Y.: Specialization of CML Message-passing Primitives. In: POPL 2007, pp. 315–326 (2007)
29. Spring, J., Privat, J., Guerraoui, R., Vitek, J.: StreamFlex: High-throughput Stream Programming in Java. In: OOPSLA 2007, pp. 211–228 (2007)
30. Lamb, A.A., Thies, W., Amarasinghe, S.: Linear Analysis and Optimization of Stream Programs. In: PLDI, pp. 12–25 (2003)
31. Rajan, H., Leavens, G.T.: Ptolemy: A Language with Quantified, Typed Events. In: Vitek, J. (ed.) ECOOP 2008. LNCS, vol. 5142, pp. 155–179. Springer, Heidelberg (2008)
32. Haller, P., Van Cutsem, T.: Implementing Joins using Extensible Pattern Matching. In: Lea, D., Zavattaro, G. (eds.) COORDINATION 2008. LNCS, vol. 5052, pp. 135–152. Springer, Heidelberg (2008)
33. Haller, P., Odersky, M.: Actors that Unify Threads and Events. In: Murphy, A.L., Vitek, J. (eds.) COORDINATION 2007. LNCS, vol. 4467, pp. 171–190. Springer, Heidelberg (2007)
34. Ericsson Computer Science Laboratory: The Erlang Pogramming Language, http://www.erlang.org
35. Milicia, G., Sassone, V.: Jeeg: Temporal Constraints for the Synchronization of Concurrent Objects. CCPE 17(5-6), 539–572 (2005)
36. Briot, J.P.: Actalk: A Testbed for Classifying and Designing Actor Languages in the Smalltalk-80 Environment. In: ECOOP 1989, pp. 109–129 (1989)
37. Chin, B., Millstein, T.: Responders: Language Support for Interactive Applications. In: Thomas, D. (ed.) ECOOP 2006. LNCS, vol. 4067, pp. 255–278. Springer, Heidelberg (2006)
38. Lin, C., Black, A.P.: DirectFlow: A Domain-Specific Language for Information-Flow Systems. In: Ernst, E. (ed.) ECOOP 2007. LNCS, vol. 4609, pp. 299–322. Springer, Heidelberg (2007)
39. Bierman, G., Meijer, E., Schulte, W.: The Essence of Data Access in Cω. In: Black, A.P. (ed.) ECOOP 2005. LNCS, vol. 3586, pp. 287–311. Springer, Heidelberg (2005)
40. Nishizawa, M.: Remote Pointcut: A Language Construct for Distributed AOP. In: AOSD 2004, pp. 7–15 (2004)

Remote Batch Invocation
for Compositional Object Services*

Ali Ibrahim[2], Yang Jiao[1], Eli Tilevich[1], and William R. Cook[2]

[1] Computer Science Department, Virginia Tech
{tilevich,jiaoyang}@cs.vt.edu
[2] Department of Computer Sciences, The University of Texas at Austin
{aibrahim,wcook}@cs.utexas.edu

Abstract. Because Remote Procedure Calls do not compose efficiently, designers of distributed object systems use Data Transfer and Remote Façade patterns to create large-granularity interfaces, hard-coded for particular client use cases. As an alternative to RPC-based distributed objects, this paper presents *Remote Batch Invocation* (RBI), language support for explicit client-defined batches. A Remote Batch statement combines remote and local execution: all the remote code is executed in a single round-trip to the server, where all data sent to the server and results from the batch are communicated in bulk. RBI supports remote blocks, iteration and conditionals, and local handling of remote exceptions. RBI is efficient even for fine-grained interfaces, eliminating the need for hand-optimized server interfaces. We demonstrate RBI with an extension to Java, using RMI internally as the transport layer. RBI supports large-granularity, stateless server interactions, characteristic of service-oriented computing.

1 Introduction

The Remote Procedure Call (RPC) has long been the foundation of language-level approaches to distributed computing. The idea is simple: replace local calls with stubs that transfer the procedure call to a remote machine for execution. RPC has been generalized for objects to create distributed object systems, including Common Object Request Broker Architecture (CORBA) [22], the Distributed Component Object Model (DCOM) [8], or Java Remote Method Invocation (RMI) [29]. Stubs are defined on a local object that acts as a proxy for a remote object. One advantage of this approach is that it does not require language changes, but can be implemented using libraries and stub generator tools.

Standard object-oriented designs, which focus on flexibility and extensibility through the use of fine-grained methods, getters and setters, and small objects, do not perform well when distributed remotely. Every method call on a remote proxy is a round trip to the server. To achieve suitable performance, remote objects must be designed according to a different set of principles[1]. Data Transfer Objects and Remote Façades are used to optimize data transfer and combine operations to reduce the number of round trips [18]. One effect of this approach is that servers and protocols are hard-coded to support specific client invocation patterns. If a client changes significantly, then the entire system, including the server and its interfaces, must be redesigned.

---

* This work was supported by the National Science Foundation under Grant CCF-0448128.

[1] Approaches using asynchronous messaging are discussed in related work.

S. Drossopoulou (Ed.): ECOOP 2009, LNCS 5653, pp. 595–617, 2009.

This paper presents *Remote Batch Invocation* (RBI), a new approach to distributed object computing. Remote Batch Invocation allows multiple calls on remote objects to be invoked in a batch, while automatically transferring arguments and return values in bulk. The following example uses a Remote Batch in Java to delete low-rated albums from a personal online music database.

```
int minimum = 5;
Service musicService = new Service("MusicCloud", Music.class);
batch (Music favoriteMusic : musicService) {
  for (Album album : favoriteMusic.getAlbums())
    if (album.rating() < minimum) {
      System.out.println("Playing: " + album.getTitle());
      try {
        album.play();
      } catch (Exception e) {
        System.out.println("error: " + e.getMessage());
}}}
```

The batch mixes local and remote computation. In this case, all the computation is remote except the two calls to `System.out`. The semantics of Java is modified within the batch to first perform all remote operations, then perform all local operations. Thus the typical ordering between local and remote statements is not necessarily preserved. For example, all of the albums are played before any of the names are printed. All loops and conditionals are executed twice: once on the server and then again on the client. Exceptions on the server terminate the batch by default, and raise the error in the analogous execution point on the client.

A remote batch transfers all data between client and server in bulk. In this case, just the `minimum` rating is sent to the server. The server returns a list of all titles of played albums. But it also returns a boolean for each album indicating whether it was played. In general, any number of primitive or serializable values can be transfered to and from the server. Remote Batch Invocation creates appropriate Data Transfer Objects and Remote Façades on the fly, involving any number of objects and methods. Standard Java objects can be published as a batch service by adding a single line of code. The semantics of the batch statement require that only a single remote invocation is made in the lexical block. This strong performance model is important, because the cost of remote invocations may be several orders of magnitude higher than local invocations.

We demonstrate Remote Batch Invocation with an extension to Java. A source-to-source translator converts the **batch** statement to plain Java which uses Batch Execution Service and Translation (BEST), our middleware library for batched execution using Java RMI. Remote Batch Invocation is not tied to RMI, but could also be implemented using other middleware transport, for example web services or mobile objects. A server can publish a remote service by making a single library call.

The performance benefits of batching operations are well-known, especially in high-latency environments. We evaluate our language extension by comparing it with other approaches to batching such as implicit batching, mobile code, and the Remote Façade pattern.

In summary, Remote Batch Invocation is a new approach to distributed objects that supports service-orientation rather than remote procedure calls and proxies. The fundamental insight is that remote execution need not work at the level of procedure calls, but can instead operate at the level of blocks, with bulk transfer of data entering and leaving the block. Unlike traditional distributed objects that maintain server side state, Remote Batch Invocation has a stateless execution model that is characteristic of service oriented computing [17,20].

2 Remote Batch Invocation

Remote Batch Invocation allows clients to combine remote operations into a single remote invocation. We will illustrate the features of Remote Batch Invocation by example. The basis of our examples is a sample remote service described by Fowler in *Patterns in Enterprise Application Architecture* [18]. This simple remote music service is comprised of three classes: Album, Artist, and Track as shown in Figure 1. The Album interface also provides the `play` method which returns the lyrics on the album and plays the album on a sound system.

```
interface Album {
  String getTitle();
  void setTitle(String title);
  Artist getArtist();
  void setArtist();
  Track[] getTracks();
  void addTrack(Track t);
  void removeTrack(Track t);
  String play();
}
```

A natural remote interface to these three classes is shown below:

```
interface Music {
  Album createAlbum(String id, String title);
  Album getAlbum(String id);
  Artist addArtist(String id, String name);
  Artist getArtist(String id);
  Track createTrack(String title);
}
```

Using the Music interface, a client can create and find artists and albums as well as create tracks. A client may update object fields using the appropriate setters. We will use this interface for our Remote Batch Invocation examples.

Unfortunately, this natural interface is too fine-grained in a system where individual method calls are expensive. Using the Remote Façade and Data Transfer patterns, Fowler wraps the Music interface:

```
interface FowlerMusic {
  String play(String id);
  AlbumDTO getAlbum(String id);
  void createAlbum(String id, AlbumDTO dto);
  void updateAlbum(String id, AlbumDTO dto);
  void addArtistNamed(String id, String name);
  void addArtist(String id, ArtistDTO dto);
  ArtistDTO getArtist(String id);
}
```

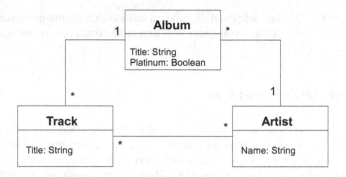

Fig. 1. Fowler Album Class Diagram

FowlerMusic is a Remote Façade for the Music interface. For example, the FowlerMusic.play method is simply calling the Music.getAlbum method followed by the Album.play method. The AlbumDTO, ArtistDTO, and TrackDTO are data transfer objects (DTO) that transfer information in bulk to and from the remote server. Fowler also defines AlbumAssembler, which maps between DTOs and objects residing on the server.

```
class AlbumAssembler {
  public AlbumDTO writeAlbum(Album subject) {
    AlbumDTO result = new ALbumDTO();
    result.setTitle(subject.getTitle());
    result.setArtist(subject.getArtist().getName());
    writeTracks(result, subject);
  }
  void writeTracks(AlbumDTO result, Album subject) { ... }
  void writePerformers(TrackDTO result, Track subject) { ... }
  public void createAlbum(String id, AlbumDTO source) {
    Artist artist = Registry.findArtistNamed(source.getArtist());
    if (artist == null) throw new RuntimeException(...);
    Album album = new Album(source.getTitle(), artist);
    createTracks(source.getTracks(), album);
    Registry.addAlbum(id, album);
  }
  void createTracks(TrackDTO[] tracks, Album album) { ... }
  void createPerformers(Track newTrack, String[] performers) { ... }
}
```

Although AlbumAssembler encapsulates the logic of mapping between DTO and model objects, it is not generic, containing a hard-coded decision about the DTO content. In the book, Fowler decides to have the Album DTO provide all the information about a single album.

The next sub-sections give examples of using Remote Batch Invocation for batch data retrieval, batch data transfer, loops, branching, and exceptions.

2.1 Batch Data Retrieval

A simple client may want to print the title and name of the artist for an album. With the fine-grained `Music` interface, the client must execute four remote calls: a call to find the album, a call to get the title of the album, a call to get the artist for the album, and a call to get the name of the artist for the album.

Using Remote Batch Invocation, the client can use the `Music` interface while still executing a single remote call. The input to the remote batch is the id of the album "1". The output of the remote batch is the title of the album and the name of the artist of the album. A remote batch can combine an arbitrary number of method calls as long as they are invoked on objects transitively reachable from the root object of the batch, in this case `music`.

```
batch (Music music : musicService) {
   final Album album = music.getAlbum("1");
   System.out.println("Title: " + album.getTitle());
   System.out.println("Artist: " + album.getArtist().getName());
}
```

The same client using the remote façade `FowlerMusic` executes a single remote method `getAlbum` which returns `AlbumDTO`. For this client, the DTO is an over-approximation of the data needed; a Remote Façade optimized for this client would need another DTO for albums that only provides the title and artist name.

```
AlbumDTO album = music.getAlbum("1");
System.out.println("Title: " + album.getTitle());
System.out.println("Artist: " + album.getArtistName());
```

For other clients, the DTO may be an under-approximation of the data needed. For example, this client prints the title of two different albums.

```
batch (Music music : musicService) {
   final Album album = music.getAlbum("1");
   System.out.println("Title: " + album.getTitle());
   final Album album = music.getAlbum("2");
   System.out.println("Title: " + album.getTitle());
}
```

`FowlerMusic` does not contain a method that matches this client pattern. Consequently, the same client using `FowlerMusic` must make an additional remote call compared to using Remote Batch Invocation. Alternatively, the `FowlerMusic` interface can be changed to include a method that takes two album IDs as input and returns a new DTO containing two fields representing the titles of the input albums. This highlights one of the disadvantages of the Remote Façade pattern; it creates a non-functional dependency between the server interface and the client call patterns.

2.2 Batch Data Transfers

Remote Batch Invocation also allows clients to transparently transfer data in bulk to the server. The following code creates `Album`, `Artist`, and `Track` objects and wires them together. The input to the remote batch is all the information about the album, artist, and track to be created and there is no output. The actual construction of the objects and method calls occur entirely on the server.

```
batch (Music music : musicService) {
  final Album album = music.createAlbum("2", "First Album");
  final Artist artist = music.addArtist("2", "John Smith");
  album.setArtist(artist);
  final Track track = music.createTrack("First track");
  track.addPerformer(artist);
  album.addTrack(track);
}
```

A client using `FowlerMusic` can also create the objects using a single remote invocation using the appropriate DTOs.

```
AlbumDTO album = new AlbumDTO("First Album");
AlbumDTO artist = new ArtistDTO("2", "John Smith");
album.setArtist(artist);
TrackDTO track = new TrackDTO("First Track");
track.addPerformer(artist);
album.addTrack(track);
music.createAlbum("2", album);
```

A drawback to using data transfer objects for creating and updating objects, is that DTO is under-specifying some of the semantics of the operation. In particular, the DTO does not tell the server whether the artist object is an artist object which should be created or if it already exists. This is a well-known problem in data mapping and commonly arises in distributed systems. A common approach and the one taken by Fowler in his book, is to specify a convention to either always create objects, always use existing objects, or create an object if it does not already exist. Another approach is to enrich the DTO with *status* fields for each normal field that specify the right semantics. Sometimes this status field is encoded into the field, for example, by using **null** as a special value. A related problem is updating objects if the client only has a partial description of the object. The client must be able to update the subset of fields which are known, but not the fields which are unknown.

The remote batch is more explicit in that specifies that the `artist` is a new `Artist` object. If the client wanted to reference an existing artist the code would be rewritten as follows:

```
batch (Music music : musicService) {
  final Album album = music.createAlbum("2", "First Album");
  final Artist artist = music.getArtist("2");
  album.setArtist(artist);
  final Track track = music.createTrack("First track");
  track.addPerformer(artist);
  album.addTrack(track);
}
```

2.3 Loops

So far, we have shown that Remote Batch Invocation supports straightline code. However, it is common for a client to need more complex logic involving branching and loops. Remote Batch Invocation allows for remoting of the enhanced **for** loop introduced in Java 1.5 if the collection can be evaluated remotely. If data from the iterations is needed locally, the remote batch constructs a data transfer object with an array of the data needed and transparently maps it on the client. Below is a simple example which shows how explicit batching can operate over arrays. The input to the remote batch is simply the id of the album and output is the title of all of the tracks, the name of all of the performers on the tracks, and the lyrics returned by the `play` method.

```
batch (Music music : musicService) {
  final Album album = music.getAlbum("1");
  System.out.println("Tracks: ");
  for (Track t : album.getTracks()) {
    System.out.print(t.getTitle());
    System.out.println(',');
    System.out.print("Performed by: ");
    for (Artist a : t.getPerformers()) {
      System.out.print(a.getName());
      System.out.print(' ');
    }
    System.out.print('\n');
  }
  System.out.println("Song: " + album.play());
}
```

The `FowlerMusic.getAlbum` method in Remote Façade nearly provides all the functionality required by this client; however, it does not include a call to the `Album.play` method.

2.4 Branching

Conditional statements, including **if** and **else**, are remoted if their condition is a remote operation. Below is a simple example that shows such a remoted conditional statement also containing the primitive operator &&.

```
batch(Music music : musicService) {
  final Album album = registry.getAlbum("1");
  if (album.getName().startsWith("A")
      || album.getName().startsWith("B")) {
    album.play();
    System.out.print("Title starts with A or B: " + album.getTitle());
  } else {
    System.out.print("Title does not start with A or B: "
        + album.getArtist().getName());
  }}
```

RBI supports boolean and numeric primitive operators, both unary and binary. Conditional code can also be included as part of operations on collections. In that case, the conditions are reevaluated on each iteration over a collection. The following example adds albums composed by Yo-Yo Ma to the favorites collection.

```
for (Artist a : t.getPerformers()) {
  if (a.getName().equals("Yo-Yo Ma")) {
    favorites.addArtist(a);
  }}
```

2.5 Exceptions

Remote Batch Invocation separates exceptions caused by failures in communication from logical exceptions that arise when executing the statements in the batch. The **batch** statement itself can raise network exceptions, which must be handled by the surrounding context. If there are no network errors, then exceptions raised by statements in the batch can be handled in the client.

Within a **batch**, a remote operation can raise an exception on the server that will terminate the batch. The thrown exception will be raised in the corresponding execution point on the client. The client must use exception handlers as in regular Java code. In addition, the execution of a remote batch may result in a RemoteException that can be handled by wrapping an entire **batch** block with a **try/catch** block.

For example, the following code extends an earlier example to include an exception handler when trying to play an album, and another handler that deals with network and communication errors raised at any point of executing the batch.

```
try {
  batch (Music favoriteMusic : musicService) {
    ...
    try {
      album.play();
    } catch (PermissionError pe) {
      System.out.println("No permission to play album"
        + album.getTitle());
    }
  } //end batch
} catch (RemoteException re) {
  System.out.println("Error communicating batch.");
}
```

The default behavior of a batch is to abort processing when an exception is thrown. As future work, we would like to be able to apply a different exception policy, for example to continue execution or restart the batch. Batches also provide a natural unit of atomic execution. In many cases it is desirable for the entire batch to succeed or fail, so that incomplete operations are never allowed. One way to achieve this is to use transactional memory on the server [7].

Even so, it is possible for the batch to succeed on the server but for a communication error to prevent the client from completing the batch. A standard two-phase commit could be used to ensure that both the server and client parts of the batch have executed to completion. These topics are beyond the scope of our current research, but we do not see any obstacles to combining RBI with distributed transactions.

2.6 Service Implementation

Implementing a Remote Batch Invocation service is much simpler than implementing a server using traditional distributed object middleware, including RMI or CORBA. There is no need to create method stubs. Instead, the server simply registers a root object with a single call after creating the server implementation object.

```
Music musicServer = new MusicImpl(...);
rbi.Server server = new rbi.Server("MusicCloud", musicServer);
```

The client connects to this service by using the same name and interface.

```
rbi.Service musicService =
  new rbi.Service("MusicCloud", Music.class);
```

As in most distributed systems, interface mismatches between client and server are detected at runtime. Standard Java interfaces define the service contract.

2.7 Service-Oriented Interaction

Remote Batch Invocation supports a service-oriented style of interaction, so it does not support object proxies. This is not a problem for many client/server interactions, which can be naturally accomplished in a single round-trip. These interactions have the following pattern:

$$\text{client} \xrightarrow{input} \text{server*} \xrightarrow{results} \text{client}$$

The client sends any number of inputs to the server, which performs multiple actions and returns any number of results to the client. There may be cases; however, when a server computation depends upon client input *and* previously defined server objects.

$$\text{client} \xrightarrow{input} \text{server*} \xrightarrow{results} \text{client*} \xrightarrow{input_2} \text{server*} \xrightarrow{results_2} \text{client}$$

This situation is easily handled in distributed object systems like CORBA and RMI, since each server operation is controlled by the client and it can use proxies to refer to the intermediate server results needed in the last step.

This interaction pattern requires some other solution in a stateless service-oriented system. The simplest approach is to have the second server batch reload or recreate the server objects that were defined in the first batch. The server may also provide public identifiers for its objects. The first *results* can include a server object identifier, which is used in the second batch to relocate the necessary server object. These patterns have been studied extensively in the context of service-oriented computing [20,17].

2.8 Allowed Remote Operations

Any Java code may appear inside the batch block; however, the compiler enforces some data flow restrictions described in Section 3. Many Java constructs such as constructor calls, casts, **while** loops, and assignments cannot be remoted; they are always executed on the client. Future work may relax some of these restrictions. If remote assignments were allowed, then it would be possible to aggregate (e.g. sum or average) over collections remotely. General loops could also be remoted without significant changes to the model.

Exceptions are a special case. The remote batch cannot catch exceptions remotely, but it does propagate them to the client in the original location of the remote operation that produced the exception. In this way, the client can catch exceptions raised remotely and handle them locally.

Keeping the remoteable constructs simple and as universal as possible increases the viability of using RBI against remote interfaces written in other languages.

3 Semantics

Our Java implementation of Remote Batch Invocation uses the following syntax:

batch (*Type Identifier* : *Expression*) *Block*

The *Identifier* specifies the name of the root remote object. The *Expression* specifies the service which will provide the root remote object. The *Block* specifies both remote and local operations. A remote operation is an expression or statement executed on the server. All remote operations inside the batch block are executed in sequence followed by the local operations in sequence. A single remote call is made which contains all of the remote operations. This is the key property as it provides a strong performance model to the programmer albeit lexically scoped. Exceptions in a remote operation are re-thrown in the local operation sequence at the original location of the remote operation. If the remote operations fail due to a network error, then an exception is thrown before any of the local operations execute. Operations inside the batch block are reordered and it is possible that the block executes differently as a batch than it normally would. The compiler does try to identify some of these cases and warn the programmer, however, it is up to the programmer to be aware of the different Java semantics inside the batch block.

Each expression in the batch is marked as *local* or *remote*. Local expressions are further subdivided into *static locals* and *non-static locals*. Remote expressions execute on the server, possibly with input from static local expressions. Local expressions execute on the client, possibly with output from remote expressions. Static local expressions are literals and variable expressions defined outside of the batch and not assigned within the batch before their use. All other local expressions are non-static.

The compiler determines the location of an expression statically. A component of this analysis is a forward flow-sensitive data-flow analysis that maps variables to locations. Locations are ordered as a small lattice where *static local* < *remote* < *non-static local*. The ⊎ operator adds or changes a mapping for a variable. The *pred* function returns the predecessors of a statement node in the control flow graph. For simplicity, we will assume in this paper that all assignments are statements; however, in Java they are actually expressions. The data flow analysis is defined in Figure 2.

The **batch** variable is remote. Variables only assigned outside the batch are static locals. Variables declared final and initialized with remote expressions are remote. All other variables inside a batch block are non-static locals. Assignments may change the mapping of a variable up the lattice of locations. For this analysis, the only case where this happens is a variable mapped as a static local may be remapped as a non-static local. It cannot happen for variables mapped as remote, because final variables cannot be reassigned.

Figure 3 defines the *location* function which maps expressions to locations. To determine the location of a variable expression, the analysis looks up the variable name in the result of the data flow analysis flowing into the statement containing the variable expression. The mutual definition of *location* and *gen* introduces a cyclic dependency which is resolved by taking the fix point of the two functions starting with the bottom value of our location lattice (static locals). The location of a primitive operation is the join of the locations of the operands. The location of an instance method call expression is the location of the target of the method call. All other expressions inside or outside the batch statement are non-static local or static local respectively.

$$n, m \in Statement$$

$$e \in Expression$$

$$inBatch(e) = \begin{cases} true & \text{e is an expression inside a batch statement} \\ false & \text{otherwise} \end{cases}$$

$$varBatch(e) = \begin{cases} v & \text{e is an expression inside a batch statement of the form } batch(T\ v : e) \\ undefined & \text{otherwise} \end{cases}$$

$$s \uplus nil = s$$

$$s \uplus [v \mapsto l] = \begin{cases} s \cup [v \mapsto l] & [v \mapsto \text{\_}] \notin s \\ (s - [v \mapsto k]) \cup [v \mapsto l] & [v \mapsto k] \in s \end{cases}$$

$$in[n] = \bigcup_{m \in pred(n)} out[m]$$

$$out[n] = in[n] \uplus gen(n)$$

$$gen(n) = \begin{cases} [v \mapsto remote] & n = [\![batch(T\ v : e)]\!] \\ [v \mapsto static\ local]) & n = [\![v = e]\!] \wedge\ !\ inBatch(n) \\ [v \mapsto non\text{-}static\ local] & n = [\![v = e]\!] \wedge\ varBatch(n) \neq v_b \\ [v \mapsto location(e)] & n = [\![final\ v = e]\!] \wedge\ varBatch(n) \neq v_b \\ nil & otherwise \end{cases}$$

Fig. 2. Analysis of Java to identify local and remote variables

$$location([\![v]\!]) = in[Stmt(v)](v)$$

$$location([\![e_1\ \mathsf{op}\ e_2]\!]) = location(e_1) \sqcup location(e_2)$$

$$location([\![o.m(\bar{e})]\!]) = location(o)$$

$$location([\![\text{\_}]\!]) = \begin{cases} non\text{-}static\ local & inBatch(\text{\_}) \\ static\ local & !\ inBatch(\text{\_}) \end{cases}$$

Fig. 3. Location of Java expressions

One important thing to note in the rules is that general assignment is not supported in the remote batch. Therefore, variables are only remote if they correspond to the **batch** variable or if they are **final** and assigned remote expressions. Java 1.5 **for** statements are executed remotely if their collection is a remote expression. A remote **for** loop is replayed locally to support local expressions or statements inside the loop. Similarly, conditional statements are executed remotely if their condition is a remote expression. A remote conditional is replayed locally to support local expressions or statements inside the **if** statement.

Data is passed by value from the client to the server and from the server to the client. For example, the remote identity function returns a copy of the local argument. This implies that all input and output values of the batch must be serializable and specifically in Java implement the Serializable interface. Remote values not used locally are not subject to this restriction. Remote expressions do have identity as long as they are part of computations on the server, and similarly local expressions have the normal notion of identity in Java.

The compiler rejects all programs in which the remote operations cannot be legally moved above the local operations. For example, parameter expressions in remote method calls cannot contain local variables defined within the batch. The compiler also rejects some programs in which moving the remote operations above the local operations might result in non-intuitive behavior. For example, parameter expressions in remote method calls should not have their value changed in the local operations. The following are considered illegal expressions by the compiler.

- Method invocations on remote values that have a parameter which is a non-static local expression or is not serializable.
- Expressions with remote locations inside of an **if** block where the condition is a local expression.
- Expressions with remote locations inside of a loop construct where the condition is local.
- Nested batch statements.

One design goal was to ensure that programmers could easily understand the semantics of the **batch** construct. To that end, our analysis uses a very simple local data flow analysis and is lexically scoped. This may allow non-intuitive programs to be accepted by the compiler, because they change the state of static local expressions via different threads, heap aliasing, or local method calls [19]. The following example shows a case where the compiler accepts a program that behaves non-intuitively from the point of view of the programmer.

```
StringBuilder sb = new StringBuilder();
sb.append("My Album");
batch(Music music : musicService) {
  m(sb);
  music.createAlbum("1", sb);
}
...
void m(StringBuilder sb) { sb.append(": Blues"); }
```

The programmer might expect that the remote method call createAlbum will be passed the string "My Album: Blues", but in a remote batch it will be passed the string "My Album", because the remote method call will occur first. Unfortunately Java reflection, virtual methods, and dynamic class loading all complicate whole program analysis. Our local lexical analysis trades off catching some non-intuitive behavior to gain simplicity, practicality, and locality.

4 Implementation

Support for Remote Batch Invocation in Java is implemented as a source to source translator which takes code containing remote batch constructs and translates them into regular Java code. The output of the source to source translator uses a script recording API that sends the remote operations as a single batch to the remote server. In the current implementation, the script recorder uses the transport layer and the service discovery mechanism of Java RMI. The support system for RBI is called BEST, which is an acronym for Batch Execution Service and Translation. BEST is implemented as a layer on top of Java RMI, without changes to the Java language or runtime. First, we discuss the translation of the batch syntax. Then, we focus on the implementation issues of BEST, its underlying techniques, and its integration with Java RMI. Section 5 quantifies BEST performance benefits.

4.1 Language Translation

The source to source translator is implemented as an extension to JastAddJ [16]. JastAddJ is a Java compiler based on JastAdd and written as a circular attribute grammar. JastAdd provides several useful features. As a circular attribute grammar, many static analyses can be expressed naturally and fixed point computations are handled by the JastAdd engine. In addition, JastAdd provides many aspect-oriented features which allow composition of different analyses and language features in a a modular fashion. The data flow analysis is implemented on top of a control flow graph module written by the authors of JastAddJ for Java 1.4. We modified the their module slightly to add support for the new **batch** construct and to support Java 1.5. For each expression, the translator computes its location as described in Section 3.

The translator traverses the program abstract syntax tree (AST) downwards starting from the root AST node. Outside of a batch, the translator does not change the Java code. Inside a batch, the translator always produces two code strings, one for the remote operations and one for the local operations. Once the entire batch is translated, some boilerplate code to setup the batch is generated first, then the remote operations are inserted, then a call to execute the batch is generated, and finally the local operations are inserted. While translating code in a batch, the translator has two different modes of operation. Initially the translator is in local mode. Expressions in local mode produce no remote operations and produce themselves as local operations. Most statements behave similarly except for remote loops and remote conditionals which produce both remote and local operations. Once the translator reaches an expression whose location is remote, it binds that remote value to a temporary variable as a remote operation and enters remote mode for that expression. The translator also adds a local operation which invokes the get method on the temporary variable. In remote mode, the translator can safely assume all sub-expressions are remote operations.

```
Service musicService = new Service("MusicCloud", Music.class);
batch(Music music : musicService) {
  final Album album = music.getAlbum("1");
  if (album.getTitle().startsWith("A")) {
    System.out.println("Tracks:");
    for (Track t : album.getTracks()) {
      System.out.print(' ');
      System.out.print(t.getTitle());
    }
  } else {
    System.out.print("Title does not start with A: "
      + album.getArtist().getName());
  }
}}
```

Fig. 4. RBI source code

```
// Remote part
Service service$ = musicService;
{ Batch batch$ = service$.getRoot();
Handle album$73751 = batch$.doInvoke(batch$,"getAlbum",
  new Class[] {String.class}, new Object[] {"1"});
Handle var$0 = batch$.doInvoke(
  batch$.doInvoke(album$73751,"getTitle", null, null),
  "startsWith", new Class[] {String.class}, new Object[] {"A"});
batch$.rIf(var$0);
cursor.Cursor t$86036$Cursor = batch$.createCursor(
        batch$.doInvoke(album$73751,"getTracks", null, null));
Handle var$1 = t$86036$Cursor.doInvoke(
                    t$86036$Cursor,"getTitle", null, null);
batch$.rElse();
Handle var$2 =
  batch$.doInvoke(batch$.doInvoke(album$73751,"getArtist", null, null),
  "getName", null, null);
batch$.rEnd();
batch$.flush();
// Local part
if((Boolean)var$0.get()){
  System.out.println("Tracks:");
  while (t$86036$Cursor.next()) {
    System.out.print(' ');
    System.out.print((String)var$1.get());
  }
} else {
  System.out.print("Title does not start with A: "
    + (String)var$2.get());
}}
```

Fig. 5. Translation of Figure 4

Figure 4 shows a RBI program which uses many of the supported features. Figure 5 shows the translation into Java code which uses BEST. An interesting part of the translation is how conditionals and loops require both remote and local operations.

4.2 BEST Client Interface

The main client interface of BEST is defined in Figure 6.

A `Batch` is a client object that represents a collection of statements. Method `flush` delineates the boundary of a batch. When `flush` is called, all the recorded statements are sent to the server in bulk, executed there, and the relevant results are returned back together. Each recorded statement returns a `Handle` which is a placeholder for a remote object, existing or created on the server. A `Handle` has two different semantics before and after `flush` is called. Before `flush`, a `Handle` serves as a placeholder for a result which has not yet been obtained. After `flush`, a `Handle` object holds a result of a remote operation that can be retrieved.

The `Batch` interface describes a script recording service. To add a method to be invoked remotely, the API provides the method `doInvoke`. The parameters of this method loosely mirror that of `Method.invoke` in the Java Reflection API. The method's parameters are deliberately weakly-typed to enable greater flexibility. This design choice

```
public interface Batch {
    public Handle doInvoke(Object obj, String method,
                           Class[] types, Object[] args);
    public Cursor createCursor(Handle value);
    public Handle unary(Ops op, Handle val1);
    public Handle binary(Ops op, Handle val1, Handle val2);
    public Handle constant(Object o);
    public Handle rIf(Handle condition);
    public Handle rElse();
    public Handle rEnd();
    public void flush();
}
```

Fig. 6. Interface to the BEST batch execution runtime

fits well the BEST programming model, in which all the calls to the script recording API are automatically generated by the source-to-source translator, thereby ensuring that the resulting code is type safe.

The `Batch` interface also provides methods to express conditional remote control flow and operators. These methods are used to express conditions and operations used in a **batch** block. The translator maps Java conditional and primitive operators into regular methods (e.g., `rIf`, `rElse`, `binary`) that are recorded for remote execution.

The `makeCursor` method takes a `Handle` parameter and returns a `Cursor`, which represents an iteration context for the collection of objects existing on the server. The assumption for calling `makeCursor` is that its `Handle` parameter represents an `Iterable` object such as a `java.util.Collection` or an array.

The `Cursor` interface is implemented as follows:

```
public interface Cursor extends Batch {
    public boolean next();
    public void setPosition(int position)
                     throws IllegalArgumentException;
    public int getPosition();
}
```

Remote operations recorded on a `Cursor` interface will be replayed on each element of an `Iterable` collection on the server. After `flush`, the `Cursor` can be iterated to retrieve the results of remote operations for every element.

The end result of recording operations using the `Batch` interface is a list of method descriptors, which are serializable objects sent to the server. Each recorded operation is assigned a sequence number which acts as an identifier for that call. The sequence numbers are sent to the server, so that method arguments can be matched to prior method return values.

4.3 Batch Execution

When the client calls `flush`, the recorded operations are sent to the server as a batch by calling a regular RMI method `batchInvoke`. To make the BEST functionality available to all RMI remote objects, the `batchInvoke` method is added to `UnicastRemoteObject`, a super class extended by RMI application remote classes.

The BEST server runtime decodes method descriptors, invokes batched methods one-by-one and returns the results back to the client. To implement conditional statements such as `if` and **else**, the BEST server interprets the operations by evaluating the specified conditional statements and changing the control flow of a batch based on their results. Similar strategy is applied to executing unary and binary operations. While at the script recording time on the client the operands are represented by handles, their actual values are obtained during the execution of a batch on the server. Then the interpretation simply operates on the actual values as was specified by the script.

Cursor operations are interpreted analogously to regular operations, with the exception that each recorded operation is executed on each element of an `Iterable` server object with the results stored in a table. The rows in the table correspond to the different variables associated with a cursor and the columns correspond to each iteration of the cursor.

4.4 Result Interpretation

For each non-cursor client `Handle`, the server returns a value, exception, or nothing. The server returns no value for a client `Handle` associated with an unexecuted remote operation. At most one `Handle` is assigned an exception, because the the remote batch is terminated by the first exception. If a `Handle` has an exception, rather than a value, then this exception is thrown when accessing its content.

For cursors, result interpretation is more complicated. Each time next is called on a `Cursor`, the `Handle` objects associated with it are assigned values from the return value array. The number of values in the array is the number of elements in the `Cursor` times the number of `Handle`'s. `Handle`'s normally do not change value after they have been assigned, with the exception when they are created within a cursor–the `Handle` values may change on each iteration of the loop.

5 Performance

In essence, *Batch Remote Invocation* is a language level mechanism that optimizes remote communication by leveraging the improved bandwidth characteristics of modern networks [23], especially in high-latency environments. Although the performance benefits of batching remote operations are well-known and have been the target of several research efforts [6,21,9], the purpose of evaluating the performance of RBI is to ensure that the overhead of its runtime, BEST, does not impose an unreasonable performance overhead. The following benchmark uses data objects with different numbers of String fields: 1, 2, 4, 8, 16, 32, and 64. The benchmark emulates a common usage scenario, in which the client retrieves the object from the server and updates its fields. This scenario was implemented and measured using three different communication styles: plain RMI, a hand-coded DTO, and RBI. Figure 7 shows the performance numbers for each version.

All the experiments were run in the Windows XP version of JDK 1.6.0_13 (build 1.6.0_13-b03), with the server running Dual Core 3GHz processors, 2 GB of RAM, and the client running Dual Core 2.4GHz Processors, 2GB of RAM, connected via a LAN

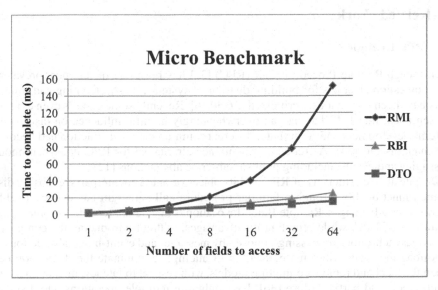

Fig. 7. Performance Comparison between RMI, RBI, and DTO versions

with a 1Gbps, 1ms latency network. The results represent the average of running each benchmark 1000 times after first running it 2000 times to warm the JVM. Warming the JVM ensured that the measured programs had been dynamically compiled before measurements.

As expected, the RMI version is the slowest, with its slope growing linearly at a fixed rate, as the number of fields increases. The DTO and RBI versions exhibit comparable performance, with DTO being faster by a small constant factor. These results are predictable, as the execution time is dominated by the number of remote calls performed by each version of the benchmark, and in most networking environments the latency of a remote call is several orders of magnitude larger than that of a local call.

The specific number of remote calls performed by each version of the benchmark is as follows. If f is the number of fields, the RMI version performs $2 * f$ remote calls (to get and set every field); the DTO version performs only 2 calls (i.e., getting and setting all fields in bulk); and finally, the RBI version performs exactly 1 remote call.

Even though the RBI version performs only one remote call, whereas the DTO version two, RBI is still slower due to the overhead imposed by its client and server runtime. To provide flexibility, BEST uses Java language features that are known to have a negative effect on performance, including reflection to locate and invoke methods as well as multiple Object arrays to pass parameters. In addition, the current implementation of BEST has not been fine-tuned for performance. Finally, the BEST overhead would be amortized more significantly in a higher-latency network environment. Compared to the hard-coded interface of DTO, RBI makes it possible to create a flexible DTO on the fly with the accompanying performance benefits due to the reduced network communication enabled by its service-oriented execution model.

6 Related Work

6.1 RPC Critique

Even though Remote Procedure Call (RPC) [32] has been one of the most prevalent communication abstracts for building distributed systems, its shortcoming and limitations have been continuously criticized [26,30,36]. Recently some experts even express the sentiment that RPC has had an overwhelmingly harmful influence on distributed systems development and wish that a different communication abstraction had become dominant instead [34]. A frequently mentioned alternative for RPC is asynchronous messaging and events, including publish-subscribe abstractions [12].

Despite all the criticisms of RPC and its object-oriented counterparts, exposing distributed functionality through a familiar procedure call paradigm has unquestionable convenience advantages. Remote Batch Invocation is an attempt to address some of the limitations of RPC, while retaining its advantages, without introducing the complications of asynchronous processing imposed by message- and event-based abstractions.

Among the main criticisms of RPC is its attempt to eliminate the distinction between the local and remote computing models, with respect to latency, memory access, concurrency, and partial failure [36]. By combining multiple operations into a single batch, RBI reduces latency. By executing all remote operations on the server in bulk, RBI maintains the local memory access model for method parameters. As future work, a transactional execution model can be combined with RBI to achieve an all-or-nothing execution property. And while batch invocations in RBI are synchronous, the resulting execution model is explicit, giving the programmer a clear execution and performance model.

6.2 Explicit Batching

Software design patterns [18] for *Remote Façade* and *Data Transfer Object* (also called Value Objects [3]) can be used to optimize remote communication. A *Remote Façade* allows a service to support specific client call patterns using a single remote invocation. Different Remote Façades may be needed for different clients. Remote Batch Invocation provides a custom Remote Façade for each client as long as the client call pattern is supported as a single batch. A *Data Transfer Object* is a `Serializable` class that provides block transfer of data between client and server. As with the Remote Façade, different kinds of Data Transfer Objects may be needed by different clients. Remote Batch Invocation constructs an appropriate value object on the fly, automatically, as needed by a particular situation. Remote Batch Invocation also generalizes the concept of a data transfer object to support transfer of data from arbitrary collections of objects.

The DRMI system [21] aggregates RMI calls as a middleware library much like BEST. DRMI uses special interfaces to record and delay the invocation of remote calls. DRMI only supports simple call aggregation and simple branching, while Remote Batch Invocation and BEST also support cursors, primitive operations, and exception handling. Like BEST, DRMI requires that the programmer partition the remote and local operations themselves. This often forces the programmer to replicate loops and conditionals manually, whereas Remote Batch Invocation offers a more flexible style of programming and relies on the source to source translator to partition the program into remote and local operations.

Detmold and Oudshoorn [15] present analytic performance models for RPC and its optimizations including batched futures as well as a new optimization construct termed *a responsibility*. Their analytic models could be extended to model the performance properties of the new optimization constructs of Remote Batch Invocation such as cursors and branching.

Sometimes a communication protocol defines batches directly, as is in the compound procedure in Network File System (NFS) version 4 Protocol [27], which combines multiple NFS operations into a single RPC request. The compound procedure in NFS is not a general-purpose mechanism; the calls are independent of each other, except for a hard-coded current filehandle that can be set and used by operations in the batch. There is also a single built-in exception policy. Web Services are often based on transfer of documents, which can be viewed as batches of remote calls [11,35].

Cook and Barfield [11] showed how a set of hand-written wrappers can provide a mapping between object interfaces and batched calls expressed as a web service document. Remote Batch Invocation automates the process of creating the wrappers and generalizes the technique to support branching, cursors, and exception handling. As a result, Remote Batch Invocation scales as well as an optimized web service, while providing the raw performance benefits of RPC [13]. Web services choreography [24] defines how Web services interact with each other at the message level. Remote Batch Invocation can be seen as a choreography facility for distributed objects.

6.3 Mobile Code

Mobile object systems such as Emerald [5] reduce latency by moving active objects, rather than making multiple remote calls. JavaParty [25] migrates objects to adapt the distribution layout of an application to enhance locality. Ambassadors is a communication technique that uses object mobility [14] to minimize the aggregate latency of multiple inter-dependent remote methods. DJ [1] adds explicit programming constructs for direct type-safe code distribution, improving both performance and safety.

Mobile objects generally require sophisticated runtime support not only for moving objects and classes between different sites, but also for dealing with security issues. A Java application can essentially disable the use of mobile code by not allowing dynamic class loading. An RBI server is fairly simple to implement. Clients only gain access to interfaces that are reachable from the service root.

Even in an environment that supports mobile code, there are advantages to Remote Batch Invocation. This can be understood by considering a translation from RBI to mobile code. A **batch** statement could be implemented using mobile code by writing two mobile classes, one that is sent from the client to the server to execute the remote operations, and another that is sent from the server back to the client to transport the results in bulk to the client. The first class would contain member variables to store all the local data sent to the server, and a method body to execute on the server. At the start of this method an instance of the second class is created and populated with data created by the remote method. At the end of the method the result object is sent back to the client. A custom pair of classes is needed for each **batch** statement in the program. While mobile code is more flexible and powerful than RBI, it can also be more work to use this power to implement common communication patterns.

6.4   Implicit Batching

Batched futures reduce the aggregate latency of multiple remote methods [6]. If remote methods are restructured to return futures, they can be batched. The invocation of the batch can be delayed until a value of any of the batched futures is used in an operation that needs its value. There are several different client invocation patterns that cannot be batched in this model. For example, unrelated remote method calls will not be batched together.

Future RMI [2] communicates asynchronously to speed up RMI in Grid environments, when one remote method is invoked on the result of another. Remote results of a batch are not transferred over the network, remaining on the server to be used for subsequent method invocations.

Yeung and Kelly [9] use byte-code transformations to delay remote methods calls and create batches at runtime. A static analysis determines when batches must be flushed.

In all of these implicit batching techniques, it is not clear how to support loops, branches, and exceptions as in Remote Batch Invocation. In addition, small changes in the program, for example introducing an assignment to a local variable, or an exception handler, can cause a batch to be flushed. This means the performance is very sensitive to the ordering of remote and local operations. On the other hand, Remote Batch Invocation automatically tries to reorder remote and local operations to maintain a single batch, while checking that the reordering makes sense.

6.5   Automatic Partitioning

Remote Batch Invocation can be seen as a language level abstraction for automatic application partitioning, a semi-automatic approach for deriving a distributed application from a centralized one.

One line of research has explored coarse grained program partitioning. The programmer, by means of a GUI or a configuration file, designates different parts of a centralized application, typically at a class or object granularity, to run on different network nodes. The resulting distribution specification then parameterizes a compiler-based tool that automatically rewrites the centralized application for distributed execution. To introduce distribution, a partitioning tool may need to both change the structure of the application (e.g., to introduce a proxy indirection) and add middleware functionality (e.g., to replace local calls with remote ones). In the Java world, recent automatic partitioning tools include Addistant [31], Pangaea [28], and one of the co-author's J-Orchestra [33]. Addistant and J-Orchestra partition programs at a class granularity; Pangaea can partition at the individual object level. J-Orchestra addresses the challenges of partitioning programs safely in the presence of unmodifiable code that comes as part of their runtime systems.

Automatic program partitioning has also been applied at finer granularaties. Swift [10] partitions Java programs into a web application backend and Javascript at the Java statement level. Constraints on the locations of statements is inferred from information flow policies and the placement of statements is optimized to minimize round-trips with respect to those constraints. Similarly, RBI infers the location of statements and expressions from a forward data-flow analysis. Some of the co-authors have previously developed Query Extraction [37]; a system for extracting database queries from Java code traversing persistent object structures. Query Extraction performs a very similar analysis to RBI to extract the code operating over persistent data and converts that code's loops and conditions to *join* and *where* clauses in database queries.

6.6   Asynchronous Remote Invocation

Another approach to optimizing distributed communication is dispatching remote calls asynchronously. One example is ProActive [4]. An asynchronous remote call in ProActive returns a future; a placeholder for to be computed results. When a client tries to resolve the future's actual value, the client blocks until the result is available.

Although asynchronous remote invocations can optimize many patterns in client-server communication, they offer no performance improvements for chains of remote calls (i.e., `o.m1().m2()`). Compared to asynchronous invocation, the RBI programming model does not involve futures and can combine chains of remote calls into a batch, thus improving their performance.

Although the current version of RBI does not take advantage of concurrent processing, in the future the script recorder could also convey dependencies between batched operations to the server, which can be used to safely introduce concurrency into the batch execution on the server.

7   Conclusion

Most of the related work discussed in Section 6 improve distributed programming using libraries and compiler optimizations. On the other hand, *Remote Batch Invocation (RBI)* addresses distributed programming with a language extension. We argue that the benefits of RBI over existing library and compiler approaches may overcome the natural inertia to changing a programming language. The benefits of RBI include:

- RBI provides a strong performance model. One server round-trip is executed for each lexical batch block.
- RBI allows multiple remote operations to be combined in a *batch* which is executed in a single round-trip to a remote server. A batch supports both control and data flow dependencies between remote operations. As a consequence, the remote server may provide a flexible fine-grained interface.
- RBI allows the programmer to mix remote and local operations naturally. The compiler separates the remote operations and takes care of transferring multiple inputs to the remote server and interpreting the multiple outputs.

RBI was implemented as a Java extension using a source to source translator and the BEST runtime middleware library. In the future, we will look at incorporating transactions and advanced failure handling approaches into RBI.

The performance of RBI was evaluated by comparing plain RMI and hand-coded DTO designs. Predictably, RBI significantly outperforms RMI and is only marginally slower than hand-optimized DTO implementations. Since RBI provides greater flexibility and control to the programmer, the small overhead imposed by its runtime is compensated by the added usability and expressiveness. RBI is also attractive compared with implicit batching because it can combine a larger set of remote operations.

RBI combines the convenience and flexiblity of fine-grained interfaces with the performance advantages of coarser-grained interfaces. In addition, the RBI stateless execution model aligns well with the increasingly prevalent service-oriented architectures, a rapidly-emerging industry standard.

Availability:

The implementation and examples discussed in the paper can be downloaded from:
`http://research.cs.vt.edu/vtspaces/best`

References

1. Ahern, A., Yoshida, N.: Formalising Java RMI with explicit code mobility. In: Proc. of OOPSLA 2005, pp. 403–422. ACM Press, New York (2005)
2. Alt, M., Gorlatch, S.: Adapting Java RMI for grid computing. Future Generation Computer Systems 21(5), 699–707 (2005)
3. Alur, D., Crupi, J., Malks, D.: Core J2EE Patterns: Best Practices and Design Strategies. Prentice Hall PTR, Englewood Cliffs (2003)
4. Baduel, L., Baude, F., Caromel, D., Contes, A., Huet, F., Morel, M., Quilici, R.: Programming, Deploying, Composing, for the Grid. In: Grid Computing: Software Environments and Tools. Springer, Heidelberg (2006)
5. Black, A.P., Hutchinson, N.C., Jul, E., Levy, H.M.: The development of the Emerald programming language. In: HOPL III, pp. 11-1–11-51 (2007)
6. Bogle, P., Liskov, B.: Reducing cross domain call overhead using batched futures. ACM SIGPLAN Notices 29(10), 341–354 (1994)
7. Brevnov, E., Dolgov, Y., Kuznetsov, B., Yershov, D., Shakin, V., Chen, D.-Y., Menon, V., Srinivas, S.: Practical experiences with java software transactional memory. In: PPoPP 2008: Proceedings of the 13th ACM SIGPLAN Symposium on Principles and practice of parallel programming, pp. 287–288. ACM, New York (2008)
8. Brown, N., Kindel, C.: Distributed Component Object Model Protocol–DCOM/1.0, Redmond, WA, 1996 (1998)
9. Cheung Yeung, K., Kelly, P.: Optimising Java RMI Programs by Communication Restructuring. In: Endler, M., Schmidt, D.C. (eds.) Middleware 2003. LNCS, vol. 2672. Springer, Heidelberg (2003)
10. Chong, S., Liu, J., Myers, A.C., Qi, X., Vikram, K., Zheng, L., Zheng, X.: Secure web application via automatic partitioning. In: SOSP 2007: Proceedings of twenty-first ACM SIGOPS symposium on Operating systems principles, pp. 31–44. ACM, New York (2007)
11. Cook, W., Barfield, J.: Web Services versus Distributed Objects: A Case Study of Performance and Interface Design. In: the IEEE International Conference on Web Services (ICWS 2006), pp. 419–426 (2006)
12. Damm, C., Eugster, P., Guerraoui, R.: Linguistic support for distributed programming abstractions. In: Proceedings of 24th International Conference on Distributed Computing Systems, pp. 244–251 (2004)
13. Demarey, C., Harbonnier, G., Rouvoy, R., Merle, P.: Benchmarking the Round-Trip Latency of Various Java-Based Middleware Platforms. Studia Informatica Universalis Regular Issue 4(1), 7–24 (2005)
14. Detmold, H., Hollfelder, M., Oudshoorn, M.: Ambassadors: structured object mobility in worldwide distributed systems. In: Proc. of ICDCS 1999, pp. 442–449 (1999)
15. Detmold, H., Oudshoorn, M.: Communication Constructs for High Performance Distributed Computing. In: Proceedings of the 19th Australasian Computer Science Conference, pp. 252–261 (1996)

16. Ekman, T., Hedin, G.: The JastAdd Extensible Java Compiler. SIGPLAN Not 42(10), 1–18 (2007)
17. Erl, T.: Service-Oriented Architecture: Concepts, Technology, and Design. Prentice-Hall, Upper Saddle River (2005)
18. Fowler, M.: Patterns of Enterprise Application Architecture. Addison-Wesley Longman Publishing Co., Inc, Boston (2002)
19. Gabriel, R.: Is worse really better? Journal of Object-Oriented Programming (JOOP) 5(4), 501–538 (1992)
20. Krafzig, D., Banke, K., Slama, D.: Enterprise SOA: service-oriented architecture best practices. Prentice-Hall, Englewood Cliffs (2005)
21. Marques, E.: A study on the optimisation of Java RMI programs. Master's thesis, Imperial College of Science Technology and Medicine, University of London (1998)
22. The Object Management Group (OMG). The Common Object Request Broker: Architecture and Specification (1997)
23. Patterson, D.A.: Latency lags bandwith. Commun. ACM 47(10), 71–75 (2004)
24. Peltz, C.: Web services orchestration and choreography. Computer 36(10), 46–52 (2003)
25. Philippsen, M., Zenger, M.: JavaParty– transparent remote objects in Java. Concurrency Practice and Experience 9(11), 1225–1242 (1997)
26. Saif, U., Greaves, D.: Communication primitives for ubiquitous systems or RPC considered-harmful. In: 2001 International Conference on Distributed Computing Systems Workshop, pp. 240–245 (2001)
27. Shepler, S., Callaghan, B., Robinson, D., Thurlow, R., Beame, C., Eisler, M., Noveck, D.: Network File System (NFS) version 4 Protocol (2003)
28. Spiegel, A.: Automatic Distribution of Object Oriented Programs. PhD thesis, FU Berlin, FB Mathematik und Informatik (2002)
29. Sun Microsystems. Java Remote Method Invocation Specification (1997)
30. Tanenbaum, A.S., Renesse, R.v.: A critique of the remote procedure call paradigm. In: EUTECO 1988, pp. 775–783. North-Holland, Amsterdam (1988)
31. Tatsubori, M., Sasaki, T., Chiba, S., Itano, K.: A Bytecode Translator for Distributed Execution of "Legacy" Java Software. In: Knudsen, J.L. (ed.) ECOOP 2001. LNCS, vol. 2072, p. 236. Springer, Heidelberg (2001)
32. Tay, B., Ananda, A.: A survey of remote procedure calls. Operating Systems Review 24(3), 68–79 (1990)
33. Tilevich, E., Smaragdakis, Y.: J-Orchestra: Enhancing Java programs with distribution capabilities. ACM Transactions on Software Engineering and Methodology (in press)
34. Vinoski, S.: RPC Under Fire. IEEE Internet Computing, 93–95 (2005)
35. Vogels, W.: Web services are not distributed objects. IEEE Internet Computing 7(6), 59–66 (2003)
36. Waldo, J., Wollrath, A., Wyant, G., Kendall, S.: A Note on Distributed Computing. Technical report, Sun Microsystems, Inc. Mountain View, CA, USA (1994)
37. Wiedermann, B., Ibrahim, A., Cook, W.R.: Interprocedural query extraction for transparent persistence. In: OOPSLA 2008: Proceedings of the 23rd ACM SIGPLAN conference on Object-oriented programming systems languages and applications, pp. 19–36. ACM Press, New York (2008)

Introduction to:
The Myths of Object-Orientation

Inviting a banquet speaker is a responsibility of the ECOOP Program Chair. The charter of the speaker is to address an audience at the juncture between information overload from a long day of conferencing and hunger from a walk around town. Thus a successful banquet speech is at the same time entertaining, thought provoking and brief. I have known James Noble for more than ten years and he certainly fits the bill for a banquet speaker. James has worked on most things OO, from the ownership types that he helped invent, to design patterns, dynamic languages and, of course, his musings on post-modernism in software construction. He is known for his wit and his ability to come up with ideas that, at first, sound crazy, then appear insane, and are, in final analysis, quite brilliant. I could not hope for a better speaker than James and was elated when he accepted my invitation.

So why am I writing this introduction to last year's ECOOP banquet speech? Well, it turns out that due to circumstances out of this PC chair's control, circumstances that involve an electric bouzouki and folk dancing, very few people got to hear James' speech in its entirety. James surmounted a defective sound system, did his best to pacify inebriated tourists, but had to give up when his microphone was summarily cut off in favor of the above mentioned bouzouki.

The following paper is a reconstruction, almost one year later, of what James had intended to say. I would like to thank James for revisiting a painful memory and writing down his notes on paper.

April 2009
Jan Vitek
West Lafayette, IN

S. Drossopoulou (Ed.): ECOOP 2009, LNCS 5653, p. 618, 2009.

The Myths of Object-Orientation

James Noble

School of Engineering and Computer Science,
Victoria University of Wellington,
New Zealand
kjx@ecs.vuw.ac.nz

Abstract. Object-Orientation is now over forty years old. In that time,
Object-Oriented programming has moved from a Scandinavian cult to
a world-wide standard. In this talk I'll revisit the essential principles —
myths — of object-orientation, and discuss their role in the evolution
of languages from SIMULA to Smalltalk to C++ to Java and beyond.
Only by keeping the object-oriented faith can we ensure full-spectrum
object-oriented dominance for the next forty years in the project for a
new object-oriented century!

In the beginning
So our myths and stories tell us
The programmer created the program
From the eternal nothingness of the void

This talk is about the myths of object-orientation: the myths, the lies that tell
the truth — the stories that were here before us, and that we will leave behind.
These are the stories we think about when we settle down in our cube to shuffle
cards, draw designs on whiteboards, to write tests, to write code, to debug. These
are the stories we think about to work out if some program is worthwhile or not,
if we will let ourselves be pleased by its shape, to measure our work against
the great programmers and designers of the past, whose names reverberate into
history and legend. These are the stories we tell our students — at least the
ones who have learned to program a little — myths to shape the programs they
write; myths to shape the way they think about the programs they write.

1 Abstraction

The founding myth of object-orientation is trinitarian. We hold these truths to
be self-evident: an object has state, behaviour, and identity:

- **identity** — an object can be distinguished from all other objects
- **behaviour** — objects communicate by sending messages; these messages
  are interpreted by the receiving object (i.e. dynamic dispatch)
- **state** — an object has mutable variables, encapsulated fields that can be
  changed from within the object.

S. Drossopoulou (Ed.): ECOOP 2009, LNCS 5653, pp. 619–629, 2009.

These truths are not, of course, self-evident — they are myths we choose to believe, to act upon, to teach. As a community, we need to share a common language. I claim — offering no support — that these three principles are what we mean when we say "my cat is object-oriented" [1]. Identity allows us to distinguish one object from another, while state and behaviour allow us to build *abstractions* using objects as components. The details of an object's state and behaviour are (or should be) hidden inside that object: an object should own its own implementation. An object's internal state and behaviour should only be visible externally by examining the results returned by message sends.

To the longstanding devotee of objects, ECOOP, and OOPSLA, something big may be missing here — *Hierarchical Program Structures* [2]: that is, *classes* and *inheritance*. While inheritance has been a feature of almost every language since SIMULA's prefixing, some important languages based on prototypes [3,4] lack classes and/or inheritance; the original version of JavaScript is probably the most popular now. Inheritance is not a large part of the story I'm telling today.

To the more recent devotee, something else is missing: *types*. Smalltalk should be a sufficient example that types are not essential to object-orientation!

2   Signification

The Scandinavians have another myth about object-orientation: *"All Programming is Simulation"*. In writing up this talk I tried to find the reference, but Google couldn't track it down! When I'm teaching object-orientation these days, I tend to use a slightly longer quote that has the virtue of actually existing:

> *A program execution is regarded as a physical model, simulating the behaviour of either a real or an imaginary part of the world.*

Object-Oriented Programming in BETA [5].

We can unpack this a little:

- **program execution** — the objects and bindings created by running program: the stack and the heap
- **physical model** — the electronic and quantum effects in the CPU and memory hardware that embody the program execution.
- **simulating the behaviour** — a program execution is designed to model, that is, to signify, a referent *outside the program itself*. As the program execution evolves over time, so should the referent.
- **part of the world** — the referent, the part of the world, the business, the context, that the program simulates.
- **real or imaginary** — the referent may predate the program (as in a manual system that is being automated) or it may be created by the program (so has to be imagined by the program's developers).

An object-oriented program is always taken as relating to something — a referent - outside the program itself. The program execution is not the main point of a program: the program execution must be taken as always referring to some other thing in the world. Here is the program, here is the bank account to which that program refers. The program plays the same part as the old ledger-books the banker's father used to write in with a fountain-pen: the numbers and signs in the ledger *signify* just how much money you have in your account. And as computers infiltrate further and further into society, the program's simulation of the world increasingly takes the place of the referent. If the bank's computer says you have no money, then you have no money, no matter what your documentation or your records or the bank's ledgers (superceded as physical models by the computer) or even your lawyer may say.

One thing — the program — stands for something else — the bank account. A program is a sign, a *semeîon* (since we are in Cyprus), a metaphor, a myth, perhaps a lie — but again, the lie that tells the "truth", that becomes the truth, that embodies the truth.

3   Dirt Is Good

What about the physical model? Is it accidental that OO is a physical model? More recently, I've been rethinking this: is there something in the physicality of it all that is essential?

Ka Mate! Ka Mate! Ka Ora! Ka Ora! We believe in life, in death, in time, in constructors and destructors and garbage collectors, change and decay in all around we see, in mutable state — because these things, this entropy and interconnectedness, is essential in the physical world. And then we leverage this physical world to make models of *itself*.

So what is it about *object-oriented* programming languages that make them good for building models? What is the big divide between object-oriented languages and their contemporary structured counterparts, such as Pascal?

Let's consider object-orientation as "where Pascal went wrong." The big gaps in Pascal (and other structured languages including C) are dynamic memory allocation with **new**, and variant records (the famous hole in Pascal's type safety). The behaviour of **new** and explicit pointers give a semantic model of individually addressable dynamically allocated memory regions; updatable memory gives us object state; and case statements or function pointers give object or type dependent behaviour.

Marxists would say this was a small example of *technological determinism*. Our myths, our aesthetics, our cultures of programming are built bottom up from enabling features of programming languages. Perhaps these features are incidental, or accidental, but it is our myths that make them essential!

4   A Digression

As an aside, other paradigms are not like this: they have other stories, other myths. If object-orientation has "world envy" — we wish to model the world — then other approaches have maths envy, or theory envy, or logic envy: they want programs to be weightless, to be insubstantial, abstract, zipless, to deny the reality with which they must somehow engage.

Consider the "utter pointlessness" of monads in lazy functional languages. These languages are designed to deny reality, to disavow entropy, to banish time, to reject any causal relationship with the world outside the program, to compute mathematically, with perfect strongly-typed abstractions. They're great for computing factorial functions — but can barely echo back user input.

And yet, the dirt of the world seeps back in — as Freud would say, the repressed unconscious will always return. If we cannot stop the world, we can at least stop the program, millions of times every second if necessary, to interact with the world outside, to read or write that dirty mutable physical state. Or we can contort our programs to simulate the mutability of the physical world.

So, if objects did not exist, we would need to (re)invent them. Consider the history of other programming languages in the last 20 years: Tcl endlessly replicating native C procedures and static data to represent widgets; Newsqueak and parallel Prolog programs using infinite loops to represent objects; and most recently, Erlang playing the same old tricks. As Suad Alagic memorably interjected during Joe Armstrong's ECOOP 2007 keynote: *"that's not a function — that's an object!"*

5 Unification

Physics lives for unification: the grand unified theory of everything is physics' holy grail. We know the unification of magnetism and electricity, of electromagnetism and the weak nuclear force, and the strange duality between waves and particles. In computer science we have our own unification and duality: code and data.

Famously, in Lisp, code and data are the same: programs are lists; data are lists; everything is a list — where list, of course, really means a cons-cell. Is this really an accidental feature of low-level models of computation (Lisp, Turing Machines, Lambda Calculus) and "homoiconic" programming languages [6,7], or something more essential?

Object-orientation goes further than Lisp; we have real data structures; everything is an object (an abstraction) not just a cons-cell; and as for code or data: who can tell? who cares? Abstraction results in unification — object-orientation unifies linked lists and arrays into collections. This is a big theoretical result: In other disciplines they give people Nobel prizes for this!

Self, Eiffel, and C♯, for example, also unify methods with fields and assignments. Java lost this, but reinvented it with JavaBeans and Eclipse's auto-generated accessors, which evolved back into the language as properties in C♯. This abstraction — or unification — is more than syntax: I think object-orientation captures something fundamental about computation, as objects abstract away the differences between data particles that exist in memory space and code waves that propagate in time.

Dynamic dispatch — rather than inheritance — enables this unification, although inheritance makes the code shorter. This is why single dispatch is essential to object-orientation, because a single dynamic dispatch is enough to ensure that as computation crosses an abstraction boundary the appropriate behaviour ensues. This is why I prefer object-oriented programming (single dispatch on abstract types) to pattern matching (multiple dispatch on concrete types).

The interesting observation here is that syntax precedes semantics; Dahl and Nygaard built simulation systems before any notion of inheritance, and Kay read the machine code of the B5000 file system before designing Smalltalk. Theorising comes along after the concrete artifacts.

Or as Karl Marx (paraphrased in the comic book "Introducing Postmodernism") puts it: *"what we produce is always miles ahead of what we think"* [8]. Myths are the result of our reflecting on our systems and our designs.

6   A Stack Is Not an Object

If object-oriented programming started with Simula, then "object-orientation" as an idea, a principle, a myth, started with Smalltalk. As Alan Kay (who did, after all, win the Turing award for this — as Nygaard and Dahl did later) puts it in the *Early History of Smalltalk* [9] (my emphasis):

> *a new design paradigm—which **I called** object-oriented.*

A little further on in that chapter, there is another quote:

> *This [object-orientation] lead to the ubiquitous stack data type example in hundreds of papers. To put it mildly, we were amazed at this.*

I was quite amazed with this quote when I first read it, and for several years later I really didn't understand what Kay meant. By that stage I'd been using and teaching object-oriented programming for several years, so of course I thought I understood it. I was especially proud of my example stack object written in Self: a `top` method, a `pop` method, a `push:` method, and I didn't even inherit from `vector`! But here is Alan Kay saying, pretty much, *"A Stack is Not an Object"*. Oops.

Fifteen years later I think I understand better what Kay was writing about. A stack is basically a data structure — an abstract data type. A good object should be more than just a data structure: it should represent something outside the program; it should be at a higher level than just a data structure; and it should unify both data and behaviour. In the terms I've used in this talk:

- **signification** — objects should be physical components of a model of something in a world outside the program.
- **abstraction** — objects should represent "higher level goals" rather than applying "procedures to data structures".
- **unification** — objects encompass both state and behaviour (and abstract both simultaneously). This is Kay's "recursion on the idea of the computer itself".

but I can't claim this insight as either novel or original. Towards the end writing out my talk notes for publication, I came across Ralph Johnson's slides for his Object-Oriented Programming and Design course [10,11]. As Ralph describes it:

> *I explain three views of OO programming. The Scandinavian view is that an OO system is one whose creators realise that programming is modelling. The mystical view is that an OO system is one that is built out of objects that communicate by sending messages to each other, and computation is the messages flying from object to object. The software engineering view is that an OO system is one that supports data abstraction, polymorphism by late-binding of function calls, and inheritance.*

Now, this seems rather better than I could manage. I'd just like to hold all three views, simultaneously — as I suspect Ralph does.

7 History, Tragedy, Farce

According to George Santayana (via Google): "Those who cannot remember the past are condemned to repeat it". To paraphrase to Karl Marx (again, and also via Google): "History repeats itself, first as tragedy, second as farce".

This is as true in software as it is in any other human endeavour. We can see it clearly with respect to object-oriented programming languages: we have SIMULA (history) followed by Smalltalk (tragedy) and finally Java (farce). This makes a great party game — choose any area of software and fill in the blanks yourself! Table 1 gives one possible set of answers: some of these are better than others.

Table 1. History, Tragedy, Farce

	History	Tragedy	Farce
Object-orientation	Simula	Smalltalk	Java
Nested object languages	Simula	BETA	Scala
Smalltalk languages	Smalltalk	Self	Newspeak
Systems languages	BCPL	C	C++
Wirth languages	Pascal	Modula	Oberon
Lisp languages	LISP	Scheme	CommonLisp
ML languages	ML	O'CAML	F♯
Languages beginning with "C"	C	ANSI C	C++
C++ languages	C++	C+@	C♯
C♯ languages	C♯1.0	C♯2.0	C♯ 3.0
BASIC languages	BASIC	VB	VB.net
Orthogonal languages	Algol-68	PL/I	Scala
Computer Companies	DEC	Sun	Oracle
Haskell	Haskell	Haskell	Haskell

8   The Power of $1\frac{1}{2}$

This leads me to the original design principle behind Java. I call it the principle of $1\frac{1}{2}$ — although perhaps the $1 + \mathcal{N}$ or $1 + \infty$ principle would be fairer, it would be less humourous and thus less memorable!

Java is not a symmetrical language. Coplien has argued symmetry-breaking is a feature of C++ [12]: I'm not so sure. In three important places, Java's design has one first class component, and then a list of second class components (that's the half). So borrowing directly from C++, Java has dynamic single dispatch (message sending) on one function argument to the left of the dot, combined with static multiple dispatch (overriding) on any number of arguments to the right of the dot.

Java's inheritance design follows this scheme: a class **extends** one first class parent — its superclass — and then **implements** any number of other second class interfaces.

Java 1.5 generics also follow this pattern. A generic type has one first class component — the underlying raw type — and then any number of type parameters that are erased at runtime. Overall, an accidental corner case of C++'s design governs much more of the design of Java.

9   Terroir

I recall, as a graduate student, having several "discussions" with Brian Boutel (then head of department) who strongly objected when — in a weak moment, I claimed *"I believe in object-orientation!"* Yea, verily, I had taken Alan Kay into my heart. While Brian was willing to concede a belief in objects may be useful in the practical art of getting real software built, as a researcher he thought that myths should be treated with a certain scepticism — as working hypotheses, not personal beliefs. On reflection, I've come to see that he was right: myths are lies we choose to believe in, knowingly and willingly. As academics, we interrogate them; as researchers, we manufacture them. On further reflection, I remember that Brian was a member of the first Haskell committee. So perhaps he had his own myths too, and was more evangelical about them than he let on.

When I was learning Smalltalk, Brian also used to complain about "Californian" programming — no types, dynamic dispatch, a relaxed interactive programming environment — much warmer, and much less bracing, than Oregon or Glasgow that gave birth to his beloved Haskell. So I wonder if, like wine, do programming languages have terroir? What influence does the environment that nurtures a programming language, or a programming principle, or a myth, have on the result? Smalltalk is Californian, Dick Gabriel has described how Unix (and C) comes from the Bell Labs engineering culture [13], but what of the rest? Can we see the clarity and austerity of Scandinavian fiords in the design of SIMULA? The interlocking relations of a social-democracy in the design of BETA? The Swiss sense of precision and cleanliness in the designs of Pascal (the Mondaine railway clock); Modula (a Tag Heuer watch); and Oberon (Swatch).

How much does a country, a city, a computing department in a city, or the bar where the graduate students drink affect the languages we all end up using?

When I was in Aarhus one year, the graduate students proudly showed me the bar (so they said) preferred by Kristen Nygaard, Bjarne Stroustrup, Anders Hejlsberg, and Mads Tofte — and where most of the best ideas in programming languages had been invented.

Bars after conferences can be good as well: Extreme programming, Aspect-Oriented programming, and Design Patterns (at least) all came from drinking sessions after conferences. And isn't that why we're all here: — to listen to the talks, to Google stuff, and to wake up with next year's ECOOP submission? I still have a vivid memory of drafting the Flexible Alias Protection paper, on a plane home, after drinking with Jan at OOPSLA '97.

Which leaves us only with the question of the origin of Java. This story — involving yet another trinity — has been relegated to the appendix, and for this, I offer neither apology or explanation.

Acknowledgements. Thanks to Jan Vitek for inviting me to give the banquet talk at ECOOP 2008, and for writing the introduction to this version; to the Bouzouki players and glass-balancers for lending me the stage for five minutes; to the English tourists for not throwing anything; to Peter Dickman for the vodka afterwards; to Ewan Tempero for comments on drafts; and to Sophia Drossopoulou for her encouragement and for printing this in the next year's proceedings.

References

1. King, R.: My cat is object-oriented. In: Object-Oriented Concepts, Databases, and Applications, Addison-Wesley, Reading (1989)
2. Dahl, O.J., Hoare, C.A.R.: Hierarchical program structures. In: Dahl, O.J., Dijkstra, E.W., Hoare, C.A.R. (eds.) Structured Programming, Academic Press, London (1972)
3. Taivalsaari, A.: A Critical View of Inheritance and Reusability in Object-oriented Programming. PhD thesis, University of Jyväskylä (1993)
4. Taivalsaari, A.: Classes vs. prototypes: Some philosophical and historical observations. In: Noble, J., Taivalsaari, A., Moore, I. (eds.) Prototype-Based Programming: Concepts, Languages and Applications. Springer, Heidelberg (1999)
5. Lehrmann Madsen, O., Møller-Pedersen, B., Nygaard, K.: Object-Oriented Programming in the BETA Programming Language. Addison-Wesley, Reading (1993)
6. Kay, A.C.: The Reactive Engine. PhD thesis, University of Utah (1969)
7. Mooers, C., Deutsch, L.: Programming languages for non-numeric processing—1: TRAC, a text handling language. In: Proceedings of the 1965 20th ACM National Conference, pp. 229–246. ACM Press, New York (1965)
8. Appignanesi, R.: Introducing Postmodernism. Icon Books Ltd (1999)
9. Kay, A.C.: The early history of Smalltalk. In: Wexelblat, R.L. (ed.) History of Programming Languages Conference (HOPL-II). ACM Press, New York (1993)
10. Johnson, R.: Object-oriented programming and design (2008), http://st-www.cs.uiuc.edu/users/johnson/598rej/

11. Johnson, R.: Erlang, the next Java (August 2007),
    http://www.cincomsmalltalk.com/userblogs/ralph
12. Zhao, L., Coplien, J.: Understanding symmetry in object-oriented languages. Journal of Object Technology 2(5), 123–134 (2003)
13. Gabriel, R.P.: LISP: Good news, bad news, how to win big. AI Expert 6(6), 30–39 (1991)
14. Kipling, R.: Just So Stories. Macmillan, Basingstoke (1902)

The Sing-Song of Old Man Java

With apologies to Rudyard Kipling [14].

Not always was Java as now we do behold him, but a Different Language with very short types. He was small and he ran slowly, and his hype was inordinate: he danced on a TV set in the middle of California, and he went to Big God Gosling.

He went to Gosling at six before breakfast, saying, 'Make me different from all other languages by five this afternoon.'

Up jumped Gosling from his fortress on the multicore and shouted, 'Go away!'

He was small and he ran slowly, and his hype was inordinate: he danced on a set-top-box in the middle of California, and he went to Middle God Steele.

He went to Steele at eight after breakfast, saying, 'Make me different from all other languages; make me, also, wonderfully popular by five this afternoon.'

Up jumped Steele from his virtual reality and shouted, 'Go away!'

He was small and he ran slowly, and his hype was inordinate: he danced on desktop in the middle of California, and he went to the Little God Gilad.

He went to Gilad at ten before dinner-time, saying, 'Make me different from all other languages; make me popular and able to run **anywhere** by five this afternoon.'

Up jumped Gilad from his office in Palo Alto and shouted, 'Yes, I will!'

Gilad called C♯ — dotNet C♯ — always hungry, just in from Redmond and showed him Java.

Gilad said, 'C♯! Wake up, C♯! Do you see that gentleman dancing in a browser? He wants to be popular and able to run anywhere. C♯, make him SO!'

Up jumped C♯ — Microsoft C♯ — and said, 'What, that hack-rabbit?'

Off ran C♯ — CLR C♯ — always hungry, grinning like a coal-scuttle, — ran after Java 1.0.

Off went the proud Java with his short little types like a bunny.

This, O Beloved of mine, ends the first part of the tale!

*   *   *

He ran on the desktop; he ran on the mainframe; he ran on the handhelds; he ran on the smartcards; he ran till his bytecodes ached.

He had to!

Still ran C♯ — Standard C♯ — always hungry, grinning like a rat-trap, never getting nearer, never getting farther, — ran after Java 1.2.

He had to!

Still ran Java — Old Man Java. He ran through the widgets; he ran through the phidgets; he ran through the applets; he ran through the servlets; he ran through the Topics of EBJ and MIDP; he ran till his parser ached.

He had to!

Still ran C♯ — ECMA C♯ — hungrier and hungrier, grinning like a horse-collar, never getting nearer, never getting farther; and they came to the J.C.P.

Now, there wasn't any proof, and there weren't any monads, and Java didn't know how to parameterise; so he stood on his types and hacked.

He had to!

He hacked through the Enums; he hacked through the Bignums; he hacked in the deserts in the middle of California. He hacked like Java 1.5

First he hacked typevars; then he hacked raw types; then he hacked wildcards; his types growing stronger; his types growing longer. He hadn't any time for rest or refreshment, and he wanted them very much.

Still ran C♯ — ISO C♯ — very much bewildered, very much hungry, and wondering what in the world or out of it made Old Man Java hack?

For he hacked like Haskell; or Eiffel or Ada; or GJ or Scala or Meta-O-CAML.

He had to!

He hacked up variance; he hacked his invariants; he stuck out modules for a balance-weight behind him; and he hacked up type inference too.

He had to!

Still ran C♯ — Dot Net's C♯ — hungrier and hungrier, very much bewildered, and wondering when in the world or out of it would Old Man Java stop.

Then came Gilad from his conference in Cyprus, and said, 'It's five o'clock.'

Down sat C♯ — ECMA Standard C♯ — always hungry, dusky in the sunshine; hung out his tongue and howled.

Down sat Java — Old Man Java — stuck out his types like a milking-stool behind him, and said, 'Thank goodness that's finished!'

Then said Gilad, who is always a gentleman, 'Why aren't you grateful to Microsoft's C♯? Why don't you thank him for all he has done for you?'

Then said Java — Tired Old Java — 'He's chased me out of the VMs of my childhood; he's chased me out of my pluggable semantics he's altered my classpath so I'll never get it back; and he's played Old Scratch with my types.'

Then said Gilad, 'Perhaps I'm mistaken, but didn't you ask me to make you different from all other languages, as well as to make you able to run anywhere? And now it is five o'clock.'

'Yes,' said Java. 'I wish that I hadn't. I thought you would do it by proofs and incantations, but this is a practical joke.'

'Joke!' said Gilad from the bar in the lobby. 'Say that again and I'll whistle up C♯ and run your primitive types off!'

'No,' said Java. 'I must apologise. Types are types, and you needn't alter 'em so far as I am concerned. I only meant to explain to Your Lordliness that I've had nothing to drink since morning, and I'm very thirsty indeed.'

'Yes,' said C♯ — ISO C♯ — 'I am just in the same situation. I've made him different from all other languages; but what may I have for my tea?'

Then said Gilad from the lobby at the conference, 'Come and ask me about it tomorrow, because I'm going to eat.'

So they were left in the middle of Cyprus, Old Man Java and Microsoft C♯, and each said, 'That's your fault.'

Author Index